NINETEENTH-CENTURY
AMERICAN
WOMEN
WRITERS

NINETEENTH-CENTURY AMERICAN WOMEN WRITERS

A Bio-Bibliographical Critical Sourcebook

Edited by Denise D. Knight
Emmanuel S. Nelson, Advisory Editor

Greenwood Press
Westport, Connecticut • London

Library of Congress Cataloging-in-Publication Data

Nineteenth-century American women writers : a bio-bibliographical
   critical sourcebook / edited by Denise D. Knight.
    p. cm.
  Includes bibliographical references and index.
  ISBN 0–313–29713–4 (alk. paper)
  1. American literature—Women authors—Bio-bibliography—
Dictionaries. 2. Women and literature—United States—
History—19th century—Dictionaries. 3. American literature—19th
century—Bio-bibliography—Dictionaries. 4. Women authors,
American—19th century—Biography—Dictionaries. 5. American
literature—Women authors—Dictionaries. 6. American
literature—19th century—Dictionaries. I. Knight, Denise D.,
1954– .
  PS217.W64N56 1997
  810.9'9287'09034—dc20
  [B]   96–35351

British Library Cataloguing in Publication Data is available.

Library of Congress Catalog Card Number: 96–35351
ISBN: 0–313–29713–4

First published in 1997

Greenwood Press, 88 Post Road West, Westport, CT 06881
An imprint of Greenwood Publishing Group, Inc.

Printed in the United States of America

The paper used in this book complies with the
Permanent Paper Standard issued by the National
Information Standards Organization (Z39.48–1984).

10 9 8 7 6 5 4 3 2

CONTENTS

PREFACE

Back in 1984, when I was a graduate student at the State University of New York at Albany, I enrolled in a course titled "American Literature, 1815–1865." The reading list from that course is still in my files; it is a crude and archaic reminder of how women writers and writers of color were relegated to the margins of American literature or forgotten altogether. Once the domain of a handful of so-called literary giants—Hawthorne, Melville, Poe, Emerson, Thoreau, and Whitman—the content and texture of our American literature anthologies have shifted dramatically in recent years. That now-passé course outline stands as evidence of how the landscape of American literature has changed; there were no writers of color taught in that graduate course, and the only woman writer included was Emily Dickinson, who was summarily discarded when the instructor had to cancel a class.

I remember not liking very much of what I was reading then. Emerson, on whom we dwelled for three long weeks, penned abstract and lofty philosophical essays; Poe's fiction emphasized the spirit of perversity and other dark themes; Hawthorne's stories examined and reexamined the themes of sin and redemption; there were no women characters to enliven Melville's tedious tales. Only Thoreau and Whitman captured my imagination; Dickinson I would have undoubtedly enjoyed, had she not been casually scratched from the syllabus. The canonical reconfiguration that has ensued since then has been remarkable, both in terms of the speed by which it is being effected and by the volume of long-forgotten literature that is being retrieved.

The pioneering work of revisionist critic Paul Lauter has changed forever the way we view nineteenth-century American literary history. No longer the sole domain of the chosen few, the canon has been revised and expanded to be far more inclusive than it was during my graduate school days. As Lauter notes in his highly acclaimed book *Canons and Contexts*, ''During the last twenty years the opportunities and challenges to teach nineteenth-century American women writers have widened almost beyond the comprehension of those trained in previous decades'' (114). Indeed, many a dusty text has been rescued from obscurity by archival researchers interested in restoring the larger literary history of the nineteenth century. Moreover, in the last two decades, numerous anthologies featuring works by nineteenth-century American women writers have been published, including Judith Fetterley's groundbreaking work *Provisions: A Reader from 19th-Century American Women* (1985), Lucy M. Freibert and Barbara A. White's *Hidden Hands: An Anthology of American Women Writers* (1985), and Elizabeth Ammons's *Conflicting Stories: American Women Writers at the Turn into the Twentieth Century* (1991). Additional studies by Nina Baym, Josephine Donovan, Jane Tompkins, Cheryl Walker, and Ann Douglas Wood have been instrumental in the recovery and reevaluation of lost texts by nineteenth-century American women writers. Mainstream anthologies from such publishers as Heath, Norton, and Prentice-Hall have taken corrective measures to reflect a more comprehensive profile of literature produced during the nineteenth century by integrating more women writers into their editions. And, not surprisingly, the once-influential voices of such culturally elitist critics as Harold Bloom, who as recently as 1994 opined that ''the current canonical crusades . . . attempt to elevate a number of sadly inadequate women writers of the nineteenth century, as well as some rudimentary narratives and verses of African-Americans'' (*The Western Canon* 540), are falling on increasingly deaf ears. Previous definitions of literary excellence are being revisited as scholars piece together a more historically accurate composite of nineteenth-century culture and literary tastes. No longer are the texts of a half-dozen or so white male writers privileged to the exclusion of other equally important voices that were silenced because they failed to adhere to the formal aesthetic tenets of works traditionally emphasized and taught.

While the revision of the canon has created the sometimes daunting dilemma about how to generate a semester-long course outline that is both representative and manageable, Bloom's complaint that ''expanding the canon . . . tends to drive out the better writers'' (540) is misguided at best; most of us who teach literature of nineteenth-century America recognize the distinct advantages of placing the works of the ''classic'' figures alongside writers who were formerly marginalized. Reading Fanny Fern's novel *Ruth Hall* along with Emerson's ''Self-Reliance'' allows us to arrive at a fuller understanding of the cultural crosscurrents at work in the deeply heterogeneous American culture. Likewise, *Walden*, with its romanticized depiction of Thoreau's life in self-imposed exile for twenty-six months provides an ironic contrast when placed next to Harriet Jacobs's autobiographical account in *Incidents in the Life of a Slave Girl* of taking refuge for seven years in an attic crawl space to avoid the sexual abuse of her brutal master. Reading the works of Rebecca Harding Davis, Margaret Fuller, Frances E. W. Harper, Harriet Beecher Stowe, and Susan Warner allows us insight into issues of domesticity, single motherhood, poverty, and hardship that were eclipsed by a heretofore woefully incomplete picture of American cultural history provided almost exclusively by male writers.

Despite both the resurgent interest in and the increasing availability of rediscovered literature, however, resources for readers have remained widely scattered. *Nineteenth-Century American Women Writers: A Bio-Bibliographical Critical Sourcebook*, then, is intended as a primary reference guide to seventy-seven American women writers of the nineteenth century. It is designed to encourage and facilitate additional research on these writers, lest they fade back into the obscurity from which they have been rescued.

The selection of writers included in this edition was a difficult one. I originally developed a tentative list of some fifty-five authors, which quickly ballooned to 75. As I began to solicit entries, researchers offered additional names of once-popular literary figures who are today virtually forgotten; hence, the list was further revised. Writers such as Civil War novelist Mary Anne Cruse, poet Sarah Piatt, transcendentalist Eliza B. Lee, and countless others, however, are omitted from this edition, not because of arbitrary judgments about their relative importance but because space constraints precluded me from including many fine writers who were brought to my attention too late. This volume, therefore, can only be *representative* of the women writers publishing during the nineteenth century—including fiction writers, poets, autobiographers, abolitionists, and essayists—rather than an all-inclusive, comprehensive edition. As archival research continues, enough additional writers will undoubtedly be recovered to comprise an entire second volume.

That being said, however, the selection process, by nature, assumes a political dimension. The figures included in this volume in no way represent the "best" or most "important" writers of the nineteenth century; indeed, while some have been assimilated into the literary canon for a considerable period of time—Dickinson, Chopin, and Stowe, for example—others, such has Henrietta Cordelia Ray, Maria Jane McIntosh, and Martha Finley, are still relatively unknown. No judgment was made about the aesthetic quality of the literature or the relative contributions of the authors included; the common denominator is that the writings of each woman aid in illuminating the social, historical, cultural, and economic climate of the nineteenth century.

Defining "women writers of nineteenth-century America" was also problematic, particularly with the contemporary trend to move away from rigidly contrived literary periods. For the purpose of this volume, nineteenth-century writers are defined as those whose best-known works were written or published during the nineteenth century. Thus, Kate Chopin (1850–1904), whose most significant publication, *The Awakening*, was published in 1899, is included; Edith Wharton (1862–1937), who wrote and published several works in the late nineteenth century but whose major works did not appear until the early twentieth century, is not included. Ethnic balance was also an important consideration; while several African-American writers are featured, the only Native American to appear is Sarah Winnemucca Hopkins; the writings of Zitkala-Sa (Gertrude Simmons Bonnin) were not published until the early twentieth century. Likewise, the only Asian-American writer I could locate from the period was Sui Sin Far, who also published after the turn of the century. It seems likely that as literary retrieval continues, more texts from writers of color will be discovered and preserved.

One further note concerns the names listed for the authors included. Since several writers published under pseudonyms, I have alphabetized using the name by which the writer is best known today, followed by the alternative name in parentheses. Thus, Sara Payson Willis Parton is located under Fanny Fern; Sarah Jane Clarke Lippincott is listed as Grace Greenwood.

Each of the seventy-seven entries in this volume follows a specific five-part format: a biography containing information about the writer's personal history; a discussion of her major works and themes; an overview of the critical studies examining the writer's works; and a two-part bibliography, featuring both works by and studies of the author. The entries are followed by a comprehensive bibliography listing resources for further study.

To everyone who made suggestions for expanding and refining my tentative list of writers, I owe special thanks. I also wish to extend my gratitude to Janet Gabler-Hover at the University of Georgia who graciously came to the rescue at the eleventh hour when one contributor dropped out of the project. I am enormously grateful for her assistance in securing replacement contributors Shelle C. Wilson Bryant and Patrick W. Bryant, who themselves deserve sincerest thanks for assuming extra work on very short notice. I also thank George F. Butler and Laura Clark, my editors at Greenwood, for their support through every phase of this project. I am indebted to Kevin J. Hayes, who allowed me to use his essay as a model for other contributors to follow. Finally, I thank my husband, Michael K. Barylski, for his unconditional support of all my research projects.

LOUISA MAY ALCOTT (1832–1888)

Gregory Eiselein

BIOGRAPHY

Louisa May Alcott, still most famous as the author of *Little Women* (1868–1869), was born in Germantown, Pennsylvania, on November 29, 1832. Her father, Amos Bronson Alcott, was an idealistic, reform-minded educator and philosopher; he was not, however, a reliable source of economic support for the family. Louisa's mother, Abigail (Abba) May Alcott, was a strong and caring woman, a supportive and practical mother, from a prominent family of New England social reformers. Louisa was the second of the Alcotts' four daughters, and these four girls, Anna, Louisa, Elizabeth, and May, would become the Meg, Jo, Beth, and Amy of *Little Women*.

In September 1834, the Alcotts moved to Boston, where Bronson opened his innovative Temple School. Following the failure of the school, the family moved to Concord, Massachusetts, in March 1840. In Concord, Bronson was closer to his friends, Ralph Waldo Emerson and Henry David Thoreau, than to his family. They seemed to respect and sympathize with the odd but enthusiastic educator. Louisa herself became a frequent visitor to the Emersons' home and an admiring, perhaps infatuated, student of Thoreau's. Louisa's foremost instructor was always her father, however, whose most resolute lessons concerned self-denial and self-control.

Out of work and depressed, Bronson traveled to England in 1842 (with monetary help from Emerson) to meet a group of English reformers impressed with his educational theories. Bronson returned with plans to establish a utopian community that would live by certain reformist principles: the "Consociate Family," communal work, vegetarianism, and other asceticisms—"high talk and low diet," as an early biographer put it (Moulton 35). Their utopia in Harvard,

Massachusetts, called Fruitlands, lasted only eight months. Louisa later parodied the community in "Transcendental Wild Oats" (1873), calling it "Apple Slump" (379), an allusion to a staple of the Fruitlands diet.

Most of the Alcotts felt relieved by the dissolution of the communal experiment, but Bronson had a nervous breakdown. Although he eventually recovered, Abba and Louisa recognized that Bronson could not provide for the family, and they took over responsibility for the family's financial and emotional support. As Bronson turned to his vegetable garden and unprofitable speaking tours, Abba took a social work position in Boston and moved the family to the city. Louisa also worked to bring an income to her financially strapped family. Besides sewing, she taught, acted for a short time, and hired herself out as a domestic servant, a companion, and a governess.

During the 1850s, Louisa Alcott found she could bring money into the family coffers by writing and selling stories. She published her first tale, "The Rival Painters" (written in 1848), in the *Olive Branch* in 1852 and earned $5. In 1849, she wrote but never published her first book, a novel titled *The Inheritance*. Alcott's first published book was *Flower Fables* (1854), a collection of fairy tales dedicated to Emerson's daughter Ellen. During the mid-1850s, Alcott began publishing short fiction in the *Saturday Evening Gazette*, and during the early 1860s in the reputable *Atlantic Monthly*. She also began writing anonymous and pseudonymous thrillers for story papers like the *American Union, Flag of Our Union, Frank Leslie's Illustrated Newspaper, Frank Leslie's Chimney Corner*, and *Frank Leslie's Lady Magazine*. Initially, these stories produced a small but much-needed income; she earned $10 for "Agatha's Confession" in 1857, for example, and $6 for "Marion Earle; or, Only an Actress!" in 1858.

During the 1850s, Louisa and her family struggled not only economically but also personally. Louisa's younger sister, Elizabeth, contracted scarlet fever in 1856 and suffered for months before dying in March 1858. Later that spring, her older sister, Anna, became engaged to John Pratt, and Louisa took the news badly. That fall—feeling lonely and looking for work, depressed about finances, Elizabeth's death, and Anna's impending marriage—Louisa despaired and, at one point, contemplated killing herself. During this period, the Alcotts returned to Concord and in 1858 moved into Orchard House.

The coming of the Civil War marked an important turning point in Alcott's career but also, unfortunately, in her health. In 1862, Alcott applied for a nursing position in Washington, D.C. Assigned to the Union Hotel Hospital in Georgetown, Alcott began a short-lived nursing career in December 1862. By January 1863, she fell ill with typhoid pneumonia. The doctors prescribed mercury-ladened calomel to treat her illness, and the resulting poisoning made her body ache, her hair fall out, and her mind restless and delirious. Bronson then traveled to Washington and brought Louisa back to Concord. Although she began to use opium as a pain reliever and sleep aid, a drug she would periodically turn to later in life, Alcott suffered the remainder of her life with the painful effects of the mercury that slowly destroyed her body.

While Alcott worked as a nurse, her sensation story "Pauline's Passion and Punishment" won a $100 prize from *Frank Leslie's Illustrated Newspaper*. Thereafter and throughout the 1860s, Alcott wrote thrillers for Leslie's periodicals and typically earned $50 to $100 per story. After convalescing for three months, Alcott began work on *Hospital Sketches* (1863), an autobiographical account of her stint as a nurse for the Union army. The book sold well and brought much-needed cash into the Alcott household; it also received favorable critical attention and helped Alcott build a reputation as a serious writer. In 1864, Alcott finished a self-consciously literary novel, *Moods*. Public response to *Moods* disappointed Alcott, however, and she turned to other kinds of work—the ever-profitable thrillers—and, in 1865, she took a position as a companion to Anna Weld, an invalid whose wealthy father hired Alcott to escort Anna on a trip to Europe. Unfortunately for Alcott, looking after Weld was frustrating, boring, and time-consuming, so the European tour was not satisfying.

Nevertheless, at Vevey, Switzerland, the trip suddenly became interesting. Alcott met Ladislas Wisniewski, a lively, young Polish refugee who would become a partial model for Laurie in *Little Women*. Alcott's journals and her later remembrances of Wisniewski suggest that she felt a sexual attraction to this dark-eyed, curly haired eighteen-year-old who played the piano, told romantic stories, and later escorted her around Paris. Although she never married and never, apparently, had a long-term sexual relationship, there is strong evidence that Alcott did have passionate, sexual feelings for men and perhaps more often for women. Late in her life, Alcott commented on her sexuality by saying: "I am more than half-persuaded that I am a man's soul, put by some freak of nature into a woman's body . . . because I have fallen in love in my life with so many pretty girls, and never once the least bit with any man" (Alcott quoted in Moulton 49). While other remarks (about Thoreau and Wisniewski, for example) suggest that she may have exaggerated her disinterest in men here, the open, unsolicited quality of this comment leaves little reason to doubt her affection for the "pretty girls."

When she returned to Concord in July 1866, Alcott again found her family in debt because, as she put it, "the money-maker was away" (*Journals* 152). Soon she began producing stories for various publishers, especially thrillers for Frank Leslie and James Elliott, editor of the *Flag of Our Union*. There were setbacks after her return: Abba was ill; Elliott rejected her book-length manuscript "A Modern Mephistopheles, or The Long Fatal Love Chase" as "too long & too sensational" (*Journals* 153); and Louisa felt despondent because her life seemed driven by the need to pay bills. Yet, as an author, Alcott was increasingly busy and successful, and in 1867, Horace B. Fuller, publisher of the children's magazine *Merry's Museum*, asked her to become the editor at a $500 a year salary.

About the time she started editing *Merry's Museum*, Thomas Niles, an editor and partner at Roberts Brothers, began pestering Alcott to write "a girl's book" (*Journals* 158) and continued to press her until she finally agreed in May 1868.

By midsummer, Alcott finished the first volume of *Little Women*. Readers loved the book, but it is difficult to know if Alcott did. In private, she called it *"dull"* (*Journals* 166); on the other hand, Alcott often took a self-deprecating attitude toward her writing. The immediately popular novel sold tens of thousands of copies that earned Alcott a small fortune in royalties. Finally, Alcott had what she had wanted all her life—financial security for herself and her family. With her new riches, she paid off bills, purchased comforts for her family (such as a modern furnace for Orchard House in 1871), and invested in railroad stocks and utilities bonds.

During the next two decades, Alcott wrote seven more juvenile novels: *An Old-Fashioned Girl* (1870), *Little Men* (1871), *Eight Cousins* (1875), *Rose in Bloom* (1876), *Under the Lilacs* (1878), *Jack and Jill* (1880), and *Jo's Boys* (1886). She also produced scores of stories for children's magazines like *The Youth's Companion* and *St. Nicholas*; these stories were collected and republished in the *Aunt Jo's Scrap Bag* series (six volumes, 1872–1882, five of which contain children's stories), *Spinning-Wheel Stories* (1884), the *Lulu's Library* series (three volumes, 1886–1889), and *A Garland for Girls* (1889). Although her books continued to be popular and lucrative, none of her works sold as well or were as widely read as *Little Women*. Alcott found fame tiring, however. She complained about her fans and their demands and said that she did not like the girls for whom she wrote. Nevertheless, around 1870, Alcott abandoned writing thrillers, which she apparently enjoyed writing, and focused her efforts on the better-paying children's books. She returned to thrillers only once, writing a new version of *A Modern Mephistopheles* in 1877.

After the publication of *An Old-Fashioned Girl*, Alcott took a second trip to Europe, traveling this time with her sister May and May's friend, Alice Bartlett. While in Rome, she learned of her brother-in-law's death and began to write a new book, *Little Men*, "so that John's death may not leave A[nna] and the dear little boys in want" (*Journals* 177). When she returned to the United States in June 1871, she found that *Little Men* had already sold 50,000 copies: It proved to be an able provider for Anna and her boys.

During her life, Alcott was an ardent supporter of various kinds of reform—feminism, dress reform, diet reform, homeopathy, peace, prison reform, child labor reform, and notably, the antislavery movement. In *Hospital Sketches*, for example, she earnestly describes herself as "a red-hot Abolitionist" (38). After joining the New England Woman Suffrage Association in 1868, Alcott became increasingly involved with the women's rights movement, its suffrage wing as well as its more conservative temperance wing. She attended women's rights conferences, made significant financial contributions, led a demonstration of women in Concord at the Centennial celebration, read the work of important feminist thinkers like Mary Wollstonecraft and Margaret Fuller, contributed pieces to the feminist *Woman's Journal*, supported other feminist writers, and led a suffrage campaign in her hometown. In 1879, she became the first woman in Concord to register to vote. Moreover, explicitly feminist themes shape many of her works from the 1870s, including, for example, *Work* (1873), which makes a narrative case for women's right to work and the dignity of single women. Alcott's temperance views take fictional shape in *Silver Pitchers* (1876).

Late in the decade, Alcott's family mourned two deaths. Abba died in November 1877, the same month the family moved into the Thoreau House. In March 1878, May surprised the family by marrying Ernest Nieriker, a Swiss bank clerk she had met in London, a man fourteen years her junior. The following year, May died in Paris less than two months after giving birth to a girl, named after Louisa and nicknamed Lulu. Louisa decided to raise her namesake, and Lulu Nieriker came to the United States in September 1880.

During the 1880s, the last years of Alcott's life, she raised Lulu and cared for her elderly father, dividing her time between Concord, Boston, and Nonquitt, Massachusetts. In October 1882, Bronson suffered a paralyzing stroke that left him disabled. Louisa herself continued to suffer from painful ill health and sought various homeopathic and mind-cure treatments while still caring for Bronson and Lulu. She also continued to write. From 1882 to 1886, she worked, sometimes to exhaustion, on her final novel, *Jo's Boys*, the third and final installment of the March family saga. She also kept producing children's stories, including three volumes dedicated to her niece, *Lulu's Library*. After a protracted illness, Bronson died on March 4, 1888. Later that day, Louisa wrote in the last letter she composed: "[A]s I dont [sic] live for myself I hold on for others, & shall find time to die some day, I hope" (*Letters* 337). Two days later, on March 6, Alcott found some time for herself and died, by herself, in her sleep.

MAJOR WORKS AND THEMES

Alcott was a prolific writer who composed in a variety of genres. She is best known for her juvenile fiction: Her first book, the last book she published in her lifetime (a volume of *Lulu's Library*), and her best-selling and most famous publications were all written for children. In between *Flower Fables* and *Lulu's Library*, however, Alcott produced thrillers and sensation stories; contributed poems, essays, and short fiction to periodicals; published two important novels for adults (*Moods* and *Work*); and recorded parts of her life in autobiographical and semiautobiographical pieces.

The apparent contradictions between the often sentimental juveniles and the thrillers have fascinated critics. In the children's novel *Under the Lilacs*, for instance, Ben Brown learns that the good influences and comforts of a properly bourgeois home are far better than unstable life in a circus. The thrillers, on the other hand, are filled with tales of desire, hatred, jealousy, violence, insanity, revenge, deception, drug addiction, aggressive female sexuality, gender subversion, sexual manipulation, and power struggles. Thus, some critics have described Alcott's career as a "double literary life" (Douglas vii).

Alcott's different audiences explain in part this double life. In *Moods* or her contributions to the *Atlantic Monthly*, for example, she wrote for a well-educated, literary audience familiar with American Transcendentalism. Alcott intended her thrillers, on the other hand, for a popular audience, seeking lively, inexpensive entertainment. Her editor pestered her for a ''girls' story'' in order to tap into a market of middle-class readers wanting respectable domestic fiction for children.

Despite the diversity of Alcott's works and the variety of genres in which she wrote, certain themes and concerns—domestic life, self-denial, deception, gender, and feminism—regularly recur. Many of her works focus on family life and strong, female characters as active nurturers, protectors, and providers; Marmee from *Little Women* is the most famous of these maternal figures, though Jo herself also becomes a maternal, nurturing character, particularly in *Little Men* and *Jo's Boys*. These characters are not, however, representatives of the passive femininity prized by middle-class discourse about the family in the nineteenth century. Some of Alcott's maternal figures—such as Faith Dane from *Moods* and ''My Contraband'' (1863) or Nan from *Little Men* and *Jo's Boys*—are neither biological mothers nor wives at all but are instead lifelong single women who devote their lives to their careers and to caring for others. Though a loving and beloved mother, Marmee is hardly passive or perfect; Marmee (like Jo) constantly struggles with anger. Alcott's domestic fiction treats not only the relationships of children to parents but also the relationships of children to siblings, to cousins, and to other (sometimes adopted) members of extended families.

Within this domestic fiction, Alcott often tells stories about the value of self-denial. From early in the novel, when the March girls give their Christmas breakfast to the poor Hummels, to late in the novel, when Jo forsakes a career as an author of sensational stories, *Little Women* is a tale of self-sacrifice and its rewards. ''Psyche's Art'' (1868) offers a similar lesson about self-denial. When Psyche Dean gives up her art studies in order to care for her family and sick sister, she is rewarded with an increase in her artistic abilities. Conversely, characters like Robert Steele, who selfishly manipulates the Carruth family in ''A Nurse's Story'' (1865–1866), or Felix Canaris, who egotistically seeks literary fame in *A Modern Mephistopheles*, are usually punished and left despairing, desperate, or dead at story's end.

In ''Behind a Mask'' (1866), on the other hand, Jean Muir successfully uses disguises and deception to lift herself out of a vulnerable position as a governess and former actress and into a position as an aristocrat's wife. As in ''Behind a Mask,'' Alcott often links a thematic emphasis on deception to settings and plots related to theater, writing, and art. Actresses like Jean Muir—as well as writers like Jo March or Felix Canaris and artists like Psyche or Diana and Percy from *Diana and Persis* or Becky and Bess from *An Old-Fashioned Girl*—appear throughout Alcott's writing.

Gender is also a prominent issue in Alcott's work. Her first juvenile novel offers children lessons about how to become ''little *women*.'' And as the representation of Jo and her painful passage from tomboyism indicates, the lessons are difficult ones. Still, Alcott's representations of gender are hardly faithful reproductions of stereotypical nineteenth-century images of femininity and masculinity. Indeed, many of Alcott's works take great delight in subversion of gender. In "My Mysterious Mademoiselle" (1869), for instance, the narrator falls for a captivating young "school-girl" and lavishly admires her feminine beauty. He later discovers, however, that the "pretty blonde school-girl" is in fact "a handsome black-haired, mischievous lad" (729) who, like Jean Muir, is good with disguises. In *Little Women*, Jo wants to marry Meg and says she is in love with Meg. Besides Jo (the girl with the boy's name) and Laurie (the boy with the girl's name), many other handsome, engaging, doubly gendered characters populate Alcott's works: John from *Hospital Sketches*, Faith Dane from *Moods*, Diana from *Diana and Persis*, and so on.

Although feminist concerns shape many of Alcott's works, particularly the thrillers, feminism becomes an explicit theme after *Little Women*. In *Work*, Alcott makes a strong case for women's right to work and the value of working women to society. As Christie tries to make her way in the world, readers see the heroine struggle with the limited job opportunities and the abuses facing working women. Alcott's feminism informs her children's novels as well. Rose Campbell, for example, the "strong-minded" orphan girl from *Eight Cousins*, returns as an outspoken, philanthropic, temperance-minded feminist in *Rose in Bloom*, where she tells her cousins that women have useful minds and that they have the right to pursue occupations and interests besides child rearing and housekeeping.

CRITICAL RECEPTION

During her lifetime, critics, reviewers, and the reading public generally appreciated and even loved Alcott's works. Although they rarely spoke specifically about her writing's aesthetic or artistic qualities, reviewers praised her children's books as delightful, charming, lively, realistic, and appealing in their rendering of valuable moral lessons. Some reviewers quoted children who expressed spontaneous enjoyment of the books and intense interest in particular characters like Jo or Laurie. Alcott's adult works, such as *Hospital Sketches* and *Work*, were also praised for their realism and moral purpose.

Although her nineteenth-century critical reception was mostly favorable, both the juvenile and adult works were also disparaged and criticized at times. In 1865, Henry James wrote a disapproving review of *Moods* for the *North American Review*, complaining that the events and characters in the book were improbable and unrealistic. Ten years later in *The Nation*, James criticized *Eight Cousins* for much different reasons: The characters in the novel were prosaic, unimaginative, vulgar, and too realistic for a children's story. In both reviews, James worried that Alcott's characters were not good moral exemplars. The ostensible immorality of Alcott's books was a common target for Alcott's detractors, who were also typically upset by her diction, including bad grammar and the use of slang by young female characters, or irritated by her focus on social problems and feminist concerns. Negative reviews of *Work*, for example, accused the novel of being inartistic and too political.

From Ednah D. Cheney's *Louisa May Alcott: The Children's Friend* (1888) through Cornelia Meigs's *Invincible Louisa* (1933) to four biographies produced in the 1950s, the critical treatment of Alcott following Alcott's death was mostly biographical. Often these accounts of Alcott's life and work focused on her career as an author of children's books; and these biographers praised her as "The Children's Friend" or "Duty's Child." Most academic literary critics paid Alcott little critical attention, except occasionally as a children's author. Like most literature for children and most works by women, Alcott was generally marginalized and ignored within the academy.

In the 1940s, however, after Madeleine B. Stern's and Leona Rostenberg's rediscovery of Alcott's thrillers, critical perspectives on Alcott began to proliferate. From the 1960s through the 1990s, scholarly interest in Alcott rapidly expanded, due in large part to the work of feminist critics. The body of feminist and historical criticism on Alcott produced during the last thirty years is immense and varied. Some of these critics, Martha Saxton and Eugenia Kaledin, for example, object to the lessons in female self-denial and submissiveness in *Little Women* and the juveniles. They see the children's texts as artistically regressive examples of Alcott's pandering to middle-class tastes and prefer the adult fiction, such as *Moods* or *Hospital Sketches*. Other critics (such as Stern, Elaine Showalter, Nina Auerbach, and Angela M. Estes and Kathleen Margaret Lant) have focused on the violent, erotic, duplicitous, subversive, and feminist elements in Alcott's sensation fiction—the dark side of Alcott's "double literary life," the "Alternative Alcott." Still other critics have emphasized the ambivalence of Alcott's work—the subversion *and* submissiveness in her fiction, the love *and* hatred of the domestic, the blurring of lines between traditional gender roles, and so on. Moreover, many postmodern feminist critics (Showalter, Elizabeth Keyser, Beverly Lyon Clark) have valued Alcott's work precisely for its rich, unresolved tensions, its contradictions, its representation of intensely emotional, subversive, queer, feminist impulses alongside male domination and the patriarchal social demand for female submissiveness. Because of renewed attention to the variety of Alcott's writings (including the thrillers) and the burgeoning feminist criticism of her work, critical debate about Alcott's life and writings has never been more varied, more controversial, or more interesting than now.

WORKS CITED

Alcott, Louisa M. *Hospital Sketches*. Boston: James Redpath, 1863.
———. *The Journals of Louisa May Alcott*. Edited by Joel Myerson, Daniel Shealy, and Madeleine B. Stern. Boston: Little, Brown, 1989.
———. "My Mysterious Mademoiselle." 1869. *Louisa May Alcott Unmasked: Col-

lected Thrillers. Edited by Madeleine Stern. Boston: Northeastern University Press, 1995. 724–732.

———. The Selected Letters of Louisa May Alcott. Edited by Joel Myerson, Daniel Shealy, and Madeleine B. Stern. Boston: Little, Brown, 1987.

———. "Transcendental Wild Oats." 1873. Alternative Alcott. Edited by Elaine Showalter. New Brunswick: Rutgers University Press, 1988. 364–379.

Douglas, Ann. Introduction to Little Women, by Louisa May Alcott. New York: New American Library, 1983. vii–xxvii.

Moulton, Louise Chandler. "Louisa M. Alcott." Our Famous Women. Hartford: A. D. Worthington & Co., 1883. 29–52.

BIBLIOGRAPHY

Works by Louisa May Alcott

Book-Length Narratives

Hospital Sketches. Boston: James Redpath, 1863.

Moods. Boston: A. K. Loring, 1864. Rev. ed. Boston: Roberts Brothers, 1882.

The Rose Family. Boston: James Redpath, 1864.

Little Women. 2 vols. Boston: Roberts Brothers, 1868–1869.

An Old-Fashioned Girl. Boston: Roberts Brothers, 1870.

Little Men: Life at Plumfield with Jo's Boys. Boston: Roberts Brothers, 1871.

Work: A Story of Experience. Boston: Roberts Brothers, 1873.

Eight Cousins; or, The Aunt-Hill. Boston: Roberts Brothers, 1875.

Rose in Bloom. Boston: Roberts Brothers, 1876.

A Modern Mephistopheles. Boston: Roberts Brothers, 1877. Published anonymously in Roberts Brothers' No Name Series.

Under the Lilacs. Boston: Roberts Brothers, 1878.

Jack and Jill: A Village Story. Boston: Roberts Brothers, 1880.

Jo's Boys, and How They Turned Out. Boston: Roberts Brothers, 1886.

Diana and Persis. Edited by Sarah Elbert. New York: Arno Press, 1978. An unfinished novella-length manuscript first published in 1978, reedited and reprinted in Alternative Alcott.

The Long Fatal Love Chase. New York: Harper and Row, 1995. A novel-length manuscript rejected by Alcott's publisher, used as a partial source for A Modern Mephistopheles, and first published in 1995.

The Inheritance. An unpublished novel-length manuscript.

Collections

Flower Fables. Boston: George W. Briggs & Co., 1854.

On Picket Duty, and Other Tales. Boston: James Redpath, 1864.

Louisa M. Alcott's Proverb Stories. Boston: A. K. Loring, 1868.

Morning-Glories, and Other Stories. Boston: Horace B. Fuller, 1868.

Hospital Sketches and Camp and Fireside Stories. Boston: Roberts Brothers, 1869.

Aunt Jo's Scrap Bag. 6 vols. Boston: Roberts Brothers, 1872–1882.

Silver Pitchers. Boston: Roberts Brothers, 1876.

Proverb Stories. Boston: Roberts Brothers, 1882.

Spinning-Wheel Stories. Boston: Roberts Brothers, 1884.

Lulu's Library. 3 vols. Boston: Roberts Brothers, 1886–1889.

A Garland for Girls. Boston: Roberts Brothers, 1889.

Comic Tragedies Written by "Jo" and "Meg" and Acted by the "Little Women." Edited by Anna Alcott Pratt. Boston: Roberts Brothers, 1893.

Behind a Mask: The Unknown Thrillers of Louisa May Alcott. Edited by Madeleine B. Stern. New York: William Morrow, 1975.

Plots and Counter-Plots: More Unknown Thrillers of Louisa May Alcott. Edited by Madeleine B. Stern. New York: William Morrow, 1976.

Alternative Alcott. Edited by Elaine Showalter. New Brunswick: Rutgers University Press, 1988.

A Double Life: Newly Discovered Thrillers of Louisa May Alcott. Edited by Madeleine B. Stern, Joel Myerson, and Daniel Shealy. Boston: Little, Brown, 1988.

Freaks of Genius: Unknown Thrillers of Louisa May Alcott. Edited by Daniel Shealy, Madeleine B. Stern, and Joel Myerson. Westport, CT: Greenwood, 1991.

Louisa May Alcott: Selected Fiction. Edited by Daniel Shealy, Madeleine B. Stern, and Joel Myerson. Boston: Little, Brown, 1991.

From Jo March's Attic: Stories of Intrigue and Suspense. Edited by Madeleine B. Stern and Daniel Shealy. Boston: Northeastern University Press, 1993.

Louisa May Alcott Unmasked: Collected Thrillers. Edited by Madeleine Stern. Boston: Northeastern University Press, 1995.

Studies of Louisa May Alcott

Bedell, Madelon. *The Alcotts: Biography of a Family*. New York: Clarkson N. Potter, 1980.

Elbert, Sarah. *A Hunger for Home: Louisa May Alcott's Place in American Culture*. Rev. ed. New Brunswick: Rutgers University Press, 1987.

Keyser, Elizabeth Lennox. *Whispers in the Dark: The Fiction of Louisa May Alcott*. Knoxville: University of Tennessee Press, 1993.

Marsella, Joy. *The Promise of Destiny: Children and Women in the Short Stories of Louisa May Alcott*. Westport, CT: Greenwood, 1983.

Payne, Alma J. *Louisa May Alcott: A Reference Guide*. Boston: G. K. Hall, 1980.

Saxton, Martha. *Louisa May: A Modern Biography of Louisa May Alcott*. Boston: Houghton Mifflin, 1977.

Stern, Madeleine B. *Louisa May Alcott*. Norman: University of Oklahoma Press, 1950.

———, ed. *Critical Essays on Louisa May Alcott*. Boston: G. K. Hall, 1984.

Strickland, Charles. *Victorian Domesticity: Families in the Life and Art of Louisa May Alcott*. Tuscaloosa: University of Alabama Press, 1985.

ANNE CHARLOTTE LYNCH BOTTA (1815–1891)

Jacquelyn N. Leonardi

BIOGRAPHY

On November 11, 1815, in Bennington, Vermont, Anne Lynch began her life as the youngest child of two and the only daughter born to Irish patriot Patrick Lynch and Charlotte Gray. Tragically, while seeking new lands in Cuba for his fellow Irishmen, Patrick Lynch died at sea only a few years after Anne's birth, leaving Charlotte alone to raise Anne and her brother. Charlotte moved the family from Windham, Connecticut, to Hartford.

At sixteen years of age, Anne entered the Albany Female Academy in Albany, New York. In 1834, after graduating with highest honors, she remained at the academy and taught for two years. She continued this livelihood at Shelter Island, New York, where she tutored three daughters of the Gardiner family.

In 1838, Lynch and her mother moved to Providence, Rhode Island, where Anne instructed young women in her home. In addition to teaching, she compiled her first book in 1841, *The Rhode-Island Book*, an anthology of prose and verse from Rhode Island citizens. Her relocation to Providence originated Lynch's literary and hostessing career as she held receptions once a week in her drawing room that attracted the "local litterateurs."

The receptions continued when she settled in New York City in the mid-1840s, but she also maintained her career in education, teaching English composition at the Brooklyn Academy for Women. At the academy, she proved herself a writer by contributing verse, travel letters, and critical articles to various periodicals including the *Democratic Review, The Christian Parlor Magazine*, and N. P. Willis's *Home Journal*.

Her reputation as writer was undermined, though, by her reputation as literary hostess. However, Lynch did not use her receptions merely to find her niche in society. The parties existed for the simple enjoyment of pleasurable company. In 1849, she opened a salon on Ninth Street in New York City. American writers such as Edgar Allan Poe, William Cullen Bryant, Horace Greeley, Ralph Waldo Emerson, George Bancroft, and Margaret Fuller attended for evenings of petty gossip and backbiting. British authors Anthony Trollope, William Thackeray, and Matthew Arnold also visited the salon. Not only did famous writers frequent the receptions, but statesmen, artists, and unknown beginners shared the jovial atmosphere of Lynch's companions and were encouraged to share their writings. Attentive listeners heard Poe read aloud "The Raven" and "The Case of M. Valdemar." An example of the salon's popularity can be seen through a Valentine's Day party that Lynch held. The invitation list included the whole "author-tribe," several artists, and military acquaintances. Bayard Taylor was appointed to write and read valentines; thus, he read one especially for Herman Melville (Leyda 272).

Nothing stopped her commitment to the salon—not even marriage. In 1855, Anne Lynch married Vincenzo Botta, who later became professor of Italian language and literature at the University of the City of New York. Although the Bottas had no children, they raised her brother's son after his death.

Continuing with her writing, Botta published a textbook in 1860 titled the *Hand-Book of Universal Literature*, a survey of various national literatures. Of the book she wrote, "This work was begun many years ago, as a literary exercise, to meet the personal requirements of the writer" (quoted in Myerson 21). Publication went through numerous editions, and a copy was found in Emerson's library. Thereafter, a newly edited and revised edition was produced in 1885. While working on the *Hand-Book of Universal Literature*, Botta died of pneumonia at the age of seventy-five in her New York home. She was buried in Woodlawn Cemetery, New York.

MAJOR WORKS AND THEMES

The Rhode-Island Book was her first major publication. The works she chose were made with "great fairness and indicate on the part of the editor a commendable liberality of sentiment and correctness of taste" (*Boston Quarterly* 134).

Besides compiling anthologies, she wrote poetry and collected her original verse in a book titled *Poems*. Her poetry does not revolve around one central theme yet reflects a "comprehensive selection of subjects" based on "devotional sentiment and the feelings akin to love and friendship" (*Literary World* 895). Some of her poetry titles include "Longing," "Aspiration," "Love," and "My Mother."

Botta's greatest and most well-known work, the *Hand-Book of Universal Literature*, is a compact manual of literary references. In this 560-page book, she surveys the field of literature, classifies the different departments, defines the periods and their developments, and sketches the great thinkers and writers who have contributed to the growth of literature (*Ladies* 57).

CRITICAL RECEPTION

Botta's works received the highest praises, which was no doubt influenced by her power and prestige from the salon. Edgar Allan Poe placed her poetry in two categories, one of merit and one of excellence. In the excellence class, he graded her two poems "The Ideal" and "The Ideal Found," stating that "I really do not know where to point out anything American much superior to them" (Poe 1207). The *Literary World* found that throughout her volume of poetry are "scattered frequent evidences of fine feeling, indicating and testifying to fineness of character in the author" (895).

Her *Hand-Book of Universal Literature* received an equal amount of acclamation; as one reviewer states, "Mrs. Botta has culled many a beautiful flower from the garden of literature which will meet with cordial recognition from the reader" (*Ladies* 57). The handbook is reviewed as "a surpassing achievement to trace the entire History of Literature, from 'The Book of Genesis,' to the 'New York Ledger,' and omit in the interval no name that time has remembered." She accomplishes this great feat "without the dryness of a catalogue" (*Christian Examiner* 70, 313).

The Rhode-Island Book that Botta compiled and edited also received high praise. One reviewer noted that the book deserves a place on the center table (*Boston Quarterly* 134). The volume "abounds in good writing" and pleasant reading "which is honorable to Rhode-Island" (*Christian Examiner* 30, 118).

The positive criticism Botta's works received was likely motivated by her influence at her salon. She provided a berth for entertainment and relaxation that many of these critics utilized, thus ensuring a warm spot in their hearts for her works.

WORKS CITED

Anonymous. Review of *Hand-Book of Universal Literature*. *Christian Examiner* 70 (1861): 312–314.

Anonymous. Review of *Hand-Book of Universal Literature*. *Ladies Repository* 21 (January 1861): 57.

Anonymous. Review of *Poems*. *Holden's* 3 (February 1849): 113–115.

Anonymous. Review of *Poems*. *Literary World* 3 (2 December 1848): 895–896.

Anonymous. Review of *The Rhode-Island Book*. *Boston Quarterly Review* 4 (1841): 134–135.

Anonymous. Review of *The Rhode-Island Book*. *Christian Examiner* 30 (March 1841): 117–119.

Leyda, Jay. *The Melville Log*. New York: Harcourt Brace, 1951.

Myerson, Joel, ed. *Dictionary of Literary Biography Vol. 3. Antebellum Writers in New York and the South*. Detroit: Gale Research, 1979.

Poe, Edgar Allan. *Essays and Reviews*. New York: Library of America, 1984.

BIBLIOGRAPHY

Works by Anne Lynch Botta

The Rhode-Island Book: Selections in Prose and Verse, from the Writings of Rhode-Island Citizens. Ed. and comp. by Anne Lynch. Providence: H. Fuller, 1841.

Poems. New York: G. P. Putnam, 1849.

Hand-Book of Universal Literature. New York: Derby and Jackson, 1860.

Studies of Anne Lynch Botta

Botta, Vincenzo, ed. *Memoirs of Anne C. L. Botta, Written by her Friends. With Selections from Her Correspondence and from Her Writings in Prose and Poetry*. New York: Tait and Sons, 1894.

Stern, Madeleine B. "The House of the Expanding Doors: Anne Lynch's Soirees, 1846." *New York History*, 23 January 1942, 42–51.

MARIA GOWEN BROOKS
(MARIA DEL OCCIDENTE)
(1794–1845)

Debbie L. Lopez

BIOGRAPHY

Maria Gowen Brooks was born in Medford, Massachusetts, the daughter of Eleanor (Cutter) Gowen and William Gowen, both of Welsh extraction. She had at least five older siblings. Though baptized Abigail Gowen, after her marriage, she legally changed her name to Mary Abigail; upon living in Cuba she would adopt the name Maria.

The Gowens lived a few miles from Harvard College, and William, a prosperous goldsmith, frequently entertained Harvard professors. Brooks was thus introduced to intellectual conversation, and she became, at an early age, interested in literature. By the time she was nine years old, she had memorized "large portions of Pope's Messiah; Milton's Comus; Addison's Cato; portions of Homer, Virgil and Ovid" (Griswold 1839, 542) and read all of Shakespeare's works. She was also proficient in music and painting and, by the age of twelve, was conversant in several modern languages. Later, her son, Horace, would recall his mother as having been throughout her life "quite a linguist. She read and wrote fluently in French, Spanish, and Italian; she also sang many songs in these tongues. . . . I remember she kept by her a Persian grammar, and often referred to it. She had a remarkable memory; and many curious facts she had stored in her mind, in scraps of poetry she had learned in her youth" (Gustafson xii–xiii).

When in 1809 Brooks's father died, bankrupt, she was sent to live with her forty-nine-year-old brother-in-law John Brooks, a widower with two sons. Over the course of the next year, the well-to-do Boston merchant would oversee the remaining year of her education and, when she left school in 1810, marry his sixteen-year-old charge. They would have two sons, Edgar (born November 25,

1811) and Horace (born August 12, 1813). Meanwhile, Brooks's husband experienced a series of financial losses, owing to his investment in several vessels
lost at sea in the War of 1812. Forced to abandon their prosperous residence,
the couple retired with one servant to a small remote house in provincial Portland, Maine. Brooks's fictionalized autobiography, *Idomen; or The Vale of Yumuri*, vividly describes her isolation during this period, as well as her fateful
meeting with the young Canadian officer with whom she fell in love early in
her unhappy marriage. The Canadian, *Idomen*'s "Ethelwald," would serve as a
romantic model in her writings.

Brooks had been writing short verses since an early age, but it was during
the Portland sojourn, at the age of nineteen, that she would make her first extensive attempt: an unpublished metrical romance in seven cantos, octosyllabic.
In 1820, in an attempt to revive her family's fortune, she published *Judith,
Esther, and Other Poems* "By a Lover of the Fine Arts," a poetic character
study of the Old Testament heroines. In 1823, when Brooks's husband died
nearly destitute, she moved with her sons and stepson to her uncle's Cuban
coffee plantation near Matanzas. On a long visit to a cousin in Canada, she
renewed her acquaintance with the Canadian officer. They were engaged but
became estranged. Upon breaking the engagement, Brooks went through a period of severe stress, twice attempting suicide by taking an overdose of opium.
Recovering, she devoted the remainder of her life to her literary career.

Upon the death of her uncle, she returned to the plantation, which she had
inherited. She had begun the first canto of her great epic poem *Zophiel; or The
Bride of Seven* four years after the publication of her first volume, wrote five
more cantos in Cuba, then accompanied her son to Dartmouth, where she made
use of the library in composing *Zophiel*'s extensive, erudite notes. She completed the manuscript in 1829, and during an 1830 visit to London, she met
Washington Irving, who submitted the manuscript to a publisher.

However, it was Robert Southey who would be her most significant benefac-
tor. Having begun a correspondence with him in 1825, shortly after the Boston
printing of the first canto of *Zophiel*, Brooks was in 1831 invited to his Keswick
home for a spring visit. The admiring Southey introduced her to Wordsworth
and Coleridge and gave her both free access to his extensive library and assistance in various translations. After her departure from England, he personally
supervised the first (London, 1833) publication of *Zophiel* by "Maria del Occidente," the new pseudonym for Brooks that he had himself coined. Reissued
in America the same year, *Zophiel* was reprinted in 1834, then again in 1879,
in an edition introduced by the poet Zadel Barnes Gustafson.

Returning to the United States, Brooks resided with her son Horace, first at
West Point, where he was a student, and then in 1843 at Fort Columbus, New
York, a military post at which her son, then a captain, was stationed. In the
summer of that year, she had printed for private circulation the romance *Idomen*,
which had first been serialized in the Boston *Saturday Evening Gazette* (1838).
In December 1843, learning of the deaths in Cuba of her stepson and her son

Edgar, she sailed for that country, where she continued composing. Among her latest productions was the "Ode to the Departed," memorializing her son. Leaving unfinished another epic, *Beatrice, the Beloved of Columbus*, she herself succumbed to tropical fever in November 1845.

MAJOR WORKS AND THEMES

A majority of Brooks's works recast biblical and classical themes in a style notable for its combination of erudition and frank sensuality. Remarking on Brooks's "daring," Thomas O. Mabbott comments: "The author's mind seems to have been perfectly free from all prudishness, and the boldness of her attitude makes what is said inoffensive" (419). Published when she was just twenty, *Judith, Esther, and Other Poems* is uneven; but the Keatsian lushness of imagery in passages such as the "Description of Holofernes" anticipates her masterful control of language in *Zophiel*.

The latter, more ambitious work explores the characteristically Romantic theme of an immortal's doomed attraction for a mortal woman. Based on a story in the apocryphal book of Tobit, *Zophiel* follows the adventures of Egla, the Jewish daughter of parents exiled during the time of the Captivity. Beloved by the fallen angel Zophiel, Egla is eventually united, instead, with her destined earthly lover but only after witnessing the murders of successive bridegrooms.

Adhering "entirely to that belief (once prevalent among the fathers of the Greek and Roman churches) which supposes that the oracles of antiquity were delivered by demons or fallen angels" ("Preface" liii), Brooks draws on her impressive knowledge of ancient history in enriching the narrative. Southey praised *Zophiel*'s "Song of Egla" as being "far, very far, superior to Sappho's celebrated ode," the "Ode to Aphrodite" (*Selections from the Letters* 156).

CRITICAL RECEPTION

Mabbott succinctly summarizes the history of Brooks's literary reception: "The critics praised—the public seems to have paid homage, but no more, and the publishers were looking for profits" (421). In England, Southey declared Brooks "the most impassioned and most imaginative of all poetesses" (*The Doctor* II, 222); in America, Rufus Griswold regarded her as "unmatched among the poets of her sex" (Gustafson xliii). Yet her work sold so poorly that, as Griswold remarked, "even the title [of her epic *Zophiel*] would have remained unknown to the common reader . . . but for occasional allusions to it by Southey and other foreign critics" (Gustafson xlii).

Brooks's first publication, *Judith, Esther, and Other Poems*, received warm but qualified praise; the *Southern Literary Messenger*, for example, appreciated the work's "striking union of strength and beauty" but noted that "by aiming at too much vigor and terseness, [Brooks] occasionally becomes obscure" (543). The collection's circulation was limited. The 1834 (Boston) edition of *Zophiel* suffered a similar fate. At the end of a month, only about twenty copies had been sold, so Brooks withdrew the remainder from the market. When she later requested Griswold to offer the copyrights to her complete works gratuitously, the publisher declined, on the grounds that they were "of too elevated a character to sell" (*Female Poets of America* 80). Only an estimated 100 copies of *Idomen* were ever printed, and her works remain unreprinted today.

WORKS CITED

Del Occidente, Maria. Preface to *Zophiel; or The Bride of Seven*, by del Occidente. Edited by Zadel Barnes Gustafson. Boston: Lee and Shepard, Publishers, 1879. liii–liv.
Griswold, Rufus Wilmot. "Biographical Sketches of Living American Poets and Novelists." *Southern Literary Messenger* 5 (1839): 541–548.
——. *The Female Poets of America*. 2nd ed. Philadelphia: Henry C. Baird, 1862.
Gustafson, Zadel Barnes, ed. "Maria del Occidente." In *Zophiel; or The Bride of Seven*, by Maria del Occidente. Boston: Lee and Shepard, Publishers, 1879. iii–xlvi.
Mabbott, Thomas Olive. "Maria del Occidente." *American Collector* (1926): 415–424.
Selections from the Letters of Robert Southey. John Wood Warter, ed. London: Longman, Brown, Green, and Longmans, 1856.
Southey, Robert. *The Doctor, &c.* 2 vols. New York: Harper & Brothers, 1836.

BIBLIOGRAPHY

Works by Maria Gowen Brooks

Judith, Esther, and Other Poems. By a Lover of the Fine Arts. Boston: Cummings and Hilliard, 1820.
Zophiel; A Poem. By Mrs. Brooks. Boston: Richardson & Lord, 1825.
Zophiel; A Poem. By Mrs. Brooks. Boston: Carter & Hendee, 1833.
Zophiel; or The Bride of Seven. By Maria del Occidente. Second American from the first London Edition. Boston: Hilliard, Gray & Co., 1834.
Idomen; or The Vale of Yumuri. By Maria del Occidente. New York: Samuel Colman, 1843.
Zophiel; or The Bride of Seven. By Maria del Occidente. Edited by Zadel Barnes Gustafson. Boston: Lee and Shepard, Publishers, 1879.

Studies of Maria Gowen Brooks

Brooks, Van Wyck. *The Flowering of New England, 1815–1865*. New York: E. P. Dutton & Company, Inc., 1936. 155–156.
Cyclopaedia of American Literature. Edited by Evert Duyckinck and Augustus Duyckinck. 2 vols. New York: Scribner, 1856. II, 198–201.
Granniss, Ruth Shepard. *An American Friend of Southey*. New York: De Vinne Press, 1913.

FRANCES HODGSON BURNETT
(1849–1924)

Gretchen Holbrook Gerzina

BIOGRAPHY

Frances Eliza Hodgson was born in Manchester, England, on November 24, 1849, and had a comfortable and conventional upbringing. Her father, Edwin Hodgson, had a profitable business selling silver tea sets, chandeliers, and other household furnishings. He died unexpectedly in 1852, leaving her mother, Eliza Boond Hodgson, two older brothers, and a younger sister in difficult financial circumstances. A fifth child was born posthumously. Her mother took over the business and saved money by moving the family to a formerly elegant neighborhood now bordered by factory workers' houses, but she ensured that her children remained in school and separate from the neighbors' children. It was in school that Frances discovered her talent for storytelling, amusing her schoolmates with her serialized romantic tales in exchange for the girls' excited attention. "If she had been a sharp, executive, business-like sort of a child," she wrote of herself later, "she might have used her juvenile power as a thing with a certain market value. She might have dictated terms, made conditions, and gained divers school-room advantages. But she had no capacities of the sort. She simply told the stories and the others listened" (*The One I Knew Best of All* 230).

When the American Civil War stopped the flow of cotton to Manchester's textile mills, other local businesses also began to fail. In 1864, Eliza Hodgson was forced to sell the family business and accept the offer of her brother, who had emigrated to America, to move the family to New Market, Tennessee, near Knoxville. It was while living first in a log cabin and later in an even smaller rural house that Frances discovered the market value of her stories. Using the money earned from picking berries to pay for return postage, she sent her first story to *Godey's Lady's Book* in 1868. Her subject matter and expression were so British that the publishers requested a second story to confirm her authorship, then accepted both with payment. From the moment that she realized she could make money with her pen, she began a lifetime of nearly constant writing to earn her living, a need that became even more pressing when her mother died in 1870 when Frances was twenty-one.

After repeated refusals, Frances agreed to marry Swan Burnett, a young Tennessee eye and ear doctor, in 1873. In what was to prove a pattern in her life, she saved her money and made a long visit first to New York to meet her new editor at Scribner, then to England to visit relatives, before returning to marry Swan. Their first son, Lionel, was born the following year. When Swan decided to further his training, the couple moved to Paris for a year, during which time their second son, Vivian (who was to be the model for her most successful novel, *Little Lord Fauntleroy*), was born. In Paris, Frances supported the family through her writing. There she wrote the first of her sixty novels, *That Lass o' Lowrie's*, drawing upon her Lancashire childhood to create a heroine who goes from being a pit girl in a coal mine to marrying a gentleman. This rags-to-riches theme would repeat itself in many of her subsequent books.

After the year in France, their fortunes changed considerably. *That Lass o' Lowrie's* became a best-seller, and the family moved to Washington, D.C., where Swan became a successful specialist and they began to move in elite social circles. President James Garfield was among their friends, and Frances's fourth book, *Through One Administration*, sandwiched in between innumerable short stories, takes Washington political life as its setting. As her literary success grew, she spent increasing amounts of time away from her husband and sons. Both her writing and her travel began to take their toll on her marriage and her health; exhausted from incessant writing, she traveled and grew emotionally distant from her husband. After the enormous success of *Little Lord Fauntleroy* in 1886, followed by *Sara Crewe* in 1888 (later expanded into *A Little Princess* in 1905 after its English stage production in 1902), Frances maintained homes in England and Italy as well as in Washington, after a time remaining married in name only.

Frances's relationship with her sons was complicated. In her time away, she persisted in writing to them as though they were far younger than they actually were. "Every day I am going to add something to the Fairy Box and we will have s'prises all winter," she wrote to Lionel when he was about sixteen (Thwaite 134). She adored them, and apparently they her, calling her "Dearest" in the way she adopted for Cedric and his mother in *Little Lord Fauntleroy*. Because she had sent her publisher a photograph of Vivian in curls and a velvet suit that became a model for Cedric, Vivian was forever plagued by his link to *Fauntleroy*. Few realized that Cedric was a robust, heroic youth in the novel, and the name became erroneously but indelibly associated with the image of a feminized milksop, an image that Vivian spend the rest of his life attempting to counter: He died in 1937 while rescuing four people after a boating accident. Even so, he realized that it was not his mother's fault that the Fauntleroy craze persisted. He wrote her first biography, *The Romantick Lady: The Life Story of an Imagination*, in 1927.

In 1888, Frances added drama to her literary accomplishments, revising some of her fiction for the stage and overseeing its production. *Little Lord Fauntleroy* had been pirated in an English stage production, and incensed at the copyright infringement, Frances hurried from Italy to London to take the author to court and produce her own version. The lawsuit was decided in her favor and set a legal precedent protecting other authors in England, who were so elated that they gave a banquet in her honor. Her second play, *Phyllis*, opened and closed quickly in 1889, and another play, *Nixie*, opened in London the following year.

That her professional ambitions took precedence over her family becomes clear in an 1889 letter from her son Lionel, still in Washington while his brother was with her in London, who wrote sadly that "I have not received a letter from you for about three weeks, but I suppose you have a great deal to do. Aunt Kate gave me the five dollars you told her to give me and I am ever so much obliged" (Carpenter 72). Back in Europe the next year, she was horrified to hear that he was extremely ill with tuberculosis and rushed home to bring him back to Europe with her, visiting specialist after specialist in a vain attempt to find a cure. Even toward the end, she kept from him the news that he was dying, and after his death in Paris in 1890, she fell into a deep depression.

Her marriage a failure and her career a great success, Frances began an ambiguous relationship with an English doctor ten years her junior, Stephen Townesend. Townesend became her business manager, but his real desire was for the theater, and Frances promoted his stage ambitions in every way she could. In 1898, she finally divorced Swan and bought an English estate, Maytham Hall, Rolvenden, Kent, where she would live for nine years and whose gardens formed the setting for her later novel *The Secret Garden* (1911). After ten years of friendship with Townesend, she married him in 1900, even though her son Vivian refused to visit whenever Townesend was present. Her biographer, Ann Thwaite, suggests that she married him under duress, quoting Frances as hoping "that when this marriage was a fixed fact, he would feel so secure that I would at least have peace," finding himself instead in "a grotesquely shackled position" (Thwaite 192). Predictably, this marriage too failed, with Frances in essence supporting him in order to keep him away from her.

From 1892 on, Frances published a book or produced a play almost every year. In 1905, after dividing her time between Washington and Europe, she became an American citizen, forty years after first moving to the United States. In 1909, she had a large house built at Plandome, Long Island. This, and a smaller house where she wintered in Bermuda, would be her last home. She died on Long Island on October 29, 1924, one month away from her seventy-fifth birthday.

MAJOR WORKS AND THEMES

Frances Hodgson Burnett's earliest works were highly conventional love stories following a ladies' magazine formula for romantic tales. However, *That Lass o' Lowrie's*, Burnett's first novel, established a number of themes and methods that she successfully repeated throughout her long writing career. While several of her books took place in the United States, or had main characters who moved between the United States and Europe, they were more often set in England and Europe and featured highly ethical, thoughtful, and independent protagonists who saw through the hypocrisies and limitations of social conventions.

Many of the plots involve a reversal of fortune or rags-to-riches theme. *That Lass o' Lowrie's*, published first as a serial in 1876, then as a novel in 1877, was based on a millworker's daughter she observed as a child from her house in Manchester. Joan Lowrie speaks in broad Yorkshire dialect, is uneducated, and has an abusive father. She is generally rough around the edges, eschewing traditional roles for women. As the novel progresses, she is asked by Fergus Derrick, a mining engineer, to marry him. In this case, as in many others of her tales, the reversal of fortune theme involves a shift in class status. Joan refuses to marry Fergus until she is properly educated for her new social position.

Little Lord Fauntleroy (1886), although involving a young American boy, also follows this format. Cedric is the son of an American mother and a deceased younger son of an English earl. When the earl's other sons also die, he sends to New York for Cedric and expects to find a young "barbarian." Instead, Cedric is honest and manly, having a natural nobility that fits him for the role society has called upon him to play. *A Fair Barbarian* (1881) also features an honest and unconventional American, Octavia Basset from Nevada, who shows the English provincial society of Slowbridge to be narrow, conventional, and humorless.

The reversal of fortune theme works somewhat differently in *The Secret Garden* and *Sara Crewe* (and its reworking as *A Little Princess*). Mary Lennox in *The Secret Garden* and Sara Crewe in the other two works both spent their early childhoods in India and moved to England after the death of their parents. (Sara's father dies after leaving her in Miss Minchin's London boarding school.) In each case, the girl loses family and fortune and becomes dependent upon others for a home. Both girls live lonely, loveless lives. Mary has been completely spoiled and needs to be reawakened to life through nature and a wholesome relationship with Yorkshire people. Sara, on the other hand, has a natural goodness and generosity that see her through illness, mistreatment, and poverty until she is restored to her "natural" state of wealth. Similarly, the wealthy protagonist of *The Dawn of a New Tomorrow* is rescued from suicide by an encounter with several pious and hopeful members of London's underclass.

CRITICAL RECEPTION

Although *The Secret Garden* and *A Little Princess* are probably the most commonly known to readers of Burnett today, it was *Fauntleroy* that was her runaway best-seller in her lifetime. It sold "over a million copies in English alone, and [was] translated into more than a dozen languages. It made Frances at least a hundred thousand dollars in her lifetime" (Thwaite 94). Praised by critics, the work took on a life of its own when mothers inspired by the novel started a fashion craze for the long curls and black velvet suit with a lace collar worn by Cedric after his move to England. Unfortunately, this image far over-shadowed the novel's portrayal of the youth in New York, running street races in red stockings and befriending a grocer and shoeshine boy. Most of its enor-mously successful stage and film productions featured girls playing Cedric's role, which further reinforced its feminine reputation.

Primarily thought of today as a writer for children, Burnett wrote in a time when such distinctions were less common and her novels attracted a wide au-dience. Her main influences, other than conventional romances, were the well-known Victorian novelists such as Dickens, Gaskell, and Thackeray. Novels like her *The Making of a Marchioness*, in which a poor woman of noble descent marries the boring Marquis of Walderhurst, display a realism about marriage and social class more commonly associated with writers like Trollope and Eliot.

BIBLIOGRAPHY

Works by Frances Hodgson Burnett

Fiction

Dolly. Philadelphia: Porter & Coates, 1877. (Retitled as *Vagabondia*. New York: Scrib-ner, 1879.)
Surly Tim and other stories. New York: Scribner, 1877.
That Lass o' Lowrie's. New York: Scribner, 1877.
Theo: A Love Story. Philadelphia: T. B. Peterson, 1877.
Earlier Stories (First Series). New York: Scribner, 1878.
Earlier Stories (Second Series). New York: Scribner, 1878.
Kathleen. Philadelphia: T. B. Peterson, 1878.
Miss Crespigny. Philadelphia: T. B. Peterson, 1878.
Our Neighbour Opposite. London: Routledge, 1878.
Haworth's. New York: Scribner, 1879.
Jarl's Daughter and other stories. Philadelphia: T. B. Peterson, 1879.
Natalie and other stories. London: Warne, 1879.
Louisiana. New York: Scribner, 1880.
A Fair Barbarian. Boston: Osgood, 1881.
Through One Administration. Boston: J. R. Osgood, 1883.
Pretty Polly Pemberton. Boston: J. R. Osgood, 1884.

Little Lord Fauntleroy. New York: Scribner, 1886.

Edith's Burglar. Boston: Jordan Marsh, 1888.

The Fortunes of Philippa Fairfax. London: Warne, 1888.

Sara Crewe. New York: Scribner, 1888.

A Woman's Will or Miss Defarge. New York: Lippincott, 1888.

The Pretty Sister of José. New York: Scribner, 1889.

Little Saint Elizabeth and other stories. New York: Scribner, 1890.

The Drury Lane Boys' Club. Washington, D.C.: Moon Press, 1892.

Giovanni and the Other. New York: Scribner, 1892. (Published in United Kingdom as
    Children I Have Known.)

Piccino and Other Child Stories. New York: Scribner, 1894.

The Two Little Pilgrims' Progress. New York: Scribner, 1895.

A Lady of Quality. New York: Scribner, 1896.

His Grace of Osmond. New York: Scribner, 1897.

In Connection with the De Willoughby Claim. New York: Scribner, 1899.

The Making of a Marchioness. New York: Stokes, 1901.

The Methods of Lady Walderhurst. New York: Stokes, 1901.

In the Closed Room. New York: McClure, 1905.

A Little Princess. New York: Scribner, 1905.

The Dawn of a New Tomorrow. New York: Scribner, 1906.

Racketty Packetty House. New York: Century, 1906.

The Troubles of Queen Silver-Bell. New York: Century, 1906.

The Cozy Lion. New York: Century, 1907.

The Shuttle. New York: Stokes, 1907.

The Good Wolf. New York: Moffat, 1908.

A Spring Cleaning. New York: Century, 1908.

Barty Crusoe and His Man Saturday. New York: Moffat, 1909.

The Land of the Blue Flower. New York: Moffat, 1909.

The Secret Garden. New York: Stokes, 1911.

My Robin. New York: Stokes, 1912.

T. Tembarom. New York: Stokes, 1913.

The Lost Prince. New York: Century, 1915.

Little Hunchback Zia. New York: Stokes, 1916.

The White People. New York: Harper, 1917.

The Head of the House of Coombe. New York: Stokes, 1922.

Robin. New York: Stokes, 1922.

In the Garden. New York: Medici Society, 1925.

Plays

That Lass o' Lowrie's. 1878.

Esmeralda. 1881. (Produced in United Kingdom as *Young Folk's Ways*, 1883.)

The Real Little Lord Fauntleroy. 1888.

Phyllis (from *The Fortunes of Philippa Fairfax*). 1889.

Nixie (from *Editha's Burglar*). 1890.

The Showman's Daughter. 1890.

The First Gentleman of Europe. 1892.

A Lady of Quality. 1897.

A Little Princess. 1902.

The Pretty Sister of José. 1903.
That Man and I (from *The De Willoughby Claim*). 1904.
Dawn of a Tomorrow. 1909.
Racketty Packetty House. 1912.

Autobiography

The One I Knew Best of All. New York: Scribner, 1893.

Studies of Frances Hodgson Burnett

Bixler, Phyllis. *Frances Hodgson Burnett*. Boston: Twayne, 1984.
———. "The Oral-Formulaic Training of a Popular Fiction Writer: Frances Hodgson Burnett." *Journal of Popular Culture* 15 (spring 1982): 42–52.
Burnett, Constance Buel. *Happily Ever After*. New York: Vanguard Press, 1969.
Burnett, Vivian. *The Romantick Lady: The Life Story of an Imagination*. New York: Charles Scribner's Sons, 1927.
Carpenter, Angelica Shirley and Jean Shirley. *Frances Hodgson Burnett: Beyond the Secret Garden*. Minneapolis: Lerner Publications Company, 1990.
Dixon, Ella Hepworth. *As I Knew Them*. London: Hutchinson, 1930.
Gohlke, Madelon S. "Re-reading *The Secret Garden*." *College English* 41 (April 1980): 894–902.
Keyser, Elizabeth Lennox. " 'The Whole of the Story': Frances Hodgson Burnett's 'A Little Princess.' " In *Triumphs of the Spirit in Children's Literature*. Hamden, CT: Library Professional Publications, 1986. 230–243.
Laski, Marghanita. *Mrs. Ewing, Mrs. Molesworth, Mrs. Hodgson Burnett*. London: Arthur Barker, 1950.
Maher, Susan Naramore. "A Bridging of Two Cultures: Frances Hodgson Burnett and the Wild West." In *Old West–New West: Centennial Essays*. Moscow: University of Idaho Press, 1993. 146–153.
Maude, Pamela. *Worlds Away*. London: John Baker, 1964.
Murray, Heather. "Frances Hodgson Burnett's *The Secret Garden*: The Organ(ic)ized World." In *Touchstones: Reflections on the Best in Childrens Literature*, vol. 1, edited by Perry Nodelman. West Lafayette, IN: Children's Literature Association, 1985. 30–43.
Phillips, Jerry. "The Mem Sahib, the Worthy, the Rajah and His Minions: Some Reflections on the Class Politics of *The Secret Garden*." *The Lion and the Unicorn* 17 (1993): 168–194.
Thwaite, Ann. *Waiting for the Party: The Life of Frances Hodgson Burnett 1849–1924*. New York: Scribner, 1974.

ALICE CARY
(1820–1871)

Laura Rogers

BIOGRAPHY

Alice Cary was born on April 26, 1820, on a farm in Hamilton County, Ohio. The nearby village, Mt. Healthy (formerly Mt. Pleasant), became the Clovernook of Cary's best-known short fiction. Cary was a prolific and popular writer; today, except for the critical attention brought to her short fiction by Judith Fetterley and her inclusion in a few anthologies, Cary's work has all but disappeared. In addition to Fetterley's work, only the biography of Mary Clemmer Ames and an article by Janice Goldsmith Pulsifer exist to call attention to her work.

Cary's biographers comment on what has been called the "Cary legend"— Alice Cary's transformation from a shy, uneducated girl from a small farming community to a woman who, at the age of thirty, moved by herself to New York City, supported herself by her writing, and made her home the center of a thriving literary and social circle. It is these aspects of Cary's life, along with the death and deprivation that marked her early years, that provide some of the pervasive themes of her work.

Alice Cary was the fourth of nine children and the fourth daughter born to Robert and Elizabeth (Jessup) Cary. Although they did not have much formal education, both parents were literate; however, books were not plentiful in the Cary household. Among the books that were available was *Charlotte Temple* by Susanna Rowson, a popular novel of the time, which may have influenced Cary's fiction (Fetterley xv).

Cary's early years were marked by the death of family members. In 1833, Lucy and Rhoda, two of Cary's sisters, died; Cary's mother died in 1835. Fetterley marks the loss of Rhoda, two years older than Alice and the sister Cary felt closest to, as perhaps the most significant event in Cary's life. It was Rhoda who encouraged Alice's early attempts at poetry and spent time with Alice telling and listening to stories. The loss of Cary's mother, in fact, did not seem as great as the loss of Rhoda. Although her public words about her mother were those of a loving daughter describing a loving mother, Cary's fiction "presents a world without mothering" (Fetterley xiv).

Robert Cary remarried in 1837 when Alice was seventeen. The nature of Cary's life while living at home with her father and stepmother has become part of the Cary legend. Critics Ames and Pulsifer present a traditionally hostile, "wicked" stepmother who made Alice and her sister Phoebe spend their time on housework instead of writing during the day and denied them candles to write by at night, forcing them to hide their manuscripts in a secret closet. Fetterley, in her rereading of the Cary legend, sees this period of Cary's life as a time when she began her career as a writer in a time and place that were helpful to her literary ambitions (xv). Mt. Healthy and its surroundings were being transformed from a farming community to a suburb of the growing city of Cincinnati.

In 1838, Cary published her first poem, "The Child of Sorrow," in *The Sentinel*, Cincinnati's Universalist newspaper. She continued to publish work without payment in local newspapers and periodicals. According to Fetterley, two events changed Alice Cary's life as a writer. Cary's professional and personal relationship with publisher and editor Rufus W. Griswold and her connections to the growing Cincinnati literary world helped her establish a national reputation as a writer.

Cary's relationship with Griswold was one of several connections she made with prominent men who helped her career. In 1848, Griswold, who had noticed Cary's poems in Western newspapers, requested some of her work to be included in his anthology *The Female Poets of America*, published in December 1849. Until Cary's death, Griswold was a major supporter and brought her work to the attention of the reading public. Fetterley notes that their relationship may, at one time, have been a romantic one. Cary was also introduced to Gamaliel Bailey, the founder of the abolitionist paper *National Era*; she had a lifelong correspondence and friendship with poet John Greenleaf Whittier.

A trip east in 1850 precipitated Cary's decision to make her home in New York; she moved in November 1850 and was soon joined by her sisters Phoebe and Elmina. A move of this magnitude for a single woman in her thirties, well past what was deemed the marriageable age, was considered most unusual, and all of Cary's biographers have speculated on the reasons for her decision. Fetterley considers that Cary "may have surmised that life as a single woman would be far more satisfactory in New York than in Mt. Healthy" (xvii). New York was already the center of the literary world and would have afforded her far more professional and literary opportunities. Ames speculates that an unhappy love affair was the reason for Cary's move; Griswold's biographer, Joy Bayless, suggests that Cary moved east specifically because of her relationship with Griswold.

Alice Cary remained in New York for the rest of her life, living with her sisters Phoebe and Elmina (who died in 1862). For over fifteen years the Carys' house became the center for Sunday evening receptions, gatherings of prominent figures in the New York literary and social world. Her relationship with Phoebe remained the primary relationship in her life. Alice and Phoebe shared a close and dependent bond; Phoebe was literally unable to survive without Alice and died shortly after Alice's death in 1871.

MAJOR WORKS AND THEMES

Alice Cary made her living as a writer; therefore, she wrote prolifically, publishing poetry, short fiction, novels, short moralistic or didactic essays, children's stories, personal essays, and articles on historical and contemporary subjects. In her lifetime she was primarily known as a poet; by ''1855, the Cincinnati *Ladies' Repository* could announce that the name Alice Cary 'has become like a household word to our eighty thousand readers' '' (Fetterley xi).

Cary thought of herself primarily as a poet and achieved her popular success with her poetry. Her volume of poetry include *Lyra and Other Poems* (1852), *Collected Poems* (1855), *Ballads, Lyrics and Hymns* (1866), and *A Lover's Diary* (1866). *The Poems of Alice and Phoebe Cary* was published in 1849. She occupied the ''poet's corner'' in the *New York Ledger*. In the 1882 edition of the collected poems of the Carys, the contents are classified under the headings of ballads and narrative poems, poems of thought and feeling, of nature and home, of grief and consolation, of love and friendship, religious poems and hymns, poems for children, and personal poems. To contemporary readers, much of Alice Cary's poetry seems indistinguishable from the work of other women poets of the day and would be read as sentimental and moralistic.

Cary published widely in some of the most popular and influential periodicals of the day including the *National Era*, the *Ladies' Repository*, the New York–based *National Magazine*, the prestigious *Atlantic Monthly*, and *Harper's Monthly*. Cary also published in a wide variety of newspapers and periodicals, including *Graham's Sartain's Union Monthly*, which was edited for a brief time by Caroline Kirkland, and Bret Harte's *The Overland Monthly*.

Cary was a prolific writer of short fiction, novels, and children's stories. Her novels include *Hagar, a Story of To-day* (1852; originally appeared in serial form in the *Cincinnati Dollar Weekly Commercial*), *Married, Not Mated* (1856), *The Bishop's Son* (1867, which was serialized in the *Springfield Republican*), and *Holly-wood* (1854; this appeared in serial form in the *Era* in 1854). *The Born Thrall*, written for the *Revolution*, was, according to Janice Goldsmith Pulsifer, a ''series of stories about women's rights and wrongs'' (27). Cary's novels are not accorded critical attention today; Pulsifer believes that they were typical of much of the contemporary fiction of the day, and indeed, they deal with the subjects of seduction, betrayal, and abandonment common to women's novels of the time (46). Cary's children's works, *Clovernook Children* (1854) and *Snow-berries* (1867), have likewise not survived and have been defined as dark stories about a world where children are not safe (Fetterley xxxv).

Cary's short fiction includes her well-known *Clovernook, or Recollections of Our Neighborhood in the West* (1852), *Clovernook, Second Series* (1853), and *Pictures of Country Life* (1859). Judith Fetterley's collection of Cary's short fiction, *Clovernook Sketches and Other Stories* (1987), part of the American Women Writers Series, served to bring her work to contemporary critical attention. Fetterley argues that Cary's best short fiction can be described as a ''sketch,'' a form in which character and consciousness are foregrounded over plot. The sketch form is ''a form that permitted her to accept and express the fragmentary and open-ended in fiction as she perceived it in life'' (Fetterley xxiv).

Cary was unique among nineteenth-century women regionalists in her interest in ''fiction as psychic exploration and dreamwork'' (Fetterley xiv). She is interested, as were other contemporary women writers, in realism, in recording the details of life in Clovernook, yet her work contains elements of the dreamlike and mystical. She examines the nature of rural lives by exploring the consciousness of characters who are often women trapped in unhappy, limiting lives or marriages. Her narratives, driven not by the conventions of plot but by the logic of interior life, echo the concerns of her male contemporaries such as Poe and Hawthorne.

In both her preface to *Clovernook* and in the conclusion to *Clovernook, Second Series*, Cary explores her own concerns and intentions for her work, defining herself both as a regionalist and as a realist, naming her subject as the rural life she knew. She argues for the worth of telling the stories of the ''simple manners and the little histories every day revealed'' and the ''shadows and sunbeams that fell about me as I came up to womanhood'' (*Clovernook* 7).

In her reading of Cary's fiction, Pulsifer defines Cary's short fiction as ''moral in tone'' and ''sentimental and rarely lightened by humor'' (54). Fetterley's work has served as a significant rereading of Cary's short fiction, especially of Cary's interest in the details of her characters' lives and the dark and melancholy tone of her work, work in which children suffer deprivation and death and women suffer unhappy and loveless marriages and limited lives.

Fetterley reads Cary's attention to detail as her attempt to create ''a 'poetics of detail,' '' so that ''Cary's narrator pays attention to those whose lives, like her own, go unmarked'' (''Entitled to'' 107). She also rereads the ''melancholy tone'' ascribed to Cary's work differently than Pulsifer, arguing that Cary's ''melancholy'' negotiated ''the relationship between her own ambition . . . and the conventions of her discourse community'' (''Entitled to'' 116).

CRITICAL RECEPTION

Alice Cary was a popular writer in her time; her name became a household word to her many readers. Yet today only her short fiction and a handful of poetry survive and have gained critical attention, almost entirely due to the efforts of her only contemporary biographer and critic, Judith Fetterley, to bring her work into the American literary canon. Yet Fetterley accords no critical attention to her poetry and novels and notes that "Cary's novels suffer from incoherence" (xx).

Although Cary was widely published as a poet in her day, critical reception of her work was varied. Pulsifer claims that her poetry is "typical of the period" (46). John Greenleaf Whittier, who worked to bring the work of Alice and Phoebe Cary to the attention of the reading public, believed, according to Pulsifer, that they were "richly gifted as poets" (46). Edgar Allan Poe commented favorably on Cary's "Pictures of Melancholy" in Griswold's *The Female Poets of America*, naming it as the "noblest poem" (Pulsifer 46) in the collection. The poem was commonly anthologized into the 1900s.

Reviews of some of Cary's other poetry were not, however, so favorable. Pulsifer reports that one reviewer wrote of Cary's *Collected Poems* (1855): " 'It is a sob in 399 parts. . . . It is a parish register of funerals, rendered into doleful verse.' " The same critic goes on to admit, however, that " 'she writes much better verse than most women who publish poetry' " (48). Another critic writes that Cary's poetry was " 'poetry of sentiment, memory and domestic affection, entirely feminine and rather tame and diffuse as a whole, but tender and sweet, cherished by many good women and dear to their hearts' " (46).

Pulsifer declares that "[i]n order to earn her living, Alice was forced to write too much" (49) and concludes that Cary's later poems are "less melancholy and show an improved technical skill" (49). She identifies Cary as part of the "feminine fifties," the group of popular women writers of the time.

To date, only Judith Fetterley has paid Cary's short stories and sketches serious critical attention; she argues convincingly that "[f]or her work in this genre Cary deserves a place in our literary history" (xx). Her rereading of Cary as a writer whose best work combines realism with the interior logic of her characters as she explores the lives of the inhabitants of Clovernook should ensure Alice Cary her place in the American literary canon.

WORKS CITED

Ames, Mary Clemmer. *A Memorial of Alice and Phoebe Cary, Some of Their Later Poems.* New York: Hurd and Houghton, 1873.

Bayless, Joy. *Rufus Wilmot Griswold: Poe's Literary Executor.* Nashville: Vanderbilt University Press, 1943.

Cary, Alice. *Clovernook Sketches and Other Stories.* Edited by Judith Fetterley. New Brunswick: Rutgers University Press, 1987.

Fetterley, Judith. "Entitled to More than 'Peculiar Praise': The Extravagance of Alice Cary's *Clovernook*." *Legacy* 10 (1993): 103–119.

———, ed. Introduction to *Clovernook Sketches and Other Stories*, by Alice Cary. New Brunswick: Rutgers University Press, 1987.

Pulsifer, Janice G. "Alice and Phoebe Cary, Whittier's Sweet Singers of the West." *Essex Institute Historical Collections* 109 (January 1973).

BIBLIOGRAPHY

Works by Alice Cary

Poetry

The Poems of Alice and Phoebe Cary. New York: Hurd and Houghton, 1849.
Lyra and Other Poems. New York: Redfield, 1852.
The Collected Poems. Boston: Ticknor and Fields, 1855.
Ballads, Lyrics and Hymns. New York: Hurd and Houghton, 1866.
A Lover's Diary. Boston: Ticknor and Fields, 1866.

Juvenile Literature

Clovernook Children. New York: John W. Lovell, 1854.
Snow-berries. Boston: Ticknor and Fields, 1867.
Ballads for Little Folk. New York: Hurd and Houghton, 1874.

Fiction

Clovernook, or Recollections of Our Neighborhood in the West. New York: Redfield, 1852.
Hagar, a Story of To-day. New York: Redfield, 1852.
Clovernook, Second Series. New York: Redfield, 1853.
Married, Not Mated. Derby and Jackson: H. W. Derby, 1856.
Pictures of Country Life. New York: Hurd and Houghton, 1859.
The Bishop's Son. New York: G. W. Carleton and Company, 1867.

Studies of Alice Cary

Armstrong, M. F. "Alice and Phoebe Cary—A Remembrance." *Woman's Journal*, 9 September 1871.
Fetterley, Judith. "Entitled to More than 'Peculiar Praise': The Extravagance of Alice Cary's *Clovernook*." *Legacy* 10 (1993): 103–119.
———, ed. Introduction to *Clovernook Sketches and Other Stories*, by Alice Cary. New Brunswick: Rutgers University Press, 1987.
Griswold, William McCrillis, ed. *Passages from the Correspondence of Rufus W. Griswold and Other Pages*. Cambridge, MA: Harvard University Press, 1939.
Mott, Frank Luther. *A History of American Magazines, 1850–1865*. Vol. 2. Cambridge, MA: Harvard University Press, 1939.
Pulsifer, Janice G. "Alice and Phoebe Cary, Whittier's Sweet Singers of the West." *Essex Institute Historical Collections* 109 (January 1973): 9–59.
Venable, W. H. *Beginnings of Literary Culture in the Ohio Valley*. Cincinnati, OH: Robert Clarke, 1891.

PHOEBE CARY
(1824–1871)

Ernelle Fife

BIOGRAPHY

Phoebe Cary was born on September 4, 1824, in comparative poverty, the sixth of nine children. The family lived in a cramped cottage on a farm north of Cincinnati. The cottage still stands looking much as it did during Phoebe's youth, maintained by the Cary Cottage Group. Cary rarely had the time to attend school, teaching herself from her parents' limited materials, primarily the family Bible. Her mother died when Phoebe was about eleven, less than two years after two of Phoebe's sisters died. When her father remarried, the children did not seem to accept their stepmother; they did not move into the new house built by Robert Cary for his new wife.

Phoebe began writing poetry at about the age of thirteen, publishing some in local newspapers. In 1849, Horace Greeley visited the Cary family, encouraging both Phoebe and her sister Alice to write; he published the first volume of their verse the following year. Phoebe moved to New York with her younger sister, Elmina, to live with Alice in 1851. Six years later, the three sisters moved to a house that Alice bought and where Alice and Phoebe held their famous Sunday evening receptions attended by writers, artists, and activists, including such notables as P. T. Barnum and Horace Greeley. The normally retiring Phoebe shone at these gatherings as a brilliant and witty conversationalist. With only the income from their writing, life was not easy, but the sisters worked diligently and tirelessly, even in the face of debilitating illness and death. Alice and Phoebe were devastated by the death of Elmina in 1862.

During her lifetime, Phoebe was, and continues to be, overshadowed by her sister Alice. In the collections of their poetry, Alice always appears first, and Phoebe is usually referred to as ''her sister.'' Alice did have more financial success and seems to have been the more public of the two; for instance, she held sole copyright to the immensely successful household edition of *The Poetical Works of Alice and Phoebe Cary*. Both sisters were abolitionists and feminists. Phoebe worked briefly for Susan B. Anthony but preferred a private role in the feminist movement, through her poetry and the Sunday evening receptions.

Phoebe had at least four marriage proposals but only one from a man she loved; she did not marry him, choosing to remain with Alice who was already succumbing to the tuberculosis that would prove terminal ten years later. Phoebe died five months after Alice, on July 31, 1871, at Newport, Rhode Island, also from tuberculosis.

MAJOR WORKS AND THEMES

Cary's poetry was wide ranging in form and theme, as the table of contents of the popular household edition of *The Poetical Works of Alice and Phoebe Cary* demonstrates: ballads and narrative poems (including parodies), poems of thought and feeling, poems of nature and home, poems of love and friendship, religious poems and hymns, poems of grief and consolation, personal poems (mostly tributes), and poems for children. Her religious poetry and her children's poetry were perhaps the most popular and, perhaps, the best poems. Much of her poetry for children contains moral lessons, as well as practical advice, couched in tales of animals or children. One notable example is "The Prairie on Fire," a poem of one boy's courage in the face of a prairie fire threatening him and his family.

Cary's poetry, while emotionally powerful, is not sentimental. She believed that married life with children was the ideal life both for a woman and for a man and seemed to value marriage between two loving, equal Christians as the highest existence possible in this life. Her love poetry, which has been overlooked, expresses this ideal. But she also recognized that a single life was better than married life to the wrong husband, to a man who was brutal or selfish or unsympathetic. As Cheryl Walker points out, several of Cary's poems are satires on marriage, such as "Dorothy's Dower," which describes a spendthrift, verbally abusive husband.

Cary was not, however, unsparing in her descriptions of the loneliness and social isolation felt by single women. Her popular verse "The Christian Woman" describes a truly Christ-like woman who, because she is single, dies alone, unmourned, and unpraised. Throughout all her poetry exists a strong, personal faith, but a faith grounded in the harsh reality of daily life. Cary believed that one's life should be filled with service, service to God and one's family—a family that includes, if possible, a husband and children. In this respect, and in her underlying wit, her poems are thematically similar to Jane Austen's novels.

CRITICAL RECEPTION

Because of its readability, Cary's poetry was extremely popular. The *Poetical Works* went through thirteen editions; *Josephine Gallery* (a collection of biographical essays) went through five editions, as did the *Last Poems*; another collection published the same year, *Poems*, had three editions. Phoebe's *Ballads* went through four editions. A collection published after the sisters' deaths with the only extensive biography of both, *The Poetical Works of Alice and Phoebe Cary with a Memorial of Their Lives by Mary Clemmer Ames*, went through six editions.

Contemporary editors were often sentimental, emphasizing the Carys' humble beginnings. A good example is Caroline May's gushing commentary on the "Sisters of the West" as possessing "a nobility and independence of thought, . . . a fervour of imagination" (552). Alice's poetry was usually deemed to be superior, although Phoebe's power of language and her concern with social issues are duly noted. Modern scholars often ignore Phoebe or mention her only in passing as Alice's sister. Emily Watts is one of the few critics who consider Phoebe to be a better poet than Alice. Only one or two of her poems have appeared in twentieth-century anthologies until recently, and there are no recent reprints of the nineteenth-century editions.

The most common reference to Phoebe is in conjunction with Alice, as if these two women wrote together, with Alice taking the leading role. For example, Susan Kissel discusses the sisters together: They "took courageous stands as women in the nineteenth century"; they published poems; they were abolitionists and feminists (25). Little effort is made to distinguish Phoebe's individual poetic style or political and social ideas. Furthermore, several critics contend that it was Alice who led the famous Sunday evening receptions, although the comments by attendees of these receptions imply that both sisters organized and participated equally. Any serious student of Phoebe Cary would do well to check all references to Alice Cary.

BIBLIOGRAPHY

Works by Phoebe Cary

Poetry

Poems. New York: Hurst, n.d.

Poems by Alice and Phoebe Cary. Philadelphia: Moss and Brother, 1850.

Poems and Parodies. Boston: Tickner, Reed, and Fields, 1854.

The Josephine Gallery. Edited with Alice Cary. Philadelphia: Lippincott, 1858.

The Poetical Works of Alice and Phoebe Cary. Household edition. Boston: Houghton Mifflin, 1865.

Poems of Faith, Hope, and Love. New York: Hurd and Houghton, 1867.

Ballads for Little Folk. Edited by Mary Clemmer. Boston: Houghton Mifflin, 1873.

The Last Poems of Alice and Phoebe Cary. Edited by Mary Clemmer Ames. New York: Hurd and Houghton; Cambridge: Riverside, 1873.

The Poems of Alice and Phoebe Cary. Edited by Mary Clemmer Ames. New York, 1873; Edited by Katherine Lee Bates. New York: Crowell, 1903.

The Poetical Works of Alice and Phoebe Cary with a Memorial of Their Lives by Mary Clemmer Ames. New York: Hurd and Houghton, 1876.

Early and Late Poems of Alice and Phoebe Cary. Boston and New York: Houghton Mifflin, 1887.

Flowers from Alice and Phoebe Cary. Boston: DeWolfe and Fiske, 1906.

Music

Our Old Homestead. Louisville, KY: Brainard, 1850.
One Sweetly Solemn Thought. New York: Lovell, 1900.

Studies of Phoebe Cary

Ames, Mary Clemmer. *A Memorial of Alice and Phoebe Cary*. New York: Hurd and Houghton, 1873.

———. *The Poetical Works of Alice and Phoebe Cary with a Memorial of Their Lives by Mary Clemmer Ames*. New York: Hurd and Houghton, 1876.

Griswold, Rufus Wilmot. *The Female Poets of America*. 2nd ed. Philadelphia: Parry and McMillan, 1859.

Hoeweller, Diane Long. "Phoebe Cary." In *American Women Writers: A Critical Reference Guide from Colonial Times to the Present*, edited by Lina Mainiero, and Langdon Lynne Faust. Vol. 1. New York: Frederick Ungar, 1979.

Kissel, Susan S. "Conservative Cincinnati and Its Outspoken Women Writers." *Queen City Heritage* 44 (1986): 20–29.

May, Caroline. *The American Female Poets: With Biographical and Critical Notes*. 2nd ed. Philadelphia: Lindsay and Blakiston, 1857.

Pulsifer, Janice. "Alice and Phoebe Cary." *Essex Institute Historical Collections* 109 (1973): 9–59.

Walker, Cheryl. "Nineteenth-Century Women Poets and Realism." *American Literary Realism* 23, no. 3 (spring 1991): 25–41.

Watts, Emily Stipes. *The Poetry of American Women from 1632 to 1945*. Austin: University of Texas Press, 1977.

CAROLINE CHESEBRO'
(CAROLINE CHESEBROUGH)
(1825–1873)

Lucy M. Freibert

BIOGRAPHY

Caroline Chesebrough, or Chesebro' as she named herself, came by the bold
and unorthodox strain in her writing naturally. Born in Canandaigua, New York,
on March 30, 1825, the fifth of eight children of Betsey Kimball and Nicholas
Goddard Chesebrough, she descended from pioneers who had founded Stoning-
ton, Connecticut, in 1649. The year after Caroline's birth, her father, a sometime
hatter, wool dealer, and postmaster, received a one-year jail sentence for joining
in a conspiracy to thwart publication of a book revealing the secrets of Free-
masonry.

Educated at the Canandaigua Seminary, Chesebro' read widely among British
and American authors. Although school records, biographical works, and bib-
liographical indexes vary the spelling of her name, she signed correspondence
"Caroline Chesebro'." In 1848, she placed her first story in *Graham's American
Monthly Magazine*. Over the next three years, while continuing to write for
Graham's, Chesebro' contributed to *Holden's Dollar Magazine*, *The Knicker-
bocker Magazine*, *Sartain's Union Magazine of Literature and Art*, *The Peterson
Magazine*, and *Godey's Lady's Book*.

By 1851, Chesebro' had gained significant recognition. J. S. Redfield published nineteen of her magazine pieces and five new stories in *Dream-Land by
Daylight, a Panorama of Romance*. In the preface, E. F. Ellet, a prominent
historian, wrote that Chesebro' deepened her sensitivity by absorbing the natural
beauty of western New York and expanded her knowledge by studying "authors
whose works display the most profound knowledge of the human heart" (viii).

After the publication of *Dream-Land*, Chesebro' placed stories chiefly in *Harper's New Monthly Magazine* but wrote also for *Appleton's Journal, Beadle's*

Monthly, Continental Monthly, The Galaxy, Lippincott's, and *Putnam's Monthly Magazine.* When *The Atlantic Monthly* began in 1857, her story "The Pure Pearl of Drover's Bay" appeared in the first volume; she continued writing for *The Atlantic* thereafter. Chesebro's published stories exceeded eighty; only a few of her poems reached print.

While building her reputation as a short fiction writer, Chesebro' also wrote novels. In 1852, when Redfield brought out the second edition of *Dream-Land,* he also published Chesebro's first novel, *Isa, a Pilgrimage,* and the following year *The Children of Light,* dedicated to her sister Catharine. Subsequent novels included *Victoria, Getting Along, Peter Carradine,* and *The Foe in the House-hold.*

In addition to writing for adults, Chesebro' also produced juvenile fiction. Her collections of moralistic stories include *The Little Cross-Bearers, The Beautiful Gate and Other Tales,* and *Blessings in Disguise* and her novels *Philly and Kit; or, Life and Raiment* and *Amy Carr; or, The Fortune-Teller.*

In 1865, Chesebro' became director of composition at Packard Collegiate Institute in Brooklyn, New York, a position she held until her death on February 16, 1873. During this period, she lived at 120 West 22nd Street in New York but also spent time with her sister and brothers who resided at Piermont, north of the city. During her years at Packard, as her correspondence indicates, Chesebro' found her teaching duties curtailing her literary output.

To provide her students an outlet for their creative work, Chesebro' initiated *The Packard Quarterly.* Shortly before her death, she proofread the issue that would carry her obituary.

MAJOR WORKS AND THEMES

Assumptions underlying Chesebro's works are the ambiguity of woman's status, woman's potential for independence, the importance of spirituality and education, and the bonding of women rather than competition between them. Themes that would inform her later works emerged in the stories collected in *Dream-Land*: the power of love, spirituality versus materialism and/or skepticism, class distinction, the artist (genius) and nature, dreams as instructive, the danger of secret marriage, and the evils of ambition.

Chesebro's unorthodoxy expands in her novels. *Isa, a Pilgrimage* combines familiar themes in a dense and somber work. Reared by a pious and wealthy foster mother, Isa develops into an educated woman and accomplished writer who aligns herself, outside the bonds of marriage, with an atheist philosopher committed to demonstrating the power of the human will. Isa's dreams lead to a complex and ambiguous conclusion.

The Children of Light, published the next year, surpasses the unconventionality of *Isa.* Combining class conflict and transcendental theories of nature and art with heterosexual and homosexual relationships, the work depicts, from childhood to maturity, the lives of three gifted women—two wealthy sisters,

Vesta and Blanche Maderon, and a working-class woman, Asia Phillips. The lesbian undertone pervading the novel emerges at the end, when Asia, rescued from suicide, receives Vesta's pledge of lifelong love and companionship.

The publication of *Peter Carradine* heralded a new direction in Chesebro's writing. The title aside, the novel focuses primarily on the community of women and the interactive lives of the whole village in which Carradine holds political eminence. When Carradine replaces the schoolteacher Miranda Roy with Mercy Fuller from Brighton, the friendship that develops between the two women, Miranda's subsequent religious conversion, and Mercy's influence on Carradine leave few villagers untouched.

The Foe in the Household, which first appeared in *The Atlantic Monthly*, was, with the possible exception of *Peter Carradine*, the best of Chesebro's novels. It interweaves multiple themes—the power of love, the danger of secret marriage, and the evil of religious rigidity. Defying the inflexible Mennonite tenet that a member might not marry outside the sect, Delia, the bishop's daughter, secretly weds a nonsectarian, thereby becoming the ''foe'' in the household, not only of her father but also, later, of the man whom she marries after her first husband's death.

CRITICAL RECEPTION

Although Chesebro's works never ranked among top sellers, she found favor with magazine editors, book publishers, and reviewers. One critic praised Chesebro's adherence ''to the inspiration of her own genius in spite of the temptation to a contrary course for the sake of popular effect'' (*Harper's* 13, 696). By the time *Dream-Land* appeared, according to *Sartain's* reviewer, Chesebro' had already ''won an enviable reputation'' by her contributions to various magazines, her work being ''rich in thought and purpose, impressed with unusual strength and poetry of imagination.'' Yet the critic found her ''bold originality of invention'' sometimes bordering on ''extravagance and startling improbability of incident'' (10, 196–197). The *Harper's* critic, on the other hand, praised her ''originality of mind'' and ''rare facility in seizing the multiform aspects of nature'' but faulted her inability to balance an ''almost masculine energy'' with a ''sweet and graceful fluency'' (4, 274).

The appearance of Chesebro's novels enhanced her reputation. Reviewers for *Harper's, Peterson's, Sartain's*, and *The Knickerbocker* all extolled the artistry of *Isa*, although some questioned its moral value. Only *The Southern Messenger* condemned it outright, calling it morally reprehensible, ''painful—shocking . . . disgusting'' (18, 319).

The Children of Light, despite its concern with seduction and the lesbian overtones of its ending, met no criticism for its morality. *Putnam's* found the novel like *Isa* in ''vigor and freshness'' but lacking ''clearness of conception'' (1, 106). *The Literary World* complained of its ''diffuseness,'' its lack of humor and character development (11, 392).

Peter Carradine met with praise everywhere. The *Harper's* reviewer considered it the "best American novel . . . written for years" and thought "no female writer in America, and not more than three in Great Britain" equal to Chesebro' in "the power of unfolding character" (27, 850).

When *The Foe in the Household* came out in book form, the reviewer for *The Atlantic Monthly* ranked it "with the very best of American fictions, . . . surpassed only by Hawthorne's romances and Mrs. Stowe's greatest work" (28, 126). *Harper's* critic agreed, writing that it "barely falls short of the first rank, at least of American novels" (43, 623).

In *A Manual of American Literature*, published in the year of her death, John S. Hart, summarizing Chesebro's twenty-year career, describes her as "rising steadily in favor." Her works, he continues, "show care and elaboration, and the improvement perceptible in the later volumes is at once evidence and fruit of honest, painstaking workmanship" (502). In 1907, reviewing his years as *Atlantic Monthly* editor, William Dean Howells placed Chesebro' among "favorites" whose excellence he recalled (100, 594). Despite these accolades, at the end of the twentieth century, Chesebro' is scarcely known; her works are out of print.

WORKS CITED

Anonymous. Review of *The Children of Light*. *The Literary World* 11 (December 1852): 392.

Anonymous. Review of *The Children of Light*. *Putnam's Monthly Magazine* 1 (January 1853): 106.

Anonymous. Review of *Dream-Land by Daylight*. *Harper's New Monthly Magazine* 4 (January 1852): 274–275.

Anonymous. Review of *Dream-Land by Daylight*. *Sartain's Magazine of Literature and Art* 10 (February 1852): 196–197.

Anonymous. Review of *The Foe in the Household*. *The Atlantic Monthly* 28 (July 1871): 126.

Anonymous. Review of *The Foe in the Household*. *Harper's New Monthly Magazine* 43 (September 1871): 623.

Anonymous. Review of *Isa, a Pilgrimage*. *The Southern Messenger* 18 (May 1852): 318–319.

Anonymous. Review of *Peter Carradine*. *Harper's New Monthly Magazine* 27 (November 1863): 850.

Anonymous. Review of *Victoria*. *Harper's New Monthly Magazine* 13 (October 1856): 696.

Ellet, E. F. Introduction to *Dream-Land by Daylight, a Panorama of Romance*, by Caroline Chesebro'. Clinton Hall, NY: Redfield, 1851.

Hart, John S. *A Manual of American Literature*. Philadelphia: Eldredge and Brother, 1873.

Howells, W[illiam] D[ean]. "Recollections of an Atlantic Editorship." *The Atlantic Monthly* 100 (November 1907): 594–606.

BIBLIOGRAPHY

Works by Caroline Chesebro'

Short Stories

Dream-Land by Daylight, a Panorama of Romance. Clinton Hall, NY: Redfield, 1851.
"The Compensation." In *The Coronal and Young Lady's Remembrancer*. Edited by Rev.
Frederic Janes. New York: James H. Pratt & Co., 1853.
"The Enigma." In *The Coronal and Young Lady's Remembrancer*. Edited by Rev. Fred-
eric Janes. New York: James H. Pratt & Co., 1853.
"The Prince at Land's End." In *Gifts of Genius: A Miscellany of Prose and Poetry, by
American Authors*. New York: C. A. Davenport, 1860.
"Victoria and Jacqueline." In *Atlantic Tales. A Collection of Stories from the Atlantic
Monthly*. No. 1. Boston: Ticknor and Fields, 1866.
"The Record of Dorcas Bently." In *Short Stories for Spare Moments. Selected from
Lippincott's Magazine*. 2nd ser. Philadelphia: J. B. Lippincott and Co., 1869.
"In Honor Bound." In *Short Stories*. Edited by Constance Cary Harrison. Distaff ser.
New York: Harper & Brothers Publishers, 1893.
"The Short Stories of Caroline Chesebro'." By Marjorie Jane Hunt. Master's thesis,
George Washington University, 1970. Contains a list of Chesebro's stories pub-
lished in magazines.

Novels

Isa, a Pilgrimage. Clinton Hall, NY: Redfield, 1852.
The Children of Light: A Theme for the Time. New York: J. S. Redfield, 1853.
Getting Along. A Book of Illustrations. New York: J. C. Derby; Boston: Phillips, Samp-
son & Co., 1855. [In two volumes. See *Susan* below.]
Susan, the Fisherman's Daughter; or, Getting Along. A Book of Illustrations. New York:
J. C. Derby; Boston: Phillips, Sampson & Co., 1855. [Two volumes in one. See
Getting Along above.]
Victoria; or, The World Overcome. New York: Derby & Jackson; Cincinnati: H. W.
Derby & Co., 1856.
Peter Carradine; or, The Martindale Pastoral. New York: Sheldon & Co.; Boston: Gould
& Lincoln, 1863.
The Fishermen of Camp's Island; or, Ye Are Not Your Own. New York: Carlton &
Porter, 1865.
The Glen Cabin; or, Away to the Hills. New York: American Tract Society, 1865.
The Foe in the Household. Boston: J. R. Osgood & Company, 1871.

Juvenile Literature

The Little Cross-Bearers. Auburn, NY: Derby & Miller; Buffalo: Derby, Orton & Mul-
ligan, 1854.
The Beautiful Gate and Other Tales. New York and Auburn: Miller, Orton, & Mulligan,
1855.
Philly and Kit; or, Life and Raiment. New York: J. S. Redfield, 1856.
Blessings in Disguise; or, Pictures of Some of Miss Haydon's Girls. New York: Carlton
& Porter, 1863.

The Sparrow's Fall; or, Under the Willow. And Other Stories. New York: Carlton & Porter, 1863.

Amy Carr; or, The Fortune-Teller. New York: M. W. Dodd, Publisher, 1864.

Studies of Caroline Chesebro'

Baym, Nina. *Woman's Fiction: A Guide to Novels by and about Women in America 1820–1870*. Ithaca: Cornell University Press, 1978. 208–230.

Blain, Virginia, Patricia Clements, and Isobel Grundy. *The Feminist Companion to Literature in English: Women Writers from the Middle Ages to the Present*. New Haven and London: Yale University Press, 1990. 201.

Fleenor, Julianne E. "Caroline Chesebro'." In Vol. 1 of *American Women Writers: A Critical Reference Guide from Colonial Times to the Present*, edited by Lina Mainiero. New York: Frederick Ungar, 1979. 346–348.

Freibert, Lucy M., and Barbara A. White, eds. *Hidden Hands: An Anthology of American Women Writers, 1790–1870*. New Brunswick, NJ: Rutgers University Press, 1985. 322–337.

Hart, John Seely. *The Female Prose Writers of America with Portraits, Biographical Notices, and Specimens of Their Writings*. Philadelphia: E. H. Butler and Co., 1852. 512–516.

Hunt, Marjorie Jane. "The Short Stories of Caroline Chesebro'." Master's thesis, George Washington University, 1970.

Meyering, Sheryl L. "Caroline Chesebro'." In *The Oxford Companion to Women's Writing in the United States*, edited by Cathy N. Davidson and Linda Wagner-Martin. New York: Oxford University Press, 1995. 164.

LYDIA MARIA CHILD
(1802–1880)

Hildegard Hoeller

BIOGRAPHY

Lydia Maria Child was born as Lydia Francis on February 11, 1802, as the youngest of five children to Convers Francis and Susannah (Rand) Francis in Medford, Massachusetts. Unlike her brother Convers, who was allowed to study at Harvard, Child never received a formal college education. She visited Miss Swan's Academy in Medford in 1814 but then, a year later, moved to Norridgewock, Maine, to live with her sister. While teaching school, Child mostly educated herself, despite her isolation, by reading classics and corresponding with her brother; she began to live with him in the summer of 1821. In 1824, and within only six weeks, Child wrote her first novel *Hobomok*, a bold depiction of miscegenation and Puritan society. The same year, she published *Evenings in New England* and met her future husband, David Lee Child. The next years saw not only her engagement to Child but also an impressive list of publications: among them many short stories, as well as *The Rebels* in 1825; *Juvenile Miscellany, Emily Parker*, and *The Juvenile Souvenir* in 1827; *Moral Lessons in Verse* (1828); and *The First Settlers of New England* (1829). By the end of 1829, when Child published her best-selling *The American Frugal Housewife*, abolitionist William Lloyd Garrison rightly called her "the first woman in the republic." This period of great popularity and success on the literary market was disrupted when Child became an outspoken abolitionist during the early 1830s. As she began to publish abolitionist short stories and finally, in 1833, *An Appeal in Favor of That Class of Americans Called Africans*, subscriptions to her *Juvenile Miscellany* dropped and forced Child to give up its publication in 1834; one year later, her library privileges at the Boston Athenaeum—which only one other woman had held during her time—were revoked. Contemporary reviewers, even when hailing her precise insight into the problems of slavery, nonetheless found it, like the public, inappropriate for a woman to take on such a strong public voice in her writing. Entering the public and "male" space of politics, Child lost her role as the "foremost lady of letters."

From there on, Child's life was dominated by writing both as a way of earning a living and as a political engagement. David Lee Child's idealistic ventures— for example, his defense of clients unable to pay for his legal services, or the plan to plant beets that would make slave labor unnecessary—left it up to Lydia to earn a living for the Child couple. While writing household advice books, children's books, and political, historical, and intellectual books, Lydia Child involved herself not only in the abolitionist movement but also in the cause of women's rights as well as the rights of Native Americans.

In 1835, David Child was arrested for debt, and Child lived the next six months with a Quaker family in New Rochelle, where she helped desegregate the village school. Later that year, she met Angelina Grimké at a meeting of the Female Anti-Slavery Society. During the 1830s Child continued to publish antislavery writing. David Child traveled to Europe to study beet sugar production. In 1838, the Childs moved to Northampton to start beet farming. In 1841, Lydia Child moved to New York to edit the *National Anti-Slavery Standard*, where she boarded with Quaker Isaac T. Hopper whose biography she later published (1853). While David Child filed for bankruptcy and moved to Washington, D.C., Lydia Child stayed in New York, published *Letters from New York*, and engaged herself in the women's rights movement. Throughout the 1840s Child continued to write both children's books such as *Flowers for Children* and political and intellectual pieces. In 1848 she began *The Progress of Religious Ideas*. In 1849 the Childs experienced a second honeymoon and moved to West Newton, Massachusetts, where they rented a farm. It was one of the very rare times in their lives that Lydia Maria Child's wishes were fulfilled and the Childs had their own household. It didn't last long. One year later, they moved to Lydia Child's father's house, where she nursed her ailing father for the next three years. In 1859, the Childs supported abolitionist John Brown by asking the governor for permission to care for him in prison; with Garrison, they organized a ceremony to honor Brown and to raise funds for the families of Brown and his men. In the early 1860s, Child's life centered around the abolitionist cause, and in 1864, Child took on the cause of the freedmen. Her *Freedmen's Book* was published in 1865. Child's political writings from then on speak for black suffrage, woman's suffrage, Native Americans' rights, and the redistribution of plantation land to provide for the freedmen. David Child died in 1874; Lydia Maria Child, six years later. She wrote until the end of her life.

MAJOR WORKS AND THEMES

Lydia Maria Child's writings impress by their sheer quantity and versatility: historical romances, short stories, political treatises, children's books, household advice books, biographies, journalistic sketches. But all of her writing seems to be informed by similar forces: a democratic mind, a keen sense of genre, and an understanding of the literary market. That Child could combine all three aspects in her writing without sacrificing one for the other is perhaps one of her most astonishing achievements. Some critics have tended to look at Child's political and domestic writing as separate, at her abolitionist writing as fundamentally different from her writing on household affairs, for example, but, in many ways, Child's entire oeuvre is connected and unified by these impulses. Child skillfully employs, manipulates, revises, even subverts available discourses to express her own convictions, to further her causes, in ways that emphasize intelligibility and relevance to most readers, not just a particular class. She must be considered as one of the most prolific, influential, talented, and truly democratic writers of her time. As such, she deserves a firm place in the American literary canon.

Her first novel, *Hobomok*, is remarkable for its daring representation of women's role in Puritan society and for its treatment of the interracial relationship between the white woman Mary and the Indian Hobomok. Child aligns the fates of Mary Conant, Hobomok, and the Episcopalian Charles Brown—the man Mary wants to marry but whom her father rejects for religious reasons—in opposition to the stern Puritan rule of Mary's father. Rather than seeing the races in opposition, Child isolates the patriarchal, Puritan community as the oppressive force that drives the plot of her novel. *Hobomok* is as remarkable for its depiction of an oppressive society and its opposing forces as it is for its complex narrative frame and different fictional genre, such as sentimental fiction and the historical romance. The novel also foreshadows Child's lifelong concern with women's rights and the rights of Native Americans; more generally, it expresses Child's interest in oppressed groups and the connecting links between them. In her next novel, *The Rebels*, set in prerevolutionary Boston, Child returns to the theme of oppression and liberation as she depicts the American colony's fight for freedom.

Often, Child's household advice books have been seen as separate and different from her fictional and political writings, and yet they are informed by similar themes. In all her work, Child is interested in making large political issues visible, intelligible, even addressable in the setting of her readers' lives. She is interested in all classes of people as they are affected by American society and tries to depict ways in which they can better their lot, find a voice, and gain their rights. Like so much of her writing, *The Frugal Housewife*, an immensely popular advice book, is an example of these concerns. A collage of recipes and general household advice, it is a specifically American book (later renamed *The American Frugal Housewife* for that reason); that is, it is unlike other books of its kind, written for "the poor." Child gives advice on household economy, trying to speak to the real and specific needs of those who are obliged to save and economize. Her specific household advice is juxtaposed with larger advice on how to "endure poverty" and manage life when one is not part of the privileged class. Both Child's democratic impulse and her desire to be both useful and reformatory are reflected in these advice books, as is Child's acute sense of the literary market. Other advice books such as *The Mother's Book* or *The Little Girl's Own Book* are equally guided by Child's realism and democratic impulse, by her desire to speak to the realities of women and not to further the cult of domesticity that painted an unrealistic and thus dangerous picture of the female sphere.

Like her household advice books, her political writings impress through their combination of realism and idealism, through their practical reformatory impulse. Although it was seen as a transgression for Child to speak out on the issue of abolition, a reviewer in the *American Monthly Review*, discussing her *An Appeal in Favor of That Class of Americans Called Africans*, felt "bound to say that Mrs. Child has treated the subject of slavery, and the collision between the Colonization and Anti-Slavery Societies, with much more temperance, with far less prejudice, and with greater ability, than Mr. Garrison or Professor Wright" (*American Monthly Review* 4 [October 1833], 298). Child's protest against slavery is based on her recognition of the humanity of the slaves, but her argument for abolition is also cold-eyed about the economical dimension of slavery. In an argument typical for her political vision, Child shows that "slavery is inconsistent with economy, whether domestic or political" (*An Appeal in Favor of That Class of Americans Called Africans* 76).

Child's political vision was one governed by the ideals of democracy and equality. For that reason, her political writings were flexible in their causes, not their principles. They encompassed the poverty of urban life, the rights of the aging, the rights of Native Americans and women, and the rights of the slaves and the freedmen.

Finally, both Child's professional situation as a writer and her democratic principles are revealed in the predominant form of her writings: that of collections, series, overviews. Her urge for democratic comprehensiveness is reflected in her intellectual interest in collecting perspectives and offering them to the reader. Just as *The Frugal Housewife* offers both a collection of specific advice and a larger vision of household economy and its relation to the "wants of the country," so does her collection of biographical writings, presented in her *Ladies' Family Library*, provide women, and men, with an impressive array of inspiring and empowering stories of women. Similarly, her collections of stories, such as her serialized *Juvenile Miscellany*, and her innovative journalistic sketches entitled *Letters from New York* both speak to the professional demands of Child's life and to her belief in the collection of perspectives, in the accumulation of specific insights to present a larger vision. Similarly, as overviews, her book *The History of the Condition of Women, in Various Ages and Nations* as well as her late book *The Progress of Religious Ideas through Successive Ages* reveal Child's characteristic interest in multiple perspectives; they parade her rare ability to connect an awareness of the relativeness of cultural ideals with, even to put at the service of, a reformatory impulse to better her own society and to critique its oppressive structures.

CRITICAL RECEPTION

Lydia Maria Child is a textbook case for the canon debate regarding nine-teenth-century American literature. Even though a major figure in her own time, Child was almost forgotten afterward. Until today, given the magnitude and importance of her writings, there has been very little criticism written on Child.

The most important critical work done on Child has been biographical. Sev-eral biographies of Lydia Maria Child bring back her life to us in full detail: Helene Baer's *The Heart Is Like Heaven* (1964), Milton Meltzer's *Tongue of Flame: The Life of Lydia Maria Child* (1965), Deborah Pickman Clifford's *Crusader for Freedom* (1992), and Carolyn Karcher's *The First Woman in the Republic: A Cultural Biography of Lydia Maria Child* (1994). These biographies have, as they should, become increasingly complex and detailed. While Meltzer and Baer laid the groundwork to give first views of Child's life, Deborah Pick-man Clifford's biography adds to the earlier ones in her use of more unpublished materials and letters by Child; interested in the paradoxes of Child's life, rather than more coherent narratives of Child as a person or role model, Clifford stresses, in her own words, the "complexity of [Lydia Maria Child's] character and the variety of her interests and concerns as a writer and reformer" (4). Carolyn Karcher's recent cultural biography is even more detailed and compre-hensive, adding close readings and detailed attention to the "historical and cul-tural matrix out of which [Child's writings] grew" (*The First Woman* xv) to Child scholarship. Both Clifford and Karcher speak to the fact that Child criti-cism is still emerging rather than established. Most of the writings on Child, with the exception of Karcher's latest biography, are still predominantly con-cerned with the necessary recovery of Child as a figure, with undoing the effect of the critical neglect that Child suffered.

Articles on Child's writing remain somewhat insular. To mention just a few, Herbert Edwards's article *The Frugal Housewife* argues in some detail that "no book was more representative of the practical and prosaic aspects of New En-gland character than Lydia M. Child's *The Frugal Housewife*" (249). It both introduces the book to the reader and places it within a historical context. Car-olyn Karcher's article "Censorship American Style" is an interesting analysis of the censorship Child encountered by publishers and the public after the pub-lication of *An Appeal*. Kirk Jeffrey's article "The Marital Experience of Lydia Maria Child" links Child's public statements to her private, marital experience, arguing that "the idiom in which Maria Child wrote about the home and women in her books and stories was the same idiom in which she thought about her own marriage" (124). Both Jennifer Fleischner's article "Mothers and Sisters" and Carolyn Karcher's article *A Romance of the Republic* discuss Child's ne-gotiation of the romance genre and the tragic mulatto figure. Discussing both *A Romance* and its precursor short story "The Quadroons," Karcher concludes that "within literary conventions that veiled the realities of race, class, and gender relations and that necessitated euphemism and obliquity, Child found it impossible to envision a truly egalitarian, multicultural society'' (100). Concentrating on "The Quadroons" and "Slavery's Pleasant Homes," Fleischner, on the other hand, stresses that Child is able to "imagine a sisterhood that can tolerate inversions of power relations" and "[to offer] an alternative view of interracial relations among women" (138).

Karcher's and Fleischner's articles begin to form a dialogue about Child's work and her relation to the romance genre. Yet, on the whole, critical readings and focused articles on Child are still few and far between; they do not yet come together as a deeply involving, coherent discussion and debate on Child's work. More work needs to be done on Child's writings; her work deserves the extended, detailed, and multifaceted critical discussions that let her writings grow in our minds and that reveal their cultural and historical as well as formal complexities.

BIBLIOGRAPHY

Works by Lydia Maria Child

Hobomok, a Tale of Early Times. Boston: Cummings, Hillard, 1824. Reprinted in *Hobomok and Other Writings on Indians.* Introduction by Carolyn Karcher. New Brunswick: Rutgers University Press, 1986.
The Rebels, or Boston before the Revolution. Boston: Cummings, Hillard, 1825.
The American Frugal Housewife. Boston: Marsh & Capen, Carter & Hendee, 1829. Current reprint of 12th ed., Boston: Applewood Books.
The Little Girl's Own Book. Boston: Carter, Hendee, and Babcock, 1831.
The Mother's Book. Boston: Carter and Hendee, 1831. Reprint, New York: Arno Press, 1972.
The Biographies of Madame de Stael and Madame Roland. Vol. I of *Ladies' Family Library.* Boston: Carter and Hendee, 1832.
The Biographies of Lady Russell and Madame Guyon. Vol. II of *Ladies' Family Library.* Boston: Carter and Hendee, 1832.
An Appeal in Favor of That Class of Americans Called Africans. Boston: Allen and Ticknor, 1833. Reprint, New York: Arno, 1968.
Good Wives. Vol. III of *Ladies' Family Library.* Boston: Carter and Hendee, 1833.
Authentic Anecdotes of American Slavery. Nos. 1–2. Newburyport, MA: Charles Whipple, 1835.
The History of the Condition of Women, in Various Ages and Nations. Vols. IV and V of *Ladies' Family Library.* Boston: J. Allen, 1835.
Anti-Slavery Catechism. Newburyport, MA: Charles Whipple, 1836.
The Evils of Slavery, and the Cure of Slavery. The First Proved by the Opinions of Southerners Themselves, the Last Shown by Historical Evidence. Newburyport, MA: Charles Whipple, 1836.
Philothea. A Romance. Boston: Otis, Broaders; New York: George Dearborn, 1836.
American Anti-Slavery Almanac for 1843. New York: American Anti-Slavery Society, 1842.
Letters from New York, First Series. New York: Charles S. Francis, 1843. *Second Series,* 1845.

Flowers for Children I, II, III. New York: C. S. Francis, 1844, 1844, 1847.

Isaac T. Hopper: A True Life. Boston: J. P. Jewett, 1853.

The Progress of Religious Ideas through Successive Ages. 3 vols. New York: C. S. Francis, 1855.

The Duty of Disobedience to the Fugitive Slave Act: An Appeal to the Legislators of Massachusetts. Boston: American Anti-Slavery Society, 1860.

The Patriarchal Institution, as Described by Members of Its Own Family. New York: American Anti-Slavery Society, 1860.

The Right Way the Safe Way, Proved by Emancipation in the British West Indies, and Elsewhere. New York: American Anti-Slavery Society, 1860.

Jacobs, Harriet A. *Incidents in the Life of a Slave Girl.* Ed. Boston: Privately published, 1861.

The Freedmen's Book. Ed. Boston: Ticknor and Fields, 1865.

Looking Toward Sunset. Ed. Boston: Ticknor and Fields, 1865.

A Romance of the Republic. Boston: Ticknor and Fields, 1867.

An Appeal for the Indians. New York: W. P. Tomlinson, 1868.

Aspirations of the World: A Chain of Opals. Ed. Boston: Roberts Brothers, 1878.

Letters of Lydia Maria Child with a Biographical Introduction by John Whittier and an Appendix by Wendell Phillips. Boston: Houghton Mifflin, 1882.

The Collected Correspondence of Lydia Maria Child, 1817–1880. Edited by Patricia Holland, Milton Meltzer, and Francince Krasno. Millwood, NY: Kraus Microform, 1980.

Lydia Maria Child: Selected Letters, 1817–1880. Edited by Milton Meltzer, Patricia G. Holland, and Francine Krasno. Amherst: University of Massachusetts Press, 1982.

Studies of Lydia Maria Child

Baer, Helene G. *The Heart Is Like Heaven.* Philadelphia: University of Pennsylvania Press, 1964.

———. "Mrs. Child and Miss Fuller." *New England Quarterly* 26 (June 1953): 249–255.

Clifford, Deborah Pickman. *Crusader for Freedom.* Boston: Beacon Press, 1992.

Edwards, Herbert. "Lydia Maria Child's *The Frugal Housewife.*" *New England Quarterly* 26 (June 1953): 243–249.

Fleischner, Jennifer. "Mothers and Sisters: The Family Romance of Antislavery Women Writers." In *Feminist Nightmares,* edited by Susan Ostrov Weisser and Jennifer Fleischner. New York: New York University Press, 1994. 125–141.

Holland, Patricia G. "*Legacy* Profile: Lydia Maria Child (1802–1880)." *Legacy: A Journal of Nineteenth Century American Women Writers* 5, no. 2 (fall 1988): 45–53.

———. "Lydia Maria Child as Nineteenth Century Professional Writer." *Studies in the American Renaissance* (1981): 157–167.

Jeffrey, Kirk. "Marriage, Career, and Feminine Ideology in Nineteenth Century America: Reconstructing the Marital Experience of Lydia Maria Child, 1828–1874." *Feminist Studies* 2 (1975): 113–130.

Karcher, Carolyn. "Censorship American Style: The Case of Lydia Maria Child." *Studies in the American Renaissance* (1986): 287–303.

———. *The First Woman in the Republic: A Cultural Biography of Lydia Maria Child.* Durham: Duke University Press, 1994.

————. "Patriarchal Society and Matriarchal Family in Irving's 'Rip van Winkle' and Child's 'Hilda Silfverling.' " *Legacy* 2, no. 2 (fall 1985): 31–44.

————. "Rape, Murder, and Revenge in 'Slavery's Pleasant Homes': Lydia Maria Child's Antislavery Fiction and the Limits of Genre." *Women's Studies International Forum* 4 (1986): 323–332.

————. "*A Romance of the Republic*: An Abolitionist Vision of America's Racial Destiny." In *Slavery and the Literary Imagination*, edited by Arnold Rampersad and Deborah E. McDowell. Baltimore: Johns Hopkins University Press, 1988. 81–103.

Meltzer, Milton. *Tongue of Flame: The Life of Lydia Maria Child.* New York: T. Y. Cromwell, 1965.

Mills, Bruce. "Lydia Maria Child and the Endings to Harriet Jacobs's *Incidents in the Life of a Slave Girl.*" *American Literature* 64, no. 2 (June 1992): 255–272.

Osborne, William S. *Lydia Maria Child.* Boston: Twayne, 1980.

Person, Leland S., Jr. "The American Eve: Miscegenation and a Feminist Frontier Fiction." *American Quarterly* 37 (1985): 668–685.

"Review of *An Appeal in Favor of That Class of Americans Called Africans,*" *American Monthly Review* 4 (October 1833): 282–298.

Streeter, Robert E. "Mrs. Child's 'Philothea'—A Transcendental Novel?" *New England Quarterly* 16 (1943): 648–654.

Yellin, Jean-Fagan. *Women and Sisters: The Anti-Slavery Feminists in American Culture.* New Haven: Yale University Press, 1989.

KATE CHOPIN
(1850–1904)

Victoria Boynton

BIOGRAPHY

Certainly, from our vantage point in the late twentieth century, Kate Chopin produced during her fifty-four years some of the most extraordinary and brilliant fiction in the American literary canon. However, this productivity began after she had lived more than two thirds of her life, embarking at thirty-nine on an extraordinary literary career. On the one hand, the first part of her life looks fairly unremarkable for where and when she lived. She did what most middle-class Southern women living during the second half of the nineteenth century did: She married, had children, and attended to her family. On the other hand, in the second phase of her life, we can see Chopin challenging convention, as does Edna Pontellier, the protagonist of her great novel *The Awakening*. By contemplating these two parts of Kate Chopin's life, we see the split between the "mother-woman" and the widow-writer, for Chopin was both loyal to normative cultural scripts and disloyal, both circumscribed by her century and her gender and actively pressing the edge of that constricting circle through her literary creation. Chopin in her twenties and thirties, married and bearing six children, was living one sort of life but quite another through her forties and early fifties, writing, publishing, and involved in literary society until her death in 1904.

In the first part of her life, although she flouted some social expectations, Chopin conformed. Nee Kate O'Flaherty, she was raised Catholic, spoke her maternal grandmother's Creole French, and read widely. At twenty, she married Oscar Chopin and moved with him to New Orleans. There, from 1870 to 1879, she lived a comfortable middle-class life, bearing five sons. During their New Orleans years, the Chopins socialized with both New Orleans Americans and

Creoles, moving across the boundaries that historically had sharply separated the people of those cultures. This culturally complex setting is key to many of the short stories and to *The Awakening*. Leaving New Orleans in 1879, Chopin was pregnant with her sixth and last child, a daughter, who was born in Natchitoches Parish, Cloutierville, where Oscar owned some small plantations and ran a general store. Cloutierville characters people the pages of her first nationally praised collection of short stories, *Bayou Folk*. Both of these Louisiana settings would be powerful influences in her fiction, but during the busy time of marriage and child rearing, Chopin was not writing.

In her 1990 biography, Emily Toth characterizes Chopin during this period as unconventional, mentioning that her smoking, flirting, and flamboyant fashion met with some disapproval from family and neighbors (20). In contrast, Per Seyersted's biography emphasizes the Chopins' popularity, both within their social class and with the poorer people of the parish. Daniel Rankin's 1932 biography paints a sunny picture of Chopin's marriage and mothering compared to Toth's feminist approach, which presents Chopin as less satisfied with the conventional role she occupied. Although biographers may differ in their slants on Chopin's married life, there is no doubt that the demands of attending to others dominated during this time of marriage and six births. In 1882, barely a decade after their marriage, Oscar Chopin died of malaria, leaving his young wife to run his business. Like Thérèse LaFirme, the hero of her novel *At Fault*, Chopin proved a capable manager. But her mother repeatedly asked her to move back to St. Louis, and in 1884, she did.

Chopin was raised in St. Louis, spent her married-mothering life in Louisiana, and returned to her mother's home in St. Louis, a widow with six children. The following year, her mother died. In the face of these deaths and within five years of her return to her home city, she began her career as a writer, quickly gaining a literary reputation, publishing her stories in regional and then national magazines. She established herself as a nationally popular writer of "local color" stories before she published *The Awakening*, and subsequently suffered the hostile reviews, and in the last four years of her life published little. Chopin died after suffering a brain hemorrhage at the World's Fair in 1904. Joyce Dyer's 1993 study describes Chopin's enthusiasm about the Fair, which was being held in St. Louis. Dyer sees the Fair as a symbol of the contradictory forces at work in Chopin's fiction, the "tension between the old and the new, between the nineteenth century and the twentieth, the traditional and the modern" (4–5). Certainly, in her life, Chopin lived through these tensions and articulated them with great beauty and keen intelligence.

MAJOR WORKS AND THEMES

Although Chopin was a translator, poet, and diarist, her greatness is defined by her fiction. As a translator of French stories, especially Maupassant's, she learned about short fiction's style and structure. As a writer of personal poetry and diaries, she exercised her expressive side. But in her fiction, her art achieves its elevated status. In this genre, she grapples with her time and place, looking deeply into her characters to discover the forces at work from within and from without.

Because she was so keenly interested in fictional locale—setting in its largest sense—an exploration of Chopin's themes makes sense only with reference to her social and historical context. Indeed, as so many scholars and reviewers have noted, she treats subjects that are "ahead of her time." And yet this very designation suggests that she is tied to her time. Like the fortune teller in "A Vocation and a Voice" who has no prescience but is especially adept at social readings of her clients, Chopin intuits the forces emerging to form the future—at once attractive, exciting, provocative, and frightening. Moreover, her themes are timely now because she so clearly wrote about issues that were only embryonic then in the thought patterns of the turn-of-the-century American.

But her treatment of these themes, most strongly articulated in her controversial work, makes clear that she was a spearhead, a hero-artist, the "courageous soul that dares and defies." Mademoiselle Reisz, the great pianist who utters this description of the artist in *The Awakening*, is the amplified echo of another musical character in Chopin's first published short story, "Wiser Than a God." Paula, the main character, decides that her music is more important than anything else, including love. She, like Mademoiselle Reisz, devotes herself to art and thus to a solitary life. Edna Pontellier, too, awakens to her own strength as an artist; however, for Edna, this artistic strength is tragically tangled with other competing and ultimately overwhelming forces, most notably erotic love, maternal care, and social duty. In any case, the devotion of these women characters to their music parallels Chopin's commitment, during the second part of her life, to her writing with its unconventional themes.

This theme of the solitary artist merges with that of the marginal character— the one whose perspective is unusual and who experiences herself as barely understood. Chopin writes about the meaning of not being understood, the feeling of isolation, the despair of the outsider and the alien spirit. Such stories as "Beyond the Bayou" and "Ma'ame Pélagie" center on marginal life, their edge-dweller protagonists physically and psychologically confined until the conclusions. Chopin, herself, was an outsider in her challenging the fictional commonplaces of her day. Initially noted as a "local colorist," paid by high-class magazines for her charming descriptive stories about the Arcadians and Creoles of Louisiana, she was increasingly conscious that artistic representation could have powerful effects. We see this critical consciousness as she investigates the artist's position in "A Gentleman of Bayou Têche." Here she critiques the artist-photographer who may rob the native Cajun of his dignity by disseminating a quaint and amusing image for the pleasure of those socially superior to him. Chopin's uncommon awareness of positioning elevates her fiction above simple local portraiture; in fact, the central theme of *The Awakening* is the evolving sense of Edna's complex position as a social subject: "In short, Mrs.

Pontellier was beginning to realize her position in the universe as a human being, and to recognize her relations as an individual to the world within and about her'' (893).

Although critical debates continue about Chopin's gender politics, she most certainly was a social critic. Though she was never allied explicitly with the strong feminist movements of her day and though she was explicitly critical of Ibsen's dramas of social commentary, Chopin is undeniably an architect of new thought about women's identity. Yet her style is nowhere didactic. Her fiction instead traces the intricate and contradictory patterns of social forces within and between particular individuals. As she draws her most forceful depictions, she unveils characters torn between urge and institution, between the need to belong and the longing to be independent, between other-love and self-love. Her best fiction shows characters negotiating these contrary and multiple forces. Thus, through Chopin's depiction of characters embedded in social setting, readers come to know the peculiar and powerful ways that social subjects evolve and operate in the world.

Though interested in characters who are men, women, boys, or girls; who were wealthy, middle class, or poor; who were black or white or combinations thereof, Kate Chopin primarily hinges her fiction on explorations of female experience. Descriptions of the social and economic positions of women permeate the work, and questions of how women negotiate the social realities of the day form an undeniable thematic complex at the core of her fiction. The key interpenetrating themes included in this complex are the conflicts between women's search for autonomy and their loyalty to the caring and nurturing roles they have held historically; the evolution of women's social and economic identities beyond their absolute dependence on men; the balancing of the imperatives of the body and the mind; and the corollary investigation of women's place in the heterosexual matrix, the biological consequences of that position, and its impact on women's sense of self and world.

We can approach this thicket of themes by looking at the women who are most independent, most strong-headed, most determined to assert their autonomy, characters such as Calixta, not as she appears in the early story ''At the 'Cadian Ball'' but in the 1898 story ''The Storm,'' and Mademoiselle Reisz and Edna Pontellier in *The Awakening*. These women act in direct opposition to social convention and make choices for themselves despite the pressure of social consequences. Some other women characters have many of the same powerful personalities but cannot sustain their autonomy in the face of their situations. For instance, Zaïda in ''A Night in Arcadie'' and Athénaïse and Charlie in the stories by those names all exhibit the potential to direct their lives as powerful, autonomous women, but each succumbs to the pressures embedded in their situations. Zaïda is finally humbled by her unfortunate choice of a man; Athénaïse is transformed from the rebel to the good wife by her pregnancy; and Charlie is converted from masculine to feminine identification to please her father. Edna Pontellier, in contrast to her foil Adèle Ratignolle, asserts her unconventional desires and takes action on them. However, Adèle, who is allied with custom and convention, lives, while Edna, who is allied with none but herself, dies. Chopin illustrates in much of her fiction how a powerful woman, seeking her own identity—that which defines her "essential" being outside of imposed social expectations—is repeatedly subjected to pressure that taxes her socially and psychologically.

This theme of independent women exploring the complications of freedom has its counterpart, the theme of dominant men who define women as possessions, attendants, and ornamental objects. In such stories as "At the 'Cadian Ball," "At Chênière Caminada," "The Gentleman from New Orleans," "In Sabine," and *The Awakening*, Chopin presents men who both consciously and unconsciously conspire with the oppressive social forces that restrict women by defining them as possessions and preventing their autonomy.

In her treatment of women's position, Chopin was especially sensitive to women's dependence on men. Although in the post–Civil War South the position of women was undergoing drastic change, the dependence of women on men powerfully shaped life's possibilities for women. In this context, many of Chopin's women characters struggle with the question of economic independence. Athénaïse, in the story by that title, runs away from her husband but sits idly with her brother's funds supporting her escape and with little possibility of working. When she tries to find work, she discovers that the little money she might earn from teaching piano would be "embarrassing." But Thérèse in *At Fault* runs her dead husband's plantation, and both Mademoiselle Reisz and Edna Pontellier in *The Awakening* are, importantly, self-sufficient and thus able to assert themselves outside of the social template. They are beyond the economic control of men that exerts itself so quietly and yet so fiercely in her fiction.

As the strict antebellum prohibitions against women's economic independence eased, the corollary notion that a woman's "true" occupation was in the home with her children—the angel of the hearth—began to break down also. Themes centering on women's position as wife and mother are central to Chopin's corpus. While, on one hand, Chopin's work seeks to demystify and to critique the romantic notions of childbearing and mothering, her fiction also cuts in another direction, reflected in her diary as she writes of her oldest son's birth: "The sensation with which I touched my lips and my finger tips to his soft flesh only comes once to a mother. It must be the pure animal sensation; nothing spiritual could be so real—so poignant" (Seyersted 40). Similarly, in the story "Regret," an older woman who has never had children is forced to care for four of them over several weeks. Their delights grow on Mamzelle Aurélie, and she is heartbroken when they go away finally with their mother. Mother-love is also clear in "Désirée's Baby," an ironic story of confused origins, racism, and reproduction in which Chopin renders the mother-child bond tenderly. The baby of the title is, importantly, Désirée's, rather than her husband's. And for Athénaïse, as soon as she realizes that she is pregnant, she is "transfigured . . . with love and rapture'' (451). Pregnancy instantly persuades Athénaïse to return to her husband and reconcile to her married state. Before her desertion, she had ''called marriage a trap'' (434), but after her return, ''her lips for the first time respond to the passion of his own'' (454).

But finally, Chopin's greatest work has a searing ambivalence about mother-child relations. The delights of motherhood, the fears of being an unfit mother, and the oppressive singularity of a mother's identity clash with one another in her most powerful fiction. *The Awakening* especially treats this theme. As Edna walks toward the Gulf about to drown herself, she recalls Adèle, who has advised her to ''think of the children,'' but Edna is torn between images of her children both as loved ones and as ''antagonists who had over come her . . . and had sought to drag her into the soul's slavery for the rest of her days'' (999).

Intricately tied to themes of women's identity as wives and mothers is the theme of sexuality. A pioneer of passion as a serious and legitimate theme, Chopin has been strongly associated with the exploration of women's sexuality. Women's embodiment and the body's desires are central themes in her later work particularly, and perhaps more than any other theme, desire has stirred strong reaction to her fiction. Stories exemplifying the theme of transgressive desire include ''A Respectable Woman'' and ''The Storm,'' both of which depict a married woman's desire outside the bounds of her marriage. But the prime example is *The Awakening*. Sensuous and straightforward in its treatment of extramarital sexuality, it shocked readers in 1899. When it was revived in the 1950s, Kenneth Eble's much-quoted line ''quite frankly the book is about sex'' indicates the continuing erotic power of the novel. Per Seyersted discusses Chopin's courage in treating sexuality: ''Revolting against tradition and authority; with a daring which we can hardly fathom today; with an uncompromising honesty and no trace of sensationalism, she undertook to give the unsparing truth about woman's submerged life'' (198). In her treatment of sexuality, again Chopin concerned herself with social conventions and the testing of their boundaries. In Chopin's fiction, women claiming their desire are women claiming themselves. However, as transgressors of the social conventions governing sexuality, they are also women at risk, just as Chopin herself was in her publishing work that dealt with such themes.

Given the social tensions amid which Chopin worked and out of which she fashioned her fiction, it is no wonder that her writing also deals with the psychological repercussions of these tensions. Depression, alcoholism, suicide, and madness are central to ''Mrs. Mobrey's Reason,'' *At Fault*, ''Her Letters,'' and *The Awakening*. Some of her most tragic and poignant stories hinge on psychological breakdown. For instance, ''Désirée's Baby'' and ''La Belle Zoraïde'' show the destructive psychological effects of racist thought and action. In the second story, the cruelly manipulative control exercised by the white woman drives her light-skinned slave mad. And in the first, the power constructed around racial background destroys a marriage. These themes that revolve around the psychologically unstable individual simply confirm the challenging social positions that characters occupy in Chopin's fiction.

CRITICAL RECEPTION

Although Chopin was a proverbial late bloomer, she established a literary reputation impressively soon after beginning to write. Having returned to St. Louis a widow, only to have her mother die the following year, she began writing on the advice of a doctor friend. After publishing her first stories— "Wiser Than a God" and "A Point at Issue!"—in 1889 in small magazines, she hungered for a wider readership. In 1890, she published her first novel, *At Fault*, at her own expense, receiving some critical acknowledgment that spurred her on to publish short stories in *Harper's* ("Boulôt and Boulotte," 1891) and *Vogue* ("A Visit to Avoyelles" and "Désirée's Baby," 1893). It was not long before she was a national success.

For Chopin, 1894 was a wonderful year. Not only did her volume of short stories *Bayou Folk* earn high praise, but other short stories, including "A No-Account Creole," were printed in *Century* and the *Atlantic*. And in the wake of the reviews, she wrote her much-anthologized "The Story of an Hour," which was published in *Vogue*. This publishing sprint initiated her literary career, followed by the 1897 publication of *A Night in Arcadie*.

Chopin was a literary success at this point. However, with the publication of *The Awakening* came a critical tempest, exemplified in Margaret Culley's collection of ten representative reviews. Willa Cather castigates the novel for its depiction of passion controlling the individual and lumps Chopin into the category of the woman author who "demands more romance out of life than God put into it." Cather, like so many others, applauds Chopin's style while denouncing the "trite and sordid" theme (Culley 153). These collected reviews call the novel "unhealthily introspective and morbid in feeling" (152), "not a healthy book" (146), "sad and mad and bad" (149), "an essentially vulgar story" (151), and "gilded dirt" (150). The *Public Opinion* reviewer states bluntly that "we are well satisfied when Mrs. Pontellier deliberately swims out to her death in the gulf" (Culley 151). These comments, and others like them, are cited in virtually all recent studies of Chopin. In fact, this novel's dramatic critical reception has fascinated Chopin scholars and may have been an element in the novel's revival. As Emily Toth argues, "Although there is no library evidence that *The Awakening* was ever banned or withdrawn (as reported by Rankin and Seyersted), the myth of book banning has done more than anything else to revive contemporary interest in Chopin's writing" ("Shadow" 287–288).

Indeed, the American imagination responds powerfully to the rebel and the iconoclast, and Chopin's image of the "courageous soul that dares and defies" draws us in. Chopin identifies herself with this rebel artist in an 1894 essay as she criticizes literary conventionality and sentimental fiction. The irony is that

Edna, unable to achieve this autonomous ideal of the artist, kills herself; similarly, the injured Chopin apologizes for Edna after the surge of hostile reviews—''I never dreamed of Mrs. Pontellier making such a mess of things'' (Culley 159)—and publishes only three stories before her death five years later.

For the fifty-plus years between her death and *The Awakening*'s resurrection, Chopin was known as a writer of local color short stories, and her posthumous literary reputation remained focused away from *The Awakening* until mid-twentieth century. John Haney's *The Story of Our Literature*, published by Scribner in 1923, provides a supplementary list of literary works including *Bayou Folk* and *A Night in Arcadie*. *The Awakening* does not appear anywhere in the volume. Nearly a decade later in 1932, Bradford Fullerton's *Selective Bibliography of American Literature 1775–1900* points to the thin critical attention to Chopin generally but praises her highly for her short stories. In 1936, *The National Cyclopedia of American Biography* raves about two of her short stories and alludes to *The Awakening*'s hostile reception in America. The next year, Joseph Reilly writes in *Commonweal*, ''She is incomparably the greatest American short story writer of her sex. Her work deserves wider appreciation'' (606–607). The 1941 edition of *The Oxford Companion to American Literature* continues to focus on the short stories as the heart of Chopin's work, referring to *The Awakening* in terms of its shocked readers and its ''morbid psychology.'' This focus on Chopin's short fiction continues in Spiller's 1948 *Literary History of the United States*, in which discussion of Chopin's work is confined to her short stories. *The Awakening* is not mentioned.

However, two years earlier, in 1946, Cyrille Arnavon published an essay that did not classify Chopin as a local colorist but instead included her in the prestigious group of American realists, including Norris and Dreiser. Also he notes connections between Chopin's work and that of Maupassant, whom she admired and translated, and Flaubert, whose *Madame Bovary* has parallels to *The Awakening*. In France, in 1952, Arnavon translated *The Awakening*, titling it *Edna* and introducing it with high praise for the power of its psychological portrait and calling for its resurrection from obscurity.

Finally, in 1952, Van Wyck Brooks cites *The Awakening*, calling it ''one small, perfect book that mattered more than the whole life work of many a prolific writer'' (341). Though he gives the novel scant space, this short discussion in *The Confident Years* signals a shift away from omission or condemnation of its disturbing themes. During the mid-1950s, Chopin's reputation continued to shift, with Kenneth Eble's call for critical resurrection in *Western Humanities Review*. His article, ''A Forgotten Novel: Kate Chopin's *The Awakening*,'' could not have had a more apt title. She is called ''a pioneer in the creative presentation of psychological realism in America'' in the 1955 edition of the *Concise Dictionary of American Literature*.

In 1969, Per E. Seyersted's *Complete Works of Kate Chopin* made available *At Fault*, Chopin's first novel, and all of the short stories, many of which had not been published before. With this publication, Chopin criticism proliferated.

Also in that year, his *Kate Chopin: A Critical Biography* was published. Since 1970, when Louis Leary edited the anthology *The Awakening and Other Stories* with Holt, Rinehart and Winston, many major publishers have printed collections of Chopin's work featuring *The Awakening*: The Feminist Press, Modern Library, Bantam, Penguin, Random House, and Norton. Culley's 1976 Norton Critical Edition, Bloom's 1987 Modern Critical Views collection, and Koloski's 1988 Modern Language Association *Approaches to Teaching Chopin's "The Awakening"* along with numerous recent book-length studies and collections make clear that Chopin's work has earned its place in the canon of major American writers.

Interestingly, in 1969, Seyersted ranked Chopin at the end of his life study: "She obviously does not come near to the breadth and stature of Dreiser, but among the American authors of second rank she occupies an important and distinctive position" (198). Seyersted has been proved wrong in his estimation. Chopin has risen through the ranks to join men like Dreiser at the apex of the American canon.

WORKS CITED

Arnavon, Cyrille. "Les Debuts du Roman Realiste Americain et l'Influence Francaise." In *Romanciers Americans Contemporains*, edited by Henri Kerst. Paris: Mason et cie, 1946. 9–35.

Brooks, Van Wyck. *The Confident Years: 1885–1915*. New York: Dutton, 1952.

Chopin, Kate. *The Complete Works of Kate Chopin*. Edited by Per Seyersted. 2 vols. Baton Rouge: Louisiana State University Press, 1969.

Culley, Margaret, ed. *The Awakening: An Authoritative Text, Contexts, Criticism*. Norton Critical Edition. New York: Norton, 1976.

Dyer, Joyce. *The Awakening: A Novel of Beginnings*. New York: Twayne, 1993.

Eble, Kenneth. "A Forgotten Novel: Kate Chopin's *The Awakening*." *Western Humanities Review* 10 (summer 1956): 261–269.

Fullerton, Bradford. *Selective Bibliography of American Literature 1775–1900*. New York: William Farquhar Payson, 1932.

Haney, John. *The Story of Our Literature*. New York: Scribner, 1923.

Hart, James. *The Oxford Companion to American Literature*. New York: Oxford University Press, 1941.

The National Cyclopedia of American Biography. New York: James T. White, 1936.

Rankin, Daniel S. *Kate Chopin and Her Creole Stories*. Philadelphia: University of Pennsylvania Press, 1932.

Reilly, Joseph. "Stories by Kate Chopin." *Commonweal* 25 (1937): 606–607.

Richards, Robert. *Concise Dictionary of American Literature*. New York: Philosophical Library, 1955.

Seyersted, Per. *Kate Chopin: A Critical Biography*. Oslo: University of Oslo Press, 1969.

Spiller, Robert, Willard Thorp, Thomas H. Johnson, Henry S. Canby, and Richard H. Ludwig, eds. *Literary History of the United States*. New York: Macmillan, 1948.

Toth, Emily. *Kate Chopin*. New York: William and Morrow, 1990.

———. "The Shadow of the First Biographer: The Case of Kate Chopin." *Southern Review* 26 (April 1990): 285–292.

Wilson, Edmund. *Patriotic Gore*. New York: Oxford University Press, 1962.

BIBLIOGRAPHY

Works by Kate Chopin

At Fault. St. Louis: Nixon-Jones Printing Company, 1890.

Bayou Folk. Boston: Houghton Mifflin, 1894.

A Night in Arcadie. Chicago: Way and Williams, 1897.

The Awakening. Chicago: Herbert S. Stone, 1899.

The Complete Works of Kate Chopin. Edited by Per Seyersted. 2 vols. Baton Rouge: Louisiana State University Press, 1969.

The Awakening: An Authoritative Text, Contexts, Criticism. Edited by Margaret Culley. New York: Houghton Mifflin, 1976.

A Kate Chopin Miscellany. Edited by Per Seyersted and Emily Toth. Natchitoches, LA: Northwestern State University Press, 1979.

A Vocation and a Voice. Edited by Emily Toth. New York: Penguin, 1991.

Studies of Kate Chopin

Bauer, Dale. "Kate Chopin's *The Awakening*: Having and Hating Tradition." In *Feminist Dialogics: A Theory of Failed Community*. Edited by Dale Bauer. Albany: State University of New York Press, 1988. 129–158.

Baym, Nina. Introduction to *The Awakening and Selected Stories*. New York: Modern Library, 1981. vii–xi.

Bloom, Harold, ed. *Kate Chopin*. Modern Critical Views Series. New York: Chelsea House, 1987.

Bonner, Thomas. *The Kate Chopin Companion, with Chopin's Translations from French Fiction*. Westport, CT: Greenwood Press, 1988.

Boren, Lynda, and Sara deSaussure Davis, eds. *Kate Chopin Reconsidered: Beyond the Bayou*. Baton Rouge: Louisiana State University Press, 1992.

Dyer, Joyce. *The Awakening: A Novel of Beginnings*. New York: Twayne, 1993.

Elfenbein, Anna Shannon. "Kate Chopin: From Stereotype to Sexual Realism." In *Women on the Color Line: Evolving Stereotypes and the Writings of George Washington Cable, Grace King, Kate Chopin*. Charlottesville: University Press of Virginia, 1989. 117–157.

Ewell, Barbara C. *Kate Chopin*. New York: Ungar, 1986.

Koloski, Bernard, ed. *Approaches to Teaching Chopin's "The Awakening."* New York: Modern Language Association, 1988.

Martin, Wendy, ed. *New Essays on "The Awakening."* Cambridge: Cambridge University Press, 1988.

Papke, Mary. *Verging on the Abyss: The Social Fiction of Kate Chopin and Edith Wharton*. Westport, CT: Greenwood Press, 1990.

Rankin, Daniel S. *Kate Chopin and Her Creole Stories*. Philadelphia: University of Pennsylvania Press, 1932.

Scaggs, Peggy. *Kate Chopin*. Twayne's United States Authors Series, ed. David J. Nor-
    dloh. Boston: Twayne Publishers, 1985.
Taylor, Helen. "Kate Chopin." In *Gender, Race and Region in the Writing of Grace
    King, Ruth McEnery Stuart, and Kate Chopin*. Baton Rouge: Louisiana State
    University Press, 1989. 138–202.
Toth, Emily. *Kate Chopin: A Life of the Author of "The Awakening."* New York: Wil-
    liam Morrow, 1990.
Walker, Nancy. *"The Awakening."* Boston: Bedford Books of St. Martin's Press, 1993.

LOUISE AMELIA KNAPP SMITH CLAPPE (DAME SHIRLEY) (1819–1906)

Samantha Manchester Earley

BIOGRAPHY

Louise Amelia Knapp Smith Clappe, who adopted the pseudonym Dame Shirley, was born to Moses and Lois (Lee) Smith in Elizabeth, New Jersey, in 1819. Her father, headmaster and teacher, moved the family from New Jersey to Amherst, Massachusetts, shortly before his death in 1832. Shirley was just thirteen years old when her father died; her mother died five years later, leaving the three brothers and four sisters under the guardianship of Amherst attorney Osmyn Baker. The care of seven orphans soon proved to be too much for one guardian, however, and the brothers and sisters scattered to boarding schools, relatives and friends, and apprenticeships around New England. Shirley and her younger sister Mary Jane (the Molly to whom the Shirley letters are addressed) remained together. In the years following her mother's death and before receiving her inheritance of $2,500, Shirley, along with Mary Jane, was enrolled in boarding school, first in Boston and later in Amherst. In school, the girls studied writing, read the standard authors, learned several foreign languages, and received music lessons.

Shirley's feeble health prompted her guardian to send her on occasional sojourns to the mountains. In a stagecoach in the hills of Vermont, she met Alexander Hill Everett, distinguished diplomat, author, and editor, and the two fell into lively conversation. After the coach trip ended, Everett, much intrigued by the beautiful, well-read young woman, struck up a correspondence with Shirley that lasted from 1839 to 1847. Everett's forty-six letters to Shirley are filled mainly with encouragement and advice from a mentor to his protégée on authors she should read and subjects about which she should write. Everett did not limit his letters to the discussion of literature, however, and when Shirley, who was

half his age, rejected him as a suitor and informed him of her decision to marry
Fayette Clappe, he reacted as a spurned, jealous lover, demanding to know all
the particulars of her bridegroom. Everett died in China in June 1847, four
months after he learned of Shirley's betrothal.

Shirley's fiance, Fayette Clappe, was originally trained in the ministry at
Brown University but after graduation decided to study medicine. He appren-
ticed himself to his older sister's husband and attended Castleton Medical College in Vermont for a period of time, then interrupted his studies to marry
Shirley and migrate to California. He received his medical degree from Castleton
in absentia in 1851.

Shirley married Clappe in 1848 or 1849, when she was thirty and he twenty-
five. The two of them suffered from weak health, but her headaches and his
"bilious attacks" indicate fragile nervous systems and possible hypochondria.
Unlikely pair that they were to rough it in the California mines, the two set sail
on the *Manilla* in 1849. Once they got to California, they spent one year in San
Francisco, waiting for Fayette's attacks to clear and his body to strengthen.
Finally, in June 1851, Fayette left for the mines, hoping that the mountain air
would restore his health and a medical practice near the miners would restore
his wallet. Shirley spent her summer on a ranch ten miles from Marysville and,
in September, joined her husband in Rich Bar on the north fork of the Feather
River.

On this fork of the Feather River, Shirley wrote twenty-three letters to her
sister Molly, six from Rich Bar and thirteen from Indian Bar, where Fayette
finally built a log cabin. The two of them lived and thrived there, until the
mining company went bankrupt. They left the mines in November 1852, narrowly escaping before the first storm of the season sealed the pass. They tried
to settle in San Francisco but soon separated. Fayette spent some time in the
Sandwich Islands, returned to Massachusetts in 1854, and located in Columbia,
Missouri, in 1855. Shirley filed for divorce in San Francisco on October 20,
1856, which was granted on April 4, 1857. Fayette remarried in Missouri around
that time.

Shirley spent the next twenty-some years of her life writing and teaching in
the San Francisco schools. She adopted and raised her niece Genevieve Stebbins
and finally retired from teaching in 1878 to go live with her niece in New York.
She continued to write, traveled to Europe, and finally moved to a retirement
home kept by Bret Harte's nieces in Morristown, New Jersey. She died there
on February 9, 1906.

MAJOR WORKS AND THEMES

Shirley had a love of the literary and wrote all her life. While a few of her
poems, including "Leverett: An Epistle from a Lady in the Country to a Distant
Friend" and " 'Alone': A Reminiscence of Margaret Fuller Ossoli," and many
of her letters, especially those to the *Marysville Herald* and *The Helmuth World*,

were published, Shirley's best-known work is her collection of letters written from the California gold mines to her sister in the East. These letters were originally published in 1854 in *The Pioneer*, a short-lived California periodical, but were later collected and published in book form in 1922, 1933, 1949, and 1970.

The Shirley Letters are one woman's description and interpretation of everyday living in the California gold mines. Her detailed depiction of the habitations of the miners and their cooking, eating, drinking, and washing practices are of great value to those curious about the living arrangements of the gold hunters. She records the menus of the celebratory meals of the camp, and she describes what they ate when the supplies began to run short (Letter Sixth). In both instances, canned oysters, canned beef, and canned ham were plentiful, but dairy products and fresh fruits and vegetables were scarce.

Shirley also provides a detailed account of the mining techniques of the time. Flumes, water systems, long-toms, and panning come under her scrutiny (Letter Fifteenth). Shirley learned how to pan for gold, which was hardly worth it, she claims, as she ruined all her clothes, sunburned her face beyond recognition, and caught a cold, all for a measly amount of gold dust (Letter Fifteenth).

Shirley also comments on male-female relationships and political battles over women's rights. Shirley's husband does not appear as a major figure in any of her letters, and when she does tell Molly about him, she is not complimentary. She is impatient with Fayette for being sick for a year in San Francisco (Letter First), irritated that he gets them lost in the mountains on their way to Rich Bar (Letter First), and exasperated when he repeatedly loses money in unsuccessful mining operations (Letter Sixth). After the sixth letter, Fayette is only mentioned in passing (he went here; he asked me to do this), and henceforth Shirley's voice and identity appear to derive from experiencing what *she* wants to experience, such as visiting a mining operation (Letter Fifteenth) or watching the Christmas and New Year revelry of the miners (Letter Twelfth). While her independent life in the wilds of California reflects the modern, "women's liberation" spirit of the "Bloomers," Shirley's few comments on these women are biting (Letter Tenth). She wonders how the Bloomers can spoil their complexions, figures, and minds by spouting ugly words, wearing men's clothing, and studying boring metaphysical treatises.

Shirley also describes and comments upon the relations between the various nationalities as they converge in California. After 1852, when gold was becoming scarce, the "Yanks" began to resent the Spaniards. According to Shirley, the Yanks were suspicious of anyone who couldn't speak English. Also, as tensions escalated with Mexico, the more violent, less enlightened Americans tended to lump all foreign speakers together and assume that they were plotting to murder the English speakers (Letters Thirteenth, Fourteenth, Sixteenth, Eighteenth, Nineteenth).

While Shirley deplores the Americans' lack of compassion and respect toward these foreigners, her account of her meetings with the Native American cultures is not so enlightened. She expresses the dominant contemporary stereotype of Native Americans as either noble savage (Letter First) or primitive animal (Letter Seventeenth).

CRITICAL RECEPTION

Most critics agree that Shirley's poetry and the letters she intended for publication are so Victorianly ornate and trite as to be unreadable and unimportant. The letters to Molly, however, the letters she intended for family eyes only, bring nothing but praise from the critics and historians. Her direct, vivid description of California wildlife—in its human and nonhuman forms—her representation of living conditions in the mines, and her commentary on national and race relations are deemed some of the best depictions and criticism of the times. These letters are considered a great resource for the study of nineteenth-century California. Richard Oglesby focuses his "Introduction" to the 1970 edition of her letters on the mining culture of the 1840s and 1850s and Shirley's apt portrayal of it. Josiah Royce also takes much of his information about California mining life from Shirley.

Shirley influenced many writers of the time, including Charles Warren Stoddard and Bret Harte. In fact, Bret Harte has been accused of plagiarizing some of his more vivid California scenes from Shirley's letters, including the death-in-the-snow scene from "The Outcasts of Poker Flats" and the funeral scene from "The Luck of Roaring Camp." Thomas Russell provides a detailed comparison of Shirley's and Harte's work in his "Printer's Forward" to the 1922 edition of her letters. Shirley's 1881 essay "Unconscious Plagiarism" attempted to clear Harte of all wrong doing, yet most critics remain convinced of Harte's guilt.

The most complete biographical reconstruction of Shirley's life is Rodman Wilson Paul's article "In Search of 'Dame Shirley.' " Sandra Lockhart's "*Legacy* Profile" of Shirley provides a fairly complete history of Shirley's life and a brief analysis of the major themes found in her letters. Lawrence Clark Powell's "California Classics Reread: The Shirley Letters" offers an overview of Shirley's life and literary endeavors.

Shirley's letters are an invaluable resource for those interested not only in the life of the California gold mines but also in an educated woman's perspective on that life—the living conditions, the special trials for women, and their solutions to those problems. Dame Shirley lived the "feminist" life that the Bloomers merely discussed.

BIBLIOGRAPHY

Works by Dame Shirley

"Leverett: An Epistle from a Lady in the Country to a Distant Friend." *United States Magazine and Democratic Review* 15 (1844): 360–362.

Letters. *Marysville Herald*, April–July 1851.

"California, in 1851." *The Pioneer* 1 (1854): 41; 2 (1854): 23; 3 (1855): 80; 4 (1855): 22.

"Unconscious Plagiarism." *The Helmuth World*, 18 June 1881, 65–66.

" 'Alone': A Reminiscence of Margaret Fuller Ossoli, by Shirley Lee." *The Shirley Letters from the California Mines in 1851–52*. Edited by Thomas C. Russell. San Francisco: Privately printed, 1922. xxxiii–xxxiv.

The Shirley Letters from the California Mines in 1851–52. Edited by Thomas C. Russell. San Francisco: Privately printed, 1922.

California in 1851–1852: The Letters of Dame Shirley. Edited by Carl I. Wheat. 2 vols. San Francisco: Grabhorn Press, 1933.

The Shirley Letters from the California Mines, 1851–1852. Edited by Carl I. Wheat. New York: Knopf, 1949.

The Shirley Letters: Being Letters Written in 1851–1952 from the California Mines. Introduction by Richard Oglesby. Salt Lake City: Peregrine Smith, 1970.

Studies of Dame Shirley

Gray, Dorothy. *Women of the West*. Millbrae, CA: Les Femmes, 1976.

Lawrence, Mary Viola Tingley. "An Appreciation." *The Shirley Letters from the California Mines in 1851–52*. Edited by Thomas C. Russell. San Francisco: Privately printed, 1922. xxvii–xxxii.

Lockhart, Sandra. "*Legacy* Profile: Louise Amelia Knapp Smith Clappe (Dame Shirley) (1819–1906)." *Legacy* 8, no. 2 (1991): 141–148.

Oglesby, Richard E. Introduction to *The Shirley Letters: Being Letters Written in 1851–1852 from the California Mines*. Salt Lake City: Peregrine Smith, 1970. v–xviii.

Paul, Rodman Wilson. "In Search of 'Dame Shirley.' " *Pacific Historical Review* 33 (1964): 127–146.

Powell, Lawrence Clark. "California Classics Reread: The Shirley Letters." *Westways* 61, no. 12 (1969): 26–29, 40.

Royce, Josiah. *California from the Conquest in 1846 to the Second Vigilance Committee in San Francisco*. Boston: Houghton Mifflin Co., 1886. 344–356.

Russell, Thomas C., ed. Foreword to *The Shirley Letters from California in 1851–52*. San Francisco: Privately printed, 1922. v–xxvi.

Wheat, Carl I., ed. Introduction to *California in 1851–1852: The Letters of Dame Shirley*. 2 vols. San Francisco: Grabhorn Press, 1933. 1, v–xviii.

———. Introduction to *The Shirley Letters from the California Mines, 1851–1852*. New York: Knopf, 1949. vii–xix.

———. "A Retrospect: Dame Shirley, Ewer, & *The Pioneer*." *California in 1851–52: The Letters of Dame Shirley*. 2 vols. San Francisco: Grabhorn Press, 1933. 2, v–xviii.

ROSE TERRY COOKE
(1827–1892)

Gail C. Keating

BIOGRAPHY

Rose Terry Cooke was born on a farm six miles outside of Hartford, Connecticut, to parents distinguished not only because of their Puritan ancestry but also
because of their impressive lineage. Her father, Henry Wadsworth Terry, a landscape gardener, was the son of a Hartford bank president and a descendant of
a Wadsworth who had come to Cambridge in 1632 before settling in Hartford
in 1636. Her mother was the daughter of John Hurlbut, the first New England
shipbuilder to sail around the world. Both parents, however, were respected
more for their heritage than for any personal accomplishments since their financial success was tenuous at best and the family lived for the most part on
inherited wealth. From her father, Terry gained a knowledge and love of nature
since, like Sarah Orne Jewett, her health was delicate, and she spent much of
her time driving through and walking in the woods and fields of Connecticut
with him. It was from her mother, who insisted she study the dictionary and
keep a daily journal, that she received her early training in literature. It was also
from her mother, a morbidly conscientious woman, that she inherited her religious nature, which brought about her conversion at sixteen, making her a devoted churchwoman. Due to her family's financial instability, they moved into
her grandmother Terry's eighteenth-century mansion in Hartford when she was
six, and it was there she became an efficient housekeeper, connecting with the
past that was so important to many New England writers. Years later, she still
held fond memories of the lavish holiday rituals celebrated at her grandmother's
and admired the efficient management of the Terry household.

Rose Terry Cooke's upbringing was typical of young women of her class in

New England. She was educated for domesticity at Catharine Beecher's Hartford Female Seminary, graduating in 1843 at the age of sixteen, after which she became a member of the Congregational Church, a religious commitment she kept throughout life. Like many intelligent, middle-class nineteenth-century women, she began supporting herself by teaching, first in Hartford, and then for three years in a Presbyterian school in Burlington, New Jersey, where she also spent a year as a governess for a clergyman's family. In 1848 she received a small inheritance from her favorite uncle, Daniel Wadsworth, which enabled her to give up teaching, return to her family in Hartford, and concentrate on her career as a writer.

Upon returning home to Connecticut, she cared for her aging parents until they died and for her deceased sister's children, always, however, finding time between her household duties for writing. In the beginning, her main interest was in verse, the traditional religious and sentimental type popular at the time. Finding it difficult, however, to find financial success in writing poetry, she soon began writing prose for magazines. Her first major piece was published in *Putnam's* in 1855, and by the time she was thirty she had gained such a reputation that she was asked to contribute the lead story for the first issue of *The Atlantic Monthly* in 1857, titled "Sally Parson's Duty." She published a great deal in the 1850s, but the 1860s were a dry period, possibly due to the ill health she suffered from all her life.

An independent woman, Cooke was proud of her ability to support herself, but the volume of work she produced in later life was mostly a result of financial need. In 1843, at the age of forty-six, she was married for the first time to Rollin H. Cooke, a widower with two children, whom she met at a boarding house in Boston when she was there to study art. They settled in Winsted, Connecticut, but the marriage created a tremendous financial burden for her. Rollin Cooke was never able to earn a steady income and moved from one job to another as bank clerk, real estate agent, genealogist, and iron manufacturer, never earning a decent living at any of them. It was his father's business failure, however, that ultimately caused her financial difficulties, since, in an attempt to save him, she lost all she had inherited and earned.

As the financial mainstay of her family, Cooke was forced to write "potboilers," selling her stories to magazines that paid the fastest. Most of her children's stories and sermonizing journalistic pieces were a result of pressure for money. Even though little is known about her marriage, all indications are that it was a good one, yet it no doubt was difficult for Cooke to lose her house and her inheritance. After moving with her husband to Pittsfield, Massachusetts, in an unsuccessful effort to improve their finances, she spent the winter of 1889–1890 in Boston, hoping to find work and waiting for him to close his business in Pittsfield. When he was unable to join her there, she returned to Pittsfield where she died of influenza in 1892.

MAJOR WORKS AND THEMES

The best work Rose Terry Cooke produced focuses not on the privileged class from which she came but on those plain, ordinary people in the little north-western corner of Connecticut who live close to the land—the farmers, their hardworking wives, country schoolteachers, deacons and ministers, general store keepers, the village loafer, and the village fool. Traveling the rural countryside as she so often did as a young girl with her father, she learned a great deal about the people and the land, which later enabled her to portray both in fiction and to earn a living by it as well. The New England landscape she describes is harsh, producing inhabitants who are lonely, hardened individuals. According to Kleitz, "The influence of the 'deep country' of New England is de-humanizing. In effect, the inhabitants Cooke describes are no longer people: the men she literally equates with animals, and the women, having lost their hearts' blood, are like the living dead, moon-struck 'lunatics' '' (129). A recurring theme is that in the nineteenth century many of the Puritan virtues had became distorted. The effect of this can best be seen in the lives of women, whose only choice is between a life of loneliness or a life of brutality.

Walker explains Cooke's perspective on women's lives when she states: "Cooke portrays New England culture as particularly devastating for women in the late 1700s and early 1800s, so often the period of her tales. Women's lives are barren, filled with endless work, and wives are subject to the whims of their husbands" (146). Newlyn agrees with Walker's thesis in her appraisal: "The pull of traditional values is evident in Cooke's stories dealing with happily self-sacrificing old maids and unbelievably romantic young girls who long only for marriage; at the other end of the spectrum are Cooke's realistic stories of New England women who lead miserably unhappy lives, women who are emotionally and physically crippled by husbands who are at best thoughtlessly cruel, and at worst, brutally and intentionally cruel" (49).

Other writers, such as Stowe, had written about strong-willed, independent women, but Cooke was the first to make her old maids heroines in their own right, thus paving the way for later writers like Sarah Orne Jewett. Cooke's single women are not weak, comic characters; rather, they lead full, useful lives, giving valuable service to their family, friends, and community at large. Even when they say they would like to marry, they are independent and proud of being able to support themselves, like Cooke herself.

Two of Cooke's best stories, "Polly Mariner, Tailoress" and "How Celia Changed Her Mind" focus on such "heroines." After Polly's mother dies, she decides to learn a trade rather than becoming a schoolteacher: "Firstly I hate damp boys: They're always gettin' damp and steamin', and I'd as lieve be choked at once. Secondly I hate boys anyway: they're nothin; but torments. An' thirdly I hate school-keepin' '' (231). Instead, Polly decides to become a tailor-ess, and even after her father dies, leaving her alone, she refuses to give up her independence and live with relatives or take in a boarder. Assuming an important position in the community, like many other women in Cooke's fiction, Polly lives her life as she chooses, free to speak her own mind without fear of its consequences for others. Uncharacteristically, however, when she is dying, Polly admits she wishes she had had "a home 'n' folks o' my own" (231), but her friend, Aunt Hanner, reassures her that "if you hain't got nobody to cry for you, you hain't got nobody to cry for, 'nd you've hed your way" (262).

Looking at "How Celia Changed Her Mind" reveals Cooke's conviction that single life is much more conducive to a woman's well-being than marriage. A spinster, Celia Barnes, wonders if her position in life might be better if she were married, only to find out the hard way after marrying Deacon Everts that it is far worse than she could have ever imagined. As the wife of a tight-fisted, cold husband, she soon learns that few married women are "more than household drudges, the servants of their families, worked to the verge of exhaustion, and neither thanked nor rewarded for their pains" (308). When her husband dies, Celia is relieved, believing she's entitled to the money he leaves her. In celebration, she vows: "[E]very year, so long as I live, I'm goin' to keep an old maids' Thanksgivin' for a kind of burnt-offering, for I've changed my mind clear down to the bottom" (315). Celia has learned what Polly understood in theory: A woman loses her dignity and self-respect in marriage. In Cooke's world, the single life, though difficult and lonely, is far superior to sacrificing one's freedom to a dictatorial man.

CRITICAL RECEPTION

Rose Terry Cooke was among the first writers to create literature out of purely local material. As a writer of realistic short stories, she is acknowledged to be a pioneer of New England regional fiction and an innovator in the use of dialect. Yet, as Susan Allen Toth points out, she is "one of the least read and most neglected of the many talented women who wrote local-color fiction for American magazines in the latter half of the nineteenth century" (19). Nonetheless, Cooke's reputation, though minor, has held firm in the twentieth century. Fred Lewis Pattee in *The Development of the American Short Story* praised the originality of Cooke's local color stories. In the 1940s, Robert Spiller's *Literary History of the United States* acknowledged the key role she played in New England realism.

Cooke's position from both a historical and a literary perspective is important because it coincided with the development of the realistic American short story at the end of the feminine 1850s when sentimental romances dominated American magazines. Cooke, along with Harriet Beecher Stowe, was a pioneer of this movement, which came to be known as the "local color" school. Cooke herself explained her mission in the preface to "Miss Lucinda," a tale about a spinster, when she wrote: "Forgive me once more patient reader, if I offer to you no tragedy in high life, no sentimental history of fashion and wealth, but only a little story about a woman who could not be a heroine" (31).

In *New England: Indian Summer*, Van Wyck Brooks praised her early efforts, stating: "Some of these tales, with their note of harsh veracity, were never to be replaced by later authors; and as tales, in their bleak finality, two or three were all but beyond comparison" (88). Scholars agree, however, that Cooke's progress as a writer was erratic; although she wrote nearly 200 stories, their quality is inconsistent, ranging from Sunday school moral tales to unusual romantic fantasies to some of the finest work produced by the local color school. According to Perry Westbrook's profile in *The Dictionary of Literary Biography*: "Not all of Cooke's approximately 200 published stories are realistic, but a number of them rank with the best realistic fiction of such New England authors . . . as Sarah Orne Jewett and Mary E. Wilkins Freeman" (95).

Surprisingly few critical studies have focused upon Cooke. Three unpublished Ph.D. dissertations of interest are Jean Downey's "A Biographical and Critical Study of Rose Terry Cooke" (1956), Susan Allen Toth's "More Than Local Color: A Reappraisal of Rose Terry Cooke, Mary Wilkins Freeman and Alice Brown" (1969), and Rodney Lee Smith's "These Poor Weak Souls: Rose Terry Cooke's Presentation of Men and Women Who Were Converts to the Social Gospel in the Gilded Age" (1978).

Recently, Cooke has been reclaimed by feminist scholars and Women's Studies advocates. Virtually all modern discussions of Cooke's life are based on three sources: Jean Downey's dissertation, Harriet Spofford's *A Little Book of Friends*, and an essay on Cooke by Spofford in Elizabeth Stuart Phelps's *Our Famous Women*. In the introduction to her 1986 collection of Cooke's stories, Elizabeth Ammons acknowledges "Cooke's biting—sometimes glumly humorous, sometimes simply grim—tales about Calvinism, about domestic violence in American society, and about life as a single woman in rural, white, middle-class New England in the late eighteenth and early nineteenth centuries" (xxiii).

There is no denying that the unevenness of Cooke's work has affected her reputation. However, the diversity of its range, from poetry to religious tracts and sentimental love stories to realistic, often bitter, exposés of a culture in decline, reveals a woman and a society in transition. Today as we approach the twenty-first century, Rose Terry Cooke's legacy allows us to look back to another era and find that many of the issues we are dealing with today have been around for quite awhile. As Katherine Kleitz states in her description of Cooke's work: "For depth of character study and realistic portrayal of a distinctive American way of life, these stories are unequalled" (127). Donovan agrees, finding Cooke's genius in her ability "to make universal comments about human nature through the use of metaphors drawn from her own environment, and yet appropriate to the speaker" (71).

WORKS CITED

Ammons, Elizabeth, ed. *"How Celia Changed Her Mind" and Selected Stories*. New Brunswick: Rutgers University Press, 1986.

Brooks, Van Wyck. *New England: Indian Summer, in Literature in New England*. Garden City: Garden City Publishing, 1944.

Cooke, Rose Terry. "How Celia Changed Her Mind." *Huckleberries Gathered from New England Hills*. Vol. 43. of The American Short Story Series. New York: Garrett Press, 1969.

———. "Miss Lucinda." *Somebody's Neighbors*. Vol. 41 of The American Short Story Series. New York: Garrett Press, 1969.

———. "Polly Mariner, Tailoress." *Somebody's Neighbors*. Vol. 41 of The American Short Story Series. New York: Garrett Press, 1969.

Donovan, Josephine. *New England Local Color Literature: A Women's Tradition*. New York: Frederick Ungar, 1983.

Kleitz, Katherine. "Essence of New England: The Portraits of Rose Terry Cooke." *American Transcendental Quarterly* 47–48 (1980): 127–139.

Newlyn, Evelyn. "Rose Terry Cooke and the Children of the Sphinx." *Regionalism and the Female Imagination* 4 (1979): 49–57.

Pattee, Fred Lewis. *The Development of the American Short Story*. New York: Harper, 1923.

Spiller, Robert, et al. *Literary History of the United States*. New York: Macmillan, 1968.

Toth, Susan Allen. "Character Studies in Rose Terry Cooke: New Faces for the Short Story." *Kate Chopin Newsletter* 2 (1976): 19–26.

Walker, Cheryl. "Rose Terry Cooke." *Legacy* 9, no. 2 (1992): 143–149.

Westbrook, Perry D. "Rose Terry Cooke." In *The Dictionary of Literary Biography*. Edited by Donald Pizer and Earl N. Harbert. Vol. 12, *American Realists and Naturalists*. Detroit: Gale Research, 1982.

BIBLIOGRAPHY

Works by Rose Terry Cooke

Poems. Boston: Ticknor and Fields, 1861.

Somebody's Neighbors. Boston: Osgood, 1881. Reprint, Vol. 41 of The American Short Story Series. New York: Garrett Press, 1969.

Root-Bound and Other Sketches. Boston: Congregational Sunday School and Publishing Society, 1885. Reprint, Americans in Fiction Series. Ridgewood, NJ: Gregg Press, 1968.

The Sphinx's Children and Other People's. Boston: Ticknor and Fields, 1886. Reprint, Vol. 42 of The American Short Story Series. New York: Garrett Press, 1969.

Poems. New York: Gottsberger, 1888.

Steadfast: The Story of a Saint and a Sinner. Boston: Ticknor and Fields, 1889.

Huckleberries Gathered from New England Hills. Boston: Houghton Mifflin, 1891. Reprint, Vol. 43 of The American Short Story Series. New York: Garrett Press, 1969.

"How Celia Changed Her Mind" and Selected Stories. Edited by Elizabeth Ammons. New Brunswick: Rutgers University Press, 1986.

Studies of Rose Terry Cooke

Brooks, Van Wyck. *New England: Indian Summer, in Literature in New England*. Garden City: Garden City Publishing, 1944.

Donovan, Josephine. *New England Local Color Literature: A Women's Tradition*. New York: Frederick Ungar, 1983.

Downey, Jean. "A Biographical and Critical Study of Rose Terry Cooke." Ph.D. diss., University of Ottawa, 1956.

———. "Rose Terry Cooke: A Bibliography." *Bulletin of Bibliography* 21 (1955): 159–163, 191–192.

Kleitz, Katherine. "Essence of New England: The Portraits of Rose Terry Cooke." *American Transcendental Quarterly* 47–48 (1980): 127–139.

Martin, Jay. *Harvest of Change: American Literature 1865–1914*. Princeton: Princeton University Press, 1967.

Newlyn, Evelyn. "Rose Terry Cooke and the Children of the Sphinx." *Regionalism and the Female Imagination* 4 (winter 1979): 49–57.

Pattee, Fred Lewis. *The Development of the American Short Story*. New York: Harper, 1923.

Phelps, Elizabeth Stuart. *Our Famous Women*. Hartford: A. D. Worthington, 1886. Includes "Harriet Prescott Spofford" by Rose Terry Cooke and "Rose Terry Cooke" by Harriet Prescott Spofford.

Sherman, Sarah Way. *Sarah Orne Jewett: An American Persephone*. Hanover, NH: University Press of New England, 1989.

Smith, Rodney Lee. "These Poor Weak Souls: Rose Terry Cooke's Presentation of Men and Women Who Were Converts to the Social Gospel in the Gilded Age." Ph.D. diss., University of Wisconsin–Milwaukee, 1978.

Spiller, Robert, et al. *Literary History of the United States*. New York: Macmillan, 1968.

Spofford, Harriet Prescott. *A Little Book of Friends*. Boston: Little, Brown, 1916.

Toth, Susan Allen. "Character Studies in Rose Terry Cooke: New Faces for the Short Story." *Kate Chopin Newsletter* 2 (1976): 19–26.

———. "More Than Local Color: A Reappraisal of Rose Terry Cooke, Mary Wilkins Freeman and Alice Brown." Ph.D. diss., University of Minnesota, 1969.

———. "Rose Terry Cooke." *American Literary Realism* 42 (1971): 170–176.

Walker, Cheryl. "Rose Terry Cooke." *Legacy* 9, no. 2 (1992): 143–149.

Welter, Barbara. *Dimity Convictions: The American Woman in the Nineteenth Century*. Athens: Ohio University Press, 1976.

Westbrook, Perry D. *Acres of Flint: Sarah Orne Jewett and Her Contemporaries*. Metuchen: Scarecrow, 1951. Rev. ed., 1981.

———. "Rose Terry Cooke." In *The Dictionary of Literary Biography*. Edited by Donald Pizer and Earl N. Harbert. Vol. 12, *American Realists and Naturalists*. Detroit: Gale Research, 1982.

INA DONNA COOLBRITH (1841–1928)

Gary Scharnhorst

BIOGRAPHY

Poet Ina Coolbrith was born in Nauvoo, Illinois, to Mormon parents. In 1851, ten years after the death of her natural father, her stepfather, St. Louis journalist and lawyer William Pickett, moved the family west to California. Her first published poem, "My Childhood's Home," appeared in the *Los Angeles Star* in August 1856.

In 1862, after a brief marriage and divorce, Coolbrith settled in San Francisco, where, mentored by Bret Harte, she soon began to earn a local literary reputation. After the founding of the *Overland Monthly*, with Harte as its first editor, in 1868, the verse of Coolbrith, Harte, and Charles Warren Stoddard was featured so often in its pages they were nicknamed "the Golden State Trinity."

By the 1870s, Coolbrith had won national renown. Her poetry regularly appeared over the course of her career in such magazines as the *Galaxy, Century, Harper's Weekly, Putnam's, Lippincott's, Munsey's*, and *Scribner's*. Though never prolific, Coolbrith had a facile style. She wrote a poem, as she once explained, "on her feet, going about her affairs until her poem is complete, and then writing it down exactly as she framed it in her mind" ("General Gossip"). In fall 1884 Coolbrith traveled to New England, where she met John Greenleaf Whittier, Oliver Wendell Holmes, and E. C. Stedman. In 1893 she visited the Columbian Exposition in Chicago and traveled to Boston and New York; and throughout the 1890s her home in the East Bay area was famous as a salon for writers and artists.

Coolbrith served as librarian of the Oakland Free Public Library from 1874 until 1893. There she met and encouraged the young Isadora Duncan, Jack London, and Mary Austin. As Austin reminisced later, "She had a low, pleasant voice; now and then a faint smile swam to the surface of her look, and passed without the slightest riffle of a laugh; and she was entirely kind and matter of fact with me'' (Austin 231). Charlotte Perkins Stetson, later Gilman, briefly lived across Webster Street in Oakland from Coolbrith in the early 1890s, and in her salon, she met the poet Joaquin Miller (who had adopted his nickname at Coolbrith's urging in 1870), Edwin Markham, Hamlin Garland, and James Whitcomb Riley (Gilman 142). After resigning from the Oakland library, Coolbrith briefly earned her living as a lecturer on such topics as "Early California Writers." She headed the Mercantile Library of San Francisco from 1898 until 1900 and, for a salary of $50 a month, the Library of the Bohemian Club from 1900 until 1906.

That year, the San Francisco earthquake and fire destroyed her home on Russian Hill, consumed her library and private papers, including the manuscript of her literary history of California, and left her without a job. "Imagine your home with every article it contains swept from you, and you left with not so much as a comb or hair pin or common pin except what might be on your person!" she wrote a friend (quoted in Rhodehamel and Wood 251). Still, her reputation was intact. She was elected president of the Pacific Coast Women's Press Association in 1910 and again in 1914, and she convened a World Congress of Authors at the Panama-Pacific International Exposition in San Francisco in 1915, the same year she was named the first poet laureate of California by vote of the state legislature. Suffering from severe rheumatism, she spent the winters between 1919 and 1923 in New York. She was awarded an honorary M.A. by Mills College in 1923. Coolbrith died in Berkeley ten days before her eighty-seventh birthday, and in 1932, a peak in Sierra County, California, was renamed "Mount Ida Coolbrith" in her honor.

MAJOR WORKS AND THEMES

Hardly an innovator, Coolbrith was a conventional lyric poet who wrote in a variety of traditional verse forms. "Longing," in the first issue of the *Overland* (July 1868), for example, restates the romantic notion that an hour in a vernal wood is more instructive than the "foolish wisdom sought in books!" Perhaps her most characteristic lyric, "In Blossom-Time," first published in the *Overland* for August 1868 and often anthologized, is an utterly conventional lyric exuberant over the approach of spring: "It's O my heart, my heart!/To be out in the sun and sing;/To sing and shout in the fields about,/In the balm and the blossoming." Occasionally, however, Coolbrith was capable of expressing raw displeasure, as in "The Captive of the White City," her ode on the plight of an Indian she saw exhibited at the Columbian Exposition in Chicago: "In the beautiful Midway Place,/The captive sits apart,/Silent, and makes no sign./ But what is the word in your heart,/O man of a dying race?" Early in the 1900s Coolbrith's verse almost always centered on an individual, usually someone she knew, as in "Paderewski," "Joseph LeConte," "With the Laurel to Edmund

Clarence Stedman on His Seventieth Birthday,'' or her eulogistic ''Bret Harte.''
After her appointment as poet laureate of the state, of course, she also produced
a vast quantity of occasional verse, much of it forgettable, such as ''Foch:
California's Greeting'' and ''The Call of the Forests.''

CRITICAL RECEPTION

With rare exceptions, Coolbrith enjoyed extremely favorable notices, particularly in the West. Her first collection of verse, *A Perfect Day and Other Poems*
(1881), contains 63 poems, 46 of them reprinted from the *Overland*. Ambrose
Bierce, not one given to idle praise, especially of women poets, commended it
in the *San Francisco News Letter*: ''a pleasant rill of song in a desert cursed by
fantastic mirages'' (quoted in Rhodehamel and Wood 156). The reviewer for
the *New York Times* (20 June 1881) similarly remarked, ''Without having a
large vocabulary or a great range of expression,'' Coolbrith ''makes pleasant
music on a few strings.'' Most reviews of Coolbrith's second collection, *Songs
from the Golden Gate* (1895), which contained exactly 100 lyrics, were also
favorable. The San Francisco journalist Henry James typically concluded, for
example, that ''California has a right to be proud of Ina Coolbrith. Sometime
it will awaken from its dreams of gold and gain and conquest to understand that
here was one who had been touched with the sacred fire'' (quoted in Rhodehamel and Wood 230). William Morton Payne, the editor of *Dial*, also praised
her verse (16 February 1896): It ''has poetic sensibility and vision, besides
command of a considerable variety of lyric forms.'' Her lyric ''Oblivion,'' he
thought, was ''sure to recall Christina Rossetti's 'Dreamland.' '' Less charitably,
however, the *New York Times* carped (24 November 1895), ''Her verse is well
written and it is readable. She is earnest, and her sincerity atones for many
faults. But, none the less, it must be said that she was not called to be a poet.''
Coolbrith's posthumous collection, *Wings of Sunset* (1929), contains 116 poems,
only 12 of which had appeared in *Songs from the Golden Gate*. Lionel Stevenson, professor of English at the University of California and Coolbrith's friend,
expressed the consensus view about her work in his review of the volume for
the *Saturday Review of Literature* (26 April 1930): ''There seems to be no doubt
that Ina Coolbrith has not yet been accorded her due place in American poetry.
Geographical isolation and infrequent publication prevented her from competing
with the crowd of minor poets who occupied the interregnum between the New
England and the Chicago dynasties. No one would think of proposing her as a
rival for the lonely independence of Emily Dickinson, but among the other
women poets she deserves a niche.''

WORKS CITED

Anonymous. ''General Gossip of Authors and Writers.'' *Current Literature* 23 (June
1898): 500.

Anonymous. Review of *A Perfect Day and Other Poems*. *New York Times*, 20 June 1881, 2.

Anonymous. "Verse Easy to Produce." Review of *Songs from the Golden Gate*. *New York Times*, 24 November 1895, 4–5.

Austin, Mary. *Earth Horizon*. Boston: Houghton Mifflin, 1932. 231.

Gilman, Charlotte Perkins. *The Living of Charlotte Perkins Gilman*. New York: Appleton-Century, 1935.

Payne, William Morton. "Recent Books of American Poetry." Review of *Songs from the Golden Gate*. *Dial*, 16 February 1896, 112–113.

Rhodehamel, Josephine DeWitt, and Raymund Francis Wood. *Ina Coolbrith: Librarian and Laureate of California*. Provo: Brigham Young University Press, 1973. 251.

Stevenson, Lionel. "Ina Coolbrith, *Wings of Sunset*." *Saturday Review of Literature*, 26 April 1930, 992.

BIBLIOGRAPHY

Works by Ina Coolbrith

Poetry

A Perfect Day and Other Poems. San Francisco: Carmany, 1881.

Songs from the Golden Gate. Boston: Houghton Mifflin, 1895.

Wings of Sunset. Boston: Houghton Mifflin, 1929.

Studies of Ina Coolbrith

Anderson, W. H. "California's First Poet Laureate." *Historical Society of Southern California Quarterly* 32 (June 1950): 105–107.

Anonymous. "Ina Coolbrith, Poet of California, Dies." *New York Times*, 1 March 1928, 5.

Cummins, Ella Sterling. *Stories from the Files*. San Francisco: Cooperative Printing Co., 1893. 149–151.

Kendall, Carlton Waldo. "California's Pioneer Poetess." *Overland Monthly*, n.s., 87 (August 1929): 229–230.

McCrackin, Josephine Clifford. "Ina Coolbrith Invested with Poets' Crown." *Overland Monthly*, n.s., 67 (November 1915): 448–450.

Purdy, Helen Throop. "Ina Donna Coolbrith, 1841–1928." *California Historical Society Quarterly* 7 (March 1928): 78.

Stevenson, Lionel. "The Mind of Ina Coolbrith." *Overland Monthly*, n.s., 88 (May 1930): 150.

Walker, Cheryl. "Ina Coolbrith and the Nightingale Tradition." *Legacy* 6 (spring 1989): 27–33.

ANNA JULIA COOPER (1858–1964)

Melanie Levinson

BIOGRAPHY

Inaccurately called "[a] quiet woman who preferred a 'lesser limelight' " (quoted in Perkins 2), Anna Julia Cooper was rather a woman who never stopped speaking out. Born a slave on August 10, 1858, in Raleigh, North Carolina, Cooper was the daughter of a slave woman, Hannah Stanley Haywood, and George Washington Haywood, her white master. When the Episcopal Church opened St. Augustine's Normal School and Collegiate Institute for newly emancipated slaves, Anna Julia was one of the first students recruited. Exceptionally bright, she became a student teacher there at the age of nine and would remain an educator the rest of her long life. St. Augustine's also formed her earliest feminist sensibilities, for she later noted that while the boys who declared an interest in theology were given every encouragement, the girls were actively discouraged from enrolling in advanced academic courses.

A boy, no matter how meager his equipment and shallow his pretensions, had only to declare a floating intention to study theology and he could get all the support, encouragement, and stimulus he needed, be absolved from work and invested beforehand with all the dignity of his far away office. While a self-supporting girl had to struggle on by teaching in the summer and working after school hours to keep up with board bills, and actually fight her way against positive discouragements to the higher education. (*Voice* 77)

In 1877, at the age of nineteen, she married the Reverend A. C. Cooper, one of those pampered theological students, who died after only two years of marriage. In 1881, Cooper continued her own education, one of very few women and even fewer African-American women to do so. She earned her Bachelor of

Arts in 1884 and her Master of Arts degree in 1887, both from Oberlin College in Ohio. While she was earning these degrees, Cooper taught college preparatory courses at Oberlin Academy to pay her keep. After earning her advanced degree in 1884, Cooper returned to her first school, St. Augustine's, to teach Latin, Greek, and mathematics. She was recruited to teach at Washington, D.C.'s M Street (later renamed Dunbar) High School in 1887, and while she was there, she published her first and best-known work, A Voice from the South (1892).

In 1901, Cooper was appointed principal of M Street, only the second woman to hold such a position. She refused to accept inferior status either for herself or for her students and battled to reject a congressional plan that would encourage young black students to learn industrial skills rather than academic ones. Though she believed in teaching trades, she also knew that there were real scholars among her pupils and convinced Harvard, Yale, and Brown to provide scholarships for some. In addition, she sent a number of them to Oberlin, Amherst, Dartmouth, and Radcliffe. Her victories did not come without cost, however. When the district reshuffled positions in 1906, she was not rehired. There was a reason that Cooper was only the second female principal in the Washington, D.C. public school system, and her aggressive advocacy for higher education flew in the face of her supervisor's theories about industrial education for children of color. Cooper fought for reinstatement, but when that concession finally came in 1910, she had been replaced as principal and was offered instead only a position as Latin teacher at a much-reduced wage.

Four years later, Cooper began to work on her doctorate at Columbia, but before she could complete the one-year residency requirement, she adopted five children and moved them all to Washington. Not long after, she began to study during the summers at Sorbonne, University of France, and requested a leave of absence in 1924 to complete the residency requirement there. As had happened many times at M Street High School, obstacles were thrown in her way. She received word from a friend that if she did not return within sixty days of her departure, she would probably be fired. Unwilling to lose the income and retirement benefits, Cooper returned to her classroom on the sixtieth day. Despite these obvious ploys to prevent her success, Cooper defended her dissertation in the spring of 1925. At the age of sixty-six, Cooper received her doctorate in history, only the fourth African-American woman to accomplish this feat. Her two French books are the result of her research while in France.

In 1929 Cooper became president of Frelinghuysen University, an evening college for working people in Washington. Again a pioneer, she was among the first educators to realize the need for such a school. Cooper was affiliated with this institution until 1941, when she retired. She died in Washington, D.C. in 1964 at the age of 105.

MAJOR WORKS AND THEMES

Cooper's primary drive was to see not only that African-American men were educated but that black women should have that opportunity as well. Only by learning and growing together, she declared, did the race as a whole have a chance to survive. While she did not often publicly decry African-American men who refused to allow that women of color could also be scholars, occasionally, she did speak out. Cooper's major work was the pioneering *A Voice from the South*, published in 1892. In it, she reports that she was asked why there were no female African-American scholars.

"Oh," I said, "so far as it is true, the men, I suppose, from the life they lead, gain more by contact; and so far as it is only apparent, I think the women are more quiet. They don't feel called to mount a barrel and harangue by the hour every time they imagine they have produced an idea." (74)

Of all her writings, this collection is the only one that is overtly feminist in tone. It is split into two parts: "Soprano Obligato" and "Tutti Ad Libitium." The latter focuses on the problems specific to black women: "Not to make the boys less, but the girls more," the former to the race as a whole (79). As Hazel Carby suggests, Cooper never confined herself to the issue of the Woman Question as such—she was interested instead in the power of the strong over the weak. Rectifying that imbalance of power was her lifelong issue.

CRITICAL RECEPTION

The *New York Independent* called *A Voice from the South* "a piercing and clinging cry which it is impossible to hear and not to understand." Her writing has been called "ambitious and . . . effectively sarcastic." Nevertheless, most critics have focused not upon her writing but upon her community activism, her commitment to the public school system, and her own personal accomplishments. This has led a few textual scholars to attempt to reclaim Cooper's writing on its own terms. In a review of *Slavery and the French Revolutionists (1788–1805)*, Cooper's own biography became the focus of the evaluation. Bob Corbett finds this "demeaning": "Certainly Cooper achieved extraordinary things, especially given her color and sex in the period she lived. But *Slavery and the French Revolutionists (1788–1805)* stands as a scholarly achievement independent of any biographical data of the author" (Internet, n.p.).

BIBLIOGRAPHY

Works by Anna Julia Cooper

A Voice from the South. Xenia, OH: Aldine Printing House, 1892.
L'Attitude de la France a L'Egard de L'Esclavage Pendant La Revolution. Paris: Imprimerie de la Cour D'Appel, 1925.
Le Pelerinage de Charlemagne: Voyage a Jerusalem et a Constantinople. Paris: A. Lahure, 1925.
Legislative Measures Concerning Slavery in the United States. Paris?: s.n., 1942.
Equality of Races and the Democratic Movement. Washington, D.C.: s.n., 1945.

The Life and Writings of the Grimke Family. n.p., 1951.
Slavery and the French Revolutionists (1788–1805). Transcripted by Frances Richardson Keller. New York: Edwin Mellen Press, 1988.
The Third Step. Cooper Papers. n.d.
Anna Julia Cooper Papers. Moorland-Springarn Research Center. Howard University, Washington, D.C.

Studies of Anna Julia Cooper

Carby, Hazel. ''On the Threshold of Woman's Era: Lynching, Empire, and Sexuality in Black Feminist Theory.'' *Critical Inquiry* 12 (1985): 262–277.

Chateauvert, Melinda. ''The Third Step: Anna Julia Cooper and Black Education in the District of Columbia, 1910–1960.'' *SAGE: A Scholarly Journal on Black Women,* Student Supplement (1988): 7–11.

Corbett, Bob. Review of *Slavery and the French Revolutionists (1788–1805),* by Anna Julia Cooper. 6 June 1995 [http://neal.ctstateu.edu/history/wo . . . istory/archives/haiti/haiti082.html], 18 March 1996.

Harley, Sharon. ''Anna J. Cooper: A Voice for Black Women.'' In *The Afro-American Woman: Struggles and Images,* edited by Sharon Harley and Rosalyn Terborg-Penn. Port Washington, NY: Kennikat Press, 1978. 87–96.

Hutchinson, Louise D. *Anna Julia Cooper: A Voice from the South.* Washington, D.C.: Smithsonian Press, 1982.

Lerner, Gerda, ed. *Black Women in White America.* New York: Pantheon Books, 1972.

Loewenberg, Bert James, and Ruth Bogin, eds. *Black Women in Nineteenth-Century American Life: Their Words, Their Thoughts, Their Feelings.* University Park: Pennsylvania State University Press, 1976.

Perkins, David. ''A Quiet Woman Who Preferred the 'Lesser Limelight.' '' *The News and Observer* (Raleigh), 29 December 1991, 2.

Washington, Mary Helen. ''Anna Julia Cooper: The Black Feminist Voice of the 1890s.'' *Legacy* 4, no. 2 (1987): 3–15.

———. Introduction. *A Voice from the South,* by Anna Julia Cooper. New York: Oxford University Press, 1988.

MARIA SUSANNA CUMMINS
(1827–1866)

Rebecca R. Saulsbury

BIOGRAPHY

Maria Susanna Cummins was born in Salem, Massachusetts, on April 9, 1827, to a family of relatively high social status and affluence. She was a descendant of Isaac Cummings, a Scottish landowner who emigrated to Massachusetts in 1638. Maria was the first child of twice-widowed David Cummins and Mehit- able Cave Cummins, and three more children would be born after her. Her father already had four children from his first two marriages. David Cummins was a Dartmouth graduate (class of 1806), lawyer, and judge; Maria's mother was the granddaughter of Dr. Thomas Kittredge, who came from a family of physicians in Andover, Massachusetts. Maria's early childhood was spent in Salem. When her father became the judge of the court of common pleas in Norfolk County, he moved the family to Dorchester, six miles from Boston's center, where Cummins spent the rest of her life.

Cummins was educated at home by her father, who recognized and encouraged her talent for writing. Such mentoring was not unusual in educated New England families. Like the fathers of Margaret Fuller and Catherine Sedgwick, David Cummins gave Maria a classical education. Later, she attended the school of Mrs. Charles Sedgwick, Catharine Maria Sedgwick's sister-in-law, at Lenox, Massachusetts. Since Sedgwick was often at the school, Cummins undoubtedly met her, and perhaps she derived inspiration from Sedgwick's intellectual ability and literary talent.

Cummins achieved early literary notice with the publication of several works in the *Atlantic Monthly*. She signed her first contract with John P. Jewett and Company, which guaranteed her ten percent royalties per copy, each to be sold for $1. In 1854, when she was twenty-seven years old, *The Lamplighter* was published. Second only to *Uncle Tom's Cabin* in sales, which was published two years earlier, *The Lamplighter* outsold even Susan Warner's best-selling novel *The Wide, Wide World*, which had appeared four years earlier. Some 40,000 copies sold in the first eight weeks, and 70,000 copies were sold by the end of its first year. *The Lamplighter* was the most talked about novel of its time; it garnered Cummins's popular success in the literary marketplace and international fame. *The Lamplighter* was translated into French, German, and Czech and was included in the Tauchnitz library of British and American authors (along with *Mabel Vaughan*, her second novel), a distinctive sign of Cummins's international popularity. Several editions were also published in London. The novel's copyright expired in the 1890s, yet cheap reprints continued to appear into the 1920s.

The huge success of *The Lamplighter* secured Cummins's position as a competitor to be reckoned with in the literary marketplace. Indeed, its success, combined with the overwhelming popularity of *Uncle Tom's Cabin* and *The Wide, Wide World*, provoked the consternation of some of America's established male writers. On January 19, 1855, Nathaniel Hawthorne, in a letter to his publisher, William D. Ticknor, remarked that "America is now wholly given over to a d—d mob of scribbling women" whose "trash" has seduced "the public taste" (*Letters* 75). Even more puzzling was the success of Cummins's first novel: "What is the mystery of these innumerable editions of the Lamplighter, and other books neither better nor worse?—worse they could not be, and better they not be, when they sell by the 100,000" (*Letters* 75). Hawthorne's opinion notwithstanding, Cummins was in great demand; the editor of the *Boston Gazette* wanted to pay her $50 for a story. Another paper, the *American Union*, asked her to state her terms. In 1857, her second novel, *Mabel Vaughan*, was published, also by Jewett and Company. Although many critics of the time felt it was structurally better than *The Lamplighter*, and while it was widely read, it did not approach her first novel in popular success and sales.

Soon after the publication of her second novel, Cummins changed publishing houses, moving to Ticknor and Fields, who paid her fifteen percent royalties. In 1860, her third novel, *El Fureidis*, was published. Four years later, her final novel, *Haunted Hearts*, appeared. Neither of her last two novels achieved the popularity of *The Lamplighter*. A few years before her death, she contributed two travel pieces to *The Atlantic Monthly*: "A Talk about Guides" (1864) and "Around Mull" (1865).

Like many of her female contemporaries, Cummins published all of her novels anonymously, a practice indicative of the literary domestics' ambivalent attitude toward writing and their reluctance to challenge the dictum that women were not meant to be published writers (Kelley 125–126). Cummins's uneasiness over her public notoriety is underscored by her cultivation of a quiet and secluded life in Dorchester, where she could give her devotion to writing and church work. Unlike most of her female literary contemporaries, however, she did not marry. Such a choice was "an anomalous and difficult situation for a nineteenth-century woman" during the age of True Womanhood, when becoming a wife and mother were deemed her chief goals and occupation (Kelley 34). In social terms, "the spinster was a forlorn, alternately ignored and disparaged figure in a society that was at a loss as to how to deal with her except to tuck her away in the home of her parents or siblings" (Kelley 34).

On October 1, 1866, at the age of thirty-nine, Cummins died of "abdominal disease." The next day, Reverend Nathaniel Hall remarked in a sermon delivered at First Church in Dorchester, "Never before, I suppose, did a writer among us, if anywhere, flame into such sudden popularity—a popularity calling for edition upon edition of her work" (quoted in Kelley 24). Cummins was remembered chiefly for her literary accomplishments.

MAJOR WORKS AND THEMES

Cummins's novels participate in two traditions much in evidence in the nineteenth century: the female bildungsroman, as seen, for example, in the works of the Brontë sisters, and the urban melodrama as, say, in Charles Dickens. Moreover, all of her works are strongly moral in their point of view, in this regard closely resembling the sentimental-domestic fiction of Catharine Maria Sedgwick, Harriet Beecher Stowe, and Susan Warner. Cummins resembles these writers in another important way: reliance upon formulas and conventions characteristic of their work and significant factors in developing large female readerships. The story of these novels by women in the antebellum period conforms to what Nina Baym terms the "overplot" or the typology of woman's fiction of that time. Briefly, the overplot presents the story of a young girl, usually abandoned or orphaned, who is left financially and emotionally destitute through a series of trials but who learns to find her way in the world. Crucial to this overplot is how the heroine perceives herself. As she overcomes the obstacles she faces and, in the process, acquires self-dependence, she learns "that women must become people to survive in a difficult world . . . women *can* become people because persons, selves, is what they all potentially are" (Baym, *Woman's Fiction* ix). The heroine's ability to deal with others and make her own way in the world is inextricably linked to her emerging piety and a religion of the heart in which she sees herself in relationship to others. All of Cummins's novels offer variations of the overplot.

The Lamplighter is a female bildungsroman that closely resembles the theme of *The Wide, Wide World* in its first 100 pages, especially in the replication of Warner's Christian ethic of submission. It tells the story of Gerty, an abandoned and mistreated orphan who is rescued at the age of eight by Trueman Flint, a lamplighter, and then by Emily Graham, a wealthy, blind, and pious young woman who shows her the path to Christian virtue and piety. Through Emily's loving guidance and a series of calamities and hardships, Gerty learns to be a self-reliant woman who trusts her own heart and resists submission to patriarchal authority. Gertrude transforms herself from the oppressed orphan living in the

slums to the educated, middle-class Christian heroine who successfully maneuvers her way through the world. Her middle-class virtue is rewarded with marriage to her childhood friend, Willie Sullivan, who is her equal both in Christian
humility and in independence. Although critics such as Alexander Cowie assert
that the novel's chief lesson "is to teach humble submission to suffering" (421),
Cummins manipulates the overplot for more subversive purposes. As Susan K.
Harris suggests, the formulaic restraints of the overplot "actually functioned as
a cover—or cover-up—for a far more radical vision of female possibilities embedded in the texts" (12–13). Specifically, Cummins textualizes two different
worldviews: one that privileges community and affectional ties, and another that
privileges submission to patriarchal authority. Gertrude's journey to adulthood
entails trying to find a way to negotiate an identity between them.

Mabel Vaughan, Cummins's second novel, features a heroine who is not an
abandoned waif but who still experiences a series of calamities and must re-
fashion herself from her "fortunate fall" from grace. Mabel Vaughan is an
heiress who enjoys the trappings of her social position, yet her life as an heiress
is a sham. Her position as a woman is purely ornamental, and thus, from Cummins's point of view, the upper class is corrupt. Mabel's fall results from a
series of melodramatic mishaps: Her brother becomes an alcoholic, her older
sister's husband goes bankrupt and dies in a train wreck, and her sister succumbs
to the shock of her husband's death. To top it all off, Mabel's father is also
bankrupted. Cummins moves the family from the affluence and corruption of
the East to the western frontier on a track of land in Illinois, their only remaining
property. On the frontier Mabel and her family must build their lives anew and
redefine themselves. Mabel is singlehandedly responsible for saving her family.
Indeed, through her hard work and new-found domestic power, Mabel comes
to serve as the novel's moral core. She rehabilitates her brother and transforms
her family's property from a useless tract of land to the center of the community.
Mabel establishes a community that privileges relational ties and an extended
kinship system. As Nina Baym notes, *Mabel Vaughan* is a utopian novel that
envisions "the national future as a matriarchy" (Introduction xxix).

Maria Cummins's third novel, *El Fureidis*, is an exotic romance novel in the
oriental mode set in Palestine and Syria. It features a romance between the
Englishman Meredith, who visits the holy land, and Havilah, a Christian Arab
woman who, because she is not constrained by Western conventions, is able to
freely express her feelings, including sexual feelings, to men. In a sense, Havilah
is also an outlaw heroine of the female adventure novel in the tradition of
Southworth's *The Hidden Hand* (1859): She combines the traditional ideology
of True Womanhood with unconventional behavior, including "physical action
and bold initiative" (Baym, Introduction xxix).

Haunted Hearts, Cummins's final work, is a historical novel set during the
War of 1812 and is her most conservative and least skilled novel. The heroine
is Angeline Cousin, a flirt, who, through her own misbehavior and thoughtless-
ness, is blamed for the apparent suicide of her lover, Gordon Rawley, an ap-

parent murderer. Angeline is subsequently ostracized by the community and redeemed only when Rawley comes back to vindicate both of them.

CRITICAL RECEPTION

The Lamplighter propelled Cummins from literary obscurity to international fame and firmly established her reputation. Critics of her time recognized Cummins's talent for rich characterization and the realistic depiction of scenes and events. A reviewer in *Harper's New Monthly* praised *The Lamplighter* for "the easy flow of its narrative, its frequent touches of pathos, and its skillful character-drawing [which] are sufficient to make it a favorite with a large class of readers" (8, 714). Another reviewer, E. P. Whipple, commended the book for its "simplicity, tenderness, pathos, and naturalness of the first one hundred pages" (quoted in Pattee 115). Several reviewers quibbled with some of the novel's extraordinary coincidences and overall conception. The *North American Review*, for example, explained that "the story did not seem . . . carefully constructed, and many of the incidents were beyond the range of even a novelist's possibility" (86, 287). But reviewers unanimously praised *The Lamplighter* for its moral point of view and edificatory piety. *Godey's Lady's Book* proclaimed "no hesitation in pronouncing it to be, in our opinion, one of the best and purest of its class that has emanated from an American mind. . . . There are, indeed, some few extravagances observable in the denouement of the plot of the 'Lamplighter'; but, notwithstanding these, the reader will be gratified, entertained, and instructed by the graphic and feeling style of the author" (49, 84). Even the *North American Review* "admired the personage that gives name to the book, and [we] could not but sympathize with the fortunes of the heroine" (86, 287).

With the publication of *Mabel Vaughan*, the reviewers at the *North American Review* reconsidered Cummins's talent as a novelist. Cummins's second novel, they proclaimed, "very far outdistances its neighbor in merit" (86, 287). In fact, this novel "has disappointed our expectations in a way in which we are glad to be disappointed" (86, 287). Unlike Cummins's first novel, *Mabel Vaughan* has a "[s]trongly conceived plot" and is realistic: "the sketches of rural, city, and Western life are wonderfully fresh, vivid, and authentic" (86, 287). The reviewers go so far as to predict for Cummins "a high and enduring place among our American novelists" (86, 287). A reviewer in *Peterson's Magazine* describes *Mabel Vaughan* as "quite up to its predecessor" (32, 363), while the reviewers at *Godey's Lady's Book* praise this novel for its "true spirit of dignity and virtue" (56, 182).

El Fureidis represents a departure of sorts for Cummins. A reviewer for *Peterson's Magazine* observed that this work should be considered a romance: "As a romance it will be generally more acceptable than if it was a novel" (28, 80). This reviewer also regarded *El Fureidis* as "much more carefully elaborated" than *The Lamplighter* and, "in every respect, superior" to it (*Peterson's* 28, 80). The romance designation notwithstanding, the reviewer praises Cummins for her characteristic realism: "The description of scenery bears evidence of being truthful; the incidents are well managed; and the tone of the book is eminently high and pure" (*Peterson's* 28, 80). Overall, however, *El Fureidis* did not enjoy the reception or sales of either *The Lamplighter* or *Mabel Vaughan*. Similarly, Cummins's last novel, *Haunted Hearts*, did not fare well in the marketplace, even though a reviewer for *Peterson's Magazine* predicted that Cummins's reputation "will be much increased . . . by the present novel" (46, 147).

In point of fact, within a few generations, Cummins's reputation sank into near oblivion. She was rescued from literary obscurity by the revival and re-habilitation of nineteenth-century women writers inaugurated in the mid-1970s by Nina Baym's *Woman's Fiction*. *The Lamplighter* was reissued in 1988 by Rutgers University Press in their American Women Writers Series. Since then, this work has received increasing scholarly attention. Yet the number of articles is still comparatively slight. Moreover, the critical revival of Cummins's work in general is relatively small in comparison to colleagues such as Fanny Fern, Harriet Beecher Stowe, and E. D. E. N. Southworth. There are, at present, no articles or studies on the corpus of Cummins's work. And although *The Lamplighter* is now a title in many course reading lists in American literary studies, her other novels have not been reissued. Much needed work remains to be done.

WORKS CITED

Anonymous. Review of *El Fureidis*. *Peterson's Magazine* 28 (January 1860): 80

Anonymous. Review of *Haunted Hearts*. *Peterson's Magazine* 46 (February 1864): 147.

Anonymous. Review of *The Lamplighter*. *Godey's Lady's Book* 49 (July 1854): 84–85.

Anonymous. Review of *The Lamplighter*. *Harper's New Monthly Magazine* 8 (April 1854): 714.

Anonymous. Review of *The Lamplighter*. *Peterson's Magazine* 25 (May 1854): 349.

Anonymous. Review of *Mabel Vaughan*. *Godey's Lady's Book* 56 (February 1858): 182.

Anonymous. Review of *Mabel Vaughan*. *North American Review* 86 (January 1858): 287.

Anonymous. Review of *Mabel Vaughan*. *Peterson's Magazine* 32 (May 1857): 363.

Baym, Nina. Introduction to *The Lamplighter*, by Maria Susanna Cummins. Edited by Nina Baym. New Brunswick: Rutgers University Press, 1988.

―――. *Woman's Fiction: A Guide to Novels by and about Women in America 1820–1870*. Ithaca: Cornell University Press, 1978. 2nd ed., Urbana and Champaign: University of Illinois Press, 1993.

Cowie, Alexander. *The Rise of the American Novel*. New York: American Book Company, 1951.

Harris, Susan K. *19th-Century American Women's Novels: Interpretive Strategies*. Cambridge: Cambridge University Press, 1990.

Kelley, Mary. *Private Woman, Public Stage: Literary Domesticity in Nineteenth-Century America*. New York: Oxford University Press, 1984.

Letters of Hawthorne to William D. Ticknor, 1851–1864. Vol. 1. Newark, NJ: Carteret Book Club, 1910. Reprint, NCR/Microcard Editions. Washington, D.C., 1972.

Pattee, Fred Lewis. *The Feminine Fifties*. New York: D. Appleton-Century Co., 1940. 115.

BIBLIOGRAPHY

Works by Maria Susanna Cummins

The Lamplighter. Boston: John P. Jewett & Co.; Cleveland: Jewett, Proctor and Worthington, 1854.
Mabel Vaughan. Boston: John P. Jewett & Co.; Cleveland: Henry P. B. Jewett; London: Sampson Low, Son & Co., 1857.
El Fureidis. Boston: Ticknor and Fields, 1860.
Haunted Hearts. Boston: J. E. Tilton and Co., 1864.

Studies of Maria Susanna Cummins

Bauermeister, Erica R. *"The Lamplighter, The Wide, Wide World*, and *Hope Leslie*: Reconsidering the Recipes for Nineteenth-Century American Women's Novels." *Legacy: A Journal of Nineteenth-Century American Women Writers* 8, no. 1 (spring 1991): 17–28.
Brown, Herbert Ross. *The Sentimental Novel in America, 1789–1860*. Durham, NC: Duke University Press, 1940.
Dobson, Joanne. "The Hidden Hand: Subversion of Cultural Ideology in Three Mid-Nineteenth-Century Women's Novels." *American Quarterly* 38 (1986): 223–242.
Mott, Frank Luther. *Golden Multitudes: The Story of Best Sellers in the United States*. New York: Macmillian Co., 1947.
Papashvily, Helen Waite. *All the Happy Endings: A Study of the Domestic Novel in America, the Women Who Wrote It, the Women Who Read It, in the Nineteenth Century*. New York: Harper, 1956.
Williams, Susan S. " 'Promoting an Extensive Sale': The Production and Reception of *The Lamplighter*." *New England Quarterly* 69 (June 1996): 179–200.

REBECCA HARDING DAVIS (1831–1910)

Lisa A. Long

BIOGRAPHY

Rebecca Blaine Harding Davis was born in the home of her maternal aunt and namesake, Rebecca Wilson Blaine, in Washington, Pennsylvania, on June 24, 1831. Rebecca and her parents, Richard Harding and Rachel (Leets) Harding, spent five years in Big Springs, Alabama, before settling in Wheeling, West Virginia, where Richard became a businessman and civic official. In her late-life autobiography, *Bits of Gossip*, Davis remembers her childhood in Wheeling wistfully, as an "isolated and calm life" (5). Her British father, a sometimes distant figure, transmitted his literary enthusiasm to his eldest daughter, reciting Shakespeare and weaving romantic tales for his children. Rebecca and her four brothers and sisters were educated at home by their mother, a member of a prominent Pennsylvania family, whom Davis ardently admired as having "enough knowledge to fit out half a dozen modern college bred women" (*Bits* 9). Davis returned to her aunt's house to attend Washington Female Seminary from 1844 to 1848. Yet while Davis's brother continued his education at Washington College, Rebecca, her class valedictorian, returned home.

Legend has it that the unknown Davis burst upon the literary scene thirteen years later with the publication of the highly acclaimed "Life in the Iron-Mills." Yet we now know that Davis spent at least some of the years between her graduation and her *Atlantic Monthly* premiere honing her craft as a poet, reviewer, and sometime editor for the *Wheeling Intelligencer*, the largest newspaper in western Virginia. James T. Fields, the renowned editor of the *Atlantic*, had nothing but praise for Davis's first "serious" effort; he sent her $50 for "Life," eagerly solicited future work, and secured an exclusive agreement with

Davis. However, publishing in the *Atlantic* evolved into a constant struggle with the powerful editor for authorial control of her work. Jean Fagan Yellin has explained how Fields's insistence that "the assembled gloom" of Davis's first novel, *Margret Howth: A Story of To-day*, be transformed into "sunlight" prompted Davis to destroy the original manuscript. Davis would wrangle with other editors throughout her career.

The Brahmin literary world responded enthusiastically to the vigorous, reformist sensibility Davis exhibited in "Life." On an 1862 tour of New England, Davis was feted by the Fields, Emerson, the Alcotts, and Oliver Wendell Holmes, among others. She was especially thrilled by her visit with the painfully solitary Nathaniel Hawthorne, whose *Twice-Told Tales* had inspired her own realistic work. Davis's literary success also drew the admiring attention of a young law student, L. Clarke Davis. The details of their courtship are sketchy, for Davis often reiterated that she "would rather tell other women's stories than [her] own" (Letter to Annie Fields, 10 January 1863). After two years of correspondence and two meetings, Clarke and Rebecca married on March 5, 1863, and settled in Philadelphia.

In 1870 Clarke abandoned his legal career altogether, becoming an editor, first of the *Philadelphia Inquirer* and then the *Philadelphia Public Ledger*. Clarke's own literary aspirations were further fulfilled with moderate success as a theater critic and fiction writer. Many critics feel that Clarke's liberal zeal encouraged the apparent hastiness and didacticism of some of his wife's work. Yet he supported Rebecca's literary career and, indeed, counted upon her income. From all that we know, the Davis marriage was a happy one, marred only by persistent economic insecurity. However, Davis also suffered from severe depression during the first year of her marriage. This illness coincided with her first pregnancy and apparently was exacerbated by the Davises' continued residence with Clarke's family. Though this was an isolated incident, the illness seems only to have cemented Davis's sympathy with those who helplessly suffer dark forces beyond their control.

While Davis's relationship with the *Atlantic* remained cordial, economic concerns compelled her to publish in other magazines. In 1861 Davis's Gothic mystery "The Murder in the Glenn Ross" appeared in the ladies' periodical *Peterson's Magazine*. She received $300 for the story, three times the amount offered for her work in the *Atlantic*. While most critics dismiss this story and similar potboilers as inferior work produced sheerly out of financial need, it proved quite popular; the protagonist of "Murder," John Page, appeared in several more of Davis's stories for *Peterson's*. Throughout her career, Davis continued to work for prestigious publications, such as *Harper's* and *Century*. She had the honor of writing serialized novels for the inaugural editions of the *Galaxy* (*Waiting for the Verdict*), *Lippincott's* (*Dallas Galbraith*), and *Scribner's* (*Natasqua*). And Davis was flattered when Harriet Beecher Stowe, whose fictional efficacy Davis greatly admired, asked her to write for *Hearth and Home*.

Yet much of her work continued to fall to more popular magazines for which, she felt and her subsequent critics concur, Davis reserved her less exploratory work.

In 1870 Davis began contributing juvenile fiction to reputable magazines such as *St. Nicholas* and *Youth's Companion*, a pursuit she would continue for the rest of her life. One might assume that Davis's interest in children's fiction evolved naturally out of her own preoccupation with her growing family. Davis had three children: Richard Harding (in 1864), Charles (in 1866), and Nora (in 1872). Both Richard and Charles followed their parents' literary lead. Richard's fame outstripped even his mother's; not only was he a successful playwright and journalist, but he served as the model for the "Gibson Man," a figure who typified American masculinity at the turn of the century. Nora never married, remaining her mother's traveling companion.

In many ways, Davis's life comes quite close to achieving the contemporary notion of "balancing" motherhood and a career. There were periods during which Davis's literary output slumped, though one could not expect otherwise from such a prolific and sustained career. For example, her production dropped off during the late 1870s and early 1880s, when her growing children would have demanded her full attention. Though many of her fictional stories would express the anguish suffered by women committed to both their professions and their families, Davis staunchly supported the primacy of the domestic sphere. During the 1880s she seldom left her home, venturing out only to spend summers with her family at their beloved retreat in New Jersey. Yet even as she advocated motherhood and wifehood, Davis ardently insisted that women must be enfranchised and self-supporting and that a career could be accommodated.

In the late 1860s and 1870s, Davis branched out into the genres that would predominate during the last twenty-five years of her career. In 1869 Davis began her twenty-year association with the *New York Tribune* as a contributing editor. In 1889 she resigned from the *Tribune* in a dispute over her First Amendment right to criticize corporate policies. But she continued her editorial work in *Putnam's Magazine*, in the *New York Independent*, and in weekly contributions to the *Saturday Evening Post*. Davis's editorial work was of a piece with her fictional writing, championing reform movements and exposing the injustices of race, gender, and class prejudice. In 1873 *Scribner's* commissioned eight local color sketches by Davis, and she increasingly added travelogues and regional essays to her repertoire; her nonfiction work reflected her daily activities and interests: narratives of journeys in Europe and the South, historically based musings on early American life, and reminiscences of the people and times she'd known. Though Davis remained active in her later years, publishing and traveling until the end of her life, her failing eyesight increasingly hampered her activities. In 1904 Clarke suffered heart failure, and on September 29, 1910, Rebecca died of a stroke.

MAJOR WORKS AND THEMES

It is perhaps impossible to accurately label a career that spanned five decades and over 500 pieces, encompassing genres ranging from realistic fiction to children's romances, from travelogues to incisive essays. Yet it is Davis's lifelong commitment to delineating the daily life of average Americans—including the injustices and the crudities—and her efforts to move her audience to social action, that typifies her oeuvre. Biographers attribute Davis's mother with instilling her reverence for factuality, and her father with awakening her sense of social responsibility. Davis herself credited Hawthorne's *Twice-Told Tales* with showing her the enchantment to be found in "commonplace folk and things" (*Bits* 30). Especially after her visit to Concord, Davis developed a view of the author, not as an inactive Emersonian prophet but as a muscular reformer. As her literary concerns sprang directly out of her everyday experience and the pressing social and political issues of her time, Davis always urged her editors to publish her "stories of to-day" as expeditiously as possible.

It is Davis's childhood in the booming industrial mill town of Wheeling, perhaps more than anything else, that shaped her social consciousness and hence her writing. In the newly chartered frontier town the young Davis was exposed to the ravages of industrial work, the disadvantages of immigrant life, and the particular plight of women. "Life in the Iron-Mills," arguably Davis's most important work, illustrates what the white, middle-class Davis garnered from her contact with the underprivileged; her emergent class consciousness is, perhaps, the most radical and consistent feature of her work. The narrator's command that the reader, too, confront his/her privilege, that s/he "come right down with me,—here into the . . . foul effluvia," distinguishes Davis's work as a forerunner of proletarian fiction. Much of Davis's subsequent fiction, such as the industrial novel, *Margret Howth*, or her exposé of the Whiskey Ring Scandal, *John Andross* (1874), continued to explore the operation of power under democratic capitalism.

Davis's professional career, which commenced in April 1861, was born, so to speak, out of the American Civil War; thus, it is not surprising that her literary aesthetic remained attuned to the regional and racial conflicts the war highlighted. Here again, geography influenced her social vision; as she wrote in *Bits*, her family's residence "on the fence" in West Virginia helped her to "see the great question from both sides" (165). War-era texts, such as "David Gaunt" (1862), evenhandedly present the war as a regional and racial family drama. "Blind Tom" (1862), a sympathetic portrayal of a disabled, African-American pianist, illustrates Davis's abolitionist sentiments and allies the oppressions of women artists and the enslaved. And *Waiting for the Verdict* (1867) is particularly remarkable for its prescience of the unresolved nature of race relations. Davis may have been the first writer to critique an American war. Her characterization of the Civil War as "general wretchedness" and "squalid misery" was applied to later conflicts in essays like "The Mean Face of War" (1899) (*Bits* 116).

Part of Davis's critique of her culture's violence entails a reaffirmation of muscular Christianity as the only motivating force behind both personal and political redemption. She continuously scourges a society that had grown too "used to money" to straighten out "relations with [its] Maker" (*Bits* 104, 106). However, Davis's religion did not fall within traditional realms; she argues that faith in the afterlife is complicit in a capitalistic machine that encourages passivity and reconciliation. In stories like "The Harmonists" (1866) and "Berrytown" (1873), utopian community leaders wield religion oppressively. In her writing, Davis reveals the tension between her aggressive Christian zeal and her pragmatic self-sacrifice that makes her reformist impulse seem so radical and some of her life choices so traditional.

Nowhere are these tensions played out more clearly than in her treatment of women's issues. Here, too, she focuses on the economic exigencies controlling Americans' lives. In 1863 Davis had the audacity to write of a child prostitute in "The Promise of the Dawn." Though the girl eventually dies, Davis's characterization is sympathetic, and her insights about the connections between moral degeneracy and economic necessity are rare for her time. Her understanding of the economics underpinning women's status continued to evolve in "In the Market" (1868) and "Earthen Pitchers" (1873), which reveal courtship and marriage as integral to a market-based economy. The incisive *A Law Unto Herself* (1878) exposes the legal basis of women's second-class status. Her essays, too, counter prevalent domestic stereotypes; "In the Gray Cabins of New England" (1895) and "Here and There in the South" (1887) expose the material and intellectual impoverishment of women, both North and South.

Though Davis clearly articulated how American society maintained women's second-class status, her relation to domestic ideology remained vexed. She repeatedly expressed her belief that women's highest rewards were to be found through the roles of mother and wife and fervently argued for the viability of a women's sphere populated by those who use only "women's methods" (*Bits* 231). Yet the frequent appearance of frustrated artists in her fiction belies the psychic expense such a position required of one so committed to her craft. "The Wife's Story" (1864), which followed close on the heels of her breakdown, dramatizes the conflict between artistic ambition and maternal duty, with the protagonist's capitulation to the latter. The fifty-year-old title character of 1889's "Anne" finds herself trapped in the domestic realm, a widowed mother who longs for the artistic passion of her youth. Even Davis's most radical essays on gender operate obliquely; in "Men's Rights" (1869) she advocates professional opportunities for women by appealing to men's right to a whole, fulfilled wife. Her work clearly reveals that Davis lived the struggles about which she wrote.

While the topics that occupied Davis's early work continued to retain her interest in the 1870s, 1880s, and 1890s—women's rights, racial and ethnic inequalities, increasing materialism, the horrors of war—Davis increasingly turned to nonfiction essays, which accommodated her emerging irony and satire more aptly. The aforementioned "Here and There in the South" features Davis's analytical skill and research ability in its depiction of the New South. Her travels in the South also provoked a revisitation of the issues preoccupying her Civil War fiction. In "Some Testimony in the Case" (1885) she articulates the economic bases of persistent racial inequality, and in "A Word to the Colored People" (1889), she argues for a racialized class consciousness. Davis continued as a writer attuned to her time and place. For example, the 1876 Bicentennial prompted historical fiction, while the 1893 Chicago World's Fair inspired essays on the "Woman Question" and the increasing materialism of the times.

Davis's relentless spotlight on social injustice suggests that little had changed for women, minorities, and the working poor during the five decades spanning her career. However, it is important to note that her fiction did yield tangible results. "Put Out of the Way" (1870), a short story dramatizing the mistreatment of the mentally ill, led to the revision of the Pennsylvania laws. And an 1899 U.S. Congressional Report incorporated "The Curse of Education," which argues that education should become part of prison reform. In her last years, Davis became more nostalgic as she reflected upon a childhood world in which "there were no railways . . . no telegraphs, no sky-scraping houses" and not a "trust or a labor union" (*Bits* 1). Her personal reminiscences were ultimately amassed in opposition to this new world in Davis's 1904 autobiography.

CRITICAL RECEPTION

Davis's critical currency rests upon her first published work of fiction, "Life in the Iron-Mills." Both in 1861 and today, "Life" has been lavishly praised for its singularity in American letters of its time: its grimy realism, its social conscience, its sensitivity to the consequences of industrial capitalism. From James T. Fields's initial enthusiasm to its present-day canonization, "Life" has rarely drawn anything but praise. Yet critical reception to Davis's body of work has remained mixed; though she was never a best-seller in her own time (her serious and sometimes unpleasant content matter daunted recreational readers), she remained well respected by the literary community throughout her life. She was consistently praised for her power of characterization and realism. *Lippincott's* review of *Waiting for the Verdict* commends Davis for avoiding heroes and instead "probing" her characters with an "unerring blade" so that they are "very like the 'vast herd' from which they are taken" (1, 118). Additionally, Davis's work neatly satisfied the literary establishment's search for a "national" literature. As early as *Margret Howth*, reviewers were praising Davis's work as disproving the "old cry" that our literature is "only a continuation of that of Europe" (*Continental Monthly* 1, 467). The unique mixture of recognition and repulsion that Davis's writing often evoked was even cited as defining American literature; a review of *A Law Unto Herself* asserts that it is because the novel shows "bad taste" that Davis "succeeds in giving a truer impression of American conditions" (*Nation* 26, 176).

While criticism of her early work was largely positive, many readers, even her friend Sophia Hawthorne, confessed a dislike for Davis's "moldy style" of "disgustful, flabby men and dried up old women" (BPL). As new schools of writers appeared on the scene and trends shifted, work that assumedly devolved into didacticism or grotesqueness was also perceived as weak. Henry James was a reliable detractor of the realistic movement Davis typified, disdainfully complaining that *Waiting for the Verdict* is in "direct oppugnancy" to the "romance" of human life and subsequently skewering *Dallas Galbraith* for "instructing us, purifying us, stirring up our pity" rather than remaining objectively interested in beauty (*Nation* 5, 410; *Nation* 7, 331). In 1892 the critical tide once again turned wholly Davis's way with the publication of her short story collection *Silhouettes of American Life*. Though praise of Davis's work was rarely as unanimously unqualified as it was for "Life in the Iron-Mills," she continued to publish and be reviewed in the best periodicals of her time.

Though Davis's important role as a pioneering realist was recognized in her own time, by 1910, the year of her death, her reputation had faded; Davis's obituary mentions that she had been an author only after distinguishing her as the mother of Richard Harding Davis. Though "Life" was commonly cited as a seminal work of American realism and naturalism during the early twentieth century, it was more often than not treated as an anomaly. Davis was also overlooked by very early feminists, perhaps because of the continued misattribution of *Pro Aris et Focis (A Plea for Our Alters and Hearths)* (1870), a deeply conservative, antisuffrage tract. Not surprisingly, Davis's contemporary critical renaissance began with the Feminist Press's 1972 reprinting of the reliable "Life in the Iron-Mills." In her influential afterward, Tillie Olsen forged a sympathetic bond—a "hunger to know"—between the seemingly oppressive life of Davis during her twenties, the poverty-stricken workers whose lives she imaginatively entered, and the lives of twentieth-century women like Olsen.

Subsequent scholarship has often revolved around issues of genre. The unique blend of realism, sentimentalism, didacticism, and naturalism that characterizes most of Davis's work continues to occupy critics who struggle to situate her among the prevalent schools of her period. Her literary aesthetic has been labelled variously as "critical realism," "literature of the commonplace," "metarealism," and so on, although Davis called herself simply a "realist." Many scholars—most notably, Sharon Harris—reconfigure the whole trajectory of nineteenth-century realism by placing Davis within it. The chameleonlike quality of Davis's life work has, perhaps, contributed to the virtual invisibility of Davis's work within the literary canon beyond "Life in the Iron-Mills."

Since the majority of Davis scholarship focuses exclusively on "Life," it tends to cluster around issues of economics, artistic possibility, and religious or secular transcendence. However, recent trends in literary and historical studies have led to a revaluation of Davis as a writer intensely engaged with the issues of her times. For example, new interest in print culture has encouraged scholars to trace Davis's professional dealings with editors and periodicals. Recent reprintings of some of Davis's lesser-known work (i.e., *Margret Howth* and Jean Pfaelzer's anthology of her magazine fiction and best nonfiction) have made more of her texts available to readers. The fine bio-bibliographical scholarship of Pfaelzer, Jane Atteridge Rose, and Sharon Harris, among others, lays the groundwork for future explorations of Davis's exhaustive body of work. Perhaps the most glaring lack in Davis criticism is the paucity of scholarship on any but a handful of her more than 500 texts. The bulk of her output, which was produced for the ladies' and children's magazines, has been unanimously classed inferior. Admittedly, Davis herself seems to have manufactured this schism between the art she submitted to literary magazines and the pulp she manufactured for economic benefit. For example, she resisted using her name in *Peterson's* bylines until 1890. However, her potboilers and children's fiction reached a much wider audience than her "serious" work; *Peterson's* alone boasted the largest circulation of any ladies' magazine in the United States. Though this work certainly appears more formulaic and "sentimental" than her experimental realism, it ably satisfied audience expectations. In light of Davis's abiding concern with representing and touching the lives of "common" people, one might view her work in popular magazines as her most effective.

The greatest tribute to Davis's influence is, perhaps, the number of women writers she has inspired to write truthfully and courageously of their own times. In "Women in Literature" (1891), she called upon women to write their own histories, to paint for future generations the "inner life and history of their time." Davis's contemporary Elizabeth Stuart Phelps answered Davis's call, explaining that Davis's work "made you feel as if she knew all about you, and were sorry for you, and as if she thought nobody was too poor, or too uneducated, or too worn-out with washing-days, and all the things that do not sound a bit grand in books, to be written about" (780). Tillie Olsen's modern-day tribute attests to the lasting legacy of Davis's work.

WORKS CITED

Anonymous. Review of *A Law Unto Herself. Nation* 26 (7 March 1878): 176.
Anonymous. Review of *Margret Howth. Continental Monthly* 1 (April 1862): 467.
Anonymous. Review of *Waiting for the Verdict. Lippincott's* 1 (January 1868): 118.
Davis, Rebecca Harding. Letter to Annie Fields. 10 January 1863. Richard Harding Davis Collection (#6109). Clifton Waller Barrett Library, University of Virginia.
Hawthorne, Sophia. Letter to Annie Fields. 25 April 1866. Boston Public Library.
James, Henry. Review of *Dallas Galbraith. Nation* 7 (22 October 1868): 331.
———. Review of *Waiting for the Verdict. Nation* 5 (21 November 1867): 410.
Phelps, Elizabeth Stuart. "At Bay." *Harper's New Monthly* 34 (May 1867): 780.

BIBLIOGRAPHY

Works by Rebecca Harding Davis

Novels

Margret Howth: A Story of To-day. Boston: Ticknor, 1862. Reprint, New York: Feminist Press, 1990.

Waiting for the Verdict. New York: Sheldon and Co., 1867. Reprint, Upper Saddle Ridge, NJ: Gregg, 1968.

Dallas Galbraith. Philadelphia: Lippincott, 1868.

John Andross. New York: Orange, 1874.

A Law Unto Herself. Philadelphia: Lippincott, 1878.

Natasqua. New York: Cassell-Rainbow, 1886.

Kent Hampden. New York: Scribner's, 1892.

Doctor Warrick's Daughters. New York: Harper, 1896.

Frances Waldeaux. New York: Harper, 1897.

Short Stories and Novellas

"Life in the Iron-Mills." *Atlantic Monthly* 7 (April 1861): 430–451.

"The Murder in the Glenn Ross." *Peterson's Magazine* 40 (November–December 1861): 347–355, 438–448.

"John Lamar." *Atlantic Monthly* 9 (April 1862): 411–423.

"David Gaunt." *Atlantic Monthly* 10 (September–October 1862): 259–271, 403–421.

"Blind Tom." *Atlantic Monthly* 10 (November 1862): 580–585.

"The Promise of the Dawn: A Christmas Story." *Atlantic Monthly* 11 (January 1863): 10–25.

"The Wife's Story." *Atlantic Monthly* 14 (July 1864): 1–19.

"The Harmonists." *Atlantic Monthly* 17 (May 1866): 529–538.

"In the Market." *Peterson's Magazine* 53 (January 1868): 49–57.

"Put Out of the Way." *Peterson's Magazine* 57 (May–June 1870): 355–367, 431–443; 58 (July–August 1870): 30–41, 109–118.

"Earthen Pitchers." *Scribner's Monthly* 7 (November 1873–April 1874): 73.

"Kitty's Choice, or Berrytown" and Other Stories. Philadelphia: Lippincott, 1873.

"Marcia." *Harper's New Monthly* 53 (November 1876): 925–928.

"Anne." *Harper's New Monthly* 78 (April 1889): 744–750.

Silhouettes of American Life. New York: Scribner's, 1892.

"Life in the Iron-Mills" and Other Stories. Edited with a biographical interpretation by Tillie Olsen. New York: Feminist Press, 1972.

A Rebecca Harding Davis Reader. Edited with a critical introduction by Jean Pfaelzer. Pittsburgh: University of Pittsburgh Press, 1995. (includes nonfiction)

Nonfiction

"Men's Rights." *Putnam's Magazine* 3 (February 1869): 212–224.

"The Middle-Aged Woman." *Scribner's Monthly* 10 (July 1875): 345–347.

"Old Philadelphia." *Harper's New Monthly* 52 (April–May 1876): 705–721, 868–882.

"Some Testimony in the Case." *Atlantic Monthly* 56 (November 1885): 602–608.

"Here and There in the South." *Harper's New Monthly* 75 (July–November 1887): 235.

"A Word to the Colored People." *Independent* 41 (12 September 1889): 1169.
"Women in Literature." *Independent* 43 (7 May 1891): 612.
"The Newly Discovered Woman." *Independent* 45 (30 November 1893): 1601.
"In the Gray Cabins of New England." *Century* 49[n.s. 29] (February 1895): 620–623.
"The Curse of Education." *North American Review* 168 (May 1899): 609–614.
"The Mean Face of War." *Independent* 51 (20 July 1899): 1931–1933.
Bits of Gossip. Boston: Houghton, 1904.

Juvenile Literature

"The Paw Paw Hunt." *Youth's Companion* 44 (9 November 1871): 353–354.
"How the 'Gull' Went Down." *St. Nicholas* 1 (June 1874): 441–444.
"Two Brave Boys." *St. Nicholas* 37 (July 1910): 835.

Studies of Rebecca Harding Davis

Boudreau, Kristin. " 'The Woman's Flesh of Me': Rebecca Harding Davis's Response to Self-Reliance." *American Transcendental Quarterly* 6, no. 2 (1992): 132–140.
Conron, John. "Assailant Landscapes and the Man of Feeling: Rebecca Harding Davis's 'Life in the Iron-Mills.' " *Journal of American Culture* 3, no. 3 (1980): 487–500.
Eppard, Phillip. "Rebecca Harding Davis: A Misattribution." *Papers of the Bibliographical Society of America* 69 (1975): 265–267.
Harris, Sharon M. *Rebecca Harding Davis and American Realism.* Philadelphia: University of Pennsylvania Press, 1991.
———. "Rebecca Harding Davis: A Bibliography of Secondary Criticism, 1958–1986." *Bulletin of Bibliography* 45, no. 4 (1988): 233–246.
———. "Rebecca Harding Davis: A Continuing Misattribution." *Legacy* 5 (1988): 33–34.
———. "Rebecca Harding Davis: From Romanticism to Realism." *American Literary Realism* 21, no. 2 (1989): 4–20.
Hersford, Walter. "Literary Contexts of 'Life in the Iron-Mills.' " *American Literature* 49 (1977): 70–85.
Hood, Richard A. "Framing a 'Life in the Iron-Mills.' " *Studies in American Fiction* (spring 1995): 73–84.
Langford, Gerald. *The Richard Harding Davis Years: A Biography of a Mother and Son.* New York: Holt, 1961.
Malzeppi, Frances. "Sisters in Protest: Rebecca Harding Davis and Tillie Olsen." *Re Artes: Liberales* 12 (1986): 1–9.
Pfaelzer, Jean. "Domesticity and the Discourse of Slavery: 'John Lamar' and 'Blind Tom' by Rebecca Harding Davis." *ESQ: A Journal of the American Renaissance* 38, no. 1 (1992): 31–56.
———. "Rebecca Harding Davis: Domesticity, Social Order, and the Industrial Novel." *International Journal of Women's Studies* 4, no. 3 (1981): 234–244.
———. "The Sentimental Promise and the Utopian Myth: Rebecca Harding Davis's 'The Harmonists' and Louisa May Alcott's 'Transcendental Wild Oats.' " *American Transcendental Quarterly* 3, no. 1 (1989): 85–99.
Rose, Jane Atteridge. "A Bibliography of Fiction and Non-Fiction by Rebecca Harding Davis." *American Realism* 22, no. 3 (1990): 67–86.

————. *Rebecca Harding Davis*. New York: Twayne Publishers, 1993.
Scheiber, Andrew J. ''An Unknown Infrastructure: Gender, Production and Aesthetic Exchange in Rebecca Harding Davis's 'Life in the Iron-Mills.' '' *Legacy* 11, no. 2 (1994): 103–117.
Seltzer, Mark. ''The Still Life.'' *American Literary History* 3, no. 3 (1991): 455–486.
Shurr, William H. '' 'Life in the Iron-Mills': A Nineteenth-Century Conversion Narrative.'' *American Transcendental Quarterly* 5, no. 4 (1991): 245–257.
Yellin, Jean Fagan. ''The 'Feminization' of Rebecca Harding Davis.'' *American Literary History* 2, no. 2 (1990): 203–219.

EMILY DICKINSON (1830–1886)

Nancy A. Walker

BIOGRAPHY

The Homestead, the Amherst, Massachusetts, house in which Emily Elizabeth Dickinson was born on December 10, 1830, had been built seventeen years earlier by her grandfather, Samuel Fowler Dickinson. With the exception of fifteen years during her childhood and early adulthood when the family lived on North Pleasant Street and a year (1847–1848) at Mt. Holyoke College, the Homestead was the only place that Dickinson lived, and a place that, as she grew into maturity, she was increasingly reluctant to leave. Although much has been made of Dickinson's reclusiveness, it can be seen as merely an extreme form of a familial tendency to stasis. For 200 years before Dickinson's birth, her ancestors had lived in New England, refusing to succumb to the lure of western lands. When Emily's brother Austin married Susan Gilbert in 1856, the couple settled in the house next door to the Homestead, the Evergreens; and like Emily, her younger sister, Lavinia (known as Vinnie), remained at the Homestead rather than marrying and starting her own family elsewhere.

If the shape of a life is measured by movement from place to place, the establishment of a family, and—in the case of a writer—the composition and publication of one's work, then Dickinson's life would seem quite unremarkable. But the first line of her poem #632, "The Brain—is wider than the Sky—," is one of the many indications in Dickinson's work that, in the words of Suzanne Juhasz, "to live in the mind is to be most thoroughly alive" (*Continent* 26). And in fact, to grow up in Amherst in the decades before the Civil War was to experience a vibrant intellectual atmosphere. Amherst Academy was founded in 1814, and Emily Dickinson's grandfather helped to found Amherst College in 1821. Dickinson's family ties to Amherst College were particularly close: Emily's father, Edward, and her brother, Austin, served as the college's treasurers for a total of sixty years; its students and faculty members were some of the family's closest associates. A substantial portion of Emily Dickinson's education therefore took place on the informal level of conversations, attendance at lectures, and cultural events. In addition, the Dickinson family prized books, giving them to each other as gifts and thus building a family library. In her poem #604, Dickinson refers to books as "Kinsmen of the Shelf."

Before she was quite five years old, Emily began attending a one-room, ungraded primary school that provided her with the rudiments of reading, writing, and arithmetic. In the fall of 1840, she and Vinnie began their studies at Amherst Academy, where the curriculum was enriched by opportunities to attend lectures at Amherst College, which was particularly strong in the sciences. While Dickinson's poetry bears numerous traces of her wide reading in literature—especially Shakespeare, George Eliot, and the Brownings—it also provides evidence of her enthusiasm for botany, zoology, and geology. In addition to formal instruction, the Academy fostered informal interaction between teachers and students, and Emily's letters from this period and later indicate that she formed close friendships during her years there. One of her Academy teachers later recalled that "her compositions were strikingly original; and in both thought and style seemed beyond her years" (Sewall 342). After seven years at Amherst Academy, Dickinson enrolled in Mt. Holyoke College in South Hadley, Massachusetts; Amherst College admitted only men, and Mt. Holyoke had been founded a decade earlier by Mary Lyon to provide higher education for young women of the area.

Although Dickinson later wrote that it was her father's decision that she not return to Mt. Holyoke after her first year, there is little evidence that she regretted her return to Amherst. She had suffered homesickness and bouts of ill health during her college year, and perhaps more important, she was unable to make a personal commitment to the Christian piety that was part of Mary Lyon's instructional agenda. The period of Dickinson's youth was one of great revivalistic fervor in New England, but while the members of her family and most of her friends joined the church, she maintained a lifelong resistance to a religious doctrine that retained much of its Puritan heritage. Such resistance gives force to much of her poetry, not only in such lighthearted statements as in poem #324 where Dickinson prefers to keep the Sabbath at home and her characterization of the antique nature of the Bible and its "faded" writers in #1545 but also in intense theological struggles with the issues of death and immortality. Lacking the security of faith, she used her poetry to explore her relationships with God, nature, and eternity.

The events of the year 1850 threw into relief Dickinson's resistance to organized religion and also pointed to her vocation as a writer. From the spring through the summer, Amherst was the site of a religious revival; in August, both Edward Dickinson and Susan Gilbert joined the First Church of Christ, and in November, Vinnie did the same, making Emily acutely conscious of remaining unconverted. Austin and Susan began a serious courtship in the spring of the year; while this was destined ultimately to bring Susan into the Dickinson family, it also marked an end to the exclusive girlhood closeness that Emily and Susan had shared—and it was to Susan that Emily had confided her fear that marriage would mean the subjection of her will to that of another. But at the same time, her skill as a writer was recognized when the Amherst College *Indicator* published her mock-serious Valentine in its "Editor's Corner." The Valentine (collected as #34 in the *Selected Letters*) features the high spirits, mocking tone, and play with language that was to characterize some of her poetry.

During the 1850s Austin received his law degree from Harvard University and thus followed his father into the legal profession. The elder Dickinson was meanwhile becoming involved in politics; he was elected to the House of Representatives in 1852, and by the end of the decade, he was considered a possible candidate for governor of Massachusetts. For a time, the public nature of the lives of the male Dickinsons did not deviate sharply from the life that Emily led. She and her sister attended a lecture in Amherst on *Hamlet* given by Richard Henry Dana and heard Jenny Lind sing in Northampton. They visited friends and relatives in Northampton and traveled to Boston, Washington, and Philadelphia. But increasingly Emily stayed home, and by 1869, she was writing to Thomas Wentworth Higginson, "I do not cross my Father's ground to any House or town" (*Selected Letters* 197). Her trips to Boston in 1864 and 1865 were necessitated by visits to an eye doctor; after that, she did not leave Amherst.

For many years scholars speculated that Dickinson's withdrawal from the larger society was the result of disappointment in love, and her letters—including the mysterious ones addressed to an unidentified "Master"—do indicate deep attachments to several individuals. It seems far more likely, however, that about the time she turned thirty she accepted the vocation of poet and consequently arranged her life to create a space for her work. Nor is it true that she withdrew completely from social contact. Through the Dickinson household swirled the controversies of the period, not least because of Edward Dickinson's political involvements: the abolition movement and impending civil war, the location of railroad lines, and religious controversies. In addition, Emily maintained a lively correspondence with family and friends—commemorating births and deaths, reporting household and community news, and discussing her reading. With such letters she sometimes enclosed brief poems; this sharing of her work constituted the major form of "publication" of her poetry during her lifetime.

During the 1850s and 1860s, the *Springfield* (Massachusetts) *Republican*, edited by Dickinson family friend Samuel Bowles, published a handful of Emily's poems. Sending poems to Bowles constituted the first of two gestures toward establishing herself publicly as a poet, both of which doomed her to disappointment. The poems that Bowles printed in the *Republican* were not the most ambitious of those she sent him; furthermore, the paper took the editorial liberty of giving the poems titles and regularizing their punctuation. Her second gesture was more audacious: After reading Thomas Wentworth Higginson's "Letter to a Young Contributor" in the *Atlantic Monthly* in the spring of 1862, Dickinson wrote to Higginson to ask whether he was "too deeply occupied to say if my Verse is alive." Higginson's letter had encouraged young writers—both male and female—to trust in the power of words and to dare to be original; unfortunately, the four poems that Dickinson enclosed with her inquiry struck Higginson as entirely *too* original for publication, but he was intrigued by what he could not fully understand, and there ensued a correspondence that lasted until Dickinson's death. Her letters cast Higginson in the role of teacher, and she signed some of them "Your scholar." It was a role for which Higginson was not well suited because he could never fully appreciate her poetic sensibility; thus, it is ironic that he coedited the first two collections of her poetry to be published after her death, in 1890 and 1891.

Despite—or perhaps even because of—Higginson's inability to recognize her poetic gifts fully, the early 1860s was the period of Dickinson's greatest productivity as a poet. Convinced of her vocation, she wrote steadily, her goal apparently no longer the publication of her work. In fact, when the poet Helen Hunt Jackson (who had spent her childhood in Amherst) tried in the 1870s to encourage Dickinson to publish her poems, she met with resistance. One of the few people at the time capable of taking Dickinson's poetry seriously on its own terms, Jackson wrote from Colorado in March of 1876, "You are a great poet—and it is a wrong to the day you live in, that you will not sing aloud" (quoted in Sewall 580). Jackson eventually convinced Dickinson to contribute a poem to a volume in the No Name Series, which published poems without attribution. When "Success is counted sweetest" appeared in *A Masque of Poets* in 1878—with several words changed—it was thought by many to be the work of Ralph Waldo Emerson.

By 1874, Dickinson's life had been punctuated with the deaths of friends and relatives—some of them young. But nothing could have prepared her for her father's death in June of that year. Always regarded as a rather stern and authoritarian figure by his children, and rendered somewhat remote by his business and political travel, Edward Dickinson was nonetheless the person around whom the household revolved, especially for his daughters. Writing to Higginson the following month, Emily summed up the power of his presence: "His Heart was pure and terrible and I think no other like it exists." Almost precisely a year later, her mother suffered a stroke and was an invalid until her death in 1882. Although Vinnie had usually been the one to care for ailing relatives, both daughters joined in the care of Emily Norcross Dickinson, and the experience seems to have brought Emily and her mother closer than they had ever been.

Meanwhile, there was family turmoil at the Evergreens next door. By the early 1880s, Austin had become engaged in a serious affair with Mabel Loomis Todd, whose husband, David, had come to teach astronomy at Amherst College.

Relations between the Homestead and the Evergreens became strained as Vinnie became an accomplice to the affair and Austin spent more and more of his time with his sisters, from whom his wife, Susan, was necessarily estranged. In the midst of what turned out to be a thirteen-year affair—lasting until Austin's death in 1895—the death of Austin and Susan's eight-year-old son Gilbert in 1883 seemed particularly tragic, especially to Emily for whom he had been a favorite nephew. Not long after Gilbert's death, she wrote to Mrs. J. G. Holland that she was suffering from what the doctor called "nervous prostration," brought on, in her words, by "the crisis of the sorrow of so many years" (quoted in Sewall 623). The only "sorrow" she mentions in her letter is Gilbert's death, but there is no question that she refers also to other deaths and to the virtual loss of Susan through Austin's marital difficulties. After late 1883, she was never really well, and she died, apparently of Bright's disease, on May 15, 1886.

Despite Emily Dickinson's self-imposed isolation, it was well known in Amherst and beyond that she was a poet. Many had read the few poems published in the *Springfield Republican*, and relatives and friends had been the recipients of her occasional poems. While it was not unusual for women to write poetry, the combination of her cryptic, difficult style and, by the 1860s, her personal invisibility had made her a mythic figure in the community. It was in precisely those terms that Mabel Loomis Todd described her in a letter shortly after her arrival in Amherst, calling her "the climax of all the family oddity" (Sewall 216). Yet following Emily's death it was Mabel Todd who instigated the preparation of selections from her poems for publication. Her entree to the poems themselves was, of course, Austin, and what had doubtless begun as curiosity on her part turned into sincere admiration as she read through more of the hundreds of poems than any other individual had seen. She convinced a reluctant Higginson to coedit a volume of the poems and a reluctant publisher to publish it. *Poems* by Emily Dickinson was published in November 1890, and by the end of 1892, it had gone through eleven printings. It was followed by another volume in 1891 and a third in 1896, and in 1894, Mabel Todd edited a two-volume collection of Dickinson's letters. Although it would be another half century before readers had access to all of Dickinson's poems without editorial alterations, the process of recognition had begun, perhaps on terms that Emily Dickinson would have approved.

MAJOR WORKS AND THEMES

When Thomas H. Johnson completed his monumental work *The Poems of Emily Dickinson* in 1955, a total of 1,775 Dickinson poems were finally made available to readers, arranged in a rough chronological order based on such evidence as changes in handwriting, the dates of letters in which poems were enclosed, and occasions in the poet's life to which they seemed to refer. An impulse to group them thematically instead would have foundered on the shoals of interpretation, for even a poem so clearly about death as the well-known

"Because I could not stop for Death—" (#712) is also a poem about courtship, the life cycle, immortality, and the timelessness of eternity. Much of the richness of Dickinson's poetry derives from its resistance to easy classification, which results partly from an elliptical style and liberties with syntax and partly from unusual combinations of images. These characteristics are, in turn, the products of a mind capable of seeing relationships between and among ideas and experiences normally considered disparate. Such a sensibility and practice were particularly at odds with prevailing poetic conventions of the nineteenth century, which favored clear messages about such topics as nature, death, and the consolations of religious faith. Dickinson's poem "A Bird came down the Walk—" (#328), for example, begins as a simple observation of the natural world, as the poet sees dew, grass, and a beetle; but as early as the first stanza, what would have been a benign scene in the hands of a more conventional poet reveals instead a confrontation with the brutal reality of nature, as the bird bites a worm in half and eats it "raw." By the end of the poem, the bird has flown into a soundless void that approximates the eternity that was so often Dickinson's subject.

Thus, although Dickinson shares with such Transcendentalists as Thoreau an affinity for and close observation of the natural world, she cannot accurately be called a "nature poet" any more than she can be called a "religious poet" or a "love poet," even though religious belief and love are frequently explored in her work. For Dickinson, concepts such as nature, faith, eternity, death, and love are complex mysteries rather than certainties, and this complexity is suggested in her yoking of the mundane and the profound and in the elliptical syntax of her poetry. A poem such as "I'm ceded—I've stopped being Theirs—" (#508) contains imagery that allows it to be read as a poem about marriage or about religious conversion—and both readings are in turn challenged by the skepticism about either state that is clear in other poems. It is this ability—or, more accurately, this necessity—to take contradictory stances that leads Alicia Ostriker to identify Dickinson's central strategy as "duplicity," which "makes possible the secret transmission of opposed messages within a single poem" (43). To call Dickinson duplicitous is not to suggest that she was unable to express strongly held views. On the contrary, she forthrightly characterizes passion in "Wild Nights—Wild Nights!" (#249) and airily dismisses the religiously secure in " 'Faith' is a fine invention" (#185). But more often she uses devices such as riddles, negative constructions, and shifts in tone of voice to tease the very concept of certainty.

Such strategies are, for example, frequently employed in the poems about death that are among her best known. Death may be a gentleman in a carriage, as in "Because I could not stop for Death—," but it may also be one term in a balancing act with an unnamed state that is worse for being less defined, as in "It was not Death, for I stood up" (#510). Death is frequently not the end of something but rather a passage to another state; Dickinson speaks of death in the past tense—"I heard a Fly buzz—when I died—" (#465)—not to point to the soul's repose in some heavenly bliss, as in the conventional poetry of the day, but to suggest the continuation of an intelligence that probes the meaning of the transition from one state to another. In the nonhuman natural world, death may be violent and capricious: A bird bites a living worm in two, and in "Apparently with no surprise" (#1624), the frost assassinates an unsuspecting flower. That this "beheading" takes place before a God who approves suggests a deity who sanctions such capricious acts of violence, and the note of irony here is similar to her calling God a "noted Clergyman" in "Some keep the Sabbath" (#324). Such a humanizing of God serves more than one purpose: It allows Dickinson to grapple with the mystery of his power on her own terms, and it also removes from him the wrath and vengeance promoted as God's attributes by the Calvinism that Dickinson rejected.

As concerned as Dickinson was with questions of belief and immortality, a great many of her poems deal with everyday secular life: love, the domestic routine, technological innovations, and political events such as the Civil War. Far from being isolated from the currents of life, Dickinson was intensely engaged with the public and private dramas of her century. Her earliest extant poems are love poems, including Valentines that young people of her day customarily sent each other in February, but as time went on, her attitudes toward conventional heterosexual love and marriage became complex and even contradictory. Even in the relatively early poem #199, which begins with the apparently proud announcement "I'm 'wife,' " the use of the quotation marks around the term hints at confinement within a category, and the sense of marriage as confinement or even the eradication of self is heightened when the matrimonial state is termed a "soft Eclipse" later in the poem. Dickinson frequently refers metaphorically to the male figure as the "sun" and the female as the "daisy," or "day's eye," which suggests an enormous hierarchical distance; as Margaret Homans has put it: "[A] flower called a day's eye is being defined not as itself but in comparison to the sun" (118). Dickinson's awareness of this unequal power relationship (which she might also have observed in her parents' marriage), coupled with her expressions of love to other women (especially Susan Gilbert, to whom she sent more than 200 of her poems), has led to speculation that Dickinson was homosexual, although the rhetoric of her letters to the unidentified "Master" would suggest otherwise, as "Daisy" yearns for the presence and approval of an unobtainable male lover.

Unlike the Transcendentalists and most women poets of her period, Dickinson embraced science and technology, and her poems are as peppered with scientific and technical language as they are with the language of nature and domesticity. In one of her "riddle" poems, in which something identified only as "it" is described, she celebrates the locomotive, which truly becomes the "iron horse" the nineteenth century termed it: "I like to see it lap the Miles—" (#585). In contrast to her domestication of the railroad, the language of technology is used to suggest the artificiality of prayer in poem #437, in which it is termed both "implement" and "apparatus." Extremes of emotion are expressed as avalanches, volcanoes, abysses, and other cataclysmic features of the geologic world. Conversely, nature peacefully observed is often dressed in domestic metaphors, as the snow in "It sifts from Leaden Sieves—" (#311) becomes face powder, smoothing the "Wrinkles" in the roadways. In such poems, Dickinson assumes the stance of the observant naturalist for whom natural phenomena are facts rather than inspiration or consolation.

Dickinson's ability to assume a number of different voices and personae both lends depth and complexity to her poetry and prevents readers from facile labeling of her philosophy or poetic practice. Her tone can be one of ecstatic joy, as it is in "I taste a liquor never brewed—" (#214). But other poems solemnly explore the emotional states of grief, despair, and loss. When Dickinson questions authority—especially religious authority—she frequently dons the mask of a child, in Barbara Clarke Mossberg's words, "using a pose of childish inquiry as a shield" (48). To this inquiring child, God is a "Curious Friend" (#564) or an "Old Neighbor" (#623) but not an awe-inspiring deity. Dickinson's adult voice can be scathingly satiric, as when she addresses the "Dimity Convictions" of proper "Gentlewomen" (#401) or the pompous minister depicted in #1207. But the adult woman's voice also appears in solemnly beautiful love lyrics such as "That I did always love" (#549) and the more openly sensual "Wild Nights—Wild Nights!" (#249). That Dickinson deliberately played a variety of roles in her poems, as if denying a unitary self, seems clear from the relatively early poem (c. 1861) that begins "I'm Nobody!" but that, because it announces her to a reader, ends by making her the "Somebody" she affects to disdain.

The "Somebody" that emerges most clearly in Dickinson's work is the poet herself. Not only is hers perhaps the most distinctive individual voice of nineteenth-century American poetry, but poetry itself is the theme of a number of her poems. For Dickinson, the true poet was endowed with the gift of special—almost holy—knowledge and the ability to interpret the world to others. Poets "light Lamps," she states in poem #883, providing a "vital Light" comparable to that of the sun. Indeed, in a list of the most important things—poets, the sun, summer, and heaven—Dickinson initially puts poets first but then decides that only they are necessary, for they "Comprehend the Whole" (#569). As a poet, Dickinson dwells in "Possibility," where her "Occupation" is to "gather Paradise" (#657). The use of religious imagery in her poems about poetry and the power of language suggests not a usurpation of divine by human activity but rather that the imagination, unfettered by doctrine, is the most powerful force she can imagine. Thus, she offers her own work as nothing less than a "letter to the World," asking that the world "judge" her "tenderly" (#441).

CRITICAL RECEPTION

To today's readers and scholars of Emily Dickinson, it may seem that for the first half century after her death the "sweet Countrymen" that she addressed in

"This is my letter to the World" judged her all too "tenderly," wrapping her in the mythology of the reclusive woman and providing her with more of a cult following than a serious appreciation of her poetic gifts. But as Richard B. Sewall notes in the final chapter of his 1974 biography of Dickinson, "myths have their uses," and those surrounding Dickinson's life and work "helped keep Emily Dickinson alive during the long years between the first flurry of interest in the 1890s and the beginning . . . of solid work toward the middle of our own century" (707). If Dickinson was misunderstood, she was at least remembered, instead of dropping out of sight as did so many other women writers of the nineteenth century.

Those close to Dickinson kept her life and work in the public eye for several decades after her death. During the 1890s, Mabel Loomis Todd and Thomas Wentworth Higginson were primarily responsible for editing volumes of her poems and letters, and as late as 1931, Todd edited yet another edition of the letters. In the intervening decades, however, the task of presenting and interpreting Dickinson to a larger public was assumed by the next generation—specifically, Dickinson's niece, Martha Dickinson Bianchi, the daughter of Austin and Susan who had shown some early promise as a poet herself. In 1924, Bianchi edited *The Life and Letters of Emily Dickinson*, a major contribution to the image of the poet as a lonely, lovesick woman, and with Alfred Leete Hampson, a volume optimistically but erroneously titled *The Complete Poems of Emily Dickinson*. Indeed, in 1945, Bianchi and Millicent Todd Bingham (daughter of David and Mabel Loomis Todd) edited *Bolts of Melody: New Poems of Emily Dickinson*.

While friends and family kept Dickinson's name alive, her work did not entirely escape the notice of the scholarly world in the early decades of the century. Most notably, she is the only woman writer considered in anthropologist Constance Rourke's 1931 *American Humor: A Study of the National Character*. Calling Dickinson "in a profound sense a comic poet" who saw "a changing universe within that acceptant view which is comic in its profoundest sense, which is part reconciliation, part knowledge of eternal disparity" (209, 211), Rourke read Dickinson in a way that could have—but did not—rescued her from her somber mythology. In fact, following Rourke's remarks, it was not until the 1980s that scholars paid serious attention to Dickinson's playfulness and her cosmic skepticism.

With the publication of three volumes of the *Poems* and the *Letters*, in 1955 and 1958, respectively, interest in and reinterpretation of Dickinson's work increased in both variety and volume, securing her place in the academic canon of American literature. In the introduction to the 1983 collection *Feminist Critics Read Emily Dickinson*, Suzanne Juhasz remarks that Dickinson "is, after all, the greatest woman poet in the English language" (1). By now, about 200 books and hundreds of articles have Emily Dickinson as their subject, including biographies, annotated bibliographies of criticism, analyses of her poetry, and musical settings of her work. The existence of the Emily Dickinson International

Society testifies to her literary stature in a number of countries, and in 1992, the Society started *The Emily Dickinson Journal*, which publishes essays on her life and work.

WORKS CITED

Homans, Margaret. " 'Oh, Vision of Language!': Dickinson's Poems of Love and Death." In *Feminist Critics Read Emily Dickinson*, edited by Suzanne Juhasz. Bloomington: Indiana University Press, 1983. 114–133.

Johnson, Thomas H. *Emily Dickinson: Selected Letters*. Cambridge: Harvard University Press, 1971.

———. *The Poems of Emily Dickinson*. Cambridge: Harvard University Press, 1955.

Juhasz, Suzanne. Introduction to *Feminist Critics Read Emily Dickinson*, edited by Suzanne Juhasz. Bloomington: Indiana University Press, 1983. 1–21.

———. *The Undiscovered Continent: Emily Dickinson and the Space of the Mind*. Bloomington: Indiana University Press, 1983.

Mossberg, Barbara Clarke. "Emily Dickinson's Nursery Rhymes." In *Feminist Critics Read Emily Dickinson*, edited by Suzanne Juhasz. Bloomington: Indiana University Press, 1983. 45–66.

Ostriker, Alicia Suskin. *Stealing the Language: The Emergence of Women's Poetry in America*. Boston: Beacon Press, 1986.

Rourke, Constance. *American Humor: A Study of the National Character*. New York: Harcourt, Brace, 1931.

Sewall, Richard B. *The Life of Emily Dickinson*. New York: Farrar, Straus and Giroux, 1974.

BIBLIOGRAPHY

Works by Emily Dickinson

The Poems of Emily Dickinson. Edited by Thomas H. Johnson. Cambridge: Harvard University Press, 1955.

The Letters of Emily Dickinson. Edited by Thomas H. Johnson. Cambridge: Harvard University Press, 1958.

Studies of Emily Dickinson

Anderson, Charles R. *Emily Dickinson's Poetry: Stairway of Surprise*. New York: Hold, Rinehart and Winston, 1960.

Bennett, Paula. *Emily Dickinson: Woman Poet*. Iowa City: University of Iowa Press, 1990.

Bingham, Millicent Todd. *Ancestors' Brocades: The Literary Debut of Emily Dickinson*. New York: Harper and Brothers, 1945.

Cady, Edwin H., and Louis J. Budd, eds. *On Dickinson* (The Best from *American Literature*). Durham: Duke University Press, 1990.

Cody, John. *After Great Pain: The Inner Life of Emily Dickinson*. Cambridge: Harvard University Press, 1971.

Dandurand, Karen. *Dickinson Scholarship: An Annotated Bibliography 1969–1985*. New York: Garland, 1988.

Duchac, Joseph. *The Poems of Emily Dickinson: An Annotated Guide to Commentary Published in English, 1890–1977*. Boston: G. K. Hall, 1979.

———. *The Poems of Emily Dickinson: An Annotated Guide to Commentary Published in English, 1978–1989*. New York: G. K. Hall, 1993.

Farr, Judith, ed. *Emily Dickinson: A Collection of Critical Essays*. Englewood Cliffs, NJ: Prentice-Hall, 1996.

———. *The Passion of Emily Dickinson*. Cambridge: Harvard University Press, 1992.

Ferlazzo, Paul J., ed. *Critical Essays on Emily Dickinson*. Boston: G. K. Hall, 1984.

Gelpi, Albert J. *Emily Dickinson: The Mind of the Poet*. Cambridge: Harvard University Press, 1965.

Johnson, Thomas H. *Emily Dickinson: An Interpretive Biography*. Cambridge: Harvard University Press, 1955.

Juhasz, Suzanne. *The Undiscovered Continent: Emily Dickinson and the Space of the Mind*. Bloomington: Indiana University Press, 1983.

Juhasz, Suzanne, Cristanne Miller, and Martha Nell Smith. *Comic Power in Emily Dickinson*. Austin: University of Texas Press, 1993.

Keller, Karl. *The Only Kangaroo among the Beauty: Emily Dickinson and America*. Baltimore: Johns Hopkins University Press, 1979.

Lease, Benjamin. *Emily Dickinson's Readings of Men and Books: Sacred Soundings*. New York: St. Martin's Press, 1990.

Lilliedahl, Ann. *Emily Dickinson in Europe: Her Literary Reputation in Selected Countries*. Washington, D.C.: University Press of America, 1981.

Loeffelholz, Mary. *Dickinson and the Boundaries of Feminist Theory*. Urbana: University of Illinois Press, 1991.

Martin, Wendy. *An American Triptych: Anne Bradstreet, Emily Dickinson, Adrienne Rich*. Chapel Hill: University of North Carolina Press, 1984.

Mossberg, Barbara Clarke. *Emily Dickinson: When a Writer Is a Daughter*. Bloomington: Indiana University Press, 1982.

Pollack, Vivian R. *Dickinson: The Anxiety of Gender*. Ithaca: Cornell University Press, 1984.

Pollitt, Josephine. *Emily Dickinson*. New York: Harper and Brothers, 1930.

Rosenbaum, Stanford P. *A Concordance to the Poems of Emily Dickinson*. Ithaca: Cornell University Press, 1964.

Sewall, Richard B. *The Life of Emily Dickinson*. New York: Farrar, Straus and Giroux, 1974.

———, ed. *Emily Dickinson: A Collection of Critical Essays*. Englewood Cliffs, NJ: Prentice-Hall, 1963.

Sherwood, William R. *Circumference and Circumstance: Stages in the Mind and Art of Emily Dickinson*. New York: Columbia University Press, 1968.

Shurr, William H., ed. *New Poems of Emily Dickinson*. Chapel Hill: University of North Carolina Press, 1993.

Smith, Martha Nell. *Rowing in Eden: Rereading Emily Dickinson*. Austin: University of Texas Press, 1992.

Taggart, Genevieve. *The Life and Mind of Emily Dickinson*. New York: Alfred A. Knopf, 1930.

Whicher, George F. *This Was a Poet: A Critical Biography of Emily Dickinson*. New York: Scribner's, 1938.

Wolff, Cynthia Griffin. *Emily Dickinson*. New York: Knopf, 1986.

Wylder, Edith. *The Last Face: Emily Dickinson's Manuscripts*. Albuquerque: University of New Mexico Press, 1971.

ALICE RUTH MOORE DUNBAR-NELSON (1875–1935)

Jean Marie Lutes

BIOGRAPHY

Alice Ruth Moore Dunbar-Nelson was born in New Orleans, Louisiana, in 1875, the daughter of a seamstress and a merchant marine. She grew up and attended public high school in New Orleans and soon became an active member of the Creole society she would use as a backdrop for much of her fiction. Of mixed black, white and Native American ancestry, she could pass as white, but she identified herself as a person of color and an advocate for African-American rights. In 1892, after graduating from a two-year teachers' program at Straight College (now Dillard University), Dunbar-Nelson took her first job as a teacher, launching a career that would often sustain her financially when her literary efforts failed to do so.

After leaving New Orleans in 1896 in search of new opportunities in the North, she lived in New York and Washington, D.C., eventually settling in Wilmington, Delaware, where she taught in a local high school for nearly twenty years. Teaching was just one of Dunbar-Nelson's many occupational titles, however; at various times, she worked as a stenographer, campaign manager, social worker, and platform lecturer. In her late thirties she began her journalistic career in earnest, writing articles and essays and working as an editor. An antilynching crusader and an ardent suffragist, she was also an organizer and lecturer in the black women's club movement. She remained politically active even when doing so impinged on her job security. In 1920, the principal of the Delaware high school where she taught locked her out of her classroom and terminated her position because of her work for the Republican Party. For the next two years, she coedited and published the Wilmington *Advocate* newspaper. She also helped to found the Industrial School for Colored Girls in Marshalltown, Delaware, where she worked as a teacher and parole officer from 1924 to 1928.

Dunbar-Nelson's book publishing career began early and ended sooner than she would have liked. She published her first book, *Violets*, a lighthearted collection of short stories, poems, and essays, when she was just twenty years old. Four years later, her second book, a short story collection titled *The Goodness of St. Rocque*, appeared. It would be her last. She never again succeeded in persuading a publisher to print a book-length volume of her fiction or poetry, although she continued to publish new stories, poems, essays, editorials, and reviews in newspapers, magazines, and literary journals. She also edited *Masterpieces of Negro Eloquence* (1914), a compilation of speeches, and *The Dunbar Speaker and Entertainer* (1920), a literary magazine.

Her ill-fated marriage to African-American poet Paul Laurence Dunbar defined her public role for most of her life. Although she left Dunbar in 1902 after only four years as his wife and was estranged from him when he died in 1906, she was still referred to as Paul Dunbar's widow two decades after his death. Yet her relationship with Dunbar was just one of the many passionate attachments she formed throughout her life. She entered into a short-lived union with Henry Arthur Callis, a teacher she married in 1910 and later divorced. She later found a more stable partnership with Robert J. Nelson, a journalist who was her husband from 1916 until her death in 1935. In addition to these heterosexual unions, Dunbar-Nelson also had at least two or three physically and emotionally intimate relationships with women. Her affair with Fay Jackson Robinson, a younger journalist and socialite, was especially intense. Despite the need to keep such involvements secret because of the prevailing intolerance toward homosexuality, evidence from Dunbar-Nelson's diary suggests the existence of an active black lesbian network in the late nineteenth and early twentieth century.

On September 18, 1935, Dunbar-Nelson died of heart trouble in Philadelphia. She was sixty years old. Her body was cremated in Wilmington, Delaware; no Philadelphia service would handle such arrangements for a person of color. Shortly thereafter, her husband honored her final wish by scattering her ashes over the Delaware River.

MAJOR WORKS AND THEMES

Dunbar-Nelson produced a tremendous range of writings that defy easy categorization, from newspaper columns to conventional lyric poetry. Although she was better recognized as a poet in her lifetime, her short fiction in the local color tradition, based on her hometown of New Orleans, is best known today. Her journalistic work, her plays, and her diary writings round out her contributions to American literature.

As an African-American woman, she confronted both sexism and racism in her struggles to be recognized as an author. Undoubtedly, her decision to retain the well-known Dunbar name, even after her subsequent marriages, earned her entry into circles that would otherwise have excluded her. A flyer for one public appearance announced: "Mrs. Paul Laurence Dunbar Coming! Mrs. Alice Dunbar-Nelson, formerly the widow of the Greatest Negro Poet" (*Give Us Each Day* 148). But her literary aspirations were always quite distinct from Dunbar's. She was a published author before she ever met him; he initiated their courtship after seeing her picture and one of her poems in a Boston magazine. He became famous for his dialect verse, while she resisted the role of the self-consciously black writer. After giving a university lecture in 1929, she noted with undisguised irritation, "My talk on the 'Negro's Literary Reaction to American Life' apparently appreciated, but of course, they would want to hear dialect Dunbar at the end. Makes me sick" (*Give Us Each Day* 303).

The white literary establishment at this time expected black authors to fulfill a particular role—namely, to write in dialect and to center their work on racial issues, as her poet-husband did. Dunbar-Nelson refused to conform to this stereotype. While she always addressed race in her nonfictional writings, she rarely made it an explicit concern of her early poetry and fiction. Her later writing expresses racial conflict much more directly. This evolution was inspired in part by the Harlem Renaissance, the exhilarating burst of African-American poetry, fiction, music, and art in the early twentieth century. Dunbar-Nelson participated in the creative outpouring not as a bold innovator but rather as a respected older writer, contributing her own voice but also helping to evaluate the new voices on the black literary scene.

Much of Dunbar-Nelson's poetry treats "universal" themes, such as unrequited love and the conflict between nature and humankind. In "Violets," a Shakespearean sonnet, she celebrates the spirituality of the natural world in a romantic meditation on her favorite flowers. Other, later poems convey her dedication to social justice, treating less traditional topics and adopting a more openly political tone. "To the Negro Farmers of the United States" praises African-American workers; the speaker of "April Is On the Way" is running from a lynch mob. In her 1920 war poem "I Sit and Sew," the female speaker yearns to join the soldiers on the field, but she must be still and quietly productive instead, as the title (also the speaker's refrain) makes clear. The poem concludes with a possible move toward rebellion: "this pretty futile seam,/ It stifles me—God, must I sit and sew?" (*Works* II, 84). As this verse illustrates, sometimes Dunbar-Nelson used poetry to explore the highly charged emotions of women trapped by domestic duties, poverty, or ambition—themes she would develop more fully in her short fiction. She portrayed the taboo subject of lesbian sexuality in "You! Inez!"—an unpublished poem dated 1921.

Her New Orleans stories, best represented in her second book, *The Goodness of St. Rocque*, offer detailed, evocative descriptions of local customs and traditions that rival those of better-known regional writers such as George Washington Cable. Set in Creole society, with characters of indeterminate race (she rarely marks them as decidedly black or decidedly white), these stories often place female characters at center stage. They follow the complexities of courtship rituals, trace the fate of jilted women, and dramatize clashes between artistic ambition and restricted female social roles. "Carnival Jangle" details the tragic fate of a young woman who cross-dresses as a male troubadour during Mardi Gras; "Sister Josepha" depicts the convent as a necessary prison for a beautiful orphan who would otherwise face sexual degradation; the title story, "The Goodness of St. Rocque," interweaves voodoo and Catholicism into the tale of two women competing for a man. "A Story of Vengeance" dramatizes female ambivalence through a disturbing dramatic monologue in which an old maid bewails her lonely, loveless existence as she looks back on her fabulously successful career as a professional singer.

Racial tension also appears at times in these early stories—in "Mr. Baptiste," a labor dispute between Irish and African-American longshoremen results in the death of an old Creole man—but it was not until much later that Dunbar-Nelson portrayed race oppression as powerfully as she portrayed gender oppression in the *St. Rocque* stories. Of course, her use of Creole characters, in and of itself, betrays her interest in race. In a 1916 essay on "People of Color in Louisiana, Part I," she explores the relation between race and language, noting "there is no such word as Negro permissible in the speaking of this State." She highlights the conflicting definitions of Creole—whites insisted that Creoles were white with French and Spanish blood, while people of color responded by saying that all natives of Louisiana were Creole, "with the African strain slightly apparent." Dunbar-Nelson concludes that "the true Creole is like the famous gumbo of the state, a little bit of everything" (reprinted in Williams, 138, 143–144).

Her journalistic writing never shrank from discussing the problems of the color line. She wrote incisively and often angrily about the damaging effects of racial discrimination and the horror of lynching, as well as the particular problems faced by women of color. In a 1928 editorial in the Washington *Eagle*, she expressed her opinion on the most recent twist in Herbert Hoover's presidential campaign. "The ultimate insult has been given to Presidential Candidate Hoover," she observed sarcastically. "He has been accused of calling upon and dancing with a colored woman!" Her anger was directed not at Hoover's accuser (one of his political opponents) but at Hoover himself, because of his outraged reaction. She concluded, "Any Negro who would vote for Mr. Hoover after his gratuitous insult to the womenkind of the race is unworthy of the trusting faith of a sister, the loyal love of a wife, or the tender self-sacrificing devotion of a mother" (*Works* II, 280). Dunbar-Nelson invested considerable creative energy in her journalism, displaying her skills as a social commentator, a political analyst, and a critic of literature, theater, and film.

The stark differences in her two published plays reflect her increasing engagement with national political issues. In *The Author's Evening At Home* (1900), a lighthearted playlet from the early part of her career, a writer's chatty wife and mother foil his repeated attempts to work in his library. The antics of the white characters in the drama seem intended solely to amuse. In contrast, Dunbar-Nelson's 1918 play, *Mine Eyes Have Seen*, clearly sets out to persuade

African Americans to support the war. The cast of mostly African-American characters decries America's history of racial injustice; a Jewish character even joins the debate on their side. The play concludes with the characters convinced that despite widespread racial discrimination, black soldiers must fight for the honor of their race and country.

Another significant aspect of Dunbar-Nelson's literary legacy is her journal, which she kept in 1921 and from 1926 to 1931. A rare find—one of the very few known journals by African-American women—it provides an insider's glimpse of major events in early twentieth-century African-American activism. Discovered, edited, and published in 1984 by Gloria T. Hull, the diary reveals a woman with a multifaceted identity, an identity that forces us to rethink rigid categories of literary authorship, as well as those of gender, race, class, and sexuality.

CRITICAL RECEPTION

Known for her physical beauty, her aristocratic bearing, and her taste for opera and art museums, Dunbar-Nelson's genteel image has often obscured her commitment to social activism—as well as the financial difficulties she encountered at almost every stage of her writing career. Her need to make money to support herself and her commitment to social reform never allowed her the luxury of writing slowly and uninterruptedly. Gloria T. Hull characterizes Dunbar-Nelson's situation aptly when she observes, "Doggedly determined to be a writer, she plied her trade, often too facilely, hastily, opportunistically, and without revision—carried forward on the flow of words that came quite easily for her" (*Works* I, xxx). Despite such haste, as Hull quickly points out, Dunbar-Nelson produced an array of writings that warrant more serious critical attention than they have thus far received.

Dunbar-Nelson's public role as a great man's wife and widow inevitably influenced critical responses to her work. Literary notices almost always identified her as Paul Dunbar's faithful helpmeet. In 1900, one reviewer even suggested that her marriage was the only reason *The Goodness of St. Rocque* appeared in print at all (New York *Evening Sun*, 11 October 1900). Most notices were less harsh. They often described her work in approving but diminutive terms, complimenting her "sympathetic and refined manner" and her "pretty" writing (New York *Evening Post*, 28 August 1900; New York *Mail and Express*, 16 December 1899; quoted in Hull, *Color* 52–54). Although she never identified herself primarily as a poet, what little serious critical attention Dunbar-Nelson received in her lifetime tended to focus on her poetry. James Weldon Johnson helped to secure her reputation when he included her in his groundbreaking 1931 anthology *The Book of American Negro Poetry*.

It is Dunbar-Nelson's fiction, however, that has garnered more attention from recent scholars. While her first book, *Violets*, is usually viewed as a juvenile precursor to her more mature work, her later collection, *The Goodness of St.*

Rocque, has attracted considerably more praise. In these stories, critics have found compelling ethnic portraits, frank portrayals of the frustrations experienced by many turn-of-the-century women, and even, as Elizabeth Ammons recently argued, a subtle, carnivalesque treatment of sexual and racial identities (Ammons 61–71).

Critics from Dunbar-Nelson's era to our own have observed that description was one of her strengths, handling plots one of her weaknesses. Her failed attempts at novels highlight this problem. In addition, she has been—and still is—criticized for maintaining a misguided division between her imaginative literature and her own historically specific experiences of racism. New readings of her work, however, suggest that she did not fully excise complex issues such as race from her fiction—even when her narratives suggest, on the surface, that she has done just that. Unfortunately, Dunbar-Nelson's diary and her extensive and spirited journalistic work have received less attention than her stories. They remain largely unexplored, despite their obvious value to literary critics and historians interested in constructing a picture of American life and letters that more accurately reflects the diversity of the American experience.

WORKS CITED

Ammons, Elizabeth. *Conflicting Stories: American Women Writers at the Turn into the Twentieth Century*. New York: Oxford University Press, 1991.

Dunbar-Nelson, Alice. *An Alice Dunbar-Nelson Reader*. Edited by R. Ora Williams. Washington, D.C.: University Press of America, 1978.

———. *Give Us Each Day: The Diary of Alice Dunbar-Nelson*. Edited by Gloria T. Hull. New York: W. W. Norton, 1984.

———. *The Works of Alice Dunbar-Nelson*. Edited by Gloria T. Hull. 3 vols. New York: Oxford University Press, 1988.

Hull, Gloria T. *Color, Sex, and Poetry: Three Women Writers of the Harlem Renaissance*. Bloomington: Indiana University Press, 1987.

BIBLIOGRAPHY

Works by Alice Dunbar-Nelson

Violets and Other Tales. Boston: Monthly Review Press, 1895.

The Goodness of St. Rocque and Other Stories. New York: Dodd, Mead, and Co., 1899.

"*The Author's Evening at Home.*" *The Smart Set* (September 1900): 105–106.

Masterpieces of Negro Eloquence. Edited by Alice Dunbar-Nelson. Harrisburg, PA: Douglass Publishing Co., 1914.

"*Mine Eyes Have Seen.*" *Crisis* 15 (1918): 271–275.

The Dunbar Speaker and Entertainer. Edited by Alice Dunbar-Nelson. Naperville, IL: J. L. Nichols, 1920.

An Alice Dunbar-Nelson Reader. Edited by R. Ora Williams. Washington, D.C.: University Press of America, 1978.

Give Us Each Day: The Diary of Alice Dunbar-Nelson. Edited by Gloria T. Hull. New
    York: W. W. Norton, 1984.
The Works of Alice Dunbar-Nelson. Edited by Gloria T. Hull. 3 vols. New York: Oxford
    University Press, 1988.

Studies of Alice Dunbar-Nelson

Ammons, Elizabeth. "The Limits of Freedom: The Fiction of Alice Dunbar-Nelson, Kate
    Chopin, and Pauline Hopkins." In *Conflicting Stories: American Women Writers
    at the Turn into the Twentieth Century.* New York: Oxford University Press, 1991.
    59–85.
Bryan, Violet Harrington. "Race and Gender in the Early Works of Alice Dunbar-
    Nelson." In *Louisiana Women Writers: New Essays and a Comprehensive Bib-
    liography,* edited by Dorothy H. Brown and Barbara C. Ewell. Baton Rouge:
    Louisiana State University Press, 1992. 120–138.
Hull, Gloria T. "Alice Dunbar-Nelson: A Personal and Literary Perspective." In *Between
    Women: Biographers, Novelists, Critics, Teachers and Artists Write About Their
    Work on Women,* edited by Carol Ascher, Louise DeSalvo, and Sara Ruddick.
    Boston: Beacon Press, 1984. 104–111.
Metcalf, E. W., ed. *The Letters of Paul and Alice Dunbar: A Private History.* Berkeley:
    University of California Press, 1973.
Shockley, Ann Allen, ed. *Afro-American Women Writers, 1746–1933: An Anthology and
    Critical Guide.* Boston: G. K. Hall, 1988.
Stetson, Erlene, ed. *Black Sister: Poetry by Black American Women, 1746–1980.* Bloo-
    mington: Indiana University Press, 1981.
Whitlow, Roger. "Alice Dunbar-Nelson: New Orleans Writer." In *Regionalism and the
    Female Imagination: A Collection of Essays.* New York: Human Sciences Press,
    1985. 109–125.

EMMA EMBURY
(1806–1863)

Janette M. Gomes

BIOGRAPHY

The first of Elizabeth Post and Dr. James R. Manley's three children, Emma Catherine Manley was born in 1806 in New York City, where she continued to reside for the fifty-seven years of her life. Despite her New York school education and the privileged status she enjoyed as the daughter of a prominent physician, Emma later wrote of the loneliness she experienced with the early development of her poetic talents, which she said were unappreciated by her family and friends (Welter 79). Nonetheless, by the age of twenty, Emma, writing under the pseudonym "Ianthe," was contributing verse to the *New York Mirror* and other periodicals.

Ianthe also began writing as "Emma C. Embury" following her marriage on May 10, 1828, to the president of the Atlantic Bank of Brooklyn, Daniel Embury. The couple established their household in Brooklyn, where Emma became the leader of a literary salon whose members included Edgar Allan Poe and Rufus W. Griswold. Daniel was praised by his contemporaries for being an intelligent man who supported his wife's literary endeavors, and Emma, who denied having a literary career, was lauded for not allowing her writing to interfere with her duties as a wife or as a mother to her three children.

The first collection of Embury's verse, *Guido, a Tale; Sketches from History and Other Poems*, was published the same year that her wedding took place. Almost all of the pieces that appeared in *Guido* and subsequent volumes of Embury's poems, stories, and essays had been previously published in popular periodicals. During the 1830s and 1840s, Embury frequently contributed to *The Knickerbocker Magazine, Sartain's Union Magazine, Godey's Lady's Book, The*

Ladies' Companion, and *Graham's Magazine*, as well as others. The latter three also listed Embury as a member of their editorial staffs during the early 1840s.

While 1848 is commonly cited as the year a serious chronic illness ended Embury's literary career and social life, her poems and stories continued to appear in periodicals as late as 1851. The symptoms of her illness progressed, however, rendering Embury a complete invalid for the two years preceding her death on February 10, 1863.

MAJOR WORKS AND THEMES

Love, along with its attendant joys and sorrows, is the predominant subject of Embury's poems and tales. *Guido*, whose title character is a poet suffering from unrequited love, was followed by another book of verse, *Love's Token Flowers* (1846), and *The Poems of Emma C. Embury*, published posthumously in 1869. Poems such as "Stanzas Addressed to a Friend on Her Marriage," in which the speaker admits to feelings of jealousy and loss, "A Lament," about the death of a brother, and "To My First-Born" indicate the range of affections Embury portrayed in her work. Her conventional, moralistic prose about love and other difficulties of life appeared in her original and reprinted collections, including *Pictures of Early Life, or Sketches of Youth* (1830), *Constance Latimer, or the Blind Girl, with Other Tales* (1838), and *Glimpses of Home Life, or Causes and Consequences* (1848).

Embury's main characters are often self-sacrificing women who remain strong and productive despite emotional upheavals and the discomforts of dissipated wealth. They are frequently village dwellers, earning Embury the nickname the "Mitford of America." In several cases, Embury's heroines are historical figures; she wrote poems about, among others, Madame de Staël and Queen Elizabeth.

Embury's work is also noted for its vivid descriptions of the environment. In *Nature's Gems, or American Wild Flowers in Their Native Haunts* (1845), Embury's prose and verse accompany an artist's renderings of American landscapes. Her depictions of the American countryside are an integral part of many of her tales and poems, a few of which were contributed to *The American Juvenile Keepsake* (1834) and praised by Rosalie V. Halsey as "some of the earliest descriptions of country life in literature for American children" (200).

CRITICAL RECEPTION

In general, Embury's contemporaries extolled her work generously. Poe, for example, wrote that her poetry was "of no common order" and, comparing her to the likes of Ann Sophia Stephens, Eliza Leslie, and Susan Sedgwick, declared that, as a story writer, Embury had "no equal among her sex in America—certainly no superior" (90–91). Later critics have admonished Embury's admirers for such lavish praise. George Harvey Genzmer, for instance, claimed that Poe and others had "habitually confused Mrs. Embury's literary achievements with her virtues as a wife and mother and her charms as a hostess" (125). Genzmer and those who agreed with his opinion did sometimes make concessions for Embury's prose. In *American Authors 1600–1900*, Embury's verse is vilified as "patently conventional and filled with far-fetched imagery," but admiration for her prose is considered "perhaps, more justifiable" (252).

Embury has also been criticized for the suffering endured by her characters. An anonymous reviewer of *Pictures of Early Life* found fault with Embury "for indulging too much in tales of sorrow, and thus drawing the picture of life in colors darker than the reality" (*North American Review* 50, 294). Halsey made similar comments about Embury's contributions to *The American Juvenile Keepsake*, calling Embury's stories "so generally gloomy . . . that one would suppose them to have been eminently successful in turning children away from the faith she sought to encourage" (200).

Most recent critics, while acknowledging Embury's shortcomings as a conventional writer, have made allowances for her position as a literary woman in nineteenth-century society. In *American Women Poets of the Nineteenth Century* (1992), Cheryl Walker credits Embury's poetry with presenting "a lively account of the attitudes a cultured, talented, intelligent woman of her time was apt to have" (79). Commentary such as Walker's suggests that Embury was successful both in the literary career she denied having and in fulfilling the other roles expected of her as a nineteenth-century American woman.

WORKS CITED

Anonymous. "Quarterly List of New Publications." *North American Review* 50 (January 1840): 289–299.

G[enzmer]., G[eorge]. H[arvey]. "Embury, Emma Catherine." In *Dictionary of American Biography*, edited by Allen Johnson and Dumas Malone. Vol. 6. New York: Charles Scribner's Sons, 1931. 124–125.

Halsey, Rosalie V. *Forgotten Books of the American Nursery: A History of the Development of the American Story-Book*. 1911. Reprint, Detroit: Singing Tree Press, 1969.

Kunitz, Stanley J., and Howard Haycraft, eds. *American Authors 1600–1900: A Biographical Dictionary of American Literature*. New York: H. W. Wilson Co., 1938.

Poe, Edgar Allan. *The Complete Works of Edgar Allan Poe*. Edited by James A. Harrison. Vol. 15. New York: George D. Sproul, 1902.

Walker, Cheryl, ed. "Emma Embury." *American Women Poets of the Nineteenth Century: An Anthology*. New Brunswick: Rutgers University Press, 1992. 78–92.

Welter, Barbara. *Dimity Convictions: The American Woman in the Nineteenth Century*. Athens: Ohio University Press, 1976.

BIBLIOGRAPHY

Works by Emma Embury

Poetry

Guido, a Tale; Sketches from History and Other Poems. New York: G. and C. Carvill,
     1828.
Love's Token Flowers. New York: J. C. Riker, 1846.
The Poems of Emma C. Embury. 1st collected ed. New York: Hurd and Houghton, 1869.

Poetry and Prose

Nature's Gems, or American Wild Flowers in Their Native Haunts. New York: D. Ap-
     pleton and Co., 1845.

Prose

Pictures of Early Life, or Sketches of Youth. New York: Harper, 1830.
*An Address on Female Education, Read at the Anniversary of the Brooklyn Collegiate
     Institute for Young Ladies.* 1831. Reprinted as "Female Education." In *Women
     and the Higher Education,* edited by Anna C. Brackett. New York: Harper and
     Bros., 1893. 47–64.
Constance Latimer, or the Blind Girl, with Other Tales. New York: Harper and Bros.,
     1838.
Glimpses of Home Life, or Causes and Consequences. New York: J. C. Riker, 1848.
     Also published under the title *The Home Offering.*
The Waldorf Family, or Grandfather's Legends. New York: J. C. Riker, 1848.
Grace Morland, or the Weight of Trifles. Boston: F. Gleason, 1849.
Selected Prose Writings of Mrs. Emma C. Embury. New York: De Vinne Press, 1893.

Studies of Emma Embury

Baym, Nina. *Woman's Fiction: A Guide to Novels by and about Women in America
     1820–1870.* Ithaca: Cornell University Press, 1978. 73.
Cleveland, Charles D. *A Compendium of American Literature.* Philadelphia: J. H. Ban-
     croft and Co., 1859. 614–616.
Griswold, Rufus Wilmot. *The Female Poets of America.* 2nd ed. Philadelphia: Parry and
     McMillan, 1856. 143–148.
Hale, Sarah Josepha. *Woman's Record: or, Sketches of All Distinguished Women from
     the Creation to A.D. 1854.* New York: Harper and Brothers, 1855. 653–657.
Hart, John S. *Female Prose Writers of America.* Philadelphia: E. H. Butler and Co.,
     1866. 139–140.
Read, Thomas Buchanan. *The Female Poets of America.* 9th ed. Philadelphia: E. H.
     Butler and Co., 1867. 87–98.
Rollins, J. A. "Mrs. Emma Catherine Embury's Account Book: A Study of Some of

Her Periodical Contributions.'' *Bulletin of the New York Public Library* 51 (August 1947): 479–485.

Rosenberg, Julia. ''Emma Catherine Manley Embury.'' In *American Women Writers: A Critical Reference Guide from Colonial Times to the Present*, edited by Lina Mainiero. Vol. 1. New York: Frederick Ungar, 1979. 594–596.

FANNY FERN
(SARA PAYSON WILLIS PARTON)
(1811–1872)

Joyce W. Warren

BIOGRAPHY

Born Sara Payson Willis in Portland, Maine, on July 9, 1811, Fanny Fern was the fifth of the nine children of Nathaniel and Hannah (Parker) Willis. The family moved to Boston when Fern was an infant, and in 1816 her father began printing the *Boston Recorder*, the first religious newspaper in the United States; in 1827, he founded the *Youth's Companion*, the first children's periodical in the country. Although her father was a professional newspaperman, Fern claimed that any talent she had for writing was inherited from her mother, who, she said, "talked poetry unconsciously" (*New Story Book* 10–13). She described her father, a converted Calvinist and deacon of the Park Street Church, as a sober man who cast a pall on the household (Ethel Parton, "Fanny Fern" 23). As a child, Fern rebelled against her father's attempts to convert her to Calvinism, and throughout her career she wrote on the cruelty of bringing up children in an oppressive and fearful religious atmosphere. In an effort to bring his spirited and rebellious daughter to a religious conversion, Willis sent her to a series of boarding schools. Consequently, Fern remained in school longer than any of her sisters and longer than most other women of the time, graduating from Catharine Beecher's Hartford Female Seminary in 1831 when she was almost twenty.

Although she did not come to conversion, Fern did receive an excellent education. According to her society's construction of women, however, her real education did not begin until she returned to her father's house, to learn, as she later said in one of her newspaper articles, the domestic arts of "bread-making and button-hole stitching" (*New York Ledger*, 26 February 1870). While at home, she also helped out her father, writing articles and proofreading copy for his papers. However, although her family regarded her domestic work with her mother as preparation for her "career" as wife and mother, no one (including Fern herself) recognized that her unpaid work for her father was providing useful training for a future career as a writer and journalist.

After six years at home, on May 4, 1837, Fern married Charles Eldredge, a cashier at the Merchants' Bank in Boston. They had three daughters, Mary (1838), Grace (1841), and Ellen (1844). Known as "handsome Charley" by his friends, Eldredge admired his wife's wit, and their marriage was apparently a happy one. However, Eldredge became involved in an unwise business venture that resulted in a long and unsuccessful (for him) lawsuit. Despite his heavy financial loss, he planned to appeal and was hopeful that he would be able to recoup his losses. But in October 1846 he died of typhoid fever at the age of thirty-five. Her husband's death was the fifth death of a close relative that Fern experienced in less than two years, and this final blow left her reeling. In 1844 her mother and younger sister Ellen had died, and the following year brought the deaths of her sister-in-law and her beloved seven-year-old daughter Mary.

Charles Eldredge died insolvent, and after his creditors were paid, his wife and children were left without money. As Fern later said, her father and father-in-law argued about who would give the least money to support her and her children (Ethel Parton, "Fanny Fern" 101). Samuel Farrington, a widower with two children, asked her to marry him, but Fern refused, telling him frankly that she did not love him. Farrington persisted in his suit, and under pressure from her father, she capitulated; they were married in January 1849. As her daughter Ellen later said in a letter that is among Fern's papers at Smith College, the marriage was "a terrible mistake." Farrington was abusive and violently jealous and used his financial power to attempt to gain control over her; she left him in January 1851, and he retaliated by spreading scandalous stories accusing her of adultery. Although his brother later retracted the stories in a letter that was carefully preserved by Fern (Sara Parton Papers, Smith College), the damage to her reputation was irremediable. Moreover, her relatives were scandalized that she would leave her husband and thus get herself talked about, and her father and father-in-law refused any financial help, hoping to force her to return to Farrington. Fern attempted to support herself and her children by working as a seamstress, and she took the Boston teachers' exam, but she did not get an appointment. Her father-in-law, Hezekiah Eldredge, threatened to rewrite his will, leaving all of his money to charity rather than to his two granddaughters unless she agreed to give up the children to him and his wife. She refused, and the will was signed in July 1851. Under the threat of this will, Fern desperately tried to earn money so that she could support her children.

It was at this point that Fern decided to try to write for the newspapers. She sent some sample articles to her brother, Nathaniel Parker Willis, a well-known writer and editor who, as owner of the New York *Home Journal*, had sponsored other struggling writers. However, Willis refused to help her and wrote back, advising her to write for the religious newspapers (which, as he well knew, paid little or no money); her articles, he said, were "vulgar" and "indecent" (letter in Warren, *Fanny Fern* 93). Angry at Willis's failure to help her when she was destitute, Fern broke off relations with her brother and later satirized him in her 1853 article "Apollo Hyacinth" and in the novel *Ruth Hall*. Resolving to be henceforth self-reliant, Fern took her little daughter Ellen by the hand and walked the streets of Boston, peddling her articles at newspaper offices. In June 1851 the Boston *Olive Branch* bought her first article, "The Model Husband"; it was printed on June 28, 1851, and Fern was paid $.50 for it. In September of that year, she began using the pseudonym of Fanny Fern, and for the rest of her life, this was the name by which she was known in both her professional and her private life.

For the next two years Fern published regularly in the *Olive Branch* and the Boston *True Flag*. Although her articles were responsible for the increased sales of these newspapers, the editors refused to pay her adequately until the editor of the New York *Musical World and Times* offered her a substantially higher rate to write for his paper. In the fall of 1852 Fern began writing a regular column for both the *True Flag* and the *Musical World and Times*, thus becoming the first American woman newspaper columnist. In 1853 her articles were collected into a book, *Fern Leaves from Fanny's Portfolio*, and she moved to New York. Also in this year Samuel Farrington obtained a divorce in Chicago on grounds of desertion. From January to April 1854 she wrote a column in the Philadelphia *Saturday Evening Post*.

In February 1854 Fern contracted to write a novel, and her autobiographical novel *Ruth Hall* was published in December. In this novel she satirized her brother, her father, her in-laws, and the editors who had exploited her. In 1855 she was paid the unprecedented sum of $100 a column to write a serialized story, "Fanny Ford," for the *New York Ledger*. In January of 1856 she began writing an exclusive column for the *Ledger*, which continued without interruption until her death sixteen years later. Also in January 1856 Fern married biographer James Parton, who was eleven years younger than she. Prior to the ceremony, the couple signed a prenuptial agreement stating that all of Fern's earnings and property belonged solely to her. Fern died of breast cancer on October 10, 1872, and is buried in Mount Auburn Cemetery in Cambridge, Massachusetts.

MAJOR WORKS AND THEMES

In addition to writing columns in the journals cited above between 1851 and 1872, Fern published two novels, *Ruth Hall* (1855) and *Rose Clark* (1856); three children's books; and six collections of her newspaper articles. Thematically, Fern was a pioneer. Her novel *Ruth Hall* is nearly unique in nineteenth-century American literature in its portrayal of a woman as the self-reliant individualist, a role that nineteenth-century Americans regarded as designed exclusively for men; like the male heroes of countless "rags-to-riches" novels of the period,

Ruth Hall realizes the American Dream—gaining wealth and success solely by her own talents and industry. And, unlike the other women's novels of the era, the novel ends not with the heroine's acquisition of a husband but with her acquisition of $10,000 in bank stock.

In her twenty-one-year career as a journalist, Fern was noted for her courageous and independent stance. She was the first woman to praise Whitman's *Leaves of Grass* in print; she wrote fearlessly on such taboo subjects as venereal disease, prostitution, birth control, and divorce; she expounded ideas on education and child rearing that have become accepted practice today; she questioned male authority and conventional marriage patterns; she condemned narrowness in religion; she urged prison reform; she criticized platitudinous religious reformers, and she sought real solutions for poverty and crime.

The underlying theme in all her work, however, was her concern for women's rights. She was not an active member of the women's rights movement; she never gave a speech or participated in a meeting. Her practical feminism derived from the exigencies of her own life experience. Most important was her advocacy of economic independence for women, a revolutionary concept at the time. Impatient with her society's double standard with respect to financial success, she wrote in the *Ledger* on June 8, 1861:

There are few people who speak approbatively of a woman who has a smart business talent or capability. No matter how isolated or destitute her condition, the majority would consider it more ''feminine'' would she unobtrusively gather up her thimble, and, retiring into some out-of-the-way place, gradually scoop out her coffin with it, than to develop that smart turn for business which would lift her at once out of her troubles; and which, in a man so situated, would be applauded as exceedingly praiseworthy.

Fern's popularity can be attributed to her original style and the vivid rendering of her ideas. Almost as important as the ideas themselves is her presentation of them in plain language and her ability to give dramatic life to the flaws she saw in society. The popularity of her columns also derived from her pungent satire. She stripped people—particularly men—of their grandiose airs and pompous self-complacency, and she satirized folly and pretension in all facets of life. Antiromantic and often cynical, Fanny Fern was the originator of the now-famous phrase ''The way to a man's heart is through his stomach.''

Fern's humor is not in the tradition of the spright playfulness of a Grace Greenwood. It is sharp and cutting. Her closest rival was Gail Hamilton, who began contributing to the newspapers some years after Fern and whose barbs Fern praised in her 1868 biographical sketch of Hamilton. The seriousness behind Fern's wit is apparent in her reply to a reader who wanted to meet her because of the humor in her articles: ''You labor under the hallucination that I felt *merry* when I wrote all that nonsense! *Not a bit of it*; it's a way I have when I can't find a razor handy to cut my throat!'' (*Olive Branch*, 31 January 1852).

CRITICAL RECEPTION

When Fern's work began appearing in the 1850s, conventional critics condemned her outspoken manner and independent stance, her "vulgar" writing, and her "indelicate" and "unfeminine" themes. In spite of these criticisms, however, she was very successful: Her works were immensely popular, and writing style was praised by the literati. The Boston papers that originally published her work found that their circulation soared after she began writing for them. Her articles were "pirated," reprinted in newspapers all over the country and in Britain, and when the first collection of her articles, *Fern Leaves from Fanny's Portfolio*, was published in 1853, it was a best-seller. A pioneer in the use of the vernacular and understatement, Fern was acclaimed by *Harper's New Monthly Magazine* in July 1854 as the welcome harbinger of a new writing style, which, the editors hoped, marked the end of the "stilted rhetoric" and "parade and pomp" of literature.

When Fern's autobiographical novel *Ruth Hall* was published in December 1854, it caused a sensation. It was reviewed in newspapers throughout the United States and Britain, and the following year it was translated into French and German. Stores advertised the "Ruth Hall bonnet," the composer Jullien wrote a dance score called "The Ruth Hall Schottishe," and a popular song, "Little Daisy," was written about Ruth's child in the novel. Until this time, Fern's identity had been kept secret, and there was much speculation about who Fanny Fern was. Was she a man or a woman? critics pondered. However, when *Ruth Hall* was published, one of the editors that she had satirized, William Moulton of the *True Flag*, did not like his portrait in the novel, and he spitefully revealed Fern's identity in the pages of his paper. Once Fern's identity was known, the novel became a roman à clef, and readers were particularly interested to see Fern's satirical portrayal of her brother N. P. Willis as the hypocritical dandy Hyacinth Ellet. Although the widespread notice of her novel and the controversy surrounding its autobiographical character helped to boost sales, the critics were not kind to Fern. The reviewers—even those who praised other aspects of the novel—castigated Fern for her "unfeminine" writing, her immodest "self-love" in her portrayal of Ruth Hall, and her "unfilial" portrayal of her father, brother, and in-laws. This criticism derived specifically from the fact that Fanny Fern was a woman. The *New York Times* on December 20, 1854, declared that if she had been a man, the revenge that she sought in satirizing her relatives would have been excusable, but in a "suffering woman," it was reprehensible. Other critics called the novel "monstrous," "abominable," "eminently evil in its tendencies and teachings" (see Warren, *Fanny Fern* 124–126).

Despite all of the public criticism of *Ruth Hall*, reviewers found much to praise in the novel: the originality and unaffectedness of Fern's style, the power of her satire, and her insight into character. Nathaniel Hawthorne, who had castigated American women writers as a "damned mob of scribbling women," revised his opinion after reading *Ruth Hall*. He wrote to his publisher in 1855:

In my last, I recollect, I bestowed some vituperation on female authors. I have since been reading "Ruth Hall" and I must say I enjoyed it a good deal. The woman writes as if the devil was in her; and that is the only condition under which a woman ever writes anything worth reading. Generally women write like emasculated men, and are only distinguished from male authors by greater feebleness and folly; but when they throw off the restraints of decency, and come before the public stark naked, as it were— then their books are sure to possess character and value. Can you tell me anything about this Fanny Fern? If you meet her, I wish you would let her know how much I admire her. (1, 78)

One measure of Fern's celebrity is the price that she could command for her articles. In 1855, when Robert Bonner, the enterprising editor of the *New York Ledger*, was looking for ways to increase the circulation of his paper, he offered Fern $25 a column to write a serialized story for him. When she refused, he increased his offer until she accepted at the unprecedented price of $100 a column—which made her the most highly paid newspaper writer of her time.

Although Fern was well known during her day, by the twentieth century her works were out of print and her name was virtually unknown. If she was referred to at all, it was to be dismissed as one of the "mob of scribbling women." Fred Lewis Pattee, for example, in his book *The Feminine Fifties* (1940), apparently without reading Fern's work, disparaged the satirical Fanny Fern as "a sentimental nonentity" (110–118), and James D. Hart in *The Popular Book* (1950) called her "the grandmother of all sob sisters" (97). In recent years, however, Fern's work has been recovered. Rutgers reprinted her novel *Ruth Hall* and a selection of 100 of her newspaper articles in *Ruth Hall and Other Writings* in 1986. Joyce Warren's biography *Fanny Fern: An Independent Woman* was published in 1992. And Fern has been the subject of numerous articles, conference papers, and doctoral dissertations.

BIBLIOGRAPHY

Papers

James Parton Papers, Houghton Library, Harvard University.
Sara Parton Papers, Sophia Smith Collection, Smith College.

Works by Fanny Fern

Periodical Publications

Boston *Olive Branch*, 1851–1855. American Antiquarian Society, Worcester, MA.
Boston *True Flag*, 1851–1855. American Antiquarian Society, Worcester, MA.

New York *Musical World and Times*, 1853–1854. New York Public Library.
Philadelphia *Saturday Evening Post*, 1853–1854. Philadelphia Public Library.
New York Ledger, 1855–1872. Watkinson Library, Trinity College, Hartford, CT.

Books

Fern Leaves from Fanny's Portfolio. Auburn: Derby and Miller, 1853.
Little Ferns for Fanny's Little Friends. Auburn: Derby and Miller, 1853.
Fern Leaves from Fanny's Portfolio. 2nd ser. Auburn and Buffalo: Miller, Orton, and
    Mulligan, 1854.
Ruth Hall. New York: Mason Brothers, 1855.
Rose Clark. New York: Mason Brothers, 1856.
Fresh Leaves. New York: Mason Brothers, 1857.
The Play-Day Book. New York: Mason Brothers, 1857.
A New Story Book for Children. New York: Mason Brothers, 1864.
Folly as It Flies. New York: G. W. Carleton, 1868.
Ginger-Snaps. New York: G. W. Carleton, 1870.
Caper-Sauce. New York: G. W. Carleton, 1872.
Ruth Hall and Other Writings. Edited by Joyce W. Warren. New Brunswick: Rutgers
    University Press, 1986.

Studies of Fanny Fern

Adams, Florence Bannard. *Fanny Fern, or a Pair of Flaming Shoes.* West Trenton, NJ:
    Hermitage, 1966.
Anonymous. *The Life and Beauties of Fanny Fern.* New York: H. Long, and Brother,
    1855.
Berlant, Lauren. "The Female Woman: Fanny Fern and the Form of Sentiment." In *The
    Culture of Sentiment: Race, Gender, and Sentimentality in Nineteenth-Century
    America*, edited by Shirley Samuels. New York: Oxford University Press, 1992.
    265–281.
Derby, James C. *Fifty Years among Authors, Books and Publishers.* New York: G. W.
    Carleton, 1884.
Eckert, Robert P., Jr. "Friendly, Fragrant Fanny Ferns." *The Colophon* 18 (September
    1934): n. p.
Harris, Susan K. "Inscribing and Defining: The Many Voices of Fanny Fern's *Ruth
    Hall.*" In *19th-Century American Women Writers: Interpretive Strategies.* Cam-
    bridge: Cambridge University Press, 1990. 111–127.
Hart, James D. *The Popular Book.* New York: Oxford University Press, 1950.
Hawthorne, Nathaniel. *Letters to William Ticknor, 1851–1969.* Edited by C. E. Frazer-
    Clark, Jr. 2 vols. Newark: Carteret Book Club, Inc., 1972. 1, 78.
Huf, Linda. "The Devil and Fanny Fern." In *A Portrait of the Artist as a Young Woman:
    The Writer as Heroine in American Literature.* New York: Ungar, 1983. 16–35.
Kelley, Mary. *Private Woman, Public Stage: Literary Domesticity in Nineteenth-Century
    America.* New York: Oxford University Press, 1984.
McGinnis, Patricia. "Fanny Fern, American Novelist." *Biblion* 2 (1969): 2–37.
Parton, Ethel. "Fanny Fern, an Informal Biography." Manuscript in the Sara Parton
    Papers, Sophia Smith Collection, Smith College.

———. "Fanny Fern at the Hartford Female Seminary." *New England Magazine* 24 (March 1901): 94–98.

———. "A Little Girl and Two Authors." *The Horn Book Magazine* 17 (March–April 1941): 81–86.

———. "A New York Childhood: The Seventies in Stuvescant Square." *New Yorker* (13 June 1936): 32–39.

Parton, James. *Fanny Fern, a Memorial Volume.* New York: G. W. Carleton, 1873.

Pattee, Fred Lewis. *The Feminine Fifties.* New York: D. Appleton-Century Co., 1940.

Schlesinger, Elizabeth Bancroft. "Fanny Fern: Our Grandmother's Mentor." *New York Historical Society Quarterly* 38 (October 1954): 501–519.

———. "Proper Bostonians as Seen by Fanny Fern." *New England Quarterly* 27 (March 1954): 97–102.

Walker, Nancy. *Fanny Fern.* New York: Twayne, 1993.

Warren, Joyce. "Domesticity and the Economics of Independence: Resistance and Revolution in the Work of Fanny Fern." In *The (Other) American Traditions: Nineteenth-Century Women Writers*, edited by Joyce W. Warren. New Brunswick: Rutgers University Press, 1993. 73–91.

———. *Fanny Fern: An Independent Woman.* New Brunswick: Rutgers University Press, 1992.

———. "Fanny Fern's *Rose Clark*." *Legacy* 8 (1991): 92–103.

———. "The Gender of American Individualism." In *Politics, Gender, and the Arts*, edited by Ronald Dotterer and Susan Bowers. Selinsgrove, PA: Susquehanna University Press, 1991.

———. "Subversion versus Celebration: The Aborted Friendship of Fanny Fern and Walt Whitman." In *Patrons and Protégées*, edited by Shirley Marchalonis. New Brunswick: Rutgers University Press, 1988. 59–93.

———. "Text and Context in Fanny Fern's *Ruth Hall*: From Widowhood to Independence." In *Joinings and Disjoinings: The Significance of Marital Status in America*, edited by JoAnna S. Mink and Janet D. Ward. Bowling Green, OH: The Popular Press, 1991. 61–76.

———. "Uncommon Discourse: Fanny Fern and the *New York Ledger*. In *Social Texts: Nineteenth-Century American Literature in Periodical Contexts*, edited by Susan Belasco Smith and Kenneth Price. Charlottesville: University of Virginia Press, 1995. 51–68.

Wood, Ann Douglas. "The 'Scribbling Women' and Fanny Fern: Why Women Wrote." *American Quarterly* 23 (1971): 3–24.

KATE FIELD
(1838–1896)

Jim Burkhead

BIOGRAPHY

Kate Field was born in St. Louis in 1838 to Joseph and Eliza (Riddle) Field, who were popular actors. Since their profession required them to travel extensively, the young Kate was educated privately in New Orleans, St. Louis, and Boston. In 1859 Field traveled with her mother to Europe, and during her three-year stay in Italy, she became friends with Robert and Elizabeth Browning, Anthony and Tom Trollope, Walter Savage Landor, and George Eliot. Anthony Trollope, like the elderly Landor, fell in love with Kate, and their friendship lasted until his death. Field's long journalistic career began during this period with a series of "press letters" from Europe for New York and Boston newspapers. She also began to contribute literary and biographical articles to *Atlantic Monthly, North American Review*, and other periodicals.

Kate Field returned to the United States in 1863 and began her diverse career as a writer, lecturer, and actress. She wrote drama criticism for many periodicals and, in 1867, began a series of theater articles for *The Atlantic Monthly*. In the same year, she published her first book, *Adelaide Ristori*, a biography of the famous Italian actress. She followed this in 1868 with two slim volumes, a translation and adaptation of Giovanni Costanza's popular Italian comedy, *Mad on Purpose*, and a strange little book on spiritualism, *Planchette's Diary*, told in first person by the wooden spirit-writing tool used in the sessions. She attended many of the lectures of Dickens's American tour and turned her descriptions and impressions of the popular novelist and his portrayal of his characters into a well-received book, *Pen Photographs of Charles Dickens's Readings*, published in 1871.

Field went on the lecture circuit and became well known in America and

England for her outspoken espousal of women's issues and controversial causes. As it had for her parents, touring became a habit of life; she spent more than half of her adult life traveling in America, England, and Europe. Field's lyceum tours and her press letters provided the subject matter for her next two books. *Hap-Hazard*, published in 1873, is a collection of essays derived from her newspaper articles about her travels in the United States, England, and France. *Ten Days in Spain*, published in 1875, chronicled Field's journey into a Spain divided by its civil war of the 1870s. Field described her trip through both monarchist and republican lines to Madrid, where she interviewed Emilio Castelar, president of the short-lived Spanish republic.

In 1874, Kate Field made her acting debut at Booth's theater in New York. She had begun writing short plays during the 1860s and now began appearing in some of her own comediettas, including *Extremes Meet, The Opera Box*, and *Caught Napping*. While acting and writing in England during 1878, Field helped Alexander Graham Bell publicize his telephone and demonstrated it to Queen Victoria and the Prince Imperial. She also found time to help lead the effort to establish a permanent Shakespeare memorial at Stratford-on-Avon.

Field returned again to the United States in October 1879 and established the Ladies Cooperative Dress Association, modeled on the co-op shops of London. She returned to writing and lecturing in 1882 and published *Charles Albert Fechter*, the biography of a popular but misanthropic Shakespearean actor. For much of the 1880s, Field traveled extensively in the American West, where she collected material for her Alaska lectures and her controversial articles and lectures about "The Mormon Menace," describing the continuing practice of polygamy and the plight of Mormon women.

In 1889, Field settled in Washington, D.C., where, starting January 1, 1890, she published, edited, and wrote for her own weekly review, *Kate Field's Washington*, a well-received publication stressing the arts, politics, and a feminist perspective on women's issues. It was the busiest, most productive time of her life, but increasing illness forced Field to cease publication in May 1895. When her illness seemed to abate, she went to Hawaii to report on the islands and on the question of Hawaiian annexation. While in the midst of giving herself totally to this cause, she fell ill once more and died of pneumonia on May 19, 1896.

MAJOR WORKS AND THEMES

Kate Field's Washington must be considered Field's most significant work. During its five-year existence, she made her weekly journal a promoter and defender of feminist issues and of Field's favorite causes, notably tariff-free art, international copyright, Mormon "treason," and Hawaiian annexation. She also championed the cause of women's letters by publishing women's fiction, nonfiction, poetry, and drama.

Field's short plays also center on themes of equality and independence for women. *Extremes Meet, Caught Napping,* and *The Opera Box* are filled with witty dialogue that often exposes male foibles and asserts female ascendency. Her travel books, *Hap-Hazard* and *Ten Days in Spain,* introduce her interest in the expansion of democracy while continuing Field's devotion to women's issues. Both are derivative and, at times, self-consciously literary; however, at their best, they are charming, sprightly entertainments. Some of Field's best prose is to be found in them, notably her memorable character descriptions, her wry humor, and her fine dialogue.

Field's two biographical works, *Adelaide Ristori* and *Charles Albert Fechter,* are satisfactory examples of contemporary biography and drama criticism. While they certainly capture the achievements of both of these popular actors, they also fall into sentimentality and idolatry.

CRITICAL RECEPTION

Though she was internationally popular during her lifetime, Kate Field is all but forgotten today, since she produced little that was not related to her journalist's career. The standard work on Field is still Lilian Whiting's 1899 biography of her intimate friend, *Kate Field: A Record,* which frustrates the modern researcher by often being secretively fastidious about her life and inordinately worshipful of her talents. Of Field's prose style, Whiting says, "She had an unusual power of presenting scenes vividly with terse condensation. Abounding in a sense of humor, she served up many a phase of life with *sauce piquante*" (151).

Almost no critical attention has been paid to Kate Field in this century. What few studies there are have been biographical, focusing on her relationship with Anthony Trollope, on her contentious encounters with Mark Twain, or on her famous attack on the Mormons and polygamy. Helen Beale Woodward reviews her life as one of a few American women of the nineteenth century who were independent, daring, and unconventional, highlighting Field's long friendship with Anthony Trollope. Michael Sadleir's 1927 biography of Trollope identifies Field as Trollope's romantic obsession, though Sadleir remarks, "He never made love to her; he was not that kind of man. But in love with her he certainly was" (210).

Karl Kiralis discusses a conflict between Field and Mark Twain over Twain's anger at Field's misquoting him in a review of Field's performance in Twain's *The Gilded Age.* He quotes a private letter in which Twain fumes, "This woman is the most inveterate sham & fraud & manipulator of newspapers I know of" (quoted in Kiralis 1). Another piece of scholarship is a lecture delivered at the University of Utah that belittles Kate Field, defends the Mormon interests she so successfully attacked, and dismisses Field as a misguided feminist crusader "detesting Mormon men, pitying Mormon women, and hating their 'hideous' religion" (Arrington 9).

WORKS CITED

Arrington, Leonard J. "Kate Field and J. H. Beadle: Manipulators of the Mormon Past."
    American West Lectures. University of Utah, Salt Lake City, 31 March 1971.
Kiralis, Karl. "Two Recently Discovered Letters: Mark Twain on Kate Field." *Mark
    Twain Journal* 20 (1980): 1–4.
Sadleir, Michael. *Anthony Trollope*. Boston: Houghton Mifflin, 1927.
Whiting, Lilian. *Kate Field: A Record*. Boston: Little, Brown & Co., 1899.

BIBLIOGRAPHY

Works by Kate Field

Caught Napping. London: G. J. Palmer, 1866.
Adelaide Ristori: A Biography. New York: John A. Gray and Green, 1867.
Mad on Purpose: A Comedy in Four Acts. New York: J. A. Gray and Green, 1868.
    Translation of *I pazzi del proaretto*, by Baron Giovanni Carlo Cosenza.
Planchette's Diary. New York: Redfield & Co., 1868.
Pen Photographs of Charles Dickens's Readings. Boston: J. R. Osgood & Co., 1871.
Hap-Hazard. Boston: Osgood & Co., 1873.
The History of Bell's Telephone. New York: Bradbury, 1874.
The Opera Box. New York: Samuel French, 1874.
Ten Days in Spain. Boston: Osgood & Co., 1875.
Extremes Meet. New York: Samuel French, 1877.
Charles Albert Fechter. New York: B. Blom, 1882.
The Drama of Glass. Toledo, OH: Libbey, 1889.
Kate Field's Washington. 1 January 1890 to May 1895.

Studies of Kate Field

Arrington, Leonard J. "Kate Field and J. H. Beadle: Manipulators of the Mormon Past."
    American West Lectures. University of Utah, Salt Lake City, 31 March 1971.
"Current Literature." Revision of *Extremes Meet*, by Kate Field. *Overland Monthly* XI
    (1873): 584–585.
Hall, N. John. *Trollope: A Biography*. New York: Oxford University Press, 1991.
Haraszti, Zoltán. "Kate Field and the Trollope Brothers." *More Books* (Boston Public
    Library) II, no. 6 (1927): 129–145.
Hutton, Laurence. "A Note on Kate Field." *The Bookman* 3 (1896): 523–524.
Kiralis, Karl. "Two Recently Discovered Letters: Mark Twain on Kate Field." *Mark
    Twain Journal* 20 (1980): 1–4.
Sadleir, Michael. *Anthony Trollope*. Boston: Houghton Mifflin, 1927.
Whiting, Lilian. *Kate Field: A Record*. Boston: Little, Brown & Co., 1899.
Woodward, Helen Beale. "The Woman in the Footnote: Kate Field." In *The Bold
    Women*. New York: Farrar, 1953. 201–214.

MARTHA FINLEY
(MARTHA FARQUHARSON)
(1828–1909)

Theresa Strouth Gaul

BIOGRAPHY

Martha Finley was born on April 26, 1828, to Dr. James Brown Finley and Maria Theresa Brown Finley in Chillicothe, Ohio. Her mother died when Finley was quite young, and Finley grew up with her father and stepfamily in Philadelphia and South Bend, Indiana. Educated in private schools, Finley briefly taught school in Indiana before beginning her literary career in Philadelphia at the age of twenty-six. In 1876, Finley moved to Elkton, Maryland, where she lived a quiet life filled with writing and church activities.

Finley published some thirty-five Sunday school stories for children between 1853 and 1875 under the pseudonym Martha Farquharson (Gaelic for Finley). Her most popular and enduring work, *Elsie Dinsmore*, was published in 1867. This book, which sold more than five million copies over six decades, initiated a series of twenty-eight Elsie books, one of the first series for girls featuring a continuing set of characters. The publication of each successive book was met by public clamor for another, and the series ended only with Finley's death in 1909 at the age of eighty. Neither her novels for adults nor a companion series, beginning with the 1878 publication of *Mildred Keith*, would ever attain the popularity of the Elsie books.

MAJOR WORKS AND THEMES

Although Finley authored nearly 100 books, her reputation rests almost solely on the Elsie Dinsmore series. Finley's heroine, a pious young girl with golden ringlets, weeps and swoons her way through a variety of situations stock to nineteenth-century children's sentimental novels. The first two books, *Elsie*

Dinsmore and *Elsie's Holidays at Roselands* (originally one volume but split into two by the publishers), set up the dominant themes of the series, religion and the father/daughter relationship. Desirous of his love and affection, Elsie attempts to offer the unquestioning obedience her father, Horace, demands. When Horace commands her to violate her religious beliefs by playing the piano or reading a novel on the Sabbath, however, pitched battles ensue, culminating in brain fevers and near-death experiences for Elsie and eventual conversion for Horace. The succeeding books follow Elsie from girlhood through grandmotherhood, continuing to emphasize her piety and her reliance on her father.

CRITICAL RECEPTION

In 1893, the *Ladies' Home Journal* proclaimed, "[T]here has been almost no character in American juvenile fiction which has attained more widespread interest and affection" (Wilson 3). While critics uniformly acknowledge the Elsie books' phenomenal success with generations of readers, their evaluations of the series and its heroine have frequently been harsh. The series has been classified as a "compound of sentimentality and masochism" (Kunitz and Haycraft 272) and "savage, neurotic realism" (Stern 52), while Elsie has been called a "nauseous little prig" (Kunitz and Haycraft 272) and a "dismal, tear-soaked, hysterical little girl" (Repplier 722). The frequency of psychoanalytic readings testifies to widespread critical agreement with G. B. Stern's statement that "careful rereading of the twenty-eight Elsie books cannot but bear out my theory that they abundantly satisfy some obscure clamor in our psychical metabolism" (54). Analyses of religion's role in the series and comparisons of Elsie to Harriet Beecher Stowe's little Eva have also been staples of Finley criticism.

Recent critics, influenced by current critical interests in women's writing and the sentimental novel, differ in their final assessment of the Elsie books. Helena Michie describes the central conflict of the novels as one in which Horace asserts control over the feminine and the maternal by enforcing his paternal law on Elsie's body. Michie sees a degree of subversion in the series, arguing that Elsie's resuscitation from death and her recovery allow her to enact a measure of revenge against her father's rule. Rather than seeing a muted protest against masculine authority, Pam Hardman argues that Finley reaffirms the need for an authoritative male presence within the home, thereby offering a profoundly conservative social vision. According to Hardman, Finley revises the sentimental formula by opening up the domestic sphere to men while shrinking the territory of women's power and control.

WORKS CITED

Hardman, Pam. "The Steward of Her Soul: Elsie Dinsmore and the Training of the Victorian Child." *American Studies* 29, no. 2 (fall 1988): 69–90.

Kunitz, Stanley, and Howard Haycraft. *American Authors, 1600–1900*. New York: The H. W. Wilson Co., 1938. 272.

Michie, Helena. " 'Dying between Two Laws': Girl Heroines, Their Gods, and Their Fathers in *Uncle Tom's Cabin* and the *Elsie Dinsmore* Series." In *Refiguring the Father: New Feminist Readings of Patriarchy*, edited by Patricia Yaeger and Beth Kowaleski-Wallace. Carbondale: University of Illinois Press, 1989. 188–206.

Repplier, Agnes. "Little Pharisees in Fiction." *Scribner's Magazine* 20 (December 1896): 718–724.

Stern, G. B. "Elsie Reread." *The New Yorker* 12 (March 14, 1936): 52–54.

Wilson, Florence. "The Author of the Elsie Books." *Ladies' Home Journal* 10 (April 1893): 3.

BIBLIOGRAPHY

Works by Martha Finley

Elsie Dinsmore. New York: Dodd, Mead, 1867; London: King, 1873.

Elsie's Holidays at Roselands. New York: Dodd, Mead, 1868; London: King, 1873.

An Old Fashioned Boy. Philadelphia: Evans, Stoddart, 1871.

Wanted: A Pedigree. New York: Dodd, Mead, 1871.

Elsie's Girlhood. New York: Dodd, Mead, 1872; London: King, 1873.

Our Fred; or, Seminary Life and Thurston. New York: Dodd, Mead, 1874.

Elsie's Womanhood. New York: Dodd, Mead, 1875; London: Routledge, 1889.

Elsie's Motherhood. New York: Dodd, Mead, 1876; London: Routledge, 1889.

Elsie's Children. New York: Dodd, Mead, 1877; London: Routledge, 1889.

Mildred Keith. New York: Dodd, Mead, 1878; London: Routledge, 1890.

Mildred at Roselands. New York: Dodd, Mead, 1879; London: Routledge, 1879.

Elsie's Widowhood. New York: Dodd, Mead, 1880; London: Routledge, 1890.

Mildred and Elsie. New York: Dodd, Mead, 1881; London: Routledge, 1890.

Grandmother Elsie. New York: Dodd, Mead, 1882; London: Routledge, 1889.

Mildred's Married Life. New York: Dodd, Mead, 1882; London: Routledge, 1890.

Elsie's New Relations. New York: Dodd, Mead, 1883; London: Routledge, 1889.

Elsie at Nantucket. New York: Dodd, Mead, 1884; London: Routledge, 1889.

Mildred at Home. New York: Dodd, Mead, 1884; London: Routledge, 1890.

The Two Elsies. New York: Dodd, Mead, 1885; London: Routledge, 1889.

Elsie's Kith and Kin. New York: Dodd, Mead, 1886; London: Routledge, 1890.

Mildred's Boys and Girls. New York: Dodd, Mead, 1886; London: Routledge, 1890.

Elsie's Friends at Woodburn. New York: Dodd, Mead, 1887; London: Routledge, 1889.

Christmas with Grandma Elsie. New York: Dodd, Mead, 1888; London: Routledge, 1888.

Elsie and the Raymonds. New York: Dodd, Mead, 1889; London: Routledge, 1890.

Elsie's Vacation. New York: Dodd, Mead, 1891; London: Routledge, 1891.

Elsie at Viamede. New York: Dodd, Mead, 1892; London: Stevens, 1892.

Elsie at Ion. New York: Dodd, Mead, 1893; London: Routledge, 1893.

Elsie at the World's Fair. New York: Dodd, Mead, 1894; London: Routledge, 1895.

Mildred's New Daughter. New York: Dodd, Mead, 1894; London: Stevens, 1894.

Elsie's Journey on Inland Waters. New York: Dodd, Mead, 1895; London: Stevens, 1895.

Elsie at Home. New York: Dodd, Mead, 1897.

Elsie on the Hudson. New York: Dodd, Mead, 1898.

Elsie in the South. New York: Dodd, Mead, 1899.

Elsie's Young Folks in Peace and War. New York: Dodd, Mead, 1900; London: Routledge, 1900.

Elsie's Winter Trip. New York: Dodd, Mead, 1902.

Elsie and Her Loved Ones. New York: Dodd, Mead, 1903.

Elsie and Her Namesakes. New York: Dodd, Mead, 1905; London: Stevens & Brown, 1905.

Studies of Martha Finley

Brown, Janet E. "The Saga of Elsie Dinsmore." *University of Buffalo Studies* 17 (July 1945): 75–129.

Dowe, Amy H. "Elsie Finds a Modern Champion." *Publishers' Weekly* 31 (31 December 1932): 2384–2387.

Hardman, Pam. "The Steward of Her Soul: Elsie Dinsmore and the Training of the Victorian Child." *American Studies* 29, no. 2 (fall 1988): 69–90.

Jackson, Jaqueline, and Philip Kendall. "What Makes a Bad Book Good: *Elsie Dinsmore.*" *Children's Literature* 7 (1978): 45–67.

Kunitz, Stanley, and Howard Haycraft. *American Authors, 1600–1900.* New York: The H. W. Wilson Co., 1938. 272.

Manthorne, Jane. "The Lachrymose Ladies." *The Horn Book Magazine* 43 (June, August, October 1967): 375–384; 501–513; 622–630.

Michie, Helena. " 'Dying between Two Laws': Girl Heroines, Their Gods, and Their Fathers in *Uncle Tom's Cabin* and the *Elsie Dinsmore* Series." In *Refiguring the Father: New Feminist Readings of Patriarchy,* edited by Patricia Yaeger and Beth Kowaleski-Wallace. Carbondale: University of Illinois Press, 1989. 188–206.

Repplier, Agnes. "Little Pharisees in Fiction." *Scribner's Magazine* 20 (December 1896): 718–724.

Shepherd, Allen. "Sweet Little Ways: Elsie Dinsmore." *Markham Review* 11 (spring 1982): 57–59.

Shinn, Thelma J. "Martha Finley." In *American Women Writers from Colonial Times to the Present: A Critical Reference Guide,* edited by Langdon Lynne Faust. Abridged ed. New York: Ungar, 1983. 216–218.

Smedman, M. Sarah. "Martha Finley." In *Dictionary of Literary Biography,* edited by Glenn E. Estes. Vol. 42. Detroit: Gale Research Co., 1985.

Stern, G. B. "Elsie Reread." *The New Yorker* 12 (March 14, 1936): 52–54.

Suckow, Ruth. "Elsie Dinsmore: A Study in Perfection, or How Fundamentalism Came to Dixie." *The Bookman* 66 (October 1927): 126–133.

Tassin, Algernon. "Martha Finley." In *Cambridge History of American Literature,* edited by William Peterfield, William Trent, John Erskine, Stewart P. Sherman, and Carl Van Doren. New York: 1927. 397–398.

Wilson, Florence. "The Author of the Elsie Books." *Ladies' Home Journal* 10 (April 1893): 3.

Wishy, Bernard. *The Child and the Republic.* Philadelphia: University of Pennsylvania Press, 1968. 87–90.

MARY ELEANOR WILKINS FREEMAN (1852–1930)

Perry D. Westbrook

BIOGRAPHY

Mary Eleanor Wilkins Freeman was born in Randolph, Massachusetts, on October 31, 1852, to Warren Wilkins, house builder, and Eleanor Lothrop. Randolph, though only fourteen miles from Boston, was in many ways a typical New England country town, churchgoing and culturally traditional. Like many of the townspeople, Freeman's parents were both descended from early colonial settlers from England. Agriculture was still important, though industry was also present in the form of shoe manufacturing in small factories and as a cottage industry in individual homes. In this environment Freeman lived during her first fifteen years, assimilating its way of life and its values. Here she received her elementary education; was indoctrinated, though perhaps not very deeply, in the moderate Calvinism of the local Congregational church; and made the most important friendship of her life with a schoolmate, Mary Wales, a farmer's daughter in whose home Freeman was a constant visitor and later lived as a permanent resident for almost twenty years.

In the 1860s Randolph's comparative prosperity drastically declined, as was happening in similar towns throughout New England. In 1867 Warren Wilkins, no longer prospering in his trade, moved with his family to Brattleboro, Vermont, where he and a partner opened a drygoods store. Brattleboro was very different from Randolph. Scenically situated on the Connecticut River, it was somewhat of a cultural center, attracting artists, writers, and musicians. After graduating from high school there in 1870, Freeman entered Mt. Holyoke Seminary, a school noted for its strict religious regimen. Like Emily Dickinson, who had attended Mt. Holyoke years before, Mary remained for only one year, dropping out because of ill health. A few courses that she took at Glenwood Seminary in West Brattleboro ended her formal education, but she was an avid reader of an impressive variety of authors, among them Goethe, Emerson, Thoreau, Thackeray, and Dickens.

Her life in Brattleboro seems to have been congenial and interesting. A friend in nearby Newfane, Evelyn Sawyer, shared her literary interests, and together they discussed the books that they had read. At the age of twenty she met and fell in love with Hanson Tyler, an ensign in the navy and a member of the most prominent local family. To Tyler, Mary was never more than a good friend, but she cherished the memory of him for the remainder of her life. However, other matters were demanding her attention. For a time she tried, unsuccessfully, to teach in a school for girls. In 1873, the same year that she met Tyler, her father's business failed, and he was forced back into his former occupation of house building. In 1876, Mary's younger sister died at the age of seventeen, and four years later, her mother died.

During this stressful decade, Freeman had been trying her hand at writing but managed to place her work only in several obscure, nonpaying periodicals. Finally in 1881 she sold a poem, "The Beggar King," for $10 to *Wide-Awake*, a children's magazine. From then on, *Wide-Awake* and the prestigious *St. Nicholas* published much of her juvenile writing, and soon she found publishers for three children's books. In 1882 her first story for adults, "The Shadow Family," won a prize of $50 in a contest conducted by the *Boston Daily Budget*. (This story is no longer extant in print or in manuscript.) Still writing poetry, she placed four poems in *Century Magazine* between 1882 and 1885, and a scattering of her verse appeared elsewhere. Her poems were conventional in style and undistinguished in subject matter, though they possessed a certain grace and facility. Yet publication in a highly respected literary magazine like *Century* was an achievement that encouraged her and impressed her fellow townspeople.

A greater achievement was the publication in 1883 of her story "Two Old Lovers" in *Harper's Bazar* (*sic*), the editor of which, Louise Booth, was until her death in 1889 Freeman's close friend and literary adviser. The story, later included in Freeman's first book, *A Humble Romance and Other Stories*, foreshadows in style and content much of her later writing. Laid in a depressed New England mill town, it is the tale of two lovers who, because of the man's inability to make a decision, never marry. It was the first of Freeman's stories to probe a subject of great apparent interest to her—the vagaries of the New England will and conscience. Henceforth, *Harper's Bazar* continued to accept much of her work. Soon even greater recognition came with the acceptance by *Harper's Monthly* of her story "A Humble Romance." However, her successes were again clouded, this time by the death of her father in 1893 in Florida, where in poor health he had found work in construction. Now, with all of her immediate family dead, Freeman at the age of thirty-two returned to Randolph to live as a paying guest with her old friend Mary Wales. She remained there until her marriage in 1902.

During her seventeen years in Brattleboro she had completed her education, experienced her first, perhaps only intense love for a man, made lifelong friends, and proved herself as an author. The Brattleboro period in her life is a presence with varying degrees of distinctness in all her writing.

A major presence from these years was the knowledge and impressions she had acquired of life in the areas of Vermont and New Hampshire surrounding Brattleboro, where a social and economic blight that affected all of New England's hill country had rendered existence a harsh, unending struggle against poverty and frustration. Waves of settlers beginning in the latter half of the eighteenth century had left down-country areas where land was already becoming scarce. In the northern hills, they cleared the rocky slopes and whatever level stretches there were along the streams and rivers. For a time, they survived by farming and sheep raising, and villages with schools and churches and an occasional small factory briefly prospered. But before the Civil War, decline set in. Crops were poor. Competition from more favored areas was ruinous. Better land available in the Middle West attracted many farm families. Laboriously cleared acres were left to revert to forest. Only the stone walls, built with incredible toil, remained to tell that the land had ever been cultivated. Washed-out roads led only to abandoned farmhouses and barns with collapsing roofs. Many people who had not migrated west left for the industrial cities in search of employment. The Civil War, of course, drew away men of fighting age. Those who survived the war often did not return to their homes, having seen the possibilities of easier and better living elsewhere. Census figures show that many of the hill towns reached their highest numbers before 1850 and declined steadily thereafter. Some towns became virtually deserted.

Yet in most communities some residents lingered, perhaps because they were more fortunate than most or, more likely, out of sheer, stubborn perseverance, but many remained either through inertia or some personal or financial disability. By the end of the century, social historians writing in periodicals like *The Atlantic Monthly* found that the deterioration in many areas bordered on degeneracy. Freeman's stories were sometimes cited to document milder but nonetheless deplorable conditions. Edith Wharton in her novel *Summer* realistically records the shocking degeneracy in Berkshire County, Massachusetts. Living in Brattleboro, one could hardly escape knowing the conditions of life in the neighboring countryside, and one way or another, Freeman did know them and in detail. Her particular interest was in the survivors—those who struggled to cope and frequently succeeded to a degree, but often with destructive effects on themselves and others. She probed deeply into her characters' psychology, often finding distorted traces of traditional Puritanism. Much of her most perceptive writing derives from her sympathetic knowledge of life in New England backcountry in her time.

Three years after her return to Randolph, the Harper company published a collection of Freeman's stories that had previously appeared in the Harper periodicals, *A Humble Romance and Other Stories* (1887). This volume was soon followed by another such collection, *A New England Nun and Other Stories*

(1891). In the stories in both these books Freeman had reached the height of her talent. For the next decade, her reputation and popularity soared, as five collections of short fiction, six novels, and one play appeared under her name, most of them issued by Harper. Though her friendship with Louise Booth of the *Bazar* ended with the latter's death, she had become well acquainted with the editor of *Harper's Monthly*, Henry M. Alden, whose home in Metuchen, New Jersey, she often visited. On one visit in 1892 she met another Metuchen resident, Dr. Charles Freeman, a nonpracticing physician, whom, after a long and somewhat rocky engagement, she married in 1902. Reputedly a man of charm, Dr. Freeman was also a heavy drinker. The marriage started off auspiciously, and Mary Freeman, urged on by her husband, continued her writing, which, it soon became apparent, the Doctor regarded as an important supplement to his income from his family's coal and lumber business. In any event, her writing declined in quality, if not quantity, as her husband sank into alcoholism and the marriage collapsed. Dr. Freeman entered a sanatorium in Trenton but remained uncured. After other such attempts, he was confined to a state hospital from which he soon escaped. Husband and wife were legally separated in 1922. Dr. Freeman changed his will in favor of his chauffer, with whom he was living. Mary Freeman and her sisters-in-law successfully contested the will after his death in 1923.

Since 1918 Freeman had all but ceased writing. However, in 1926 she received two honors: the American Academy of Letters awarded her the William Dean Howells Gold Medal for Fiction in recognition of her realistic stories of rural New England life, and the American Institute of Arts and Letters elected her to membership. These honors came none too soon, for on March 13, 1930, she died in Metuchen after a long illness. She was buried in a cemetery in nearby Plainfield, New Jersey.

MAJOR WORKS AND THEMES

In a British edition of stories that had appeared in Freeman's *A Humble Romance*, she wrote in a foreword: "These little stories were written about the village people of New England. They are studies of the descendants of the Massachusetts Bay colonists, in whom can still be seen traces of those features of will and conscience, so strong as to be almost exaggerations and deformities, which characterised their ancestors" (quoted in Westbrook 16–17). This brief statement applies to most of her best writing, whether stories or novels. Her settings are for the most part in villages and rural New England where the inhabitants were of the old English stock, and she emphasized and analyzed the effects of a lingering Puritanism on these people's wills and consciences, which, as she stated, after 200 years or more, often had become warped or downright psychopathic. Yet such was not always the case, as she recognized in her fiction. In some of her characters a strong will and a sensitive conscience proved to be assets that produced useful and spiritually beneficial results. Finally, in some cases, Freeman's characters are handicapped by a *lack* of willpower or conscience or both.

Freeman's concern with the presence of a residual Puritanism in the behavior and attitudes of her characters may have had its roots in her own upbringing in the Congregational Church, which in somewhat diluted strength still preached the Calvinist doctrines on which it had been founded. But beyond question, she had observed firsthand the oddities and excesses of will and conscience exhibited in her psychologically convincing probing of her characters' motivations. That these people happened to be located in New England fitted the reading public's notion that the region fostered eccentricity. For example, the term *New England conscience* has long carried a denotation of abnormality. The popular appeal, then, of Freeman's writing was that of local color at a time when that genre was at the height of its popularity. Freeman would rightly be considered a local colorist, and her frequently eccentric characters would, also rightly, be taken as part of the local color. But a thoughtful reader would also see in them evidence of their creator's insights into the ways in which people in general, not just in New England, cope with a difficult social and economic environment combined with personal problems of varying severity.

Two of Freeman's stories (both in *A New England Nun*) in which a strong will coupled with a sensitive conscience motivates successful action against formidable odds are "The Revolt of 'Mother' " and "Louisa." In the first, a wife's concern for her children's well-being thwarts the plans of her stubborn and greedy husband, who builds a fine new barn for his farm animals while his family lives in a house not much better than a hovel. The second story, "Louisa," recounts the determined efforts of a young woman who supports herself and her mother by cultivating their tiny farm rather than the daughter's marrying a man she neither loves nor respects. A story in which will and conscience border on the pathological is "An Honest Soul" in *A Humble Romance*. In it, an impoverished seamstress, making a trifling mistake in sewing a customer's patchwork quilt, persists in doing and redoing her work until, having attained perfection, she falls to the floor in exhaustion and hunger. In another such story, "A Conflict Ended," also in *A Humble Romance*, a man's disagreement regarding a theological point prompts him to sit in protest on the steps of his church, thereby losing the respect of the woman he had hoped to marry. As often happens in Freeman's stories, the woman resolves the situation, in this case, by leading him hand in hand into the church.

In other stories the protagonists are almost totally passive. One such is "A New England Nun," perhaps Freeman's most profound character study. In it, Louisa Ellis, the main character, and Joe Dagget have been engaged for fifteen years. During this time, he has long been in Australia, where he has been working to provide money for his marriage. Meanwhile, Louisa has devoted herself to the care of a supposedly vicious dog and a canary and fussing with her

daintily appointed cottage. When her fiancé finally returns, the two find themselves temperamentally far apart. He seems determined to keep his promise but
becomes attracted to another more vivacious woman. Accidentally becoming
aware of this, Louisa releases her betrothed from his vows and continues to live
the existence to which she had become accustomed. Any regrets she may have
vanish as she settles into her accustomed way of life, which to her is a satisfactory substitute for marriage.

A very different sort of passivity is that of the defeated, utterly despairing
inmates of a poorhouse in the story "Sister Liddy" in *A New England Nun*,
one of Freeman's most striking achievements in realism. Contrasting with Freeman's passive characters is the protagonist in "A Village Singer" in *A New
England Nun*. A contralto in her church choir, Candace Whitcomb is replaced
by a younger woman. Far from accepting her dismissal, Candace reacts with a
defiant rage that reaches emotional heights that Freeman asserts are latent, if
seldom unleashed, in outwardly reserved New Englanders.

Themes relating to conscience and will inform most of Freeman's writing and
underlie the conflicts on which her plots are based. Frequently, they are embodied in stories involving marriages in which a deadlock has developed, or the
standoff may be between lovers. Resolutions of these conflicts occur when one
of the contenders becomes activated by a force other than a stubborn will or an
exaggerated conscience. Love is sometimes the solvent, but not always.

Themes, situations, and character types similar to those found in Freeman's
short fiction recur in her better novels—especially in *Jerome, Jane Field*, and
Pembroke. All three deal with village life, but *Pembroke* surpasses the other
two with its full cast of village characters interacting in such a way as to create
a sense of the community itself as an organic whole, and achieving this with a
realism unique at the time in New England fiction. Another novel with a very
different setting is *The Portion of Labor*, in which the central action involves a
labor strike in a mill town, the strikers' cause being championed and to some
extent led by a young woman with a Puritan sense of duty and justice combined
with a passionate nature comparable to that of the protagonist of "A Village
Singer."

CRITICAL RECEPTION

At the time of the publication in 1887 of Freeman's *A Humble Romance and
Other Stories*, William Dean Howells wrote in *Harper's New Monthly*: "Who-
ever loves the face of common humanity will find pleasure in [these stories].
They are peculiarly American and they are peculiarily 'narrow' in a certain way,
and yet they are like the best modern work everywhere in their directness and
simplicity" (640). As an advocate of realism, Howells found Freeman's writing
very satisfying, despite occasional lapses into sentimentality. Oliver Wendell
Holmes, James Russell Lowell, and Henry James also recognized the realistic

strength of Freeman's work. From a different viewpoint, Rollin Lynde Hartt in an article in the *Atlantic*, "A New England Hill Town," commended Freeman's accuracy in depicting people living in New England's backcountry. In another *Atlantic* article, "Miss Wilkins: An Idealist in Masquerade," Charles M. Thompson drew attention to Freeman's Puritan background and its influence on her writing and notes her insights into the sometimes pathological working of the human will. He also sees in her work an underlying strain of Emersonian idealism and hints of mysticism.

Freeman's preoccupation with the residual Puritanism that she detected in her New Englanders inevitably gave rise to comparisons with Hawthorne. In an essay, "Hawthorne: Looking Before and After," Paul Elmer More placed Freeman at the end of a line of Puritan authors beginning with Cotton Mather. In her work, he thought the final debilitating and distorting effects of a dying Calvinism were dealt with, and he discussed the story "Two Old Lovers" as illustrative of this. In *Jerome*, which he considered her best novel, he saw her breaking with her Calvinish concerns. In a somewhat similar vein, Fred Lewis Pattee included in his book *Sidelights on American Literature* a chapter titled "The Terminal Moraine of New England Puritanism," in which he described Freeman as an accurate recorder of the detritus left, as he implies, by a Puritan ice age. F. O. Matthiessen, concentrating less on the Puritan elements in Freeman's work, wrote in 1931: "The struggle of the heart to live by its own strength alone is her constant theme, and the sudden revolt of a spirit that will endure no more provides her most stirring dramas" (408).

Freeman's work was widely read and received serious critical attention in the United Kingdom. Typical was a notice in the *London Spectator* on *A New England Nun*: "The stories are among the most remarkable feats of what we may call literary impressionism in our language, so powerfully do they stamp on the reader's mind the image of the classes of individuals they portray without spending on the picture a single redundant word" (quoted in Pattee 187). British author Arthur Machen, best known for his stories of fantasy and the supernatural, approvingly describes Freeman as depicting "a society in which each man stands apart, responsible only for himself and to himself, conscious only of himself and his God." To Machen, Freeman's strong-willed characters, even if their actions are absurd, illustrate what is to him "the everlasting truth that, at last, each man must stand or fall alone and that if he would stand, he must to a certain extent live alone with his soul" (173–176). Machen gave special praise to Freeman's novel *Pembroke*, as did another British author, Sir Arthur Conan Doyle, in an article, "Mary E. Wilkins Freeman," in *Harper's Weekly* (1903). Doyle considered *Pembroke* comparable to *The Scarlet Letter* in power and artistry.

To a lesser extent, Freeman attracted attention in France, where in 1896 an essay "Un Romancier de la Nouvelle-Angleterre" appeared in *Revue des Deux Mondes*, written by Thérèse Blanc, who was on the editorial staff of that periodical. The essay contains praise for Freeman's stylistic skill but warns that French readers will be puzzled by the strangeness of the echoings of Puritanism in her writings. The French, she thought, might be at a loss to understand *Pembroke*. With her essay, Blanc included a translation of "A New England Nun."

In 1956 Edward Foster published the first biography of Freeman, and ten years later, Perry D. Westbrook published a critical study of her writing. (Westbrook's book appeared in a revised edition in 1988.) Both authors recognized in Freeman a skilled observer of the mores and conditions of New England village life. A recent, extremely valuable contribution is Brent L. Kendrick's *The Infant Sphinx: Collected Letters of Mary E. Wilkins Freeman*. Its main introduction along with introductions to the successive periods in which the letters were written and its copious annotations constitute the fullest and most detailed study of Freeman's life and career yet to appear.

In the 1960s, as the country became increasingly concerned with the status and rights of women in our society and courses in women's studies began to appear in colleges and universities, a keen interest developed in women writers, especially those writing extensively about women. Among such authors, Freeman drew close attention, mainly from women critics. Two collections of her stories appeared, one edited by Michelle Clark and the other by Marjorie Pryse, both with critical introductions. A third volume, edited by Barbara H. Solomon, with a lengthy introduction, contains selected stories by Sarah Orne Jewett as well as by Freeman. Other critics and scholars discussed Freeman in parts of books or in periodical articles, among them Alice Glarden Brand, Leah Blatt Glasser, Susan Allen Toth, and Ann Douglas Wood. With these writers the focus has been primarily on the efforts, successful more often than not, of Freeman's women to overcome harsh social or economic handicaps through their own inner strengths, which they may have long been aware of or which they have not come to realize until a time of crisis. In addition, some of these critics deal perceptively with Freeman's literary skills, for example, in her use of symbols, her creation of atmosphere, and her development of theme and character. After comparative neglect during at least two decades following her death, this renewal of interest in Freeman has restored her reputation to its rightful place among nineteenth-century American authors.

WORKS CITED

Howells, William Dean. "The Editor's Study." *Harper's New Monthly* 75 (September 1987): 640.
Machen, Arthur. *Hieroglyphics*. 1902. Reprint, London: Unicorn Press, 1960. 173–176.
Matthiessen, Francis Otto. "New England Stories." In *American Writers on American Literature*, edited by John Macy. New York: Horace Liveright, 1931. 399–413.
Pattee, Fred Lewis. *Sidelights on American Literature*. New York: Century, 1915. 187.
Westbrook, Perry D. *Mary Wilkins Freeman*. Rev. ed. Boston: Twayne Publishers, 1988. 16–17.

BIBLIOGRAPHY

Works by Mary Wilkins Freeman

Adult Writings

A Humble Romance and Other Stories. New York: Harper & Brothers, 1887.
A New England Nun and Other Stories. New York: Harper & Brothers, 1891.
Giles Corey, Yeoman: A Play. New York: Harper & Brothers, 1893.
Jane Field. New York: Harper & Brothers, 1893.
Pembroke. New York: Harper & Brothers, 1894.
Madelon. New York: Harper & Brothers, 1896.
Jerome, a Poor Man. New York: Harper & Brothers, 1897.
The People of Our Neighborhood. Philadelphia: Curtis Publishing Company, 1898.
Silence and Other Stories. New York: Harper & Brothers, 1898.
Evelina's Garden. New York: Harper & Brothers, 1899.
The Jamesons. New York: Doubleday and McClure Company, 1899.
The Heart's Highway, a Romance of Virginia. New York: Doubleday, Page & Company, 1900.
The Love of Parson Lord and Other Stories. New York: Harper & Brothers, 1900.
The Portion of Labor. New York: Harper & Brothers, 1901.
Understudies. New York: Harper & Brothers, 1901.
Six Trees. New York: Harper & Brothers, 1903.
The Wind in the Rose-Bush and Other Stories of the Supernatural. New York: Doubleday, Page and Company, 1903.
The Givers. New York: Harper & Brothers, 1904.
The Debtor. New York: Harper & Brothers, 1905.
By the Light of the Soul. New York: Harper & Brothers, 1906.
"Doc" Gordon. New York: Authors and Newspapers Association, 1906.
The Fair Lavinia and Others. New York: Harper & Brothers, 1907.
The Shoulders of Atlas. New York: Harper & Brothers, 1908.
The Whole Family, a Novel by Twelve Authors [including Freeman, William Dean Howells, Henry James, et al.]. New York: Harper & Brothers, 1908.
The Winning Lady and Others. New York: Harper & Brothers, 1909.
The Butterfly House. New York: Dodd, Mead & Company, 1912.
The Yates Pride: A Romance. New York: Harper & Brothers, 1912.
The Copy-Cat and Other Stories. New York: Harper & Brothers, 1914.
An Alabaster Box [with Florence Morse Kingsley]. New York: D. Appleton and Company, 1917.
Edgewater People. New York: Harper & Brothers, 1918.
The Best Stories of Mary E. Wilkins Freeman. Introduction by W. W. Lanier. New York: Harper & Brothers, 1927.
The Collected Ghost Stories of Mary E. Wilkins Freeman. Edited by Edward Wagenknecht. Sauk City, WI: Arkham House, 1974.
The Revolt of Mother and Other Stories. Edited by Michelle Clark. Old Westbury, NY: Feminist Press, 1974.
Selected Stories of Mary E. Wilkins Freeman. Edited with an introduction by Marjorie Pryse. New York: W. W. Norton, 1983.

The Infant Sphinx: Collected Letters of Mary E. Wilkins Freeman. Edited by Brent L. Kendrick. Metuchen, NJ: Scarecrow Press, 1985.

Juvenile Writings

Decorative Plaques. Designs by George F. Barnes. Poems by Mary E. Wilkins. Boston: D. Lothrop and Company, [1883].

The Cow with the Golden Horns and Other Stories. Boston: D. Lothrop and Company, [1884].

The Adventures of Anne: Stories of Colonial Times. Boston: D. Lothrop and Company, [1886].

The Pot of Gold and Other Stories. Boston: D. Lothrop and Company, [1892].

Young Lucretia and Other Stories. New York: Harper & Brothers, 1892.

Comfort Pease and Her Gold Ring. New York and Chicago: Fleming H. Revell Company, 1895.

Once Upon a Time and Other Child Verses. Boston: Lothrop Publishing Company, [1897].

The Green Door. New York: Moffat Yard and Company, 1910.

Studies of Mary Wilkins Freeman

Blanc, Thérèse [Mme. Thérèse Blanc-Bentzon]. "Un Romancier de la Nouvelle-Angleterre." *Revue des Deux Mondes* 136 (1 August 1896): 544–569.

Blanck, J. N. "Mary E. Wilkins Freeman." In *Bibliography of American Literature.* Vol. 3. New Haven: Yale University Press, 1959. 324–343.

Brand, Alice Glarden. "Mary Wilkins Freeman: Misanthropy as Propaganda." *New England Quarterly* 50 (March 1977): 83–100.

Donovan, Josephine. *New England Local Color Literature: A Woman's Tradition.* New York: Continuum, 1988.

Foster, Edward. *Mary E. Wilkins Freeman.* New York: Hedrick House, 1956.

Glasser, Leah Blatt. "Mary E. Wilkins Freeman: The Stranger in the Mirror." *Massachusetts Review* 25 (summer 1984): 323–339.

Hamblen, Abigail Ann. *The New England Art of Mary E. Wilkins Freeman.* Amherst, MA: Green Knight Press, 1966.

Hirsch, David E. "Subdued Meaning in 'A New England Nun.'" *Studies in Short Fiction* 2 (spring 1965): 124–136.

Howells, William Dean. "Editor's Study." *Harper's New Monthly* 74 (February 1887): 482–486.

Johns, Barbara. "Some Reflections on the Spinster in New England Literature." In *Regionalism and the Female Imagination,* edited by Emily Toth. New York: Human Sciences Press, 1985. 29–64.

Marchalonis, Shirley. *Critical Essays on Mary Wilkins Freeman.* New York: Macmillan, 1991.

Oaks, Susan. "The Haunting Will: The Ghost Stories of Mary Wilkins Freeman." *Colby Library Quarterly* 21 (December 1985): 208–220.

Pryse, Marjorie. "The Humanity of Women in Freeman's 'A Village Singer.'" *Colby Library Quarterly* 19 (June 1983): 69–77.

————. "An Uncloistered New England Nun." *Studies in Short Fiction* 20 (fall 1983): 289–295.

Reichardt, Mary R. "Mary Wilkins Freeman: One Hundred Years of Criticism." *Legacy* 4 (fall 1987): 31–44.

―――. *A Web of Relationships: Women in the Short Fiction of Mary Wilkins Freeman.* Jackson: University Press of Mississippi, 1992.

Romines, Ann. "A Place for 'A Poetess.' " *Markham Review* 12 (summer 1983): 61–64.

Sherman, Sarah W. "The Great Goddess in New England: Mary Wilkins Freeman's 'Christmas Jenny.' " *Studies in Short Fiction* 17 (spring 1980): 157–164.

Thompson, Charles M. "Miss Wilkins: An Idealist in Masquerade." *Atlantic Monthly* 83 (May 1899): 665–675.

Toth, Susan Allen. "Defiant Light: A Positive View of Mary Wilkins Freeman." *New England Quarterly* 46 (March 1973): 82–93.

―――. "Mary Wilkins Freeman's Parable of Wasted Life." *American Literature* 42 (January 1971): 464–467.

Warren, Austin. *The New England Conscience.* Ann Arbor: University of Michigan Press, 1966. 157–169.

Westbrook, Perry D. *Acres of Flint: Sarah Orne Jewett and Her Contemporaries.* Rev. ed. Metuchen, NJ: Scarecrow Press, 1981. 86–104.

Westbrook, Perry D., *Mary Wilkins Freeman.* Rev. ed. Boston: Twayne Publishers, 1988.

Wood, Ann Douglas. "The Literature of Impoverishment: The Women Local Colorists in America, 1865–1914." *Women's Studies* 1 (1972): 3–40.

MARGARET FULLER
(1810–1850)

Susan Belasco Smith

BIOGRAPHY

Sarah Margaret Fuller was born in Cambridgeport, Massachusetts, on May 23, 1810, to Timothy Fuller, a Harvard-educated lawyer who served in the Massachusetts state legislature and the United States Congress, and Margarett [*sic*] Crane Fuller, who taught school briefly in her hometown of Canton, Massachusetts, before her marriage. Raised in a household that stressed middle-class New England values as well as Unitarian rationalism, Margaret Fuller was educated carefully and rather unusually for a young woman of her time. Her father served as her teacher in her early years, and Fuller was reading Latin at age six. Located between Harvard College and the bridge to Boston, Cambridgeport was a neighborhood of academics and young professionals, and the Fullers mixed easily with both. When her father's career was too demanding for him to continue his work on her education, Fuller was tutored by members of the college, and in 1823–1825, she attended schools in Boston, Cambridgeport, and finally the Young Ladies Seminary of Groton. Her letters from her childhood and years at school reveal a high degree of conscientiousness and absorption in her studies, as well as some anxiety about pleasing her father, who could be sternly disapproving.

When Fuller returned home from school to Boston in 1825, she possessed a preparatory education that would have been the envy of a bright young man. But as a woman, Fuller could not go on to Harvard, and instead, she stayed at home and embarked on her study of Italian and German literature, interests that remained with her throughout her life. She was especially engaged by Petrarch, by Dante, and by Germaine de Staël, whose *Corinne* became a favorite of hers. In addition, she was part of the social and intellectual world of Harvard and made friendships with a number of young men who went on to notable careers, especially James Freeman Clarke, Frederic Henry Hedge, George T. Davis, William Henry Channing, and Oliver Wendell Holmes, as well as young women such as Eliza Farrar, Ellen Sturgis, and Anna Barker.

Her most important friendship of this period was with James Freeman Clarke, who would later become a Unitarian minister as well as the editor of the Unitarian journal *The Western Messenger*. With Clarke, Fuller studied Goethe, reading *Torquato Tasso, Faust*, and *Wilhelm Meisters Lehrjahre*. She began working on translations and tried writing essays and poems; she also developed an intense interest in the self-cultivation that Goethe advocated. Her father's political career ended in 1833, and Timothy Fuller moved his family to a farm in Groton. Devastated by the separation from her friends and from her beloved Cambridge, Fuller tutored her younger siblings and worked on her own writing. She published her first essay, "In Defense of Brutus," in the *Boston Daily Advertiser* on November 27, 1834. In 1835, she published three reviews in Clarke's *Western Messenger*. Encouraged by these publications, Fuller began to think of the possibility of writing a life of Goethe and happily accepted an invitation to travel to Europe with her friend Eliza Farrar and her husband John, a Harvard mathematics professor. The trip was canceled when Timothy Fuller died of cholera on September 30, 1835, leaving the family in serious financial distress.

Fuller had little choice but to assume the role of manager of her family's affairs and as well as partial breadwinner. Determined, however, to continue her association with the intellectual world of Boston and becoming increasingly influenced by the literary movement of Transcendentalism, Fuller also wanted to meet and know Ralph Waldo Emerson, author of *Nature* (1836) and founder (with Henry David Thoreau) of the loose association known as the Transcendental Club. In the summer of 1836, Fuller had her chance through the encouragement of their mutual friends, Frederic Henry Hedge and Harriet Martineau, who had toured the United States in 1835 and made Fuller's acquaintance during her visit to Cambridge. Emerson invited Fuller to visit him and his wife, Lidian, in Concord in July. Her visit lasted three weeks and marked a turning point in the careers of both. Emerson would say after Fuller's untimely death in 1850 that with her demise he had lost his audience. To Fuller, Emerson represented the mature, intellectual companion she needed. The meeting with Emerson also helped Fuller think of new ways in which she might continue her literary career and assist her family as well.

Alternating between living in Groton and staying with friends in Boston, Fuller kept writing. Her two-part essay "Modern British Poets" appeared in the *American Monthly Magazine* in September and October. In addition, she offered German, French, and Italian literature to young women in Boston in the fall of 1836 and was also invited to teach at Bronson Alcott's Temple School. Although Fuller admired Alcott and his radical approach to teaching, he was unable to pay her, and Fuller was forced to look for work elsewhere. She accepted a position at Hiram Fuller's Green Street School in Providence, Rhode Island, and spent the next two years there. Although Fuller was a popular teacher, she missed the livelier intellectual and social life of Boston and felt that her students took time away from her own writing. In the spring of 1838, Fuller left her position in Providence and promptly completed her first book, her translation of Eckermann's *Conversations with Goethe*, and continued her research on a biography of Goethe.

At this time, Fuller accepted Emerson's offer to become the editor of the *Dial*, which she edited from July 1840 until July 1842. As editor, Fuller published a variety of literary experiments in prose and poetry, reflecting the speculative nature of Transcendentalism. She printed the work of Emerson, Bronson Alcott, Theodore Parker, George Ripley, Henry David Thoreau, and Elizabeth Peabody. She also published her own work: Her essay on the letters of two German intellectuals, "Bettine Brentano and Her Friend Günderode" (January 1842); a review of Nathaniel Hawthorne's *Twice-Told Tales* (July 1842); and "The Great Lawsuit: Man *versus* Men. Woman *versus* Women" (July 1843), the essay that formed the basis of *Woman in the Nineteenth Century* (1845). The editorship of the *Dial*, however, could not provide an income, and Fuller initiated "Conversations" for women in Boston, a series that she led from 1839 until 1844. Designed to help women understand concepts in the arts, mythology, history, and even the intellectual potential of women, the classes included Lidian Emerson, Sophia Hawthorne, Elizabeth Peabody, Sarah Clarke, Caroline Sturgis, and Lydia Maria Child (Capper 511). During these years in Boston, Fuller established herself as a major literary figure who was teaching and writing serious work.

Accepting an invitation from James Freeman Clarke and his sister, Sarah, Fuller had an opportunity to travel to what was then the American West in the summer of 1843. Fuller and the Clarkes journeyed to Niagara Falls by train and then to Illinois, Wisconsin, and Ohio by boat and stagecoach. Deeply impressed by her travels and by the plight of the Native Americans and wives of settlers she had met, Fuller determined to write a book of her journey. Fuller received permission to read and study in the Harvard College library (the first woman to do so) and, with the encouragement of Thoreau and Emerson, finished her manuscript, *Summer on the Lakes, in 1843*. Emerson helped her publish it in 1844, and after Horace Greeley, editor of the increasingly successful *New York Tribune* read it, he offered her a job as literary editor. By this time, Fuller's friendship with Emerson was growing difficult, her potential suitor Samuel Ward had decided to marry Anna Barker, and Fuller was undoubtedly chafing under the geographical and intellectual constraints of Boston and Transcendentalism. To the surprise of her family and friends, she accepted the job and made plans to move to New York. At Greeley's suggestion, she first revised her *Dial* essay "The Great Lawsuit" for publication as a book, *Woman in the Nineteenth Century*, which Greeley's company published in 1845.

From December 7, 1844, until July 1846, Fuller wrote some 250 articles and reviews and selected and edited other literary pieces for about a fourth of each issue of the *Tribune*. At the *Tribune*, she was in the middle of the large national and international news stories of the day. The controversy over the annexation of Texas was much in the news, as was the ongoing issue of slavery. Fuller wrote reviews of *The Narrative of the Life of Frederick Douglass*, Poe's *Tales*, and a translation of Goethe's *Essays on Art*. She also wrote articles on the "Asylum for Discharged Female Convicts," the "Water Cure," and the plight of Irish immigrants, as well as a commentary on the anniversary of the Emancipation of Slaves in the British West Indies in an article entitled "First of August, 1845." By any measure, Fuller was covering a great many social and cultural events and interpreting them for a large public audience, far greater than the readership of *The Western Messenger* or even the *Dial*, for which she had previously written. In addition to her work at the *Tribune*, Fuller also prepared and published her fourth book, a collection of her essays and reviews, *Papers on Literature and Art* (1846). During this time, she fell in love with James Nathan, a German businessman. But Nathan went abroad in early 1846, and Fuller was left in New York, feeling deserted and humiliated. When Marcus and Rebecca Spring, a wealthy philanthropic couple, invited her to accompany them on a European tour, Fuller proposed that Greeley engage her as a foreign correspondent. He agreed, and she sailed for England with the Springs on August 1, 1846.

Fuller and the Springs traveled first to England, Scotland, and France, spending the fall and winter touring the countryside and visiting the principle cities. They arrived in Italy in March 1847 and traveled throughout the spring and summer from Genoa to Rome, Florence, Cologna, Ravenna, and finally to Venice. In July 1847, the Springs left Fuller in Venice and went on to Germany. Fuller wanted to see more of Italy, especially Rome, and determined to stay on her own. Throughout this first year, Fuller wrote her dispatches for the *Tribune;* her first appeared in the *Tribune* on September 24, 1846. The early dispatches were accounts of her travels and of the people she met such as Thomas Carlyle and George Sand, but when she and the Springs arrived in Italy, they found themselves in the midst of efforts to free and unite Italy. The spirit of revolution was everywhere, and Fuller became deeply involved. She also met Marchese Giovanni Ossoli, an Italian Catholic of modest means who participated in the struggle for Italian independence as a member of the republican army. Although no records survive of a legal marriage between Fuller and Ossoli, she eventually took his name, and they lived together as much as possible beginning in late 1847. Increasingly, the subject of Fuller's dispatches became the revolution, and events moved swiftly forward. But the revolutionaries were no match for the war machinery of the Austrians and the French, and despite heroic efforts, the fragile republic in Italy that had been created in 1848 was obliterated by the summer of 1849. Fuller continued to write her dispatches (albeit irregularly) during these years, covering many of the major events of the revolution from the scene in Rome. She would eventually write thirty-seven dispatches, which appeared until January 6, 1850. She wrote friends that she was working on a manuscript, "The History of the Late Revolutionary Movements in Italy," her own account of the failed efforts of the Italian nationalists to gain independence and unity, based on her dispatches and additional material. Fuller was also pregnant; her son, Angelo, was born on September 5, 1848, but she said nothing of his existence in letters to her family and friends until the summer of 1849.

During the early part of 1850, Fuller and Ossoli lived in Florence, where they were friendly with Robert and Elizabeth Barrett Browning. After making a series of difficult arrangements, they secured passage on a small ship, the *Elizabeth*, and sailed for the United States on May 17, 1850. Arriving near New York on July 19, 1850, a violent storm caused the *Elizabeth* to break up on a sandbar, just off the coast of Fire Island. Fuller, Ossoli, and their son died in the shipwreck. No trace of Fuller's body was ever discovered.

MAJOR WORKS AND THEMES

Despite the fact that Fuller died when she was barely forty years old, she published over 300 short works in periodicals as well as six books, including two translations, a travel book, a treatise on the status of women in society, and a collection of published and unpublished reviews and essays. Concerned throughout with the promotion of an American literature, the necessity of increased rights for women, the importance of education and self-cultivation for all, and the politics of power within the state, Fuller saw herself as an interpreter of the sign and symbols of human culture.

Fuller's earliest book-length works were translations of Johann Peter Eckermann's *Conversations with Goethe* (1839) and Bettina von Arnim's *Die Günderode* (1842). Although Fuller had been taught Greek and Latin, she taught herself to read German, and these works reflect her early interests in German romanticism, pedagogy, interpretation, and the position of women in society (Zwarg 463–464). In her preface to *Conversations with Goethe*, Fuller used the biographical materials she had been gathering to shed new light on the less well known details of Goethe's later life and, at the same time, introduced Goethe to her Transcendental friends, many of whom, including Emerson, could not read German. Building on the popularity of the English translation of Bettina von Arnim's fictionalized *Goethe's Conversations with a Child* (1838), Fuller translated *Die Günderode*, an epistolary novel about the exchange of letters between von Arnim and another woman writer. The novel is both a debate and an exchange about the nature and power of female friendship.

Fuller's third book, *Summer on the Lakes, in 1843*, was partly a response to the numerous travel books written by European visitors, including Frances Trollope's *Domestic Manners of the Americans* (1832), Harriet Martineau's *Society in America* (1837), and Charles Dickens's *American Notes* (1842). Although Fuller was ostensibly writing an account of her travels to the American West, she also wrote an "exploration of American culture, both as it was and as she hoped it might be, and her personal search for ways of thought and action that would give her a voice in the definition of that culture'' (Smith 191). Beginning with her impressions of Niagara Falls, a popular tourist destination in the mid-nineteenth century, Fuller records her reactions to a variety of experiences on her largely circular tour: Niagara, Buffalo, Chicago, Mackinac Island, Sault Ste. Marie, Milwaukee, central Illinois, and returning to Buffalo. Fuller saw settlements of Native Americans as well as the small farms of pioneers. Shocked by the conditions of the Indians, she was also struck by the weariness of the wives of white settlers; as some scholars have argued, the frontier meant a much more restricted life for women than it did for men (Kolodny 112–130). *Summer on the Lakes* is also autobiographical; while Fuller was absorbed by the geography of her journey, she also includes a variety of dialogues that explore her interest in a life of action, over and above the contemplative life of self-cultivation that she had known in New England.

Before she moved to New York in 1844 to take the position of literary editor for Greeley's *New York Tribune*, she revised her essay for the *Dial* ''The Great Lawsuit: Man *versus* Men. Woman *versus* Women'' into her next book, *Woman in the Nineteenth Century* (Reynolds 17). Challenging and erudite, *Woman in the Nineteenth Century* is Fuller's statement on the status of women in society: economic, political, intellectual, and sexual. Arguing for increased vocational opportunities for women, Fuller attacked the hypocrisies she saw in her society and called for a reexamination of the rigid roles prescribed for men and women. Fuller's departure points are the Transcendental notion of the perfectibility of human beings and Emersonian self-reliance; she uses those positions to examine the implications for women (Steele 101). She illustrates her points with a variety of examples from mythology, history, and literature, all designed to suggest the potential that women can realize if they are free of the barriers of patriarchal convention. Anticipating campaign for the reform of marriage laws that would come later in the century, she offers a specific critique of the institution of marriage and offers examples for how equality would improve the lives of married couples. Anecdotal, digressive, and often difficult, *Woman in the Nineteenth Century* is nonetheless the first American feminist manifesto. Elizabeth Cady Stanton felt that it led the way to the Seneca Falls Women's Rights Convention of 1848.

While *Woman in the Nineteenth Century* was in press, Fuller was busy at her new job as literary editor of the *Tribune*. For the next two years, she wrote articles and reviews and edited the works of others for the literature section of the paper. During the course of her work, Fuller posed what may be viewed as a series of challenges to an Emersonian conception of individualism and of the scholar's proper role in society. Her articles became increasingly concerned with social problems and concerns, and she took an active role in promoting new American literature whenever she could. Evert A. Duyckinck, an editor and responsible for the ''Library of Choice Reading'' and the ''Library of American Books,'' published by Wiley and Putnam, encouraged her to collect her articles and reviews, and her *Papers on Literature and Art* was published in 1846. This two-volume collection included one unpublished essay, "American Literature: Its Position in the Present Time, and Prospects for the Future." The book caught the attention of Walt Whitman, who reviewed it for the *Brooklyn Daily Eagle* on November 9, 1846: "We think the female mind has peculiarly the capacity, and ought to have the privilege, to enter into the discussion of high questions of morals, taste, &c. We therefore welcome Miss Fuller's papers, right heartily" (Chevigny, *The Woman* 507).

Fuller's last works were the thirty-seven dispatches she wrote as the *Tribune*'s foreign correspondent from 1846 to 1850. Begun as travel letters, they became an account of the political upheaval in Europe. When Fuller arrived in Italy in 1847, it was divided into three parts: Lombardy and Venezia, governed by Austria; the Papal States, ruled by the current Pope, Pius IX; and Naples and Sicily, controlled by the French. Italian patriots were united in their hatred of foreign domination and their wish for Italian unification; they were, however, divided about how a united Italy might be accomplished. For her *Tribune* readers, Fuller wrote about the efforts of Joseph Mazzini who favored a republic as well as those who favored a federation of states under the leadership of the pope. She also wrote movingly about the establishment of a Roman Republic on February 9, 1849, and its sad end a few months later on July 1. Fuller's dispatches, written as they were on the scene as the drama of the failed revolutions throughout Europe played out, may not be the "History" that Fuller intended, but they do constitute an important chronicle of the people and events during a tumultuous time in European history. As America's first woman foreign correspondent, Fuller ended her career as a Transcendentalist thinker turned radical.

CRITICAL RECEPTION

With the publication of *Summer on the Lakes* and *Woman in the Nineteenth Century*, Margaret Fuller became a fairly famous woman in New England and even enjoyed some celebrity abroad, especially in Paris where *Woman* had been translated into French. But reviewers sometimes found her work difficult. When Caleb Stetson published his review of *Summer* for the *Christian Examiner*, he called the book a "work of varied interest, rich in fine observation, profound reflection and striking anecdote" but was simultaneously reserved about the "high degree" of subjectivity in the book (274). Although Edgar Allan Poe admired some of Fuller's works (and especially her unwillingness to write glowingly of the popular Henry Wadsworth Longfellow), he noted rather ambiguously that *Woman in the Nineteenth Century* is "a book which few women in the country could have written, and no woman in the country would have published, with the exception of Miss Fuller" (7–8). Lydia Maria Child, author of *Hobomok* (1824) and editor of the *National Anti-Slavery Standard* (1841–1843), wrote of Fuller's courage in writing *Woman in the Nineteenth Century*: "The book in question is written in a free energetic spirit. It contains a few passages that will offend the fastidiousness of some readers; for they allude to subjects which men do not wish to have discussed, and which women dare not approach'' (97).

When Fuller died in 1850, Walter Savage Landor published a poem, a "lament of her untimely end," in which he recognized Fuller's "glorious soul,/ Renowned for strength of genius." Landor's tribute was not the only one; in 1852, James Freeman Clarke, Ralph Waldo Emerson, and William Henry Channing collected Fullers letters and journals and prepared the *Memoirs of Margaret Fuller Ossoli*. The purpose of the collection was to create a memorial and to recreate Fuller's life, in accordance with their own recollections (Chevigny, "Long Arm" 451). It sold well, and for a time, it was the best-selling biography of the decade. Editions of Fuller's works appeared, one edited by her brother Arthur Fuller in 1856 and another by Horace Greeley in 1869. In the 1880s, two biographies were published, one by Julia Ward Howe and one by Thomas Wentworth Higginson. Julian Hawthorne's biography *Nathaniel Hawthorne and His Wife* (1884) included a scathing passage from Hawthorne's journal in which he denigrated Fuller's intelligence. These events notwithstanding, in the decades following Fuller's death, her renown faded and her works went quietly out of print.

Because of recent reconstructions of the literary canon and the consequent shifts in literary interpretations, scholars no longer view Margaret Fuller as Emerson's brightest student or as a minor figure in the Transcendental circle. Rather, feminists and other scholars interested in cultural studies have emphasized Fuller's vital contributions to the literature that constitutes the American Renaissance and restored her works to a place of prominence. Today, Margaret Fuller and her works are at the center of midnineteenth century American studies.

WORKS CITED

Capper, Charles. "Margaret Fuller as Cultural Reformer: The Conversations in Boston." *American Quarterly* 39 (1987): 509–528.

Chevigny, Bell Gale. "The Long Arm of Censorship: Myth-making in Margaret Fuller's Time and Our Own." *Signs: Journal of Women in Culture and Society* 2 (1976): 450–460.

———. *The Woman and the Myth: Margaret Fuller's Life and Writings*. Rev. ed. Boston: Northeastern University Press, 1994.

Child, Lydia Maria. "Woman in the Nineteenth Century." *Broadway Journal*, 15 February 1845, 97.

Kolodny, Annette. *The Land before Her: Fantasy and Experience of the American Frontiers, 1630–1860*. Chapel Hill: University of North Carolina Press, 1984.

Poe, Edgar Allan. "*Woman in the Nineteenth Century*." In *Complete Works of Edgar Allan Poe*. New York: G. P. Putnam's Sons, 1902. 2: 7–8.

Reynolds, Larry J. "From *Dial* Essay to New York Book: The Making of *Woman in the Nineteenth Century*." In *Periodical Literature in Nineteenth-Century America*, edited by Kenneth M. Price and Susan Belasco Smith. Charlottesville: University Press of Virginia, 1995. 17–34.

Smith, Susan Belasco. "*Summer on the Lakes*: Margaret Fuller and the British." *Resources for American Literary Study* 17 (1991): 191–207.

Steele, Jeffrey. *The Representation of the Self in the American Renaissance*. Chapel Hill: University of North Carolina Press, 1987. 100–133.

[Stetson, Caleb]. "Notice of Recent Publications." *Christian Examiner* 37 (1844): 274–276.

Zwarg, Christina. "Feminism in Translation: Margaret Fuller's *Tasso*." *Studies in Romanticism* 29 (1990): 463–490.

BIBLIOGRAPHY

Works by Margaret Fuller

Conversations with Goethe in the Last Years of His Life, Translated from the German of Eckermann. Boston: Hilliard, Gray and Co., 1839.

Die Günderode. Boston: E. P. Peabody, 1842.

Summer on the Lakes, in 1843. Boston: Little and Brown, 1844.

Woman in the Nineteenth Century. New York: Greeley and McElrath, 1845.

Papers on Literature and Art. New York: Wiley and Putnam, 1846.

Editions of Margaret Fuller's Works

Hudspeth, Robert N., ed. *The Letters of Margaret Fuller, 1817–1850*. 6 vols. Ithaca: Cornell University Press, 1983–1994.

Kelley, Mary, ed. *The Portable Margaret Fuller*. New York: Penguin Books, 1994.

Mitchell, Catherine C., ed. *Margaret Fuller's New York Journalism*. Knoxville: University of Tennessee Press, 1995.

Reynolds, Larry J., ed. *Woman in the Nineteenth Century*. New York: Norton, 1996.

Reynolds, Larry J., and Susan Belasco Smith, eds. *"These Sad but Glorious Days": Dispatches from Europe, 1846–1850 by Margaret Fuller*. New Haven: Yale University Press, 1991.

Smith, Susan Belasco, ed. *Summer on the Lakes, in 1843*. 1844. Reprint, Urbana: University of Illinois Press, 1991.

Steele, Jeffrey, ed. *The Essential Margaret Fuller*. New Brunswick: Rutgers University Press, 1992.

Wade, Mason. *The Writings of Margaret Fuller*. New York: Viking, 1941.

Studies of Margaret Fuller

Allen, Margaret Vanderhaar. *The Achievement of Margaret Fuller*. University Park: Pennsylvania State University Press, 1979.

Blanchard, Paula. *Margaret Fuller: From Transcendentalism to Revolution*. New York: Dell, 1978.

Capper, Charles. *Margaret Fuller: An American Romantic Life*. Vol. 1, *The Private Years*. New York: Oxford University Press, 1992.

Chevigny, Bell Gale. *The Woman and the Myth: Margaret Fuller's Life and Writings.* Rev. ed. Boston: Northeastern University Press, 1994.

Deiss, Joseph Jay. *The Roman Years of Margaret Fuller.* New York: Thomas Y. Crowell, 1969.

Dickenson, Donna. *Margaret Fuller: Writing a Woman's Life.* New York: St. Martin's Press, 1993.

Ellison, Julie. *Delicate Subjects: Romanticism, Gender, and the Ethics of Understanding.* Ithaca: Cornell University Press, 1990.

Emerson, Ralph Waldo, William Henry Channing, and James Freeman Clarke. *Memoirs of Margaret Fuller Ossoli.* 2 vols. Boston: Phillips, Sampson, 1852.

Higginson, Thomas Wentworth. *Margaret Fuller Ossoli.* 1884. Reprint, New York: Confucian Press, 1980.

Howe, Julia Ward. *Margaret Fuller.* 1883. Reprint, New York: Haskell House, 1968.

Myerson, Joel. *Critical Essays on Margaret Fuller.* Boston: G. K. Hall, 1980.

———. *Margaret Fuller: A Descriptive Bibliography.* Pittsburgh: University of Pittsburgh Press, 1978.

Reynolds, Larry J. *European Revolutions and the American Literary Renaissance.* New Haven: Yale University Press, 1988.

Robinson, David. ''Margaret Fuller and the Transcendental Ethos: *Woman in the Nineteenth Century.*'' *PMLA* 97 (1982): 83–98.

Stern, Madeleine B. *The Life of Margaret Fuller.* 2nd ed. Westport, CT: Greenwood Press, 1991.

Urbanski, Marie Mitchell Olesen. *Margaret Fuller's Woman in the Nineteenth Century.* Westport, CT: Greenwood Press, 1980.

von Mehren, Joan. *Minerva and the Muse: A Life of Margaret Fuller.* Amherst: University of Massachusetts Press, 1995.

Watson, David. *Margaret Fuller: An American Romantic.* New York: Berg, 1988.

Zwarg, Christina. *Feminist Conversations: Fuller, Emerson, and the Play of Reading.* Ithaca: Cornell University Press, 1995.

CHARLOTTE PERKINS GILMAN (1860–1935)

Catherine J. Golden

BIOGRAPHY

Charlotte Anna Perkins Gilman, now considered a revolutionary in feminist circles, was fittingly born on the eve of America's Independence Day in 1860 in Hartford, Connecticut. "If only I'd been a little slower," Gilman confides in her autobiography, "and made it the glorious Fourth!" (*Living* 8). The only daughter of Frederick Beecher Perkins and Mary Fitch Westcott, Gilman was the third of four children (two died in infancy); her parents married in 1857 and divorced in 1873. Both came from prominent families, but Gilman was most proud of her father's distinguished relatives: reformer/authors Catharine Beecher and Harriet Beecher Stowe (her great-aunts) and evangelist Lyman Beecher (her great-grandfather).

Her talented but undisciplined father had difficulty sustaining his endeavors—career and family. Gilman never experienced the security of the home, which she later criticized in her theoretical works. Frederick Perkins left when Gilman was a child, stigmatizing the family by his desertion. Though he visited the family periodically, Gilman states in her autobiography "that my childhood had no father" (*Living* 5). She experienced chronic poverty and frequently sparred with her emotionally undemonstrative mother. Mary Perkins moved her family nineteen times in eighteen years.

Precocious, Gilman taught herself to read before age five; by age eight, she wrote imaginative tales, which, she admits in her autobiography, respond to the loneliness of her early life. Her formal education was limited, but she was an avid reader, stirred by Emerson's essays, Dickens's and Eliot's novels, James Freeman Clarke's *Ten Great Religions*, and John Stuart Mill's *The Subjection of Women*. In 1880, she completed a two-year course of study at the Rhode

Island School of Design. By age twenty-one, she was earning a modest income as a freelance commercial artist and private teacher but longing for independence and a literary and artistic life. During this period, she shared a close friendship with Martha Luther, bringing Gilman her "first deep personal happiness" (*Living* 48). Luther, however, married in 1881. Gilman recounts the keen loss of her friendship with Martha Luther in her final diary entry of 1881.

A month later, she declined the first proposal of marriage from Charles Walter Stetson, an aspiring artist whom Gilman describes in her autobiography (written forty-five years later) as "quite the greatest man, near my own age, that I had ever known" (*Living* 82). She was torn between convention—the ideals of marriage and motherhood—and her conviction to devote her life to her work; this struggle plagued her ten-year marriage to Stetson, whom she apprehensively married on May 2, 1884.

In her autobiography and her diaries, Gilman describes Stetson as a devoted and tender man who tried to understand her. She objected to the conventions of marriage, not to Stetson per se. Her misgivings about the private home and her disdain for domestic drudgery and women's subjugation in marriage found their way into her early poetry, such as "In Duty Bound" and "To the Young Wife" (in *In This Our World*).

Gilman's apprehensions about matrimony and the home intensified following the birth of her daughter Katharine Beecher Stetson on March 23, 1885. The despondency of this period reverberates in Gilman's autobiography and diary entries; she notes: "Every morning the same hopeless waking. Every day the same weary drag. To die mere cowardice. Retreat impossible, escape impossible" (*Diaries* 332). Gilman was depressed, spiritless, weak, and hysterical. Stetson offered to let her "go free" (*Diaries* 332), and they underwent a trial separation. She took a trip west, visiting her brother and father and staying with her old friend Grace Ellery Channing in Pasadena. Independent of husband and child, Gilman recovered fully from her depression. But she grew despondent again within a month of her return home: "[F]or now I saw the stark fact— that I was well while away and sick while at home" (*Living* 95).

During the spring of 1887, when Gilman was twenty-six, she agreed to undergo a one-month "rest cure" treatment at the Philadelphia sanitarium of Dr. S. Weir Mitchell, who diagnosed her condition as "neurasthenia" or "nervous prostration," a breakdown of the nervous system. Key to Mitchell's treatment (which aimed to heal the mind by healing the body) were complete inactivity and seclusion. When she left his sanitarium, Mitchell provided this much-quoted advice: " 'Live as domestic a life as possible. Have your child with you all the time. . . . Lie down an hour after each meal. Have but two hours' intellectual life a day. And never touch pen, brush or pencil as long as you live' " (*Living* 96).

Following this regimen, Gilman found herself on the brink of a total breakdown. She and Stetson agreed to separate in the fall of 1887. To Gilman, the effects of her breakdown were long lasting, ever affecting her powers of concentration. However, she began to heal when she gained her independence and moved to Pasadena with her daughter. Two months later, Stetson came to Pasadena for a year, but the two never reconciled; they divorced in 1894. It was in California that Gilman launched her professional career.

Her satirical poems and her Nationalist verse established her career as a public lecturer (for a fee) and by 1891 earned her a reputation as a poet. Gilman curtailed her involvement in Nationalism in 1892 to devote her energies to areas of reform for women. To manage as a single mother, she also produced short articles and short stories. Her landmark short story indicting patriarchy, "The Yellow Wall-Paper," was written during this period; it was first published in the January 1892 issue of *New England Magazine*.

In 1893 she lost her mother to cancer, brought forth her first collection of poetry (*In This Our World*), began to edit the short-lived *Impress* (a magazine sponsored by the Pacific Coast Women's Press Association [PCWPA]), and gained influential literary admirers. Longing to dedicate her whole life to serving her community at large, Gilman sent her daughter Katharine east in May 1894 to live with her father and Channing, whom Stetson married in June 1894. Gilman considered Channing her daughter's "co-mother," but this untraditional parenting arrangement provoked public scandal. That same month, she and fellow Nationalist Helen Campbell assumed ownership of and expanded *The Impress*. *The Impress* failed, however, when it lost its backing by the PCWPA; Gilman, a divorced woman and an "unnatural mother," was seen as a liability to backers.

Not discouraged, Gilman continued lecturing at home and in England and wrote short stories, poems, and essays—all with a social purpose. After years of planning and thinking, she quickly drafted *Women and Economics* (1898), in which she argues against women's economic dependence on men. By 1899 *Women and Economics* had earned Gilman an international reputation.

She had no intention of marrying again but changed her mind in 1897 after renewing her acquaintance with her first cousin Houghton Gilman, a New York patent attorney. Like other contemporary feminist activists such as Elizabeth Cady Stanton and Carrie Chapman Catt, Gilman found a way to balance marriage and career. Before marriage, they worked out an arrangement allowing her freedom to travel and time to devote to her work. Throughout their thirty-four-year marriage (they married in Detroit in June 1900), Houghton did not actively participate in the movements that occupied Gilman's efforts, but he was her avid supporter; he attended her lectures, read her work, and assisted with her research.

The decade following her second marriage was one of extreme productivity. During this major phase of her literary career, Gilman wrote several book-length treatises: *Concerning Children* (1900), *The Home: Its Work and Influence* (1903), *Human Work* (1904), and *The Man-Made World; Or, Our Androcentric Culture* (1909–1910). Between 1899 and 1910, she regularly contributed to major magazines including *The Saturday Evening Post, Scribner's, Woman's Home Companion*, and *Harper's Bazar* [sic]. In these works and in the *Forerunner*,

Gilman presents several broad themes that form the basis of much of her writing and lecturing: economic emancipation of women; socialized housekeeping, including kitchenless homes; the enactment of a social motherhood, featuring trained child care experts; and the gynecocentric theory of sexual differentiation contesting male dominance, indebted to the work of Lester Ward.

In 1909 Gilman launched her monthly magazine the *Forerunner*, which has a marked socialist slant and reflects Gilman's commitment to the rights of women. Gilman was publisher, editor, and sole author of the *Forerunner* (1909–1916) during its seven-year-and-two-month run. She established herself as a novelist as well as a writer of poetry, short story, and essay; her novels published serially in *Forerunner* include *What Diantha Did* (1910) (her first complete novel) as well as her utopian fiction *Moving the Mountain* (1911) and *Herland* (1915).

Gilman ended the *Forerunner* in 1916 because her readership was waning, and she felt she had conveyed all she had to say. At age fifty-six, she largely retreated from the public. In 1919, she contributed a regular column to the *New York Tribune*, drawing a regular salary for the first time in her life. She continued to tour as a lecturer, but in 1922 she retired to Connecticut; *His Religion and Hers* (1923), her final social treatise, received a mixed response.

Gilman's reputation slowly declined. During her final years, she wrote her autobiography, *The Living of Charlotte Perkins Gilman*, which was completed just before her death and published posthumously. She also completed a detective novel, *Unpunished*, and revised *A Study in Ethics* but could place neither with a publisher. After Gilman's death, her friend Amy Wellington tried unsuccessfully to secure a publisher for a new anthology of Gilman's verse entitled *Here Also*.

In January 1932, Gilman was diagnosed with inoperable breast cancer, but Houghton died first, rather suddenly in May 1934, from a cerebral hemorrhage. Gilman returned to Pasadena, her former home, to be near her family; Grace Channing Stetson, now a widow, joined her there. As her own disease progressed, Gilman planned her suicide by chloroform. She took her life on Saturday, August 17, 1935, leaving a typed suicide note: "When all usefulness is over, when one is assured of unavoidable and imminent death, it is the simplest of human rights to choose a quick and easy death in place of a slow and horrible one" (*Living* 333). Making a rational choice, Gilman elected to die as she lived—with dignity.

MAJOR WORKS AND THEMES

Deemed a leading feminist in her own time (along with Olive Schreiner and Ellen Key), Gilman, ironically, repudiated the term *feminist* when it came into use in her later years. Rather, she called herself a humanist. Her world was masculinist, men having usurped human traits as their own, and Gilman wanted to restore an equal gender balance, to emancipate women from "house service" to promote the best development of society. Unencumbered by domestic servitude, women could serve and benefit the world.

Gilman's books were reviewed widely, and she had an international reputation, but she earned her living primarily as a lecturer, not as an author. Moreover, she began her public career as a poet—which launched her lecturing career—and throughout her life, she wrote nearly 500 poems as a means of social criticism. A three-part collection, *In This Our World* contains poems for diverse audiences. Influential editors like William Dean Howells were enthusiastic about her socialist/nationalist agenda, traditionalists were drawn to her more moderate poems, and women could find comfort, wisdom, and even empowerment in her feminist verses.

An equally prolific author of short fiction, Gilman wrote nearly 200 short stories. While some of the stories such as "Dr. Clair's Place" (1915) and "Making a Change" (1911) resemble her utopian fiction and might best be seen as feminist fantasies, others like "Mrs. Elder's Idea" (1912) urge for women's personal and economic independence. Gilman's best-known and best-written "The Yellow Wall-Paper" focuses on the consequences of women's subordination in marriage. Intentionally didactic, "The Yellow Wall-Paper" graphically depicts the crippling limitations of a patriarchal society, driving the female protagonist to madness. Partly drawn from Gilman's own life experience (as was much of her short fiction and poetry), this story of a wife and mother undergoing a three-month "rest cure" for postpartum depression was written "to reach Dr. S. Weir Mitchell, and convince him of the error of his ways" (*Living* 121). Ironically, Gilman had difficulty placing "The Yellow Wall-Paper," for which she is best known today.

Women and Economics established Gilman's reputation as an authority on female subjugation. Like Thorstein Veblen, she advances that female oppression dates to prehistoric times. Gilman criticizes the "sexuo-economic" relation that leaves women economically and socially dependent on men. To Gilman, men and women would not be truly emancipated until women were freed from domestic bondage to contribute to the work of the world. In *The Home* and *Concerning Children*, Gilman elaborates and refines her historical and sociological analysis of men and women and her ideas about "social motherhood" and socialized housekeeping. As Ann J. Lane argues in *To Herland and Beyond*, "to know only *Women and Economics* is to be familiar with only part of her ideas. It is to settle for a view of the ground floor and to neglect the enticing staircase that leads to more elaborate and intriguing rooms above" (254).

Gilman founded the *Forerunner* because she felt constrained by the limited market for expressing "important truths, needed yet unpopular" (*Living* 304). In her words, " 'If the editors and publishers will not bring out my work, I will!' " (*Living* 304). Gilman estimated that each yearly volume of the *Forerunner* contained the equivalent of four books of 36,000 words and cost $3,000 to publish. The magazine shows Gilman's range as a writer, for it includes editorials, serial articles, book reviews, sermons, comments, and observations on current events ranging from dress reform to child labor laws and women's suffrage, advertisements, poems, humor, short stories, and installments of her novels.

Set in 1940, *Moving the Mountain* shows men and women (no longer prisoners of the private home) participating fully in the socialized economy of this "baby Utopia," as Gilman called it. True of other utopian romances, *Moving the Mountain* includes more dialogue than plot. Moving one step further, *Herland* envisions a socialized motherhood in a radical Utopia with no men at all; the children are raised by a genuine community of women who reproduce parthenogenetically. The three male companions (one a sociologist) who discover this lost civilization are initially blind to the wonders of the advanced Herlanders, but two of the male intruders essentially convert to socialism and feminism by the end of the novel. Reprinted in 1979, *Herland* is now acclaimed as a feminist utopian novel; the sequel entitled *With Her in Ourland* (1916) was also serialized in *Forerunner*.

CRITICAL RECEPTION

Gilman's satirical verse within *In This Our World* enjoyed a near cult following among socialists in the United States and England. Her satirical lyric "Similar Cases" earned her the praise of contemporary luminaries such as Upton Sinclair, George Bernard Shaw, Lester Ward, Woodrow Wilson, and Howells, who ranked Gilman's "Similar Cases" and her other "civic satire" with James R. Lowell's *The Biglow Papers* (1848). Her feminist treatise *Women and Economics* was translated into seven languages and had an enormous immediate impact on reform writers and critics.

In the early twentieth century, she lectured in England, Germany, Scandinavia, and throughout the United States and wrote prolifically. Although the circulation of *Forerunner* was small (Gilman had to lecture and publish outside the magazine to meet expenses), subscribers came from Europe, India, and Australia as well as across the United States.

Gilman's fame dwindled following the end of World War I; as Lane notes in her introduction to Gilman's reissued autobiography, "A vision of a better world that had sustained the socialist movement and the women's movement dimmed. . . . Charlotte Gilman continued to espouse her communitarian, socialist commitment to a life of productive, social purpose, whereas young women of this time sought a different kind of womanhood, one stressing personal, emotional, and sexual satisfactions" (xvii). By 1930, Gilman lamented her fallen popularity. She received no lecture invitations, and she could not place her last books. Gilman hoped that her biography with a foreword by prominent author Zona Gale might revive interest in her work; published posthumously, it sold poorly.

Although Gilman believed her life was marked by failure and died feeling neglected, the field of Gilman scholarship has grown steadily since the late 1960s. Carl Degler's 1956 *American Quarterly* essay inaugurated the revival of interest in Gilman's work, and in 1966, Degler brought forth a reprinting of *Women and Economics*. The entire run of the *Forerunner* was reprinted in 1968 as part of Greenwood's series of radical U.S. periodicals.

Resurrected among the works by overlooked late nineteenth-century American and British women writers, "The Yellow Wall-Paper" was reprinted by the Feminist Press in 1973, with an "Afterword" by Elaine Hedges. From its first publication until the early 1970s, it was virtually unknown; it is now part of the contemporary canon, hailed in feminist circles, and reprinted in major anthologies. "The Yellow Wall-Paper" is considered the best written of her short stories, which often fail aesthetically while serving an ideological point. Since the story's republication in 1973, there have been well over two dozen critical essays written about it, many reprinted in casebooks on "The Yellow Wall-Paper" by Catherine Golden (*The Captive Imagination*) and Thomas L. Erskine and Connie L. Richards (*The Yellow Wallpaper*).

In 1979, Lane brought forth a modern edition of *Herland*, and in 1980, Lane edited *The Charlotte Perkins Gilman Reader*, making accessible short stories and excerpted novels from *Forerunner*. Other collections by Denise D. Knight, Carol Farley Kessler, Barbara Solomon, and Larry Ceplair attest to the rising interest in reprinting Gilman's work. Beginning in the 1980s, biographers Mary A. Hill, Gary Scharnhorst, and Lane have examined her life and work, giving particular emphasis to her feminist convictions. And her diaries, edited by Knight, are now available.

Today, Gilman's prodigious output of theoretical studies, articles, and fiction stands as a major theoretical contribution to modern feminist thought.

BIBLIOGRAPHY

Works by Charlotte Perkins Gilman

Verse

In This Our World. Oakland: McCombs & Vaughn, 1893. London: T. Fisher Unwin, 1895. 3rd ed. Boston: Small, Maynard & Co., 1898. Reprint, New York: Arno, 1974.

Fiction

"The Yellow Wall-Paper." *New England Magazine* 5 (January 1892): 647–656. Reprint, with afterword by Elaine Hedges, Old Westbury: Feminist Press, 1973.
The Yellow Wallpaper. Boston: Small, Maynard & Co., 1899.
Moving the Mountain. Forerunner 2 (1911). Reprint, New York: Charlton, 1911.
Herland. Forerunner 6 (1915). Reprint, with introduction by Ann J. Lane, New York: Pantheon Books, 1979.
The Charlotte Perkins Gilman Reader. Edited, with introduction by Ann J. Lane. New York: Pantheon Books, 1980.
"The Yellow Wall-Paper" and Selected Stories by Charlotte Perkins Gilman. Edited,

with introduction by Denise D. Knight. Newark: University of Delaware Press, 1994.

Nonfiction

Women and Economics: A Study of the Economic Relation between Men and Women as a Factor in Social Evolution. Boston: Small, Maynard & Co., 1898. Reprint, with introduction by Carl N. Degler, New York: Harper & Row, 1966.

Concerning Children. Boston: Small, Maynard & Co., 1900.

The Home: Its Work and Influence. New York: McClure, Phillips & Co., 1903.

Human Work. New York: McClure, Phillips, 1904.

Forerunner 1–7 (1909–1916). Reprint, with introduction by Madeleine B. Stern, New York: Greenwood, 1968.

The Man-Made World; Or, Our Androcentric Culture. Forerunner 1 (1909–1910). Reprint, New York: Charlton, 1911.

His Religion and Hers: A Study of the Faith of Our Fathers and the Work of Our Mothers. New York: Century Company, 1923.

The Living of Charlotte Perkins Gilman: An Autobiography. With foreword by Zona Gale. New York: D. Appleton-Century Co., 1935. Reprint, New York: Arno Press, 1972, and Harper & Row, 1975. Reprint, with introduction by Ann J. Lane, Madison: University of Wisconsin Press, 1990.

Charlotte Perkins Gilman: A Nonfiction Reader. Edited, with introduction by Larry Ceplair. New York: Columbia University Press, 1992.

The Diaries of Charlotte Perkins Gilman. 2 vols. Edited, with introduction by Denise D. Knight. Charlottesville: University Press of Virginia, 1994.

Studies of Charlotte Perkins Gilman

Golden, Catherine, ed. *The Captive Imagination: A Casebook on The Yellow Wallpaper.* New York: Feminist Press, 1992.

Hill, Mary A. *Charlotte Perkins Gilman: The Making of a Radical Feminist, 1860–1896.* Philadelphia: Temple University Press, 1980.

Karpinski, Joanne B. *Critical Essays on Charlotte Perkins Gilman.* Boston: G. K. Hall, 1992.

Knight, Denise D. *Charlotte Perkins Gilman: A Study of the Short Fiction.* Boston: Twayne, 1997.

Lane, Ann J. *To Herland and Beyond: The Life and Work of Charlotte Perkins Gilman.* New York: Pantheon Books, 1990.

Scharnhorst, Gary. *Charlotte Perkins Gilman.* Boston: Twayne, 1985.

———. *Charlotte Perkins Gilman: A Bibliography.* Metuchen, NJ: Scarecrow Press, 1985.

ANNA KATHARINE GREEN
(1846–1935)

Timothy R. Prchal

BIOGRAPHY

Anna Katharine Green was born in Brooklyn, New York on November 11, 1846. After graduating from Vermont's Ripley College, Green aspired to be a poet. She wrote to Ralph Waldo Emerson to ask for advice, and he cautioned her of the sacrifices needed to succeed. Still, she wrote a detective novel, *The Leavenworth Case* (1878), to garner the clout necessary to have her poems published. The novel was so popular—winning international praise in a genre generally deemed to be masculine territory—that Green redirected her literary ambitions. Though one collection of her poetry was published, her more than thirty volumes of detective fiction would earn her contemporary renown and the title "the Mother of Detective Fiction."

Green's detective fiction was more profitable than the efforts of her husband, Charles Rohlfs, whom she married in 1884. Rohlfs found fame after surrendering stage acting for furniture design. He later starred in the stage adaptation of *The Leavenworth Case*, a clue that the marriage was bolstered by creative cooperation. The two settled in New York State, where Green bore three children and lived most of her life. (After her marriage, Green used the name Rohlfs on her published works. Subsequently, her works are sometimes indexed by that name.)

Green died in Buffalo, New York, on April 11, 1935, at the age of 88.

MAJOR WORKS AND THEMES

Among Green's accomplishments was the development of a series detective whose popularity rivaled—and predated—Sherlock Holmes. Ebenezer Gryce, a

New York City police detective, was introduced with *The Leavenworth Case*. Here, we learn that the plump, unassuming Gryce defies the expectations of a master crime-solver. His eye, for instance, does not "plunge into the core of your being and pounce at once upon its secret" but is "an eye that never pounced, that did not even rest—on you" (7). Regardless, by carefully compiling evidence, Gryce sees through the ruses of his guilty quarry. He also cooperates with other sleuths rather than remaining a solitary genius like Poe's Dupin or Doyle's Holmes. In *That Affair Next Door* (1897), Gryce comes to appreciate the investigative skills of Amelia Butterworth, a high-society spinster often cited as a model for Agatha Christie's Miss Marple. She reappears with Gryce in *Lost Man's Lane* (1898) and *The Circular Study* (1900). Logical, independent, and accommodating, Butterworth is "the first woman detective in American literature to challenge the accepted role of women" (Ross 78). Green's other notable woman detective is Violet Strange, whose cases are recounted in *The Golden Slipper and Other Problems for Violet Strange* (1915). Strange evinces something of a New Woman ethos by being a professional investigator, covertly financing the training for her sister's singing career after her father disowns the sister for marrying against his wishes. Though Green created other detectives, these three have made the most significant mark in detective fiction history.

Underlying Green's fiction is, in Patricia Maida's words, "a religious orientation that specifically identifies sin as the cause of crime and grace as a force in establishing harmony" (*Mother* 78). This is despite Green's accuracy in detailing the material world. Green brought a new sense of realism to detective fiction, very likely facilitated by her father's acquaintances on the New York City police force. Her work is embellished with ballistics and coroner's reports, floor plans, even the mechanical gadgetry of her industrial era. Like Edith Wharton, Green often located her realistic worlds within the upper echelons of American society.

CRITICAL RECEPTION

From her first novel onward, Green enjoyed critical and popular acclaim. Wilkie Collins and Agatha Christie saluted her work. President Woodrow Wilson and British Prime Minister Stanley Baldwin were among her fans. However, Green's reputation suffered as twentieth-century modernism blurred nineteenth-century distinctions between good and evil. (Perhaps moral ambiguity came to be better reflected in hard-boiled detective fiction.) Attention to Green's work dwindled, leading Barrie Hayne to conclude that Green now "dwells in the house of detective fiction as a Victorian cabinet portrait towards the rear of the mantelpiece, . . . rarely taken down and dusted anymore" (152). Growing academic interest in women writers and in popular genres, though, has begun to reestablish Green's place in American literary history.

Feminist critics particularly have addressed Green's work, debating if she was conservative or progressive in regard to women characters. Maida points out that her early novels place women in passive roles, but works such as *The Circular Study*, published at the turn of the century, exhibit "provocative change." In this particular novel, the rape of a young woman "reveals a shocking, though real, evil," one Maida sees as alerting readers to the authentic crimes endured by women (*"Legacy"* 56). However, the sexual ruin of an innocent woman is a novelistic convention older than *Charlotte Temple*, and when Green's victim wastes away and dies from her dishonor, one might question the extent to which Green is accurately representing women's experience. Similarly, Hayne counters the claim that Violet Strange's secret motive for crime-solving subverts patriarchy by contending that Strange repeatedly reinforces essentialist assumptions of feminine intuition and instinctual disdain of sordid affairs (174). Hayne and others see Amelia Butterworth as the more reliably feminist detective.

WORKS CITED

Green, Anna Katharine. *The Leavenworth Case*. New York: Putnam's, 1878.

Hayne, Barrie. "Anna Katharine Green." In *10 Women of Mystery*, edited by Earl F. Bargainnier. Bowling Green, OH: Bowling Green University Popular Press, 1981. 150–178.

Maida, Patricia D. "*Legacy* Profile: Anna Katharine Green (1846–1935)." *Legacy: A Journal of American Women Writers* 3, no. 2 (1986): 53–59.

———. *Mother of Detective Fiction: The Life and Works of Anna Katharine Green*. Bowling Green, OH: Bowling Green University Popular Press, 1989.

Ross, Cheri L. "The First Feminist Detective: Anna Katharine Green's Amelia Butterworth." *Journal of Popular Culture* 25, no. 2 (1991): 77–86.

BIBLIOGRAPHY

Works by Anna Katharine Green

Novels

The Leavenworth Case. New York: Putnam's, 1878.
A Strange Disappearance. New York: Putnam's, 1880.
The Sword of Damocles. New York: Putnam's, 1881.
Hand and Ring. New York: Putnam's, 1883.
XYZ. New York: Putnam's, 1883.
The Mill Mystery. New York: Putnam's, 1886.
7 to 12. New York: Putnam's, 1887.
Behind Closed Doors. New York: Putnam's, 1888.
The Forsaken Inn. New York: R. Bonner's Sons, 1890.
A Matter of Millions. New York: R. Bonner's Sons, 1890.
Cynthia Wakeham's Money. New York: Putnam's, 1892.
Marked "Personal." New York: Putnam's, 1893.

Miss Hurd: An Enigma. New York: Putnam's, 1894.
The Doctor, His Wife, and the Clock. New York: Putnam's, 1895.
Dr. Izard. New York: R. Bonner's Sons, 1895.
That Affair Next Door. New York: Putnam's, 1897.
Lost Man's Lane. New York: Putnam's, 1898.
Agatha Webb. New York: Putnam's, 1899.
The Circular Study. New York: McClure, Phillips, 1900.
One of My Sons. New York: Putnam's, 1901.
The Filigree Ball. Indianapolis: Bobbs-Merrill, 1903.
The Amethyst Box. Indianapolis: Bobbs-Merrill, 1905.
The Millionaire Baby. Indianapolis: Bobbs-Merrill, 1905.
The Chief Legatee. New York: Authors and Newspapers Association, 1906.
The Woman in the Alcove. Indianapolis: Bobbs-Merrill, 1906.
The Mayor's Wife. Indianapolis: Bobbs-Merrill, 1907.
The House of the Whispering Pines. New York: Putnam's, 1910.
Three Thousand Dollars. Boston: R. G. Badger, 1910.
Initials Only. New York: Dodd, Mead, 1911.
Dark Hollow. New York: Dodd, Mead, 1914.
To the Minute, Scarlet and Black. New York: Putnam's, 1916.
Mystery of the Hasty Arrow. New York: Dodd, Mead, 1917.
The Step on the Stair. New York: Dodd, Mead, 1923.

Short Story Collections

The Old Stone House and Other Stories. New York: Putnam's, 1891.
A Difficult Problem and Other Stories. New York: F. M. Lupton, 1900.
The House in the Mist. New York: New York Book, 1905.
Masterpieces of Mystery. New York: Dodd, Mead, 1913.
The Golden Slipper and Other Problems for Violet Strange. New York: Putnam's, 1915.

Poetry

The Defense of the Bride and Other Poems. New York: Putnam's, 1882.

Drama

Risifi's Daughter, a Drama. New York: Putnam's, 1887.

Studies of Anna Katharine Green

Cornillon, John. "A Case for Violet Strange." In *Images of Women in Fiction: Feminist Perspectives*, edited by Susan K. Cornillon. Bowling Green, OH: Bowling Green University Popular Press, 1973. 206–215.
Giffuni, Cathy. "A Bibliography of Anna Katharine Green." *Clues: A Journal of Detection* 8, no. 2 (1987): 113–133.
Hayne, Barrie. "Anna Katharine Green." In *10 Women of Mystery*, edited by Earl F. Bargainnier. Bowling Green, OH: Bowling Green University Popular Press, 1981. 152–178.
Maida, Patricia D. *"Legacy* Profile: Anna Katharine Green (1846–1935)." *Legacy: A Journal of American Women Writers* 3, no. 2 (1986): 53–59.

————. *Mother of Detective Fiction: The Life and Works of Anna Katharine Green.* Bowling Green, OH: Bowling Green University Popular Press, 1989.

Ross, Cheri L. "The First Feminist Detective: Anna Katharine Green's Amelia Butterworth." *Journal of Popular Culture* 25, no. 2 (1991): 77–86.

Welter, Barbara. "Murder Most Genteel: The Mystery Novels of Anna Katharine Green." In *Dimity Convictions: The American Woman in the Nineteenth Century.* Athens: Ohio University Press, 1976. 130–144.

SARAH PRATT McLEAN GREENE (1856–1935)

Karen L. Kilcup

BIOGRAPHY

"He knew, of course, that the names were real . . . but he said that the names were good and the place remote, and he was sure no trouble would follow, and I believe that he was as magnificently innocent and undesigning in the matter as we" (*Book News* 37). In an 1893 interview, Sarah Pratt McLean Greene made this observation about her publisher and the lawsuit that followed the 1881 publication of her first novel, *Cape Cod Folks*. This suit, the first libel action for fiction in the United States, brought the young author immediate national fame.

The book itself was the result of a term teaching in Cedarville, a village of Plymouth, Massachusetts, after Greene's departure from Mt. Holyoke Female Seminary, which she attended in 1871–1872 and 1873–1874. Living with a local family, the Fishers, in their house called the "Ark," Greene was immersed in the life and personalities of the local community. When she left the community and returned to her Simsbury, Connecticut, home, she wrote down her semiautobiographical recollections of the experience. Her brother-in-law, delighting in her letters to him, convinced Greene to send her manuscript to an editor friend of his in Boston; after staying up all night reading the novel, the editor persuaded her to let him publish it immediately. When news of the book reached the "remote" Cape Cod community, several of the characters portrayed in the novel filed libel suits against both the author and her publisher, A. Williams & Co., which published a formal apology, averring its ignorance of the author's use of real names for some of her characters. In spite of this apology and the publisher's change of the characters' names in subsequent editions, the plaintiffs pursued their suit; one, Lorenzo Leonard Nightingale, sought the sum of $10,000 in damages. In February 1884, he was awarded $1,095, a significant amount for the time. The trial was surrounded by garish publicity, which ironically helped increase sales of the novel. By the end of 1882, its second year of publication, *Cape Cod Folks* had already gone through eleven printings, making the author the talk of the nation's literary community. Greene was both surprised and horrified at the response of the people she portrayed (*Book News* 37–38).

The rural Cape Cod community was very different from the relatively sophisticated and affluent environment in which the author was born on July 3, 1856. One of five children, Greene was a member of a distinguished and well-educated family; among her ancestors were several Presbyterian pastors. Her brother would eventually be elected governor of Connecticut and the state's U.S. senator. Gaining encouragement and assistance from her mother in particular, Greene took advantage of the family's substantial library to prepare herself for her later studies in South Hadley, where she studied a variety of subjects that included algebra, physiology, and botany (Howe 262–263; *Thirty-Fifth Annual Catalogue* 20).

By the time that she married a former Annapolis midshipman in 1887, at the age of thirty-one, Greene was an established writer, having published two novels (*Cape Cod Folks* and *Towhead: The Story of a Girl*) and one collection of sketches (*Some Other Folks*). Our knowledge of her movements after this time is sketchy; we do know that she and her husband moved west, living at various times in Mexico, Washington Territory, and California. During this period, she wrote two very conventional western novels—*Lastchance Junction* and *Leon Pontifex*—and (in 1888) gave birth to twin sons who died in their infancy. When her husband also died, in 1890, Greene returned to New England, the source of her best and most interesting fiction. During the next twenty-four years, she would write several more novels and publish poems and sketches in periodicals. Finally settling in Lexington, Massachusetts, Greene died there in 1935 at the age of seventy-nine. She was acknowledged by obituaries in the *Boston Globe*, the *Boston Transcript*, and the *Mount Holyoke Alumnae Quarterly*, as well as in the local newspaper, which highlighted the praise she received from writers as diverse as Mark Twain, John Greenleaf Whittier, and Sarah Orne Jewett. Finally, much of her life remains mysterious. Recalling her stay on Cape Cod, one resident who knew the author when she taught in Cedarville was to observe: "She would go over by that sea everytime she got a chance, when it stormed, and in dark nights. She would lie there on the rocks like a seal for hours, and nobody ever knowed what she was doing there" (*Literary World* 309).

MAJOR WORKS AND THEMES

Rural communities were the focus of most of Greene's best work. Beginning with *Cape Cod Folks* and continuing with *Towhead: The Story of a Girl* (1883), *Vesty of the Basins* (1892), *Flood-Tide* (1901), *Winslow Plain* (1902), and *Power Lot* (1906), Greene explored the dynamics of these communities and of their relationship with the world at large. Many of these novels have one or (as in the case of *Flood-Tide*) more heroines who mediate between the healthy rural communities and the larger, corrupt world, which is often represented by a man in flight from that world. *Vesty of the Basins*, the author's second most popular novel, tells the story of a self-sacrificing rural women who, when her wealthy lover betrays her by marrying someone else, eventually marries the crippled narrator who has come to the community to escape from his worldly life.

In *Power Lot*, a temperance novel, the wealthy alcoholic Rob Hilton comes from the city to the country where he is cured via the agency of the powerful (and humorously portrayed) Mrs. Byjo, who is "as able-bodied at the mixin' bowl as . . . at the plow" (216), and sentimental heroine Mary Stingaree, a well-educated woman who gives up a career as a college president to care for her dying mother and alcoholic brother. Mary is only one example of the New Woman, who is sometimes ambivalently portrayed in Greene's fiction; Dr. Margaret Langthorne and "bookwriter" Mrs. Temple of *Flood-Tide* are others. On one level, the women favored by Greene often represent traditional feminine virtues such as self-sacrifice, love for others, and mild virtue; on another level, those who are too self-sacrificing, such as Infra in *Flood-Tide*, eventually die.

Another important subject for Greene is motherhood, whether the mother is literal, as in the case of Dorna Gleeson in *Flood-Tide*, or figurative, as with Vesty, the exemplary heroine of *Vesty of the Basins*. Whether metaphorical or real, this motherhood is often the means by which the author makes a point and rescues or transforms a character. In *Vesty*, the title character, whose name comes from the Roman goddess of the hearth, is the community's mother. In the latter novel, Dorna is the harassed mother of "bad boy" Dinny. In spite of her partly successful efforts to make him more well behaved—at one point, he causes a row in the community for "tinking ducks" with stones—he dies in an accident caused, ironically, by his attempt to rescue his pet dove from danger. Dorna's mothering is transferred to Dinny's friend, the orphan "Little Everywheres."

A key feature of much of Greene's most important work is its humor; even mothering can be expressed in comic terms. One day, Dorna chides Everywheres for sprinkling her cats with water, and he protests that " 'Sprinklin' don't make 'em suffer.' " Dorna responds, " 'No, but it gives 'em a mean aspect, and they seem to take it more to heart 'n as if their necks was clean broke off an' taggin' along after 'em' " (*Flood-Tide* 315). This passage suggests the voice that informs Greene's work in significant ways, sometimes serving as an antidote to the writer's sentimentalism and sometimes working in concert with it. In many instances, the writer's humor develops over a period of time, making quotation difficult; as Nancy Walker observes, women are not known for "one-liners"; they are "*story*tellers," not "*joke* tellers" (Walker xii).

Marriage is another theme that Greene explores, often representing it affirmatively and sentimentally in her explicit portraits but at times undermining this perspective. In spite of her name, Mrs. Byjo in *Power Lot* has no husband, nor does she need one. Grandma Fisher in *Cape Cod Folks* offers a humorous portrait of a keen and witty woman who is needed to keep her wayward husband on the path of virtue. And Aunt Rocksy Tate, in *Flood-Tide*, offers the following observation at a wedding: "Gettin' married has allas seemed to me in some ways like dyin' or other harissments. When it's over, it's over, and hain't got to be gone through with no more. I wish ye sufficient jiy" (*Flood-Tide* 173). While her overt portrayals of marriage are positive, Greene sometimes undercuts these depictions to reveal other perspectives.

Class, ethnic, and race relations enter into a number of novels. In *Power Lot*, one of the interesting pairings is between a wealthy urban alcoholic and his rural counterpart, Bate Stingaree, who together scheme to buy some alcohol. Suggesting the lack of opportunity for poor, rural individuals and the corruption that can follow, Greene eventually shows how Bate is killed for his criminal scheming, while Rob recovers. *Cape Cod Folks* includes a Native American character, and *Towhead*, an African-American woman who, in spite of her stereotypical role as cook, is at times appealingly quirky. In more central ways, *Stuart and Bamboo* (1897) and *Everbreeze* (1913) investigate the relationship between immigrants and their communities. New England communities and New England natives remain at the center of Greene's focus in all of her most significant work.

CRITICAL RECEPTION

Reviewers of Greene's era did not know what to make of her formal interactions; combining humor, realism, regionalism, and sentimentalism, her work makes classification difficult. One review of *The Moral Imbeciles* (1898) (not her best) echoed a comment that others iterated about her writing more generally: "The novels of Mrs. Sarah Pratt McLean are quite unclassifiable. They violate the ordinary rules of fiction at every turn" (*The Outlook* 89). In general, her peers received her with strong praise; *Cape Cod Folks* provoked comments such as that made by a Boston critic, who asserted, "[The] novel [is] so thoroughly original, that it will provide the most jaded readers of fiction with a series of new and delightful sensations" (Scrapbook n.p.). The jacket notes for Greene's second novel *Towhead* include the following raves: "Every chapter is fresh and sparkling with life and humor, and we cannot help but eulogize the author for her masterly hand and genius of storytelling" (*N.Y. Star*); "It is a phenomenal work" (*Portland Transcript*); "It contains more and better character-writing than any book of its kind we have seen for many a day" (*Chicago Inter-Ocean*) (all from *Towhead* jacket notes).

In the wake of the libel suit for *Cape Cod Folks*, many readers took sides. Most highlighted Greene's sympathy for Cape Cod people, and one asserted that the author "tells her own story with a keen sense of her own failings as well as those of the Cape Codders" (Scrapbook n.p.). *The Literary World* published two essays examining the court case, concluding that ''we do not defend Miss McLean, but we have no sympathy with the suit and no approbation for the verdict'' (*Literary World* 56). Her controversial beginning seems not to have influenced other writers' opinions of her work; Greene corresponded with other writers such as Stowe and Twain; Twain had six of her books in his Hartford, Connecticut, library and read her with appreciation. In a letter responding to Greene's gift of *Cape Cod Folks*, Twain wrote, ''I am just as much obliged to you, all the same, but I have *already* read it—months ago—& vastly enjoyed & admired it, too; as did the rest of this family & the visitor within its gates. There was but one regret—that there wasn't more of it'' (Clemens n.p.). The measure of her contemporary popularity comes from anthologist of women's humor Kate Sanborn, who excluded Greene from *The Wit of Women*, her survey of nineteenth-century humorists, on the basis of the author's familiarity to contemporary readers: ''The very best bit from Miss Sallie McLean would be how 'Grandma Spicer gets Grandpa Ready for Sunday-school,' from 'Cape Cod Folks;' [*sic*] but why not save space for what is not in everybody's mouth and memory'' (*The Wit of Women* 69).

Some of the recent writing on Greene has been done by journalists or non-specialists, such as Helen Estes and Edward B. Hinckley, who focus mostly on her life and the fame of her libel suit. Although Greene is not included in the collection, Judith Fetterley and Marjorie Pryse's *American Women Regionalists* provides some insight into her work. Fetterley and Pryse distinguish between the detachment of the narrators in local color writing and the sympathy of regionalist writers' narrators: ''regionalist texts allow the reader to view the regional speaker as subject and not as object and to include empathic feeling as an aspect of critical response'' (xvii). In her own time often classed as a local colorist, Greene was at pains to distinguish herself from this category, writing to Fred Lewis Pattee in 1914 that she in effect considered herself a realist.

With the ongoing development of feminist criticism in such areas as sentimentalism and humor, as well as regionalism, the writer can again be appreciated more fully. A recent *Legacy* profile by Karen Oakes discussing Greene's life and work compares her to other New England regionalists and draws a distinction between the women-centered communities in writers such as Stowe and Jewett and those of Greene; Oakes observes that Greene ''chooses instead to focus more attention on female-male and cross-class relationships'' (59–60). By the same author, another essay, '' 'She had not precisely the air of a man': Theorizing Gender in the Humor of Stowe and Greene,'' compares the humor of the two writers and assesses the ways in which their work confirms or complicates current theories of women's humor (Kilcup xx).

As our knowledge about the complexity and interaction of genres in nineteenth-century literature becomes more substantial, Greene's work, without which any survey of late nineteenth- and early twentieth-century humor and regionalist fiction is incomplete, is beginning to receive renewed attention.

WORKS CITED

" 'Cape Cod Folks' and Its Author." *Book News* 12, no. 134 (1893): 37–38.

Clemens, S. L. Letter to Miss S. P. McLean, Hartford. 12 December 1881. Alderman Library, University of Virginia.

Estes, Helen. "First Fiction Libel Suit." *Yankee* (October 1971): 82–85.

Fetterley, Judith, and Marjorie Pryse, eds. *American Women Regionalists, 1850–1910.* New York: Norton, 1992.

Hinckley, Edward B. *Harvard Graduates Magazine* (June 1931): 453–467.

Howe, Julia Ward. *Representative Women of New England.* Boston: New England Historical Publishing Company, 1904.

The Literary World, 23 February 1884, 56.

The Literary World, 8 March 1884, 74–75.

McLean, Sally Pratt. Review from *Literary World,* 16 July 1881. Scrapbook. Boston Public Library Rare Books Collection.

Review of *The Moral Imbeciles. The Outlook,* 3 September 1898, 89.

Sanborn, Kate. *The Wit of Women.* New York: Funk and Wagnalls, 1900.

Thirty-Fifth Annual Catalogue of the Mount Holyoke Female Seminary, in South Hadley, Mass., 1871–72. Northampton: Bridgman and Childs, 1872.

Walker, Nancy A. *A Very Serious Thing, Women's Humor and American Culture.* Minneapolis: University of Minnesota Press, 1988.

BIBLIOGRAPHY

Works by Sarah Pratt McLean Greene

Cape Cod Folks. By Sally Pratt McLean. Boston: A. Williams, 1881.

Towhead: The Story of a Girl. By Sally Pratt McLean. Boston: A. Williams, 1883. (Jacket notes)

Some Other Folks. By Sarah Pratt McLean. Boston: Cupples, Upham, 1884.

Lastchance Junction. "By the author of 'Cape Cod Folks.' " Boston: Cupples and Hurd, 1889.

" 'Beauty' Faulkner." *Harper's Weekly,* 9 August 1890, 622–623.

Leon Pontifex. Boston: DeWolfe, Fisk, 1890.

Vesty of the Basins. New York: Harper, 1892.

"Peter-Patrick." In *Selections from the Writings of Connecticut Women.* Norwalk, CT: Literary Committee Connecticut Board of Lady Managers for the Columbian Exposition, 1893.

Stuart and Bamboo. New York: Harper, 1897.

"The Wind." *Overland Monthly* (November 1897): 416.

The Moral Imbeciles. New York: Harper and Brothers, 1898.

Flood-Tide. New York: Harper, 1901.

Winslow Plain. New York: Harper, 1902.

"The Flower." *Harper's Weekly,* 10 December 1904, 55.

Power Lot. New York: Baker and Taylor, 1906.

The Long Green Road. New York: Baker and Taylor, 1911.

Everbreeze. New York: Appleton, 1913.

Studies of Sarah Pratt McLean Greene

James, Edward T., ed. *Notable American Women, 1607–1950.* Vol. 2. Cambridge: Belknap–Harvard University Press, 1971. 86–87.

Kilcup, Karen L. " 'She had not precisely the air of a man': Theorizing Gender in the Humor of Stowe and Greene." *Studies in American Humor,* n.s., no. 3 (1996): 20–30.

The Literary World, 10 September 1881, 309.

The Literary World, 18 November 1882, 393.

Mount Holyoke Alumnae Quarterly 20, no. 1 (1936): 53.

Oakes, Karen. "*Legacy* Profile: Sarah Pratt McLean Greene." *Legacy: A Journal of American Women Writers* 11, no. 1 (1994): 55–64.

Twain, Mark. Mark Twain–Howells Letters: *The Correspondence of Samuel L. Clemens and William D. Howells, 1872–1910.* Edited by Henry Nash Smith and William M. Gibson. Vol. 2. Cambridge: Belknap–Harvard University Press, 1960.

GRACE GREENWOOD
(SARA JANE CLARKE LIPPINCOTT)
(1823–1904)

Kevin J. Hayes

BIOGRAPHY

Sara Jane Clarke was born in Pompey, New York, on September 23, 1823, the youngest daughter of Thaddeus Clarke, physician, and Deborah (Baker) Clarke. Not long after her birth, the family moved to nearby Fabius and later to Rochester, where Sara was educated. While in her teens, she began contributing verse to the local papers. In the *Fredonia Censor* (1840), for example, she published ''The Doomed Soldier of Fort Meigs,'' a treatment of a young deserter sentenced to be hanged who was reprieved at the last moment. Her sentimental and sympathetic portrayal of the soldier anticipates much of her subsequent work. In 1842, the family moved to New Brighton, Pennsylvania, and Sara joined them there the following year.

In 1844, she began contributing letters to the *New York Mirror* and *Home Journal*, signing them ''Grace Greenwood,'' a name that she began to use socially as well. These contributions secured her literary reputation, and she began to write for some of the most important periodicals of the day: *Godey's Lady's Book, Graham's American Monthly Magazine, Sartain's Union Magazine of Literature and Art*, and the *Saturday Evening Post*. Her contributions ranged from sentimental fiction and verse to comments on the current state of literature and politics. Perhaps most noteworthy are her remarks concerning the international copyright issue, written as burlesques of contemporary authors. Her spoof of Edgar Allan Poe pokes fun at the overly rational, Dupinesque narrator as well as many of Poe's characteristic motifs. Her spoof of Herman Melville's *Typee* idealized the poet's life. Describing a South Pacific poet laureate, she wrote:

The place of all the world for your Shelleys and Byrons were Typee. In festivals and public processions I observed that his bardship took precedence of valiant chiefs and venerable divines; and for a reason, I think, the poet being created by Heaven, priests and warriors by circumstance. I have no doubt, furthermore, but that as those of his *genus* are given to epicurism, the choice bit is awarded him when an enemy is dished up. I also ascertained that no man was allowed to play critic in Typee, unless himself a poet. (Thorp 457).

To be sure, Greenwood's burlesque of *Typee*, like her other parodies, was good-hearted. In a contribution to Nathaniel P. Willis's *Home Journal*, she had fondly appreciated Melville's first book: "Why I never chanced upon Mr. Melville's work before, is one of the inscrutable mysteries of my fate. While luxuriating in its perusal, I looked back upon myself in my ante-Typee-cal existence, with positive commiseration" (Leyda 220).

In 1849, Greenwood became an editorial assistant for *Godey's Lady's Book*, but Louis Godey dismissed her the following year for an antislavery essay she contributed to the *National Era*. Gamaliel Bailey, the editor of the abolitionist *National Era*, subsequently offered her a position and asked her to move to Washington. She accepted the position and simultaneously became the Washington correspondent for the *Saturday Evening Post*. She would continue her association with the *Post* until the late 1890s.

Starting in 1850, Greenwood began gathering and publishing her periodical contributions as separate works. *Greenwood Leaves* (1850), first series, was the earliest of her many popular books. *Poems* (1851), a collection of periodical verse, and *History of My Pets* (1851), her first work of juvenile literature, soon followed. An 1852–1853 European tour allowed her to contribute numerous travel reports to the *National Era* and the *Saturday Evening Post*. Her European sojourn prompted a travel narrative, *Haps and Mishaps of a Tour in Europe* (1854), and another work for children, *Merrie England: Travels, Descriptions, Tales and Historical Sketches* (1855). While in England, she ingratiated herself to the London literati, most notably Martin Farquhar Tupper, who later inscribed a copy of his *Proverbial Philosophy* to her.

On October 17, 1853, Grace Greenwood married Leander K. Lippincott with whom she had one daughter, Annie. That same year, she and her husband began *The Little Pilgrim*, one of America's first children's magazines, an effort that one reviewer called "the best work of the kind we have ever seen" (*Graham's* 44, 234). Though their periodical venture was a success, their marriage proved unhappy. Lippincott was often rumored to be unfaithful, and his association with the U.S. government was fraught with controversy. He acquired a position with the government and rose to the chief clerkship of the General Land Office, only to be dismissed from the post and indicted on a charge concerning fraudulent Indian land claims in 1876. After the indictment, Lippincott fled prosecution, abandoning his wife and daughter.

Throughout the 1850s, Greenwood continued to publish a steady stream of books, mostly collections gathered from *The Little Pilgrim* and from her numerous other periodical contributions. During the late 1850s, she joined the lecture circuit and spoke for various humanitarian reforms. Before the war, she argued vigorously for abolition. After the war, she argued for prison reform and against capital punishment, among many other causes. From the 1870s, she frequently vacationed overseas and out West. Her overseas journeys prompted *Stories and Sights of France and Italy* (1867) and another work for children, *Bonnie Scotland: Tales of Her History, Heroes, and Poets* (1861). Her excursions to Colorado inspired *New Life in New Lands: Notes of Travel* (1873), a work extolling the charm and beauty of the Rocky Mountains. From 1870, she served as correspondent for the *New York Tribune* and the *New York Times* as well as for other newspapers in Philadelphia and Chicago. Before her death in 1904, she lived alternately in New York and Washington and continued to travel and write.

MAJOR WORKS AND THEMES

Greenwood Leaves, the first series, Grace Greenwood's earliest separately published work, contained sentimental sketches (e.g., "Sly Peeps into the Heart Feminine") that, though popular in their time, seem stale and clichéd a century and a half later. *Greenwood Leaves*, however, also included the literary burlesques and Greenwood's insightful journalistic letters, works that will prove her most lasting. Perhaps recognizing that her letters excelled her tales and sketches, Greenwood included proportionately more letters in her next collection of periodical work, *Greenwood Leaves: A Collection of Sketches and Letters: Second Series* (1852).

Haps and Mishaps of a Tour in Europe, Greenwood's first collection of travel essays, portrayed the eminent authors she met, described the Italian and English scenery, commented on works of art, and attempted to delineate the British national character. *Haps and Mishaps* is a little too tame and uneventful to survive as a classic American travel narrative, but Greenwood's story of western travel, *New Life in New Lands: Notes of Travel*, a collection of letters that originally appeared in the *New York Times*, provides memorably vivid descriptions of Chicago, Colorado, Utah, Nevada, and California.

To survive as a woman of letters during the nineteenth century, Greenwood had both to be prolific and to write prose and verse gushing with sentimentalism. Her numerous sentimental books, however, have rightly doomed much of her work to obscurity. Her most lasting works are those that transcend the literary conventions of the day, her burlesques of contemporary literati, her tough-minded journalistic correspondence, and her appreciation of the landscape of the American West.

CRITICAL RECEPTION

Greenwood Leaves firmly established Grace Greenwood's reputation. Reviewing the book, John Greenleaf Whittier found Greenwood's "freedom, freshness, and strong individuality . . . fully developed" (197). Another reviewer found that Greenwood had "sufficient force of being and character to write in all varieties of mood without parting with her personality"; her mind appeared "fresh, active, powerful and impassioned" (*Graham's* 36, 286). Another found the volume an excellent mixture of seriousness and humor. Greenwood's seriousness marked her sympathy with humankind; her humor sprang from her "keenness of intellect, fulness of imagination, kindliness of temper, and playfulness of spirit" (*Holden's* 6, 502). *Greenwood Leaves . . . Second Series* elicited similarly enthusiastic comments. The *Christian Examiner* appreciated Greenwood as one of the literary leaders of the American woman. Their reviewer found that she availed herself of the "largest liberty now claimed for her sex in matters of opinion and in the expression of it" (52, 156). In his *Cyclopaedia of American Literature*, Evert Duyckinck found her prose writings "animated by a hearty spirit of out-of-door life and enjoyment, and a healthy, sprightly view of society" and her poems "the expressions of a prompt, generous nature" (654).

Greenwood's good-hearted writing was ideal for her works for children, but it was less effective for her travel writings. The *Southern Quarterly Review*, reviewing her *Haps and Mishaps*, found that she saw "all things abroad pretty much through a rose-coloured medium." Her book the reviewer found "slight and full of superlatives," and her often rapturous descriptions were sometimes "ludicrous" (10, 242).

While Greenwood deserves credit as one of America's early female newspaper correspondents, she never really escaped the pervasive sentimentalism of her day. Reviewing one of her early works, a writer for *Graham's Magazine* found that she had "not yet obtained the faculty of viewing things as they are in themselves, independent of the feelings they excite in her own soul" (40, 219). Though Greenwood's works remained popular throughout the nineteenth century, never did she escape the feelings of "her own soul" to describe her subjects "as they are in themselves."

WORKS CITED

Anonymous. Review of *Greenwood Leaves*. *Graham's American Monthly Magazine* 36 (April 1850): 286.

Anonymous. Review of *Greenwood Leaves*. *Holden's Dollar Magazine* 6 (August 1850): 501–502.

Anonymous. Review of *Greenwood Leaves . . . Second Series*. *Christian Examiner* 52 (January 1852): 156.

Anonymous. Review of *Greenwood Leaves... Second Series. Graham's American Monthly Magazine* 40 (February 1852): 219.

Anonymous. Review of *Haps and Mishaps of a Tour in Europe. Graham's American Monthly Magazine* 44 (February 1854): 234.

Anonymous. Review of *Haps and Mishaps of a Tour in Europe. Southern Quarterly Review* 10 (July 1854): 242–243.

Duyckinck, Evert, and George Duyckinck. *Cyclopaedia of American Literature.* 1855. Reprint, Detroit: Gale, 1965. 653–658.

Leyda, Jay. *The Melville Log.* 1951. Reprint, New York: Gordian Press, 1969.

Sherman, W. J. "The Doomed Soldier of Fort Meigs." *Ohio Archaeological and Historical Publications* 34 (1925): 203–205.

Thorp, Willard. " 'Grace Greenwood' Parodies *Typee." American Literature* 9 (January 1938): 455–457.

W[hittier]., J[ohn]. G[reenleaf]. Review of *Greenwood Leaves. National Era* 3 (13 December 1849): 197.

BIBLIOGRAPHY

Works by Grace Greenwood

Poetry

Poems. Boston: Ticknor, Reed, and Fields, 1851.

Tales and Sketches

Greenwood Leaves: A Collection of Sketches and Letters. Boston: Ticknor, Reed and Fields, 1850.

Greenwood Leaves: A Collection of Sketches and Letters: Second Series. Boston: Ticknor, Reed and Fields, 1852.

Recollections of My Childhood, and Other Stories. Boston: Ticknor, Reed and Fields, 1852. Also published under the title *Stories of My Childhood.*

Haps and Mishaps of a Tour in Europe. Boston: Ticknor, Reed and Fields, 1854.

A Forest Tragedy, and Other Tales. Boston: Ticknor and Fields, 1856.

Records of Five Years. Boston: Ticknor and Fields, 1867.

Stories and Sights of France and Italy. Boston: Ticknor and Fields, 1867.

New Life in New Lands: Notes of Travel. New York: J. B. Ford, 1873.

Stories for Home-Folks, Young and Old. New York: J. B. Alden, 1884.

Stories and Sketches. New York: Tait, Sons & Company, 1892.

Europe: Its People and Princes.—Its Pleasures and Palaces. Philadelphia: Hubbard, n.d.

Juvenile Literature

History of My Pets. Boston: Ticknor, Reed, and Fields, 1851.

Merrie England: Travels, Descriptions, Tales and Historical Sketches. Boston: Ticknor and Fields, 1855.

Old Wonder-Eyes; and Other Stories for Children. With Leander K. Lippincott. New York: J. Miller, 1857.

Stories and Legends of Travel, for Children. Boston: Ticknor and Fields, 1857.

Stories from Famous Ballads. Boston: Ticknor and Fields, 1860.

Bonnie Scotland: Tales of Her History, Heroes, and Poets. Boston: Ticknor and Fields, 1861.

Nellie, the Gypsy Girl. New York: General Protestant Episcopal Sunday School Union and Church Book Society, 1863.

Stories of Many Lands. New York: Hurst, 1866.

Heads and Tails: Studies and Stories of Pets. New York: American News Co., 1874.

Treasures from Fairy Land. With Rossiter Worthington Raymond. New York: American News Company, 1879.

Queen Victoria: Her Girlhood and Womanhood. New York: J. R. Anderson and H. S. Allen, 1883.

Studies of Grace Greenwood

Beasley, Maurine. "Pens and Petticoats: Early Women Washington Correspondents." *Journalism History* 1 (winter 1974–1975): 112–115.

Carlson, A. Cheree. "Limitations on the Comic Frame: Some Witty American Women of the Nineteenth Century." *Quarterly Journal of Speech* 74 (1988): 310–322.

Mott, Frank Luther. *A History of American Magazines.* Vols. 1–4. Cambridge: Belknap Press of Harvard University Press, 1930–1957.

Pattee, Fred Lewis. *The Feminine Fifties.* New York: D. Appleton-Century Co., 1940. 276–282.

Thorp, Margaret Farrand. *Female Persuasion: Six Strong-Minded Women.* New Haven: Yale University Press, 1949. 143–178.

ANGELINA GRIMKÉ
(1805–1879)

Lynn Domina

BIOGRAPHY

Born on February 20, 1805, Angelina Grimké was the youngest child of Judge John Faucheraud Grimké and Mary (Smith) Grimké. Hers was a prominent slaveholding family in Charleston, South Carolina. Angelina's sister, Sarah Grimké, was her godmother and the sibling to whom she was closest. As a girl, she attended Charleston Seminary, where she was introduced to the moral circumstances of her culture when she witnessed the back of a small boy covered with scars and scabs; Angelina fainted at the sight. Because she did not agree with the content of the required prayers, she refused confirmation into the Episcopal Church in 1818 and joined a Presbyterian congregation in 1826. In 1827, Angelina became interested in Quakerism, partly through Sarah's influence, and began attending the Quaker meeting in Charleston. Because of her opposition to slavery, her relationship with her family was strained, and she left Charleston in 1829 for Philadelphia, where Sarah had been living for several years.

Angelina began to assume a more activist stance toward abolitionism, attending lectures sponsored by the Philadelphia Anti-Slavery Society, which she formally joined during the spring of 1835. At the end of the following summer, she wrote William Lloyd Garrison a letter expressing her views; when Garrison printed this letter without her permission in *The Liberator*, Angelina was urged to retract her opinions, but she refused. Subsequently, Angelina received an offer from the American Anti-Slavery Society to speak to women's sewing circles in New York. At this point, she decided to write her *Appeal to the Christian Women of the Southern States* (1836)—the only abolitionist text written by a Southern woman to other Southern women. When copies of this *Appeal* reached Charleston, her family was warned that if Angelina set foot in the city, she would be arrested. Despite her discomfort with the propriety of women assuming such public roles, Sarah agreed to accompany Angelina to New York, and the two sisters often spoke on the same platform, though Angelina was the more charismatic speaker. The following year, Angelina published her *Appeal to the Women of the Nominally Free States* (1837). Also in 1837, Angelina participated in the first public debate between a man and a woman, and she addressed the Massachusetts State Legislature on slavery.

In May of that year, Angelina married Theodore Weld, an event that led to both Angelina's and Sarah's expulsion from the Quakers. Sarah lived with the Welds after their marriage and for most of her remaining life, separating from them for only a brief period because of tension created by a debt owed by the Welds to her and by her assertion of a dominant role in child care.

In 1853, the Welds decided to join the Raritan Bay Union, an experimental communal organization, though it didn't actually open until the following year. After the union folded in 1856, the sisters remained teaching in its school for several years.

After the Civil War, Angelina read of a student surnamed Grimké who attended Lincoln University; she eventually discovered that he and a brother were the sons of her own brother Henry and a slave woman. Angelina attended Lincoln University's commencement in order to meet her nephews, and she and Sarah attempted to support them through law school.

In 1870 both sisters became vice presidents of the newly formed Massachusetts Woman Suffrage Association, and that March both voted illegally in an organized protest for women's suffrage. Angelina died on October 26, 1879, after having been paralyzed by several strokes.

MAJOR WORKS AND THEMES

Nearly all of Angelina Grimké's published work addresses issues of slavery and abolitionism. Her *Appeal to the Christian Women of the Southern States* relies extensively on biblical argument, and she refutes commonly made proslavery assertions based on the Bible. She extensively compares American with Hebrew slavery and documents several differences that position Hebrew slavery as less brutal. Similarly, her *Letters to Catherine E. Beecher*, originally published in newspapers and revised in book form, assumes that her readers are Christian and that they are concerned to reconcile the moral imperatives of Christianity with the apparent economic imperatives of slavery. She declines to excuse the North for its implicit and explicit participation in the slave system. Toward the conclusion of these letters, she moves into a discussion of women's rights, understanding race and sex to be analogous in the pursuit of human rights.

Her speeches address these issues also. She occasionally begins by justifying her presence at the podium, and she sometimes refers to those who protest the content of her speech, indicating perhaps that she was enough at ease to make spontaneous comments. Her speeches are particularly energetic and continue to convey their power as forceful documents.

CRITICAL RECEPTION

Most who heard Angelina lecture agree that she was a dynamic speaker. Catherine H. Birney quotes several witnesses, including one who "speaks of the gentle, firm, and impressive voice which could ring out in clarion tones" (190). Her lectures were crowded, not only because she was a woman speaking publicly on abolition but because she performed so effectively.

Her writing was received equally enthusiastically, at least by those who agreed with her stance. Birney describes her *Appeal to the Women of the Nominally Free States* as "remarkable in its calm reasoning, sound logic, and fervid eloquence" (173). In her more recent biography, Gerda Lerner describes the *Appeal to the Christian Women of the Southern States* as "remarkable . . . for its simple and direct tone, the absence of fashionable rhetoric and its bold logic which in the name of righteousness advises even lawbreaking with Garrisonian unconcern" (141). Very little contemporary critical work has been done on Angelina Grimké. Nearly all critics consider Angelina and Sarah together, and most also consider their individual speeches and printed texts in the broader context of their life work.

WORKS CITED

Birney, Catherine H. *The Grimké Sisters: Sarah and Angelina Grimké, the First American Women Advocates of Abolition and Women's Rights.* Boston: Lee & Sheppard, 1885. Reprint, New York: Haskell House, 1970.
Lerner, Gerda. *The Grimké Sisters from South Carolina: Pioneers for Woman's Rights and Abolition.* New York: Shocken Books, 1971.

BIBLIOGRAPHY

Works by Angelina Grimké

Published Writing

Slavery and the Boston Riot: A Letter to Wm. L. Garrison. Philadelphia: 30 August 1835. Broadside.
Appeal to the Christian Women of the Southern States. New York: American Anti-Slavery Society, 1836.
An Appeal to the Women of the Nominally Free States; Issued by an Anti-Slavery Convention of American Women & Held by Adjournment from the 9th to the 12th of May, 1837. New York: W. S. Door, 1837.
Letters to Catherine E. Beecher, in Reply to an Essay on Slavery and Abolitionism, Addressed to A. E. Grimké. Boston: Isaac Knapp, 1838.

Letter from Angelina Grimké Weld, to the Woman's Rights Convention, Held at Syracuse, September, 1852. Syracuse: Master's print, 1852.
Letters of Theodore Dwight Weld, Angelina Grimké Weld and Sarah Grimké: 1822–1844. Edited by G. H. Barnes and D. W. Dumond. 2 vols. New York: D. Appleton-Century Co., 1934.
With Sarah Grimké. "A Sketch of Thomas Grimké's Life Written by His Sisters in Philadelphia and Sent to His Friends in Charleston for Their Approbation." *The Calumet, Magazine of the American Peace Society* (January–February 1835).
With Sarah Grimké, eds. *An Inquiry into the Accordancy of War with the Principles of Christianity . . . with Notes by Thomas Grimké*, by Jonathan Dymond. Philadelphia: I. Ashmead & Co., 1834.

Published Speeches

Speech before the Legislative Committee of the Massachusetts Legislature, 21 February 1838. *The Liberator*, 2 May 1838.
Speech in Pennsylvania Hall, 16 May 1838. In *History of Woman Suffrage*, by Elizabeth C. Stanton, Susan B. Anthony, and Matilda J. Gage. 6 vols. New York: Fowler & Wells, 1881–1922. I: 334–336.
Speech before Woman's Loyal League, 14 May 1863. In *History of Woman Suffrage*, by Elizabeth C. Stanton, Susan B. Anthony, and Matilda J. Gage. 6 vols. New York: Fowler & Wells, 1881–1922. II: 54–56.
"Address to the Soldiers of Our Second Revolution." Resolution read and adopted by the Business Meeting of the Woman's Loyal National League, 15 May 1863, written by Angelina Grimké Weld. In *History of Woman Suffrage*, by Elizabeth C. Stanton, Susan B. Anthony, and Matilda J. Gage. 6 vols. New York: Fowler & Wells, 1881–1922. II: 890–891.

Studies of Angelina Grimké

Austin, George Lowell. "The Grimké Sisters." *The Bay State Monthly* (August 1885).
Birney, Catherine H. *The Grimké Sisters: Sarah and Angelina Grimké, the First American Women Advocates of Abolition and Woman's Rights.* Boston: Lee & Sheppard, 1885. Reprint, New York: Haskell House, 1970.
Ceplair, Larry. *The Public Years of Sarah and Angelina Grimké: Selected Writings, 1835–1839.* New York: Columbia University Press, 1991.
DuBois, Ellen. "Struggling into Existence—The Feminism of Sarah and Angelina Grimké." *Women: A Journal of Liberalism* 1 (1970): 4–11.
Lerner, Gerda. *The Grimké Sisters from South Carolina: Pioneers for Women's Rights and Abolition.* New York: Shocken Books, 1971.
Lumpkin, Katherine Du Pre. *The Emancipation of Angelina Grimké.* Chapel Hill: University of North Carolina Press, 1974.
Melder, Keith E. "Forerunners of Freedom: The Grimké Sisters in Massachusetts, 1837–38." *Essex Institute Historical Collections* 103 (1967): 223–249.

SARAH GRIMKÉ
(1792–1873)

Lynn Domina

BIOGRAPHY

The sixth child of Judge John Faucheraud Grimké and Mary (Smith) Grimké, Sarah Grimké was born on November 26, 1792, into a prominent slaveholding family in Charleston, South Carolina. When she was four years old, she witnessed the whipping of a slave, an incident to which she later ascribed the genesis of her abolitionist thought. As a young child, she was closest to her brother Thomas; although her formal education reflected a feminine curriculum—for example, French, music, embroidery—she also studied the more academic subjects Thomas pursued until Judge Grimké forbade her to study Latin.

When Sarah was twelve, the last of her siblings, Angelina Emily Grimké, was born. Sarah became Angelina's godmother and cultivated a maternal relationship with her; Angelina addressed Sarah as ''mother'' into their adulthood. Through their speaking and writing on abolition and women's rights, these two Grimké sisters would eventually become closely associated in the public mind.

As an adult, Sarah experienced a series of religious conversions, the first in 1817 when she converted to Presbyterianism from her family's Episcopalianism. The following year, Judge Grimké became ill and was advised to consult a physician in Philadelphia. Sarah accompanied him there in 1819 and subsequently to the New Jersey shore where Judge Grimké died on August 8. Following his death, Sarah remained two months in Philadelphia, boarding with a Quaker family. Although she seems not to have expressed interest in Quakerism then, she began to explore its principles the following year.

In 1821, Sarah made the unconventional decision as a single woman (although she was initially accompanied by her recently widowed sister Anna) to leave Charleston, returning only for sporadic visits. She began regularly attending

Friends meetings and applied for membership in the Fourth and Arch Street Meeting of the Philadelphia Society of Friends during February of 1823. Her application was accepted on May 29. Partly under Sarah's influence, Angelina also began exploring Quaker beliefs and moved to Philadelphia in 1829.

In 1835, Angelina became heavily involved in the abolitionist movement, joining the Philadelphia Female Anti-Slavery Society. Sarah initially resisted political activism, considering such a public identity inappropriate for women. Yet by October of 1836, Sarah agreed to accompany Angelina to New York for a convention held by the American Anti-Slavery Society. Soon thereafter, the two Grimkés exercised public courage in becoming the first female abolitionist agents in the United States. Although Angelina was often the main attraction at their public lectures, Sarah generally also took the platform despite her discomfort in speaking.

In December, Sarah wrote *An Epistle to the Clergy of the Southern States*, and in 1837, *An Address to Free Colored Americans* was published by the Anti-Slavery Convention of American Women. During this period, Sarah became increasingly interested in the question of women's roles in public and private life and began her *Letters on the Equality of the Sexes*. With Angelina, she delivered a series of lectures in Boston early in 1838 addressing this subject.

Two months after these lectures, Angelina married Theodore Weld, an event that led not only to Angelina's expulsion from the Society of Friends, since Weld was not a Quaker, but also to Sarah's because she had attended the ceremony. Sarah would continue to live with her sister and brother-in-law, despite some tense incidents, for much of her life. When the Welds decided to join the Raritan Bay Union, an experimental communal organization, in 1853, the sisters decided to separate; debts owed by the Welds to Sarah as well as Sarah's assumption of a dominant role in raising Angelina's children had become sources of frustration for Angelina. The separation was short-lived, however; by the time the Union actually opened during the summer of 1854, Sarah had returned to the household.

After the Civil War, Angelina discovered the existence of two mulatto nephews, the sons of Henry Grimké and one of his slaves, Nancy Weston. With the hope of contributing to the education of these two nephews, Sarah wrote a novel concerning interracial love, but it never sold.

In 1870 both sisters became vice presidents of the newly formed Massachusetts Woman Suffrage Association, and that March both voted illegally in an organized protest for women's suffrage. Sarah remained an officer of the Association until her death on December 23, 1873.

MAJOR WORKS AND THEMES

During her lifetime, Sarah Grimké published two independently authored works, *An Epistle to the Clergy of the Southern States* in 1836 and *Letters on the Equality of the Sexes and the Condition of Woman* in 1838; she also published a translation of Lamartine's *Joan of Arc: A Biography* in 1867. Her *Epistle* is a pamphlet-length letter heavily reliant on biblical imagery, quotation, and style. Slavery, she argues, has "trampled the image of God in the dust" (Ceplair 92). After citing several scriptural references that appear to condemn slavery, she refutes American slaveholders' major arguments.

Her *Letters* are similarly based on her rereading of Christian scripture: "I shall depend solely on the Bible to designate the sphere of woman, because I believe almost every thing that has been written on this subject, has been the result of a misconception of the simple truths revealed in the Scriptures" (Ceplair 204). Within these letters, she argues that men and women are created equally in the image of God, and she critiques social and professional limitations placed on women. Rather than argue against Christianity, she attempts to use its foundational text as a liberating document.

CRITICAL RECEPTION

Even by those who agreed with her principles, Sarah was not admired as a public speaker. Catherine H. Birney describes her oratory as "never very fluent. . . . [T]he language was unvarnished, sometimes harsh, while the manner of speaking was often embarrassed" (191). Many audience members apparently tolerated Sarah in order to hear Angelina. Others, of course, objected to the very fact of a woman speaking publicly.

Her writing was received more sympathetically. Birney describes the *Epistle* as "written in a spirit of gentleness and persuasion, but also of firm admonition" (161). In her more recent biography, Gerda Lerner suggests, "Although her style was not as fluid and lucid as Angelina's and she showed no originality of style, her arguments were well-reasoned. Her boldness in directly challenging the church . . . was a sign of her intellectual and personal growth" (156). Contemporary readers would certainly find her style lacking in fluidity. What little critical work that has been done on her writing examines it in terms of its political and historical ramifications rather than as pieces that were ever read primarily for aesthetic pleasure.

WORKS CITED

Birney, Catherine H. *The Grimké Sisters: Sarah and Angelina Grimké, the First American Women Advocates of Abolition and Woman's Rights*. Boston: Lee & Sheppard, 1885. Reprint, New York: Haskell House, 1970.

Ceplair, Larry. *The Public Years of Sarah and Angelina Grimké: Selected Writings 1835–1839*. New York: Columbia University Press, 1991.

Lerner, Gerda. *The Grimké Sisters from South Carolina: Pioneers for Woman's Rights and Abolition*. New York: Shocken Books, 1971.

BIBLIOGRAPHY

Works by Sarah Grimké

An Epistle to the Clergy of the Southern States. New York: n.p., 1836.

An Address to Free Colored Americans. New York: Anti-Slavery Convention of American Women, 1837.

Letters on the Equality of the Sexes and the Condition of Woman; Addressed to Mary Parker, President of the Boston Female Anti-Slavery Society. Boston: Isaac Knapp, 1838.

Letters of Theodore Dwight Weld, Angelina Grimké Weld and Sarah Grimké: 1822–1844. Edited by G. H. Barnes and D. W. Dumond. 2 vols. New York: D. Appleton-Century Co., 1934.

Lamartine, Alphonse M. L. de Prat de. *Joan of Arc: A Biography.* Translated by Sarah Grimké. Adams & Co., 1867.

With Angelina Grimké. ''A Sketch of Thomas Grimké's Life Written by His Sisters in Philadelphia and Sent to His Friends in Charleston for Their Approbation.'' *The Calumet, Magazine of the American Peace Society* (January–February 1835).

With Angelina Grimké, eds. *An Inquiry into the Accordancy of War with the Principles of Christianity . . . with Notes by Thomas Grimké,* by Jonathan Dymond. Philadelphia: I. Ashmead & Co., 1834.

Studies of Sarah Grimké

Austin, George Lowell. ''The Grimké Sisters.'' *The Bay State Monthly* (August 1885).

Bartlett, Elizabeth Ann. *Liberty, Equality, Sorority: The Origins and Interpretation of American Feminist Thought: Frances Wright, Sarah Grimké, and Margaret Fuller.* Brooklyn: Carlson, 1994.

Birney, Catherine H. *The Grimké Sisters: Sarah and Angelina Grimké, the First American Women Advocates of Abolition and Woman's Rights.* Boston: Lee & Sheppard, 1885. Reprint, New York: Haskell House, 1970.

Ceplair, Larry. *The Public Years of Sarah and Angelina Grimké: Selected Writings, 1835–1839.* New York: Columbia University Press, 1991.

DuBois, Ellen. ''Struggling into Existence—The Feminism of Sarah and Angelina Grimké.'' *Women: A Journal of Liberalism* 1 (1970): 4–11.

Lerner, Gerda. *The Grimké Sisters from South Carolina: Pioneers for Woman's Rights and Abolition.* New York: Shocken Books, 1971.

Melder, Keith E. ''Forerunners of Freedom: The Grimké Sisters in Massachusetts, 1837–38.'' *Essex Institute Historical Collections* 103 (1967): 223–249.

SARAH JOSEPHA HALE
(1788–1879)

Aleta Cane

BIOGRAPHY

The third child of Gordon and Martha Whittlesey Buell, Sarah Josepha was born on October 24, 1788. That was the year Washington assumed the presidency of the United States. Sarah was educated at home, in Newport, New Hampshire, with her older brothers Charles and Horatio. When Horatio went off to Dartmouth, he shared his notes and texts with Sarah, thus affording her more education than most women of her time. She conducted a dame school for six years until her marriage to David Hale in 1813. An ambitious lawyer and a Freemason, Hale encouraged Sarah to continue her studies and to write. Several of her poems were published by *The New Hampshire Spectator*, Newport's weekly newspaper. Sarah Hale bore five children during her happy nine-year marriage. David died suddenly, in 1822, and Hale tried the millinery trade to support herself and her children while continuing to write stories and poems. David's Freemason lodge paid for the publication of Sarah's first book of poems, *The Genius of Oblivion and Other Original Poems* (1823). Although not a critical success, the book sold well, allowing Hale to write full-time. *The Atlantic Monthly, The Literary Gazette*, and *The Spectator and Ladies' Album* published her poems and stories. She submitted winning entries to several poetry contests. In 1826, *The Spectator and Ladies' Album* published seventeen of Hale's poems, two short stories, and one literary review. Four of her poems appeared in the fashionable gift book *The Memorial* in 1827.

That same year her novel *Northwood* was published to enthusiastic reviews, launching Hale's national literary career. John Lauris Blake invited her to edit his new publication, *The Ladies' Magazine*. Although she tried editing the journal from Newport, she had to move to Boston to continue her work. Leaving her four older children to continue their educations in the homes of their aunts and uncles, Hale vowed to earn enough money to support and educate all of them. She succeeded.

The magazine that Hale envisioned was to contain only well-written, original materials. She particularly encouraged women authors to submit their writings. Desire for originality forced Hale to write many of the stories and poems for the first issues of the magazine herself. Later contributors included Lydia Sigourney, Maria Fuller, Elmira Hunt, and Sarah Whitman. Hale's magazine encouraged the education of women, published American authors writing about American scenes and themes, and promoted the good works of its readers.

Part of Hale's campaign of good works in *The Ladies' Magazine* supported the Perkins School, the first school for the blind; organized a mammoth fair that raised the funds to complete the Bunker Hill Monument; founded the Seaman's Aid Society; and promoted a school for the children of poor working women.

Although Hale supported poor women who had to work, she publicly espoused the notion that men and women had separate spheres of influence and that women, the morally purer of the two sexes, would be polluted by entering into the public sphere that men inhabited. In the February 1832 issue of *The Ladies' Magazine*, she opined: ''I consider every attempt to induce women to think they have a right to participate in the public duties of government as injurious to their best interests and derogatory to their character. Our empire is purer, more excellent and spiritual'' (87). Thirty-seven years later, she denounced the woman's suffrage movement on the same grounds.

In 1830, Marshall Lowell, a composer and a friend of Hale's, asked her to write verses for children, which he then set to music, thus making them easy to learn and remember. *Poems for Our Children* (1830) were metrically regular poems with a different moral message as the theme of each one. ''Mary Had a Little Lamb'' was one of these poems.

The Ladies' Magazine and Louis Godey's *Lady's Book* merged in 1836. Hale and Godey made the new magazine, which kept the name *Lady's Book*, the most influential and most widely circulated periodical of its era. The magazine's hand-tinted fashion plates and sentimental poems and stories raised the number of subscribers to 150,000 just prior to the Civil War.

In 1841 Hale moved to Philadelphia to be close to the publisher of the *Lady's Book*. Philadelphia was the home of many well-known magazines such as *Graham's Magazine*. Both Godey and Graham realized the value of publishing original works by well-known authors. In 1854, both magazines took out copyrights on their contents. Newspapers and publishers of gift books railed against their actions, but Hale defended the copyrights as protection for American authors and publications.

During the 1840s and 1850s, Hale championed daily bathing, psychologically sound child-rearing practices, playgrounds for city children, the career of the first female doctor, Elizabeth Blackwell, healthful clothing styles for women, and the rehabilitation of Washington's home at Mt. Vernon, which became a national monument. She advised Matthew Vassar on the opening of Vassar College and lobbied the college's trustees to hire female faculty members. In 1863, Hale encouraged President Lincoln to declare the third Thursday of November to be a day of national thanksgiving.

When the Union was rent by arguments concerning slavery, Hale republished *Northwood* (1852), reminding abolitionists in her introduction that "the master is their brother as well as the servant" (Finley 175). Her novel *Liberia* (1853) makes the case for educating slaves before their liberation and subsequent repatriation in Liberia.

The year 1853 was a prolific one for Hale. She published the encyclopedic *Woman's Record: or Sketches of All Distinguished Women*. It was revised twice, in 1855 and 1876. In December 1877, Hale retired from *Godey's Lady's Book*, writing in her final editorial column, "I must bid farewell to my countrywomen, with the hope that this work of half a century may be blessed to the furtherance of the happiness and usefulness in their Divinely appointed sphere" (254). Sixteen months later, at the age of ninety, she died peacefully.

MAJOR WORKS AND THEMES

Hale's novels *Northwood* (1827, 1852) and *Liberia* (1853) dealt with the differences in life and industry between the Northern and Southern states and the question of slavery. Hale sought to teach her readers that there were more similarities than differences among Americans. She supported education and liberation of slaves and their repatriation in Africa.

In her editorial writings in *The Ladies' Magazine* and the subsequent *Lady's Book*, Hale asserted her most repeated theme: the differentiation of the sexes. Men are physically stronger, and women show greater moral and religious strength. That these two spheres of influence are of equal importance, she had no doubt. To Hale they were also divinely designated as separate. She reiterated this theme in *Woman's Record* (1853, 1855, 1876), which *Notable American Women* characterizes as "an ambitious biographical encyclopaedia containing 2500 entries and an early effort to remedy the neglect of women in most such works" (114). Nina Baym describes the book as "a conflation of the progress of Christianity with that of women. The Christian message is precisely the superiority of women" ("Onward Christian Women" 253).

Hale's other major themes are the encouragement of women's education and the support of organizations for social improvement. She declared that women's education and the promotion of women as teachers were her favorite themes. She averred that women are natural teachers and that they would happily work for lower wages, which would make universal education affordable to all.

Hale supported Godey's policy that forbid political or religious issues from appearing in the pages of their magazine. Godey feared alienating any reader, and Hale concurred. When the war broke out, Hale wrote that she wanted to make the *Lady's Book* "an oasis in the desert" (December 1862).

Articulating that women at home wielded moral suasion, which would help to end the war, she elided her conservative social ideology and editorially neutral position in the wartime pages of the *Lady's Book*. She promoted the moral education of children, which she believed was a mother's most important task. Her etiquette, homemaking, and recipe books also demonstrate her interest in making woman's work at home more scientific and more praiseworthy.

CRITICAL RECEPTION

Critically, Hale has been viewed more as an important social force than as a prominent author. When *Northwood* was first published, it received positive reviews including one in the *United States Review and Literary Gazette* by William Cullen Bryant, who wrote that the book was "another proof to many already existing that neither talents nor materials were wanting in the United States" (Finley 38).

The North American Review (1853) declared that *Woman's Record* was unbalanced, in that, of the four sections, the section on contemporary women and their writings was too long and the other sections too brief. The anonymous writer also takes issue with Hale's inclusion of snippets of writings by women, which the writer felt was not in keeping with the encyclopedia's genre. As to woman's moral superiority, the same reviewer notes, "[W]e have now high domestic authority for saying it is very sensitive doctrine indeed, and as true as the book" (260). Like *The Genius of Oblivion* (1823), *Woman's Record* may not have received critical acclaim, but both were well received by the book-buying public.

Current criticism centers around the question of whether Hale was a proto-feminist, through the example of her own life, or a retrograde force due to her conviction that separate spheres for the sexes were divinely ordained. While early biographers, such as Ruth Finley (1931) and Isabelle Webb Entrikin (1946), argue that Hale was the consummate feminist, Ann Douglas, Nina Baym, and Patricia Okker agree that Hale's ideology marked her as an adherent to standards of Victorian womanhood that sought to keep women out of the public realms of politics, commerce, and ideas. Hale's strong antisuffrage rhetoric is also seen by contemporary critics as evidence of her valorization of an ideology that limited, rather than liberated, her loyal readers.

BIBLIOGRAPHY

Works by Sarah Josepha Hale

Books

The Genius of Oblivion and Other Original Poems. Concord, NH: Jacob B. Moore, 1823.
Northwood: A Tale of New England. 2 vols. Boston: Bowles and Dearborn, 1827.

Sketches of American Character. Boston: Putnam and Hunt, 1829.
Poems for Our Children. Boston: R.W. Hale, 1830.
Flora's Interpreter: or The American Book of Flowers and Sentiments. Boston: Marsh,
    Capen and Lyon, 1832.
The Ladies Wreath: A Selection from the Poetic Writers of England and America. Boston:
    Marsh, Capen and Lyon, 1837.
Northwood: or Life North and South Showing the Character of Both. 2nd ed. New York:
    H. Long and Parather, 1852.
*Woman's Record: or Sketches of All Distinguished Women from "The Beginning" till
    A.D. 1850.* New York: Harper and Brothers, 1853.
Liberia; or Mr. Peyton's Experiments. New York: Harper and Brothers, 1853. Reprint,
    Upper Saddle River, NJ: Gregg Press, 1968.
Manners: or Happy Homes and Good Society All the Year Round. Boston: J. E. Tilton
    and Co., 1867.
Love; or A Woman's Destiny, a Poem. Philadelphia: Duffield Ashmead, 1870.

Periodicals Hale Edited

The Ladies' Magazine. Vols. 1–3. Boston: Putnam and Hunt, 1828–1830. Vol. 4. Boston:
    Marsh, Capen and Lyon, 1831.
The Ladies' Magazine and Literary Gazette. Vols. 5–6. Boston: Marsh, Capen and Lyon,
    1832–1833.
The American Ladies' Magazine. Vols. 7–9. Boston: James B. Dow, 1834–1836.
Godey's Lady's Book. Vols. 14–95. Philadelphia: Godey, January 1837–December 1877.

Studies of Sarah Josepha Hale

Baym, Nina. "At Home with History: History Books and Women's Sphere before the
    Civil War." *Proceedings of the American Antiquarian Society* 101 (1991): 275–
    295.
——. "Onward Christian Women: Sarah J. Hale's History of the World." *New En-
    gland Quarterly* 63 (June 1990): 249–270.
Douglas, Ann. *The Feminization of American Culture.* New York: Alfred A. Knopf,
    1977.
Entrikin, Isabelle Webb. *Sarah Josepha Hale and "Godey's Lady's Book."* Lancaster,
    PA: Lancaster Press, 1946.
Finley, Ruth. *The Lady of Godey's: Sarah Josepha Hale.* Philadelphia: J. B. Lippincott,
    1931.
Hoffman, Nicole Tonkovich. "*Legacy* Profile: Sarah Josepha Hale." *Legacy: A Journal
    of 19th Century American Women Writers* 7 (fall 1990): 47–55.
Okker, Patricia. *Our Sister Editors: Sarah J. Hale and the Tradition of Nineteenth-
    Century American Women Editors.* Athens: University of Georgia Press, 1995.
Rogers, Sherbrooke. *Sarah Josepha Hale: A New England Pioneer 1788–1879.* Gran-
    tham, NH: Tompson and Rutter, 1985.
"Sarah Josepha Hale." In *Notable American Women, 1607–1950,* edited by Edward T.
    James. Cambridge, MA: Belknap Press, 1971.
Scott, Ernest L., Jr. "Sarah Josepha Hale's New Hampshire Years, 1788–1828."
    Historical New Hampshire 49, no. 2: 59–96.

GAIL HAMILTON
(MARY ABIGAIL DODGE)
(1833–1896)

Robert E. Kanter

BIOGRAPHY

Mary Abigail Dodge, better known to her readers as Gail Hamilton, was born on March 31, 1833, in Hamilton, Massachusetts, the youngest of seven children born to James Brown Dodge, a prosperous farmer, and Hannah (Stanwood) Dodge, who had been a teacher before she was married. Both parents were members of the Congregational Church, which was a central point of family life. Hamilton's childhood was by all accounts a happy one; her longtime friend Harriet Prescott Spofford wrote: "She loved her immediate family with an intensity that sought in every way to promote their happiness, and in return they adored her" (93). Hamilton was particularly close to her sister, Hannah Augusta, who collected and edited volumes of Hamilton's correspondence and poetry after her death.

Hamilton's education was strong for a girl of her time. As a young child, she attended the West District School in Hamilton, and she was sent to boarding school in Cambridge, Massachusetts, when she was twelve. At thirteen she began a three-year course of study at Ipswich Female Seminary, where her training included French, Latin, German, algebra, history, chemistry, and philosophy (Coultrap-McQuin, Introduction xiv). She graduated from the seminary in 1850 and began work as a teacher there soon after. Hamilton was an excellent teacher, well liked by her colleagues and pupils, but by the spring of 1853 she was anxious to broaden her horizons. "I am so tired of Ipswich," she wrote to her brother at this time, "not of teaching, for I like it, not of Mr. and Mrs. Cowles, for I love them, but of the same white houses and the same black barns, the dreary, monotonous intolerable sameness" (*Life in Letters* 1, 46). She left Ipswich to begin teaching at the Hartford Female Seminary in February 1854, then took a teaching post at the Hartford High School in September of the same year, where she stayed until 1858.

In January 1856, while still at Hartford High School, Hamilton took the first decided steps in her career as a professional writer by submitting an essay and some poems to Gamaliel Bailey, editor of the widely circulated antislavery paper, the *National Era*. (The *Era* is perhaps best remembered now as the paper in which Harriet Beecher Stowe's *Uncle Tom's Cabin* was first published.) The forthright tone and humor displayed in her letter to Bailey are characteristic of her writing and convey a sense of her personal character:

I wish to measure myself by a new standard. I have been flattered from my youth up till I have perhaps learned to flatter myself. May I beg that your practised eye glance over the pages that accompany this and see whether they be of sufficient merit to interest your readers, or whether the hand that wrote them is capable of producing anything of real worth?

I hope I am not misunderstood. I do not ask for charity, nor for a friendly judgment, but for a just one. If you think the pieces worthless, you will not hesitate to say so and I promise not to drown myself thereupon. (*Life in Letters* 1, 107–108)

Bailey accepted the pieces, praising her in his reply with the remark that ''your pen is not a commonplace one'' and offering to pay $50 at the end of the year for whatever prose sketches she would send (*Life in Letters* 1, 118). In addition to her work for the *Era*, Hamilton also began to contribute to the *Independent*, an important and widely circulated Christian newspaper.

In the autumn of 1858 Hamilton left Hartford and the demands of teaching for Washington, D.C., to live with the family of Gamaliel Bailey as governess to his children. This arrangement allowed her time to observe the political life of the capital, and residence with the Baileys brought her into contact with many public figures as well. Despite some initial shyness and anxiety about her appearance, she became comfortable in society, and she was known for her intelligence and wit. As she wrote to her sister, in characteristically unapologetic terms: ''I tell you I could 'cut a dash' if I should set out! Sometimes I think I will. Most women are so stolid. They stand and expect to be entertained. I circulate and talk wild and make 'em laugh and am natural and so people get round me'' (*Life in Letters* 1, 279). While living with the Baileys, Hamilton continued to write for the *Era* and contributed book reviews and opinion columns to the *Independent* and the *Congregationalist*. She also wrote political commentary for the latter under the pen name of ''Cunctare,'' Latin for ''hesitate'' or possibly ''dodge'' (Beasley 89). Gamaliel Bailey died in June 1859, and Hamilton stayed with the family until the following spring, when she returned to Massachusetts, partly because Mrs. Bailey could no longer afford to pay her and partly because her mother was concerned for her safety as the threat of war increased.

At home Hamilton was able to concentrate more fully on writing, with a degree of success indicated by the prestige of her publishers. Her essays began to appear in *The Atlantic* in 1860, and her first book, *Country Living and Country Thinking*, was brought out by Ticknor and Fields in 1862. Over the next six years, she published seven more books with Ticknor and Fields on a wide range of topics: on the roles of men and women in marriage, writing as an occupation, religion, and her travels in the United States, mostly from material that had first appeared in periodicals. As Coultrap-McQuin has pointed out, Hamilton set herself apart from many other women writers by the forms in which she worked: "Although by the 1850s and 1860s women were prominent as fiction writers, Hamilton was unusual as an essayist and political commentator" (Introduction xvi).

Hamilton enjoyed a friendly relationship with her publisher, James T. Fields, until 1867, when she discovered that their agreement on royalties for her books yielded her a smaller percentage than the industry norm. Fields would not settle the matter on terms agreeable to her, and the dispute dragged on until the spring of 1869, when by mutual agreement an arbitrator settled the matter, finding that the publisher had not defrauded Hamilton intentionally and awarding her a far smaller sum than she had sought. As Coultrap-McQuin asserts, however, the battle between Hamilton and Fields had broader implications for the literary marketplace: "[Hamilton] made a significant contribution to the history of professional (women) writers, and she exposed the Gentleman Publisher's market for what it really was: a relationship based on power, even when conducted as a friendship" (*Literary Business* 134). Hamilton wrote a slightly fictionalized account of the matter in *A Battle of the Books* (1870), which she published at her own expense; naturally, she published nothing further with Ticknor and Fields or in *The Atlantic*, which was owned by the firm.

After 1871 Hamilton spent a good deal of time with the family of her cousin Harriet Stanwood Blaine, who was married to politician James G. Blaine. She lived with them in Washington during the winter, helping to entertain and to take care of the children, and she traveled with them to Europe in 1877–1888. She also assisted James Blaine with a book he wrote on Congress and helped him with his political speeches. With her return to Washington, Hamilton resumed her newspaper correspondence, becoming, as Maurine Beasley notes, "one of a group of noteworthy women journalists in the Capitol during the 1870s" that included her friend and mentor "Grace Greenwood" (pseudonym of Sara J. Lippincott) (94).

In 1889 Hamilton took up the cause of an American woman, Florence Chandler Maybrick, whom she believed had been wrongly convicted for the murder of her English husband. She was finishing a biography of James Blaine when she suffered a stroke in 1895 that left her in a coma for seven weeks. In her final book, *X Rays* (1896), she argued for the existence of an afterlife based on her near-death experiences. Hamilton died at home in Massachusetts on August 17, 1896.

MAJOR WORKS AND THEMES

Although Hamilton's most important work consists of essays and political commentary, Janice Goldsmith Pulsifer notes that her published writing "takes all forms: essays, sketches, juvenile fiction, poetry, biography, a novel, a satire, articles on topics of the day" (169). The wide range of the forms Hamilton worked in is matched by the wide range of the subject matter she took on, despite the objections of critics who would have had women limit themselves to domestic topics. Addressing that issue, she wrote in the essay "My Book": "I shall not confine myself to my sphere. . . . Wherever I see the symptoms of a pie, thither shall my fingers travel. Wherever a windmill flaps, it shall go hard but I will have a tilt at it" (*Skirmishes and Sketches* 432–433). She published five books of what Pulsifer classifies as "country sketches" prior to 1874: *Country Living and Country Thinking* (1862), *Gala Days* (1863), *Skirmishes and Sketches* (1865), *Summer Rest* (1866), and *Twelve Miles from a Lemon* (1874). There are also three books that treat conduct of the sexes, and relations between men and women, especially with regard to marriage: *A New Atmosphere* (1865), *Woman's Wrongs* (1868), and *Woman's Worth and Worthlessness* (1872). A third important category is constituted by her works that treat religion and theology: *What Think Ye of Christ?* (1877), *Sermons to the Clergy* (1876), and *A Washington Bible Class* (1890).

Hamilton's writing on gender issues is particularly interesting to literary critics and historians looking back at her work. Her feminism, evident both in works that address women's issues directly, such as *Woman's Wrongs* and *Woman's Worth and Worthlessness*, and in pieces on other topics, such as "My Garden," was based on the assumption that women and men were different by nature, so that there was always some distinction in the capabilities and tendencies of the sexes. But she also argued that her society constructed an artificially limited ideal for women, which discouraged them from developing their true potential. That potential, in her terms, included characteristics that had been wrongly reserved for men, particularly strength of mind and body. Unlike some of her contemporaries who were also fighting for improvements in women's lives, Hamilton opposed suffrage for women, on the grounds that the vote would not lead directly to the social changes most needed to improve women's lives: better educational opportunities and better wages. Although her positions on such questions put her somewhere in the middle of the spectrum of American feminism in the nineteenth century, her strong belief in the importance of self-improvement put her in line with the dominant Victorian ideal of character. Coultrap-McQuin sums up Hamilton's vision of feminism well: "[Her] message to women is loud and clear: make something of yourself, despite the discrimination and disadvantages imposed on your lives by society" (Introduction xxvii).

The humor that runs through much of Hamilton's work is also of interest to modern scholarship, as Coultrap-McQuin has pointed out. Writing of "My Garden'' (which is reprinted in a 1992 selection of Hamilton's work), Coultrap-McQuin cites play with sex stereotypes, exaggeration, and self-mockery, along with more subtle aspects of style and organization, as the important elements of Hamilton's humor.

Hamilton's writing about the profession of authorship, which, in addition to teaching, seemed to her an appropriate occupation for women, is also interesting. "My Book," from *Skirmishes and Sketches*, "illustrates the way the new woman as writer responds to a critical world" (Coultrap-McQuin, Introduction xxx). In addition, Hamilton's satiric version of her dispute with James T. Fields in *A Battle of the Books* provides interesting material for scholars concerned with the development of authorship as a profession in nineteenth-century America or the evolution of author-publisher relationships.

CRITICAL RECEPTION

Early assessments of Hamilton's writing show appreciation for her style and tone, although they are marked by the double standard of criticism for men and women that Hamilton herself spoke against. For example, Edwin Percy Whipple, who held considerable authority as a critic in his day, uses sexist terms that connote disagreeableness in a woman to describe Hamilton's style, even as he recommends her work:

Miss Mary A. Dodge (Gail Hamilton) might be styled an essayist, but that would be but a vague term to denote a writer who takes up all classes of subjects, is tart, tender, shrewish, pathetic, monitory, objugatory, tolerant, prejudiced, didactic, and dramatic by turns, but always writing with so much point, vigor, and freshness that we can only classify her among "readable" authors. (quoted in Pulsifer 172)

There has been relatively little modern critical treatment of Hamilton's writing as yet, perhaps because views such as her opposition to women's suffrage might seem to indicate that her writing would not hold much interest for late-twentieth-century readers. But it would be a mistake for contemporary readers to let Hamilton's relative conservatism turn them away from what Coultrap-McQuin calls her "strikingly modern critique of discrimination against women in society" (Introduction xxi). Coultrap-McQuin details the strengths of that critique well:

She presents a clear analysis of the impact of cultural stereotypes on the self-concept and expectations of women. She points out the negative results on women of those stereotypes, including poor health, excessive attention to fashion, and bad marriages. She astutely describes double standards in language usage and literary criticism. She is sensitive to class differences among women and empathizes with the poor. These views alone make her worth reading today. (Introduction xxix–xxx)

Recently, other feminist critics have taken up Coultrap-McQuin's challenge. In her book *The Disobedient Writer*, which explores the way selected women writers have responded to various literary traditions, Nancy A. Walker argues that Hamilton employs the Genesis story as a "convenient and familiar trope" to make "pointed comments about the relationship between women and literary tradition" (31). In a similar vein, Sherry Lee Linkon examines elements of Hamilton's later works that constitute what she terms a "gendered Jeremiad." "Like most Jeremiads," Linkon writes, "Hamilton's messages are usually conservative, but they also reveal her efforts to resist and revise her culture's dominant ideas about gender."

While criticism of Hamilton's published writing focusing on gender represents an important step in the reevaluation of her work, other important aspects remain to be explored, chief among them her use of humor and her vision of Christianity. Hamilton's letters also offer opportunities for further scholarly work, as she kept up a regular correspondence not only with her family but with many literary and intellectual figures of her day, including Grace Greenwood (Sara Jane Lippincott), John Greenleaf Whittier, and Henry James, Sr. These letters, together with her literary work, represent a rich and largely untapped resource for literary critics and historians.

WORKS CITED

Beasley, Maurine. "Mary Abigail Dodge: 'Gail Hamilton' and the Process of Social Change." *Essex Institute Historical Collections* 116, no. 2 (1980): 82–100.

Coultrap-McQuin, Susan. *Doing Literary Business: American Women Writers in the Nineteenth Century.* Chapel Hill: University of North Carolina Press, 1990.

———, ed. Introduction to *Gail Hamilton: Selected Writings.* New Brunswick: Rutgers University Press, 1992.

Hamilton, Gail [Mary Abigail Dodge]. *Gail Hamilton's Life in Letters.* Edited by H. Augusta Dodge. 2 vols. Boston: Lee and Shepard, 1916.

———. *Skirmishes and Sketches.* Boston: Ticknor and Fields, 1865.

Linkon, Sherry. "In Other Words: Nineteenth-Century American Women Essayists." Unpublished manuscript.

Pulsifer, Janice Goldsmith. "Gail Hamilton, 1833–1896." *Essex Institute Historical Collections* 104, no. 3 (1968): 165–216.

Spofford, Harriet Prescott. *A Little Book of Friends.* Boston: Little, Brown, 1916.

Walker, Nancy A. *The Disobedient Writer: Women and Narrative Tradition.* Austin: University of Texas Press, 1995.

BIBLIOGRAPHY

Works by Gail Hamilton

Country Living and Country Thinking. Boston: Ticknor and Fields, 1862.
Gala Days. Boston: Ticknor and Fields, 1863.

Stumbling Blocks. Boston: Ticknor and Fields, 1864.
A New Atmosphere. Boston: Ticknor and Fields, 1865.
Skirmishes and Sketches. Boston: Ticknor and Fields, 1865.
Summer Rest. Boston: Ticknor and Fields, 1866.
Wool-Gathering. Boston: Ticknor and Fields, 1867.
Woman's Wrongs: A Counter-Irritant. Boston: Ticknor and Fields, 1868.
Memorial. Mrs. Hannah Stanwood Dodge. Cambridge, MA: Riverside, 1869.
A Battle of the Books. Cambridge, MA: Riverside, 1870.
Woman's Worth and Worthlessness. New York: Harper and Bros., 1872.
Twelve Miles from a Lemon. New York: Harper and Bros., 1874.
Nursery Noonings. New York: Harper and Bros., 1875.
Sermons to the Clergy. Boston: W. F. Gill, 1876.
First Love Is Best. Boston: Estes and Lauriat, 1877.
What Think Ye of Christ? Boston: Estes and Lauriat, 1877.
Our Common School System. Boston: Estes and Lauriat, 1880.
The Insuppressible Book. Boston: S. E. Cassino, 1885.
A Washington Bible Class. New York: D. Appleton, 1890.
Biography of James G. Blaine. Norwich, CT: Henry Bill Publishing Co., 1895.
X Rays. Gail Hamilton: Hamilton, MA, 1896.
Gail Hamilton's Life in Letters. Edited by H. Augusta Dodge. 2 vols. Boston: Lee and
    Shepard, 1901.
Chips, Fragments and Vestiges. Boston: Lee and Shepard, 1902.
Gail Hamilton: Selected Writings. Edited by Susan Coultrap-McQuin. New Brunswick:
    Rutgers University Press, 1992.

Studies of Gail Hamilton

Beasley, Maurine. "Mary Abigail Dodge: 'Gail Hamilton' and the Process of Social
    Change." *Essex Institute Historical Collections* 116, no. 2 (1980): 82–100.
Coultrap-McQuin, Susan. *Doing Literary Business: American Women Writers in the
    Nineteenth Century.* Chapel Hill: University of North Carolina Press, 1990.
Fern, Fanny [Sara Payson Parton]. "Gail Hamilton—Miss Dodge." In *Eminent Women
    of the Age: Being Narratives of the Lives and Deeds of the Most Prominent
    Women of the Present Generation,* edited by James Parton, 2 vols. Hartford, CT:
    S. M. Betts, 1869. I: 202–220.
Langworthy, Margaret Wyman. "Mary Abigail Dodge." In *Notable American Women,
    1607–1950,* edited by Edward T. James, 3 vols. Cambridge, MA: Harvard Uni-
    versity Press, 1971. I: 493–495.
Pulsifer, Janice Goldsmith. "Gail Hamilton, 1833–1896." *Essex Institute Historical Col-
    lections* 104, no. 3 (1968): 165–216.
Spofford, Harriet Prescott. "Biographical Sketch." In *Gail Hamilton's Life in Letters,*
    edited by H. Augusta Dodge. 2 vols. Boston: Lee and Shepard, 1901.
———. "Gail Hamilton." In *A Little Book of Friends.* Boston: Little, Brown, 1916. 87–
    115.

MARION HARLAND (MARY VIRGINIA HAWES TERHUNE) (1830–1922)

Lee Hunter

BIOGRAPHY

During her long and successful writing career, Marion Harland published over seventy books of fiction, domestic advice, history, and biography; indeed, at her death in 1922, her name was "as well known in . . . America as that of the president of the United States" (Smith, "Marion Harland" 2). Born December 21, 1830, in Amelia County, Virginia, Mary Virginia Hawes was the third of eight children of Samuel Pierce Hawes, a transplanted merchant from Dorcester, Massachusetts, and Judith Anna Smith, the daughter of an aristocratic Virginia planter. Although Mary Virginia completed her formal schooling with two years at a girls' seminary in Richmond, she was educated largely at home, studying independently and with tutors. At thirteen, Mary Virginia went with her sister to live with a relative, Ann Rice, in Hampden-Sidney, Virginia; there, a student at Union Theological Seminary tutored the two girls. Samuel Hawes had directed the tutor to educate his daughters "as if they were boys and preparing for college." Years later, Marion Harland would write about this time of intensive education, "Were I required to tell what period of my nonage had most to do with shaping character and coloring my life, I should reply, without hesitation, 'The nine months passed at Rice Hill' " (*Autobiography* 97).

At age fifteen, Mary Virginia began publishing short moral treatises in two Richmond religious weeklies, "using a male pseudonym to lend authority to her evangelical essays and . . . to protect herself from the curiosity of friends and neighbors" (Smith, "*Legacy* Profile" 52). In 1853, the *Southern Era* published her story "Kate Harper," written under the pseudonym Marion Harland, and awarded her a $50 prize for the "best temperance serial" (*Autobiography* 240). Pleased with her success, Mary Virginia "dragged out the rough copy" of the novel she had written at age sixteen, began revising, and completed it within two months (*Autobiography* 241–242). Although a local publisher rejected the manuscript, Samuel Hawes arranged to have *Alone* published in Richmond in 1854 at his expense (*Autobiography* 238, 245). Two years later, J. C. Derby republished the popular novel in New York; in fact, *Alone* would eventually sell over 100,000 copies (Derby 564).

In 1856, Harland married Edward Payson Terhune, a New Jersey native and a Presbyterian clergyman. The couple first lived in rural Virginia, but in 1859, Terhune accepted a pastorate in Newark, New Jersey. Although Harland reluctantly left her native state (*Autobiography* 355–356), she would live in the North the rest of her life. During their fifty-year marriage, the Terhunes had six children, three of whom survived to adulthood. Despite her responsibilities as a minister's wife and a mother, Harland continued to write at an almost feverish pace, publishing over a dozen novels between 1856 and 1870, including *Moss-side* (1857); *Nemesis* (1860); *Miriam* (1862); *Husks* (1863); *Sunnybank* (1866); and *Phemie's Temptation* (1869). In addition to her novels, Harland also wrote for magazines, primarily *Godey's Lady's Book* and *Peterson's* (Mott 224), and by 1870, she "had established herself among the nation's top-selling authors of popular women's fiction" (Smith, "*Legacy* Profile" 52).

As "the heyday of woman's fiction began to fade" in the late 1860s, Harland shifted her focus from writing fiction to writing cookbooks and handbooks of domestic instruction (Smith, "*Legacy* Profile" 52). Ultimately, Harland published some twenty-five books of cookery and advice, including *Breakfast, Luncheon and Tea* (1875), *Common Sense in the Nursery* (1885), and *Eve's Daughters; or Common Sense for Maid, Wife, and Mother* (1882). *Common Sense in the Household* (1871), Harland's first cookbook, offered various recipes as well as advice ("Familiar Talks") to young and inexperienced wives. Although Scribner's considered the book a risk, *Common Sense* sold over a million copies and remained in print for fifty years (Smith, "*Legacy* Profile" 53). Additionally, Harland wrote articles on homemaking for various magazines, including *Ladies' Home Journal* and *Good Housekeeping*, and briefly held editorial positions at two, *St. Nicholas* (1876) and *Babyhood* (1884–1886); she also established and edited *The Home-Maker* magazine from 1888 to 1890.

By 1885 Harland had become "one of the premier domestic authorities in the country," and "[b]y the mid-1890s, she had won herself such a following that anything with her name on it was a guaranteed seller" (Smith, "*Legacy* Profile" 53). Harland's popularity enabled her to publish, in addition to her fiction and domestic advice, over a dozen books of travel, history, biography, and autobiography. *Home of the Bible* (1895) details her travels through the Middle East with her son, and *Some Colonial Homesteads and Their Stories* (1897) provides historical information about specific Virginia estates. Charlotte Brontë, John Knox, and William Cowper all figure as subjects of Harland's book-length biographies, and she published her own autobiography, *Marion Harland's Autobiography; The Story of a Long Life*, in 1910. Harland urged her readers to "[s]elect your vocation—but have one! Be too busy and too happy in your chosen labor to count the years as they go by" (*Looking Westward* 16). Indeed, Harland's life reiterates her injunction: In addition to her writing, she lectured throughout the eastern United States for the Chautauqua Association (1891–1894). She also wrote a syndicated advice column for the Philadelphia *North American* (1900–1910) and the *Chicago Tribune* (1910–1917). Harland continued writing as long as her health allowed; in fact, she dictated her last novel—*The Carringtons of High Hill* (1919)—at age eighty-nine in a state of almost total blindness. On June 3, 1922, at the age of ninety-one, Harland died at her home in Brooklyn, New York.

MAJOR WORKS AND THEMES

Marion Harland's novels primarily focus on the domestic and religious lives of women. Although the fiction often contains a romantic plotline, Harland emphasizes the inner lives of her protagonists, young women who undergo great trials and who learn strength, acceptance, religious piety, and the importance of women's domesticity. Harland portrays educated, articulate women in her fiction, and although she argues for recognition of women's intellectual capabilities, she upholds the notion of separate sexual spheres. Rather than participate in the business of man, woman should fulfill her divine calling through feminine vocations, such as teaching or homemaking. Harland's woman must serve as a "moral and spiritual guide" to others and, through them, provide "a powerful influence for good in the community" (Smith, "Marion Harland" 180).

Alone (1854), Harland's first novel, focuses on a young woman's struggles to assume her proper role in society. Orphaned at fifteen and under the influence of a misanthropic guardian, Ida Ross grows dangerously cynical and emotionless. Although loving friends enable Ida to escape her cynicism, she discovers inner strength and acceptance only through a powerful religious conversion. Religion provides comfort, but it does not supplant the need for human love; significantly, Ida finds true happiness only when she marries Morton Lacy at the end of the novel. In *Alone* Harland portrays both the fulfillment women can find in domesticity and the power inherent in domestic roles, a power that religious piety strengthens. As a friend tells Ida, "Yet woman has her sphere, no less than man; and if he conquers in his by might of purpose and brute strength, she guides, instead of rules in hers, by love and submission" (34).

In Harland's third novel, *Moss-side* (1857), Grace Leigh, like Ida Ross, must withstand adversities in order to learn acceptance and religious piety; only after her trials does Grace marry happily. In this novel, Harland articulates her view of the ideal marital relationship, depicted metaphorically through the relationship of ivy to an oak tree. Far from a "parasite" on the masculine oak, the feminine "ivy has its root in the earth that imparted life to the forest giant; and grow with, and twine into the oak as it will, it retains its individuality" (150). Although woman could live without man, marriage best suits her and offers her the most opportunities. For Harland, without the support of the oak, the ivy, though "hardy," represents merely "a dwarfed, stubborn apology for a tree." However, "if left to Nature's guidance, . . . it might have climbed almost to the clouds" (430). Although Harland delineates marriage as a partnership rather than a patriarchal institution (Baym 203), she clearly envisions man as the dominant partner.

In her cookbooks and domestic advice books, Harland's "mission—closely paralleling the domestic feminism of Catharine Beecher—was to redeem women's profession, to elevate housework from drudgery to a divinely-ordained vocation" (Smith, "*Legacy* Profile" 53). Although Harland acknowledged the problems associated with housekeeping and sympathized with homemakers, she urged women to recognize that it was a high honor to be the custodian of other's welfare and happiness. Similarly, motherhood embodies a divinely appointed responsibility; mothers act as "God's deputies upon earth in the work of training immortal souls" (*Breakfast* 401).

In *Eve's Daughters* (1882), Harland advises mothers on the care of young women, from babies to adulthood, advocating "rational, athletic, educated lives for girls." For example, parents should allow girls to run and play outdoors, to eat heartily, and to dress comfortably (Smith, "Marion Harland" 436–437). Moreover, girls should receive a broad education composed of geometry and algebra as well as Latin and German (*Eve's Daughters* 154–156). Because young women might one day need "to meet reverses and override poverty" (259), they should also learn a profession: "Choose now a special line of study and of thought, bearing directly upon whatever profession, trade or avocation you may select as the business of your life. Choose Something to Do [*sic*], *and do it!*" (258). However, woman's most important role remains that of wife and mother: "Absorption in your chosen art or profession, however worthy it may be in itself, becomes a fault when it ignores the claims of others upon time and consideration" (338).

CRITICAL RECEPTION

Almost all of Harland's books sold well, and by the end of her career, "[h]er name on a book cover or a byline was an instant guarantee of sales" (Smith, "Marion Harland" 2). Contemporary reviewers usually commented favorably on Harland's work, although they recognized that Harland wrote "for the multitudes" (Review of *Sunnybank*). *Alone*, Harland's best-selling novel, earned praise for its "[l]ively scenes, spirited descriptions and sage discussions of important moral questions." Although the reviewer faults Harland for her "grandiloquence and learnedness" (Review of *Alone* 728, 731), he also states: " 'Alone,' viewed as a whole, is as deserving as it has been successful" (732). Two later novels set in the antebellum South, *Judith* (1883) and *His Great Self* (1892), earned the praises of Thomas Nelson Page, who favorably compared Harland to E. D. E. N. Southworth, Augusta Evans, and Caroline Hentz (quoted in Smith, "Marion Harland" 474). Harland's cookbooks and domestic advice books were also well received by critics. For example, the *New York Times* found *Eve's Daughters* to be "a useful book," "cleverly written," and the Springfield *Republican* declared it "frank, sensible, and brimful of womanly intuitions, information, and advice" (quoted in Smith, "Marion Harland" 440).

Despite their popularity (or perhaps because of it), Harland's works were largely ignored after her death. With the rise of feminism in the 1970s, literary critics began including Harland in their discussions of nineteenth-century women writers, but, to date, no book-length study of Harland has been published. Three recent works, however, do include important critical information on Harland. In *Woman's Fiction* (1978), Nina Baym discusses Harland's early fiction, particularly *Alone, The Hidden Path*, and *Moss-side*; Baym notes that although Harland held "a clear domestic ideology," it was not without "significant strains and ambivalences" (181). Mary Kelley's *Private Woman, Public Stage* (1984), a study of twelve nineteenth-century woman writers, offers a more complex examination of Harland, combining literary analysis and biography to explore the lives of women writers who, despite their belief in the supremacy of the domestic sphere, acted as public figures, "creators of culture" (xii). Kelley explores the "continuing crisis of identity" these writers faced as they struggled to bridge "the gulf between a private domestic experience and a public literary career" (111, xi). In *Domestic Novelists in the Old South* (1992), Elizabeth Moss focuses on five popular nineteenth-century Southern women writers, including Harland, who used "their prose to respond to northern and sometimes southern criticism" (2). Moss examines Harland's early fiction in the context of "southern domestic novels [which] fused the conventional *Bildungsroman* . . . with the rhetoric of proslavery, veiling an explicitly political message" (13).

Additional information on Harland can be found in two works by Karen Smith, the short but useful "*Legacy* Profile" of Harland and her unpublished 1990 dissertation, "Marion Harland: The Making of a Household Word." Smith's dissertation, a narrative biography of Harland, offers the most exhaustive analysis of Harland's life as well as the most complete primary bibliography of her works (Smith notes that Harland's "works occupy more than 15 pages of the *National Union Catalogue*" [7]). Although Harland seems to be garnering more attention from critics, a great deal remains to be done. Literary critics have largely ignored Harland's later novels and short fiction, as well as her cookbooks and domestic advice books. Additionally, many traditional feminists have overlooked Harland's seemingly benign portrayals of woman's sphere. However, with our growing critical awareness of the multiplicity of voice in feminists ideology, Harland's work is ripe for further analysis.

WORKS CITED

Anonymous. Review of *Alone*. *Southern Literary Messenger* 20 (1854): 726–732.
Anonymous. Review of *Eve's Daughters*. *New York Times*, 2 May 1882, 7.

Anonymous. Review of *Sunnybank*. *New York Times*, 16 November 1866, 2.

Baym, Nina. *Woman's Fiction: A Guide to Novels by and about Women in America 1820–1870*. 1978. 2nd ed. Ithaca: Cornell University Press, 1993.

Derby, J. C. *Fifty Years among Authors, Books, and Publishers*. New York: G. W. Carleton and Co., 1884.

Harland, Marion. *Alone*. Richmond: A. Morris, 1854.

———. *Breakfast, Luncheon and Tea*. New York: Scribner, Armstrong, 1875.

———. *Eve's Daughters; or Common Sense for Maid, Wife, and Mother*. New York: Charles Scribner's Sons, 1882.

———. *Looking Westward*. New York: Charles Scribner's Sons, 1914.

———. *Marion Harland's Autobiography; The Story of a Long Life*. New York: Harper and Brothers, 1910.

———. *Moss-side*. New York: Derby and Jackson, 1857.

Kelley, Mary. *Private Woman, Public Stage: Literary Domesticity in Nineteenth-Century America*. New York: Oxford University Press, 1984.

Moss, Elizabeth. *Domestic Novelists in the Old South: Defenders of Southern Culture*. Baton Rouge: Louisiana State University Press, 1992.

Mott, Frank Luther. *A History of American Magazines*. Vol. 3. Cambridge: Harvard University Press, 1938.

Smith, Karen. "*Legacy* Profile: Marion Harland." *Legacy* 8 (1991): 51–57.

———. "Marion Harland: The Making of a Household Word." Ph.D. diss., University of Massachusetts, 1990.

SELECTED BIBLIOGRAPHY

Works by Marion Harland

See also Works Cited.

Novels

The Hidden Path. New York: J. C. Derby, 1855.
Sunnybank. New York: Sheldon, 1866.
Phemie's Temptation. New York: Carleton, 1869.
Judith: A Chronicle of Old Virginia. Philadelphia: Our Continent Publishing Co; New York: Fords, Howard, and Hulbert, 1883.
His Great Self. Philadelphia: J. B. Lippincott, 1892.

Advice Manual and Cookbook

Common Sense in the Household, a Manual of Practical Housewifery. New York: Charles Scribner's Sons, 1871.

Travel, Biography, History

Home of the Bible: A Woman's Vision of the Master's Land. Chicago: Monarch, 1895.
Some Colonial Homesteads and Their Stories. New York: G. P. Putnam's Sons, 1897.
Charlotte Brontë at Home. New York and London: G. P. Putnam's Sons, 1899.

Studies of Marion Harland

See also Works Cited.
Bolton, Sara Knowles. *Successful Women*. Boston: Lothrop, 1888. 90–109.
Halsey, Francis W., ed. *Women Authors of Our Day in Their Homes*. New York: J. Pott, 1903. 19–29.
McCandless, Amy Thompson. ''Concepts of Patriarchy in the Popular Novels of Antebellum Southern Women.'' *Studies in Popular Culture* 10, no. 2 (1987): 1–16.
Orgain, Kate Alma. *Southern Authors in Poetry and Prose*. New York: Neale Publishing Co., 1908. 186–193.

FRANCES E. W. HARPER
(1825–1911)

Gretchen Holbrook Gerzina

BIOGRAPHY

Frances Ellen Watkins was born in Baltimore, Maryland, to free, middle-class black parents who both died by the time she was three. She was taken in and raised by her aunt and uncle, Henrietta and William Watkins, who were educated, free blacks living in Baltimore and part of its abolitionist community. A shoemaker by trade, as well as an African Methodist Episcopal minister who ran a black literary society, her uncle founded a school, the Watkins Academy, in 1820, where Frances was educated in all the standard academic subjects. She was also a friend to and influence upon the famous abolitionist William Lloyd Garrison (Bacon 22–23).

At fourteen, Frances left the Watkins Academy and went to work for a white family named Armstrong. Although she was employed as a seamstress and nursemaid, she had the run of the Armstrongs' bookshop and their encouragement in her interest in writing. At the age of twenty or twenty-one she collected her poems into a volume called *Forest Leaves*, no copies of which survive.

In 1850 or 1851, she moved to Ohio to teach sewing at another school for free blacks, Union Seminary outside of Columbus, which would later move and become Wilberforce University. There she was the first female instructor, and as with her earlier employment, she was hired for her domestic rather than academic or literary skills. A year or two later she moved to another teaching position in York or Little York, Pennsylvania.

Her lifelong involvement with abolitionism, and the passage of the Fugitive Slave Act and Fugitive Slave Law in the 1850s, led her to question whether her real calling lay in teaching or activism, and she finally wrote to the antislavery activist William Still that she chose the latter (Still 757). For two years Harper lived with the Stills in an apartment over the Philadelphia antislavery office and was involved with those running the Underground Railroad; there she wrote poetry, some of which was later printed as *Poems on Miscellaneous Subjects* (1854). William Lloyd Garrison wrote the introduction, and it "proved such a success that it was reprinted at least five times with some twenty editions between 1854 and 1871, and earned [her] the reputation as the most popular black poet before Paul Dunbar" (Bacon 25).

In August 1854 Frances and her cousin William Watkins traveled to Boston's antislavery office, and that month in New Bedford, Massachusetts, she commenced what would be her career as a social reform speaker. She gave a speech called "The Elevation and Education [or 'Education and Elevation'] of the Negro Race," which was so well received that she was hired as a traveling lecturer by the Maine Anti-Slavery Society, living for the first time in an all-white world. In 1857 she moved back to Pennsylvania and traveled as a lecturer in that state and New Jersey.

At a time when public lectures were popular public entertainment, Harper was praised for her voice, grammar, composure, and gentle but persuasive rhetoric. Her audiences included whites and blacks, and she was so successful, she wrote to Still, that some believed she must either be a man or a white person painted black (Still 772). In 1858 she began speaking in the Midwest, where one Detroit listener said that "the whites and colored people here are just crazy with excitement about her. She is the greatest female speaker as ever was here" (Bacon 28–29). As the antislavery movement expanded in the late 1850s following the famous Dred Scott Decision, the demand for Harper's speeches increased, as did her income, most of which she donated to the Underground Railroad.

The loneliness and physical effort of unceasing travel lecturing began to take its toll on her health, and when she married a free black widower named Fenton Harper in 1860 in Cincinnati, they moved with his three children outside of Grove City, Ohio, to a farm that she purchased with the savings from her lecture earnings. Here she intended to live the retired life of a farmer's wife who made and sold butter and raised a family. Her only daughter, Mary, was born during this period. Unfortunately, Fenton Harper died after only four years of marriage, leaving her with four children and the appalling discovery that he had been in overwhelming debt. Frances lost everything, including her bed and the butter tubs she used to earn a living (Bacon 32). Out of financial necessity, she returned to lecturing.

Her long and perhaps best-known poem "Moses: A Story of the Nile" was written over a two-year period while Harper once again lived with the Stills (the children were now living with other families). Published in 1869, the poem is described by Maryemma Graham in her introduction to the Oxford edition of Harper's poetry as "a forty-page biblical allegory in blank verse" (*Complete Poems* xliv). A departure from her usual ballad style, it obviously resonates to the black experience in the United States. In this as in all her writing, the connection between her dedication to social reform and art is clear.

A new phase of Harper's life and work began in 1866, when she spoke at the Eleventh Woman's Rights Convention in New York, drawing upon her personal and financial losses after her husband's death. "Had I died instead of my husband," she said, "how different might have been the result . . . no administrator would have gone into his house, broken up his home, sold his bed, and taken away his means of support" (*Proceedings, Eleventh Woman's Rights Convention*, quoted in Bacon 21).

Her long association with women's rights groups, however, was a troubled one. White women pressed for women's suffrage at the exclusion of racial issues, a position with which Harper, along with Frederick Douglass and other black activists, vehemently disagreed. In her view, blacks were in immediate and desperate need of the vote in order to prevent being drawn back into slavery. It was well known that a number of feminists, including Elizabeth Cady Stanton, resisted championing votes for blacks. In any case, Harper was not convinced that "giving the woman the ballot is immediately going to cure all the ills of life. I do not believe that white women are dewdrops just exhaled from the skies" (*Proceedings* 46). However, over the years she aligned herself with a number of women's groups, including the American Woman's Suffrage Association (AWSA) and the Woman's Christian Temperance Union (WCTU). In both of these associations she was the only well-known black woman in a powerful and public position. She helped found the National Association of Colored Women and served as its vice president. Because of all of these positions, and because of her reputation as a writer, she was in great demand as a speaker.

Using Philadelphia as a base, Harper continued to lecture throughout the South, adding issues concerning the black family, temperance, and Christianity to her repertoire. She was particularly concerned that black women, so long separated by slavery from education and the moral mainstream, learn to care for their families in all aspects of life. Furthermore, they were in her view the most oppressed group of people in the country. Supporting herself by staying with families along the way and selling her poetry to her audiences, she nonetheless refused payment for the separate talks she gave to black women in churches and meeting halls. The themes on which she spoke to them appeared in her fiction, not only in her poems and her famous novel *Iola Leroy* (1892) but in her other three novels, *Minnie's Sacrifice, Sowing and Reaping*, and *Trial and Triumph*, all published serially in the *Christian Recorder* between 1869 and 1889. The recent discovery and republishing of these three novels by Frances Smith Foster challenges much of the modern criticism of *Iola Leroy*, which seemed to stand alone as her sole novel, addressing exclusively the theme of the tragic mulatto.

Harper and her daughter Mary lived from 1870 on in a house she purchased in Philadelphia at 1006 Bainbridge, the publishing location given for many of her later works. Here she wrote a book of poems on the South and Southerners encountered in her travels, *Sketches of Southern Life* (1872). In addition to her numerous books of poetry, she published articles regularly in black and white magazines and newspapers. Speaking and writing until the end of her life, Harper died in 1911.

Iola Leroy, her novel published in 1892, was taken for many years by modern critics to be the first novel published by an African-American woman. The recent discovery of Harriet Wilson's *Our Nig* changed that view, but modern criticism has been slow to realize just how prolific, widely read, and influential Harper was in her own time. She was, quite simply, "the most important black woman writer during the last half of the nineteenth century" (Lauter 28).

MAJOR WORKS AND THEMES

It is widely accepted that Harper's poetic influences were Longfellow and Whittier; in fiction, Harriet Beecher Stowe is often cited as a model, partly because of the antislavery emphasis and partly because Harper published a poem called "Eliza Harris" based upon Stowe's novel *Uncle Tom's Cabin*.

Harper's literary themes, echoing those in her public speaking, can be divided into three major areas, all of which fall roughly under the umbrella of "uplift": the situation of black people in ante- and postbellum America, moral choices, and temperance. These themes often overlap, as in *Trial and Triumph* and *Minnie's Sacrifice* and in many of the poems. Because she was always overt in her expression of these themes, her work has often been dismissed by modern critics as being overly didactic, despite the demonstrated appeal of her work to her contemporaries.

Most of her poetry took the ballad form, with simple rhyme schemes and straightforward themes. It is crucial to recognize, however, that she drew upon the oral tradition of African America, incorporating the recitation of her poetry into her speeches and lectures. In this respect the derivation of the poetic structure and its intended audience intertwined in important ways. She also preceded Paul Laurence Dunbar in her use of dialect. Far from being an expression of contempt for Black English or of the superiority of her own standard pronunciation, it was meant as a visible reminder of the varieties of black speech and the inherent wisdom of those who had survived slavery and devised methods of subverting it. For example, her "Aunt Chloe" poems, dramatic monologues of a former slave during Reconstruction, use irony and pathos as their major tools:

> If freedom seem'd a little rough
>   I'd weather through the gale;
> And as to buying up my vote,
>   I hadn't it for sale. ("The Deliverance")

Similarly, in *Iola Leroy*, she provides a variety of examples of black speech patterns in order to emphasize the multiplicity of African-American experiences.

Some of her themes, notably temperance and the importance of making and standing by moral decisions, transcend race. Of her three recently discovered novels, *Sowing and Reaping*, like her earlier short story "The Two Offers," involves protagonists who are white. *Sowing and Reaping* describes the evils of alcohol and gambling, and the importance of hard work, abstinence, and Christian values in overcoming these evils and building a life worth living. Women who overlook the addictive qualities of these vices and marry men who participate in them always live to regret it. While Harper was exceedingly concerned about the problems alcohol and gambling created for the black community, she was careful not to present them as exclusive to the black community.

The issue of passing, or more correctly those who were unwittingly made to pass, for white forms one of the subjects of both *Minnie's Sacrifice* and *Iola Leroy*. In each, young mixed-race Southerners are raised as white and only informed as they near or reach adulthood of their true racial heritage. How they choose to participate in the education and life of the black community forms the central dilemma for these protagonists.

CRITICAL RECEPTION

Critical response to Harper's work has had several distinct phases. In many ways the most recent articles on her work have been the most problematic. In her own time, Harper was an enormously popular and successful writer. Her contemporaries would have been surprised to learn of her later obscurity, particularly as a poet. Even accepting shifts in public taste, it is troubling that those earlier critics who charged themselves with writing histories of African-American literature either ignored or dismissed her work. The reason for this neglect of black women's writing in general, according to Mary Helen Washington in *Invented Lives*, is that the "single distinguishing feature of the literature of black women [is that it is] about black women" (xxi). Paul Lauter goes a step further in discussing the neglect of Harper's work by pointing out that she, like many others of her time, did not separate "the social functions of fiction" from its artistic form; "indeed they were dominant when Harper was growing up, especially among her abolitionist colleagues" (29).

Modern criticism by black women has taken Harper to task for another reason. Harper's best-known work in the late twentieth century is her 1892 novel *Iola Leroy*. Until extremely recently it was thought not only to be the earliest novel by a black woman but Harper's only novel. In that context, it was seen as problematic because of the "tragic mulatto" protagonist, Iola, who only discovers after her mother's death that she is partly black and has been sold back into slavery, and for its use of dialect. For example, Kimberly A. C. Wilson condemns Harper, saying that "[b]y painting Iola as the traditionally beautiful, blond, blue-eyed, and fair heroine, Harper devalues her own brown hair, brown eyes, and brown skin" (105).

Such criticism has been effectively answered by critics like Hazel Carby, who finds not only that the mulatto figure in general stands for an expression of the often problematic history of black and white in America but that Iola herself is far from being the real, or at least only, heroine of the novel. A number of dark-skinned characters are given intellectual prominence in the book, and what ''Harper acknowledged was the need to forge a new, alternative vision, a new role for black intellectuals. In this regard, *Iola Leroy* was a textbook for the educated black person in the crisis of disenfranchisement, lynching, and the Jim Crow laws'' (Carby 93).

Furthermore, *Iola Leroy* now needs to be read in the context of Harper's other three novels, unknown at the time that this criticism was written. Of the three novels, one has white protagonists, one has mulatto protagonists, and the third has an entirely black cast of characters, grappling with the problems of the emerging black middle class without any discussion of mixed-race characters at all. As critics begin to recast their opinions in light of this important literary discovery, new approaches will certainly emerge.

BIBLIOGRAPHY

Works by Frances E. W. Harper

Fiction

''The Two Offers.'' *Anglo-African Magazine*, 1859.
Minnie's Sacrifice. First published serially in *The Christian Recorder*, 1869.
Sowing and Reaping. First published serially in *The Christian Recorder*, 1876–1877.
Trial and Triumph. First published serially in *The Christian Recorder*, 1888–1889.
Iola Leroy; or, Shadows Uplifted. Philadelphia: Garrigues Brothers, 1892.

Poetry

Forest Leaves. N.p., 1835 (?).
Poems on Miscellaneous Subjects. Boston: J. B. Yerrinton & Son, 1854.
Moses: A Story of the Nile. Philadelphia: Merrihew & Son, 1869.
Poems. Philadelphia: Merrihew & Son, 1871.
Sketches of Southern Life. N.p., 1872.
The Martyr of Alabama and Other Poems. N.p., 1894.
Atlanta Offering: Poems. Philadelphia: Ferguson, 1895.
Atlanta Offering: Poems. Philadelphia: 1006 Bainbridge Street, 1896.
Idylls of the Bible. Philadelphia: 1006 Bainbridge Street, 1901.
Complete Poems of Frances E. W. Harper. New York: Oxford University Press, 1988.
''For the Twenty-fifth Anniversary of the Home for Aged and Infirm Colored Persons'' and ''For the Dedication of the Parker Annex to the Home for the Aged and Infirm Colored Persons.'' In ''Frances Harper and the Old People: Two Recently Discovered Poems.'' *The Griot* (Southern Conference on Afro-American Studies) 4 (winter–summer 1995): 52–56.
The Sparrow's Fall and Other Poems. N.p., n.d.

Studies of Frances E. W. Harper

Ammons, Elizabeth. ''*Legacy* Profile: Frances Ellen Watkins Harper (1825–1911).'' *Legacy: A Journal of Nineteenth-Century American Women* 2 (fall 1985): 61–66.

Bacon, Margaret Hope. " 'One Great Bundle of Humanity': Frances Ellen Watkins Harper (1825–1911)." *Pennsylvania Magazine of History and Biography* 113 (January 1989): 21–43.

Carby, Hazel. *"Of Lasting Service for the Race": The Work of Frances Ellen Watkins Harper.* New York: Oxford University Press, 1987. 62–94.

Elkins, Marilyn. "Reading beyond the Conventions: A Look at Frances E. W. Harper's *Iola Leroy, or Shadows Uplifted.*" *American Literary Realism, 1870–1910* 22 (winter 1990): 44–53.

Ernest, John. "From Mysteries to Histories: Cultural Pedagogy in Frances E. W. Harper's *Iola Leroy.*" *American Literature* 64 (September 1992): 497–518.

Griffin, Jasmine Farah. "Frances Ellen Watkins Harper in the Reconstruction South." *SAGE: A Scholarly Journal on Black Women* (Student Supplement 1988): 45–47.

Hill, Patricia Liggins. " 'Let Me Make the Songs for the People': A Study of Frances Watkins Harper's Poetry." *Black American Literature Forum* 15 (summer 1981): 60–65.

Lauter, Paul. "Is Frances Ellen Watkins Harper Good Enough to Teach?" *Legacy: A Journal of Nineteenth-Century American Women* 5 (spring 1988): 27–32.

Scheick, William J. "Strategic Ellipsis in Harper's 'The Two Offers.' " *Southern Literary Journal* 23 (spring 1991): 14–18.

Still, William. *The Underground Rail Road: A Record of Facts, Authentic Narratives, Letters, Etc.* Philadelphia: Porter and Coates, 1872.

Tate, Claudia. "Allegories of Black Female Desire; or, Rereading Nineteenth-Century Sentimental Narratives of Black Female Authority." In *Changing Our Own Words.* New Brunswick, NJ: Rutgers University Press, 1989. 98–126.

Washington, Mary Helen. *Invented Lives: Narratives of Black Women 1860–1960.* Garden City, NY: Anchor Press, 1987.

Wilson, Kimberly A. C. "The Function of the 'Fair' Mulatto: Complexion, Audience, and Mediation in Frances Harper's *Iola Leroy.*" *Cimarron Review* 106 (January 1994): 104–113.

Young, Elizabeth. "Warring Fictions: *Iola Leroy* and the Color of Gender." *American Literature* 64 (September 1992): 273–297.

CAROLINE LEE WHITING HENTZ (1800–1856)

Melanie Levinson

BIOGRAPHY

Caroline Lee Whiting was born on June 1, 1800, in Lancaster, Massachusetts. At the age of twenty-four she married Nicholas Marcellus Hentz, a French political refugee. From 1826 to 1830 they lived in Chapel Hill, where he held a professorship in modern languages at the University of North Carolina. In 1830, for reasons that remain unclear, Professor Hentz left the university. He subsequently established a number of schools for girls, but the family always struggled financially. Though Caroline was busy assisting Nicholas by providing room and board for the students, in 1843 she wrote *De Lara; or, The Moorish Bride* for the Tremont Theater in Boston. She published *Lovell's Folly* in 1833, *Aunt Patty's Scrap Bag* in 1846, and *The Mob Cap* in 1848. When Nicholas's health failed in 1849, Caroline was left to provide for her family. Soon after, she began to publish regularly.

By the time of her death from pneumonia in 1856, Hentz had published eight novels. *Linda; or, The Young Pilot of Belle Creole* (1850) was her most popular. The next year, she published *Rena, the Snowbird* (1851). These were followed by *Marcus Warland* (1852), *Eoline* (1852), *Helen and Arthur* (1853), *The Planter's Northern Bride* (1854), *Robert Graham* (1855), and *Ernest Linwood* (1856). *Love after Marriage; and Other Stories of the Heart* appeared posthumously in 1857.

In his unpublished ''Autobiography,'' Hentz's son, Dr. Charles Hentz, described his parents in the following way:

She was possessed of one of the most lovely, sunny dispositions that ever existed—was charming in person & conversation, and was always a center of attraction wherever she went, and the attention she drew inevitably, always excited my poor, dear father's jealous temperament to a frenzy—My earliest recollections are associated with scenes of this kind, to which I was often a bewildered and frightened listener. (C. Hentz 18–19)

This picture of the Hentz's domestic life provided by their son allows the reader to speculate upon the reasons for the family's frequent moves. Perhaps more important, however, it highlights certain wish fulfillment and autobiographical elements in Caroline Hentz's fiction, including women who escape the restraints of socially approved female roles, and the jealous men who try to confine them.

MAJOR WORKS AND THEMES

Hentz's first novel, *Linda*, was also the most popular, going through thirteen editions in two years. It deals with themes and characters that would become standard in her novels, including a daring heroine and her mistrust of jealous men. Rather than accept marriage to her stepbrother, whom she does not love, Linda runs away and has a series of wild adventures. Hentz does not, however, glorify Linda's trials; she does not accept the nineteenth-century literary convention that suffering increases feminine beauty. Suffering simply makes Linda very ill.

Though she subverts this convention, Hentz was to support others. While she never owned a slave, she became a powerful voice for maintaining the institution. In its defense, she wrote *The Planter's Northern Bride* (1854), which is interesting both for its direct response to Harriet Beecher Stowe's *Uncle Tom's Cabin* (1852) and for its deviation from the adventurous, wild, and ultimately tamed heroine, though that figure does appear in the narrative.

In *Bride*, Moreland, a Southern planter escaping to the North to recover from a nasty divorce, meets and initiates a romance with Eulalia Hastings, the daughter of a staunch abolitionist. After overcoming her father's objections and getting married, the two return to Moreland's Southern plantation where Eulalia takes both Effie, first wife Claudia's wayward daughter, and the house slaves in hand.

The "angel" Eulalia assimilates herself with great ease and rapidity into the life of the Southern slave mistress and, though reared in a staunchly abolitionist household, is hurt and offended when "Mammy" would rather attend a church service than stay home to help her with the baby. "She missed the respectful, affectionate, spontaneous obedience which had made the relation of mistress and servant hitherto so delightful" (480). In describing this change, Hentz evidently is unaware that "gentle," angellike Eulalia is being characterized as missing the power a slave mistress possesses.

If we see female courage and pride in this novel, it is not in Eulalia, who becomes a staunch supporter of the Southern status quo, but in Claudia. Though she has committed no sin other than enjoying the company of people not of Moreland's class (among them her biological mother), she proudly refuses to answer when Moreland questions her fidelity. She later reveals to him that she would rather suffer the consequences of a sin she had not committed than to ease his unreasonable jealousy. She makes this confession on her deathbed, surrounded by the chaos that Hentz indicates is inflicted by undisciplined and ill-trained slaves.

It would seem that in the interest of supporting the Southern institution of slavery, Hentz was willing to recreate the wild heroine of other stories into a crazed ex-wife whose refusal to give up that freedom once wed has disastrous consequences for her soul.

Though Mrs. Elmwood says in *Lovell's Folly* that the Sutherlands are "no more responsible" for slavery than someone who "lives near, or in the vicinity of, a volcano," by the end of *Bride*, Hentz's narrator is warning the North not to interfere lest that volcano should erupt:

We love the North. . . . But, should the burning lava of anarchy and servile war roll over the plains of the South, and bury, under its fiery waves, its social and domestic institutions, it will not suffer alone. (579)

CRITICAL RECEPTION

Contemporary critics of Hentz's work were generally encouraging. Though some were wary about her use of sentimentalism, many felt that she balanced "spontaneousness and freedom" with "refinement, delicacy, and poetic imagery" (Baym 127). *The Planter's Northern Bride*, one contemporary reviewer asserted, maintained the "wisdom of loving the whole country," a view most felt was missing in Stowe's work (quoted in Schillingsburg 149). Although some critics felt that the South was portrayed unrealistically, in that Hentz had taken up none of its faults to balance its advantages, most were relieved to have a well-known writer responding to Stowe's overwhelmingly successful novel.

Most recent criticism has focused on Hentz's feminist heroines, her support of slavery, or more generally, her place in the tradition of sentimental novels. Critics by turns find her subversive and conventional, rebellious and complacent.

BIBLIOGRAPHY

Works by Caroline Lee Whiting Hentz

Lovell's Folly. Cincinnati: Hubbard and Edmands, 1833.
De Lara: or, The Moorish Bride. Tuscaloosa, AL: Wodruff & Olcott, 1843.
Aunt Patty's Scrap Bag. Philadelphia: Carey & Hart, 1846.
The Mob Cap; and Other Tales. Philadelphia: T. B. Peterson, 1848.
Linda; or, The Young Pilot of Belle Creole. Philadelphia: A. Hart, 1850.
Eoline; or, Magnolia Vale. Philadelphia: T. B. Peterson, 1852.
Marcus Warland; or, The Long Moss Spring, a Tale of the South. Philadelphia: A. Hart, 1852.
The Planter's Northern Bride. 2 vols. Philadelphia: Parry & McMillian, 1854.

Robert Graham. Philadelphia: Parry & McMillian, 1855.
Courtship and Marriage; or, The Joys and Sorrows of American Life. Philadelphia: T. B. Peterson, 1856.
Ernest Linwood. Boston: J. P. Jewett, 1856.
Love after Marriage; and Other Stories of the Heart. Philadelphia: T. B. Peterson, 1857.

Studies of Caroline Lee Whiting Hentz

Bakker, Jan. "Twists of Sentiment in Antebellum Southern Romance." *Southern Literary Journal* 26, no. 1 (1993): 3–13.

Baym, Nina. *Woman's Fiction: A Guide to Novels by and about Women in America, 1820–1870.* Urbana: University of Illinois Press, 1993.

Ellison, Rhoda C. Introduction to *The Planter's Northern Bride*, by Caroline Lee Whiting Hentz. Chapel Hill: University of North Carolina Press, 1970.

———. "Mrs. Hentz and the Green-Eyed Monster." *American Literature* 22 (1950): 345–350.

Hentz, Charles. [Unpublished autobiography]. Manuscript Department; Wilson Library, University of North Carolina, Chapel Hill, NC.

Papashvily, Helen Waite. *All the Happy Endings: A Study of the Domestic Novel in America, the Women Who Wrote It, the Women Who Read It, in the Nineteenth Century.* New York: Harper, 1956.

Schillingsburg, Miriam J. "The Ascent of Woman, Southern Style: Hentz, King, Chopin." In *Southern Literature in Transition.*, edited by Philip Castille and William Osborne. Memphis: Memphis State University Press, 1983.

———. "Caroline Lee Hentz." In *Antebellum Writers in New York and the South*. Edited by Joel Myerson. Detroit: Gale Research Company, 1979. 148–149.

MARIETTA HOLLEY
(JOSIAH ALLEN'S WIFE)
(1836–1926)

Kate H. Winter

BIOGRAPHY

On July 16, 1836, Marietta Holley was the seventh and last child born into a farm family in rural upstate New York near a village then known as Bear Creek. In an area that was still New York's frontier, her father, John Milton Holley, and her mother, Mary Taber, managed a modest living with the help of their children, and as a girl, Marietta learned domestic skills and farm work while she furtively wrote poems and stories on whatever scraps of paper she could find. At fourteen she finished her formal schooling in the one-room district school and began a lifelong habit of wide reading that fed her literary ambitions and enlarged her world. When her brothers left for the California gold fields in the 1850s, Holley helped support her sisters and aging parents by giving music lessons and bartering handcrafts. Innately shy, and nearly silenced by a speech impediment, she continued to write poetry in the popular style. At the age of twenty-one she saw her first work in print in the local newspaper, appearing under the pseudonym "Jemyma," the first of her pen names. Later she more boldly used "M. H." and the British spelling of her father's name, "Hawley." In 1867, *Peterson's* magazine first published one of her poems with "Marietta Holley" appended to it, and she began to realize a small income from her writing. Heartened by the response to her work, in 1869 she sent out two short stories written in the style of the dialect humorists and bearing her newest pseudonym "Josiah Allen's Wife." The choice of name was a shrewd one, disguising Holley herself and making her outspoken protagonist—a woman's rights advocate—seem less threatening than the zealous suffragists, thereby gaining a new audience for their feminist arguments. From that point on, her work appeared regularly in *Peterson's* as well as in the *New York Home Journal*, the *Christian Herald, Lippincott's*, and *Ladies' Home Journal*.

Her sense of herself as a professional writer was formed in part by the success of other women writers from the region: Frances Whitcher, Grace Greenwood, and Fanny Forester. With increasing confidence, Holley submitted a packet of verse and fiction to Mark Twain's publisher, Elisha Bliss at the American Publishing Company, and offered to write a book for him. He immediately recognized a new voice in the tradition of dialect writers and commissioned her to write *My Opinions and Betsey Bobbet's* (1873). Upstate New York had long had a tradition of political and feminist activism. Elizabeth Cady Stanton and Susan B. Anthony had brought the question of woman's rights to the center of public consciousness with the 1848 convention in Seneca Falls, New York, and Dr. Mary Walker and Frances E. Willard were both activists born and raised in the north country. Holley blended the impulse to reform with her literary aspirations and created a character who advocated the vote for women as the cure for most of society's ills.

The enormous success of her first book—five printings in the first year and simultaneous publication in Britain—launched a career that lasted over forty years, long after the peak of dialect humor was past. Holley's pseudonym became a household word as ''Betsey Bobbet Clubs'' and dramatic renditions of her comedy spread her humor and her message (Graulich 187). She remained on the family homestead, never leaving the county until her first journey when she was in her forties, halfway through her life. Thereafter she traveled regularly but not widely, venturing to Saratoga and New York City, Washington and Virginia, but preferring to have her friends and admirers visit her at ''Bonnie View,'' the grand Victorian house she built for herself in 1888 on the land her father had farmed. Despite repeated invitations to attend social and literary gatherings and to speak before audiences including the U.S. Congress on woman's rights, she refused public appearances. A solitary sort except for devoted family members, her friend Clara Barton, and an adopted daughter, Holley never married, choosing the writing life over matrimony, as she said. When she died on March 1, 1926, at nearly ninety years old, she had helped gain the vote for women not by petitions but by her pen. Among the local folk, initial feelings of distrust and envy had given way to pride in their region's writer, the woman who had given their voices and her vision to the world.

MAJOR WORKS AND THEMES

Holley's life could hardly have been more outwardly different from that of her extravagantly talkative heroine, Samantha Smith Allen, the rustic philosopher known to her reading public as ''Josiah Allen's Wife.'' Samantha, large and loquacious, turns her sturdy common sense to political and social matters, countering the prevailing arguments against temperance and woman's suffrage in a vernacular that underscored their absurdities and her own rock-solid country values. Her pragmatic feminism was dressed in the style of the masculine tradition of the vernacular humorists or "Literary Comedians" with its peculiar spellings, puns, fractured proverbs and biblical quotations, incongruous catalogs, anticlimax, extravagant images, and exaggerated dialect. In *My Opinions and Betsey Bobbet's* (1873), she introduces the indomitable farm wife as stalwart commentator on the injustices and indignities of women's roles within the genteel tradition. Samantha's right-minded philosophy is set off by the figures of the simpering, love-starved spinster and poetess Betsey Bobbet and the foolish patriarch Josiah Allen whose argument is always that woman's place is on a pedestal to keep her from the polls. Betsey Bobbet represents what Holley saw as the pathetic product of America's diminished role choices for women: Vain and silly, her only goal is marriage and the social status and economic security it might bring. She has no means of making a living and so spends her time writing dreadful sentimental poetry and looking for a husband. Josiah is ironically portrayed as having conventionally feminine traits as well: He is illogical, vain, submissive to his spouse, and full of genteel pretensions. It is Samantha who manifests the political savvy, independence, and fortitude that readers identified as masculine. Thus, she opened up the stereotypes of earlier comedy and fiction and undermined the assumptions that kept women from participation in government.

Holley created the first sympathetic comic female figure in American literature. In addition, hers was the first overtly feminist humor written by an American. In *My Opinions and Betsey Bobbet's*, Holley set the pattern for her remaining twenty-one books of fiction: After taking care of a series of crises in fictional Jonesville and the seasonal imperatives on the Allen farm, Samantha sallies forth on a tour or "tower," usually to assist some errant friend or family member. Her travels provide the opportunity for her to poke fun at the foibles of American middle-class culture and admonish and advise the social and political figures she inevitably encounters, for example, Horace Greeley and Victoria Woodhull. In her "episodin' and allegorin' "—her storytelling and commentary—she confronts the grim realities of women's lives after the Civil War and proposes pragmatic solutions based in law and Christian morality. Holley shrewdly put the arguments for the vote into the mouth of a successfully married woman, taking the marriage conventions of the domestic fiction of the time and showing how romance and lawful wedlock were incompatible, given the legal status of women. At the same time, she offered women readers a new kind of heroine: wiser, older, firm in her political convictions, and busy with the business of the world while still managing the domestic sphere with skill.

The formula was so successful that the next novel, *Josiah Allen's Wife as a P.A. and P.I.: Samantha at the Centennial* (1877), was devised as a travel book from the start. Holley was asked to visit the centennial exhibition in Philadelphia but refused, writing the book entirely from maps, guidebooks, and news accounts. Though she kept to the family homestead, her concern with her anonymity abated somewhat, and she included her own name in parenthesis under Josiah Allen's Wife on the title page of *My Wayward Pardner* (1880). Like the novel in verse that followed it, *The Lament of the Mormon Wife* (1880), *Wayward Pardner* critiques Mormon beliefs, especially polygamy. Having at last ventured outside the narrow limits of her region, she also declared herself as an author separate from Samantha by including her photograph with her signature in the front of her 1883 collection of stories, *Miss Richard's Boy*. As successful as the ventures were, the public preferred the comic sketches of the country wife encountering America in its finery and diversity, and Holley returned to the pattern. Her later books covered the World's Fair (1893), a grand tour through Europe (1895) and around the world (1905), the St. Louis Exposition (1904) and New York's resorts, Saratoga (1887) and Coney Island and the Thousand Islands (1911), these last three being the only places she actually visited.

In her remaining works, she tackles directly the social issues of most concern to her: race, children's rights, and the legal and social place of women in America. Holley's—and Samantha's—solution to America's social ills was to give women the vote. Holley pressed for reform in many of the areas women activists were working for. In *Sweet Cicely* (1885), she wrestled with the effect of alcohol on the lives of women and children. *Samantha among the Brethren* (1890) takes up gender and politics in the Protestant church. In *Samantha on the Race Problem* (1892), she considers racial politics after manumission. Her 1887 best-seller *Samantha at Saratoga* exposes the folly of fashion and gentility for women. Holley ended her career with *Samantha on the Woman Question* (1913) and *Josiah on the Woman Question* (1914). Samantha's humor won even resisting readers and made the principles of human rights and temperance accessible and palatable to a wide audience.

CRITICAL RECEPTION

Mark Twain called Holley's second Samantha book, *Samantha at the Centennial*, "brilliant, a great improvement on the first" (*Woman's Journal* 22 [1878]). It was the sort of backhanded praise that marked most reviewers' responses to her work. Rarely more than a brief notice rather than a penetrating commentary, the reviews were generous and warm, patronizing and condescending, sometimes within the same sentence. The sales of her books, the solicitations to lecture, and the advances from publishers all indicate that her work was immensely popular, and it was that feature that reviewers often focused on. One in the *Critic* in 1886 commented that hers was "the kind of humor which is 'popular,' though not destined to be immortal" (n.s., 5:93). Kate Sanborn excluded Holley from her 1885 anthology *The Wit of Women* because "every one who enjoys that style of humor knows [it] by heart'' (68) and " 'Samantha' is a family friend from Mexico to Alaska'' (69). Reviewers often referred to Samantha's popularity as though it made her work unworthy of serious comment. One wrote, ''Admirers of the rather obvious humor of 'Josiah Allen's Wife' (Miss Marietta Holley [*sic*])—and they are legion—will rejoice'' at the publication of a new book (*Dial* 47 [1909]:464). The appearance of *Around the World with Josiah Allen's Wife* (1905) evoked a similar response: " 'Samantha's' journeyings on this side of the ocean have amused thousands of readers, and they will doubtless be happy to accompany her on her foreign travels'' (*Critic* 47 [1905]:580). There is often a certain critical disdain as in this review from *The Athenaeum* in which her style is described as ''unbridled dialect and high-falutin' melodrama'': ''Afflicting as she is in her humorous moments, her strivings after pathos—and they are numerous and prolonged—are even more productive of acute mental dyspepsia'' (97 [1891]:50). Her critics misunderstood the way Holley was blending the vernacular humor tradition with the conventions of women's sentimental fiction and local color and travel writing, sometimes all in one book. Occasionally, a reviewer recognized the reformer at work, as in the editor's comments on *Samantha in Europe* where he lauds her ''common-sense philosophy and the high religious and ethical teachings'' that are clothed in ''such simple, quaint, and humorous garb'' (*The Arena* 15 [1896]: 688–689). Her poetry fared slightly better. In a letter to Holley, John Greenleaf Whittier pronounced one of her poems ''perfect,'' and reviewers were generally more gentle and less condescending when handling her verse, preferring it to her comedy. Her volume *Poems* met with the *New York Tribune* reviewer's moderated enthusiasm: ''We are inclined to put her poetry above her prose, though no doubt from a practical point of view there is no room for comparison'' (5 September 1888, 8). As twentieth-century literary values imposed different aesthetic standards, Samantha's narratives were seen more as burlesque than humor, droll dogma strung on a barely perceptible strand of plot. One reviewer commenting on *Samantha at the St. Louis Exposition* dismissed her work as ''satire and weakly witty garrulity'' (*Independent* 58 [1905]:212). In the spirit of Samantha's characteristic moderation, most critics recognized some virtue in the work, as this *Critic* reviewer concluded that Holley's ''eloquence has lost some of its freshness. Yet in these latest controversies with Josiah the humor is genuine, and, as usual, there is much good sense mingled with it'' (49 [1906]: 286).

WORKS CITED

Graulich, Melody. " 'Wimmen is my theme, and also Josiah': The Forgotten Humor of Marietta Holley.'' *American Transcendental Quarterly* (summer–fall 1980):187–197.

Sanborn, Kate. *The Wit of Women*. New York: Funk and Wagnalls, 1885.

BIBLIOGRAPHY

Works by Marietta Holley

My Opinions and Betsey Bobbet's: Designed as a Beacon Light, to Guide Women to Life, Liberty and the Pursuit of Happiness, but Which May Be Read by Members of the Sterner Sect, Without Injury to Themselves or the Book. Hartford, CT: American Publishing Co., 1873.

Josiah Allen's Wife as a P.A. and P.I.: Samantha at the Centennial. Hartford, CT: American Publishing Company, 1877.

Betsey Bobbet: A Drama. Adams, NY: W. J. Allen, 1880.

The Lament of the Mormon Wife. Hartford, CT: American Publishing Co., 1880.

My Wayward Pardner; or My Trials with Josiah, America, the Widow Bump, and Etcetery. Hartford, CT: American Publishing Co., 1880.

Miss Richard's Boy and Other Stories. Hartford, CT: American Publishing Co., 1883.

Sweet Cicely: Josiah Allen as a Politician. New York: Funk and Wagnalls, 1885.

Miss Jones' Quilting and Other Stories. New York: J. S. Ogilvie, 1887.

Poems. New York: Funk and Wagnalls, 1887.

Samantha at Saratoga or Flirtin' with Fashion. Philadelphia: Hubbard Brothers, 1887.

Samantha among the Brethren. New York: Funk and Wagnalls, 1890.

Samantha on the Race Problem. New York: Dodd, Mead, 1892; republished in 1898 as *Samantha among the Colored Folks.*

Tirzah Ann's Summer Trip and Other Sketches. New York: F. M. Lupton, 1892.

Samantha at the World's Fair. New York: Funk and Wagnalls, 1893.

Widder Doodle's Love Affair and Other Stories. New York: F. M. Lupton, 1893.

Josiah's Alarm and Abel Perry's Funeral. Philadelphia: Lippincott, 1895.

Samantha in Europe. New York: Funk and Wagnalls, 1895.

Samantha at the St. Louis Exposition. New York: G. W. Dillingham, 1904.

Around the World with Josiah Allen's Wife. New York: G. W. Dillingham, 1905.

Samantha vs. Josiah: Being the Story of the Borrowed Automobile and What Became of It. New York: Funk and Wagnalls, 1906.

Samantha on Children's Rights. New York: G. W. Dillingham, 1909.

Josiah's Secret. Watertown, NY: Hungerford-Holbrook, 1910.

"How I Wrote My First Books." *Harper's Bazaar* (September 1911).

Samantha at Coney Island and a Thousand Other Islands. New York: Christian Herald, 1911.

Samantha on the Woman Question. New York: Fleming H. Revel, 1913.

Josiah Allen on the Woman Question. New York: Fleming H. Revel, 1914.

"The Story of My Life," published serially. *Watertown Daily Times* (Watertown, NY), 5 February to 9 April 1931.

Studies of Marietta Holley

Blyley, Katherine Gillette. "Marietta Holley." Ph.D. diss., University of Pittsburgh, 1936.

Butler, Ellis P. "Marietta Holley." *Mark Twain Quarterly* (fall 1937):13.

Curry, Jane. "Women as Subjects and Writers of Nineteenth Century American Humor." Ph.D. diss., University of Michigan, 1975.

————, ed. *Samantha Wrastles the Woman Question*. Champaign: University of Illinois Press, 1983.

Graulich, Melody. " 'Wimmen is my theme, and also Josiah': The Forgotten Humor of Marietta Holley." *American Transcendental Quarterly* (ATQ) (summer–fall 1980):187–197.

Gwathmey, Gwendolyn B. " 'Who Will Read the Book, Samantha?' ": Marietta Holley and the 19th Century Reading Public." *Studies in American Humor*, series 3, no. 1: 28–50.

Morris, Linda Ann Finton. "Women Vernacular Humorists in Nineteenth Century America: Ann Stephens, Frances Whitcher, and Marietta Holley." Ph.D. diss., University of California at Berkeley, 1978.

Ross, Cheri L. "Nineteenth Century American Feminist Humor: Marietta Holley's Samantha Novels." *Journal of the Midwest Modern Language Association* 22, no. 2 (fall 1989): 12–25.

Williams, Patricia. "The Crackerbox Philosopher as Feminist: The Novels of Marietta Holley." *American Humor* 7, no. 1 (1980): 16–21.

Williamson, Mary Celeste. "Marietta Holley's Samantha." Master's thesis, Catholic University of America, 1946.

Winter, Kate H. "Marietta Holley, 'Josiah Allen's Wife.' " *Legacy* 2, no. 1 (spring 1985):3–5.

————. *Marietta Holley: Life With "Josiah Allen's Wife."* Syracuse, NY: Syracuse University Press, 1984.

MARY JANE HAWES HOLMES (1825–1907)

Lisa Logan

BIOGRAPHY

Mary Jane (Hawes) Holmes was born in Brookfield, Massachusetts, on April 5, 1825, the fourth daughter and fifth of nine children of Preston and Fanny (Olds) Hawes. Encouraged by an intellectual father and a mother who loved literature, and perhaps by her uncle, Rev. Joel Hawes, a Hartford minister widely known for his essays and sermons, Holmes came to writing early. She attended school at age three, began studying grammar at six, and taught school at thirteen; Holmes's first story was published when she was sixteen.

In 1849, she married Daniel Holmes, a Yale graduate from Brockport, New York, and the two moved to Versaille, Kentucky; there they had charge of Glen's Creek district school from 1850 to 1852. The couple then returned to Brockport; while her husband practiced law, Holmes began writing fiction, drawing on her experiences of rural life in Kentucky to produce her first novel, *Tempest and Sunshine* (1854). Thereafter, Holmes continued to write at the rate of approximately one novel per year, completing thirty-nine novels before her death. Her fiction appeared in the following periodicals, often in serial form: *People's Home Journal, Lippincott's, Good Literature, Ladies' Home Journal*, and *Woman's Home Companion*.

Holmes's novels were tremendously popular. In 1865 the *New York Weekly*, competing with the *Ledger*'s E. D. E. N. Southworth, ran *Marian Grey* and boosted its circulation by 50,000. Holmes's arrangement with the *Weekly* was also profitable for her; she received between $4,000 and $6,000 per story and even retained copyrights. Her books were in such demand that some libraries circulated twenty to thirty copies of each title. Her publisher, G. W. Carleton, issued many editions of each title, including inexpensive paperbacks.

While her literary success allowed Holmes and her husband to travel in England, Russia, France, the Mediterranean, and the Far East, she remained committed in her literary and personal pursuits to local small town life. In addition to producing an enormous body of fiction, she taught Sunday school, established a village reading room, was active in Brockport literary clubs, and entertained neighborhood girls with her talks on art, literature, and travel. Holmes died of a stroke on October 6, 1907, shortly after returning from her summer home at Oak Bluffs, Massachusetts. Her best-known works are *Tempest and Sunshine* (1854), *The English Orphans* (1855), *'Lena Rivers* (1856), *Meadow Brook* (1857), *Dora Deane* (1858), and *Marian Grey* (1863).

MAJOR WORKS AND THEMES

Holmes's novels portray the daily domestic life of young, white, marriageable, middle-class women with simplicity and humor to readers who were apparently hungry for her subject matter. They depict with realism and appreciation small towns in rural America and the manners and morals of nineteenth-century middle-class women. In her fiction Holmes includes scenes from her own background, including life in backwoods Kentucky (*Tempest and Sunshine, Marian Grey*) and in rural New England (*'Lena Rivers, Meadow Brook*, and *Dora Deane*), as well as scenes of historical interest to readers today, such as life in a poorhouse and at Mt. Holyoke Seminary (*The English Orphans*). *Meadow Brook*'s Rosa Lee seems based on Holmes herself; the novel ends with its heroine married to a wealthy planter and writing a novel that she believes will be a best-seller.

Holmes's plots are considered somewhat hackneyed today for their happy endings, rather clichéd Byronic heroes and sensitive or rebellious heroines, missed communications and letters gone astray, long-lost relatives found again. But they evidently spoke to a wide audience, who bought her books more than those of any other nineteenth-century writer, save Harriet Beecher Stowe.

In all of Holmes's novels, deserving heroines marry their handsome, older, wiser, and wealthier suitors. What makes them deserving is that they come from the country, are opposed to fashion and urbanity, and are, by nineteenth-century standards of femininity, good women; that is, they are self-sacrificing, modest, obedient, attractive, and possessed of common sense. Frequently, heroines seem based on the author herself. In *Meadow Brook*, for example, the heroine Rosa Lee is ambitious to become a schoolteacher, a goal that she achieves, like the author, by age thirteen. One of her best-known heroines, Lena Rivers, received her very practical education in the New England common schools, such as where Holmes taught as a girl. Holmes said of her own works, "I try to avoid the sensational, and never deal in murders, or robberies, or ruined girls; but rather in domestic life as I know it to exist. I mean always to write a good, pure, natural story, such as mothers are willing their daughters should read, and such as will do good instead of harm" (cited in Urness 208).

To emphasize her opinions about womanhood, Holmes often pits women, including sisters, against each other. For example, *Tempest and Sunshine* (1854) contrasts the rebellious, disobedient sister Julia (Tempest) with the kind, good, subservient sister Fanny (Sunshine). Fanny gets the husband, while Julia, finally tempered by experience, earns only the right to take care of their father. In other novels, the penniless but beautiful and simple heroine competes for her suitor with wealthier yet less pure women.

Lucy Brashear has described the purpose of these stories as "education for wifehood." According to Brashear, Holmes wrote to "advise young women to conform to the manners and morals prescribed by society" (19). A bad marriage of spinsterhood constitutes failure, and this failure is necessarily the *woman's* fault (and her poverty is therefore deserved). Arguing that Holmes's work is antifeminist, Brashear traces in these novels a three-pronged prescription for success, including physical beauty, personality, and academics (Brashear 21–23). Nina Baym, however, believes that Holmes's work self-consciously parodies generic elements of domestic fiction and advances ideas of women's independence (see *Woman's Fiction* 188–197).

Holmes's subjects and themes earned her a formidable place in the American literary marketplace of her time. Her treatment of everyday life, the middle class, and women's coming of age places her squarely in the tradition of what Nina Baym has called "woman's fiction." Perhaps what distinguishes her from many of her counterparts is her simple, straightforward style and her sense of humor.

CRITICAL RECEPTION

With few exceptions, Holmes's work was not reviewed in the better periodicals of her day, such as *Harper's* or *The Atlantic*, suggesting that her status, even then, was not quite "literary." A reviewer in *Appleton's Journal* observed this lack of critical attention, comparing her to Southworth, Stephens, and Evans, all of whom, "if statistics were given, would be found, we think, to have an immense constituency in all the small towns and rural districts, such as no English writer possesses here" (cited in Mott 246). Holmes's regular appearances in the *Weekly*, which was an inexpensive story-paper with a less-than-intellectual audience, perhaps only confirmed this status.

Holmes's work was praised, however, for its realism and its excellence in the standards of domestic fiction. For example, the *North American Review* (January 1858) appreciated *The English Orphans*, which "inculcates without intruding" (cited in Baym, *Novels, Readers, and Reviewers* 127). This reviewer also approved of its local color, writing, "the picture of rural and village life . . . deserve[s] to be hung up in perpetual memory as types of humanity fast becoming extinct" (cited in Papashvily 147). Another reviewer praised the domestic scenes in *Tempest and Sunshine* (1854), which are "written as only a woman could write" (cited in Baym, *Novels, Readers, and Reviewers* 207).

Her novels were at once praised and criticized for what readers have now come to associate with the virtues and pitfalls of nineteenth-century domestic fiction. While a reviewer in *Harper's* praised *Tempest and Sunshine* for its depiction of "life in Kentucky" and a plot "wrought with considerable skill," it noted "marks of haste" and "want of finish." This reviewer found "isolated passages of great power"; while the review commended the outlines of characters "admirable given," it also noted that they lacked "thorough elaboration" (278).

Finally, reviewers liked Holmes's good humor and lack of sensationalism. The *North American Review* said that *The English Orphans* "stops short of mawkishness" and that its "comic vein is worked with equal success and moderation" (cited in Papashvily 147). Her serial fiction, despite its lack of prominence in reviews in literary periodicals, is credited with having saved the *New York Weekly*. In 1888 Holmes authored an essay whose title best attests to her position in nineteenth-century readers' minds: "Men, Don't Be Selfish; a Talk to Husbands by the Ladies' Favorite Novelist."

WORKS CITED

Anonymous. Review of *Tempest and Sunshine*. *Harper's* (July 1854): 278.
Baym, Nina. *Novels, Readers, and Reviewers: Responses to Fiction in Antebellum America*. Ithaca: Cornell, 1984.
Brashear, Lucy. "The Novels of Mary Jane Holmes: Education for Wifehood." In *Nineteenth-Century Women Writers of the English-Speaking World*, edited by Rhoda B. Nathan. New York: Greenwood, 1986.
Mott, Frank Luther. *A History of American Magazines*. Cambridge: Harvard, Belknap, 1957.
Papashvily, Helen Waite. *All the Happy Endings: A Study of the Domestic Novel in America, the Women Who Wrote It, the Women Who Read It, in the Nineteenth Century*. New York: Harper, 1956.
Urness, Carol. "Mary Jane Holmes." In *Notable American Women 1607–1950: A Biographical Dictionary*, edited by Edward T. James. Vol. 2. Cambridge: Belknap Press of Harvard, 1971.

BIBLIOGRAPHY

Works by Mary Jane Hawes Holmes

Tempest and Sunshine; or Life in Kentucky. New York: Appleton, 1854.
The English Orphans; or, A Home in the New World. New York: Appleton, 1855.
The Homestead on the Hillside and Other Tales. New York: Miller, Orton, Mulligan, 1855.
'Lena Rivers. New York: Miller, Orton, Mulligan, 1856.
Meadow Brook. New York: Miller, Orton, Mulligan, 1857.
Dora Deane; or, The East India Uncle. New York: G. W. Carleton, 1858.
Maggie Miller; or Old Hagar's Secret. New York: A. L. Burt, 1858.
Hugh Worthington, a Novel. New York: G. W. Carleton, 1859.

Cousin Maude and Rosamond. New York: G. W. Carleton, 1860.
Marian Grey; or, The Heiress of Redstone Hall. New York: G. W. Carleton, 1863.
Darkness and Daylight. New York: G. W. Carleton, 1864.
The Cameron Pride; or, Purified by Suffering. New York: G. W. Carleton, 1867.
The Christmas Font, a Story for Young Folks. New York: G. W. Carleton, 1868.
Rose Mather: A Tale of the War. New York: G. W. Carleton, 1868.
Ethelyn's Mistake; or, The Home in the West; a Novel. New York: G. W. Carleton, 1869.
Millbank; or, Roger Irving's Ward. A Novel. New York: G. W. Carleton, 1871.
Edna Browning, or, The Leighton Homestead. New York: G. W. Carleton, 1872.
West Lawn, and the Rector of St. Mark's. New York: G. W. Carleton, 1874.
Edith Lyle, a Novel. New York: G. W. Carleton, 1876.
Mildred. A Novel. New York: G. W. Carleton, 1877.
Daisy Thornton and Jessie Graham. New York: G. W. Carleton, 1878.
Forrest House: A Novel. New York: G. W. Carleton, 1879.
Chateau d'or, Norah, and Kitty Craig. New York: G. W. Carleton, 1880.
Red-Bird. A Brown Cottage Story. New York: G. W. Carleton, 1880.
Madeline. A Novel. New York: G. W. Carleton, 1881.
Queenie Hetherton. New York: G. W. Carleton, 1883.
Bessie's Fortune. New York: J. W. Dillingham, 1885.
Christmas Stories. New York: G. W. Carleton, 1885.
Gretchen: A Novel. New York: J. W. Dillingham, 1887.
Marguerite. New York: J. W. Dillingham, 1891.
Doctor Hathern's Daughters. A Story of Virginia, in Four Parts. New York: J. W. Dillingham, 1895.
Mrs. Hallam's Companion and The Spring Farm and Other Tales. New York: J. W. Dillingham, 1896.
Paul Ralston. A Novel. New York: J. W. Dillingham, 1897.
The Tracy Diamonds. New York: J. W. Dillingham, 1899.
The Crompton's. New York: J. W. Dillingham, 1902.
Rena's Experiment. New York: J. W. Dillingham, 1904.
The Abandoned Farm, and Connie's Mistake. New York: J. W. Dillingham, 1905.

Studies of Mary Jane Hawes Holmes

Baym, Nina. *Woman's Fiction: A Guide to Novels by and about Women in America 1820–1870.* Ithaca: Cornell University Press, 1978. 175–207.
Brashear, Lucy. "The Novels of Mary Jane Holmes: Education for Wifehood." In *Nineteenth-Century Women Writers of the English-Speaking World*, edited by Rhoda B. Nathan. New York: Greenwood, 1986. 19–25.

PAULINE ELIZABETH HOPKINS (1859–1930)

Janet Gabler-Hover

BIOGRAPHY

Pauline Elizabeth Hopkins was born in Portland, Maine, to Sarah and Northrup Hopkins. Sarah Hopkins's second husband was William A. Hopkins, a tailor and Civil War veteran. Hopkins was related through her mother to the Paul family of Baptist ministers, who founded the first black church in Boston. She was also the grandniece of the poet James Whitfield. In her youth, Hopkins moved with her stepfather and mother to Boston, where she attended the Boston Girls' High School. She began her remarkable career at fifteen by writing a prize-winning essay on the "Evils of Intemperance and Their Remedies." She was awarded $10 in gold by William Wells Brown, author of the first "Tragic Mulatto" novel *Clotel* (1853). Hopkins also sang opera with her family's theatrical company "The Hopkins's Colored Troubadours." She wrote plays for the company as well, including *Peculiar Sam; or, The Underground Railroad* (1879).

Discouraged from playwrighting by a local theater manager (*Colored American Magazine* [*CAM*] [January 1901]:216), Hopkins worked four years as a stenographer for the Massachusetts Bureau of Statistics. Meanwhile, she lectured on black history at churches and schools and read drafts of her fiction to women's clubs. Hopkins's literary career began with *Contending Forces; or, A Romance Illustrative of Negro Life North and South*, the first and only surviving publication of the Colored Co-operative Publishing Company (Boston, 1900). Most of her other work appeared in the Co-operative's *Colored American Magazine (CAM)*, sometimes under her mother's maiden name, Sarah A. Allen.

Flanked by famous contributors, *CAM*, the first African-American general interest magazine, covered literary, social, historical, and political subjects of concern to African Americans. Hopkins is often acknowledged as the general editor of *CAM* from its outset, but she was not listed on the masthead until 1903. In 1904, new management connected to Booker T. Washington purchased *CAM* and moved it to New York, at which time Hopkins was fired under the guise of ill health. Likely sources of irritation for Washington were Hopkins's pro-DuBois agitationist politics and her endorsement of multiple societal roles for women. Sadly, she spent her final years in obscurity as a stenographer at Massachusetts Institute of Technology and died tragically when the bandages she wore to ease her neuritis caught fire from a nearby stove.

MAJOR WORKS AND THEMES

Hopkins adapts the popular form of sentimental fiction to pursue the theme of racial miscegenation in her fiction at a time when white racist ethnographers warned against the dangers of racial hybridity and argued the innate superiority of the Caucasian race. The ideological complexity of sentimental fiction, as well as the power of the African-American experience to transform superficial sentimental conventions into profoundities, justifies viewing Hopkins's works as American classics. By the end of Hopkins's first serialized novel, *Hagar's Daughter*, both a white and darker complected heroine are revealed to be mulatto; the sentimental trapping of secret identity becomes a profound metaphor for American race distinctions that are simultaneously revealed to be arbitrary and unjust determinants of human worth. In *Contending Forces*, hidden identity unravels to reveal the ''sin''—illegitimate child—of the near-white heroine who nevertheless marries happily. Her ''crime'' was not her own; she was raped by her lascivious white uncle. Antebellum black slave women were not ''essentially'' promiscuous but sexually brutalized by violent white men.

In her second serial novel, *Winona*, Hopkins's increasing hopelessness about white America's ability to transcend racial prejudice is shown by the removal of the mixed-race hero and heroine to England, although racially tolerant England is a fictive rather than literal landscape. Hopkins's final novel, *Of One Blood*, embraces Pan-Africanism by constructing an alternative history for the African race when her mulatto hero explores his unconscious and discovers the ancient Ethiopian city of Meroe, the cradle of all civilization. Hopkins uses William James's psychology to explicate the journey (Otten).

Throughout her career, Hopkins wrote on African history and African-American achievement, empowered black women, and appealed to the imaginative vision and moral nature of her white audience to break the bounds of their prejudice through acknowledgment of a common identity. But Hopkins's audience was small, and her eloquent appeals went unheard.

CRITICAL RECEPTION

The only contemporary reviews of Hopkins's published novel *Contending Forces* occurred in the *Colored American Magazine* and were predictably praiseworthy. There are no known reviews of Hopkins's serial fictions and little way of knowing how widely they were read. In the Harlem Renaissance, Hopkins was dismissed as a writer of sentimental as opposed to serious fiction. Neglect of Hopkins continued until Ann Elizabeth Shockley's 1972 essay "Pauline Elizabeth Hopkins: A Biographical Excursion into Obscurity" and the publication of Hopkins's four novels by the Oxford Schomburg Library in the late 1980s. A collection of her short fiction is also available from Schomburg and listed below. There are some puzzling blanks in the listing of Hopkins's final work for the *New Era*, which Hopkins coedited in Boston in 1916 with Walter Wallace, a founding member of the *Colored American Magazine*. For instance, Dorothy Porter lists "Topsy Templeton" as an article, while Ann Shockley and Jane Campbell describe it as a fiction serial. No bibliographical specifics beyond the 1916 date are provided, and the *New Era* seems largely unavailable.

Several issues predominate in Hopkins criticism. Critics question whether Hopkins's use of the sentimental form undermines the quality of her fiction. In addition, Hopkins's use of the near-white heroine is both indicted because of the Anglo-European standard employed to praise black womanhood and understood as Hopkins's attempt to gain empathy from her white audience. The future of Hopkins criticism appears promising as recent scholars begin to address Hopkins's complicated ideology, sophisticated narrative strategy, and scholarly eclecticism such as the use of modern psychology.

BIBLIOGRAPHY

Works by Pauline Elizabeth Hopkins

Published and Serial Novels

Contending Forces; Or, A Romance Illustrative of Negro Life North and South. New York: Oxford University Press, 1988; Reprint from Boston: The Colored Cooperative Publishing Co., 1900.

[Allen, Sarah A.] *Hagar's Daughter. A Story of Southern Caste Prejudice. The Magazine Novels of Pauline Hopkins*. New York: Oxford University Press, 1988. Reprint from *Colored American Magazine* (March 1901–January–February 1902).

Winona. A Tale of Negro Life in the South and Southwest. The Magazine Novels (see above) (May 1902–October 1902).

Of One Blood. Or, The Hidden Self. The Magazine Novels (see above) (November 1902–November 1903).

Short Fiction in Colored American Magazine

"The Mystery within Us." (May 1900): 14–18.
"Talma Gordon." (October 1900): 271–290.
"General Washington. A Christmas Story." (December 1900): 95–104.
"A Dash for Liberty." (August 1901): 243–247.
"Bro'r Abr'm Jimson's Wedding. A Christmas Story." (December 1901): 103–112.

[Allen, Sarah A.] "The Test of Manhood. A Christmas Story." (December 1902): 114–119.
"As the Lord Lives, He Is One of Our Mother's Children." (November 1903): 795–801.

Selected Nonfiction in *Colored American Magazine*

"Famous Men of the Negro Race. Charles Lenox Remond." (May 1901): 34–39.
"Booker T. Washington." (October 1901): 436–441.
"Famous Women of the Negro Race" [Series]. "I: Phenomenal Vocalists" (November 1901): 45–53; "II: Sojourner Truth" (December 1901): 124–132; "III: Harriet Tubman ('Moses')" (January–February 1902): 210–223; "IV: Some Literary Workers" (March 1902): 277–280; "V: Literary Workers" (April 1902): 366–371; "VI: Educators" (May 1902): 41–46; "VII: Educators" (June 1902): 125–130; "VIII: Educators" (July 1902): 206–213.
"Club Life among Colored Women." (August 1902): 273–277.
"Higher Education of Colored Women in White." (October 1902): 445–450.
[Allen, Sarah A.] "Latest Phases of the Race Problem in America." (February 1903): 244–251.
"Reminiscences of the Life and Times of Lydia Maria Child." (February 1903): 271; (March 1903): 353; (May–June 1903): 465.
"Venus and Apollo Modelled from Ethiopians." (May–June 1903): 465.
"How a New York Newspaper Man Entertained a Number of Colored Ladies and Gentlemen at Dinner in the Revere House, Boston, and How the Colored American League Was Started." (January 1904): 151–160.
"In the Editor's Sanctum." (April 1904): 297.

Other Dated Nonfiction

"The New York Subway." *Voice of the Negro* (December 1904): 605, 608–612.
"Dark Races of the Twentieth Century" [Series]. *Voice of the Negro* (February 1905): 108; (March 1905): 187; (May 1905): 330; (June 1905): 415; (July 1905): 459.
A Primer of Facts Pertaining to the Early Greatness of the African Race and the Possibility of Restoration by Its Descendants. Cambridge, MA: P. E. Hopkins & Co., 1905.

Plays

Slaves' Escape: or The Underground Railroad, 1879; later titled *Peculiar Sam, or, The Underground Railroad*. A Musical Drama in 4 Acts. Boston: N.p., 1879.
One Scene from the Drama of Early Days. N.p., n.d.

Anthologies, Bibliographies, and Collections

Ammons, Elizabeth, comp. *Short Fiction by Black Women, 1900–1920*. New York: Oxford University Press, 1991.
Pauline E. Hopkins Papers, Negro Collection, Fisk University Library.
Yellin, Jean Fagan, and Cynthia D. Bond, comp. *The Pen Is Ours. A Listing of Writings by and about African-American Women before 1910 with Secondary Bibliography to the Present*. New York: Oxford University Press, 1991.

Studies of Pauline Elizabeth Hopkins

Campbell, Jane. "Pauline Elizabeth Hopkins." In *Afro-American Writers before the Harlem Renaissance*. Vol. 50 of *Dictionary of Literary Biography*, edited by Trudier Harris and Thadious M. Davis. Detroit: Bruccoli Clark, 1986. 182–189.

Carby, Hazel V. Introduction to *The Magazine Novels of Pauline Hopkins*. New York: Oxford, 1988. xxix–l.

Gillman, Susan. "The Mulatto, Tragic or Triumphant? The Nineteenth-Century American Race Melodrama." In *The Culture of Sentiment: Race, Gender, and Sentimentality in Nineteenth-Century America*, edited by Shirley Samuels. New York: Oxford University Press, 1992. 221–243.

Johnson, Abby Arthur, and Ronald M. Johnson. "Away from Accommodation: Radical Editors and Protest Journalism, 1900–1910." *Journal of Negro History* 62 (October 1977): 325–338.

Otten, Thomas J. "Pauline Hopkins and the Hidden Self of Race." *ELH* 59 (spring 1992): 227–256.

Porter, Dorothy B. "Pauline Elizabeth Hopkins." In *Dictionary of American Negro Biography*, edited by Rayford W. Logan and Michael R. Winston. New York: W. W. Norton, 1982. 325–326.

Shockley, Ann Elizabeth. *Afro-American Women Writers, 1746–1933*. Boston: G. K. Hall, 1988.

———. "Pauline Elizabeth Hopkins: A Biographical Excursion into Obscurity." *Phylon* 33 (spring 1972): 22–26.

Yarborough, Richard. Introduction to *Contending Forces*. New York: Oxford University Press, 1988. xxvii–xlviii.

SARAH WINNEMUCCA HOPKINS (1844–1891)

Shelle C. Wilson Bryant and Patrick W. Bryant

BIOGRAPHY

Born in 1844 near Humboldt Lake in what is now Nevada, Thocmetony or ''Shell Flower'' is known to history as Sarah Winnemucca—a spokesperson for her people, the Piute Indians of the Great Basin. Sarah was born the fourth child and second daughter of Old Winnemucca (so called to distinguish him from Sarah's cousin Young Winnemucca). Highly regarded by his people, he became, with Sarah's help, ''Big Chief of the Piutes,'' as she recognized an opportunity in the white emigrants' desire to deal with only a few leaders with the authority to speak for her people (Canfield 4). Her mother, Tuboitonie, died at the Pyramid Lake Reservation in the spring of 1865 and does not figure prominently in Sarah's autobiography or other accounts of her life. Sarah's father and her maternal grandfather, Captain Truckee, however, were prominent figures in her life and the life of the Piutes. Captain Truckee, for whom the Truckee Rivers in California and Nevada are named, is said to have been an early guide to the emigrants who crossed the Great Basin (specifically, the Stevens-Townsend-Murphy party of 1844 and Captain Joseph Aram in 1846).

Captain Truckee fought with Fremont against the Mexicans and was known for his desire to live peaceably with the whites. He returned from his many travels to California with guns and ammunition and tales of the great towns and houses built by the white man. Sarah, however, who often heard stories of the violence of whites, developed an intense fear of them (Winnemucca, *Life* 11). Her fears were reinforced by a traumatic childhood experience. Rumors of approaching whites sent her tribe on the run. Burdened by two young children, Sarah's mother and aunt could not keep up, so they buried the children up to their necks in the sand and covered their heads with brush to protect them from the sun. Left there for the day, Sarah was extremely frightened, "thinking every minutes that I was to be unburied and eaten up by the people that my grandfather loved so much" (12). When she was still young, and still very much afraid of whites, she became ill from eating too much cake (a gift from a white family). During her illness, she was visited daily by a white woman her mother described as an angel—an experience that enabled Sarah to overcome her fears and, in her own words, come "to love the white people" (33).

As a preadolescent, Sarah was "adopted" by a white woman named Mrs. Stockton. During this time away from the Piutes, she worked for several white families and probably received her Christian name. In 1857, at age thirteen, Sarah and her younger sister Elma lived with the family of Major William M. Ormsby in Genoa on the eastern side of the Sierra. Sarah and Elma were expected to earn their keep as housekeepers and companions to Major Ormsby's daughter Lizzie. It was here that Sarah learned to read and write English, which quickly became her principal tongue (she learned Spanish by the age of ten).

In September 1859, Old Winnemucca requested that Sarah and Elma come home, as he was concerned by the increase in emigrant activity spurred by the discovery of silver in the area. Also in 1859, Captain Truckee became ill and asked, as a dying request, that Sarah and Elma be sent to California to be educated by the sisters in San Jose. According to Sarah, his wish was honored, and she and her sister left for the convent in the spring of 1860; however, they stayed only three weeks before being forced to leave when white parents complained about having Indians in school with their children. (There is some discrepancy regarding the historical accuracy of this memory [see Canfield 31].) In that same year, the growing discontent between the settlers along the Carson River Valley and the Piutes led to a bloody conflict known as the Piute War of 1860.

The Piute Reservation on Pyramid Lake was established as a result of this conflict. In 1865, the Piutes stole some cattle from the white settlers, and another conflict ensued. While the Piute men were gone, the whites set fire to the camps, killing women and children. Sarah lost a younger brother and shortly thereafter her mother and older sister.

In 1868, Sarah and her brother Natchez accepted an invitation from Captain Jerome to move to Camp McDermit in northeastern Nevada. There, Sarah served as post interpreter between 1868 and 1871. On January 29, 1871, Sarah was married to First Lieutenant Edward C. Bartlett by a justice of the peace in Salt Lake City (her marriage would not have been legal in Nevada, as there was a law against miscegenation). Bartlett, an alcoholic, squandered their income, and, disillusioned, Sarah left Bartlett and returned to Camp McDermit with her brother. She was officially divorced on September 21, 1876. Sarah would marry twice more: first to Joseph Satwaller on November 13, 1778 (there is no record of this or her marriage to Bartlett in her autobiography) and finally to Lewis H. Hopkins on December 5, 1881.

In 1876, the Malheur Reservation was established in southeastern Oregon.

Three years later, Sarah accepted the invitation of the agent in charge, Samuel Parrish, to work as his interpreter and later as a teacher. Parrish was well liked by the Piutes, and they begged him to stay when the government replaced him in 1876 with Major Rinehart, who mistreated the Indians. When Sarah reported his conduct, she was banished from the agency. Many Piutes also fled the agency, and some joined the Bannock tribe, who were eager for war.

When the Bannock war began in June of 1878, Sarah offered her help to the army. She demonstrated her courage by risking great danger to ride 223 miles on horseback and by wagon in just three days to reach her father and return him and his people and valuable information to the troops. She also served as interpreter, scout, and guide for General Oliver Howard during this conflict.

After the Bannock war, Sarah began to lecture, exposing the wrongs her people suffered at the hands of the government "Indian" agents. Her first lecture, in 1879, began a series of lectures across the northeastern states. Elizabeth Palmer Peabody and her sister Mary Tyler Mann took up Sarah's cause and introduced her to many prominent figures: John Greenleaf Whittier, Ralph Waldo Emerson, and Justice Oliver Wendell Holmes.

Sarah spoke boldly. She did not hesitate to enumerate the wrongs done her people and was not afraid to hold the government responsible. While she lectured, Sarah found time to write her autobiography, *Life among the Piutes: Their Wrongs and Claims*, her only book-length publication.

On July 6, 1884, the Senate passed a bill requiring all Piutes to return to Pyramid Lakes, and Sarah knew her work to secure a place for them at Camp McDermit was lost and with it her cause. She turned her attention to education and established, on her brother's farm, "The Peabody Indian School" (named for Elizabeth Peabody) for Piute children. The school faced financial trouble. It did not qualify for funds from the government because it was controlled by an Indian, and Lewis Hopkins squandered what money Sarah, with the help of Elizabeth Peabody, was able to raise for the school. Despite this economic hardship and an antagonistic political environment, Sarah managed not only to keep the school open for four years but to achieve some critical acclaim from visiting educators.

Lewis Hopkins died on October 18, 1887. Sarah soon retired to her sister Elma's home in Monida, Montana, herself in ailing health. She died on October 17, 1891.

MAJOR WORKS AND THEMES

Sarah Winnemucca's single prominent work, *Life among the Piutes: Their Wrongs and Claims*, has inscribed in its title the major themes and conflicts of her life and work. The title identifies the work as autobiographical and reveals its focus on vindicating the Piute people, but it also shows Sarah's struggle to appeal to a white audience without compromising her Native American values.

This struggle, tied as it is to Sarah's political goals for her people, permeates the fabric of her narrative.

Throughout her work, Sarah grapples with the rhetorical challenge of establishing points of identity between her and her audience of predominantly white women (see Georgi-Findlay) while maintaining her authenticity as a spokesperson for the "other"—the Piutes. The title of her book invokes this conflict by implicitly positioning her outside Piute culture through pronoun reference—"*Their* Rights and Claims"—and by referring to her life "among" them as if differentiated from her "current" life. Memoirs by white settlers writing about their experience with Indians have similar titles. General Oliver Howard, for example, uses the title *My Life and Experience among Our Hostile Indians* for his 1907 memoir, in which he devotes an entire chapter to Sarah.

Sarah and her editor, Mary Mann, consciously nurture the reader's affinity for *Life among the Piutes*'s narrator both thematically and extratextually. Mann frames the narrative with an introduction and appendices praising Sarah's moral virtue. Within the narrative, Sarah invokes bourgeois Victorian values by depicting herself as "lady-like" (e.g., riding side-saddle, 153), by claiming "I am powerless, being a woman" (139), and by portraying sexual violence as a threat to womanly respectability (Georgi-Findlay 236, 238).

In spite of her appeals to Victorian "respectability," however, Sarah does not pander to white Christians by portraying a conversion to "civilized ways" (Ruoff, "Three" 263). In fact, she is harshly critical of Christian hypocrisy with regard to Indian agents and their treatment of her people: "You have not got the first part of a Christian principle about you, or you would leave everything and see that my poor, broken-hearted people get home" (Hopkins, *Life* 239). Additionally, she cleverly inverts the imputation of savagery by alluding early in her book to cannibalism among white settlers. She further subverts white claims of moral virtue through the specter of sexual violence in the narrative. She couches her fear of being raped in ostensible terms of protecting her virtue, but it also functions thematically to show white men as potential predators. She reinforces her rhetorical stance by referring to would-be rapists as "white savages" (243–244). Nor does she appeal strictly to moral virtue to deliver her from such dangers; she relies on her own physical power: "If such an outrageous thing is to happen to me, it will not be done by one man or two, while there are two women with knives, for I know what an Indian woman can do" (228). By way of example, she tells of bloodying a cowboy's nose for touching her unsolicited (231).

Sarah Winnemucca's work is important in its condemnation of government policies toward Native peoples and its frank criticism of racism, and it is effective in its rhetorical strategy of appealing to a white audience to gain its readers' sympathy for the author's culture. The book is not expertly written; the prose is generally stilted and awkward, prone to melodrama, and often self-contradictory. But the narrative conveys an important voice of "otherness" in

American society that was crucial to nineteenth-century reforms and still resonates powerfully today.

CRITICAL RECEPTION

Prior to the publication of her book, Sarah was under critical attack from the press for her frank criticism of governmental policies in regard to the Indians. As she wrote, "My reputation has been assailed, and it is done so cunningly that I cannot prove it to be unjust" (Canfield 206). Elizabeth Peabody, who privately published her work *Life among the Piutes: Their Wrongs and Claims*, hoped it would act to garner support for Sarah's cause, show her to be virtuous and honest, and finally influence the Indian policies under consideration by the Congress. In fact, in an effort to boost the book's reputation, she wrote to the editor of the *Boston Daily Advertiser*, "I heard that there was an unfavorable notice of Sarah Winnemucca's book in the Advertiser when it first came out. . . . I want the Daily Advertiser to recognize her and her cause—and think you will agree" (Peabody 415).

Sarah's reputation was not primarily literary—she was known more for her lectures and political influence than for her writing. Her book was sold for $1 per copy in the lecture halls and homes where she spoke and through the mail. All profits helped defray the cost of the lecture tour and provided income for the Hopkins. Though the book was popular among reformists who heard Sarah speak (John Greenleaf Whittier and Mrs. Ralph Waldo Emerson each purchased $10 worth), the book apparently received little attention in the literary press.

WORKS CITED

Howard, Oliver O. *My Life and Experiences among Our Hostile Indians*. Hartford, CT: A. T. Worthington & Co., 1907. Reprint, New York: Da Capo Press, 1972.
Peabody, Elizabeth Palmer. *Letters of Elizabeth Palmer Peabody: American Renaissance Woman*. Edited by Bruce A. Ronda. Middletown, CT: Wesleyan University Press, 1984.

BIBLIOGRAPHY

Works by Sarah Winnemucca Hopkins

"The Pah-Utes." *The Californian* 6 (1882): 252–256.
Life among the Piutes: Their Wrongs and Claims. Edited by Mary Mann. Boston, 1883. Reprint, Bishop, CA: Chalfant Press, Inc., 1969.

Works about Sarah Winnemucca Hopkins

Brimlow, George F. "The Life of Sarah Winnemucca: The Formative Years." *Oregon Historical Quarterly* (2 June 1952): 103–134.

Brumble, H. David. *American Indian Autobiography*. Berkeley: University of California Press, 1988.

Canfield, Gae Whitney. *Sarah Winnemucca of the Northern Paiutes*. Norman: University of Oklahoma Press, 1983.

Fowler, Catherine S. "Sarah Winnemucca, Northern Paiute, 1844–1891." In *American Indian Intellectuals*, edited by Margot Liberty. St. Paul: West Publishing, 1978. 33–42.

Gehm, Katherine. *Sarah Winnemucca: Most Extraordinary Woman of the Paiute Nation*. Phoenix: O'Sullivan, 1975.

Georgi-Findlay. "The Frontiers of Native American Women's Writing: Sarah Winnemucca's *Life Among the Piutes*." Arnold Krupat, ed. *New Voices in Native American Literary Criticism*. Washington and London. Smithsonian Institution Press, 1993. 222–252.

Payer, Bernd C. "Autobiographical Works Written by Native Americans." *Amerikastudin/American Studies* 26, nos. 3–4 (1981):386–402.

Ruoff, A. LaVonne Brown. "Old Traditions and New Forms." In *Studies in American Indian Literature*, edited by Paula Gunn Allen. New York: MLA, 1982. 147–168.

———. "Three Nineteenth-Century American Indian Autobiographers: William Apes, George Copway, and Sarah Winnemucca." In *Redefining American Literary History*, edited by A. LaVonne Ruoff and Jerry Ward. New York: MLA, 1990. 251–269.

———. "Western American Indian Writers, 1854–1960." In *Literary History of the American West*, edited by The Western Literature Association. Fort Worth: Texas Christian University Press, 1987. 1038–1057.

Sands, Kathleen Mullen. "American Indian Autobiography." In *Studies in American Indian Literature*, edited by Paula Gunn Allen. New York: MLA, 1982. 55–65.

JULIA WARD HOWE
(1819–1910)

Nancy R. Wurzel

BIOGRAPHY

Born in New York City on May 27, 1819, Julia Cutler Ward was raised in an environment of wealth and distinction. Her mother, Julia Rush Cutler Ward, was the grandniece of General Francis Marion, the "Swamp Fox" of South Carolina, and her father, Samuel Ward, claimed descent from two early governors of Rhode Island. The Wards provided a happy, nurturing home for their six children, but when Julia Ward died following childbirth in 1824, the tenor of the household changed. In accord with his Calvinistic views, Samuel Ward raised his family, especially the three girls, in an austere atmosphere of virtual isolation. As much as she admired her "dear father['s]" philanthropic work and appreciated his generosity, Julia still perceived him as her "jailer" (*Reminiscences* 49). Nevertheless, she had almost seven years of formal education before opting for home study, and Samuel Ward provided excellent tutors. Unlike most girls of the antebellum era, Julia continued her education past the age of sixteen, and her diverse curriculum included French, German, Italian, Latin, history, piano, chemistry, mathematics, and philosophy.

Julia's academic accomplishments, seclusion, and religious training encouraged her "introspective tendency" (*Reminiscences* 57) as well as her love of literature. Like her mother, she composed religious verses, and a selection of her poems was published in the *American* by the time she was fourteen (Clifford 23). Only as an adult did Julia discover that her mother had also written and published poetry, a bold decision for the era. In fact, Rufus Griswold later included the work of each in *The Female Poets of America* (1849).

After her father's death in 1839, Julia observed a two-year period of mourning. Nevertheless, the marriage of her brother into the Astor family in 1838 increased her opportunities to travel and to develop her social and intellectual interests. She found companions who encouraged her literary efforts as well as her explorations of liberal Christianity. Julia thus became acquainted with many at the center of midnineteenth-century literary culture: Margaret Fuller, Charles Dickens, Ralph Waldo Emerson, George Ticknor, Elizabeth Peabody, and Henry Wadsworth Longfellow.

An intelligent, wealthy, and attractive young woman, Julia received several proposals of marriage, yet her selection of a husband appears to have been unfortunate. In 1843, Julia married the renowned physician Samuel Gridley Howe, who was eighteen years her senior. Director of the Perkins Institute for the Blind, abolitionist, philanthropist, and social reformer, Samuel Howe was less benevolent to his wife than to those whose predicaments he worked to remedy. He insisted that Julia devote all her energy to the family, and he restricted her intellectual endeavors, her social activities, and her financial independence. Each apparently loved the other, but their union was characterized by conflict, and Julia suffered through several periods of severe depression, especially from 1843 to 1853 (Grant 64).

Though the Howes traveled to Europe and often spent summers in Newport, Rhode Island, their home was in Boston, site of the Perkins Institute. For the first decade of her marriage, Julia was absorbed in raising her family and trying to please her husband. Despite her joy in the children, she felt isolated, as if her "voice [was] frozen" (quoted in Grant 76–78). By the mid-1850s, however, she had formed a friendship with Theodore Parker and renewed her acquaintance with Longfellow, both of whom influenced her to resume writing poetry. In 1854, Ticknor, Reed & Fields published *Passion Flowers*, her first and most successful volume of verse. Plays, travel narratives, other volumes of poetry, and essays on social and religious topics followed, as did regular publication of her poetry in the *Atlantic Monthly* after its inception in 1857.

Julia was raised with a distrust of the antislavery movement, but Samuel Howe's involvement with reform work changed her views, and she joined him in the abolitionist cause by the mid-1850s. Interestingly, Samuel did not mind Julia's writing in service of causes he adopted, and in 1855, when he became the editor for the *Commonwealth*, an abolitionist journal, Julia wrote editorials, reviews, and essays for him. Though she did not find the work artistically satisfying, it was well received.

Indeed, the Civil War provided the context for her supreme literary success: "The Battle Hymn of the Republic." In 1861, Julia's husband was commissioned for a medical examination of the troops, and she accompanied him to Washington. One day, when Julia and friends were returning from a review of the troops, they began to sing battle songs, and James Freeman Clarke urged Julia to write lyrics for "John Brown's Body." She agreed that she had always wanted to compose words for that "stirring tune." Later that night, Julia awakened and scribbled the words that had formed in her mind (*Reminiscences* 274–

275). She was pleased with the verses, which appeared in the *Atlantic* in February 1862.

In 1863, the youngest child and only son of the Howes died. Julia lapsed into a depression, followed by an exploration of philosophy, particularly Spinoza and Hegel, and she joined the Unitarian Church, for which she had a long-standing affinity. She felt called to share her religious views, and in the wake of the poor reception of *Later Lyrics* in 1866, she was drawn toward public speaking. After the Civil War, Julia adopted the cause of woman's suffrage, as did many of the abolitionists, although she had initially distanced herself from the movement. Her limited association with educated women predisposed her to believe that women required the direction of male authority, but her experience working with women in the antislavery movement persuaded her that women had intellectual potential on a par with men (Clifford 169–171).

Thus began Julia's career as a public speaker. Urged by Thomas Wentworth Higginson, Julia attended her first woman's suffrage gathering in 1868 and became president of the New England Woman Suffrage Association at the conclusion of that very convention. Julia was committed for the remainder of her life to woman's suffrage, but she was never a radical feminist. She sought to expand the educational and economic opportunities for women rather than transform their perceived roles as wives and mothers (Clifford 178). As a moderate, Julia worked to unite local suffrage organizations and helped found the American Woman's Suffrage Association (AWSA) in 1869. Involvement in social causes again brought journalist responsibilities, and Julia became editor of the AWSA's weekly, the *Woman's Journal*, for which she wrote articles and editorials.

Julia's career as a speaker flourished, and her interests expanded. In 1870 she became president of the New England Woman's Club, which she had helped to organize, and in 1871, she was chosen president for an American chapter of the Women's International Peace Association. She also worked for the ministry of women, an effort encouraged by Theodore Parker. Additionally, she joined the Association for the Advancement of Women (AAW) in 1873, an organization to foster the education of women. Julia often delivered papers for the AAW and served as president for almost twenty years. Although Samuel Howe objected strenuously to Julia's public life and her speaking engagements, he became more supportive of her work, for he also endorsed woman's suffrage. During Samuel's final years, Julia traveled with him, nursed him, and provided the companionship he desired. Despite continued quarrels, they resolved their difficulties and enjoyed more peaceful relations in the weeks before Samuel's death in 1876.

Julia was once a wealthy woman, but Samuel gained control of her resources, invested them unsuccessfully, and bequeathed his estate directly to the children. Consequently, Julia was left in a precarious financial situation, and she relied on public speaking for her livelihood. At home and abroad, she focused on the problems of modern materialism, and she worked to improve the welfare of middle-class women, especially their limited opportunities in the workplace and substandard pay.

Julia's reputation as a speaker increased as she aged (and coincidentally began to resemble Queen Victoria). Her personal dignity combined with her learned manner reflected favorably on the cause of woman's suffrage, and when she began an extensive tour in 1888, she found that her lectures on literature were in less demand than her talks on women and society. Nevertheless, she was treated as a distinguished literary figure. She served as a vice president of the Association of American Authors, and in 1908, she was elected to the American Academy of Arts and Letters, the first woman to achieve the honor. She died on October 17, 1910.

MAJOR WORKS AND THEMES

According to Julia Ward Howe, *Passion Flowers* "dealt partly with the strong questions of the time" (*Reminiscences* 229–230), including political struggles in Italy and the condition of the slaves in the United States. The poems also explore Howe's inner life with meditations on philosophy, personal relations, and nature. The verses are sentimental and romantic as the title "What I Said to the Dying Rose, and What She Said to Me" indicates. *Words for the Hour* (1857), by contrast, centers primarily on public events, and *Later Lyrics* (1866) explores Civil War themes as well as philosophic and religious issues.

Howe's drama, *Leonora, Or the World's Own*, depicts the seduction and betrayal of a village maiden by a soldier and their mutual ruin. For revenge, Leonora falsely accuses her lover of being a traitor to the crown, and he is hanged. Thus, Howe boldly presents sexual passion and portrays a woman exacting revenge instead of suffering remorse for her sexuality.

As Deborah Clifford observes, in "The Battle Hymn of the Republic," Howe expresses the "religious and nationalistic fervor" of the Union, enhanced by the conviction that God would support their righteous cause (147).

In *Margaret Fuller* (1883), Howe pays tribute to an early mentor and presents Fuller's life as that of an exemplary woman, a role model for the future. For Howe, Fuller epitomizes the independent woman who relies on her intellect, moral dignity, and pride as she joins the public discourse. Howe's autobiography, *Reminiscences*, embodies a similar endeavor, and she provides an intimate and detailed portrait of her own girlhood, marriage, and struggle for self-expression.

The individual lectures and essays of Howe encompass a variety of themes related to the social, political, economic, and spiritual position of women. The issue of woman's suffrage provides the focal point around which Howe's ideas constellate.

CRITICAL RECEPTION

Published anonymously, *Passion Flowers* was Howe's most successful volume of poetry; for example, George Ripley, the critic for the *New York Tribune*, relished the "spiritual history too passionate and intense for concealment." The critic for the *Southern Quarterly Review* praised the "wide and deep reflection," the "sorrow, yearning, love, care, delight, and all the elements of real, and thoughtful, and earnest life" (180–181). Howe also recorded favorable personal responses from Emerson and John Greenleaf Whittier but claimed the supreme compliment was hearing Parker quote her verses "from the pulpit" (*Reminiscences* 228). Indeed, the poems appealed to many, and when the book went into a second printing, Howe was identified as the author. The editor of *Putnam's*, George Williams Curtis, told Howe that *Words for the Hour* was a stronger volume than *Passion Flowers* but warned it would be less successful (*Reminiscences* 230). Few shared his opinion regarding its merits, and his predictions were correct. *Later Lyrics* was received even less generously. For instance, the reviewer for the *North American Review* enjoyed the war poems but lamented the frequent "introduction of some recondite fancy or some transcendental allusion" (644).

Nonetheless, Howe was encouraged by the publication of her verses and fulfilled her ambition to write for the stage. Performed in both New York and Boston, *Leonora* shocked audiences with its sexual imagery and challenges to traditional morality. One New York critic declared it "full of literary merits and of dramatic defects" (quoted in *Reminiscences* 230).

According to Howe's modest estimation, the "Battle Hymn of the Republic" was "somewhat praised on its appearance" (*Reminiscences* 275), but actually it soon became the theme song for both Union soldiers and civilians. No other work of Howe has been awarded such acclaim. Reviews of *From Sunset Ridge* (1898) cite "Battle Hymn" as its chief merit (Payne 52), and the lyrics, which were frequently recited at Howe's lecture appearances, remain her chief literary accomplishment.

Margaret Fuller appealed to the contemporary audience, although Emerson, Clarke and W. H. Channing's *Memoirs of Margaret Fuller Ossoli* was widely read. Writing for the *Dial*, Sara A. Hubbard noted its "purity of purpose and a capacity and effectiveness which have bestowed fresh honor upon womanhood" ("Life" 161). Perhaps not surprisingly, given the color and scope of Howe's life, *Reminiscences* was the most generously received of her books. Hubbard praised its "rich treasury of facts, anecdotes, and observations, relating to eminent persons and events of the last eighty years" ("Reminiscences" 79).

WORKS CITED

Anonymous. Review of *Later Lyrics*. *North American Review* 104 (April 1867): 644–646.

Anonymous. Review of *Passion Flowers*. *Southern Quarterly Review* (July 1854): 180–191.

Clifford, Deborah. *Mine Eyes Have Seen the Glory: A Biography of Julia Ward Howe*. Boston: Little, Brown, 1979.

Grant, Mary H. *Private Woman, Public Person: An Account of the Life of Julia Ward Howe from 1819 to 1868*. Brooklyn: Carlson, 1994.

Howe, Julia Ward. *Later Lyrics*. Boston: J. E. Tilton, 1866.
———. *Reminiscences*. 1899. Reprint, New York: New American Library, 1969.
Hubbard, Sara A. "The Life of a Noble Woman." *Dial* 4 (1883): 161–164.
———. "The Reminiscences of Mrs. Howe." *Dial* 28 (January 1900): 79–82.
Payne, William Morton. Review of *From Sunset Ridge*. *Dial* 36 (January 1899): 52.
Ripley, George. Review of *Passion Flowers*. [New York] *Tribune*, 10 January 1855.

BIBLIOGRAPHY

Works by Julia Ward Howe

Passion Flowers. Boston: Ticknor, Reed & Fields, 1854.
Leonora, Or the World's Own: A Tragedy in Five Acts. New York: Baker & Godwin, 1857.
Words for the Hour. Boston: Ticknor & Fields, 1857.
A Trip to Cuba. 1860. New York: Praeger, 1969.
Later Lyrics. Boston: J. E. Tilton, 1866.
From the Oak to the Olive: A Plain Record of a Pleasant Journey. Boston: Lee & Shepard, 1868.
Margaret Fuller. 1883. Reprint, Westport: Greenwood, 1970.
From Sunset Ridge: Poems Old and New. Boston: Houghton, 1898.
Reminiscences. 1899. New York: New American Library, 1969.

Work Edited by Julia Ward Howe

Sex and Education: A Reply to Dr. E. H. Clarke's "Sex in Education." 1874. Reprint, New York: Arno, 1972.

Studies of Julia Ward Howe

Clifford, Deborah. *Mine Eyes Have Seen the Glory: A Biography of Julia Ward Howe*. Boston: Little, Brown, 1979.
Grant, Mary H. *Private Woman, Public Person: An Account of the Life of Julia Ward Howe from 1819 to 1868*. Brooklyn: Carlson, 1994.
Hall, Florence Howe, ed. *Julia Ward Howe and the Woman Suffrage Movement*. 1913. Reprint, New York: Arno, 1969.
Richards, Laura Elizabeth. *Two Noble Lives: Samuel Gridley Howe and Julia Ward Howe*. Boston: Dana, 1906.

HELEN HUNT JACKSON
(1830–1885)

Kelli Olson

BIOGRAPHY

Born on October 14, 1830, Helen Maria Fiske spent her early years in Congregationalist Amherst, Massachusetts. There she would meet Emily Dickinson and become a lifelong correspondent with her. To her parents' consternation, Helen was a high-spirited, inquisitive child, unlike her more sedate, younger sister Ann. Her mother, Deborah Vinal Fiske, wrote her cousin: "Helen learns very well, but I do not drive her very much to make her very literary—she is quite inclined to question the author of everything; the Bible she says does not feel as if it were true" (Banning 11).

Deborah Fiske, creative in her own right, sent her young daughter letters from their household cat that Jackson later in life would edit and collect in the children's story *Letters from a Cat* (1879). Her father, Nathan Welby Fiske, was a professor of languages at Amherst College. Formally a Congregationalist minister, he espoused the Calvinist faith, which Jackson discarded later in life. When her mother became sick with tuberculosis, Jackson at age nine was sent to a series of boarding schools as her parents looked for an environment with enough discipline for her. By the age of nineteen, Jackson had lost both parents to tuberculosis and attended six schools. This frequent moving and traveling began a lifelong pattern for Jackson. Under her maternal grandfather's care, she transferred to the Abbott (later Springer) Institution in New York, boarded with the John Abbott family, and finally excelled scholastically.

At a ball in Albany, New York, Jackson met the governor's brother Army Lieutenant Edward B. Hunt, an engineer and physicist with great potential. They were married in 1852, and during their eleven-year marriage, she led an active social life, meeting many contacts who later would help her during her literary career. Such was the case when visiting Anne Lynch Botta's literary salon in New York City; there she met Parke Godwin, the assistant editor of the *New York Evening Post*, who would publish her first poem and prose piece.

Transferred to several New England posts, the Hunts were stationed four times in Newport, Rhode Island, a small artists' colony, and when her husband was transferred to less desirable locations, Jackson returned to Newport. There she socialized with the literati, including such distinguished writers as Henry Wadsworth Longfellow, William Cullen Bryant, and leading women writers like Caroline Kirkland, Margaret Fuller, and Lydia Maria Child. A friend and literary mentor, Moncure Conway remembered her: "Socially she was very attractive, brilliant in appearance and conversation, and with a charming play of humor, which in her early life had possessed a perilous tendency toward sarcasm" (271).

Her first child, a son born in 1853, died just under the age of one. Two years later, her second son, Rennie, was born. Thirty years later she would incorporate her child-rearing techniques into *The Training of Children* (1882). On October 2, 1863, tragedy struck the family. Her husband, then a major in the Union army, died in an accident while testing his invention, one that fired projectiles under water. In less than two years, Rennie was dead of diphtheria.

Alone at age thirty-five and independent by nature, Jackson turned to literary endeavors to support herself. Living with the Abbotts, she isolated herself and dealt with the grief of her son's death by writing poetry. She sent these poems under the pseudonym "Marah," and they were published in the *New York Evening Post* and *Nation*. After spending some time in her favorite town of Bethlehem, New Hampshire, she wrote a sketch and sent it to the *New York Evening Post*, which printed it with her pseudonym "H.H." The *New York Evening Post*, *Nation*, and the *New York Independent*, a liberal weekly, were her chief publishing outlets, although she soon broadened her base to the *Atlantic Monthly*, *The Christian Union*, and various children's magazines.

To accelerate her budding career further, she moved back to Newport in 1866 and into the same boarding house as Thomas Wentworth Higginson and his wife. Higginson became a lifelong mentor to Jackson, reading and commenting on most of her work and serving as her agent when she traveled to Europe in 1868. Through him, she met such influential people as Ralph Waldo Emerson, Julia Ward Howe, and Theodore Tilton, editor of the liberal weekly *New York Independent*.

Jackson was a quick learner and a versatile writer. Early in her career, she focused on poetry and travel sketches, using the pseudonym "H.H." In 1870, Fields, Osgood and Co. of Boston published her *Verses* with the agreement that she would pay for the plates. Her second book, *Bits of Travel* (1872), was published under the same arrangement. After the success of these two, she had little trouble publishing again. She began writing short stories for *Scribner's Monthly* under the pseudonym Saxe Holm; these stories were eventually collected into two volumes. Only a few knew she was the author, and the controversy over the author's identity increased sales. For only two of her works did Jackson consent to use her name rather than a pseudonym—*Ramona* (1884) and *A Century of Dishonor* (1881).

When negotiating prices for her works, Jackson quickly became a shrewd businesswoman. As she wrote James T. Fields, "I never write for money, I write for love, then after it is written, I *print* for money" (Banning 90). She would ask for the return of her manuscript if an editor did not pay the market price and then send it elsewhere. Once Scribner's refused to pay $800 for her first novel intended as a Saxe Holm story, *Mercy Philbrick's Choice* (1876). She offered the novel to Roberts Brothers, where Thomas Niles accepted it for his No Name Series, which marketed itself by the mystery of the authors. Jackson wrote another story for this anonymous series entitled *Hetty's Strange History* (1877). Finding a mutually rewarding relationship, she settled on Roberts Brothers, where twenty-two of her books were eventually published.

In 1872, Jackson spent two months in California, where she wrote sixteen installments for the *New York Independent* that were later included in *Bits of Travel at Home* (1878). Like many women writers, Jackson wrote for children. Her first book, printed in 1867, was a translation from French of Florain's *Bathmendi: A Persian Tale*. Published in the *Riverside Magazine* and *St. Nicholas*, she collected these stories in *Bits of Talk in Verse and Prose for Young Folks*, printed in 1876. Two years later, she published a book for older children, *Nelly's Silver Mine* (1878). In the 1880s, she published her cat stories.

In 1878, Johnsons Brothers published *Masque of Poets* as part of its No Name Series. Jackson contributed some of her own poems and persuaded Emily Dickinson to let her submit "Success." Perhaps the only one of Dickinson's contemporaries to appreciate Dickinson's brilliance, Jackson repeatedly encouraged her to publish. Jackson wrote her, "You are a great poet—and it is wrong to the day you live in, that you will not sing aloud. When you are what men call dead, you will be sorry you were so stingy" (Banning 225).

Plagued with chronic bronchial infections, Jackson moved to Colorado Springs in 1873. There she wrote many sketches of the territory, later collected in *Bits of Travel at Home*. In 1875 she married railroad prospector and banker William S. Jackson, six years her junior. They made Colorado Springs their home, yet Jackson traveled frequently. She traveled to the East to edit her work and discuss business with publishers and to California and the Southwest to research her sketches. Both Jacksons were active and often apart.

In the fall of 1879, Jackson attended a gathering that changed the direction of her life. At a reception of the Omaha Indian Committee, she heard Chief Standing Bear of the Poncas of Nebraska recount the experiences of his tribe with the U.S. government. Like many Native Americans in the nineteenth century, the government moved the Poncas from land legally their own to unproductive land. Although Jackson once ridiculed those who took up causes, she spent the last six years of her life as an advocate for the Poncas and other Native Americans. As a woman with a "hobby," she lectured and collected funds on behalf of the Poncas and helped organize the Boston Indian Citizenship Association. Putting her pen to work, she attacked Secretary of the Interior Carl Schurz in a series of letters to the editor and wrote essays arousing public sympathy for the plight of the Poncas. She wrote a friend: "I shall be found with 'Indians' engraved on my brain when I am dead.—A fire has kindled within me which will never go out" (Mathes 5).

Spending several months in New York's Astor Library, Jackson researched the relations between Native Americans and the United States. She wrote a stirring indictment of American policy in *A Century of Dishonor*, published in 1881. At her own expense, she sent copies bound in blood-red jackets to every congressman. Ben Franklin's words were emblazoned on the cover: "Look at your hands! They are stained with the blood of your relations" (quoted in Mathes 36). She then met with congressmen to lobby for justice for the Native Americans.

Her trip to California in the spring of 1883 was in the capacity of special commissioner of Indian Affairs in southern California to report on conditions of the Mission Indians. With her friend and interpreter Abbot Kinney, who called her "General," she toured southern California for a month to research and write the "Report on the Conditions and Needs of the Mission Indians." Her influence obtained legal resources for the southern California Native Americans to protect their property rights. Unfortunately, the Mission Indian bill, based on her report, did not pass in Congress, and most of her other recommendations were not effected until after her death.

In an effort "to move people's hearts," Jackson wrote her historical romance *Ramona* (Banning 200). In Colorado Springs, the plot had flashed through her mind in less than five minutes, and in New York, she wrote the novel from December 1883 to March 1884 with great passion and zeal, succumbing twice to "nervous prostration" and plagued by a persistent cold. She found herself writing 2,000 to 3,000 words a morning and working late into the night. She drew upon her trips to California for plot, scenery, and characters. In a letter to a friend, she wrote: "If I can do one-hundredth part for the Indians as Mrs. Stowe did for the Negroes, I will be thankful" (Banning 202).

Ramona was serialized in the *Christian Union* and published by Roberts Brothers in 1884. Certainly her most successful novel, *Ramona* received effusive praise and sold well, yet it did not spur the reforms that Jackson had hoped. However, since it was first published, *Ramona* has gone through over 300 reprintings.

In 1884, having written *Ramona* and returned from New York, Jackson fell down the steps of her home in Colorado Springs and broke her leg. When the bone did not heal properly, Jackson returned to California, hoping the climate would improve her health. She corresponded with naturalist John Muir about a possible camping expedition, but shortly thereafter, she died of cancer on August 12, 1885, in San Francisco. Dickinson wrote Jackson's husband: "Helen of Troy will die, but Helen of Colorado, never" (Banning 225).

Two years after her death, Congress passed the Dawes Act, the first comprehensive piece of legislature to establish a protective Indian policy.

MAJOR WORKS AND THEMES

During the last six years of Jackson's life, she championed Native Americans,
working in fiction and nonfiction on their behalf. Best known for her historical
romance *Ramona*, Jackson creates a Mexican Indian heroine who loves and
marries a noble Indian, Alessandro. Together they suffer intense hardships ranging from displacement from their village to the death of their child because of
the reservation doctor's neglect. Alessandro, mentally unstable from the injustices he has suffered, is killed for stealing a horse he mistook as his own. Jackson
based her plot on people and incidents discovered during her California trips
and hoped "to move people's hearts" (Banning 200). However, the harshness
of Jackson's message is softened when Ramona's "cousin" rescues and marries
her, and they sail to Mexico City to a new life. Clearly, Jackson is working
within the conventions of the domestic novel: She idealizes her heroine, promotes Christian virtues, and concludes with a marriage.

Working in nonfiction, Jackson wrote *A Century of Dishonor* to record the
injustices inflicted upon Native Americans by the U.S. government. Focusing
on seven tribes, she cites official reports, legal authorities, and treaties, showing
the broken promises of 100 years. She concludes by encouraging protection of
Native Americans and their right to property until the law would protect them
as citizens.

As a special commissioner of Indian Affairs, Jackson with Abbot Kinney
wrote *Report of Mrs. Helen Hunt Jackson and Abbot Kinney on the Conditions
and Needs of the Mission Indians in 1883* (1887). The many recommendations
were largely ignored; however, the report did lead to U.S. legal representation
on behalf of Native Americans to protect their lands. The report is most valuable
today for its historical information about the Mission Indians.

Besides being a crusader for Native American rights, Jackson throughout her
career wrote travel sketches that were first published in the *New York Evening
Post, New York Independent,* and *Atlantic Monthly.* Her European travel
sketches were collected in *Bits of Travel* (1872), and her sketches about her
native New England, Colorado, and California were collected in *Bits of Travel
at Home* (1878). Her sketches of the West particularly gave Easterners an entertaining glimpse into the territories and new states. After her death, Roberts
Brothers collected Jackson's sketches in *Glimpses of Three Coasts* (1886), *Father Junipero and the Mission* (1902), and *Glimpses of California and the Missions* (1902). Jackson's sketches reveal a sense of humor and a sharp eye for
nature and detail.

Jackson wrote most of her fiction under the pseudonym Saxe Holm. These
short stories, first published by *Scribner's,* tend to incorporate the conventions
of domestic fiction, celebrating the virtues of the hearth. A marriage or a re-

constituted happy home concludes most stories. Her heroines are idealized as pure, angelic, wise beyond their years, and just. However humble and self-effacing these heroines are in their speech, they are moral and/or spiritual leaders of their families and sometimes of the community. Jackson's novels *Mercy Philbrick's Choice* and *Hetty's Strange History* were published in the Johnsons Brothers' No Name Series. In these novels, she explores the sacrifices of her heroines, providing a character study and perhaps even questioning the absurdity of extreme self-sacrifice.

Beginning her career as a popular poet, Jackson worked within the confines of traditional feminine verse. She specialized in lyrical poetry, as did most women poets. Her topics range widely, beginning with poems on the death of her child and moving to nature themes. According to Emily Stipes Watts, Jackson contributes to American poetry by emphasizing stanzaic form to control feeling and thought in direct opposition to Whitman's "poetic excesses" (142–143).

CRITICAL RECEPTION

Jackson's first book of poems entitled *Verses* received glowing reviews by *Scribner's Monthly* and Higginson in the *Atlantic Monthly*. Emerson included five of her poems in his collection of American poetry *Parnassus*. In the introduction, Emerson wrote: "The poems of a young lady who contents herself with the initials 'H.H.' . . . have rare merit of thought and expression, and will reward the reader for the careful attention they require" (Whitaker 20).

With the publication of her second book, *Bits of Travel*, a collection of travel sketches, her reputation was firmly established. A reviewer for the *Literary World* found her style of writing "piquant, epigrammatic, and sometimes really witty" and praised her "sharp sense of the odd and ludicrous." A collection later published, *Bits of Travel at Home* was similarly praised, although a reviewer for the *Atlantic* found her too effusive about nature (42, 777–778).

Jackson's Saxe Holm stories drew much speculation about the author's identity. The first harsh reviews came with the No Name Series novel *Mercy Philbrick's Choice*. The *Nation* likened it to a Sunday school tract, while the *Saturday Review* called it "an elaborate mistake" (Whitaker 20). The *Literary World* found it "extravagantly ideal" and lacking in "naturalness" (7, 79–80). However, the novel sold well—8,000 copies in four months. Roberts Brothers published another of Jackson's books, *Hetty's Strange History*, in its No Name Series that also received negative reviews. A reviewer for *Harper's* noted that novels like *Hetty's Strange History* and *Mercy Philbrick's Choice* "tend to develop a morbid self-consciousness, a diseased introspection, and a dyspeptic appetite of the affection in the reader" (55, 939).

Jackson turned to children's literature with greater critical approval. *Nelly's Silver Mine* was praised by the *Atlantic* as a "grateful relief" from children's literature that deals with "the more barbaric side of Western frontier life" (42, 779–780). Typically, reviewers warmly praised her children's books.

Ramona was an instant success. First serialized in the *Christian Union, Ramona* was printed in book form the same year of 1884, selling 15,000 copies. To Jackson's disappointment, critics overwhelmingly praised the novel as a romance rather than as a deliberation on the plight of Native Americans. The *Critic* reviewed it as "one of the most tender and touching [love stories] we have read for a considerable period," and another reviewer described it as "a prose Evangeline" (Shinn 323). A few critics, such as H. E. Scudder for the *Atlantic Monthly*, found "the wrongs sink deeper into the mind than if they had been the subject of the most eloquent diatribe" (130). However, another reviewer criticized the novel as "no burning appeal, no crushing arraignment, no such book as Uncle Tom's Cabin" (*Overland Monthly* 5, 330). Beyond its critical acclaim, *Ramona* spawned a body of literature about the heroine and California.

After Jackson's death, publishers rushed to print her unpublished works as well as new collections of her writings.

WORKS CITED

Anonymous. "Book Reviews." *Overland Monthly* 5 (March 1885): 330.

Anonymous. "Current Criticism: Something Very Rare." *Critic* 3 (10 January 1885): 22.

Anonymous. "Editor's Literary Record." *Harper's* 55 (November 1877): 939.

Anonymous. Review of *Bits of Travel*. *Literary World* 2 (1 January 1872): 118–119.

Anonymous. Review of *Nelly's Silver Mine*. *Atlantic Monthly* 42 (December 1878): 779–780.

Anonymous. [Untitled] *Literary World* 7 (November 1876): 79–80.

Banning, Evelyn I. *Helen Hunt Jackson*. New York: Vanguard Press, 1973.

Conway, Moncure. "Mrs. Jackson." *Athenaeum*, no. 3018 (29 August 1885): 271.

Mathes, Valerie Sherer. *Helen Hunt Jackson and Her Indian Reform Legacy*. Austin: University of Texas Press, 1990.

[Perry, T. S.] "Recent Literature." *Atlantic Monthly* 42 (December 1878): 777–778.

Scudder, H. E. "Recent American Fiction." *Atlantic Monthly* 55 (January 1885): 130.

Shinn, Milicent. "The Verse and Prose of 'H.H.'" *Overland Monthly* 6 (September 1885): 323.

Watts, Emily Stipes. *The Poetry of American Women from 1632 to 1945*. Austin: University of Texas Press, 1977.

Whitaker, Rosemary. *Helen Hunt Jackson*. Boise, ID: Boise State University, 1987.

BIBLIOGRAPHY

Works by Helen Hunt Jackson

Poetry

Verses. Boston: Fields, Osgood and Co., 1870.

Verses. New and enlarged edition. Boston: Roberts Brothers, 1873.

Sonnets and Lyrics. Boston: Roberts Brothers, 1886.
Poems. Boston: Roberts Brothers, 1892.

Sketches and Nonfiction

Bits of Travel. Boston: Osgood, 1872.
Bits of Talk about Home Matters. Boston: Roberts Brothers, 1873.
Bits of Travel at Home. Boston: Roberts Brothers, 1878.
A Century of Dishonor: A Sketch of the United States Government's Dealings with Some of the Indian Tribes. New York: Harper and Brothers, 1881.
The Training of Children. New York: New York and Brooklyn Publishing Co., 1882.
Report of Mrs. Helen Hunt Jackson and Abbot Kinney on the Conditions and Needs of the Mission Indians in 1883. With Abbot Kinney. Washington, D.C.: Government Printing Office, 1883.
Glimpses of Three Coasts. Boston: Roberts Brothers, 1886.
The Procession of Flowers in Colorado. Boston: Roberts Brothers, 1886.
Father Junipero and the Mission. Boston: Little, 1902.
Glimpses of California and the Missions. Boston: Little, 1902.

Fiction

Saxe Holm's Stories. 1st ser. New York: Charles Scribner's Sons, 1874.
Mercy Philbrick's Choice. Boston: Roberts Brothers, 1876.
Hetty's Strange History. Boston: Roberts Brothers, 1877.
Saxe Holm's Stories. 2nd ser. New York: Charles Scribner's Sons, 1878.
Ramona; A Story. Boston: Roberts Brothers, 1884.
Zeph. Boston: Roberts Brothers, 1885.
Between Whiles. Boston: Roberts Brothers, 1887.

Juvenile Literature

Bathmendi: A Persian Tale. Boston: Loring, 1867.
Bits of Talk in Verse and Prose for Young Folks. Boston: Roberts Brothers, 1876.
Nelly's Silver Mine: A Story of Colorado Life. Boston: Roberts Brothers, 1878.
Letters from a Cat: Published by Her Mistress, "H.H." Boston: Roberts Brothers, 1879.
Mammy Tittleback and Her Family: A Story of Seventeen Cats. Boston: Roberts Brothers, 1881.
The Hunter Cats of Connorloa. Boston: Roberts Brothers, 1884.
Pansy Billings and Popsy. Boston: Lothrop, 1898.

Studies of Helen Hunt Jackson

Banning, Evelyn I. *Helen Hunt Jackson*. New York: Vanguard Press, 1973.
Byers, John R., Jr., and Elizabeth S. Byers. "Helen Hunt Jackson (1830–1885): A Critical Bibliography of Secondary Comment." *American Literary Realism, 1870–1910* 6 (summer 1973): 197–241.
Coultrap-McQuin, Susan. " 'Very Serious Literary Labor': The Career of Helen Hunt Jackson." In *Doing Literary Business: American Women in the Nineteenth Century*. Edited by Susan M. Coultrap-McQuin. Chapel Hill: University of North Carolina Press, 1990. 137–166.

Higginson, Thomas Wentworth. "Helen Jackson ('H.H.')." In *Contemporaries*. Boston and New York: Houghton, Mifflin and Co., 1900. 142–167.

Mathes, Valerie Sherer. *Helen Hunt Jackson and Her Indian Reform Legacy*. Austin: University of Texas Press, 1990.

Odell, Ruth. *Helen Hunt Jackson (H.H.)*. New York: D. Appleton-Century Company, 1939.

Schmudde, Carol E. "Sincerity, Secrecy, and Lies: Helen Hunt Jackson's No Name Novels." *Studies in American Fiction* 21, no. 1 (spring 1993): 51–66.

Whitaker, Rosemary. *Helen Hunt Jackson*. Boise, ID: Boise State University, 1987.

———. "*Legacy* Profile: Helen Hunt Jackson (1830–1885)." *Legacy: A Journal of American Women Writers* 3, no. 1 (spring 1986): 56–62.

HARRIET A. JACOBS
(LINDA BRENT)
(C. 1813–1897)

Terry J. Martin

BIOGRAPHY

Harriet Ann Jacobs, the great-granddaughter of a white South Carolina planter, was born a mulatto slave in Edenton, South Carolina, in 1813. Her mother, Delilah, was, in Jacobs's words, "noble and womanly[,] . . . a slave merely in name" (7). Her father, Daniel Jacobs, was a carpenter who, though himself a slave, was permitted to hire out his time. Her brother, John, was born two years later. Raised in a comfortable home, Jacobs was unaware that she was a slave until she was six years old, when, upon the death of her mother, she was placed in the care of her mistress, Margaret Horniblow. Horniblow taught her to read, write, and sew, promoted her Christian faith, and raised her "almost like a mother" (Jacobs 7). Jacobs expected to be emancipated by her. Yet when Jacobs was twelve years old, Horniblow died and bequeathed Jacobs to her niece Mary Matilda Norcom.

As Mary's property, Jacobs came under the power of Mary's father, Dr. James Norcom, who ceaselessly cajoled and threatened Jacobs to submit to him sexually. Jacobs turned in desperation to a sympathetic white neighbor, the young lawyer Samuel Tredwell Sawyer, who she hoped would buy her and free her and with whom she eventually bore two children, Joseph and Louisa Matilda. Norcom permitted Jacobs's children to stay with her grandmother Molly Horniblow, a manumitted slave who owned a house and sold baked goods for a living. However, Norcom refused to sell Jacobs, and when she overheard him plotting to send her children to his son's farm to be broken in and kept to prevent her from escaping, Jacobs took to hiding in the hopes that Norcom would give up his plan and eventually sell her children (whom she thought to purchase through an agent). After taking temporary refuge with both black and white neighbors, she remained secretly for seven years in her grandmother's garret, a narrow space with little air or light. Jacobs sewed, read, wrote, crawled for exercise, and watched her children and other visitors through a small hole in the wall that she had made with a gimlet. Her long confinement and exposure to heat and cold led to serious ailments from which she occasionally suffered the rest of her life.

While in hiding, Jacobs had letters posted to Norcom from New York and other cities to convince him that she had escaped to the North. She also succeeded in a ruse to have her children purchased from him by Sawyer. However, the latter did not subsequently free them as he had promised. Jacobs remained anxious about their susceptibility to being reclaimed as slaves by Sawyer, especially after he married and left to pursue a political career in Washington. Unwilling to leave the South without her children, yet increasingly alarmed at the danger to which she was subjecting her grandmother and family by remaining, Jacobs finally fled north by boat in 1842 after her near discovery by a neighbor. Louisa was already staying in Brooklyn with relatives of Sawyer, to whom Jacobs was later told she had been "*given*" (166).

In New York, Jacobs met her brother John, who had also escaped from his master. She found employment as a live-in baby nurse for the family of magazine writer and editor Nathaniel Parker Willis. Willis's wife, Mary Stace Willis, was a well-educated English woman who made special accommodations for Jacobs's fragile health and fugitive status. Jacobs was forced to flee with John to Boston on two occasions when she was apprised of Norcom's arrival in New York. However, she arranged for her son to be sent there, and she persuaded Sawyer's relatives to allow her daughter to leave New York with her. For the first time, she lived together with her family in relative freedom. Jacobs supported them by sewing and taught Louisa to read and write, while Joseph attended school.

When Mrs. Willis died in 1845, Willis persuaded Jacobs, who was attached to the baby and who sought better wages than her sewing yielded, to accompany his family to England. In her ten months in England, Jacobs was impressed by the virtual absence of racial prejudice, and she claimed later to have experienced grace in the household of a clergyman of Steventon. She returned to Boston where she lived for two years with her daughter. (Her son had meanwhile embarked on a whaling ship after suffering racially motivated harassment as a printer's apprentice.) Later she placed Louisa in a boarding school in New York and went to Rochester, New York, with John to open an antislavery reading room located above the office of Frederick Douglass's newspaper, *The North Star*. She lived there for nine months with Quaker reformers Isaac and Amy Post, participated in abolitionist sewing and discussion groups, and read abolitionist literature. Jacobs eventually confided her history to Amy Post, who suggested that she publish it for the abolitionist cause.

When the reading room failed to attract enough business, Jacobs returned to New York and met Willis's new wife Cornelia Grinnell Willis, who employed her to care for her baby. However, the passage of the Fugitive Slave Law in 1850 made Jacobs's situation precarious, for it made her liable to sudden seizure and legislated punishment for anyone caught aiding a fugitive slave. Nevertheless, when Norcom and later his daughter Mary Norcom Messmore and her husband came to New York to try to seize her, Mrs. Willis helped hide her. Then, after secretly negotiating with the Messmores, Mrs. Willis purchased Jacobs for $300 and emancipated her. Jacobs felt both grateful to Mrs. Willis and galled that her freedom, to which she believed herself naturally entitled, had been attained by purchase.

With her children's and her own future now secure, Jacobs turned her attention to her own autobiography. She at first tried to persuade Harriet Beecher Stowe to write it for her. However, Stowe angered Jacobs by a racist comment about Louisa, and Stowe wanted to include Jacobs's history in her *Key to Uncle Tom's Cabin* rather than writing it as an individual work. Therefore, Jacobs chose to write it herself. She sharpened her writing skills by sending letters to the *New York Tribune*. Convinced that her employer Nathaniel Willis was proslavery, she wrote secretly and at night, and her autobiography took five years to complete. After various difficulties finding a publisher, Jacobs finally published it herself in 1861 with editorial aid from Lydia Maria Child and black abolitionist William C. Nell.

Jacobs devoted herself during the remainder of the Civil War to relief work for black fugitives in the South. She used her new-found fame as an author to channel supplies gathered by abolitionist societies in the North to camps of refugee slaves, among whom she founded schools and orphanages and encouraged self-reliance. In 1868 she traveled to England to raise funds for them. In addition, her letters describing conditions in the refugee camps were published in the North. By 1870 she and her daughter returned to Massachusetts, where she was employed as Matron of the Women's Club in Boston. By 1878 she had moved to Washington, D.C., where, confined to a wheelchair, she was cared for by her daughter until her death in 1897.

MAJOR WORKS AND THEMES

"Slavery is terrible for men," Jacobs wrote, "but it is far more terrible for women" (77). *Incidents* (1861), the sole work on which Jacobs's literary reputation rests, was the first narrative by an African-American woman to deal openly with the theme of sexual exploitation of slave women by white masters. As a mulatto, Jacobs typified a class of slave women generally regarded as more desirable and therefore especially prone to sexual harassment. Yet *Incidents* challenges the stereotypical view of the slave girl as the helpless, ravaged victim at the mercy of the slave master's whim. Instead, Jacobs depicts her persona Linda Brent with, in Nina Baym's words, "intelligence, will, resourcefulness, and courage" (22)—qualities associated with the male protagonists of slave narratives. Brent's master's progressive attempts to coerce and dominate her only increase her will to resist, and in tricksterlike fashion, she outwits and outmaneuvers him at every step. With aphoristic irony, Jacobs concludes, "He that is *willing* to be a slave, let him be a slave" (26). *Incidents* forms the loosely disguised account of Jacobs's own heroic resistance to the dehumanization of slavery, and as such, the book is itself an eloquent assertion of her inviolable humanity.

Incidents shares many features in common with previous slave narratives. It presents a familiar (though nonetheless shocking) litany of abuses by slave owners, including the exploitation of workers; the separation of families; the deprivation of food, clothing, and shelter suffered by slaves; and even torture—often for purely whimsical and arbitrary motives; *Incidents* similarly portrays the corruption of white slave owners. In addition, it employs the first-person singular narrative voice, which was believed to add authenticity to such accounts, and it seeks to provide a factual document in which the narrating self is at the periphery rather than at the center of attention.

Yet *Incidents* also redefines the genre in significant ways. In what is widely regarded as the paradigmatic slave narrative, *The Narrative of Frederick Douglass* (1845), freedom is attained through physical struggle, education, and self-reliance. Of course, Jacobs, alias Brent, never physically overpowers her master, nor does her education constitute a definitive moment of liberation, as it does for Douglass (although her literacy does prove crucial in outwitting Norcom, alias Flint). Moreover, Jacobs emphasizes the importance of interdependence rather than self-reliance. Far from being an individual effort, her liberation depends upon a network of people who risk either their lives or well-being for her. In return, she dedicates herself to the slave community by discreetly sharing information (such as the dangerous nature of the muster following Nat Turner's rebellion) or by carefully guarding secrets (such as her knowledge of the whereabouts of Fanny) so as to ameliorate the condition of others. In addition, Jacobs brings a maternal ethic to the slave narrative: As a mother, she will not seek freedom at the expense of her own children. Jacobs chooses to remain in the South and watch over her children until she is sure that her own removal to the North will not place them in jeopardy. By the same token, Jacobs most honors women such as her grandmother, whose maternal care and protection extend to so many others both within and beyond her own nuclear family. It is, after all, with the memory of her grandmother that Jacobs concludes the book. *Incidents* thereby replaces the solitary heroic fugitive of so many male slave narratives with the image of the outraged and dedicated mother (Braxton 382), and it emphasizes the need for a communal response to oppression.

Jacobs also transforms the slave narrative by bringing a uniquely feminist perspective to her work. She places slavery in a more pervasive and insidious context when she refers to it as the "patriarchal institution" (146). The work's epigraph, a quotation from Isaiah 32:9, not only warns contextually against alliances with Egypt but also suggests that women who fail to protect their sisters in bondage may end up enslaved themselves. Jacobs shows that under patriarchy all women are oppressed. She documents how even the (white) wives and daughters of the slave owners suffer from the male prerogative to have concubines and sell the offspring. What is most painful to Jacobs, besides Flint's harassment, is the inability of her mistress to rise above her anger and jealousy to sympathize with Jacobs's misery as the unwilling victim of Flint's attentions. Jacobs similarly laments the readiness of slaves such as Jenny to betray her in order to gain favor with their masters. Patriarchy, Jacobs suggests, sows enmity and mistrust between those who ought to be natural allies in fighting against it.

Nevertheless, Jacobs offers a number of hopeful instances of communities of women working together (sometimes secretly) to check the worst abuses of patriarchy: The sister of her grandmother's deceased mistress pays $50 to emancipate Jacobs's grandmother when the aptly named Flint puts her, despite her long and loyal service, up for sale; a neighboring white woman and her loyal black cook hide Jacobs in their house to save her from Flint; Jacobs's grandmother likewise hides her for seven years; Jacobs is befriended, given shelter, and protected by both the first and the second Mrs. Willis (alias Bruce), and she is eventually purchased and emancipated by the latter. Although men such as Brent's uncle Phillip, friend Peter, and brother William are sometimes instrumental in helping Jacobs to escape and to cope afterward, Jacobs offers a new paradigm to counter patriarchy in the formation of communities of women based on mutual sympathy and aid. Indeed, *Incidents* makes explicit appeals to women readers (e.g., ''Oh, you happy free women'' [16]; see also 54, 55), whom Jacobs judges more likely to be compassionate both with her sexual harassment and with the plight of her children.

Incidents similarly constitutes a critique of the patriarchal concept of True Womanhood prevalent in Jacobs's day. As defined by popular sentimental and seduction fiction, women were expected to be submissive, pure, pious, and domestic (Welter 21). Jacobs, of course, rejects submissiveness outright: Submissiveness in a slave girl can only entail her corruption at the hands of the rapist slave master, while submissiveness in his wife merely aids and abets the crime (Jacobs cites the determined resistance of her mistress to her master's intended concubinage as an inadvertent source of protection to Jacobs herself). Although Jacobs to a certain extent values purity, or chastity, she nevertheless boldly justifies her own transgression: ''There is something akin to freedom in having a lover who has no control over you, except that which he gains by kindness and attachment'' (55). Jacobs thereby contextualizes purity into a relative, rather than an absolute, virtue and suggests that its rigid observance may actually be self-limiting and harmful to women. Of the qualities of True Womanhood, Jacobs most retains piety, yet not to the point that she will refuse to question God's justice in permitting slavery or overlook the fact that certain forms of piety can be misguided and pernicious, such as her grandmother's naive faith that God ''had seen fit to place [Jacobs and her brother] under such circumstances; and though it seemed hard, [they] ought to pray for contentment'' (17). Similarly, Jacobs's piety is qualified by her unwillingness to forgive Flint, for whom Jacobs confesses openly vengeful feelings (196). Finally, despite Jacobs's ceaseless striving for the domestic bliss of "a hearthstone of [her] own, however humble" (201), she acknowledges that her "story ends with freedom; not in the usual way, with marriage" (201). In fact, Jacobs's narrative emphasizes the need for economic independence and political justice (Doriani 207), without which domestic happiness has no firm foundation.

Jacobs's relation to her readers is highly problematic. Her tone oscillates between conciliation and defiance and between confession and self-vindication. Her self-abasing appeal, "Pity me, and pardon me, O virtuous reader!" (55), shades into the assertive declaration, "I knew what I did, and I did it with deliberate calculation" (54). Jacobs's ambivalence stems in part from her desire at once to woo Northern readers to the abolitionist cause and to expose the extent of the racism and sexism that she had encountered in the North. Thus, although her narrative sought to appeal to a white, Northern, educated audience, it also exposed many unpleasant facts about them: Northerners were uncompassionate (29), ignorant (55), easily duped by Southerners (73–74, 146–147), and silent before the South's moral outrages (29–30); in addition, the North was not truly free soil (158), for it merely aped the customs of the South (163) and demeaned itself in returning Southern slaves (28, 35–36, 44). Ironically, Northerners themselves were "proverbially the hardest masters" (44).

By the same token, Jacobs both upholds and daringly subverts the bourgeois moral standards of her readers. Although she couches much of her narrative in conventional moral terms (e.g., "I wanted to keep myself pure . . . [but] made a plunge into the abyss" [53]), she nevertheless claims that moral categories such as purity are inapplicable to slaves, who, she affirms, "ought not to be judged by the same standard as others . . . [for] the condition of a slave confuses all principles of morality, and, in fact, renders the practice of them impossible" (55, 56). Thus, Jacobs confesses her "sorrow and shame" (53) at having taken a lover out of wedlock even as she justifies the act and warns Northern readers not to sit in judgment on slaves whose situations they cannot understand. For Jacobs, the ethical value of any act is radically dependent upon its context, and the systemic abuse suffered by slaves in particular exempts them from the need to respect the rules of the system. Thus, it is no crime for a slave to steal food from the owner who has stolen his labor from him (48), and slaves are not bound to respect "the laws . . . of robbers" (187). Such statements contain profoundly subversive implications.

Incidents contains many other innovations as well, which no one has summarized better than Jean Fagan Yellin:

In [Jacobs's] hand, the pathetic seduced "tragic mulatto" of white fiction is metamorphosed from a victim of white male deception and fickleness into an inexperienced girl making desperate choices in her struggle for autonomy; the "mammy" of white fiction becomes not the white babies' nurse but the nurturer and liberator of her own children. In her hand, the madwoman in the attic sanely plots for her freedom; instead of studying self-control within a domestic setting, the young woman learns to engage in political action. (Introduction xxxiv)

Incidents is revolutionary in spirit. It is thus one with the genius of its age, the American Renaissance, which produced so many masterpieces concerned with the liberation of self and society. Yet as the work of a writer doubly oppressed as a woman and as an African-American slave, its contribution is unique, and it remains an insightful and compelling critique of American ideologies and institutions.

CRITICAL RECEPTION

The publication of *Incidents* made Jacobs a small celebrity within abolitionist circles. The book was published with testimonials by Lydia Maria Child, Amy Post, and George W. Lowther. It was reviewed in the *Anti-Slavery Bugle, Weekly Anglo-African*, and *National Anti-Slavery Standard*, and on February 16, 1861, a letter appeared in the *National Anti-Slavery Standard* praising the author for her veracity and "vivid dramatic power" but disapproving of her excessive moralizing.

Jacobs's authorship did not come to be widely doubted until the twentieth century, when it was believed that Lydia Maria Child had ghostwritten the work for her. However, in 1981 Jean Fagan Yellin documented that Jacobs was indeed the author on the basis of Jacobs's correspondence with Amy Post and Lydia Maria Child (see "Written by Herself"). As a result, Jacobs's work has enjoyed a resurgence of critical interest in the twentieth century. Critics disagree over whether Jacobs's use of the form and rhetoric of sentimental domestic fiction (including the Richardsonian seduction plot) ultimately restricts her or whether, by combining the form and rhetoric of sentimental fiction with that of the masculine slave narrative, she transcends and transforms both genres. (The first position is argued by Annette Niemtzow; the second, by Beth Doriani, Valerie Smith, and others.) However, critics agree that *Incidents* is the best slave narrative written by an African-American woman and that it significantly transformed the genre.

WORKS CITED

Anonymous. Letter. *National Anti-Slavery Standard*, 16 February 1861.
Anonymous. Review of *Incidents. Anti-Slavery Bugle*, 9 February 1861.
Anonymous. Review of *Incidents. National Anti-Slavery Standard*, 23 February 1861.
Anonymous. Review of *Incidents. Weekly Anglo-African*, 13 April 1861.
Baym, Nina. *Woman's Fiction: A Guide to Novels by and about Women in America 1820–1870*. Ithaca: Cornell University Press, 1978.
Doriani, Beth Maclay. "Black Womanhood in Nineteenth-Century America: Subversion

and Self-Construction in Two Women's Autobiographies.'' *American Quarterly* 43, no. 2 (June 1991): 199–222.

Smith, Valerie. *Self-Discovery and Authority in Afro-American Narrative*. Cambridge, MA: Harvard University Press, 1987.

Welter, Barbara. *Dimity Convictions: The American Woman in the Nineteenth Century*. Athens: Ohio University Press, 1976.

Yellin, Jean Fagan. Introduction to *Incidents in the Life of a Slave Girl, Written by Herself*, by Harriet A. Jacobs. Cambridge, MA: Harvard University Press, 1987. xiii–xxxiv.

———. ''Written By Herself: Harriet Jacobs' Slave Narrative.'' *American Literature* 53, no. 3 (1981): 479–486.

BIBLIOGRAPHY

Work by Harriet Jacobs

Incidents in the Life of a Slave Girl, Written by Herself. Edited by Jean Fagan Yellin. Cambridge, MA: Harvard University Press, 1987.

Studies of Harriet Jacobs

Andrews, William L. *To Tell a Free Story: The First Century of Afro-American Autobiography*. Urbana: University of Illinois Press, 1986.

Braxton, Joanne M. ''Harriet Jacobs' *Incidents in the Life of a Slave Girl*: The Re-Definition of the Slave Narrative Genre.'' *Massachusetts Review* 27 (1986): 379–387.

Yellin, Jean Fagan. *Women and Sisters: The Antislavery Feminists in American Culture*. New Haven: Yale University Press, 1989.

Zafar, Rafia, and Deborah Garfield, eds. *Harriet Jacobs and Incidents in the Life of a Slave Girl: New Critical Essays*. Cambridge and New York: Cambridge University Press, 1996.

SARAH ORNE JEWETT (1849–1909)

Perry D. Westbrook

BIOGRAPHY

Sarah Orne Jewett was born in South Berwick, Maine, on September 3, 1849, the second of three daughters of Theodore Herman Jewett, a country doctor, and Caroline Frances (Perry) Jewett of Exeter, New Hampshire. Descended on both sides from families prominent in their towns and states from colonial times to the present, Jewett was by birth a member of the so-called Brahmin class of New England, and she was fully aware and appreciative of her status as such.

Though she lived for extended periods in Boston, Jewett retained a deep and unchanging devotion to her native town. South Berwick was her home first and always. "I am proud to have been made of Berwick dust," she wrote ("Old Town" 609). As a child and throughout her life, Jewett suffered from rheumatoid arthritis, which intermittently interrupted her schooling and some of her activities as an adult. She received her elementary education at a local private school, after which she attended, with many periods of absence, Berwick Academy, from which she graduated in 1865. At home she read widely in contemporary and classic English and American literature. But more important in her education than the schools was her father, who was deeply attached to her and as a doctor understood her illness and her consequent emotional and intellectual needs. He was a strong influence on her throughout his life and hers. Often as a girl she would accompany him on his rounds among his patients in the nearby countryside, and in this way, she accumulated impressions of a large variety of people, some poor but others not, which served her later in her writing.

When Jewett was eighteen, her first published story, "Jenny Garrow's Lovers," appeared under a pseudonym in 1868 in *Flag of Our Nation*. It was of little consequence, but she soon placed a better story in the *Atlantic Monthly* after much revising as required by editors James T. Fields and William Dean Howells, both of whom served her well as literary mentors. "Mr. Bruce," as the story is called, is a tale of courtship laid in Boston and is untypical of Jewett's work. Her next story, "The Shore House," also published in the *Atlantic*, with its setting in the fictional port of Deephaven, is the first of her works to reflect her sensitivity to the people and places of Maine both past and present, which is the strength of her best writing. Other stories with Deephaven settings continued to appear in the *Atlantic* until 1877 when Jewett, on Howells's urging, combined and published them, augmented by some fresh material, in a loosely constructed novel with the title *Deephaven*. Reviews were favorable; Jewett's many literary friends in Boston were delighted; her career was launched. Book after book appeared for the next twenty-five years. Many of them were collections of previously published stories and sketches, for example, *Country By-Ways* (1881), *A White Heron and Other Stories* (1886), and *The Queen's Twin and Other Stories* (1899). There were also novels—*A Country Doctor* (1884), *A Marsh Island* (1885), *The Tory Lover* (1901)—and a few books for young people. The height of her achievement came in 1896 with the publication of *The Country of the Pointed Firs*, an American classic.

Jewett was a prominent figure in Boston literary circles, and she developed friendships not only among her editors but among such authors as Thomas Bailey Aldrich, James Russell Lowell, Harriet Beecher Stowe, John Greenleaf Whittier, Willa Cather, and Henry James. Some of these offered, and she accepted, useful literary advice, though she had developed her own distinctive style and tone. But her deepest friendships were with women, and the deepest of all, the most intense of all, was with Annie Fields, the wife of James Fields, the publisher. After James Fields's death in 1881, Jewett spent part of each winter in Boston with Annie Fields and part of each summer in Annie's cottage at Manchester-by-the-Sea north of Boston. The two traveled together four times to Europe, where they visited literary acquaintances. They were in fact almost inseparable. Attachments like theirs have been described as "Boston marriages," whether the term is appropriate or not. In any event, there is no record that Jewett was ever in love with a man or that at any time in her life she considered marriage a desirable goal. Recently the issue of lesbianism has arisen regarding Jewett and Fields. As close an answer as is possible is given by Paula Blanchard in her recent biography of Jewett: "Sarah Orne Jewett's love for other women was as passionate and absorbing as any heterosexual man's, but from all available evidence it never led to direct sexual expression" (Blanchard 54).

In 1902 Jewett suffered a serious injury in a fall from a carriage. Recovery was never complete, and her writing, other than letters, ceased. But she still spent time with Annie Fields. On June 24, 1909, she died of a stroke in the family home in South Berwick.

MAJOR WORKS AND THEMES

A formative influence on Jewett's writing can be traced to the teaching of the Swedish mystic Emanuel Swedenborg. She had been introduced to Swedenborg's thought by a retired Harvard professor, Philophilus Parsons, who was her friend during the early 1870s. Jewett had been brought up in the Congregational Church but had later become an Episcopalian. She did not embrace Swedenborg's complex and puzzling theology, but she was impressed by two of his teachings. One of these was an injunction to put to use to the best of one's ability the talents that God had given one to use as His instrument. The second and corollary teaching was that these talents should be employed for the benefit of humanity. Parsons, who for a time seemed almost a father figure in Jewett's life, read her work and praised or criticized it on the basis of these precepts, which exerted a strong influence on her writing from then on, though usually their presence was unobtrusive.

In a preface to an 1894 edition of *Deephaven*, Jewett revealed the extent of Parson's Swedenborgian influence. First she states in her preface that she had had a very definite purpose in writing *Deephaven*. She had been disturbed by the fact that summer visitors to Maine failed to appreciate or understand the local inhabitants. It saddened her that "timid ladies mistook a selectman for a tramp, because he happened to be crossing a field in his shirtsleeves" (3). Such attitudes, she thought, must be corrected, and she quoted Plato to support her purpose: " '[T]he best thing that can be done for the people of a state is to make them acquainted with one another' " (3). As a further support for her purpose, she quoted at length from George Sand's *Legendes Rustiques* to the effect that in the lives of rural folk, or peasants, we may catch glimpses into the past, even into prehistory. Jewett adds that there exists a "class of country people who preserve the best traditions of culture and of manners, from divine inborn instinct toward what is simplest and best and purest, who know the best because they themselves are of kin to it" (5–6). Though motivated by these purposes, Jewett was enough of a natural storyteller and literary artist not to let them render her work didactic. In *Deephaven* she was not concerned only with the town's admirable fisherfolk and farmers. Like many of an actual small New England seaport, Deephaven had once had a class of gentry who lived by "tradition and time-honored custom" (4) but whom changing times were sweeping away.

Deephaven is actually a series of stories or episodes held together by a loosely constructed frame narrative. Two upper-class city-bred young women pass a summer vacation in a mansion once owned by the deceased aunt of one of them. As the days pass, the two experience a gradual and pleasant discovery of an unfamiliar way of life, mainly through the many acquaintances they readily make. They have easy access to the homes of the former gentry. They chat with fishermen, farmers, and retired sea captains. They are welcomed by many women of the town. Most remarkable among them is the versatile Mrs. Patton, whose talents and achievements bring to mind Elmira Todd, the chief character in *The Country of the Pointed Firs*. Several other women, living alone, impress the girls (as Jewett calls them) with their ability to find contentment despite their material poverty. Jewett leads the girls and her readers through all the economic and social strata of Deephaven society. Included is a meeting with an impoverished farmer outside of town, whose misery and finally his funeral Jewett describes in poignant detail.

In a collection of essays, *Country By-Ways* (1881), Jewett, dropping any pretense of fiction, takes the reader on outings in her native Berwick, focusing on the past as well as the present. One essay, "River Driftwood," describes the author's leisurely progress in a rowboat downstream on the Pisquataqua River. As she drifts along with the tide, she muses on various sites that figured largely in Berwick's history. She gives close attention to the Hamilton House, a stately prerevolutionary mansion that once had been the home of a family with the way of life that she praised in *Deephaven*. The second sketch of major interest in *Country By-Ways*, "An October Ride," tells of a horseback ride that Jewett takes in the fields and woods near Berwick. She describes the overgrown meadows and pastures, the deserted farms, the cellar holes, of a region abandoned by its population. A house on the verge of ruin is central to the sketch. Caught in a rain shower, the author finds shelter in the house. She escorts the reader through it, commenting on its still-discernible former attractions. It had been the home of a beloved and venerated minister, long dead, who had presided over a now-extinct parish. Waiting out the shower, the narrator lights a fire on the hearth, bringing back a moment of warmth into the chill of decay.

Jewett's nostalgia for the past is best expressed in sketches like these and the ones in *Deephaven*. Two books in which she attempts to deal with history more objectively were less successful. In *The Story of the Normans* (1887), written for young people, her theme is the arguable one that the greatness of England and the English (she was an ardent Anglophile) is attributable to the Normans. Her efforts were largely unconvincing. She was also far from her best in her only historical novel, *The Tory Lover*, laid during the American Revolution with some of the action occurring in Berwick. Henry James, on reading it, urged her to return to her customary themes and subjects.

In truth, Jewett was inept at writing novels of the traditional sort. She was best in writing short stories and sketches either as separate pieces or ones loosely strung together as in *Deephaven* and *Pointed Firs*. However, in addition to *The Tory Lover*, two of her efforts at lengthy, plotted fiction deserve notice. *A Country Doctor* (1884), drawing in part from Jewett's own experiences, is the story of an orphaned girl who, taken into the home of a doctor, accompanies him on his rounds, as Jewett had done with her father. The girl develops an ambition to become a doctor herself (as Jewett may have temporarily done), but she has a suitor who wishes to marry her. Marriage would, of course, be the socially more acceptable choice for a young woman at that time, but she defies conventional opinion and pressures and chooses to study medicine. *A Country Doctor* was soon followed by another novel, *A Marsh Island* (1885). As in much of Jewett's writing, place, or setting, dominates in it. Here the setting is an area of dry land, an island, in the midst of one of the salt marshes in southwestern Maine. On the island lives a farming family who works the land and harvests the salt hay. The plot is rather uneventful, with a minimum of conflict. Primarily, it is a paean to the beauty of the marsh and a celebration of the harmony between those who live there and their natural surroundings. Jewett shared with her father the Emersonian conviction that nature is a source of moral and spiritual strength in human lives.

That Transcendental conviction is central to one of Jewett's most admired and most frequently anthologized stories, "A White Heron." In it a young girl, brought up in a city but now living with her grandmother on a lonely farm, passes her time wandering in the woods and fields, for there are no playmates. One day an ornithologist, a young man armed with a gun, appears. He is seeking a white heron that he has heard is nesting in that area, and he offers the girl $10 if she can tell him the whereabouts of the nest. The girl is attracted by the offer and could give the man, to whom she is drawn, the information he seeks. Thus, a conflict occurs in the girl's mind. Before dawn of the day after the man's arrival, she slips out of the house and into the woods, where she climbs to the top of a mighty pine tree. The tree seems to envelop her almost lovingly in its branches as she makes her way upward. From the top, as the sun rises over the ocean, she sees the heron flying to its nest. That morning, when the man questions her again, he gets no answer. The child has developed a loyalty to nature that in this instance is stronger than her loyalty to her own kind.

In 1896 Jewett's masterpiece *The Country of the Pointed Firs* was published by Houghton Mifflin. In it she has created a world in miniature, a little coastal village where the inhabitants embody in their lives and characters all that Jewett valued most or considered most significant in the human condition. The location of her fictional village, Dunnet Landing, is on a section of the Maine coast where Jewett and Fields had vacationed. The setting is lovely and is described lovingly and fully—the rocky shoreline, the pointed firs, the islands offshore, human dwellings that look as much a part of the landscape as the boulders and ledges cropping out of the cleared land.

The narrator, an author, had come to Dunnet Landing to find solitude in which to write, but she soon becomes a part of its life and is deeply impressed by what her involvement reveals to her. Almost at once she and her landlady—the widow Elmira Todd—become close friends. Mrs. Todd is an herbalist, actually an herbal doctor, who ministers to the townspeople. Though there is a medical doctor, with whom she is on good terms, her services are in constant demand. In the village, she is respected as possessing a profound and time-honored knowledge. As the narrator suggests, she enjoys the respect that a sibyl would command in a more primitive society. Growing some of her herbs in her own garden and gathering others in the fields and woods, Mrs. Todd seems privy to powers of nature not known to ordinary humanity.

The narrator becomes acquainted with many local people, all of them distinct individuals, held together by ties of community and a common, shared past. The most striking among them are women, all of them strong in character and self-reliance, especially Mrs. Todd. Others are Mrs. Blackett, Mrs. Todd's mother, who lives with her sixty-year-old son on a nearby island; Esther Hight, who succeeds at farming land where men had failed; Joanna Todd, who for years has chosen to live alone on an outer island, pathetic perhaps but accepted, as the narrator points out, in the same way an anchorite would have been in the Middle Ages.

In the life of Dunnet Landing age-old rituals persist. Most impressive in the narrator's view is a family reunion, that of the Bowden family, which she attends with Mrs. Todd and Mrs. Blackett. By sailboat and by buggy, members of the Bowden family, to which almost everyone in the region seems connected, converge on the original Bowden homestead. The feast that is the main event is held in a grove to which the people repair in solemn procession. As Jewett puts it, they

might have been a company of ancient Greeks going . . . to worship the god of harvests. . . . It was strangely moving to see this and to make a part of it. The sky, the sea, have watched poor humanity at its rites so long; we were no more a New England family celebrating its own existence and simple progress; we carried the tokens and inheritance of all such households from which this had descended, and we were only the latest of our line. (90)

Jewett thus finds in the life of Dunnet Landing a timelessness that is related to its strength. But it draws its strength from another source as well. On the drive to the reunion, Mrs. Todd points to a flourishing ash tree in a field as they pass by. Previously, she remarks, the tree had seemed to be dying. She readily explains its renewed vigor: "Grown trees act that way sometimes, same's folks. . . . There's sometimes a good hearty tree growin' right out of the bare rock, out o' some crack that holds the roots. . . . You lay your ear down to the ground an' you'll hear a little stream runnin'. Every such tree has got its own livin' spring; there's folks made to match 'em" (84). And she might have added that there are communities like Dunnet Landing, indeed, the human community as a whole, that must find the living waters that nature provides if they hope to flourish.

CRITICAL RECEPTION

Early reviewers approved of Jewett's work for its local color. The intention of local color writing in general was to reveal the ways of life in a certain region to people living elsewhere. Jewett herself had stated that this was one of her incentives. But soon other themes appeared in her writings. Her reputation was established by *Deephaven*, which was reviewed favorably by William Dean

Howells. A champion of literary realism, he was especially pleased by the book's capture of ''the very tint and form of reality . . . while over the whole is cast a light of the sweetest and gentlest humor and of a sympathy as tender as it is intelligent'' (Nagel 25). If he detected any trace of sentimentality, as other critics have done, Howells did not mention it.

Two years later in the *Atlantic*, Horace E. Scudder, reviewing Jewett's collection of stories and sketches *Old Friends and New* (1879), did hint at a tendency toward the sentimental when he referred to ''the womanly kindness which pervades her writings'' (Nagel 127). He also comments on her predilection for writing about elderly women whom she presents ''in their dignity and homely truthfulness'' but lets ''us smile quietly with her at their quaintness.'' He notes that ''the motive of love as a passion between the young is almost wholly absent from these stories'' (Nagel 28).

The first comprehensive critique of Jewett's writing, Charles Miner Thompson's ''The Art of Miss Jewett,'' appeared in the *Atlantic* in May 1904. Thompson's approach is through Jewett's biography. He points out that she was a member of a long-established class of cultured New Englanders about whom she wrote realistically and sympathetically. But she also lived in a small town and was well acquainted with humbler folk and wrote about their lives with accuracy and respect. From this background, Thompson believes, Jewett was able to create an integrated picture of New England. He praises her avoidance of sentimentality, her restrained humor, and the simplicity of her style. Though she is sensitive to suffering, Thompson notes, she shuns tragedy and ugliness.

In the meantime, Jewett had been receiving attention in France. A member of the staff of *Le Revue des Deux Mondes*, Thérèse Blanc, who was keenly interested in American literature and culture, wrote a thoughtful essay on Jewett's *A Country Doctor*, titled ''Le Roman de la Femme-Médicin'' for *Le Revue*, drawing notice to the heroine as an example of a New Woman. Blanc also translated one of Jewett's stories and found a translator for *A Country Doctor*. In another essay in *Le Revue*, ''Le Naturalisme aux Etats-Unis,'' she expressed admiration of ''A White Heron'' and *Country By-Ways*.

In America almost a decade after Thompson's essay, an article by Edward M. Chapman, ''The New England of Sarah Orne Jewett,'' in the *Yale Review* rather closely paralleled what Thompson had already written. Fred Pattee, a professor of literature, in his book *A History of American Literature since 1870* (1915) gives Jewett close attention, emphasizing her nostalgia for the past of a rapidly changing New England and compares her to Hawthorne in the simplicity of her style and her interest in the past. He singles out ''A White Heron,'' ''Miss Tempy's Watchers,'' and ''The Dulham Ladies'' as examples of her writing at its best but detects a tone of patrician aloofness in her attitude toward her rural characters. Edward Garnett in his book *Friday Nights* (1922) also finds resemblances in Jewett's work to Hawthorne's, especially in her success in demonstrating that the lives of her rural coastal folk are influenced by their environment and heritage. Martha H. Shackford in 1932 in an article, ''Sarah Orne

Jewett,'' in *The Sewanee Review* also notes the influence of environment on Jewett's characters and suggests an echoing of Wordsworth in her admiration of rural folk. More negative than most was C. Hartley Grattan's article in 1929, ''Sarah Orne Jewett,'' in *The Bookman*. Grattan faults Jewett for having no sense of tragedy and for being out of touch with the modern world.

The most quoted critique of Jewett's writing is that of Willa Cather in an often reprinted preface to *The Best Short Stories of Sarah Orne Jewett* (1925). Jewett, during the last two years of her life, had been Cather's friend and literary adviser. Cather's preface is favorable to the point of adulation. She assures the reader that the stories she has gathered, if ''read by an eager student fifty years from now, will give him the characteristic flavor, the spirit, the cadence, of an American writer of the first order—and of a New England which will then be a thing of the past'' (in Jewett, *Best Short Stories* 8). She ends the preface with the remark: ''If I were asked to name the three American books which have the possibility of a long, long life, I would say at once, *The Scarlet Letter, Huckleberry Finn*, and *The Country of the Pointed Firs*'' (10).

In 1929 Francis O. Matthiessen, a Harvard professor, published the first biography of Jewett. It was appreciative but somewhat skimpy and occasionally inaccurate. In 1960 John Eldridge Frost published a much fuller biography. An extremely important study is Richard Cary's *Sarah Orne Jewett* (1962), which is primarily concerned with tracing Jewett's development as an author and analyses of her writings. Cary is unquestionably the outstanding Jewett scholar and critic, having, among other contributions, edited her letters and certain of her works and compiled a volume of writings of various critics about her. Another more recent and highly important biographical-critical study, *Sarah Orne Jewett* (1980), is the work of Josephine Donovan, who has written frequently on Jewett from a feminist point of view. Another book with a feminist theme is Sarah Way Sherman's *Sarah Orne Jewett: A New England Persephone* (1989).

In 1994 the most inclusive book thus far on the subject, *Sarah Orne Jewett: Her World and Her Work*, by Paula Blanchard, was published in the Radcliffe Biography Series. Blanchard's scholarship and critical acumen are of the highest order, based as they are on the extensive published writing about Jewett and on sizable accumulations of unpublished material. Blanchard is particularly effective in her coverage of feminist writing on Jewett. The feminist critics have had several focuses on Jewett: her attitude toward marriage; the significance of her close relationship with Annie Fields; the bonding of Mrs. Todd and the narrator in *Pointed Firs*; the mother-daughter relationship, for example, that between Mrs. Todd and her mother. Some of these critics touch also on the Transcendental or even mystical elements in Jewett's writing: a sharing of consciousness, suggestive of extrasensory perception—Blanchard calls it a ''fluidity of consciousness'' (96)—as pointed out by Marjorie Pryse and Marcia McClintock Folsom, among others. The perception of Jewett as primarily a local colorist has long been abandoned in favor of her recognition as a nineteenth-century author of important psychological and spiritual insights.

WORKS CITED

Blanchard, Paula. *Sarah Orne Jewett: Her World and Her Work*. Reading, MA: Addison-Wesley, 1994.

Jewett, Sarah Orne. *The Country of the Pointed Firs and Other Stories*. Preface by Willa Cather. Garden City, NY: Doubleday & Company, 1956. Anchor Books edition.

———. "The Old Town of Berwick." *New England Magazine* 10 (July 1894): 585–609.

———. Preface to *Deephaven*. Boston: Houghton, Mifflin & Company, 1894.

Nagel, Gwen L. *Critical Essays on Sarah Orne Jewett*. Boston: G. K. Hall, 1984.

BIBLIOGRAPHY

Works by Sarah Orne Jewett

Deephaven. Boston: James R. Osgood & Co., 1877.

Play Days. Boston: Houghton, Osgood & Co., 1878.

Old Friends and New. Boston: Houghton, Osgood & Co., 1879.

Country By-Ways. Boston: Houghton, Mifflin & Co., 1881.

A Country Doctor. Boston: Houghton, Mifflin & Co., 1884.

The Mate of the Daylight, and Friends Ashore. Boston: Houghton, Mifflin & Co., 1884.

A Marsh Island. Boston: Houghton, Mifflin & Co., 1885.

A White Heron and Other Stories. Boston: Houghton, Mifflin & Co., 1886.

The Story of the Normans. New York: G. P. Putnam's Sons, 1887.

The King of Folly Island and Other People. Boston: Houghton, Mifflin & Co., 1888.

Betty Leicester, a Story for Girls. Boston: Houghton, Mifflin & Co., 1890.

Strangers and Wayfarers. Boston: Houghton, Mifflin & Co., 1890.

Tales of New England. Boston: Houghton, Mifflin & Co., 1890.

A Native of Winby and Other Tales. Boston: Houghton, Mifflin & Co., 1893.

Betty Leicester's Christmas. Boston: Houghton, Mifflin & Co., 1894.

The Life of Nancy. Boston: Houghton, Mifflin & Co., 1895.

The Country of the Pointed Firs. Boston: Houghton, Mifflin & Co., 1896.

The Queen's Twin and Other Stories. Boston: Houghton, Mifflin & Co., 1899.

The Tory Lover. Boston: Houghton, Mifflin & Co., 1901.

An Empty Purse. Boston: Merrymount Press, 1905.

Letters of Sarah Orne Jewett. Edited by Annie Fields. Boston: Houghton, Mifflin & Co., 1911.

Verses. Edited by M. A. De Wolfe Howe. Boston: Merrymount Press, 1916.

The Best Stories of Sarah Orne Jewett. Boston: Houghton, Mifflin, 1925.

Sarah Orne Jewett Letters. [*sic*] Edited by Richard Cary. Waterville, ME: Colby College Press, 1958.

The World of Dunnet Landing. Edited by David Bonnell Green. Lincoln: University of Nebraska Press, 1962.

The Uncollected Stories of Sarah Orne Jewett. Edited by Richard Cary. Waterville, ME: Colby College Press, 1971.

Books edited by Sarah Orne Jewett

Stories and Poems for Children. By Celia Thaxter. Boston: Houghton, Mifflin & Co., 1895.

The Poems of Celia Thaxter. Boston: Houghton, Mifflin & Co., 1896.

Letters of Sarah Wyman Whitman. Boston: Houghton, Mifflin & Co., 1907.

Studies of Sarah Orne Jewett

Blanc, Thérèse. "Le Naturalisme aux Etats-Unis." *La Revue des Deux Mondes* 83 (15 September 1887): 428–451.

Brooks, Van Wyck. *New England Indian Summer (1865–1915)*. New York: E. P. Dutton, 1940. 347–353.

Cary, Richard. "Miss Jewett and Madame Blanc." *Colby College Quarterly* 7 (September 1967): 467–487.

———. *Sarah Orne Jewett*. New York: Twayne Publishers, 1962.

———, ed. *Appreciation of Sarah Orne Jewett*. Waterville, ME: Colby College Press, 1973.

Chapman, Edward M. "The New England of Sarah Orne Jewett." *Yale Review* 3 (October 1913): 157–172.

Crumpacker, Laurie. "The Art of the Healer: Women in the Fiction of Sarah Orne Jewett." *Colby Library Quarterly* 3 (September 1983): 155–166.

Donovan, Josephine. *New England Local Color Literature: A Woman's Tradition*. New York: Continuum, 1988.

———. *Sarah Orne Jewett*. New York: Ungar, 1980.

———. "A Woman's Vision of Transcendence: A New Interpretation of the Works of Sarah Orne Jewett." *Massachusetts Review* 21 (summer 1980): 365–380.

Folsom, Marcia McClintock. "Tact as a Kind of Mind-Reading: Empathic Style in Sarah Orne Jewett's *The Country of the Pointed Firs*." *Colby Library Quarterly* 18 (March 1982): 66–78.

Frost, John Eldridge. *Sarah Orne Jewett*. Gundalow Club Kittery Point, ME: 1860.

Garnett, Edward. *Friday Nights*. New York: Alfred A. Knopf, 1922. 189–198.

Grattan, C. Hartley. "Sarah Orne Jewett." *The Bookman* 49 (May 1929): 296–298.

Held, George. "Heart to Heart with Nature: Ways of Looking at 'A White Heron.' " *Colby Library Quarterly* 18 (March 1892): 55–65.

Howard, June. *New Essays on "The Country of the Pointed Firs."* New York: Cambridge University Press, 1995.

Matthiessen, Francis Otto. *Sarah Orne Jewett*. Boston: Houghton Mifflin, 1929.

Mayer, Charles W. " 'The Only Rose': A Central Jewett Story." *Colby Library Quarterly* 17 (March 1981): 83–90.

Mobley, Marilyn E. *Folk Roots and Mythic Wings in Sarah Orne Jewett and Toni Morrison*. Baton Rouge: Louisiana State University Press, 1994.

Nagel, Gwen L., ed. *Critical Essays on Sarah Orne Jewett*. Boston: G. K. Hall, 1984.

Nagel, Gwen L., and James Nagel. *Sarah Orne Jewett: A Reference Guide*. Boston: G. K. Hall, 1978.

Pattee, Fred Lewis. *A History of American Literature Since 1870*. New York: The Century Co., 1915.

Piacentino, Edward J. "Local Color and Beyond: The Artistic Dimension of Sarah Orne
    Jewett's 'The Foreigner.' " *Colby Library Quarterly* 21 (June 1985): 92–98.
Pryse, Marjorie. Introduction to *The Country of the Pointed Firs and Other Stories*, by
    Sarah Orne Jewett. New York: W. W. Norton, 1982.
———. "Women 'at Sea': Feminist Realism in Sarah Orne Jewett's 'The Foreigner.' "
    American Literary Realism 15 (autumn 1982): 244–252.
Renza, Louis A. *"A White Heron" and the Question of Minor Literature*. Madison:
    University of Wisconsin Press, 1984.
Roman, Margaret. *Sarah Orne Jewett: Reconstructing Gender*. Tuscaloosa: University
    of Alabama Press, 1992.
Sherman, Sarah Way. *Sarah Orne Jewett: A New England Persephone*. Hanover, NH:
    University Press of New England, 1989.
Smith, Gayle L. "The Language of Transcendence in Sarah Orne Jewett's 'A White
    Heron.' " *Colby Library Quarterly* 9 (March 1983): 37–44.
Thorp, Margaret Ferrand. *Sarah Orne Jewett*. Pamphlets on American Writers, no. 61.
    Minneapolis: University of Minnesota Press, 1966.
Waggoner, Hyatt H. "The Unity of *The Country of the Pointed Firs.*" *Twentieth Century
    Literature* 5 (July 1959): 67–73.
Weber, Carl J. "New England through French Eyes Fifty Years Ago." *New England
    Quarterly* 20 (September 1947): 385–395.
Weber, Clara Carter, and Carl J. Weber. *A Bibliography of the Published Writings of
    Sarah Orne Jewett*. Waterville, ME: Colby College Press, 1949.
Westbrook, Perry D. *Acres of Flint: Sarah Orne Jewett and Her Contemporaries*. Me-
    tuchen, NJ: Scarecrow Press, 1981.
———. *The New England Town in Fact and Fiction*. Rutherford, NJ: Fairleigh Dick-
    inson University Press, 1982.
Wood, Ann Douglas. "The Literature of Impoverishment: The Women Local Colorists
    in America, 1865–1914." *Women's Studies* 1 (1972): 3–40.

GRACE ELIZABETH KING (1852–1932)

Laura E. Skandera-Trombley

BIOGRAPHY

Grace Elizabeth King was born in New Orleans, Louisiana, on November 29, 1852, the third child and eldest of four girls in a family of eight children. Her father, William Woodson King, a Georgia native, was a successful jurist and served in the Louisiana state legislature but lost his money with the defeat of the Confederacy. King's mother, Sarah Ann Miller, was her father's second wife. She was of Georgia ancestry though born and raised in New Orleans. Of Protestant religious faith, she grew up immersed in New Orleans' French-speaking, Catholic Creole society. Sarah King, known as a "charming *raconteuse*," would entertain her daughters with stories of Creole society (James 331). Grace King was educated first by governesses and then was a student in Creole schools. During the Civil War the family fled to their plantation in St. Martin's parish where they remained for four years. Upon their return to the city at the end of Union occupation, Grace matriculated at the Institute St. Louis, described in her story "Monsieur Motte," where she became so proficient in French that she won a prize in competition and graduated at age sixteen. She then was educated by the Misses Cenas, and under the tutelage of Héloise Cenas, she developed an interest in writing.

After her father's death in 1881, King's writing aspirations grew stronger, and her first essay appeared in 1885, "Heroines of Fiction," delivered before the Pan-Gnostic Society. At a party in 1885, King met Richard Watson Gilder, editor of the *Century* magazine and publisher of George Washington Cable. After hearing her criticism of Cable's portrayals of Creole society, Gilder challenged her to improve upon Cable's work by writing her own stories. King immediately composed "Monsieur Motte," and Charles Dudley Warner, an acquaintance of King's family, sold the story to the *New Princeton Review*, where it appeared in January 1886. This story and three others were published as *Monsieur Motte* in 1888.

At Warner's invitation, King traveled to Hartford, Connecticut, in June 1887. There she met Samuel Clemens (Mark Twain) and his wife Olivia, who would become her lifelong confidant. King also was introduced to Isabella Beecher Hooker, an ardent feminist, and she later commented in her autobiography: "Isabella Hooker . . . talked to me about 'Woman's Rights' and converted me to her point of view" (*Memories of a Southern Woman of Letters* 77). Despite her pleasant visit and the friends she made there, King never lost her Southern sympathies and on the whole heartily disliked the North. In 1888 she published a novelette, "Earthlings," for which Clemens had high praise, calling it a "masterpiece" (Bush 41–42).

Although King was decidedly cool in her observations about the North, such Yankee monthlies as *Harper's Bazaar* and *Century* praised and published her short stories. Successfully launched upon her literary career, King wrote about what she knew best, portraying women characters living in the South, namely, Louisiana. Most of her works were set during the antebellum period and recaptured the days of upper-class Creole glory. King considered herself a realist writer and viewed her writings as sentimental only when they depicted what she viewed was a sentimental era. King also wrote several stories depicting the supposed evils of Reconstruction and its disastrous effects on the Old South and its supporters.

King had long been interested in the history of the territory and then the state of Louisiana, and from 1892 to 1898, she wrote a series of historical works chronicling past events and individuals. King was commissioned to write a biography of the Canadian founder of New Orleans and Mobile, and in 1892, she published *Jean Baptiste le Moyne, Sieur de Bienville*. She went on to publish a high school textbook in 1893, in collaboration with J. R. Ficklen, titled *A History of Louisiana*, and wrote a history of the city, *New Orleans: The Place and the People*, published in 1895. In 1898 King finished and published *DeSoto and His Men in the Land of Florida*. In addition to her writing career, King was a longtime member of the Louisiana Historical Society and held the office of recording secretary and served on the advisory board of the society's journal *Quarterly* (James 331).

After meeting Isabella Hooker in 1887, King became actively interested in women's writing and sought out and became friends with such authors as Annie Fields, Sarah Orne Jewett, and Ruth McEnery Stuart (Taylor 40). King never married; she traveled widely, and her mother and sisters, Nan and Nina, took care of her personal affairs and functioned as secretarial support. At one point in her career, King functioned as a literary agent for French writers who desired to publish in America. She was rewarded for this service by being made an *Officier de l'Instruction Publique* by the French government in 1915. King was also elected as a Fellow of the Royal Society of Arts and Sciences in England, and Tulane University awarded her an honorary doctorate. During the last twenty years of her life, King wrote two novels and several short stories. Her autobiography, *Memories of a Southern Woman of Letters*, was published post-humously in 1932. King died of nephritis at her home at age seventy-eight.

MAJOR WORKS AND THEMES

Grace King's fictional writing was concerned principally with issues of race and gender. King's treatment of African Americans in her work is confined to the mulatto, like George Washington Cable, yet unlike Cable, King made the mulatto woman her focus. In "Monsieur Motte," King was most immediately reacting to Cable's critical portrayals of the white South and his belief in the superiority of African Americans in general. King, in short, took the other view, and her work served as an expression of her white supremacist assumptions. In her first collection of short stories, *Monsieur Motte*, King portrayed the desta-bilized Southern family that emerged following the end of the Civil War. The war had permanently changed business and cultural norms and created the need for new definitions of class, race, and gender.

King's next collection of short stories was titled *Tales of a Time and Place* (1892) and continued the motifs outlined in *Monsieur Motte*: a revered ante-bellum past, the chaos brought on by Reconstruction, redefined racial relation-ships, and the new role of women during Reconstruction. *Balcony Stories* (1893), King's third collection of stories, was her most critically acclaimed and most popular work. The emphasis in this collection was women's lives. Once again, King explored how kinship is reflected in terms of class, race, and gender; and of the thirteen stories, eleven portray a central female character.

The Pleasant Ways of St. Médard (1916) has been recognized as the most autobiographical of King's works, concerned with the Reconstruction period in New Orleans and white women's response to their changed environment. The book received excellent reviews; however, few copies were purchased by the public, and it appeared that the vogue for local color and Civil War prose had ended. King would never again enjoy the kind of popularity she had for her first three collections.

In order to survive as a woman of letters during the turn of the century, King wrote fiction, biographies, textbooks, and histories of Louisiana. Considering such a productive output in so many different genres, King's exclusion from most standard works on Southern literature and history is a sad indicator of the marginality women writers occupy. King's most lasting works are those prose texts that feature women, and some of her collections have recently been re-printed; perhaps with this recent spate of publications, both primary and critical, King will reemerge from a critical and literary purgatory.

CRITICAL RECEPTION

Before the turn of the century, King was a respected author of realist fiction and biographical and historical studies. Her stories were favorably received and well regarded by critics. After 1900, King's reputation gradually declined, and her reputation was summed up in 1980 as that of "a competent realist" (Mainiero 458). More recent critical works on King have once again reevaluated her literary merits. Helen Taylor states that King's works "are of considerable relevance to modern literary scholars, since she is one of the very few American women writers who have confronted the problems of race and gender in relation to regional political and social concerns" (28). Critic Linda Coleman expands upon Taylor's claim and concludes: "When the complex links between sexism and racism are understood as a compounding of materials and spiritual difference and deprivation . . . King appear[s] in an at once more sympathetic and more critical light" (33). Coleman goes on to acknowledge that although King was a significant figure in her day, until recently she had been ignored at least in part because of her "white-apologist position on race" (33). Based on the wealth of recent critical works on King, it appears as though she is having a revival at present.

WORKS CITED

Bush, Robert. "Grace King and Mark Twain." *American Literature* 44 (March 1972): 31–51.

James, Edward T., ed. *Notable American Women 1607–1950*. Vol. 2. Cambridge: Belknap Press of Harvard University Press, 1971.

King, Grace. *Memories of a Southern Woman of Letters*. New York: Macmillan Company, 1932.

Mainiero, Lina, ed. *American Women Writers: A Critical Reference Guide*. Vol. 2. New York: Frederick Ungar Publishers, 1980.

Taylor, Helen. *Gender, Race, and Region in the Writings of Grace King, Ruth McEnery Stuart, and Kate Chopin*. Baton Rouge: Louisiana State University Press, 1989.

BIBLIOGRAPHY

Works by Grace Elizabeth King

"Earthlings." *Lippincott's Monthly Magazine* 42 (1888): 599–679.
Monsieur Motte. New York: A. C. Armstrong and Son, 1888.
Jean Baptiste le Moyne, Sieur de Bienville. New York: Dodd, Mead and Company, 1892.
Tales of a Time and Place. New York: Harper and Brothers, 1892.
Balcony Stories. New Orleans: L. Graham Co., 1893.
A History of Louisiana. With J. R. Ficklen. Baton Rouge: University Publishers, 1893.
New Orleans: The Place and the People. New York: Macmillan Company, 1895.
DeSoto and His Men in the Land of Florida. New York: Macmillan Company, 1898.

Stories from Louisiana History. With J. R. Ficklen. New Orleans: L. Graham and Son, 1905.

The Pleasant Ways of St. Médard. New York: Henry Holt and Company, 1916.

Creole Families of New Orleans. New York: Macmillan Company, 1921.

Madame Girard, an Old French Teacher of New Orleans. New Haven: n.p., 1922; reprinted from the *Yale Review*.

La Dame de Sainte Hermine. New York: Macmillan Company, 1924.

A Splendid Offer: A Comedy for Women. [one-act play] N.p., 1926.

Mount Vernon on the Potomac: History of the Mt. Vernon Ladies' Association of the Union. New York: Macmillan Company, 1929.

Memories of a Southern Woman of Letters. New York: Macmillan Company, 1932.

Grace King of New Orleans: A Selection of Her Writings. Edited by Robert Bush. Baton Rouge: Louisiana State University Press, 1973.

Studies of Grace Elizabeth King

Bush, Robert. *Grace King: A Southern Destiny*. Baton Rouge: Louisiana State University Press, 1983.

———. "The Patrician Voice: Grace King." In *Literary New Orleans: Essays and Meditations*, edited by Richard S. Kennedy. Baton Rouge: Louisiana State University Press, 1992. 8–15.

Coleman, Linda S. "At Odds: Race and Gender in Grace King's Short Fiction." In *Louisiana Women Writers: New Essays and a Comprehensive Bibliography*, edited by Dorothy H. Brown and Barbara C. Ewell. Baton Rouge: Louisiana State University Press, 1992. 33–56; 270–271.

Elfenbein, Anna Shannon. *Women on the Color Line: Evolving Stereotypes and the Writings of George Washington Cable, Grace King, Kate Chopin*. Charlottesville: University Press of Virginia, 1994. 74–116.

Juncker, Clara. "Grace King: Feminist, Southern Style." *Southern Quarterly* 26, no. 3 (spring 1988): 15–30.

Kirby, David. *Grace King*. Boston: Twayne, 1980.

Taylor, Helen. "The Case of Grace King." *Southern Review* 18, no. 4 (fall 1982): 685–702.

———. *Gender, Race, and Region in the Writings of Grace King, Ruth McEnery Stuart, and Kate Chopin*. Baton Rouge: Louisiana State University Press, 1989. 28–83.

CAROLINE KIRKLAND
(1801–1864)

Nancy A. Walker

BIOGRAPHY

Caroline Matilda Stansbury was born on January 11, 1801, in New York City. The eldest child of Eliza Alexander Stansbury and Samuel Stansbury, she became part of a family that prized literature and education. Her paternal grandfather, Joseph Stansbury, a Tory sympathizer during the Revolutionary War, wrote satiric poetry. Her mother was the author of both poetry and fiction, and her father's sister, Lydia Mott, ran a Quaker school that Caroline began attending at the age of eight. She took good advantage of educational opportunities unusual for young women in the early decades of the nineteenth century, learning to read French, Latin, and German as well as English literature—accomplishments that are evident in the many literary allusions in her own work. She was also receptive to the religious and moral teachings of Lydia Mott's Quaker philosophy, and by the early 1820s, she was teaching in a school her aunt owned in Clinton, New York. After Samuel Stansbury died in 1822, Caroline's mother moved the family to Clinton, where Caroline's income helped to support them.

While in Clinton, Caroline met William Kirkland, a young man with similar background and interests. Following graduation from Hamilton College, which his grandfather had helped to found, William aspired to be a college teacher, but when he suffered an accidental loss of hearing, he went to Germany to study for a time. Caroline and William Kirkland were married the day before her twenty-seventh birthday, in 1828, and embarked upon a life of collaborative work that ran counter to an increasingly insistent ideology of separate spheres of activity for women and men. During the first year of their marriage, the Kirklands established a girls' school near Utica, New York, and shared responsibilities for their infant daughter. In 1835, they moved to Detroit, Michigan, to jointly administer the Detroit Female Seminary.

The fact that Michigan in the 1830s was frontier territory led to the Kirklands' next venture and ultimately to Caroline Kirkland's career as a writer. William Kirkland purchased 800 acres of land west of Detroit, and in 1837, the family moved there to help found the village of Pinckney. Removed from the educated culture with which she had long been familiar, Caroline Kirkland wrote entertaining letters to friends in the East, who in turn encouraged her to describe her experiences for publication. The result was Kirkland's first book, *A New Home— Who'll Follow?* (1839), published under the pseudonym Mary Clavers in order to avoid revealing her identity to her Pinckney neighbors. Kirkland's persona and narrator, Mrs. Clavers, is, like Kirkland herself, an educated and sophisticated Easterner transplanted to a frontier culture that she initially finds dismayingly crude and makeshift but in which she discovers values of community and cooperation necessary for survival in an unsettled area and capable of blurring class distinctions. Indeed, one of Kirkland's purposes in *A New Home* is to counter the emphasis on rugged individualism that characterized most of the period's writing about the western frontier, including the novels of James Fenimore Cooper.

Kirkland's use of a pseudonym and her naming of the town of Pinckney "Montacute" did not suffice to disguise her identity, and the satiric tone of portions of *A New Home* angered her Pinckney neighbors; their response convinced Kirkland to be more restrained in her subsequent writing, including her second book about the frontier experience, the 1842 collection of sketches *Forest Life*. By the time *Forest Life* was published, the Kirklands' Michigan sojourn was coming to an end; Pinckney had not become the thriving metropolis envisioned by its founders, and in 1843, Caroline and William Kirkland moved their family—which by then included five children—back to New York City, where William became an editor for the New York *Mirror* and Caroline wrote for the paper. The Kirklands quickly became part of a New York literary circle that included Edgar Allan Poe, Nathaniel P. Willis (brother of Sara Willis Parton, better known as "Fanny Fern"), Lydia Maria Child, Lydia Sigourney, and William Cullen Bryant. By this point, Caroline Kirkland was publishing stories and sketches in such periodicals as *Graham's, Knickerbocker, Godey's Lady's Book*, and *Yankee Doodle*. In 1845 she published her third collection of sketches about frontier life, *Western Clearings*.

Like many other nineteenth-century American women writers, Caroline Kirkland had thus far written for publication with the twin motivations of professional vocation and economic necessity. The latter became paramount after 1846, when William was accidentally drowned, leaving her to support her large family. She accomplished this in part by returning to teaching in girls' schools, but writing and editing remained her major occupations. She served briefly as editor of a Unitarian newspaper that William had edited before his death, and in 1847 she became editor of the *Union Magazine* (later *Sartain's*), which was dedicated to literature and the arts. Kirkland's prolific production of stories and sketches for this and other periodicals led to the Scribner's publication of three collections of her magazine pieces in the 1850s.

While the titles of these collections—for example, *A Book for the Home Circle* (1853) and *Autumn Hours and Fireside Reading* (1854)—suggest a domestic, familial audience well within the acceptable sphere of influence of the woman writer, Kirkland's interests were by no means limited to manners and morals. As befitted her education, she was involved in the world of belles lettres, preparing an edition of Spenser's *Faerie Queene* for publication in 1847. And due both to her Quaker training and the reformist spirit of the times, she wrote on a number of social issues. Although never an activist in the cause of female suffrage, she wrote an introduction to the 1845 publication of Mrs. Hugo Reid's *A Plea for Women*, and in 1853, she addressed the rehabilitation of female convicts in *The Helping Hand, Comprising an Account of the Home for Discharged Female Convicts and an Appeal in Behalf of that Institution*. Kirkland's last major publication, *Personal Memoirs of Washington* (1857), was a biography of George Washington designed to emphasize both his personal, domestic life and his opposition to slavery.

The last years of Kirkland's life were occupied with building a new home in New Jersey and with supporting abolition before the Civil War and the Union during it. She organized fund drives for the Union army and was a member of the United States Sanitary Commission, which would later become the Red Cross. Two days after organizing a fund-raising event for the Sanitary Commission, she died of a stroke on April 6, 1864.

MAJOR WORKS AND THEMES

Caroline Kirkland never left behind her initial career as a teacher. In one way or another, everything she wrote during twenty-five years as a published author was intended to educate her readers. Even in her first book, *A New Home— Who'll Follow?*, whose witty, often satiric style makes it in Sandra A. Zagarell's characterization an ''exuberant book'' (xv), Kirkland imagines as readers others who might migrate to the frontier and offers them descriptions of what to expect and cautions about their behavior. As part of her attempt to counter the masculine accounts of settlement that glorified frontier freedom and independence, Kirkland wrote as a woman who encountered muddy roads, alcoholics who abused their wives, and unscrupulous land speculators and who discovered that the cupboard shipped from New York would not fit into her log cabin and so ''did yeoman's service long afterwards as a corn-crib'' (*Home* 45). In contrast to accounts of western settlement that promoted opportunities for individual heroism, Kirkland insisted that the frontier community was dependent upon sharing and cooperation for its very survival. Her chapter on her neighbors' habits of borrowing everything from livestock to flour sifters becomes almost slapstick comedy, but she is quite serious in pointing out that social class snobbery is counterproductive on the frontier: "If I treat Mrs. Timson with neglect to-day can I with any face borrow her broom to-morrow? And what would become of me, if in revenge for my declining her invitation to tea this afternoon, she should decline coming to do my washing on Monday?" (*Home* 65). Perhaps Kirkland's most direct (and most amusing) attack on the masculine mythology of the frontier is her account in chapter VII of a trip from Detroit embarked upon by "Mr. Clavers" and several other men—"a tour with a view to the purchase of one or two cities" (*Home* 25). Despite being outfitted with compasses, blankets, boots, coats, and brandy, these "gentlemen who have been for many years accustomed to pavements and gaslamps" (*Home* 27) get lost, must depend upon the scanty hospitality of a family of settlers, and return weary and bedraggled.

Like other women writers of the antebellum period, such as Lydia Maria Child and Fanny Fern, Kirkland adopted the stance of the commonsense moralist, and especially in *A New Home*, she used satire and wit to convey her messages about pretension, indolence, and unethical behavior in much the same ways as did Fern in her columns for the New York *Ledger*. Eloise Fidler, who visits Montacute, is Kirkland's target not only because she writes deplorably sentimental poetry but also because her fancy clothes render her unfit to participate in the work of the household. But Kirkland's concerns go beyond the domestic to take in swindlers who start banks with no collateral and those who sell unsuspecting pioneers land that turns out to be under water.

Michigan readers who objected to the satiric tone of *A New Home* evidently missed the way that Kirkland makes fun of herself in the persona of Mary Clavers and shows her gradually coming to appreciate the beauty of Michigan and the stamina and hospitality of many of its inhabitants. As her portrayal of Eloise Fidler indicates, the book deals in large measure with her education in the realities of frontier life—a leaving behind of cultural pretensions and expectations to embrace the cooperative spirit of community building. Her next collections of sketches about the West, *Forest Life* and *Western Clearings*, are far more restrained in their social critique, more apt to dwell on the picturesque features of landscape than on the human drama of settlement. When her husband died and she became reliant on her pen for a livelihood, the need for a wide, consistent reading audience acted as a further brake on the tone and style of her cultural observations.

Nonetheless, Kirkland's overriding goal remained social reform, ranging from matters of manners to the status of women and the abolition of slavery. Whereas in her travel writings—letters to *Sartain's* magazine published as *Holidays Abroad, or, Europe from the West* in 1849—she preferred art to politics, writing for example, "I had always cared far more about Italian pictures than Italian politics" (1, 182), in her own country she entered fully, if decorously, into the political scene, expressing her views on everything from the need for women's clothing reform to the rehabilitation of female prisoners. Indeed, one of the hallmarks of Kirkland's career as a writer is her capacity for empathy with women in a wide variety of social classes and circumstances. Although herself the product of a certain level of privilege—especially in terms of education and culture—she took to heart her Quaker training and the democratic lessons of her years in frontier Michigan, calling for humane reforms on behalf of all women.

Kirkland's solid position as a woman writer and editor by 1850 informs the sprightly tone of her essay "Literary Women," published that year in *Sartain's*. The essay is primarily a witty, sometimes even sarcastic defense of the "blue-stocking," as intellectual women were derogatorily termed. Kirkland argues that literary women are not so numerous as to pose a threat ("hardly more abundant than dodos"), that a woman's love of pen and ink need not interfere with domestic responsibilities, and that intellectual pursuits do not render women unattractive—thus countering some of the major cultural objections to the blue-stocking. But, characteristically, Kirkland's essay takes on issues far larger than its announced subject. It begins as a spirited indictment of all prejudice, which "is fond of whirling a sword horizontally, and feel quite clear of any guilt when heads are sliced off" ("Literary" 193)—including prejudice against old maids and stepmothers.

By writing *Personal Memoirs of Washington*, Kirkland's most ambitious book in terms of research, she endeavored to participate in writing the history of America in ways that Nina Baym discusses in *American Women Writers and the Work of History, 1790–1860*. As Baym points out, in the early decades of the Republic, history was thought to be one of the most appropriate subjects for women to study: "Since the march of history had created a nation in which home was coextensive with the body politic, knowledge of history would show republican women in republican homes who they were and what their work was" (13). For many women, it was a short step from reading history to writing history, and in her biography of Washington, Kirkland attempted to rewrite the story of the nation's first president to emphasize his domestic as opposed to his public life—to, in Zagarell's words, reject the "value system in which true manhood and the fully public life are one" (xxiv). In her effort to counter the image of George Washington presented by biographers such as Jared Sparks and Washington Irving, Kirkland undertook a project similar to that of *A New Home*: recasting a national narrative in terms that reflected women's perspectives and values.

CRITICAL RECEPTION

Like scores of other nineteenth-century women writers, Caroline Kirkland enjoyed both popular and critical success during her lifetime, only to be consigned to the much-maligned category of "sentimental" female authors by the critical tastes and practices of the late nineteenth and early twentieth centuries. Like many of her contemporaries, Edgar Allan Poe responded enthusiastically to *A New Home—Who'll Follow?* In "The Literati of New York," Poe praised the work's realism in depicting "the *home* and home-life of the backwoodsman" (1181). At midcentury, she was well respected as both author and editor, both publishing her own work with distinguished publishing houses and attracting the era's best-known authors to *Sartain's*. But by the time of William Rose Benét's *The Reader's Encyclopedia* in 1948, Kirkland was listed as the author of "pioneer books," and her son, William Kirkland, author of *Zury* (1887), was given four times as much space and hailed as one of the earliest writers of realistic literature. By the time of the 1962 *Reader's Encyclopedia of American Literature*, Caroline Kirkland was accorded fuller treatment and cited as a forerunner of Sinclair Lewis in her treatment of small-town life, but true scholarly attention awaited the republication of *A New Home* in 1990 in the Rutgers University Press American Women Writers Series, with an introduction by Sandra A. Zagarell.

WORKS CITED

Baym, Nina. *American Women Writers and the Work of History, 1790–1860*. New Brunswick: Rutgers University Press, 1995.

Benét, William Rose. *The Reader's Encyclopedia*. New York: Thomas Y. Crowell, 1948.

Herzberg, Max J. *The Reader's Encyclopedia of American Literature*. New York: Thomas Y. Crowell, 1962.

"Literary Women." In *A New Home*. New Brunswick, NJ, n.d.

Poe, Edgar Allan. "The Literati of New York." In *Essays and Reviews*. New York: Library of America, 1984.

Zagarell, Sandra A. Introduction to *A New Home—Who'll Follow? or, Glimpses of Western Life*, by Mrs. Mary Clavers, an actual settler [Caroline Kirkland]. New Brunswick: Rutgers University Press, 1990. xi–l.

BIBLIOGRAPHY

Works by Caroline Kirkland

A New Home—Who'll Follow? or, Glimpses of Western Life, by Mrs. Mary Clavers, an actual settler. New York: C. S. Francis, 1839.

Forest Life, by the Author of *A New Home*. 2 vols. New York: C. S. Francis, 1842.

Introduction to *A Plea for Women*, by Mrs. Hugo Reid. New York: Farmer and Daggers, 1845.

Western Clearings. 2 vols. New York: Wiley and Putnam, 1845.

Spenser and the Faerie Queene. New York: Wiley and Putnam, 1847.

Holidays Abroad, or, Europe from the West. 2 vols. New York: Baker and Scribner, 1849.

Preface to *Dahcotah, or, Life and Legends of the Sioux around Fort Snelling*, by Mrs. Mary Eastman. New York: John Wiley, 1849.

The Evening Book, or, Fireside Talk on Morals and Manners, with Sketches of Western Life. New York: Charles Scribner, 1852.

A Book for the Home Circle, or, Familiar Thoughts on Various Topics, Literary, Moral, and Social. A Companion for the Evening Book. New York: Charles Scribner, 1853.

The Helping Hand, Comprising an Account of the Home for Discharged Female Convicts and an Appeal in Behalf of that Institution. New York: Charles Scribner, 1853.

Autumn Hours and Fireside Reading. New York: Charles Scribner, 1854.

Personal Memoirs of Washington. New York: D. Appleton, 1857.

The School-Girl's Garland. New York: Charles Scribner, 1864.

Patriotic Eloquence: Being Selections from 100 Years of National Literature. New York: Charles Scribner; Cleveland: Ingham and Bragg, 1866.

Studies of Caroline Kirkland

Baym, Nina. *Woman's Fiction: A Guide to Novels by and about Women in America 1820–1870.* Ithaca: Cornell University Press, 1978.

Davidson, Cathy N., and Linda Wagner-Martin, eds. *The Oxford Book of Women's Writing in the United States.* New York: Oxford University Press, 1995.

Donovan, Josephine. *New England Local Color Literature: A Women's Tradition.* New York: Frederick Ungar, 1983.

Fetterley, Judith, ed. *Provisions: A Reader from 19th-Century American Women.* Bloomington: Indiana University Press, 1985.

Keyes, Langly Carlton. "Caroline Matilda Kirkland: A Pioneer in American Realism." Ph.D. diss., Harvard University, 1935.

Kolodny, Annette. *The Land before Her: Fantasy and Experience of the American Frontiers, 1630–1860.* Chapel Hill: University of North Carolina Press, 1984.

Leverenz, David. *Manhood and the American Renaissance.* Ithaca: Cornell University Press, 1989.

Osborne, William S. *Caroline M. Kirkland.* New York: Twayne, 1972.

Pattee, Fred Lewis. *The Feminine Fifties.* New York: D. Appleton-Century Co., 1940.

Riordan, D. G. "The Concept of Simplicity in the Works of Mrs. Caroline Matilda Kirkland." Ph.D. diss., University of North Carolina, 1973.

Roberts, Audrey. "Caroline Matilda Stansbury Kirkland." In *American Women Writers: A Critical Reference Guide.* New York: Ungar, 1988.

———. "The Letters of Caroline M. Kirkland." Ph.D. diss., University of Wisconsin, 1976.

Spencer, Stacy L. "Literary Profile: Caroline M. Kirkland." *Legacy* 8, no. 2 (fall 1991): 133–140.

Walker, Nancy A. *The Disobedient Writer: Women and Narrative Tradition.* Austin: University of Texas Press, 1995.

Warren, Joyce W., ed. *The (Other) American Traditions: Nineteenth-Century Women Writers.* New Brunswick: Rutgers University Press, 1993.

LUCY LARCOM
(1824–1893)

Susan Alves

BIOGRAPHY

Born on March 5, 1824, in Beverly, Massachusetts, Lucy Larcom was the seventh child of the eight born to her father, Benjamin Larcom, and his second wife, Lois Barrett Larcom. Larcom's father, a retired sea captain, was a merchant of East Indian goods in Beverly. In 1832 Benjamin Larcom died, leaving the large family in Lois Larcom's care. While the older children found work in such trades as tailoring, Lois Larcom brought the younger children to Lowell where she found work managing a mill boardinghouse for female factory operatives.

In 1835, soon after her mother and sisters arrived in Lowell, Lucy Larcom began work as a doffer. For the next two years, Larcom would work nine months in the mills and attend school for the remaining three months. At age fifteen, with her formal schooling ended and still employed in the mills, Larcom joined her older sister Emeline at the ''factory girls'' Improvement Circle meetings. There, Larcom's poetry and stories drew the attention of Harriet Farley, the editor of a new literary magazine, *The Lowell Offering*. This periodical was run by female factory workers and funded by the Lowell mill owners. Larcom became a regular contributor to the magazine, eventually attracting the attention of John Greenleaf Whittier, who became her lifelong friend and mentor.

Lucy Larcom went west to the Illinois prairie in 1846. For six years she worked as a schoolteacher. During this time, she saved enough money to pay for her tuition at Monticello Academy in Godfrey, Illinois, a place where she would cultivate her love for learning, writing, and spiritual development. These were productive years for Larcom. She continued contributing to Farley's periodical, now entitled *The New England Offering*, as well as to local New England newspapers and to Whittier's abolitionist weekly, the *National Era*.

Having turned down a long-standing marriage offer in 1852, Larcom returned to New England. Now formally trained as a teacher and needing a steady income, Lucy Larcom began the first of many years at Wheaton Seminary for Women in Norton, Massachusetts. These were years of great stress and personal turmoil. The energy she expended in teaching seemed at cross purposes to her writing and studying. Still, she managed not only to meet her responsibilities at Wheaton, cultivating warm and loyal relationships with her students there, but to continue writing as well.

While a full-time faculty member at Wheaton, Lucy Larcom achieved literary success and notoriety. Her intellectual and artistic pursuits brought Larcom into the milieu of the middle class, while the reality of this independent woman's economic situation kept her among the working classes. For the rest of her life, Lucy Larcom tried to balance the demands of her financial needs with the social and creative requirements of her writing.

The editorship of Ticknor and Fields' *Our Young Folks* gave Lucy Larcom a steady income, allowed her to leave teaching, put her into contact with other women writers such as Harriet Beecher Stowe and Lydia Maria Child, and provided enough quiet time between editions for Larcom to write and to find refreshment by traveling to the mountains of New Hampshire. Larcom wrote that these were among the happiest years of her life. When the magazine folded, Lucy Larcom went on to work for Houghton Mifflin as an editor and also oversaw collection and editorial matters on three children's poetry anthologies with Whittier in the late 1870s.

From the mid-1870s until her death, Lucy Larcom, a former "factory girl," was able to support herself with her writing in the style of the middle class. She had become widely known and celebrated by the public and by such renowned male poets as Longfellow and Whittier. Her death in 1893 was noted in most major newspapers. She is buried in a family plot in Beverly, Massachusetts.

MAJOR WORKS AND THEMES

The publication of four poems drew Lucy Larcom into the inner circle of the New England literati. Notably, Rufus Griswold included "Elisha and the Angels" and "The Burning Prairie" as well as a biography of Larcom written by Whittier in his anthology *Women Poets of America* (1854). In 1857 the prominent art periodical *The Crayon* published "Hannah Binding Shoes." A few years later, in 1861, "The Rose Enthroned" was issued in the prestigious *Atlantic Monthly*. These poems exhibit the range of Larcom's poetic themes from piety to local color infused with a didactic handling of current social issues such as the abolition of slavery and the personal cost of the waning cottage industries.

CRITICAL RECEPTION

Two of Lucy Larcom's four books of poetry, *Wild Roses of Cape Ann* (1880) and *Poems*, the Household Edition (1884), attracted the attention of the general reading public and literary luminaries such as James Fields and William Dean Howells. Oliver Wendell Holmes wrote to Larcom that "I have been reading your poems at all the spare moments I could find" (Addison 197). In a letter to Larcom, Longfellow enthusiastically wrote: "I always liked your poetry; and now like it more than ever" (Addison 198). By publishing the collected volume of Larcom's poetry as a household edition, Houghton Mifflin asserts Lucy Larcom's rightful place in a dominant middle-class American culture. Like the major poets of her age, Larcom was marketed to a growing and literate population.

Only one of Lucy Larcom's two books focusing on industrial labor in Lowell received a positive critical reception. The long narrative poem *An Idyl of Work* (1875), which is rooted in American idealism and romanticism, was harshly criticized at publication. For this poetic subject, Larcom's choice of genre and her use of blank verse are anachronistic. In the preface, the poet admits that "[t]he routine of such a life is essentially prosaic" (vii). The evocation of Lowell in the 1840s as well as the details of industrial labor and of white working-class women's lives are among the poem's greatest strengths. When she took up similar themes and subjects in the autobiographical *A New England Girlhood* (1889), Larcom was far more successful. The prose of autobiography is better suited to the purposes of representing life experiences in the industrial age. The text is only one of a few that recount women's lives in antebellum industrial America.

In the twentieth century, Lucy Larcom's poetry and prose have enjoyed some critical attention, particularly from feminist scholars seeking to uncover a women's poetic tradition. Notably, Cheryl Walker locates Larcom within this concept of an American women's poetic tradition. Shirley Marchalonis's extensive biography of Lucy Larcom (*Worlds* 1989) considers not only the poet in a literary tradition but the significance of her life within the context of nineteenth-century American culture and history. Although Lucy Larcom's writing and literary career provide a nexus for the critical analysis of gender, class, and race, few scholars offer sustained consideration of Larcom's literary production.

WORKS CITED

Addison, Daniel Dulany. *Lucy Larcom: Life, Letters, and Diary.* Boston: Houghton Mifflin, 1894.
Larcom, Lucy. *An Idyl of Work.* Boston: Osgood, 1875.

BIBLIOGRAPHY

The following is only a partial listing. For a more complete bibliography of Lucy Larcom, including the location of archival collections, see Shirley Marchalonis's *The Worlds of Lucy Larcom, 1824–1893* (1989).

Major Works by Lucy Larcom

Similitudes, from the Ocean and Prairie. Boston: Jewett, 1853.
Poems. Boston: Fields, Osgood, 1868.
Childhood Songs. Boston: Osgood, 1875.
An Idyl of Work. Boston: Osgood, 1875.
Landscape of American Poetry. New York: D. Appleton, 1879.
Wild Roses of Cape Ann and Other Poems. Boston: Houghton Mifflin, 1880.
Larcom's Poetical Works [Lucy Larcom's Poems]. Household Edition. Boston: Houghton
    Mifflin, 1884.
A New England Girlhood. Boston: Houghton Mifflin, 1889.
At the Beautiful Gate. Boston: Houghton Mifflin, 1892.

Studies of Lucy Larcom

Addison, Daniel Dulany. *Lucy Larcom: Life, Letters, and Diary.* Boston: Houghton Mif-
    flin, 1894.
Alves, Susan. " 'Faint Reminiscences of Yesterday among the Looms': Lucy Larcom's
    Production and Revision of an American Factory Girl Subjectivity." "A Thou-
    sand Times I'd Rather Be a Factory Girl: The Politics of Reading American and
    British Female Factory Workers' Poetry, 1840–1914." Ph.D. diss., Northeastern
    University, 1996.
Dublin, Thomas. *Women at Work: The Transformation of Work and Community in Low-
    ell, Massachusetts, 1826–1860.* New York: Columbia University Press, 1979.
Marchalonis, Shirley. "Lucy Larcom, 1824–1893." *Legacy* 5, no. 1 (1988): 45–52.
———. *The Worlds of Lucy Larcom, 1824–1893.* Athens: University of Georgia Press,
    1989.
———, ed. *Patrons and Protegees: Gender, Friendship and Writing in Nineteenth-
    Century America.* New Brunswick, NJ: Rutgers University Press, 1988.
Rollar, Stephany. "Lucy Larcom. A Portrait of Nineteenth-Century America." Senior
    thesis, Wheaton College, 1962.
Walker, Cheryl. *The Nightingale's Burden.* Bloomington: University of Indiana Press,
    1982.
Ward, Susan Hayes, ed. *The Rushlight: Special Number in Memory of Lucy Larcom.*
    Trustees of Wheaton Seminary. Boston: Ellis, 1894.

ROSE HAWTHORNE LATHROP (MOTHER MARY ALPHONSA) (1851–1926)

Patricia Dunlavy Valenti

BIOGRAPHY

Born in 1851 in Lenox, Massachusetts, Rose Hawthorne Lathrop was the youngest child of Nathaniel and Sophia Hawthorne. Lathrop spent part of her childhood in England, Portugal, and Italy, and after the family returned to the Wayside, her father died. Seeking a better life for her children, Sophia Hawthorne moved them first to Dresden, then to England, where she died in 1871. Within months, Rose Hawthorne married George Parsons Lathrop (later to become the editor of Nathaniel Hawthorne's works). The couple returned to the United States and had one child, Francis, whose death in 1881 was followed by their separation for almost a year. Between 1875 and 1892, Lathrop published fiction and poetry. In 1891, George and Rose Lathrop converted to Roman Catholicism, and during the next five years, she abandoned imaginative writing to explore biographical subjects and issues of social justice. In 1896, Lathrop left her husband to found an order of nuns dedicated to the care of indigents dying of cancer. Mother Mary Alphonsa, as she was known for the rest of her life, died in 1926. The Servants of Relief for Incurable Cancer flourishes to this day.

MAJOR WORKS AND THEMES

Lathrop's imaginative works may be classified according to genre and theme: fiction for or about children; fiction dealing with the relationships between the sexes; poetry about male-female relationships; and poetry on the subjects of death and grief.

Lathrop's earliest published stories frequently employ children as main characters, incorporate events from her youth ("Lindie's Portrait" [1887]), and have children as their intended audience ("The Owl That Stared" [1876] appeared in the children's periodical *St. Nicholas Magazine*). "Princess Roundabout" (1875), "Toy Mysteries" (n.d.), and "Fun Beams" (1884) each explore some aspect of initiation into adulthood. These sentimentalized depictions of young people, protected by wise, loving parents, suggest Lathrop's nostalgia for childhood.

Her depictions of adult male-female relationships, however, are not so placid as these narratives of childhood. In "Browning the Meerschaum" (1874), Lathrop examines again the loss of innocence, specifically in the context of a young man's painful infatuation with an elusive woman. This story establishes a recurring situation in Lathrop's stories ("For a Lord" [1892], "Troth" [1892], and "Saagenfreed" [1876]) about men and women: A women is pursued, often by more than one man, but her affections remain unattainable.

"Prisoners!", published in two installments in 1883 during the Lathrops' separation, is her fullest development of this theme, as well as her longest, most complex, and most interesting story. James Wentworth woos Clover Guerrinar as part of a perverse plan to avenge his friend Stein, who died from unreciprocated love for Clover. Wentworth's fantasies about this revenge metaphorically suggest psychological rape. Wentworth needs to dominate, and Clover needs to remain free—a freedom she defines in terms close to Wentworth's own notion of domination. "Prisoners!" raises the disturbing possibility that neither sex is capable of mutually satisfactory relationships.

Lathrop's stories about children and male-female relationships raise interesting thematic issues, often at the expense of successful narrative structure. Flawed as well are those poems ("Hidden History," "Lost Battle," "Looking Backward," "Unloved," "The Fault-Demon," and "A Ballad of the Mist") where Lathrop employs hackneyed medieval settings to romanticize the idea of lost or unrequited love. Imitative in style and form, conventional in content, these poems are the exercises in literature typical of "accomplished" nineteenth-century women.

Other groups of poems that deal with the relations between the sexes are, however, innovative in technique and daring in content. "A Wooing Song," Lathrop's first published poem, clearly reflects marital joy with none of the fear of loss of identity voiced by the heroine of "Prisoners!". "Morning Song," a brief lyric that describes the pleasures of awakening in the arms of a beloved, and "Violin," in which that musical instrument symbolizes yielding to sexual impulse, move romance into the domain of eros.

Yet another group of poems, set in the contemporary beau monde, depict male-female relationships as one aspect of the overall frivolity and lifelessness of society. Using a female persona, "At the Breakfast Table: Our Modern Amazon" makes extensive use of military metaphors to produce a spirited satire of the coquette. More often, Lathrop assumes a male voice to assail the emptiness of society in poems such as "The Lover's Fate," "Just Bloomed," "The Girls

We Might Have Wed," "Used Up," and "Youth's Suicide." Well executed and penetrating though these poems are, Lathrop's most skillful, subtle, and complex handling of the theme of the vacuity of social mores is entitled "Neither." Published only in *Along the Shore*, "Neither" anticipates T. S. Eliot's "The Love Song of J. Alfred Prufock." Like Prufrock, the speaker in "Neither" is a man whose self-deprecating monologue in the manner of Laforgue questions identity at a crossroad. He is, however, "Doomed to mere fashionable ways" in a society devoid of grander schemes for damnation. Issues of moment succumb to the trivialities of "cigarettes, and tea, / Sighs, mirrors, and society."

Far less interesting are Lathrop's elegiac poems, though they poignantly remind the reader of her grief over the death of her son ("Francie") and her father ("Power against Power"). "The Roads That Meet"—divided into sections on art, love, and charity—hint at the shift her life would take after her conversion to Catholicism.

In the early 1890s, partly from financial necessity, Lathrop turned her pen to biographical subjects. She published a series of articles on her father that she eventually turned into *Memories of Hawthorne* (1897). With her husband, she wrote *A Story of Courage: Annals of the Georgetown Convent of the Visitation of the Blessed Virgin Mary* (1894), a history of the Visitation Nuns in America. Both of these works indicate as much about Lathrop's burgeoning commitment to social justice as they do about their ostensible subjects.

CRITICAL RECEPTION

Along the Shore, Lathrop's collection of poems that appeared in 1888, received mixed reviews, as did many of her short stories. Without a doubt, the most consistently generous critics of her poetry and fiction were her brother, Julian Hawthorne, and her husband, George Parsons Lathrop. Both of these men enjoyed flourishing literary careers of their own and considerable sway among publishers. Lathrop's biographical works about her father, although they too met with some mixed reviews, were enthusiastically received by the general public and highly marketable. Lathrop had discovered a profitable métier at the very moment she decided to abandon it for another calling entirely.

BIBLIOGRAPHY

Works by Rose Hawthorne Lathrop

Books

Along the Shore. Boston: Houghton Mifflin, 1888.
A Story of Courage: Annals of the Georgetown Convent of the Visitation of the Blessed Virgin Mary. With George Parsons Lathrop. Boston: Houghton Mifflin, 1894.
Memories of Hawthorne. Boston: Houghton Mifflin, 1897. New ed., Boston: Houghton Mifflin, 1923.

Short Fiction

"Browning the Meerschaum." *Harper's Bazar* (1874). Clipping file, Archives of the Servants of Relief for Incurable Cancer, Hawthorne, NY.

"Princess Roundabout." *Independent* (1875). Clipping file, Archives of the Servants of Relief for Incurable Cancer, Hawthorne, NY.

"The Owl That Stared." *St. Nicholas Magazine* IV (1876): 16–18.

"Saagenfreed." *Appleton's Journal*, 10 June 1876, 741–745.

"An Up Country Titania." 12 July 1879. Clipping file, Archives of the Servants of Relief for Incurable Cancer, Hawthorne, NY.

"Huff and Tiff." *Harper's Weekly*, 2 September 1882, 554.

"Prisoners!" *Harper's New Monthly Magazine* LXVII (1883): 503–511, 696–705.

"Fun Beams." *St. Nicholas Magazine* XI (1884): 225–231.

"Lindie's Portrait." *St. Nicholas Magazine* XIV (1887): 512–514.

"For a Lord." *Harper's Bazar*, 30 July 1892, 613–615.

"Troth." *Harper's New Monthly Magazine* LXXXV (1892): 341–350.

"Toy Mysteries." *Independent* (n.d.). Clipping file, Archives of the Servants of Relief for Incurable Cancer, Hawthorne, NY.

Poetry Not Appearing in Along the Shore

"The Lover's Fate." *Appleton's Journal* XIX (January 1878): 50.

"The Fault-Demon." *New Country Magazine* V (1883–1884): 798.

"The Greater World." *Scribner's Magazine* V (1889): 536.

"Just Bloomed." *Century* XXXVIII (1889): 480.

"The World Runs On." *Harper's New Monthly Magazine* LXXXI (1890): 845.

"At the Breakfast Table: Our Modern Amazon." 20 July 1891. Clipping file, Archives of the Servants of Relief for Incurable Cancer, Hawthorne, NY.

"The Choice." *Catholic World* LVI (October 1892): 17.

Articles

"My Father's Literary Methods." *Ladies' Home Journal* XI (March 1894): 371–375.

"Hawthorne as Worker." *Cambridge Magazine* II (June 1896): 68–79.

"Some Memories of Hawthorne." *Atlantic Monthly* LXXVII (1896): 173.

"A Cheerful View of a Hard Problem." *Catholic World* LXVIII (February 1899): 659–696.

Studies of Rose Hawthorne Lathrop

Culbertson, Diane, ed. *Rose Hawthorne Lathrop: Selected Writings*. New York: Paulist Press, 1993.

Valenti, Patricia Dunlavy. "*Memories of Hawthorne*: Rose Hawthorne Lathrop's Auto/Biography." *A/B: Auto/Biography Studies* 8 (spring 1993): 1–15.

———. *To Myself a Stranger: A Biography of Rose Hawthorne Lathrop*. Baton Rouge: Louisiana State University Press, 1991.

EMMA LAZARUS (1849–1887)

Carolyn A. Statler

BIOGRAPHY

Emma Lazarus was born in New York City on July 22, 1849, the fourth of seven children, to a close-knit, wealthy Jewish family. The children were probably tutored privately in the classical tradition—literature, the arts, mythology, and languages. The family belonged to a synagogue, but "the religious side of Judaism held little interest for Miss Lazarus or . . . her family" (Cowen 241).

Biographers have relied heavily on a memoir written by her sister Josephine for information about Lazarus's life. Lazarus is painted as shy and retiring so that "one hesitates to lift the veil and throw light upon a life so hidden and a personality so withdrawn" (1), and as a "true woman, too distinctly feminine to wish to be exceptional" (9).

However, she was also "much sought after in cultured society in New York" (Cohen 321) and always "on fire about something" (Cowen 240). This shy woman sent her first book, *Poems and Translations Written Between the Ages of Fourteen and Sixteen* (1866), to Ralph Waldo Emerson, whom she had met at the home of a friend. Emerson became her literary mentor, and Lazarus dedicated her second book, *Admetus and Other Poems* (1871), to him. When Emerson did not include her work in *Parnassus*, his collection of British and American poetry, Lazarus wrote, expressing her disappointment and questioning his omission.

A personal and literary turning point came with her response to the persecution of Russian Jews (1881–1882) and the subsequent immigration of many Jews to the United States. She visited the immigrants on Ward's Island, helped establish the Hebrew Technical Institute to provide training for immigrants, and wrote "strident poetry and prose in behalf of Eastern European Jews" (Young 43).

In her recent treatment of Lazarus's life and work, Diane Lichtenstein suggests that Lazarus created a persona that "permitted her entry into the American literary nation by veiling or protecting her" (*Writing* 42). Lazarus did achieve entry through correspondence and many literary connections; her friend and well-known critic E. C. Stedman thought her a "natural companion of scholars and thinkers" (264). At her death on November 19, 1887, the *American Hebrew* published a memorial issue with tributes from Walt Whitman, Harriet Beecher Stowe, Robert Browning, and John Greenleaf Whittier, among others. Whittier said that "the Semitic race never had a braver singer" (quoted in Lichtenstein, *Writing* 58).

MAJOR WORKS AND THEMES

Lazarus's best-known lines, the last five lines of "The New Colossus," begin: "Give me your tired, your poor." The sonnet was written for a literary auction to raise money for a pedestal for the Statue of Liberty. James Russell Lowell wrote to her, "Your sonnet gives its subject a 'raison d'etre' which it wanted before quite as much as it wanted a pedestal" (quoted in Vogel 159).

Lazarus was a respected and talented translator, particularly of the work of Heinrich Heine, as well as a poet. Other translations include the work of medieval Spanish Jewish poets, Goethe, Hugo, Petrarch, and Leopardi. She wrote two works of fiction, *Alide* (1874), based upon Goethe's account of a youthful affair, and a short story, "The Eleventh Hour"; she wrote one drama, *The Spagnoletto*, based on the life of a seventeenth-century Spanish artist.

Lazarus's early work is largely drawn from classical themes or deals with destiny, greatness, the artist, nature, and beauty. In her work, Lazarus moved from "worshipping at the Greek shrine" (Vogel 159) to more contemporary, particularly Jewish, themes: anti-Semitism and the establishment of a Jewish state. She was also an ardent proponent of an American national literature freed from European influence.

As a spokesperson for Jewish causes, Lazarus was a prolific contributor of essays, reviews, and poems to newspapers and periodicals. Three notable essays are "Is Lord Beaconsfield a Representative Jew?" which argues that Disraeli is representative; "Russian Christianity vs. Modern Judaism," which responds to a newspaper article that denied the persecution of Russian Jews; and "The Jewish Problem," which suggests resolution in the establishment of a Jewish state. The *American Hebrew* published her fifteen-part series *An Epistle to the Hebrews* (1882–1883), an appeal to Jews to "reflect on their history" and "preserve their special identities" (Lichtenstein, *Writing* 47).

Lichtenstein places Lazarus in the tradition of Jewish women writers because Lazarus addresses the themes of that tradition: "ideals of womanhood, of Jewishness, of Americanness and the fusion of those identities" (*Writing* 37).

CRITICAL RECEPTION

Sixteen years after her death, the *New York Tribune* characterized Lazarus as the "most talented woman the Jewish race has produced in this country" (quoted in Young 15). Praised as a "Miriam" and a "Deborah," discussion of her work often focuses on her gender and religion, which Lichtenstein suggests is the reason that her work is often ignored.

Her work was apparently taken seriously by Emerson and praised by Ivan Turgenev and Robert Browning. Her first book, written in her teens, was well received, although Vogel suggests with a "good deal more kindness than the pervading unoriginality of most of the pieces called for" (43).

Although William Dean Howells rejected "Admetus" for publication in the *Atlantic Monthly*, it was praised by London reviewers, who compared her work favorably to Browning's. Whittier said of her that "she often has the rugged strength and verbal audacity of Browning" (quoted in Lichtenstein, *Writing* 58).

Lazarus's "magnum opus" (Cowen 229), "The Dance to Death," is written in blank verse, which is often stronger than her rhymed verse. Like her other work, it has had varied response. This five-act tragedy is described as a "strangely powerful drama" (Stedman 264), "full of sonorous, graceful passages" (*The Critic* 293). However, Jacobs dismisses it as "an ill-conceived intrigue . . . the whole love story is . . . unconvincing and dull" (150). Her last work, "By the Waters of Babylon," in a form she called "Little Poems in Prose," is seen by Schappes as a "beautiful summation of her character and ideals of her most mature style" (*Selections* 24) but by Jacobs as the "failing effort of a failing spirit" (197).

Today, "The New Colossus" is probably Lazarus's only work that is remembered. Widely known and widely read in her lifetime, she may have been "more beloved than studied" (Vogel 162). Young suggests that her work has not survived because "her talent was not a major one," and her work "no longer rings true" (xv). However, Vogel believes that she "presaged the spiritual odyssey" of twentieth-century Jewish writers (preface). Schappes, who has done much to preserve Lazarus's work, says that the reason to read Lazarus today is that "she can still delight, stir, inspire and instruct" (*Selections* 15).

BIBLIOGRAPHY

Works by Emma Lazarus

Poems and Translations Written Between the Ages of Fourteen and Sixteen. New York: Printed for private circulation, 1866.
Admetus and Other Poems. 1871. Reprint, Upper Saddle River, NJ: Literature House, 1970.
Alide, an Episode in Goethe's Life. Philadelphia: Lippincott, 1874.
Poems and Ballads of Heinrich Heine. New York: R. Worthington, 1881.

Songs of a Semite: The Dance to Death and Other Poems. 1882. Reprint, Upper Saddle River, NJ: Literature House, 1970.
An Epistle to the Hebrews. 1882–1883. Edited by Morris U. Schappes. Centennial Edition. New York: Jewish Historical Society of New York, 1987.
The Poems of Emma Lazarus. 2 vols. New York: Houghton Mifflin, 1888.
Schappes, Morris U., ed. *The Letters of Emma Lazarus 1868–1885.* New York: New York Public Library, 1949.
———. *Emma Lazarus: Selections from Her Poetry and Prose.* New York: Emma Lazarus Federation of Jewish Women's Clubs, 1967.

See Vogel for an extensive listing of works in periodicals, uncollected works, and unpublished works in manuscript.

Studies of Emma Lazarus

Baym, Max I. "Emma Lazarus and Emerson." *Publications of the American Jewish Historical Society* 38 (1949): 261–287.
———. "A Neglected Translator of Italian Poetry: Emma Lazarus." *Italica* 21, no. 4 (1944): 175–185.
Cohen, Mary M. "Emma Lazarus: Woman; Poet; Patriot." *Poet-Lore: A Magazine of Letters* 5 (1893): 320–331.
Cowen, Philip. "Recollections of Emma Lazarus." *American Hebrew,* 5 July 1929, 229.
Jacob, Heinrich Eduard. *The World of Emma Lazarus.* New York: Schocken Books, 1949.
Lazarus, Josephine. Introduction to *The Poems of Emma Lazarus.* New York: Houghton Mifflin, 1888.
Lichtenstein, Diane. "Emma Lazarus." In *Jewish American Women Writers: A Bio-Bibliographical and Critical Sourcebook,* edited by Ann R. Shapiro. Westport, CT: Greenwood Press, 1994.
———. "Words and Worlds: Emma Lazarus's Conflicting Citizenships." *Tulsa Studies in Women's Literature* 6, no. 2 (1987): 247–263.
———. *Writing Their Nations: The Tradition of Nineteenth Century Women Writers.* Bloomington: Indiana University Press, 1992. 36–59.
Merriam, Eve. *Emma Lazarus: Woman with a Torch.* New York: Citadel Press, 1956.
"Miss Lazarus' Life and Literary Work." *The Critic,* 10 December 1887, 293–295.
"Miss Lazarus's Translations of Heine." *The Century,* 8 March 1882, 785–786.
Pauli, Hertha, and E. B. Ashton. *I Lift My Lamp.* New York: Appleton-Century-Crofts, 1948.
Ruchames, Louis. "New Light on the Religious Development of Emma Lazarus." *Publications of the American Jewish Historical Society* 42 (1952): 83–88.
Stedman, E. C. *Genius and Other Essays.* 1911. Reprint, Port Washington NY: Kennikat Press, 1966. 264–267.
Vogel, Dan. *Emma Lazarus.* Boston: Twayne Publishers, 1980.
Young, Bette Roth. *Emma Lazarus in Her World, Life and Letters.* Philadelphia: Jewish Publication Society, 1995.

MARIA JANE McINTOSH
(1803–1878)

Jennifer Hynes

BIOGRAPHY

Maria Jane McIntosh was born in 1803 in Sunbury, Georgia, to Mary Moore (Maxwell) and Lachlan McIntosh, the descendant of a prominent Scottish family and a wealthy plantation owner and lawyer who died when Maria was just a few years old. McIntosh was educated at home by her mother and at two schools: a coeducational academy in Sunbury and Baisden's Bluff Academy in McIntosh County. After her mother died in 1823, McIntosh began managing the plantation. In 1835 she sold the property and moved to New York to live with a half brother, naval Captain James McKay McIntosh. She invested her fortune in securities but lost it in the Panic of 1837.

McIntosh's financial crisis led her to attempt a writing career, beginning with a series of moral children's stories that were published using the pseudonym "Aunt Kitty." By the early 1840s she had turned to writing moral fiction for adults and novels that Nina Baym classifies as "woman's fiction," publishing anonymously until 1846. McIntosh was a prolific writer, and her novels were successful enough, appearing both in American and British editions, to afford her an independent living.

McIntosh spent 1859 living in Geneva, Switzerland, with the wife of a nephew, John Elliott Ward. After she returned to New York, she taught at a school run by Henrietta B. Haines. After publishing her final novel, *Two Pictures; or, What We Think of Ourselves, and What the World Thinks of Us* (1863), she held for a time a fashionable salon in New York. After suffering a yearlong illness, McIntosh died at the home of her niece and namesake, Maria McIntosh Cox (who was also a writer), in Morristown, New Jersey, on February 25, 1878.

MAJOR WORKS AND THEMES

McIntosh began her literary career with moral juvenile stories modeled on Samuel Griswold Goodrich's popular ''Peter Parley'' tales. From this work, she made a smooth transition to writing moral fiction for young men with her first novels for adults: *Conquest and Self-Conquest; or, Which Makes the Hero?* (1843) and *Praise and Principle; or, For What Shall I Live?* (1845). Both of these early works contrast an upright, hardworking, temperate hero with his lazy, self-indulgent friend, with the hero benefiting from his efforts and restraint.

McIntosh would continue the formula of contrasting characters and situations in her later novels, most of which focus on the trials and fortunes of a struggling heroine in the style of ''woman's fiction.'' For example, *Two Lives; or, To Seem and to Be* (1846), the first novel published under McIntosh's own name, deals with a pair of dissimilar heroines. The impulsive, emotional, dependent Grace Elliott contrasts with her cousin, self-aware, independent, orphaned Isabel Duncan, to represent both the dangers of dependence and the dangers of excess independence for women. Likewise, in her proslavery novel *The Lofty and the Lowly; or, Good in All and None All-Good* (1853), McIntosh portrays the virtues of a chivalrous South against the vices of an enterprising North. But both the slave economy of the plantation and the factory system of the urban North— along with the societies that they create—come in for criticism from McIntosh, who seems to advocate a happy medium. Finally, McIntosh follows the nineteenth-century tradition of creating pairs of heroines whose outward appearances signify inner differences. In *The Lofty and the Lowly*, the blonde Alice is a delicate, obedient, submissive, devout Christian, while her brunette cousin, Isabelle, is a proud, passionate, fashionable belle.

Although McIntosh tended, particularly early in her career, to employ some of the standard elements of popular fiction, her individual stamp resulted in ingenious plot maneuvers and complex character development. For example, while one of her earliest novels, *Woman an Enigma; or, Life and Its Revealings* (1843), depicts convent life and the French Revolution, she weaves her components into a psychological study of female character development. Thus, as Baym argues, McIntosh was one of the earliest novelists to emphasize the interior life of heroines rather than spinning melodramatic tales.

McIntosh was also an apologist for slavery, in 1853 writing both her proslavery novel *The Lofty and the Lowly* and an essay, ''Letter on the Address of the Women of England to Their Sisters of America, in Relation to Slavery.'' The novel, which was written in answer to Harriet Beecher Stowe's blockbuster antislavery novel, *Uncle Tom's Cabin* (1852), pits a vicious, exploitive system of Northern factory labor against a family-centered plantation economy that values slaves and teaches them to live as Christians. Likewise, McIntosh's essay, which appeared first in the *New York Observer* before its publication in pamphlet form, was written in reaction to ''An Affectionate and Christian Address of Many Thousands of Women of Great Britain and Ireland to Their Sisters the

Thousands of Women of the United States of America,'' an abolitionist plea that was entrusted to Stowe by a group of British women during her 1853 visit to England. McIntosh's essay argues that slaves are happy and well cared for under a plantation system run by nurturing, humane Christians.

McIntosh's only other nonfiction, *Woman in America: Her Work and Her Reward* (1850), outlined her conservative position on the nineteenth-century woman question. In this piece, she criticizes the women's rights movement, taking a stand for domestic feminism to argue that women should use their position of spiritual and moral superiority to reform American society. Like the heroines in her fiction, the ideal for women is put forth not as independence and self-assertion but as a proud, virtuous dependence on the strength of men.

CRITICAL RECEPTION

Although she began her writing career with pseudonymous children's stories and followed with anonymous adult works, McIntosh became a popular author when she finally began publishing under her own name in 1846 with *Two Lives; or, To Seem and to Be*. By 1855 she was included in Sarah Josepha Hale's *Woman's Record*; Hale lauded McIntosh's ''originality and freshness of mind,'' as well as her ''unusual power in depicting the passions and interesting the feelings'' (742). Hale also noted the trait that most strongly characterized nineteenth-century opinion of McIntosh: her ''pure morality and religion'' (742). She was cited in the 1875 edition of Evert A. and George L. Duyckinck's *Cyclopaedia of American Literature* as the creator of fiction characterized by ''truthfulness and happy style'' (2:206). Even as late as the 1890s, Julia Colles applauded McIntosh's work for its nobility and high ''spirituality'' (2:176).

While many popular nineteenth-century women writers have enjoyed a resurgence of interest during the past two decades, McIntosh has received little attention in terms of scholarly articles, republication of her work, or inclusion in anthologies. In spite of efforts by Nina Baym, Bashar Akili, and Elizabeth Moss to offer a thorough analysis of McIntosh's works, she is generally remembered as one of the many creators of flowery, sentimental melodrama popular during the midnineteenth century. McIntosh also tends to inflame twentieth-century critics because of her proslavery stance.

WORKS CITED

''An Affectionate and Christian Address of Many Thousands of Women of Great Britain and Ireland to Their Sisters the Thousands of Women of the United States of America.'' 1853. Reprinted in Forrest Wilson, *Crusader in Crinoline: The Life of Harriet Beecher Stowe*. Philadelphia: Lippincott, 1941. 342–343.

Colles, Julia Keese. ''Miss Maria McIntosh.'' In *Authors and Writers Associated with Morristown. With a Chapter on Historic Morristown*. 2nd ed. Morristown, NJ: Vogt Brothers, 1895. 174–176.

Duyckinck, Evert A., and George L. Duyckinck. *Cyclopaedia of American Literature*. 2 vols. Philadelphia: William Rutter & Co., 1875.

Hale, Sarah Josepha. *Woman's Record*. New York: Harper & Brothers, 1855.

BIBLIOGRAPHY

Works by Maria Jane McIntosh

Blind Alice; or, Do Right If You Wish to Be Happy, as by Aunt Kitty. New York: Dayton and Saxton, 1841.

Florence Arnott; or, Is She Generous?, as by Aunt Kitty. New York: Dayton and Saxton, 1841.

Jessie Graham; or, Friends Dear, but Truth Dearer, as by Aunt Kitty. New York: Dayton and Saxton, 1841.

Ellen Leslie; or, The Reward of Self-Control, as by Aunt Kitty. New York: Dayton and Newman, 1842.

Grace and Clara; or, Be Just as Well as Generous, as by Aunt Kitty. New York: Dayton and Saxton, 1842.

Conquest and Self-Conquest; or, Which Makes the Hero? (anon.) New York: Harper & Brothers, 1843.

Woman an Enigma; or, Life and Its Revealings. (anon.) New York: Harper & Brothers, 1843; London: Novel Newspaper, no. 326, 1843. Also published as *Louise de la Valiere*.

The Cousins: A Tale of Early Life, as by Aunt Kitty. New York: Harper & Brothers, 1845.

Praise and Principle; or, For What Shall I Live? (anon.) New York: Harper & Brothers, 1845.

Two Lives; or, To Seem and to Be. New York: D. Appleton & Co., 1846.

Aunt Kitty's Tales. New York: D. Appleton & Co., 1847.

Charms and Counter-charms. New York: D. Appleton & Co., 1848.

Woman in America: Her Work and Her Reward. New York: D. Appleton & Co., 1850.

Evenings at Donaldson Manor; or, The Christmas Guest. New York: D. Appleton & Co., 1851.

Letter on the Address of the Women of England to Their Sisters of America, in Relation to Slavery. New York: T. J. Crowen, 1853. Originally appeared in the *New York Observer*, 28 April 1853.

The Lofty and the Lowly; or, Good in All and None All-Good. New York: D. Appleton & Co., 1853. Republished as *Alice Montrose; or, The Lofty and the Lowly: Good in All and None All Good*. London: R. Bentley, 1853.

Meta Gray; or, What Makes Home Happy. New York: D. Appleton & Co., 1853.

Emily Herbert; or, The Happy Home. New York and London: D. Appleton & Co., 1855.

Rose and Lillie Stanhope; or, The Power of Conscience. New York: D. Appleton & Co., 1855.

Violet; or, The Cross and the Crown. Boston: John P. Jewett and Co., 1856.

A Year with Maggie and Emma: A True Story. New York and London: D. Appleton & Co., 1861.

Two Pictures; or, What We Think of Ourselves, and What the World Thinks of Us. New York: D. Appleton & Co., 1863.

Violette and I, as by Cousin Kate. Boston: Loring, 1870.

The Children's Mirror: A Treasury of Stories, as by Cousin Kate. London and New York: T. Nelson, 1887.

Studies of Maria Jane McIntosh

Akili, Bashar. "Maria Jane McIntosh, a Woman in Her Time: A Biographical and Critical Study." Dissertation, University of Technology, Loughborough, United Kingdom, 1990.

Baym, Nina. "Maria McIntosh." In *Woman's Fiction: A Guide to Novels by and about Women in America 1820–1870.* 2nd ed. Urbana and Chicago: University of Illinois Press, 1993. 86–109.

Chew, Martha. "Maria Jane McIntosh." In *American Women Writers: A Critical Reference Guide from Colonial Times to the Present*, edited by Lina Mainiero. Vol. 4. New York: Frederick Ungar, 1982. 96–98.

Colles, Julia Keese. "Miss Maria McIntosh." In *Authors and Writers Associated with Morristown. With a Chapter on Historic Morristown.* 2nd ed. Morristown, NJ: Vogt Brothers, 1895. 174–176.

Moss, Elizabeth. *Domestic Novelists in the Old South: Defenders of Southern Culture.* Baton Rouge: Louisiana University Press, 1992.

Moss, Sara Elizabeth. " 'Our Earnest Appeal': The Southern Domestic Novelists and Their Literary Defense of Southern Culture, 1833–1866." Ph.D. diss., Washington University, 1989.

ADAH ISAACS MENKEN
(1835–1868)

Gary Scharnhorst

BIOGRAPHY

Born Ada Bertha Theodore near New Orleans to a Creole father and a Jewish-Irish mother, the actor and poet Adah Isaacs Menken was best known to nineteenth-century audiences for her performances in *Mazeppa*, a melodrama loosely based on Byron's verse romance. Despite her impoverished circumstances, Menken received a classical education, and in 1855, she began to publish poetry and appear in local theatricals in east Texas. By 1857, she was an established actor on the New Orleans stage and an occasional contributor of verse to the Cincinnati *Israelite*. After her New York debut in 1859, she frequented Whitman's circle at Pfaff's. The next year, depressed by a divorce from her first husband and separation from her second, heavyweight boxer John Carmel Heenan, and by the deaths of a son and her mother, Menken contemplated suicide and plumbed the depths of her despair in a series of poems eventually collected in her posthumously published volume *Infelicia*. She resumed her career in 1861, performing *Mazeppa* for the first time in Albany on June 3. In 1862 she married humorist Robert Henry Newell ("Orpheus C. Kerr"), and in the summer of 1863 they sailed for San Francisco, where she performed *Mazeppa* at Maguire's Opera House over a period of four months for upward of half the box office receipts. While in California, she also joined the coterie of writers who produced the literary weekly *Golden Era*, among them Joaquin Miller, Mark Twain, Bret Harte, Charles Warren Stoddard, and Artemus Ward. Miller later wrote, "Her fascination lay in her beauty of mind, her soul and sweet sympathy, her sensibility to all that was beautiful in form, color, life, heart, humanity" (quoted in Jacobson 199). In his essay "A Full and Reliable Account of the Extraordinary Meteoric Shower of Last Saturday Night," Twain alluded to her western theatrical tour: "[T]he whole constellation of the Great Menken came flaming out of the heavens like a vast spray of gas-jets, and shed a glory abroad over the universe as it fell!" (Harte and Twain 153). On his part, Harte modeled a character in his nouvelle *The Crusade of the Excelsior* (1887) upon Menken. In March 1864, while she was staging *Mazeppa* in Virginia City, the miners there named an outcrop of the Comstock Lode "the Menken" and founded the Menken Shaft and Tunnel Company to drill for ore.

In October 1864, Menken opened in *Mazeppa* at Astley's Amphitheatre in London, where she again attracted a circle of literary admirers, including Charles Reade, Algernon Swinburne, and Dante Gabriel Rossetti. After divorcing Newell in 1865, she married James Paul Barkley, a former Confederate officer, at her New York mansion Bleak House in August 1866. Three days later, Menken sailed alone to Paris, where she bore a short-lived son in November who was christened in honor of his godmother, George Sand. Shortly before the end of the year, she performed triumphantly in *Les Pirates de la Savane* at the Théatre de la Gaité in Paris, and her salon was soon frequented by such figures as Théophile Gautier and the elder Alexandre Dumas. Her affairs with Swinburne and Dumas, who traded in the rumors by authorizing the sale of photographs of them together, invited ridicule, though they hardly dampened her popularity. Menken died in Paris in August 1868 from an ailment variously diagnosed as consumption, cancer, and a ruptured appendix. Visited on her deathbed by Henry Wadsworth Longfellow, she urged her friends not to grieve: "I have lived more than a woman of a hundred years of age; it is only justice I should go to where they carry the old" (quoted in Mankowitz 237). Initially buried in the Jewish section of Père Lachaise, her body was removed at the instructions of her agent Edwin James to Montparnasse the next year.

MAJOR WORKS AND THEMES

The collection *Infelicia* contains thirty-one of Menken's "wild soul poems," about half of her total production. These lines were often written, as she once explained, "in the stillness of midnight and when waking to the world the next day they were to me the deepest mystery. I do not see in them as a part of myself; yet I know that the soul prompted every word and that every line is somewhere within me" (quoted in Lesser 215). Such sentimental poems as "Resurgam" and the sonnet "Aspiration," first published in the *Golden Era* in 1863, dramatize "the cruel and harsh victimisation of women in mid-nineteenth-century social life. Women could recognise the truths contained in her writing, even if they attributed the extremity of the Menken's experience of them, to her moral laxity" (Mankowitz 80). In them, the poet declares her independence, her refusal ever again to rely upon men for a livelihood. In the lines that close the volume, "Infelix," first published in the *Golden Era* on January 3, 1864, the poet indulges in the luxury of regret: "I can but own my life is vain/A desert void of peace;/I missed the goal I sought to gain." Elsewhere, as in "Judith," she indicts moral hypocrites: "Stand back, ye Philistines!/Practice what ye preach to me;/I heed ye not, for I know ye all./Ye are living burning lies, and profanation to the garments which with stately steps ye sweep your marble palaces." Such vers libre clearly betrays the influence of Whitman, whose "poetic form . . . brought her a medium in which she could express the full fire of her passion and emotion. Although she never became a slavish imitation of his free verse form, she was unquestionably the first and probably the only American poet at the time who dared to follow along the path Whitman had opened" (Lesser 64).

CRITICAL RECEPTION

Dedicated with his permission to Charles Dickens, Menken's *Infelicia* was continuously in print between 1868 and 1902. In a review of the first American edition, the *New York Tribune* dismissed her poetry as "little more than an echo of Walt Whitman, Ossian, and other suspicious models, with no assuring proof of originality or even of sincerity. . . . The tone of the volume is for the most part sad, often cynical, even desperate, but the smell of foot-lights and burnt rosin pervades the whole composition" (6). On a more sympathetic note, however, the *New York Times* allowed that while the poet's "whole life was passed in violation of social law," the poems "show that there was left in her" a "grace of virtue," that "she was conscious of the better way" (4). Similarly, Rossetti thought some of the writing "really remarkable" (quoted in Mankowitz 200). Though Swinburne reportedly wrote across the page proofs of the book, "Lo, this is she that was the world's delight," he later told Theodore Watts-Dutton that her poems were "the greatest rubbish ever written" (quoted in Lesser 212). Before 1950, a pair of master's theses were devoted to Menken's verse; however, her poetry has attracted little critical attention even during the canon reformation of the past generation. Menken's best biographer Allen Lesser has opined, "The poems Menken wrote during this storm and stress period of her life [in 1860–1861], more revealing than those which any other female American poet had ever dared publish, disclose her growing bewilderment, her indignation, and finally the crushing sense of humiliation that followed" (62). In all, however, he concludes, "She lacked the critical perspective to see that her poems expressed the very essence of the American spirit in their bold rhythms and lurid images. In their broad splashes of color and extravagant self-dramatizations they were completely alien to the trend toward decadence of contemporary English literature" (215).

WORKS CITED

Anonymous. "Adah Isaacs Menken's Poems." *New York Tribune*, 29 September 1868, 6:2–3.
Anonymous. Review of *Infelicia*. *New York Times*, 21 October 1868, 4.

Harte, Bret, and Mark Twain. *Sketches of the Sixties*. San Francisco: Howell, 1926. 151–157.

Jacobson, Pauline. *City of the Golden Fifties*. Berkeley: University of California Press, 1941.

Lesser, Allen. *Enchanting Rebel: The Secret of Adah Isaacs Menken*. New York: Beechurst Press, 1947.

Mankowitz, Wolf. *Mazeppa: The Lives, Loves and Legends of Adah Isaacs Menken*. London: Blond & Briggs, 1982.

BIBLIOGRAPHY

Work by Adah Isaacs Menken

Infelicia. London and Paris: Hotten; Philadelphia: Lippincott, 1868.

Studies of Adah Isaacs Menken

Anonymous. "Adah Isaacs Menken." *New York Times*, 12 August 1868, 4:6.

Anonymous. "Infelix." *Brooklyn Eagle Supplement*, 25 June 1882, 2.

Falk, Bernard. *The Naked Lady: A Biography of Adah Isaacs Menken*. London: Hutchinson, 1952.

Foster, Barbara M., and Michael Foster. "Adah Isaacs Menken: An American Original." *North Dakota Quarterly* 61 (fall 1993): 52–62.

———. "Adah Isaacs Menken Wins the West." *Journal of the West* 33 (October 1994): 76–82.

Menken, Adah Isaacs. "Notes of My Life." *New York Times*, 6 September 1868, 3.

Rowland, Andrea. "Tilley and Menken: Male Impersonators in the Popular Theater of Nineteenth-Century England." *Theatre Annual* 44 (1989): 11–20.

ANNA CORA OGDEN MOWATT (RITCHIE) (1819–1870)

Lois Josephs Fowler

BIOGRAPHY

Anna Cora Mowatt was born in 1819, ninth of fourteen children of Samuel and Eliza Ogden, both descended from patrician American families. She spent the first six years of her life in southern France because her father's shipping business demanded that he be there. When her family returned to New York City, she enrolled in boarding school. In her *Autobiography of an Actress* (1854), she writes about moving from a very strict boarding school to one more playful, where learning was fun, and she attributes the change to the good sense of her mother, who recognized the disadvantages of too much discipline.

From the time she was small, Mowatt exhibited a precocious love of learning and of writing. She wrote amateur plays that her sisters and brother performed at family functions. Then, when she was only fifteen, and despite her family's disapproval that she marry at such a young age, she eloped with a young lawyer, James Mowatt. Reconciliation with her family soon took place, however, and she continued to stage amateur productions of her own. In 1835, she published her first play, *Gulzara*, in *The New World*, a magazine considered to be genteel for the publication of a work written by refined, talented young ladies. *Fashion; or Life in New York* (1849), the best known of her plays and one that is still produced today, was written much later in her career.

Mowatt's husband lost his business investments in the depression of the late 1830s, and his sight became greatly impaired by an unexpected illness. With his support and that of her father, Mowatt began giving public readings of poetry in order to earn an income. These attempts were met with enthusiasm by audiences who, despite her patrician background, were receptive to Mowatt, and she soon began to augment this income by publishing stories, novels, and plays.

She continued to work as a writer and performer, and between 1845 and 1854, she won acclaim both for the successful staging of her plays and for her appearances as a leading actress in America and England. As a woman of her class, Mowatt worried about appearing on stage, but the need for money prevailed. She starred not only in her own well-known play *Fashion* but also in Shakespearean comedies, in Sheridan's plays (especially *The School for Scandal*), and in popular nineteenth-century sentimental dramas, such as *The Lady of Lyons*.

After suffering ill health for several years, her husband died in England in 1851. In 1854, Mowatt gave up her career in theater to marry William F. Ritchie, an editor of the *Richmond Examiner*, in Richmond, Virginia, where she became active in the highly conservative social life. Her marriage to Ritchie, however, had many difficulties; not only did she suspect him of having an affair with a slave, but in the sectional crisis preceding the Civil War, she was unable to take sides with him against the Union. Shortly before the outbreak of war, Mowatt and Ritchie separated, and she eventually returned to England. Despite the popularity of *Fashion*, the legal ambiguities involved in the payment of royalties left Mowatt with little money. In her later years, she became too ill to continue writing, and she died in England in 1870.

MAJOR WORKS AND THEMES

Fashion, Mowatt's major work as a playwright, was a satire of manners that illustrates her debt to restoration comedy in style but not in substance; it focuses on the importance of American morality and criticizes attempts by the new rich to copy European customs. The heroine is Gertrude Trueblood, who marries the hero at the end; the satire focuses on Mrs. Tiffany, who mistakes a French butler for a count, spends her husband's money frivolously until he is bankrupt, and copies what she takes to be European style and "fashion." The play continues to arouse laughter even with contemporary audiences. It was one of the more successful American plays of its time and virtually the only one of the period still produced and appreciated today.

Mowatt's *Autobiography of an Actress, or, Eight Years on the Stage* (1854) presents the central image of a woman of vivid personality playing out a drama influenced by her breach of social convention. In need of money and with many debts from her husband's long illness, Mowatt had financial worries and hoped that publication of her autobiography would prove profitable. Her purpose in writing it, however, is stated in a conventional way: to fulfill a promise made to her late husband to describe the experiences of a woman in acting. Yet the autobiography betrays feminist feelings; Mowatt describes herself as a struggling sister who challenges the public image of what women can and must do. She demonstrates rebellion against conformity by illustrating how women can escape from their traditional positions of legal and social inferiority. She also presents evidence of understanding the broader history of her times, including details of her own importance as a woman who transformed her place in society by becoming a public figure and risking a challenge to her reputation. The treatment of her own successful experiences with hypnotism for illnesses, and her identification with the philosopher Swedenborg, also provides insight into nineteenth-century medical and intellectual interests. Mowatt's autobiography is also literary in its consciousness of self, a confessional genre that has become popular in contemporary letters.

It is not clear why Mowatt waited until after her husband's death in 1851 to publish her memoirs; what is clear is her desire to protect him from any more disappointments or shame than he had already endured by his illness and financial ruin.

CRITICAL RECEPTION

Despite her prolificacy, Mowatt's work has garnered little critical attention in recent years. In addition to her plays, she wrote minor pieces of fiction and travel accounts, but her reputation today rests primarily on her autobiography and the popularity of *Fashion*, which was well received by both British and American audiences and is still anthologized and performed today.

According to accounts by critic Eric W. Barnes, "the press reports [of *Fashion*], both in terms of space allotted and liberality of encomiums, exceeded anything heretofore offered New Yorkers by way of dramatic criticism" (110). J. W. S. Hows, for example, declared that "Mrs. Mowatt may lay claim to having produced the best American comedy in existence" (quoted in Barnes 110), and the daily New York *Express* review was equally enthusiastic. Although there were "two or three dissenting voices" among the critics covering the opening night performance, including one by Edgar Allan Poe, who dismissed *Fashion* as a bad imitation of *The School for Scandal* (111), Barnes concludes that "it is probably quite safe to say that no play ever written by an American is comparable to *Fashion* in the immediate sensation which it created" (111). Likewise, critic Lee A. Jacobus applauds *Fashion* as "a true American statement" (33).

Of the autobiography, feminists such as Elizabeth Cady Stanton argued for its importance as a document that spoke for women's acceptance in all occupations. Generally, however, active feminists of the time focused their energy and reading on the more militant work by women who addressed issues such as unfair marriage laws and suffrage. Dr. Mary Walker, however, wrote "the only negative criticism of the *Autobiography* in *The Evangelical Review* (Barnes 258), when she refuted Mowatt's contention that "there was nothing in the theatrical profession itself which was absolutely conducive to immorality" (258). Nathaniel Hawthorne, on the other hand, was so impressed with Mowatt's memoirs that he suggested it as recommended reading to his friend Richard Monckton Milnes (258). Indeed, "almost without exception" critics reacted favorably to the book (257). As late as 1954, Barnes maintained that Mowatt's

Autobiography "is still a very remarkable book. It gives us the most important picture of the theatre of the forties and fifties which we possess" (258).

BIBLIOGRAPHY

Works by Anna Cora Ogden Mowatt

Pelayo, of the Cavern of Covadonga. New York: Harper, 1836.

Gulzara, or the Persian Slave. New York: S. French, 1841.

The Fortune Hunter, or the Adventures of a Man about Town: A Novel of New York Society. New York: J. Winchester, New World Press, 1844.

The Lady's Work-Box Companion: Being Instructions in All Varieties of Canvas Work. New York: Burgess, Stringer, and Co., 1844.

Life of Goethe: From His Autobiographical Papers and the Contributions of His Contemporaries. New York: J. Mowatt, 1844.

Evelyn, or a Heart Unmasked: A Tale of Domestic Life. Philadelphia: G. B. Zieber, 1845.

Armand; or the Peer and the Peasant. New York: S. French, 1847.

Fashion; or Life in New York. New York: S. French, 1849.

Autobiography of an Actress, or, Eight Years on the Stage. Boston: Ticknor, Reed, and Fields, 1854.

Twin Roses: A Narrative. Boston: Ticknor and Fields, 1857.

Fairy Fingers: A Novel. New York: Carleton, 1865.

The Mute Singer: A Novel. New York: Carleton, 1866.

Italian Life and Legends. New York: Carleton, 1870.

Studies of Anna Cora Ogden Mowatt

Barnes, Eric Wollencott. *The Lady of Fashion: The Life and Theatre of Anna Cora Mowatt.* New York: Scribner, 1954.

Butler, Mildred Allen. *Actress in Spite of Herself: The Life of Anna Cora Mowatt.* New York: Funk & Wagnalls, 1966.

Jacobus, Lee A. "Anna Cora Mowatt: *Fashion.*" In *The Longman Anthology of American Literature.* Edited by Lee A. Jacobus. New York: Longman, 1982. 33–34.

Matthews, Brander. *Macready and Forrest and Their Contemporaries.* New York: Cassell, 1886.

McCaslin, Nellie. *Leading Lady.* Studio City, CA: Players Press, 1993.

MARY NOAILLES MURFREE (CHARLES EGBERT CRADDOCK) (1850–1922)

Jennifer A. Gehrman

BIOGRAPHY

Mary Noailles Murfree was born at Grantland, the family plantation near Murfreesboro, Tennessee, on January 24, 1850, the second of three children born to William Law Murfree and Fanny Priscilla (Dickinson) Murfree. When she was only four years old, she suffered from a dangerously high fever that left her with permanent, minor paralysis. During her convalescence, she nurtured an already voracious reading habit supported by the family's extensive private library. In 1855 the Murfrees began a fifteen-year tradition of vacationing in the Cumberland mountains at Beersheba Springs, the resort that would later become the model for Murfree's fictional New Helvetia Springs. Here Mary was first exposed to the lifestyles and mannerisms of the mountain folk who would inhabit so much of her fiction. In 1857 the family moved to Nashville, where Mary and her sister Fanny attended the Nashville Female Academy. The family remained in Nashville for the duration of the Civil War, during which Grantland was burned to the ground in the 1862 battle of Stone River—an incident Murfree later used as the basis for her first novel, *Where the Battle Was Fought* (1884).

Shortly after the end of the war, the Murfrees sent Mary and Fanny for a two-year sojourn at the Chegary Institute, a continental-style girl's finishing school in Philadelphia. They returned to Nashville in 1869, remaining until 1872 when the entire family moved back to the outskirts of Murfreesboro and the recently completed New Grantland. There Mary first began to write with publication in mind, strongly encouraged by her father and perhaps prompted by the family's thinning financial resources. "Flirts and Their Ways," an essay by R. Emmet Embury, appeared in the May 1874 issue of *Lippincott's*, followed just over one year later by "My Daughter's Admirers," published under the same pseudonym. Both are examples of biting social satire in which Murfree exposes the pettiness and subterfuge rampant in genteel society; she meticulously pins down and classifies each genus of the species social butterfly.

"The Dancin' Party at Harrison's Cove" appeared in the *Atlantic Monthly* in May 1878 under the pseudonym Charles Egbert Craddock, inaugurating Murfree's career as a leader in Southern regionalist writing. This was not, however, her first account of Tennessee mountain life; two earlier works, "Taking the Blue Ribbon at the County Fair" and "The Panther of Jolton's Ridge," had been accepted by *Appleton's Weekly* in 1876, but the magazine went out of circulation before either of the stories appeared in print. "The Dancin' Party," a portrait of Southern mountain folk as seen through the eyes of a worldly outsider, set the pattern for the kind of fiction Murfree would write for the next two decades. She followed it with seven more stories in the pages of the *Atlantic Monthly*, publishing all eight in an 1884 collection called *In the Tennessee Mountains*, a volume that met with immediate and sustained success.

In 1881 the entire family moved to St. Louis, where Mary's brother, William, was already practicing law. She continued to write highly popular short stories and novels throughout the next decade. One of her most popular novels, *The Prophet of the Great Smoky Mountains*, began a serialized run in the *Atlantic Monthly* in January 1885, several months before Murfree ever actually saw the Smokies. Before her first landmark visit to Montvale Springs in the summer of 1885, Murfree used the comparatively tame Cumberlands as the pattern for her fictional mountain landscapes. That same year, Mary, her sister Fanny, and their father traveled to Boston to meet with Murfree's publishers for the very first time. New England literati were astounded to discover that such "virile" stories, filled with violent, gun-toting, hard-drinking mountaineers, had been written by a petite, refined Southern gentlewoman with a slight limp. Murfree was at the apex of her popularity, publishing seven more short stories and six more novels set in the mountains of Tennessee over the next twelve years.

Mary and Fanny returned with their parents to New Grantland in 1890, suffering the devastating loss of their father just two years later. Both family finances and the market for local color writing began to wane rapidly at this time, prompting Murfree to turn her talents to the increasingly more profitable genre of historical romance. In 1897 the editors at Macmillan invited Murfree to contribute to their Stories from American History Series. Murfree began two years of painstaking research culminating in *The Story of Old Fort Loudon* (1899), a novel documenting interactions between the native Cherokee population and British and French pioneers during the mideighteenth century in Tennessee. Murfree followed this venture with two more historical novels, *A Spectre of Power* (1903) and *The Amulet* (1906), and seven short stories over the next seven years.

After the death of their mother in 1902, Mary and Fanny moved into Murfreesboro where they remained for the rest of their lives. Murfree continued to write for many years, publishing her second Civil War novel, *The Storm Centre*

(1905), several more mountain-based short stories, and two novels about life in the Mississippi Delta, *The Fair Mississippian* (1908) and *The Story of Duciehurst* (1914). In spite of her unflagging productivity, Murfree's writing met with less and less success. In 1912 Murfree began touring and lecturing around Tennessee as state regent of the Daughters of the American Revolution. Shortly after her two-year tenure ended, Murfree's health declined, leaving her confined to a wheelchair and eventually blind. The University of the South awarded her an honorary doctoral degree in June 1922. Unable to attend the ceremony due to her last serious illness, Murfree died on July 31, 1922.

MAJOR WORKS AND THEMES

Of Murfree's eighteen novels and more than fifty short stories, fully half focus on the peoples and landscapes of the Tennessee mountains. Of these, the eight stories composing *In the Tennessee Mountains* are still considered her best work. In many of these stories, Murfree employs a city-dweller, usually a guest at New Helvetia Springs, as a foil to accentuate the exotic qualities of the local mountain population. Although she approached her favorite subjects as an outsider, Murfree clearly respected mountain people, their customs, and the grandeur of their homeland. Rough and unlettered, her mountain characters usually possess a level of dignity and pride based on self-sufficiency unmatched by their sophisticated urban counterparts.

Murfree's mountain men are invariably tall, strong, and potentially dangerous, dressed in ill-fitting, worn-out suits of brown jeans. Her married women are usually prematurely aged, highly competent mothers with huge broods of tow-headed children. They are the hubs of activity in households presided over by shiftless husbands who work little, drink heavily, and frequently beat them. Her most famous character type is the "mountain-flower." These young women are usually pale, ethereal creatures, with masses of curling yellow hair. They frequently suffer an unrequited love for a sophisticated stranger, such as Celia Shaw in "The Star in the Valley" or Loralinda Byars in "A Chilhowee Lily" (1912). Other mountain-flowers risk their lives in valiant attempts to save the unworthy mountain men they love. Clarsie Giles in "The Harnt That Walks Chilhowee" (1884) and Cynthia Ware, who goes "Drifting Down Lost Creek" (1884) to save her lover from jail, are both representatives of this type.

The most prominent theme running through all of Murfree's fiction is an unwavering belief in a common humanity transcending economic and social class. For example, in "The Star in the Valley," Reginald Chevis believes himself quite magnanimous in his amused pity for Celia Shaw. He is somewhat appalled by her coarse ways and the fact that she encourages her male relatives to drink themselves into a stupor. When he learns that Celia has used their drunkenness to prevent them from committing murder and sacrificed her life riding through a winter storm to warn her neighbors, Chevis begins to understand that "despite all his culture, his sensibility, his yearnings toward humanity, he was not so high a thing in the scale of being."

Many stories such as "Over on the T'Other Mounting" (1884) and especially "The Harnt That Walks Chilhowee" underscore the superiority of mountain life. In "The Romance of Sunrise Rock" (1884), for example, two vacationing urbanites, John Cleaver and Fred Trelawney, discuss the merits and drawbacks of mountain life; by the end of the story, Trelawney has happily decided to remain, while Cleaver returns to his stress-filled, moribund existence in the city.

Murfree juxtaposes the grandeur and imposing permanence of extravagantly described mountain landscapes to the relative insignificance and transcience of her human characters to create a strong sense of naturalistic determinism. Most characters, Hiram Kelsey and Rick Tyler from *The Prophet of the Great Smoky Mountains*, Mink Lorey from *In the Clouds* (1886), Fee Guthrie from *In the "Stranger People's" Country* (1891), and many others struggle in vain against their fates. Their futile struggles are played out against the majestic backdrop of the unchanging mountains, seemingly impervious to time and tempest.

CRITICAL RECEPTION

Murfree's ability to paint vivid pictures of mountain landscapes was in some ways her fatal flaw. Initially, audiences welcomed the long, meticulously crafted descriptive passages that made the mountains such an all-pervasive presence in her stories. As time went on, however, readers wearied of the "amethystine mists" surrounding Murfree's mountain peaks and began to criticize the exuberance, floridity, and redundancy of her descriptions with increasing disdain. According to Fred Lewis Pattee, Murfree's Tennessee mountains "take on the proportions of the Canadian Rockies or the Alps" (311). One favorite target of critics became derrogatorily known as "Mary's moon." Richard Cary, however, has defended Murfree's copious descriptions by comparing them to Hawthorne's use of setting as a vehicle to convey the emotional and moral states of human characters. Murfree's malevolent characters move in a landscape dominated by gloom and darkness, while heroes and heroines appear bathed in bright sunshine or iridescent moonglow.

During her lifetime and throughout the first half of the twentieth century, critics compared Murfree favorably with Bret Harte for her ability to recreate distinctive regional details and with Joel Chandler Harris and George Washington Cable for her ability to capture the unique dialect of southern Appalachia. When she moved beyond regionalism, critics and the reading public alike lost interest rapidly. Although "The Harnt That Walks Chilhowee" and "The Dancin' Party at Harrison's Cove" continue to find their way into anthologies, very little scholarly attention has been paid to Murfree's works in recent decades. A brief flurry of interest surrounded the University of Tennessee's reprint of *In the Tennessee Mountains* in 1970 but quickly died away. While this is not surprising, it is unfortunate. Murfree's perspective as a Southern woman of powerful intellect and literary talent makes not only her mountain stories but her depictions of the Civil War and her analyses of the challenges confronting the survivors on both sides deserve further study.

WORK CITED

Pattee, Fred Lewis. *A History of American Literature Since 1870.* New York: Century, 1921. 308–316.

BIBLIOGRAPHY

Works by Mary Murfree

Novels

Where the Battle Was Fought. Boston: J. R. Osgood & Co., 1884.
Down the Ravine. Boston: Houghton, Mifflin & Co., 1885.
The Prophet of the Great Smoky Mountains. Boston: Houghton, Mifflin & Co., 1885.
In the Clouds. Boston: Houghton, Mifflin & Co., 1886.
The Story of Keedon Bluffs. Boston: Houghton, Mifflin & Co., 1887.
The Despot of Broomsedge Cove. Boston: Houghton, Mifflin & Co., 1888.
In the "Stranger People's" Country. New York: Harper & Brothers, 1891.
The Juggler. Boston: Houghton, Mifflin & Co., 1897.
The Story of Old Fort Loudon. New York: Macmillan Company, 1899.
The Champion. Boston: Houghton, Mifflin & Co., 1902.
A Spectre of Power. Boston: Houghton, Mifflin & Co., 1903.
The Amulet. New York: Macmillan Company, 1906.
The Windfall. New York: Duffield & Co., 1907.
The Fair Mississippian. Boston: Houghton, Mifflin & Co., 1908.
The Ordeal; A Mountain Romance of Tennessee. Philadelphia: J. B. Lippincott Company, 1912.
The Story of Duciehurst; A Tale of the Mississippi. New York: Macmillan Company, 1914.

Short Story Collections

In the Tennessee Mountains. Boston: Houghton, Mifflin & Co., 1884.
The Bushwackers, and Other Stories. Chicago: Herbert S. Stone & Co., 1899.
The Mystery of Witchface Mountain, and Other Stories. Boston: Houghton, Mifflin & Co., 1895.
The Phantoms of the Foot-Bridge, and Other Stories. New York: Harper & Brothers, 1895.
The Young Mountaineers. Boston: Houghton, Mifflin & Co., 1897.
The Frontiersmen. Boston: Houghton, Mifflin & Co., 1904.
The Raid of the Guerilla, and Other Stories. Philadelphia: J. B. Lippincott Company, 1912.

Studies of Mary Murfree

Carleton, Reese M. ''Mary Noailles Murfree (1850–1922): An Annotated Bibliography.''
    American Literary Realism, 1870–1910 7 (autumn 1974): 293–378.

Cary, Richard. *Mary N. Murfree.* New York: Twayne, 1967.

Parks, Edd Winfield. *Charles Egbert Craddock (Mary Noailles Murfree).* Chapel Hill:
    University of North Carolina Press, 1941.

Quinn, Arthur Hobson. *American Fiction.* New York: D. Appleton-Century, 1936.

Williams, Cratis D. ''Charles Egbert Craddock and the Southern Mountaineer in Fic-
    tion.'' *Appalachian Journal* 3 (1976): 134–162.

Wright, Nathalia. Introduction to *In the Tennessee Mountains*, by Mary Noailles Murfree.
    Knoxville: University of Tennessee Press, 1970. 5–33.

ELIZABETH OAKES SMITH
(1806–1893)

Leigh Kirkland

BIOGRAPHY

Elizabeth Oakes Prince was born in North Yarmouth, Maine, on April 18, 1806, the second daughter of sea captain David Prince and Sophia Blanchard. Her father was lost at sea when she was two; her mother remarried, and Elizabeth grew up in Portland.

In 1823, she married thirty-six-year-old Seba Smith, editor and publisher of the *Eastern Argus* and the *Portland Courier*, later the author of a popular political satire, *The Jack Downing Letters*. Four sons survived to adulthood. Although Oakes Smith "hazard[ed] little scraps of prose and poetry for her husband's newspaper" (Neal xxiv), her first outside encouragement came from John Neal, when he published her unsigned poem in the *New England Galaxy* in 1835.

Seba Smith sold his newspaper, then met with financial ruin through land speculation in the 1830s. After an ill-fated journey south to market a gin for Sea Island cotton, the Smiths returned to New York in 1839 to write, Oakes Smith with more success than her husband. In the same year, "Mrs. Seba Smith" published *Riches without Wings* (1839), a didactic children's story.

By the early 1840s, Mrs. Seba Smith was publishing both as Elizabeth Oakes Smith and Ernest Helfenstein. During the 1850s, she became well known as a writer, lyceum lecturer, social reformer, and woman's rights activist. Her poems, criticism, and essays appeared regularly in *Ladies' Companion, Southern Literary Messenger, Graham's*, and *Godey's Lady's Book*. Later she wrote outside the mainstream, in *Religio Philosophical Journal* and for *The Lily* and *Una*, among emerging women's magazines.

Her work appeared in the ubiquitous gift books, and Oakes Smith edited the

1846 and 1847 volumes of *The May Flower*, soliciting work from friends in the New York literary salons.

In 1842, her seven-canto "The Sinless Child," an extremely popular narrative romance, appeared in the *Southern Literary Messenger*. *The Western Captive*, a historical romance, was serialized in *The New World* and published as a novel. Poetry collections followed: *The Sinless Child and Other Poems* (1843), as well as *The Poetical Writings of Elizabeth Oakes Smith* (1845) and *The Keepsake* (1845), a republication of *The Poetical Writings*. Children's books, *The True Child* (1845) and *Rosebud* (1845), include Indian stories as well as traditional fare. Her poetry was collected in the standard anthologies of women's verse, while *The Salamander* (1848), a Germanic tale of the supernatural, and "The Sagamore of Saco," set in seventeenth-century Maine and serialized in *Graham's*, established Oakes Smith as a fiction writer.

In 1849, she and a woman companion climbed Mt. Ktaadn in Maine, the first white women to do so. Apparently, she never published any account of the experience. Another juvenile collection, *The Dandelion*, appeared the same year; the fourth, *The Moss Cup*, in 1853. A historical play, *The Roman Tribute; or, Attila the Hun*, opened in Philadelphia in 1850 (Hale 786); although the text is lost, plot summary survives in Griswold's *Poetry of American Women* (Baym, *American Women* 187).

At this time, Oakes Smith made public her concern with woman's rights. A revised version of her *New York Tribune* series *Woman and Her Needs*, published by Fowler and Wells (1851), was reprinted several times. From 1851, at the age of forty-five, till 1857, she took to the lecture circuit. One of the first American women to speak publicly for abolition and woman's rights, Oakes Smith shared platforms throughout the Northeast with the likes of Emerson and Wendell Phillips and lectured as far west as Chicago. According to her biographer, her family objected strenuously, and conservative friends, including Sarah Hale, spurned her for abandoning a woman's place. However, others, including Lucretia Mott and Paulina Wright Davis, encouraged her.

She and Seba Smith, with their sons Appleton, Alvin, Sidney, and Edward Oaksmith, published and wrote most of the copy for a magazine, which changed names several times between 1854 and 1858: *The United States Magazine of Science, Art, Manufactures, Agriculture, Commerce and Trade* became *Emerson's United States Magazine*, then *Emerson's Magazine and Putnam's Monthly*. Oakes Smith was coeditor of their final magazine, in 1859, *The Great Republic*.

During the 1850s the Smith family was in turmoil. Seba was often ill. Their eldest son Appleton was accused of (in 1852 and 1861) and imprisoned for nine months for participating in the slave trade. Three sons joined the mercenary army of William Walker, the American filibusterer who took over Nicaragua in 1856. Even so, the decade was one of Oakes Smith's most productive. She reflected contemporary speculation about the occult with *Shadow Land* (1852), which deals with spiritualism, clairvoyance, dreams, and psychic abilities (including her own). An advice book, *Hints on Dress and Beauty* (1852), calls for abandoning fashion for practicality. Paradoxically, though she was a delegate to National Woman's Rights Conventions from 1850, in the movement's history she is reduced to an anecdote. Following Susan B. Anthony's castigation of Oakes Smith's and Paulina Wright Davis's attire at the 1852 Syracuse convention as inappropriate, Oakes Smith was denied the presidency of the group. In 1868, she became a charter member of Sorosis, New York's first woman's club.

Although her own marriage was infelicitous, she opposed divorce on the grounds that the marriage sacrament was inviolable. A pamphlet extracted from *Woman and Her Needs*, "The Sanctity of Marriage" (1853), calls for opportunity for women in order to restore marriage to a spiritual union rather than an economic necessity.

She ventured further into drama with *Old New York; or, Democracy in 1689* (1853) and speculative fiction with *Bertha and Lily* (1854). *The News-Boy* (1854), published anonymously, sparked social reform by publicizing the plight of New York newsboys.

After radical changes in the literary marketplace following the Civil War, she wrote for *Beadle's Monthly, Baldwin's Monthly,* and *Home Journal,* republishing work and writing literary biographical essays. Tragedy struck her family repeatedly. Edward, her youngest, died in Cuba of yellow fever in 1865. In July 1868, Seba died in Long Island, and in December, Sidney was lost at sea. She published three novels for Beadle's Dime Novel series: *Black Hollow* (1864), *Bald Eagle, or the Last of the Ramapaughs* (1867), and *The Sagamore of Saco* (1868), expanded from the 1848 serial.

After Seba's death, Oakes Smith moved to North Carolina to live with Appleton. She continued to write nostalgic memoirs for Maine newspapers and to work on the autobiography promised in magazines, unpublished in her lifetime. In 1887, at age seventy-one, she served as minister to an Independent congregation in Canastota, New York. She died in November 1893.

MAJOR WORKS AND THEMES

Oakes Smith employs largely conventional and impersonal nineteenth-century themes, except in her nonfiction. The nonfiction prose exhibits more vitality and originality, likely because taking up political subjects constituted more risk for a woman than writing poetry or fiction. Her writing was market driven, but Oakes Smith objected to writers representing women as completed by love and marriage.

"The Sinless Child" illustrates the moral superiority of women rather than the civil equality advocated in her political writings. The heroine is female Christ and "Emerson's self-reliant person" (Watts 103) rather than biblical Eve. The shorter poems rarely stray from the "archetypes" identified by Walker in *Nightingale's Burden,* a mark of their conventionality.

Bertha and Lily (1854) imagines the capabilities of a woman outside convention. The protagonist Bertha is freed by dark knowledge and forbidden experience that result in angelic, illegitimate Lily. Bertha, reunited with Lily, becomes a minister, superseding feckless pastor Ernest Helfenstein. *The Salamander* (1848) is presented as written by the "late" Helfenstein and as edited and with an introduction by Oakes Smith, thus killing off her alter ego. The text contains multiple levels of fictionality, in the style of Irving.

Oakes Smith's novels are usually set in the historical past, possibly stemming from the emphasis of Congregationalist background on exemplary lives. She employs Native American characters; with the exception of *Bertha and Lily*, the novels are more Cooperesque than domestic. *The Western Captive* (1842) contains the "most openly romantic relationship between a white woman and a Native American man in women's historical fiction" (Baym, *American Women Writers* 160).

Arguably her most interesting work, the 600-page manuscript autobiography, heralded as imminent for twenty years before her death, is available only in a partial and highly corrupt 1924 edition.

CRITICAL RECEPTION

"The Sinless Child" established Oakes Smith's reputation as a poet, although the language used by reviewers seems applicable to any of her contemporaries. Edgar Allan Poe, in *Godey's*, remarks that when first published "The Sinless Child" attracted attention from "the novelty of its conception and the general grace and purity of its style" (907). The poem exhibits "elevated moral design and delicate beauty of imagery" (Tuckerman xxviii); its "inspiration seems drawn from the purest well-springs of thought and fancy" (Keese xi). Her poetry is "characterized rather by a passionate and lofty imagination than by fancy, and a subtle vein of philosophy more than sentiment" (Read 23). Poe writes that while the "conception [of 'The Sinless Child'] is original," "the conduct, upon the whole, is feeble, and the *denouement* is obscure, and inconsequential" (*Broadway Journal* 221).

A frequent criticism of Oakes Smith's writing is the lack of polish; she wrote too quickly. Poe is caustic about this failing, "With a good deal more . . . of what is termed in the school-prospectuses, composition, Mrs. Smith would have made of 'The Sinless Child' one of the best, if not the very best of American poems" (*Godey's* 911). Others are more apologetic—"A higher finish and more careful revision would render the fruits of her pen more tasteful and permanent . . . these defects are ascribable to circumstances" (Tuckerman xxx)—or amazed at "how few of her pieces display the usual carelessness and haste of magazine articles" (Griswold 6).

As professional writer and feminist, Oakes Smith was atypical of middle-class white women, yet exemplary of social change in the nineteenth century. She is part of the 1850s surge of women writing for magazines, of the woman suffrage movement, of reform movements, and also of often-ignored cultural phenomena like spiritualism that run counter to what we have chosen to see as dominant trends.

BIBLIOGRAPHY

Works by Elizabeth Oakes Smith

Poetry

"Stanzas." *The New-England Galaxy* 18, no. 1 (21 February 1835): 1.

The Sinless Child and Other Poems. Edited by John Keese. New York: Wiley & Putnam; Boston: W. D. Ticknor, 1843.

The Keepsake: A Wreath of Poems and Sonnets. By Mrs. Seba Smith. New York: J. S. Redfield, 1845; Leavitt and Company, 1849.

The Poetical Writings of Elizabeth Oakes Smith. New York: J. S. Redfield, 1845; 2nd ed., 1846.

The Female Poets of America: With Portraits, Biographical Notices, and Specimens of their Writing. Ed. Thomas Buchanan Read. Philadelphia, 1848. 7th ed. Philadelphia: E. H. Butler, 1857.

Juvenile

Riches without Wings, or The Cleveland Family. By Mrs. Seba Smith. Boston: George W. Light, 1838; 3rd ed., 1839.

Rosebud. Boston: Saxton & Kelt, 1845.

The True Child. Stories for Real Children. By Mrs. E. Oakes Smith. Boston: Saxton & Kelt, 1845. 4th ed. Auburn: Derby, Miller & Co., 1849.

The Dandelion: Stories Not for Good Children, Nor Bad Children, But for Real Children. Buffalo: G. H. Derby & Co., 1849; Auburn: Derby & Miller; Buffalo: Derby, Orton & Mulligan; Cincinnati: Henry W. Derby, 1853.

The Moss Cup. By Mrs. E. Oakes Smith. Auburn: Derby & Miller; Buffalo: Derby, Orton & Mulligan; Cincinnati: Henry W. Derby, 1853.

Novels

The Western Captive; or, The Times of Tecumseh. New York: J. Winchester, 1842.

The Salamander: A Legend for Christmas. Found Amongst the Papers of the Late Ernest Helfenstein. Edited by E. Oakes Smith. New York: George P. Putnam, 1848. Reprinted as *Mary and Hugo; or The Lost Angel, a Christmas Legend*, by Elizabeth Oakes Smith. New York: Derby and Jackson, 1857.

Bertha and Lily; or, The Parsonage of Beech Glen: A Romance. New York: J. C. Derby; Boston: Phillips, Sampson & Co.; Cincinnati: H. W. Derby, 1854.

The News-Boy. By Anonymous. New York: J. C. Derby, 1854.

Black Hollow. New York: Beadle and Adams, 1864.

Bald Eagle, or the Last of the Ramapaughs. A Romance of Revolutionary Times. New York: Beadle & Adams, 1867; London, 1870.

The Sagamore of Saco. Beadle's Dime Novels 142. New York: Beadle & Co., 1868.

Nonfiction

Woman and Her Needs. New York: Fowler and Wells, 1851. Reprint, New York: Arno
    Press, 1970.
Hints on Dress and Beauty. New York: Fowler and Wells, 1852.
Shadow Land; or, The Seer. New York: Fowler and Wells, 1852.
Old New York; or, Democracy in 1689. A Tragedy, in Five Acts. New York: Stringer &
    Townsend, 1853.
"The Sanctity of Marriage" 1–10. *Woman's Rights Commensurate with Her Capacities
    and Obligations. A Series of Tracts* 5. Syracuse: J. E. Master, 1853.
The Romance of Nature; or, The Poetical Language of Flowers, by Thomas Miller.
    Edited by Elizabeth Oakes Smith. New York: J. C. Riker, [1852].

Autobiography

The Autobiography of Elizabeth Oakes Smith. Edited by Mary Alice Wyman. Lewiston,
    ME: Lewiston Journal Co., 1924.
*"A Human Life: Being the Autobiography of Elizabeth Oakes Smith": A Critical Edition
    and Introduction.* Ed. Leigh Kirkland. Ph.D. diss., Georgia State University, 1994.

Studies of Elizabeth Oakes Smith

Baym, Nina. *American Women Writers and the Work of History, 1790–1860.* New Bruns-
    wick: Rutgers University Press, 1995.
———. *Woman's Fiction: A Guide to Novels by and about Women in America 1820–
    1870.* Ithaca: Cornell University Press, 1978.
Douglas, Ann. *The Feminization of American Culture.* New York: Alfred A. Knopf,
    1977.
Griswold, Rufus T. Preface to *The Poetical Writings of Elizabeth Oakes Smith.* New
    York: J. S. Redfield, 1845. 5–8.
Hale, Sarah Josepha. *Woman's Record; or, Sketches of All Distinguished Women.* 2nd
    ed. New York: Harper & Brothers, 1855. Reprint, New York: Source Book Press,
    1970.
Neal, John. Preface to *The Sinless Child and Other Poems,* by Elizabeth Oakes Smith.
    New York: Wiley & Putnam, 1843. xv–xxvi.
Pattee, Fred Lewis. *The Feminine Fifties.* New York: D. Appleton-Century Co., 1940.
Poe, Edgar Allan. Review of *The Poetical Writings of Elizabeth Oakes Smith. Broadway
    Journal,* 23 August 1845. Reprinted in *Edgar Allan Poe: Writings in* The Broad-
    way Journal: *Nonfictional Prose.* Edited by Burton R. Pollin. New York: Gordian
    Press, 1986. 1: 221–222.
———. Review of *The Poetical Writings of Elizabeth Oakes Smith. Godey's Lady's
    Book* (December 1845). Reprinted in *Edgar Allan Poe: Essays and Reviews.* New
    York: Library of America, 1984. 906–917.
Russo, Ann, and Cheris Kramarae. *The Radical Women's Press of the 1850s.* New York:
    Routledge, 1991.
Tuckerman, H. T. Preface to *The Sinless Child and Other Poems,* by Elizabeth Oakes
    Smith. New York: Wiley & Putnam, 1843. xxvii–xxxii. (First appeared in *Gra-
    ham's*)
Tyler, Alice Felt. "Elizabeth Oakes Smith." In *Notable American Women, 1607–1950:*

A Biographical Dictionary, edited by Edward T. James. Cambridge: Harvard University Press, 1971. 3:309.

Walker, Cheryl, ed. *American Women Poets of the Nineteenth Century: An Anthology.* New Brunswick: Rutgers University Press, 1992. 66–77.

———. *The Nightingale's Burden: Women Poets and American Culture before 1900.* Bloomington: Indiana University Press, 1992.

Watts, Emily Stipes. *The Poetry of American Women from 1632 to 1945.* Austin: University of Texas Press, 1977. 83–120.

Wiltenburg, Joy. "Excerpts from the Diary of Elizabeth Oakes Smith." *Signs* 9 (1984): 534–548.

Wyman, Mary Alice. *Two American Pioneers: Seba Smith and Elizabeth Oakes Smith.* New York: Columbia University Press, 1927.

FRANCES SARGENT LOCKE OSGOOD (1811–1850)

Shelle C. Wilson Bryant and Patrick W. Bryant

BIOGRAPHY

Poet Frances Sargent Locke was born in 1811 to a Boston merchant and his second wife. She spent her childhood in Hingham, Massachusetts, with her older sister, Anna Maria Wells (also a poet) and a brother. Educated mostly at home, Frances was a published poet by her early twenties and would have more than six books of poetry published over her lifetime. Her first poems were published before her marriage to Charles Stillman Osgood in October of 1835, whom she had met in 1834 when he painted her portrait. After marrying, the couple immediately moved to London and welcomed the birth of their first daughter, Ellen, in July of 1836.

Both Frances and Charles enjoyed great success in England where they were members of London's high society. Frances published two books of poetry while there, *A Wreath of Wild Flowers from New England* (1838) and *The Casket of Fate* (1839). After five years, and pregnant a second time, Frances returned to America with Charles and gave birth to another daughter, May.

The 1840s were productive for Osgood; she wrote or edited six books, including *The Poetry of Flowers and Flowers of Poetry* (1841), *Puss in Boots and the Marquis of Carabas* (1844), *Poems* (1846), and *Cries of New York* (1846), and contributed poetry and short fiction to many journals of the day, including *Graham's Magazine*, *Ladies Magazine*, and *Broadway Journal*. During this creatively successful period, she again moved in elite circles, attending meetings at many of New York's literary salons. However, while her poetry met with popular success, her marriage was in jeopardy, and she and Charles separated in 1844. Much of her poetry around this time alludes to Charles's infidelity, though no proof has surfaced.

In March of 1845, during her separation from Charles, Osgood met Edgar Allan Poe and embarked on a controversial and widely discussed literary friendship. Poe publicly praised her work and published her poems regularly in the *Broadway Journal*, a periodical he edited. In fact, Osgood was the first woman to have a poem published in the front of the *Journal*, a position most often reserved to promote either Poe himself or one of his friends (De Jong, "Lines" 39). It is clear that they admired one another, and though their poems often read as amorous correspondence, there is some dispute as to the extent of their involvement. John Evangelist Walsh argues in *Plumes in the Dust* that they had a sexual relationship. He credits Poe with paternity of Osgood's third child, Fanny Mae, who died in 1847, one year after her birth. Others argue that Poe and Osgood had a platonic relationship and were merely "mutual admirers and literary allies" (De Jong, "Lines" 31).

Shortly before Fanny Mae's death, Frances was briefly reunited with Charles, but in 1849, after Poe's death, Charles left once again, this time for the California gold rush. Soon after, Frances appointed Rufus Griswold her literary executor and dedicated her last book, *Poems* (1850), to him.

Following Fannie Mae's birth, Osgood was confined to bed. Three years later, on May 12, 1850, she died of tuberculosis. Osgood's daughters were fourteen and eleven at the time of her death and soon succumbed to the disease themselves.

MAJOR WORKS AND THEMES

Frances Osgood's poetry is often characterized by the clichés that pervade so much of nineteenth-century America's sentimental writing. Indeed, many of her poems reflect the mediocrity that dominated the popular magazine trade. However, in the widely ranging and voluminous corpus of Osgood's writing lie more than a few poems of surprising freshness and vigor. Clichés and sentimentality aside, Frances Osgood's poems are often rebellious, witty, confrontational, acerbic, and perhaps even playfully sexual. In "Ah! Woman Still," Osgood implies she composed in the improvisational style often considered the special province of the "poetess" (De Jong, "Her Fair Fame" 269). The conventional model of womanly feeling stoking the divine fire of her poetry, as depicted in this verse, may drive the bulk of Osgood's work, but in her best poems, she drops such pretense in favor of a raw and sometimes disquieting honesty.

Even when she is working in conventional modes, Osgood often thwarts expectations. One popular motif she adopts is effusive praise of "purity." Yet, consistent with Cheryl Walker's suggestion that Frances and Charles were sexually active before their marriage ("Profile" 7), Osgood's treatment of purity sometimes strays from her society's moral rigidity. In "Purity's Pearl; or the History of a Tear," for example, Osgood indulges the typical dichotomy between "Purity's snow-white pearl" (virginity) and "Love's ruby" (sexual experience); however, in contrast with nineteenth-century mores, she does not portray "Purity's pearl" as the exclusive prize of sexual innocence. Instead, the poem's heroine, apparently jaded by love, flings away her ruby and cries for her pearl's return. Mercy (here a feminine personification) emerges from the sea and grants her request. By departing from the more common theme of irrecoverable virtue, Osgood suggests "Purity" and sexual experience are not mutually exclusive. Though subtle, the poem's departure from social norms is surprising compared with typical morally didactic poetry.

In many other poems, Osgood expresses radical sentiments under a veil of whimsy. The speaker of "Caprice" categorically refuses to subject to anyone's authority but her own, yet she salves her rebellion by playfully invoking "caprice" as woman's divine right. Similarly, in "Woman," Osgood labels bluntly women's status as a toy, a doll, and a slave. But then she assures her reader she's not a subversive and ends the poem in ostensible submission to a prescribed feminine stereotype.

Verses like these indicate that Osgood was capable of sophisticated and subtle rhetoric in her poems. In light of this, some of her imagery may be less "innocent" than her popular reputation would suggest. Cheryl Walker, for example, reads Osgood's "The Cocoa-Nut Tree" as "an example of blatant phallus worship" (*American Women Poets* 107). Likewise, the poem "To an Idea that Wouldn't 'Come' " may contain more than a simple homage to other writers when Osgood suggestively couples allusions to Whitman's "pen" and Greenwood's "lip."

Osgood's break with tradition is not always subtle, however. Her love poetry's darker side is often abrupt and frankly confrontational. In the four-line "Impromptu, To—" she writes with bitterness, and in the more fully developed poem "To—," the speaker sarcastically mocks the self-important "lofty feelings" of the poem's object. As many readers have commented, in works like these, Osgood gives vent to feelings she could not express otherwise.

Frances Osgood stands out among popular sentimental poets of the nineteenth century not because of her skillful wordplay and powerful imagery but because of her honesty and the often daring realism of her poetic voice. In light of so much moralistic and didactic verse from other poets of her era, Osgood's poems are refreshingly human. While she joins others in lauding virtue, fidelity, duty, and truth, she also portrays those who contemplate adultery, whose marriages fail, who grow impatient with society—those who, to be true to themselves, have to break the rules.

CRITICAL RECEPTION

Frances Osgood was extremely popular in the 1840s both as a poet and as a literary personality. Apparently by her own design, Osgood's literary and social reputations were linked for a number of years to Edgar Allan Poe, who publicly praised her work. While many Poe scholars scoff at the idea that he could have really liked her work (see De Jong, "Lines"), there is no reason to assume his compliments were disingenuous. De Jong points out in "Her Fair Fame" that nineteenth-century critics, including Poe, held women poets to a different and more narrowly defined standard than they did male poets. Given the limitations of these strictures—the mandate to praise modesty, sincerity, virtue, etcetera— much of Osgood's poetry is quite good. While usually adhering to the trappings of the "lady poet," she often rhetorically subverts them. It does not seem un- likely that Poe appreciated her ability to transcend the very conventions he helped reinforce for women's writing.

Poe was not the only contemporary of Osgood's who admired her work. Rufus Griswold, too, thought highly enough of her to write a long, complimen- tary sketch, "Frances Sargent Osgood," which he published several times in the late 1840s. While the basis of his judgment may seem dubious—he tries to smooth the more unconventional edges of Osgood's life and works to make her better fit the "poetess" mold—his admiration is genuine. Griswold's sketch appeared again in a memorial of Osgood edited by Mary Hewitt: *Laurel Leaves: A Chaplet Woven by the Friends of the Late Mrs. Osgood.* Comprising works by Hewitt, Sarah Helen Whitman, and Nathaniel Hawthorne, among others, the book stands as a testimony to the strength of Osgood's reputation among her contemporaries.

Ironically, the mutually promotional relationship between Osgood and Poe has continued to dominate Osgood's reputation since her death. As a conse- quence, Osgood's work has received little critical attention through the years except as it bears on her canonical literary ally. She has recently come to be included in anthologies and discussions of women writers, but to date, there is no critical edition of her work and no book-length biography. Frances Osgood's work and life clearly merit further and closer attention.

BIBLIOGRAPHY

Works by Frances Sargent Locke Osgood

A Wreath of Wild Flowers from New England. London: Edward Churton, 1838.
The Casket of Fate. London: C. Whittingham, 1839.
Flower Gift, a Token of Friendship for All Seasons. Chambersburg, PA: Shryock, Reed & Co., 1840.
Puss in Boots and the Marquis of Carabas. New York: Benjamin & Young, 1844.
Cries of New York. New York: J. Doggett, Jr., 1846.
Poems. New York: Clark and Austin, 1846.
The Floral Offering, a Token of Friendship. Edited by Frances Sargent Locke Osgood. Philadelphia: Carey and Hart, 1847.
A Letter about the Lions. New York: Putnam, 1849.
Poems. Philadelphia: Carey & Hart, 1850.
The Poetry of Flowers and Flowers of Poetry. Edited by Frances Sargent Locke Osgood. New York: Derby & Jackson, 1859.
Osgood's Poetical Works. New York: Leavitt & Allen Brothers, 1880.

Studies of Frances Sargent Locke Osgood

De Jong, Mary G. "Her Fair Fame: The Reputation of Frances Sargent Osgood, Woman Poet." In *Studies in the American Renaissance*, edited by Joel Myerson. Charlottesville: University Press of Virginia, 1987. 265–287.

———. "Lines from a Partly Published Drama: The Romance of Frances Sargent Osgood and Edgar Allan Poe." In *Patrons and Protégées: Gender, Friendship, and Writing in Nineteenth-Century America*, edited by Shirley Marchalonis. New Brunswick: Rutgers University Press, 1988. 31–58.

Dobson, Joanne. "Sex, Wit, and Sentiment: Frances Osgood and the Poetry of Love." *American Literature* 65, no. 4 (1993): 631–650.

Hewitt, Mary E., ed. *Laurel Leaves: A Chaplet Woven by the Friends of the Late Mrs. Osgood*. New York: Lamport, Balkeman & Law, 1854.

Hunnewell, Fannie. "The Life and Writings of Frances Sargent Osgood." Master's thesis, University of Texas, 1924.

Jones, Buford, and Kent Ljungquist. "Mrs. Osgood's 'The Life-Voyage' and 'Annabel Lee.' " In *Studies in the American Renaissance*. edited by Joel Myerson. Charlottesville: University Press of Virginia, 1983. 275–280.

Ostriker, Alicia Suskin. *Stealing the Language: The Emergence of Women's Poetry in America*. Boston: Beacon Press, 1986.

Pollin, Burton R. "Poe and Frances Osgood, as Linked through 'Lenore.' " *Mississippi Quarterly* 46, no. 2 (1993): 185–197.

Reilly, John E. "Mrs. Osgood's 'The Life-Voyage' and 'Annabel Lee.' " *Poe Studies* 17, no. 1 (1984): 23.

Walker, Cheryl. *The Nightingale's Burden: Women Poets and American Culture before 1900*. Bloomington: Indiana University Press, 1982.

———. "Profile of Frances Osgood." *Legacy* 1, no. 2 (1984): 5–7.

———, ed. *American Women Poets of the Nineteenth Century: An Anthology*. New Brunswick: Rutgers University Press, 1992.

Walsh, John Evangelist. *Plumes in the Dust: The Love Affair of Edgar Allan Poe and Fanny Osgood*. Chicago: Nelson-Hall, 1980.

Watts, Emily Stipes. *The Poetry of American Women from 1632 to 1945*. Austin: University of Texas Press, 1977.

ELIZABETH STUART PHELPS
(1815–1852)

Cynthia J. Davis

BIOGRAPHY

When Rebecca Harding Davis died in 1910, not one literary journal noted her passing (Olsen 152). An obituary in the *New York Times* appeared under this header: "Mother of Richard Harding Davis Dies at Son's Home in Mt. Kisco, aged 79" (Olsen 153). Thankfully, such neglect has been corrected in the past few decades: Davis has not only been rediscovered but even canonized (while her journalist son's star has plummeted). This has not, however, been the case with Elizabeth Stuart Phelps, another woman writer ultimately eclipsed by her more famous child. Although Phelps's daughter took her mother's name in hopes of perpetuating her memory—and although, of course, no one would want to marginalize this rightly famous daughter—it is regretfully true that one reason Elizabeth Stuart Phelps (1815–1852) has not retained her rightful place in literary history is that Elizabeth Stuart Phelps (Ward) (1844–1911) has, albeit with the best of intentions, usurped it.

Literary scholars seem only to have contributed to this confusion. Rutgers Press's edition of *The Story of Avis* lists the author's name as Elizabeth Stuart Phelps and not as Elizabeth Stuart Phelps Ward, the latter name being the conventional means of distinguishing the daughter from her mother. Carol Farley Kessler's Twayne critical edition on the daughter's career also refers to its titular subject without appending her married surname.

In certain respects, the lives and not just the names of mother and daughter are similar. Both married fairly late for their respective time periods, both were writers, both explored the conflicts experienced by women who had artistic aspirations in their fiction. But in other ways—for which the mother might have been glad, had she lived to see her daughter into her adult years—their lives were vastly different, especially when it came to artistic autonomy.

Elizabeth Stuart was the fifth of nine children born to Abigail Clark and Moses Stuart in Andover, Massachusetts, on August 13, 1815. Her father taught sacred literature at Andover Theological Seminary and suffered from insomnia. Her mother was already a chronic invalid by the time her first daughter was born. The temperaments of both parents—along with Elizabeth's persistent fear that her mother would die and her abiding desire for her father's approval—had a profound effect on the young girl in her formative years. Even after she had grown up, married, and achieved her first literary success, her husband Austin contended that the keenest pleasure his wife ever received was her father's "hearty 'Well Done' after the publication of one of her simple stories" ("Memorial" 19).

Elizabeth was apparently a precocious child; at the age of ten she was already writing stories to amuse her sisters and the servants. She also showed a talent for painting and at a later point even briefly considered it as a career, but she would ultimately choose writing as the profession most amicable to domestic responsibilities (her daughter's *The Story of Avis* is loosely based on her mother's frustrated career as an artist).

Elizabeth Stuart began her formal education at Abbott Academy in Andover. At age sixteen she moved to Boston in order to attend the Mount Vernon School. There she lived in the home of the school's director, Jacob Abbott, who would later gain some fame as a children's author. At the time his young ward and pupil lived with him, Abbott was the editor of a religious periodical, and it was here that Elizabeth published her first pieces under the pseudonym H. Trusta (*Trusta* being an anagram for her last name).

Religion was very much on the girl's mind at the time, and as she grew in faith, she eventually disavowed literary work as not sufficiently "solid and useful" ("Memorial" 37). Since Stuart was at this time already suffering from the illness that would plague and ultimately end her life, her decision to renounce writing may also have stemmed from the medical belief that for a woman a life of the mind invariably crippled the life of the body.

By 1834, at the height of her religious fervor, Stuart's health had so deteriorated that she was forced to leave Boston and return to Andover. She was diagnosed with "cerebral disease," with symptoms including constant headaches, temporary paralysis, partial blindness, and nervous prostration. And yet, despite medical convictions that writing and women's health were antithetical, it was only when Elizabeth decided to pick up her pen again that, she claimed, she was able to regain both health and happiness and say, "Goodbye to doctors" ("Memorial" 38). Unfortunately, this was a farewell that was to be short-lived.

Her illness was not so debilitating, however, that it prevented her from marrying Austin Phelps, one of her father's students from Andover, in 1842. Austin and his new wife soon thereafter moved to Boston, where he became the minister of the Pine Street Church in Boston. Elizabeth would later recall the six years the Phelpses remained in Boston as the happiest time in her life. There she gave birth to her only daughter, Mary Gray (who later took her mother's name) and soon thereafter, a son, Moses Stuart, known as "Stuart."

In order to entertain her children, Phelps wrote and illustrated stories, many of which were posthumously collected in *Little Mary; or Talks and Tales for Children* (1854). In addition, up until the end of her life, she regularly and anonymously contributed fiction to adult magazines (many posthumously collected in *The Last Leaf from Sunny Side* [1853] and *The Tell-Tale; or, Home Secrets Told by Old Travellers* [1854]) and wrote a series of children's books featuring "Kitty Brown" for the American Sunday School Union.

The relatively full life Phelps was able to lead in Boston, however, was not to last; it was with a good deal of dread and sadness that she greeted Austin's 1848 decision to return to Andover so that he could join the Academy's faculty. Her misgivings notwithstanding, these last four years of her life were her most successful literary ones. The year before she died, she published her most popular novel, *The Sunny Side; or, The Country Minister's Wife* (1851), which was apparently based upon the life of her deceased friend and daughter's namesake, Mary Gray, and which sold some 100,000 copies during its first year in print. The last year of her life saw the publication of her personal favorite, *A Peep at "Number Five"; or, A Chapter in the Life of a City Pastor* (1852), based upon her own life experiences.

And yet literature and its successes were not the only things on Phelps's mind in 1852. This same year, Phelps struggled through her son Stuart's serious, though not ultimately fatal, illness; her father's unexpected death (Phelps's invalid mother would actually outlive both her husband and her daughter by several years); and the birth of her third child, Amos Lawrence. A little more than three months after Amos was born, Phelps died. As Phelps's daughter, Mary a.k.a. Elizabeth Stuart Phelps (Ward), would reflect in her autobiography near the end of her own life, "Her last book and her last baby came together and killed her" (*Chapters from a Life* 12; see also Kessler as the source for biographical information).

In 1854, Austin Phelps married his deceased wife's sister, Mary Stuart, who was suffering from tuberculosis. Although their aunt proved a good surrogate mother to the children, she succumbed to her disease only two years into the marriage. Austin would remarry one more time, a woman Elizabeth's daughter respected, even loved, but never saw as supplanting her biological mother. Thus, the irony that the daughter's attempt to insure her mother would not be forgotten—by taking her name, some sources say at the very moment of the mother's death—ultimately resulted in the supplanting she so dreaded.

MAJOR WORKS AND THEMES

Elizabeth Stuart Phelps's early literary contributions were primarily juvenalia and/or religious writings. Many of these were formulaic, and Phelps had a difficult time recognizing in them the expression of her own artistic talent. As her husband Austin recounts in his "Memorial" to his deceased wife, "She herself was often unable to recognize with confidence her own volumes, after years had passed since she wrote them. She has several times been seen bending over the counter of a bookstore, in perplexity as to the authorship of some little book which she held in her hand, seeming to detect some familiar traces of her former self, and yet unable at last to decide whether she were the author of it or not" (58).

Perhaps this disconnection between authorial self and authored text explains why she took such pleasure in both *The Sunny Side* and her second novel, *A Peep at "Number Five"; or, A Chapter in the Life of a City Pastor* (1852), as both were based in real life. As Nina Baym points out, the two novels read as companion pieces: The former depicts the lives of a country minister and his wife and the latter of a city minister and his wife (Baym 1978, 246). Classified by most critics as works of domestic realism (despite their rather idealistic portrayals of ministers' wives), these novels pay close attention to the details of everyday life, the nuances of dialogue, the turmoils and joys of characters hitherto not necessarily recognized as worthy subjects of literature. In *The Sunny Side*, Phelps goes beyond merely representing women's lives to proselytizing about improving those lives: Over the course of the novel, she recommends that every adult woman train herself informally and daily in reading and writing and that each should also have the opportunity of a formal education.

Many of Phelps's articles and pieces published in journals over the course of her life were posthumously published in two collections: *The Last Leaf from Sunny Side* (1853), prefaced by her husband's memorial tribute to his wife; and *The Tell-Tale; or, Home Secrets Told by Old Travellers* (1853). The latter includes within it "The Husband of A Blue," one of Phelps's several stories that explores a woman's devotion to writing. Many of the stories Phelps wrote to entertain her children and, primarily, her only daughter are collected in *Little Mary; or Talks and Tales for Children* (1854).

Feminist critics have paid most attention to a story by Phelps originally published in 1852 as a Christmas book and entitled "The Angel over the Right Shoulder." And little wonder. It is an incredibly powerful and ultimately disheartening story of a wife's desire to expand the conventional definition of a woman's work (which is "never done") in order to include within it intellectual pursuits—that is, reading and writing. Distracted day in and day out by numerous household cares, the protagonist Mrs. James finds herself increasingly frustrated at never being able to attend to such pursuits and hence increasingly concerned that her life is devoid of any real meaning, substance, or purpose. When Mr. James patronizingly instructs his wife to set aside two hours out of every day for study but then proceeds to interrupt her as frequently and freely as do the nanny, her children, and so on, we begin to see how futile such aspirations may have been for married bourgeois women at midcentury, as well as why, to borrow from Virginia Woolf, there was no female Shakespeare.

A happy resolution to such a dilemma, at least in Phelps's worldview, was not possible in reality. And yet the author's/character's apparent need for such a resolution was so great that she resorts to dreaming it into existence. After a particularly wearying day, Mrs. James falls asleep, only to dream that her every gesture is recorded by two angels: one who sits over her right shoulder, entering her every good deed in his ledger, the other on her left, transcribing in his ledger her every bad—the latter, fortunately, capable of being erased by the tears this angel sheds every time she redeems herself. When Mrs. James awakes from this dream, she no longer has to fret that her life is insignificant: If she can't be a writer, at least she knows that she is the written, and in a text where God and not one frail woman serves as the author. In other words, as Judith Fetterley concludes, "Phelps attempts to resolve the conflict by allowing her protagonist to substitute the role of object for that of subject, the role of character for that of author'' (207).

CRITICAL RECEPTION

International recognition came to Elizabeth Stuart Phelps with the publication of *The Sunny Side*; and yet critical essays on Phelps are so scarce that what is remarkable about her critical reception is the lack thereof. Searches through periodical indexes unearthed only one brief review of *The Sunny Side* in a journal called *The New Englander*. Nina Baym's helpful *Novels, Readers, and Reviewers* cites a September 1852 review of *The Sunny Side* in the *Christian Examiner*, which praises the depiction of the minister's wife: "Her character is beautifully drawn. The cheerer of her husband in despondency, the kind and wise guide of her children in the right way, with modesty prompting the wish to shrink from publicity, but high principle curbing the indulgence of that wish, she appears the true pastor's wife, ready when occasion calls to be the friend and counsellor of those around her, but finding her peculiar sphere of duty in her own home'' (102). Baym also cites a July 1853 review of *A Peep at "Number Five"* that appeared in the *Ladies' Repository*, praising the novel and recommending it to "those who would have a faithful daguerrotype of a city preacher's trials and enjoyments'' (156).

Phelps fares no better in scholarly monographs. Despite the popularity of *The Sunny Side* and *A Peep at "Number Five,"* Phelps is not even mentioned in such canon-forming books as Fred Lewis Pattee's *The Feminine Fifties* (1940). Nina Baym's *Woman's Fiction* does devote two pages to Phelps, succinctly summarizing her career and the "bourgeois realism'' of such works as *The Sunny Side* and *A Peep at "Number Five."* Jane Tompkins in her groundbreaking *Sensational Designs* makes only a passing mention of Phelps as an author unjustly overlooked—and then proceeds to overlook her (123). Judith Fetterley defies convention and includes a selection from the mother and not the daughter in her reader of nineteenth-century American women's fiction, providing a helpful introduction to Phelps's life and themes. Carol Farley Kessler is the only other contemporary critic who has paid Phelps serious attention, including an article on the relationship between mother and daughter. However, even she is more interested in the daughter than the mother, as evidenced by her critical edition on the former. For scholars in search of yet another "lost" woman writer worthy of rediscovery, Elizabeth Stuart Phelps should prove a prime candidate and a rich find.

WORKS CITED

Anonymous. Review of *The Sunny Side*. *The New Englander* 10 (1851): 236.

Baym, Nina. *Novels, Readers, and Reviewers: Responses to Fiction in Antebellum America*. Ithaca: Cornell University Press, 1984.

———. *Woman's Fiction: A Guide to Novels by and about Women in America 1820–1870*. Ithaca: Cornell University Press, 1978.

Fetterley, Judith, ed. "Elizabeth Stuart Phelps (1815–52)." In *Provisions: A Reader from 19th-Century American Women*. Bloomington: Indiana University Press, 1985. 203–209.

Kessler, Carol Farley. *Elizabeth Stuart Phelps*. Boston: Twayne, 1982.

Olsen, Tillie. "A Biographical Interpretation." In *Life in the Iron Mills*, by Rebecca Harding Davis. New York: Feminist Press, 1972. 69–174.

Pattee, Fred Lewis. *The Feminine Fifties*. D. Appleton-Century Co., 1940.

Phelps, Austin. "Memorial." In *The Last Leaf from Sunny Side*, by Elizabeth Stuart Phelps. Boston: Phillips, Sampson, 1853.

Phelps (Ward), Elizabeth. *Chapters from a Life*. Boston: Houghton Mifflin, 1896.

Tompkins, Jane P. *Sensational Designs: The Cultural Work of American Fiction, 1790–1860*. New York: Oxford University Press, 1985.

BIBLIOGRAPHY

Works by Elizabeth Stuart Phelps

Short Stories

"The Angel over the Right Shoulder." 1852. Reprinted in *Provisions: A Reader from 19th-Century American Women*. Edited by Judith Fetterley. Bloomington: Indiana University Press, 1985. 209–215.

The Last Leaf from Sunny Side. Boston: Phillips, Sampson, 1853.

The Tell-Tale; or, Home Secrets Told by Old Travellers. Boston: Phillips, Sampson, 1853.

Novels

A Peep at "Number Five"; Or, A Chapter in the Life of a City Pastor. Boston: Phillips, Sampson, 1852.

The Sunny Side; Or, The Country Minister's Life. Philadelphia: American Sunday School
    Union, 1851.

Juvenile Literature

Kitty Brown and Her City Cousins. Philadelphia: American Sunday School Union, 1852.
Kitty Brown and Her Little School. Philadelphia: American Sunday School Union, 1852.
Kitty Brown Beginning to Think. Philadelphia: American Sunday School Union, 1853.
Little Kitty Brown and Her Bible Verse. Philadelphia: American Sunday School Union,
    1851.
Little Mary; or Talks and Tales for Children. Boston: Phillips, Sampson, 1854.

Studies of Elizabeth Stuart Phelps

Baym, Nina. *Woman's Fiction: A Guide to Novels by and about Women in America
    1820–1870.* Ithaca: Cornell University Press, 1978.
Culley, Margo. "Vain Dreams: The Dream Convention and Women's Fiction." *Frontiers*
    1 (1976): 94–102.
Fetterley, Judith, ed. "Elizabeth Stuart Phelps (1815–52)." In *Provisions: A Reader from
    19th-Century American Women.* Bloomington: Indiana University Press, 1985.
    203–209.
Kessler, Carol Farley. "A Literary Legacy: Elizabeth Stuart Phelps, Mother and Daugh-
    ter." *Frontiers* 5 (fall 1980): 28–33.
———. *Elizabeth Stuart Phelps.* Boston: Twayne, 1982.

HENRIETTA CORDELIA RAY (1849?–1916)

Elizabeth A. Moorehead

BIOGRAPHY

H. Cordelia Ray, as she signed her name, was born into a clerical family, the youngest of three surviving daughters of the influential abolitionist and activist Reverend Charles Bennett Ray and Charlotte Augusta Burrough. Reverend Ray was the editor of the *Colored American* and active in the abolition, temperance, suffrage, and education movements, besides serving as minister in the Congregational Church for twenty years. Dates listed in various sources for Cordelia Ray's birth range from 1849 to 1852. Raised in an educated and prominent African-American family, Ray studied Greek, Latin, French, and German at the Sauveneur School of Languages. In 1891, she earned a master's degree in pedagogy from the University of the City of New York. She taught in the New York public schools and tutored students in languages, English literature, music, and mathematics. After Ray retired from public school teaching, she continued tutoring individuals and small groups from her home in Woodside, Long Island.

Ray received her widest public recognition as a poet when her long ode, "Lincoln; Written for the Occasion of the Unveiling of the Freedmen's Monument in Memory of Abraham Lincoln, April 14, 1876," was read at the unveiling of the monument in Washington, D.C. Her poem circulated widely and was eventually published in 1893. Ray published two books of poetry, *Sonnets* in 1893 and *Poems* in 1910. Many of the poems in *Sonnets* appear also in *Poems*. In addition, she published poems in periodicals. With her sister Florence, Ray also wrote a biography of her father, *Sketch of the Life of the Reverend Charles B. Ray*, published in 1887. This public collaboration between the sisters expresses their lifelong private collaboration; neither married, and they lived together until Florence's death. Ray never sought public acclaim, preferring to live quietly within the circle of her friends, her books, and her family. Her early biographer, Hallie Q. Brown, notes of Ray: "There was a transfiguring light that radiated from her, for she bore herself as one endowed with an innate sense of things divine" (171).

Ray's life remains significant not only for her publication and recognition as a poet but also for her scholarly accomplishments in a time when these public attainments were difficult for women and for African Americans. Ray was not the only woman of achievement in her family; Florence received a master's of pedagogy from the University of the City of New York (1891) and also taught in New York public schools, and Ray's sister Charlotte was the first African-American woman to be admitted to the District of Columbia Supreme Court bar, after receiving a law degree from Howard University in 1872. Ray's family was the core influence of her life and her work.

MAJOR WORKS AND THEMES

Ray's greatest poetic influences are religion and classic literature. Traditional in form and theme, Ray's *Poems* contains 135 selections arranged under ten headings, some according to form and some according to theme: A Rosary of Fancies; Meditations; Sonnets; Champions of Freedom; Ballads and Other Poems; Chansons D'Amour; Quatrains; The Procession of the Seasons; The Seer, the Singer and the Sage; and Heroic Echoes. The poems' major themes are the duties and responsibilities of the human condition, nature, Christian optimism and idealism, and love.

Her poetry expresses more originality and intensity when she writes of the people and ideals she cared about most, such as her father, her sister Florence, as in "Verses to My Heart's-Sister," or when she writes about the influence of prominent figures such as in her elegy "In Memorium: Frederick Douglass." Other influences in Ray's work are classic authors, including Goethe, Milton, Tennyson, and Thoreau. Several poems reveal Ray's perception of nature's soothing effects on the spirit and mind, as an earthly revelation of divine grace, for example, in "Wood Carols." Ray's control of technique and form remains impressive throughout her poems, and she often experiments with stanza form and rhyme scheme.

A member of an influential and activist family, Ray's poetry might be expected to contain themes of African-American or women's rights, but Ray chose to express her concerns through an intellectualized and sentimental approach. Though several poems address the debt owed to activists and "champions of freedom," the tone of the poems remains forward looking and optimistic, permeated with her religious faith, as "daring souls are needed e'en to-day" ("In Memorium: Frederick Douglass" 163). Ray consistently maintains the image of the genteel woman poet, addressing issues within the boundaries of her sheltered reality and only connecting with a less privileged reality through the filter of the nineteenth-century sentimental tradition.

CRITICAL RECEPTION

Perhaps the most glowing accolades for Ray's poetry come from Hallie Q. Brown: "Cordelia Ray's poetry . . . may be likened to the quaint touching music of a shell murmuring of the sea—a faint yet clear note sounding all the pathos and beauty of undying life" (171). The delicacy and restraint displayed in Ray's poetry seemed the fitting tone for a woman of the nineteenth century, and Ray received a modicum of local recognition during her lifetime. Jessie Fauset's contemporaneous review of her *Poems* comments, "The quality of the verse is uneven, perhaps, but much of it is very, very good" (183).

Ray's work most recently has been recognized by inclusion in several anthologies. In common with many nineteenth-century poets, Ray focused on the techniques of her craft rather than the expression of feeling or unacceptably blatant political commentary. Not considered experimental by today's criterion, Joan R. Sherman comments: "[Ray] suppressed natural feeling and thoughtful scrutiny of human relationships, actions and ideas to serve a Muse for whom poetry was more a skill than an art, more a penmanship exercise than a new, complex creation of heart and mind" (134). Nevertheless, Ray's poetry contains moments of inspiration when her work escapes the boundaries of craft and achieves a delicate artistry.

WORKS CITED

Brown, Hallie Q. *Homespun Heroines and Other Women of Distinction.* Xenia, OH: Aldine, 1926. Introduction by Randall K. Burkett. New York: Oxford University Press, 1988. 171.

Fauset, Jessie. Review of *Poems.* "What to Read." *Crisis* 4 (August 1912): 183.

Sherman, Joan R. *Invisible Poets: Afro-Americans of the Nineteenth Century.* Urbana: University of Illinois Press, 1974. 134.

BIBLIOGRAPHY

Works by Henrietta Cordelia Ray

Sketch of the Life of the Reverend Charles B. Ray. With Florence T. Ray. New York: Little, 1887.

Sonnets. New York: Little, 1893.

Poems. New York: Grafton, 1910.

Studies of Henrietta Cordelia Ray

Brown, Hallie Q. *Homespun Heroines and Other Women of Distinction.* Xenia, OH: Aldine, 1926. Introduction by Randall K. Burkett. New York: Oxford University Press, 1988. 169–175.

Kapai, Leela. "Henrietta Cordelia Ray." In *Afro-American Writers before the Harlem*

Renaissance, edited by Trudier Harris. Vol. 50 of Dictionary of Literary Biography. Detroit: Gale, 1986. 233–237.

Robinson, William H., ed. *Early Black American Poets: Selections with Biographical and Critical Introductions*. Dubuque, IA: Brown, 1969. 138–144.

Sherman, Joan R., ed. *African-American Poetry of the Nineteenth Century: An Anthology*. Urbana: University of Illinois Press, 1992. 265–281.

———. *Invisible Poets: Afro-Americans of the Nineteenth Century*. Urbana: University of Illinois Press, 1974. 129–135.

Shockley, Ann Allen. *Afro-American Women Writers, 1746–1933: An Anthology and Critical Guide*. New York: Penguin, 1988. 327–333.

Walker, Cheryl, ed. *American Women Poets of the Nineteenth Century: An Anthology*. New Brunswick: Rutgers University Press, 1992. 352–363.

LIZETTE WOODWORTH REESE (1856–1935)

Denise D. Knight

BIOGRAPHY

The lyric poet Lizette Woodworth Reese was born along with her twin sister, Sophie, on January 9, 1856, in Waverly, Maryland, during one of the worst snowstorms of the season. Her father, David Reese, was of Welsh ancestry; her mother, Louisa Gabler, was a native of Saxony, Germany. As a child she read and enjoyed Poe's "The Raven" and developed an appreciation of such English writers as Shakespeare, Emily Brontë, Thackeray, and Hardy. Her favorite American poets included Whittier and Emerson. Reese eschewed the writings of Wordsworth and Tennyson, whose wordiness she found boring. In 1873, she graduated from Eastern High School in Baltimore and, at the age of seventeen, began a career in teaching at St. John's Parish School in Waverly. From that point on, she enjoyed dual careers as both teacher and poet. Her first poem, "The Deserted House," was published in *Southern Magazine* in June 1874. From 1877 until 1881, Reese taught at a black high school in Baltimore. It was also in 1877 that her first of fourteen books, *A Branch of May*, was published. By the age of thirty-two, Reese was receiving public accolades for her poetry; in 1890, she became one of the founding members of the Women's Literary Club in Baltimore, where she served as chair of the poetry section until her death some forty-five years later. Her most famous poem, "Tears," appeared in *Scribner's* in 1899, and in 1901, she began a twenty-year stint as an English teacher at Western High School in Baltimore. In 1922, the year following her retirement from forty-eight years of teaching, Reese became honorary president of the Edgar Allan Poe Society in Baltimore, a post she held until her death. On the eve of her seventy-fifth birthday, Reese published *A Victorian Village: Reminiscences of Other Days* (1929), and in 1931, she won the Mary L. Keats

Memorial Prize for her lifelong literary contributions. That same year she was named poet laureate of Maryland and one of the three "greatest living women in America" (Dietrich 118); she was also awarded an honorary doctorate of literature by Goucher College in Baltimore. One acquaintance described Reese as "shy, modest [and] possessing a keen whimsical sense of humor" while maintaining a "staunch loyalty to her ideals, founded upon her boundless faith in God" (120). Reese remained single throughout her life and died in Baltimore from the effects of a kidney infection on December 17, 1935, just shy of her eightieth birthday. She is interred in St. John's Church graveyard in Waverly, Maryland.

MAJOR WORKS AND THEMES

The titles of half of her published poetry volumes—*A Branch of May* (1887), *A Handful of Lavender* (1891), *A Quiet Road* (1896), *Wild Cherry* (1923), *White April* (1930), *Pastures* (1933), and *The Old House in the Country* (1936)— reveal Reese's thematic emphasis on the simple beauty of the rural countryside. As Robert J. Jones notes, Reese wrote about what she "saw and felt in language and images that were sharp and real. . . . She tried to say *old* things in fresh ways. Her poetry was about common things, universal emotions, and she worked to find different ways and words to express them" (2, 6). Indeed, Reese often looked to the natural world as a sanctuary where she could find and celebrate simple pleasures. The quiet elegance of her language effectively captured the common aspects of nature: the cobwebbed thorn, the crooked lane, the jeweled bough, the ancient pear tree. Her rural roots strongly shaped the content and texture of the verse she produced. In her book of reminiscences, *A Victorian Village* (1929), Reese described in particular the influence of a "wide-spreading lovely old hawthorn bush" that "took the measure of all the poetry which was in me. More than anything else did[,] it held for me the essence and the substance of all loveliness" (101).

Unrequited love is another theme explored by Reese, although there is no concrete evidence to suggest that she had ever been romantically involved. When asked by a young writer whether she had even been in love, Reese's response was curt and evasive (Jones 73). The degree of passion evident in some of the love poems, however, including "Lover to Lover," "The Kiss," "Bound," "Renunication," and "A Song of Separation," bespeaks a woman experienced in the joy and pain of being in love.

Religious lyrics and elegies were also produced in abundance by Reese. Her traditional Christian beliefs are apparent in such verses as "Lord, Oft I Come," "Good Friday," "A Carol," "Bible Stories," and "A Christmas Folk-Song." Reese's best-known sonnet, "Tears," celebrates hope in the face of death. Elegies were written to commemorate such public figures as Robert Herrick, John Keats, and Robert Louis Stevenson; Reese also memorialized several family members and friends in her poetry. *Little Henrietta* (1927) is a long, traditional elegy written about the death from diptheria of Reese's six-year-old cousin,

Henrietta Matilda. She also wrote dozens of occasional poems; "The Deserted House," "Early Dusk," "A Foggy Afternoon," and "In Praise of Common Things" are among her finest.

Reese published two prose works: *A Victorian Village* appeared in 1929, followed by *The York Road* in 1931. It is her autobiographical account *A Victorian Village* that provides most of what we know about Reese's childhood, teaching career, and acquaintances with other literary figures. Her only attempt at fiction writing was the posthumously published *Worleys* (1936), a partially completed and rather conventional novel that recounts the effects of the Civil War on an eight-year-old girl whose badly wounded father dies after returning home from the war.

CRITICAL RECEPTION

While Reese's work is only now being revisited as a result of the ongoing reassessment of American literary history, she enjoyed enormous popularity during her lifetime. In addition to her volumes of poetry, Reese's work regularly appeared in such periodicals as *Scribner's, Atlantic, Century, Lippincott's, Harper's, Bookman*, and *Ladies' Home Journal*. A dinner held in her honor in December 1926 was attended by such noted writers as Robert Frost, Sara Teasdale, Edwin Markham, Elinor Wylie, and William Rose Benét (Jones 11). Along with winning the Keats prize, Reese was also the recipient of the coveted Shelley Memorial and the Harper's National Poetry prize.

Criticism of Reese's work is almost universally positive. American novelist Hervey Allen applauded Reese's poetry as "pure gold" (vi) and "the music of life" (viii). He was particularly pleased that she "refrained from elaborating upon the general dolors of being a female or from harping upon some peculiarly sensitive difficulty of her own personality" (vi). Louis Untermeyer praised her work for its "undercurrent of intensity beneath its quiet contours" (109) and characterized her verse as "fresh" and "never banal" (110). "Hers is a singing that is not dependent on a fashion," Untermeyer wrote (110). Emily Stipes Watts, in *The Poetry of American Women from 1632 to 1945*, remarked that Reese was "one of the best women poets" of her time and author of "several excellent sonnets" (145–146). Robert P. Harriss insisted that Reese "influenced American lyric poetry as no other woman has done" (200). Robert J. Jones characterized Reese as "one of the world's true poets" (2), and an article in the *Baltimore Sun* in 1987 expressed the hope that someone would rescue "her poetry from undeserved oblivion" (quoted in Jones 4).

BIBLIOGRAPHY

Works by Lizette Woodworth Reese

Verse

A Branch of May. Baltimore: Cushing and Bailey, 1887. Reprint, Portland: Thomas B. Mosher, 1909.

A Handful of Lavender. Boston: Houghton, Mifflin and Co., 1891. Reprint, Portland: Thomas B. Mosher, 1915, 1919.
A Quiet Road. New York: Houghton, Mifflin and Co., 1896. Reprint, Portland: Thomas B. Mosher, 1916, 1924.
A Wayside Lute. 1909. Reprint, Portland: Thomas B. Mosher, 1916, 1922, 1929.
Spicewood. Baltimore: Norman Remington Co., 1920.
Wild Cherry. Baltimore: Norman Remington Co., 1923.
The Selected Poems of Lizette Woodworth Reese. New York: George H. Doran Co., 1926.
Little Henrietta. New York: George H. Doran Co., 1927.
White April and Other Poems. New York: Farrar & Rinehart, 1930.
Pastures and Other Poems. New York: J. J. Little and Ives Co., 1933.
The Old House in the Country. New York: Farrar & Rinehart, 1936.

Prose

A Victorian Village: Reminiscences of Other Days. New York: Farrar & Rinehart, 1929.
The York Road. New York: Farrar & Rinehart, 1931.

Fiction

Worleys. New York: Farrar & Rinehart, 1936.

Studies of Lizette Woodworth Reese

Allen, Hervey. Introduction to *The Old House in the Country*, by Lizette Woodworth Reese. New York: Farrar & Rinehart, 1936.
Dietrich, Mae. "Lizette Woodworth Reese." *Emily Dickinson Bulletin* 15 (1970): 114–122.
Hahn, H. George. "Twilight Reflections: The Hold of Victorian Baltimore on Lizette Woodworth Reese and H. L. Mencken." *Southern Quarterly: A Journal of the Arts in the South* 22, no. 4 (summer 1984): 5–21.
Harriss, Robert P. "April Weather: The Poetry of Lizette Woodworth Reese." *South Atlantic Quarterly* 29, no. 2 (April 1930): 200–207.
Jones, Robert J. *In Praise of Common Things: Lizette Woodworth Reese Revisited.* Westport, CT: Greenwood Press, 1992.
Mearns, Hughes. *The Pamphlet Poets: Lizette Woodworth Reese.* New York: Simon and Schuster, 1928.
Rittenhouse, Jessie. *The Younger American Poets.* 1914. Reprint, Freeport, NY: Books for Libraries, 1968.
Untermeyer, Louis. *Modern American Poetry.* New York: Harcourt, 1930.
Walker, Cheryl. *The Nightingale's Burden: Women Poets and American Culture before 1900.* Bloomington: Indiana University Press, 1982.
———. ed. *American Women Poets of the Nineteenth Century: An Anthology.* New Brunswick: Rutgers University Press, 1992.
Watts, Emily Stipes. *The Poetry of American Women from 1632 to 1945.* Austin: University of Texas Press, 1977.
Wirth, Alexander C. *Complete Bibliography of Lizette Woodworth Reese.* Baltimore: Proof Press, 1937.

CATHARINE MARIA SEDGWICK
(1789–1867)

Rebecca R. Saulsbury

BIOGRAPHY

Catharine Maria Sedgwick was born on December 28, 1789, in Stockbridge, Massachusetts, where she spent most of her life. She was the third daughter and sixth child of Theodore Sedgwick and Pamela (Dwight) Sedgwick, who had seven children in all, including four sons. The Sedgwicks and Dwights were among the first settlers of New England. Indeed, the Dwight family was one of the most prestigious and aristocratic families in the Connecticut River Valley, and Theodore Sedgwick, Catharine's father, was one of the early Republic's staunchest and most influential Federalists.

But her father came from more humble beginnings. He was born in 1746 to a family of New England farmers and tavern keepers on a barren country farm in a small Connecticut hill town. Nevertheless, he attended Yale College, where he briefly studied theology before turning to law. Thereafter, he rapidly rose in social stature to that associated with the Dwight family. He was a member of the Continental Congress and the House of Representatives, becoming its Speaker. He also served as a senator from Massachusetts and eventually became chief justice of the Massachusetts Supreme Court.

Catharine's mother stayed at home and did her best to fulfill the most important role accorded to women in the late eighteenth century: Republican motherhood. Pamela Sedgwick's bouts with depression, however, coupled with her husband's frequent and lengthy absences, made her role as manager of the domestic sphere particularly difficult for her and her children. Pamela's depression became increasingly severe; she spent her last years as an invalid.

Catharine's formal education was typical for New England's elite daughters. After a brief stay in Stockbridge's public schools, she enrolled at several private boarding schools, including Mrs. Bell's school in Albany at age thirteen and Mrs. Payne's finishing school in Boston at age fifteen. Looking back on her formal education, Catharine regarded it as a waste. In her journals she remarked, " 'Education in the common sense, I had next to none' " (quoted in Beach 13). But she valued her education at home facilitated by her father and brothers. Her father had assumed the role of mentor in her informal training, a role not unusual in New England's educated families. He had read the works of Hume, Butler, Shakespeare, and Cervantes aloud to her and instilled a passion for reading. He also encouraged her to read challenging material, such as Rollins's *Ancient History*. She learned to emulate the daily intellectual habits and pursuits of her father and brothers.

Like her home education, Sedgwick's Federalist and Calvinist background significantly shaped her views and the authorial role she would assume as a culture builder. Although she could not follow in her father's political footsteps, she adapted the goals that her father had intended for his sons by capitalizing on the doctrine of women as superior moralists and used it to become an arbiter of moral and national culture. Certainly her intellectual background and social position encouraged her to seek an active role in a democratic society.

In 1807, Catharine's mother died; two years later, her father remarried, and she, now nineteen years old, left Stockbridge to live with relatives in Albany and New York for the next six years, returning in 1813 to an ill father who would die that year. Shortly before her return he confessed his liberal religious beliefs to William Ellery Channing. At this time, Catharine began to record in her journals and letters her own doubts and criticisms of Calvinism. Eight years later, she joined the Unitarian Church in September 1821, as did her brothers Theodore and Henry, both of them lawyers and advocates of social reform. All three were among the founders of the first Unitarian Church in New York City. Sedgwick's family and friends, however, were deeply troubled by her conversion. Shortly after she joined the Unitarians, one of her favorite aunts reportedly told her, " 'Come and see me as often as you can, dear, for you know, after this world we shall never meet again' " (quoted in Beach 28). Ironically, it was Sedgwick's religious convictions that prompted her to begin writing. In 1822, she wrote a small pamphlet protesting religious intolerance, particularly that of New England Calvinism. This piece eventually evolved into her first novel, *A New-England Tale*, which she published anonymously. Anonymity notwithstanding, she worried that her novel would offend friends and neighbors in Stockbridge. In a letter to Susan Channing, she wrote: " 'I could not endure the idea that I had written myself out of the affections of my own people' " (quoted in Clements xi). The success of this work increased her concern. Her brother Harry reported in a letter to her that the novel " 'was going off very rapidly . . . and would soon be entirely exhausted' " (quoted in Clements xi). Four months after the first printing, a second printing was ordered, which subsequently sold in two months. In fact, *A New-England Tale* was a best-seller in Britain and America and received critical acclaim in both countries.

Sedgwick's move from Calvinism to Unitarianism coupled with the publication of *A New-England Tale* were defining moments in her life and career in that she created "for herself a dynamic role in both the moral and literary development of the emerging American character and [set] out on what would be a long, distinguished career as a writer" (Clements xv). In the preface to the first edition, written on March 30, 1822, Sedgwick explained that *A New-England Tale* constituted her "humble effort to add something to the scanty stock of native American literature" (7).

With the publication of her second novel, *Redwood*, in 1824, Sedgwick achieved popular and critical success on a par with her contemporaries James Fenimore Cooper and Washington Irving. Maria Edgeworth declared that Sedgwick's characters were " 'to America what Scott's characters are to Scotland, valuable as original pictures' " (quoted in Beach 30). A second edition of *Redwood* was published in the same year and republished in England. Moreover, it was translated into German, Swedish, Italian, Spanish, and French. The success of *Redwood* and her next three novels established Sedgwick as the most popular author in America and the most popular female novelist before Harriet Beecher Stowe.

Hope Leslie, Sedgwick's third novel and first historical romance, was published in 1827. Critics universally proclaimed it an American masterpiece, and Sedgwick secured national and international fame. Fame, however, was not something to which she aspired. In a journal entry for June 10, 1827, she explained that she only wanted her literary efforts to " 'produce some good moral feeling' " (quoted in Kelley, "Introduction" ix). She also revealed, " 'My author existence has always seemed something accidental, extraneous, and independent of my inner self' " (quoted in Beach 33).

Clarence and *The Linwoods* followed *Hope Leslie* in 1830 and 1835, respectively. Set in Revolutionary New York, *The Linwoods* was Sedgwick's second and last historical romance. It featured such prominent figures as George Washington, and it celebrated the colonists' struggle for independence. In the second half of her career, she achieved fame as an author of didactic stories for children and working-class people. Her most famous didactic novels comprised a trilogy that included *Home* (1835), *The Poor Rich Man, and the Rich Poor Man* (1836), and *Live and Let Live* (1837). All three were enormously successful and went through fifteen, sixteen, and twelve editions, respectively. In 1841, she published *Letters from Abroad to Kindred at Home*, a two-volume collection of her letters written during a fifteen-month tour of Europe in 1839 and 1840 with her brother Robert and other family members. Twenty-two years elapsed between *The Linwoods* and the publication of her sixth and final novel, *Married or Single?* in 1857. During this interim period, she published a steady stream of tales and sketches in annuals, gift books, and periodicals such as *Godey's, Graham's*, and *Harper's*. These pieces established her reputation as a skilled writer. Twenty-one of these works appeared in two volumes published in 1835 and in a second series in 1844.

In addition to being a prominent author, Sedgwick was an active philanthropist. She founded the Society for the Aid and Relief of Poor Women and organized the first free school in New York, primarily for Irish immigrant children. She worked for many years with the Women's Prison Association of New York and served as its president from 1848 to 1863. Sedgwick was also involved with the Isaac T. Hopper Home for women released from prison, who received room and board, help with finding employment, and Bible instruction (Kelley, *Private Woman* 296). Despite her commitment to social reform, however, Sedgwick was never a reformer in the conventional sense. Although she abhorred slavery and supported property rights for women, she never participated in the woman's movement or joined the abolitionists. She believed that women's political and social enfranchisement could be achieved only when women attained intellectual equality with men.

In contrast to nine out of ten women in antebellum America, Sedgwick made a conscious decision not to marry. Instead, she divided her time among her brothers' and other Sedgwick family homes in Stockbridge, Lenox, and New York City. In effect, her brothers Robert and Charles served as surrogate spouses and helped to husband her literary career. She had friends in the most prominent literary and social circles in New York City and New England , including Cooper, Hawthorne, Bryant, Emerson, and Melville. Despite her own happiness, however, Sedgwick did not recommend the single life to other women. In her journal she wrote enigmatically, " 'From my own experience I would not advise any one to remain unmarried, for my experience has been a singularly happy one' " (quoted in Beach 23).

Sedgwick died in Roxbury, Massachusetts, on July 31, 1867, at age seventy-eight. Hawthorne declared her America's "most truthful novelist." Fanny Kemble Butler, Sedgwick's friend of almost thirty years, described her as "one of the most charming, most amiable, and most excellent persons" she had known. William Cullen Bryant, her lifelong friend, gave the following tribute: " '[Sedgwick's] unerring sense of rectitude, her love of truth, her ready sympathy, her active and cheerful beneficence, her winning and gracious manners . . . make up a character . . . I would not exchange for anything in her own interesting works of fiction' " (quoted in Beach 39).

MAJOR WORKS AND THEMES

Sedgwick conceived all of her works in moral terms, an important factor in establishing the sentimental-domestic tradition in which Maria Susanna Cummins, Susan Warner, and Harriet Beecher Stowe would follow. Yet her most significant contributions to American literary history are not moral but cultural. Sedgwick had an intense belief in the democratic experiment, and her works are examples of an aesthetic nationalism: They articulate and define a national American literature. By taking up such a role, "Sedgwick recreated early American dialects, settings, historical events, social issues, and ideological debates in her novels'' (Davidson vii). In contrast to her male counterparts, however, Sedgwick complicates conceptions of American community and citizenship by making women central characters in her novels. Through a domestic setting and moral framework, she uses female characters to foreground the heterogeneity of America as a nation by showing how race, gender, religion, social, and ideological issues figure into American identity.

A New-England Tale is set in the New England countryside and features the elements of the overplot that would come to define the American domestic novel. Jane Elton, a virtuous orphan girl, is the novel's protagonist reluctantly taken in by Mrs. Wilson, her tyrannical and hypocritical Calvinist aunt who regularly mistreats her. Despite the trials and hardships she endures, Jane's virtue, generosity, and selflessness are rewarded with marriage to Mr. Lloyd, a Quaker whose religious views mirror her own. Jane's Christianity is held up against her aunt's faith and others who, despite appearances, are false Christians. Further, the novel questions parental authority and warns its readers against rigid Calvinist doctrine. It also presented to readers the contemporary landscape and manners of New England. As Victoria Clements argues, *A New-England Tale* "presages the role that will be played by woman's fiction in the general interrogation of religious, political, and social authority that will characterize the first half of the century and generate the liberal reform activity of the ensuing thirty years'' (xxvi).

Hope Leslie, Sedgwick's first attempt at historical romance, is undoubtedly her finest novel. She negotiates the boundaries of historical romance and sentimentalism to confront authorized history and offer a correlative to the Puritans' ethnocentric view of the Pequot War and the displacement of Native Americans. Sedgwick revisions Puritan historiography through the lens of those traditionally marginalized from and oppressed by it—women and Native Americans. *Hope Leslie* tells the story of Faith Leslie, her sister Hope, and Magawisca, a Pequot Indian. Early in the novel, Faith is captured by Indians and eventually marries Magawisca's brother. Magawisca saves Hope's fiancé, Fletcher Everell, and Hope defies patriarchal authority to secure the release of Magawisca and Nelema, an Indian woman unjustly accused of witchcraft. Magawisca functions as the alternative historian of the Pequot War, while Hope "actively resists her male superiors in order to act on the good impulses of her heart'' (Nelson 193). Sedgwick questioned Puritan historiography on the basis that the Puritans' "bigotry, their superstition, and above all their intolerance, were too apparent on the pages of history to be forgotten'' (quoted in Nelson 193). She explored the possibilities for a more inclusive conception of American identity.

The publication of *Home* was Sedgwick's first didactic narrative and represented a departure from her concentration on the romance novel. Her belief in the importance of the American home to the survival of the Republic dominated *Home* as well as *The Poor Rich Man, and the Rich Poor Man* and *Live and Let Live*, which rounded out her didactic trilogy. Echoing the theme of *Live and Let Live, Means and Ends* (1839) praised "domesticity as a worthy locus for a woman's identity and emphasized preparation for her marital role" (Kelley xxxvi). *Married or Single?*, her final novel, addressed the problem of spinsterhood and assured women that marriage was not essential to women's happiness. Sedgwick's didactic tales functioned as a vehicle to express her reformist impulses and were "intended to provide solutions for social injustices which existed in . . . America" (Foster 116). These works also represented her attempt to ameliorate "the abyss which she believed a difference in manners had created between social classes" (Foster 124).

CRITICAL RECEPTION

Critics of her time ranked Sedgwick with Irving, Cooper, and Bryant as one of the founders of American literature. *Harper's New Monthly Magazine* included her among "those who first created an American literature worthy [of] the name" (43, 826). Harriet Martineau argued that Sedgwick's books "are a sign of a new and a better time. . . . Here we have . . . the vigorous beginning of a national literature; the first distinct utterance of a fresh national mind" (65). Sedgwick was praised for her combination of realism and romance and for being one of America's first novelists to take up the landscape and manners of the country as her subject matter.

Maria Edgeworth declared *Redwood* " 'a work of superior talent, far greater than even "The New-England Tale" gave me reason to expect' " (quoted in Dewey 169). But William Cullen Bryant's review of *Redwood* for the *North American Review* was a mixed one. Sedgwick deviates from conventional historical romance, he declared, by locating her narrative in real life, rather than going back to "the infancy of our country" (Bryant 245–246). She has not "made any use of the incidents of our great national struggle for independence" (Bryant 245–246). Rather, Bryant argues, *Redwood* is more like a domestic romance in which the manners and ideas of America are "connected in real life, with much that is ennobling and elevated" (272). Although Bryant is initially somewhat doubtful of Sedgwick's abilities as a romance writer in *Redwood*, he still proclaims that her domestic romance exalts "our national reputation abroad, and . . . improve[s] our national character at home" (272). Harriet Martineau expressed similar views, and she praised the realistic character of Deborah Lenox and "the sketches of American life": She "could not have existed anywhere but in New England; she is the true offspring of the place and time" (50).

Hope Leslie received critical accolades. The *North American Review* judged this work "the best" of Sedgwick's first three novels (1828, 411). It underscored her triumph as a historical romance writer: "She has had the industry to study the early history of New England . . . and the talent to . . . present us the whole, a beautiful work, to verify our theories, to enliven our ancestral attachments, to delight, instruct, and improve us" (1828, 413).

The *Western Monthly Review* was more reserved in its approval for *Hope Leslie*. Although they spared no praise in comparing her novelistic ability to Ann Radcliffe and Maria Edgeworth, they objected to Sedgwick's construction of Magawisca as a moral character. "From our knowledge of her race," the reviewer explained, "we should have looked in any place for such a character, rather than in an Indian wigwam" (1, 295). In their view, the romance genre did not give Sedgwick permission to create a heroine who, they believed, could not actually exist: "Magawisca is the first genuine Indian angel, that we have met with. . . . Dealers in fiction have privileges; but they ought to have foundation, some slight resemblance to nature" (295).

Clarence, Sedgwick's fourth novel, did not achieve the critical success of its predecessors. While the *North American Review* admired it for its "pictures of natural scenery" that ranked with "the distinct pencil of Cowper," this work's greatest faults were its overly convoluted and complicated plot (32, 74). She was further criticized for her attempt "to give a highly romantic interest to events occurring in our own prosaic age and country" (1831, 84).

But the *North American Review* believed Sedgwick had come into her own as a writer of historical romances with the publication of *The Linwoods*. This work, as they noted, "carries us back to the period of the revolutionary war, the heroic age of our country . . . and consequently offers the finest scenes and materials for romance" (1836, 161).

Home, The Poor Rich Man, and the Rich Poor Man, and *Live and Let Live; or, Domestic Service Illustrated*, Sedgwick's trilogy titles, garnered her unqualified praise. The *Southern Literary Messenger* proclaimed her "the Edgeworth of America. . . . [O]ur country-woman has, in our judgment, no equal on this side of the Atlantic" (3, 331). Harriet Martineau praised the trilogy as her "best productions. . . . Sedgwick gives readers American manners informed and actuated by American life. . . . She gives us perhaps the first true insight into American life; and for this we should owe her hearty thanks" (59–60).

This praise and her enormous reputation notwithstanding, Sedgwick disappeared into literary obscurity by the end of the nineteenth century. Twentieth-century literary histories barely mention her. Van Wyck Brooks refused to consider her as a significant figure in American literary history. Regardless of her literary merits, "no one could have supposed that her work would live" (Brooks 188). But Brooks allowed that she "prepared the way for the writers who followed by stimulating the interest of her readers in her own landscape and manners" (188). Brooks's statement was an accurate assessment of Sedgwick's low literary stature until the revival and rehabilitation of nineteenth-century women writers inaugurated in the mid-1970s by Nina Baym's *Woman's Fiction*. In 1987, *Hope Leslie* was reissued by Rutgers University Press in its American Women Writers Series. In 1995, Oxford University Press reissued *A New-England Tale* in its Early American Women Writers Series. Approximately twenty-five scholarly articles have been written about Sedgwick's work in the last decade alone, most of them on *Hope Leslie*. She is also the subject of at least eight doctoral dissertations in the last decade. These examine her critical reputation and reception, her experience in the literary marketplace, her uses of genres, and her relationship to other nineteenth-century women writers. This acknowledgment of Sedgwick's importance in early American literary history and her contributions to the creation of a national literature is long overdue.

WORKS CITED

Anonymous. Review of *Clarence; or, A Tale of Our Own Times. North American Review* 32 (January 1831): 73–95.

Anonymous. Review of *Hope Leslie; or, Early Times in the Massachusetts. North American Review* 26 (April 1828): 403–420.

Anonymous. Review of *Hope Leslie; or, Early Times in the Massachusetts. Western Monthly Review* 1 (September 1827): 289–295.

Anonymous. Review of *The Linwoods. North American Review* 42 (January 1836): 161–195.

Anonymous. "A New England Village." *Harper's New Monthly Magazine* 43 (November 1871): 826.

Anonymous. Review of *The Poor Rich Man, and the Rich Poor Man. Southern Literary Messenger* 3 (1837): 331–334.

Beach, Seth Curtis. *Daughters of the Puritans: A Group of Brief Biographies.* Freeport, NY: Books for Libraries Press, 1905.

Brooks, Van Wyck. *The Flowering of New England, 1815–1865.* New York: Dutton, 1937.

Bryant, William Cullen. Review of *Redwood, a Tale. North American Review* 20 (April 1825): 245–272.

Clements, Victoria. Introduction to *A New-England Tale; or, Sketches of New-England Character and Manners,* by Catharine Maria Sedgwick. Edited by Victoria Clements. 1822. Reprint, New York: Oxford University Press, 1995. xi–xxvii.

Davidson, Cathy N. Preface to *A New-England Tale; or, Sketches of New-England Character and Manners,* by Catharine Maria Sedgwick. Edited by Victoria Clements. 1822. Reprint, New York: Oxford University Press, 1995.

Dewey, Mary E., ed. *Life and Letters of Catharine M. Sedgwick.* New York: Harper & Brothers, 1871.

Foster, Edward Halsey. *Catharine Maria Sedgwick.* New York: Twayne Publishers, 1974.

Kelley, Mary. Introduction to *Hope Leslie; or, Early Times in the Massachusetts,* by Catharine Maria Sedgwick. 1827. Reprint. Edited by Mary Kelley. New Brunswick, NJ: Rutgers University Press, 1987. ix–xxxvii.

———. *Private Woman, Public Stage: Literary Domesticity in Nineteenth-Century America.* New York: Oxford University Press, 1984.

Martineau, Harriet. "Miss Sedgwick's Works." *Westminster Review* 28 (October 1837): 42–65.

Nelson, Dana. "Sympathy as Strategy in Sedgwick's *Hope Leslie.*" In *The Culture of Sentiment: Race, Gender, and Sentimentality in Nineteenth-Century America,* edited by Shirley Samuels. New York: Oxford University Press, 1992. 191–202.

Sedgwick, Catharine Maria. *A New-England Tale; or, Sketches of New-England Char-*

acter and Manners. Edited by Victoria Clements. 1822. Reprint, New York: Oxford University Press, 1995.

BIBLIOGRAPHY

Major Works by Catharine Maria Sedgwick

Novels

A New-England Tale; or, Sketches of New-England Character and Manners. New York: E. Bliss & E. White, 1822.
Redwood, a Tale. New York: E. Bliss & E. White, 1824.
Hope Leslie; or, Early Times in the Massachusetts. New York: White, Gallaher, and White, 1827.
Clarence: or, A Tale of Our Own Times. Philadelphia: Carey & Lea, 1830.
Home: Scenes and Characters Illustrating Christian Truth. Boston: J. Munroe, 1835.
The Linwoods; or, "Sixty Years Since" in America. New York: Harper & Brothers, 1835.
The Poor Rich Man, and the Rich Poor Man. New York: Harper & Brothers, 1836.
Live and Let Live; or, Domestic Service Illustrated. New York: Harper & Brothers, 1837.
Means and Ends, or Self-Training. Boston: Marsh, Capen, Lyon & Webb, 1839.
Married or Single? New York: Harper & Brothers, 1857.

Tales and Sketches

Tales and Sketches. Philadelphia: Carey, Lea, and Blanchard, 1835.
Tales and Sketches. 2nd ser. New York: Harper & Brothers, 1844.

Letters

Letters from Abroad to Kindred at Home. 2 vols. New York: Harper & Brothers, 1841.
Life and Letters of Catharine Maria Sedgwick. Edited by Mary E. Dewey. New York: Harper & Brothers, 1871.

Studies of Catharine Maria Sedgwick

Castiglia, Christopher. "In Praise of Extra-Vagant Women: *Hope Leslie* and the Captivity Romance." *Legacy* 6 (fall 1989): 3–16.
Fick, Thomas H. "Catharine Sedgwick's 'Cacoethes Scribendi': Romance in Real Life." *Studies in Short Fiction* 27 (fall 1990): 567–576.
Garvey, T. Gregory. "Risking Reprisal: Catharine Sedgwick's *Hope Leslie* and the Legitimation of Public Action by Women." *The American Transcendental Quarterly (ATQ)* 8, no. 4 (December 1994): 287–298.
Gossett, Suzanne, and Barbara Ann Bardes. "Women and Political Power in the Republic: Two Early American Novels." *Legacy* 2 (fall 1985): 13–30.
Gould, Philip. "Catharine Sedgwick's 'Recital' of the Pequot War." *American Literature* 66, no. 4 (December 1994): 641–662.
Harris, Susan K. *19th-Century American Women's Novels: Interpretive Strategies*. Cambridge: Cambridge University Press, 1990.
Kelley, Mary. *The Power of Her Sympathy: The Autobiography and Journal of Catharine*

Maria Sedgwick. Boston: Massachusetts Historical Society. Distributed by Northeastern University Press, 1993.

Singley, Carol J. "Catharine Maria Sedgwick's *Hope Leslie*: Radical Frontier Romance." In *Desert, Garden, Margin, Range: Literature on the American Frontier*, edited by Eric Heyne. New York: Twayne Publishers, 1992. 110–122.

Zagarell, Sandra A. "Expanding 'America': Lydia Sigourney's *Sketch of Connecticut*, Catharine Sedgwick's *Hope Leslie*." *Tulsa Studies in Women's Literature* 6, no. 2 (fall 1987): 225–245.

LYDIA HOWARD HUNTLEY SIGOURNEY (1791–1865)

Karen L. Kilcup

BIOGRAPHY

One of nineteenth-century America's best-known and most popular poets was born in Norwich, Connecticut, into what were unlikely circumstances for a major writer: Her father, a Revolutionary War veteran, was the gardener for an influential family, the Lathrops. The precocious Sigourney, who could reputedly read at an early age, acquired a better education than many women of her period, enjoying the support and encouragement of her parents and of Mrs. Jerusha Lathrop, the wife of her father's employer. After the death of Mrs. Lathrop when Sigourney was thirteen, she continued her education independently and, through the assistance of Mrs. Lathrop's family, eventually opened a school for young ladies and published her successful first volume *Moral Pieces, in Prose and Verse* (1815). This volume was the prelude to a fifty-year publishing career that would finally include thousands of periodical publications and more than fifty separate books, many of which were reprinted more than once. Sigourney's writing encompassed poetry, autobiography, advice writing, children's literature, sketches, history, and travel (*Dictionary of Literary Biography* 264–266).

One important motivation for her writing was to earn a living and to support her parents. Looking back on her career, Sigourney willingly acknowledged the economic motivations for her writing; she observed, "[O]riginating in impulse, and [in] those habits of writing that were deepened by the solitary lot of an only child, it gradually assumed a financial feature which gave it both perseverance and permanence." She added, "This, which at first supplied only my indulgences, my journeyings, or my charities, became gradually a form of subsistence" (*Letters of Life* 378). In contrast, she claims, "[F]ame, as a ruling motive, has not stimulated me to literary effort" and in a sentence makes clear the force behind her aesthetic: "[T]he only adequate payment are the hope and belief that, by enforcing some salutary precept, or promoting some hallowed practice, good may have been done to our race" (*Letters of Life* 379).

The financial concerns of her birth family dissipated briefly when in 1819 she married Charles Sigourney, an apparently prosperous local merchant and bank official, joining his large household that included three children from a previous marriage, along with other family members and servants. Not only did the marriage require her to relinquish her successful career as a teacher, but her husband, regarding her writing profession as too public an occupation for a lady, permitted her to continue it only as a genteel avocation and only anonymously. Sigourney admitted the emotional cost of this prohibition when she reflected on her early married life: "Among the disturbing forces that conflicted with this somewhat dreamy period of my existence, was the thought that I could no longer, by my own earnings, add to the comfort of my parents. It had been the purest, most unmixed pleasure, that I had ever tasted. How could I possibly resign it?" (*Letters of Life* 258). In spite of his decree of anonymity, Charles did help his wife revise the footnotes to her epic poem *Traits of the Aborigines of America*, which was published in 1822, five years after it was written. Sometime in 1833, possibly owing to pressure on the family's economic situation, perhaps because she made a decision to defy her husband's wishes, or for some combination of these and other reasons, Sigourney began to use her name again on her published work.

This name was to acquire significant value in the era of literary annuals and magazine publication, as Sigourney herself, a shrewd businesswoman, recognized, selling it to such popular periodicals as *Godey's Lady's Book* and *Godey's Lady's Companion*, on whose mastheads she appeared as editor, though she did not appear to have had any responsibilities. Other editors, such as Edgar Allan Poe, vied for her work for their publications. Part of her success can be attributed to her skill as a self-publicist, equal in the nineteenth century perhaps only to Whitman. As part of this effort, during her travels to Europe in the early 1840s, she attempted to forge connections with famous British writers, and at home she fostered comparisons between herself with popular British poet Felicia Hemans. "The Sweet Singer of Hartford," as she was pleased to be known, was adept at packaging and marketing previously published materials into new volumes, keeping her name prominent in the public eye.

Sigourney's autobiography reveals a woman who was to some degree eager to confirm the public perception of her as virtuous and pious, a model wife and mother. It also reveals the author's wit and her dedication to her profession. She tells readers that "my epistolary intercourse is extensive, and exceeds a yearly exchange of two thousand letters. It includes many from strangers, who are often disposed to be tenacious of replies, and to construe omission as rude neglect" (*Letters of Life* 377). The writer handled this vast correspondence often without assistance; that she possessed a keen sense of humor is evident in her recording the various requests that she received from strangers: "Epitaphs for a man and two children, with warning that only two hundred and fifty letters must be allowed in the whole, as the monument was not large enough to contain more''; ''The owner of a canary-bird, which had accidentally been starved to death, wishes some elegiac verses''; ''A monody for the loss of a second wife, fortified by the argument that I had composed one at the death of the first'' (*Letters of Life* 371, 373, 374).

The author's apparently unhappy marriage led to the birth of five children, three of whom died at a young age. The younger of the surviving two, Andrew, died in 1850 at the age of nineteen. Although age moderated her prolific output in the 1850s and early 1860s, it could not prevent her from writing her auto-biography, which she completed just before her death in 1865. At the end of her life, she acknowledged, ''My literary course has been a happy one. Its encouragements have exceeded both my expectations and desserts'' (*Letters of Life* 378). She also admitted the labor that such a prolific career necessitated: ''If there is any kitchen in Parnassus, my Muse has surely officiated there as a woman of all work, and an aproned waiter'' (*Letters of Life* 376).

MAJOR WORKS AND THEMES

Sigourney's writing ranged across many genres and explored a variety of issues, but certain forms and attitudes were characteristic. Beginning with *Moral Pieces*, which was written partly for schoolroom use in her early work as a teacher, and continuing with *Letters to Young Ladies* (1833) and *Letters to Mothers* (1838), she pursued one strand, domestic and advice writing. Essentially conventional in this mode, she emphasizes morality and piety for women; in *Lucy Howard's Journal* (1858), a mixed autobiography/novel/conduct book, she affirms that women's ''truest joy'' lies ''in making others happy'' (145). Throughout her autobiography, Sigourney acknowledged the overriding concern with moral improvement that motivated much of her work.

Among her diverse works were travel writing (*Pleasant Memories of Pleasant Lands* [1842]), historical writing (*Evening Readings in History* [1833]), temperance writing (*The Intemperate, and the Reformed* [1833]; *Water-drops* [1848]), and children's writing (*Poetry for Children* [1834]). Concentrating on famous people and places, present and past, the first two genres look at the public world, while the latter more often focus on motherhood, family, proper behavior, and Christian virtues. Sigourney herself, however, points implicitly to the links between public and private worlds when she notes that *Water-drops* was ''particularly addressed to females, to propitiate their influence against a foe that lays waste their dearest hopes, and to quicken them in impressing upon the tender minds committed to their charge the subjugation of the appetites, and the wisdom and beauty of self control'' (*Letters of Life* 354).

One of the writer's most important texts is the five-canto, 4,000-lines-plus epic poem *Traits of the Aborigines of America* (1822), which addresses the historic wrongs committed by European settlers in relation to their Native American counterparts and the continuing racism inflicted by the former on the latter. Sigourney highlights this theme repeatedly in her work, from some of the sketches in *Sketch of Connecticut, Forty Years Since* (1824) to many individual poems and sketches, including "Indian Names," "Oriana," and "Funeral of Mazeen." Sigourney was later to say, "[O]ur injustice and hard-hearted policy with regard to the original owners of the soil has ever seemed to me one of our greatest national sins" (*Letters of Life* 327).

Sketch of Connecticut also critiques the dominant culture's relationship to other nondominant and culturally vulnerable groups, such as African Americans (both slaves and free blacks), the poor, the working class, and women. Women's moral power, a favorite Sigourney theme, is embodied here in the person of Madame L——, who rules charitably and benevolently over the community in a kind of energetic, matriarchal Christian democracy. This volume was intended in part as "an offering of gratitude to her whose influence, like a golden thread, had run through the whole woof of my life," her early patron Mrs. Lathrop (*Letters of Life* 329).

Sigourney's poetry frequently considers death and dying, interwoven with depictions of the home and motherhood, as in a famous poem like "Death of an Infant," which mourns the loss of a child from the mother's perspective as it celebrates the child's reunion with God. Similarly, "A Father to His Motherless Children" enters into the sentimental genre prevalent in nineteenth-century literature. A poem like "Hebrew Dirge" highlights the sympathy that should be given to the mother of a dead infant, insisting, "O! for the *living* spare those tears / Ye lavish on the *dead*." As her correspondence indicates, she was famous—and sought after—for her elegiac poems, of which she composed thousands. But Sigourney's poetry as emphatically considers nature and nationhood; "Niagara," "Indian Names," and "Connecticut River" celebrate the power of the American landscape and acknowledge the awe that it inspires. As does much of her work, the latter, like "The Western Emigrant," brings together apparently disparate public and private worlds. Along with "Connecticut River," "The Western Emigrant" also explores the role of women in American history; Sigourney envisages pioneer women in affirmative and sometimes idealistic terms. Her sense of humor reemerges in a poem like "To a Shred of Linen," which expresses with wit and energy the conflicts between a literary and a domestic life, as well as exploring the changing values of contemporary society.

CRITICAL RECEPTION

Criticism of Sigourney has been divided from the beginning. Her mostly positive contemporaries praised her piety, virtue, and domesticity; Edgar Allan Poe remarked, "Among those high qualities which give her, beyond doubt, a title to the sacred name of the poet are an acute sensibility to natural loveliness—a quick and perfectly just conception of the moral and physical sublime—a calm and unostentatious vigor of thought—a mingled delicacy and strength of expression—and above all, a mind nobly and exquisitely attuned to all the gentle charities and lofty pieties of Life'' (Poe 113). At the same time, Poe, like many of his contemporaries, criticized her for being imitative, most notably of Mrs. Hemans (112). Many also chided her for casualness and lack of care in composition. But even Poe's criticism was tempered by high praise; citing lines from ''Zinzendorff,'' he affirms, ''[T]he lines are glowing all over with the radiance of poetry. The image in italics is perfect. Of the versification, it is not too much to say that it reminds us of Miltonic power'' (114).

By the turn of the century, the more positive tone of contemporary reviews had changed to virtually unmitigated disparagement; one critic observed that ''she was in the main a hack writer, and the greater number of her works are potboilers'' (Collin 29). Only Louise Bogan sounded a note of mild respect, in an essay of 1947, when she pointed out that Sigourney ''managed to put feminine verse-writing on a paying basis, and give it prestige; even Poe did not quite dare to handle her work too roughly'' (Bogan 426). Kenneth Andrews's view reflects the dominant tone and content of twentieth-century appraisals of Sigourney until very recently: ''Though her own international fame established her supremacy, dozens of Hartford housewives competed with her during the sentimental forties and fifties in the manufacture of pathos out of weddings, funerals, train wrecks, early death, widows in distress, and little babies, dead or alive, whose tiny shoes were never put away'' (147).

Criticism of the past twenty-five years echoes the mix of earlier voices, although the most recent considerations have tended to be more affirmative. Ann Douglas Wood reads beyond the poet's sentimentality and piety to discover a capable self-publicist who used poetry as a means of sublimating her desires for greater cultural power and freedom for women. Explaining Sigourney's numerous poems about dying and death, Emily Stipes Watts notes that ''with the infant and maternal death rate still high . . . it is not surprising that nineteenth-century poets, both men and women, continued to write many elegies'' (85); she highlights the difference between many male poets and Sigourney, who ''was attempting to deal honestly and in fairly real terms with the emotions, frustrations, and tragedies of the deaths of real children and their real mothers. Unlike her contemporary Bryant, she was simply not satisfied by the general thought that we all die'' (86). Watts also uncovers Sigourney's contributions to American poems about domesticity and the family, and she emphasizes the quality of her children's verse (95–96). Noting that ''her very success seems held against her'' (107), Judith Fetterley cites the writer's subversive affirmation of femininity and her reversal (and implied critique) of ''the sexual imperialism of traditional American fiction in which male writers inhabit and speak through female characters'' (110). Sandra Zagarell provides an appreciative discussion of the ambitiousness and innovation of Sigourney's *Sketch of Connecticut*.

Perhaps the most positive contemporary reappraisals are those of Annie Finch and Nina Baym. The former highlights Sigourney's representation of a different kind of American self and a different relation to nature, and she argues for the power of the writer's nature poetry. Baym, also arguing for the power and continuing importance of Sigourney's poems, asserts that *Traits of the Aborigines of America* "might be thought of as a belated entry in the competition for 'the American epic'" and highlights how "it is uniquely structured from an Indian point of view" (396). We are still in the early stages of recovering, understanding, and reappraising the significance of Sigourney's diverse and massive body of work.

WORK CITED

Bowles, Dorothy A. "Lydia H. Sigourney." In *Dictionary of Literary Biography*. Vol. 73, *American Magazine Journalists, 1741–1850*, edited by Sam G. Riley. Detroit: Gale Research Co., 1988. 264–274.

BIBLIOGRAPHY

Works by Lydia Sigourney

Poetry

Traits of the Aborigines of America, a Poem. By Anonymous. Cambridge, MA: Hilliard & Metcalf, 1822.
Poems. Boston: Samuel G. Goodrich, 1827.
Poems. Philadelphia: Key & Biddle, 1834.
Poetry for Children. Hartford, CT: Robinson & Pratt, 1834.
Zinzendorff, and Other Poems. New York: Leavitt, Lord, 1835.
Pocahontas, and Other Poems. New York: Harper, 1841.
The Poetical Works of Mrs. L. H. Sigourney. Edited by F. W. N. Bayley. London: Routledge, 1850.

Sketches, Fiction, Nonfiction Prose, and Mixed Genre

Moral Pieces, in Prose and Verse. Hartford: Sheldon & Goodwin, 1815.
Sketch of Connecticut, Forty Years Since. By Anonymous. Hartford: Oliver D. Cooke, 1824.
Evening Readings in History. By Anonymous. Springfield, MA: G. & C. Merriam, 1833.
The Intemperate, and the Reformed. New York: Sleight & Van Norden, 1833.
Letters to Young Ladies. By Anonymous. Hartford: P. Canfield, 1833.
Sketches. Philadelphia: Key & Biddle, 1834.
Tales and Essays for Children. Hartford: F. J. Huntington, 1835.
Letters to Mothers. Hartford: Hudson & Skinner, 1838.
Pleasant Memories of Pleasant Lands. Boston: James Munroe, 1842.
Myrtis, with Other Etchings and Sketches. New York: Harper, 1846.
Water-drops. New York: Robert Carter, 1848.
Past Meridian. New York: Appleton, 1854.
Lucy Howard's Journal. New York: Harper, 1858.
Letters of Life. New York: Appleton, 1866.

Studies of Lydia Sigourney

Andrews, Kenneth R. *Nook Farm, Mark Twain's Hartford Circle*. Cambridge: Harvard University Press, 1950.

Baym, Nina. "Reinventing Lydia Sigourney." *American Literature* 62, no. 3 (1990): 385–404.

Bogan, Louise. "The Heart and the Lyre." In her *A Poet's Alphabet: Reflections on the Literary Art and Vocation*. Edited by Robert Phelps and Ruth Limmer. New York: McGraw-Hill, 1970.

Collin, Grace Lathrop. "Lydia Huntley Sigourney." *New England Magazine* 27, no. 1 (1902): 15–30.

Day, Betty Harris. " 'This Comes of Writing Poetry': The Public and Private Voice of Lydia H. Sigourney." Ph.D. diss., University of Maryland, 1993.

De Jong, Mary G. "*Legacy* Profile: Lydia Howard Huntley Sigourney." *Legacy* 5, no. 1 (1988): 35–43.

Fetterley, Judith, ed. *Provisions: A Reader from 19th-Century American Women*. Bloomington: Indiana University Press, 1985. 105–116.

Finch, Annie. "The Sentimental Poetess in the World: Metaphor and Subjectivity in Lydia Sigourney's Nature Poetry." *Legacy* 5, no. 2 (1988): 3–18.

Haight, Gordon S. *Mrs. Sigourney: The Sweet Singer of Hartford*. New Haven: Yale University Press, 1930.

Petrino, Elizabeth A. " 'Feet so precious charged': Dickinson, Sigourney, and the Child Elegy." *Tulsa Studies in Women's Literature* 13, no. 2 (1994): 317–338.

Poe, Edgar Allan. Review of *Zinzendorff, and Other Poems*. *Southern Literary Messenger* 2, no. 12 (1836): 112–117.

Watts, Emily Stipes. "1800–1850: Sigourney, Smith, and Osgood." In *The Poetry of American Women from 1632 to 1945*. Austin: University of Texas Press, 1977. 83–97.

Wood, Ann Douglas. "Mrs. Sigourney and the Sensibility of the Inner Space." *New England Quarterly* 45, no. 2 (1972): 163–181.

Zagarell, Sandra A. "Expanding 'America': Lydia Sigourney's *Sketch of Connecticut*, Catherine Sedgwick's *Hope Leslie*." *Tulsa Studies in Women's Literature* 6, no. 2 (1987): 225–245.

E. D. E. N. SOUTHWORTH (EMMA DOROTHY ELIZA NEVITTE SOUTHWORTH) (1819–1899)

Amy E. Hudock

BIOGRAPHY

A news clipping in the files of the Washington Historical Society in Washington, D.C. reports that early in her marriage Emma Southworth and her new husband, Frederick, called a one-room log cabin on the wild frontiers of Wisconsin home. On their first night in the dilapidated cabin, Frederick, having found they had no matches to light the fire, left Southworth sitting outside the front door, enjoying the beautiful spring evening, when "[a]ll at once a sense of the appalling stillness abroad startled her, when a long, low murmur like the winds in the tree tops, so filled her with dread that she rushed into the house and barred the door. Pulling the cotton curtain carefully aside she looked out and saw the scintillating hungry eyes of a pack of wolves" (undated clipping, Southworth Papers, Washington Historical Society). Realizing that they desired a recently butchered piece of meat, she moved the temptation to a more secure part of the cabin as the hungry wolves continued to dig and claw at the weak perimeter for over an hour before her husband and his gun returned to liberate Southworth and the fresh meat. The image of Southworth keeping a pack of howling wolves at bay indicates the essence of her personality: She responded to threats to her happiness and livelihood with typical courage and perseverance.

Despite the social conditioning that might have birthed a more passive, dependent, and submissive young woman, Southworth's life lessons taught her strength enough to ward off wolves—both real and metaphorical. Her mother, Susannah Georgia Wailes, married Charles L. Nevitte, a forty-five-year-old established Washington, D.C. businessman, when she was only fifteen years old. The age difference, Susannah's mother's move into her son-in-law's home, and Southworth's later withering portrayal of such unions in her fiction suggest the marriage was designed to provide both the young daughter and the widowed mother with security, a plan that ultimately failed because the husband died a rather quick death. Knowing the circumstances of her parents' marriage and her mother's swift remarriage for the same financial reasons, Southworth learned early how women's financial dependence can create mismatched, and even misguided, marriages as well as how precarious such arrangements can be.

As her attitudes developed concerning women's limited economic roles, so did the intellectual ability that would ultimately allow her to express her outrage. Despite the neglect she and her sister experienced in the home of their new stepfather, Mr. J. C. Henshaw did provide them with a solid classical education at the school he and Mrs. Henshaw ran out of the first floor of their home. The author of an 1860 biographical sketch identified as only THY (possibly Southworth herself) claims, "Here Emma first discovered that she possessed some mental power—a discovery quite as surprising to herself as it was to others" (35). Her early success created a lifelong fascination with books and storytelling, and she spent much of her free time perusing the family library, which helps explain the many literary allusions in her novels.

After graduating from Henshaw's school in 1835 at the age of sixteen, Southworth taught in Washington public schools until her marriage to Frederick in 1840. Apparently, however, she left the unhappiness of her stepfather's home for even a more difficult situation. In 1844, Frederick left his family in Washington under the pretense of making his fortune in Brazil. "In those sad days," Southworth wrote to her daughter, "I used to go to the post office in hopes of getting a letter from Brazil and, [day] after day, and & week [after week] come home crushed and disappointed" (Library of Congress, 19 January 1894). He did not return until his wife possessed the money and fame he craved for himself, but by that time, Southworth had learned to thrive without him.

Once she realized her husband would not return, she sought a means to support herself and her two children after discovering no help forthcoming from her family. Southworth did teach again in the school system but eventually found writing more inspiring and financially stable. Her first short story, "The Irish Refugee" (1846), was published in the abolitionist newspaper *The Baltimore Saturday Visiter*, which eventually became the *National Era*. She published six short stories before her first full-length novel, *Retribution*, appeared in 1849 to much critical and popular acclaim. Henry Peterson of the *Saturday Evening Post* wooed her onto his contributor list, where she remained, writing for the *Era* and the *Post*, until 1857, when Robert Bonner of the *New York Ledger* made an exclusive arrangement with Southworth for everything her pen produced. Her relationship with Bonner proved lucrative and satisfying: He provided few editorial suggestions; he marketed her well; and together they helped make the *Ledger* one of the most popular story weeklies. As her success in the serial papers swelled, so did the sales figures of her books, published and marketed by T. B. Peterson. Finally, Southworth achieved the financial security and independence she needed, although she never fully allowed herself to trust its stability.

Through the course of her long fiction writing career (1846–1890), Southworth's novels and short story collections consistently topped sales lists and drew readers to the serial papers featuring her seemingly magical name. She published approximately forty-three novels and eight short story collections, many appearing in multiple editions and translations throughout the world. Theaters produced at least four of her novels, including one of the most popular plays of the period, *The Hidden Hand*, which appeared in over forty cities and towns in the United States as well as running three versions consecutively in London. Southworth once said of her writing: "I have always tried to please the multitude and satisfy the cultured; and with what success others may judge. I know that I number among my readers some professors of colleges, ministers of the gospel, and senators on one hand—schoolboys and girls and little street gamins on the other—& a vast multitude in between" (Perkins Library, 24 March 1887). And most readers did judge her favorably, writing positive reviews, sending her adoring letters, keeping her novels in demand until 1930.

Southworth's final new publication in the *Ledger*, *A Deed without a Name*, ran from January 2, 1886, to October 30, 1886. After this novel, only reprints of earlier stories appeared. In 1886, the author began to receive warnings that the new *Ledger* staff, particularly Bonner's sons, who were replacing their father as the head of the publishing empire, found her work dated and unsatisfying to changing tastes. For the first time in her association with the *Ledger*, Southworth's weekly submissions began to be inspected by a "reader" who apparently criticized Southworth's writing style, for she or he prompted the following defensive reply: "I always do my very best; but it is utterly impossible for me to write in any other way than my own. As I do like criticism, I must accept the adverse as willingly as the favorable—if I can" (Perkins Library, 24 March 1887). Southworth seems to have been unable to alter her style to reflect the new mood of the *Ledger*; the story that prompted this correspondence never appeared in print.

In the letters dating from 1887, Southworth wrote Bonner as she had done for thirty years, and Bonner, it appears, continued to pay her and accept her copy long after the decision had been made to cut her from the contributor's list. No letters to Bonner seem to remain from the period June 13, 1887, to December 30, 1889; thus, no record reveals how Bonner informed Southworth her services were no longer required, nor how she handled the news. But since Southworth's identity was intimately intertwined with her role as a writer, and she had planned to write for the *Ledger* for the rest of her life, this news must have been painful. She seems to have survived, however, because her later years were spent living in Georgetown, enjoying her dogs and sharing her life with her son, Richmond, and his wife, Blanche. When she died in 1899, a country mourned as the *New York Times* front-page obituary spread the news.

MAJOR WORKS AND THEMES

Discussing Southworth's "major works" is difficult because of her incredible productivity and the current unavailability of her work to a wide readership. Today, readers and critics tend to address Southworth's most enduring novel *The Hidden Hand*, originally serialized in the *New York Ledger* (1859, 1868–1869, 1883), first published in book form in 1888, and available in a 1988 reprint from Rutgers University Press. However, critics do examine other out-of-print works, including *The Deserted Wife* (1850), *The Discarded Daughter* (1852), and *The Curse of Clifton* (1852), but we need further inquiry before we herald her "major" works. Thus, while subjective, identifying a few particularly fascinating ones will, nonetheless, help guide readers through the apparent maze of Southworth publications. While *The Hidden Hand* clearly ranks as an important Southworth novel, revealing Southworth's humor, sense of adventure, and eagerness to challenge traditional gender definitions, it is not the only novel or short story worth reading. For instance, Southworth's second novel *The Deserted Wife* stands as one of her finest novels, offering raw emotion, finely detailed development of the main character (up until the point her editor demanded she finish the novel quickly), and an insightful depiction of the breakdown of a marriage. Also, the novel *Fair Play* (1868) and its sequel, *How He Won Her* (1869), should be read for their reflections of the Civil War through a focus on a woman who dresses as a man for battle.

In addition, her short stories also deserve attention, especially the collections *Old Neighborhoods and New Settlements* (1853, also called *The Wife's Victory*) and *The Haunted Homestead* (1860), which address Southworth's major themes and favorite genres. Such short stories as "Neighbors Prescriptions," a story reminiscent of the sharp wit of Fanny Fern, show the sarcastic side she often hid in her more conventional novels. "New Year in the Rough-Cast House" explores one of her favorite topics, temperance, by realistically depicting the effects of alcoholism. In her continual effort to teach her readers humanistic lessons, she writes in "The Thunderbolt to the Hearth" of capital punishment's moral failure. She attacks the gender socialization that makes women easy victims in such stories as "The Temptation." In her gothic ghost stories, such as "The Haunted Homestead" and "The Specter Reveals," the author examines the distinctions between fact and fiction, reality and illusion, and universal and individual perception. And finally, in "The Presentiment," Southworth addresses the slavery issue with a story of two men, raised together, black and white, slave and master, in which this power imbalance creates a criminal out of a good, decent man. Her short stories, then, reveal the issues and questions that concerned Southworth and that she expanded in her novels.

Ultimately, she is best known as a vivid storyteller with a mission; she wanted to entertain and change the world, particularly for women. As Joanne Dobson argues in her introduction to the 1988 reprint of Southworth's novel *The Hidden Hand* (1888), "As a talented writer and woman passionate about the injustices perpetrated upon women in a society that allowed them little other than symbolic power, she inevitably helped shape the popular perception of women's status'' (xxi). Although Southworth would never have called herself a feminist, many critics recognize the powerful influence the examples of her life and her fiction possessed in empowering women of the nineteenth century.

CRITICAL RECEPTION

In Southworth's own day, readers tended to find her work delightful. Nina Baym explains that among the hundreds of authors she surveyed, Southworth was one of only three who were consistently praised for stylistic variations (*Novels* 134). Although the author was at first questioned for her stylistic excesses, later, these excesses became, in the reviewers' eyes, the reason for her popularity (135). At the turn of the century, she became one of the authors condemned by the rising ''realists'' as too sentimental. For twentieth-century critics, as well, critical assessment of Southworth's style changes from ''excessive'' to ''expressive.'' Early in the century, critics such as Fred Lewis Pattee (1940) criticize Southworth for her ''sentimentality,'' saying that she was a good example of the overglorification of bad writers; later, however, critics such as Mary Noel (1954) claim that Southworth's popularity and value were genuine, saying that Southworth successfully combined the ''sweetest sentiment with the blow of a well-directed fist'' in her use of coverplots (conventional story lines) to disguise harsh and angry messages protesting the victimization of women (1). Helen Papashvily (1956) views Southworth as the high priestess of a cult that challenges male authority. Nina Baym (1978) readily claims what many considered Southworth's greatest weakness, her decorative and overstated prose, as a flamboyant rejection of the female decorum of other writers of her time. Joanne Dobson (1988) notes the difference modernist attitudes makes in twentieth-century critics. And Susan K. Harris (1990) abandons the term *sentimentality* altogether and refers to Southworth's work as ''exploratory'' because it thematically explores alternatives for women's lives. Currently, Southworth is receiving more attention, with recent dissertations, chapters in larger works, and scholarly articles examining her work and her place in literary tradition. Southworth reflected on the social realities of her day, particularly for women, and, in doing so, captured the imaginations of generations of readers. She stands, then as now, as a vital figure in the development of fiction in the United States.

WORKS CITED

Baym, Nina. *Novels, Readers, and Reviewers: Responses to Fiction in Antebellum America*. Ithaca: Cornell University Press, 1984.
———. *Woman's Fiction: A Guide to Novels by and about Women in America 1820–1970*. Ithaca: Cornell University Press, 1978.

Dobson, Joanne. Introduction to *The Hidden Hand*, by E. D. E. N. Southworth. New Brunswick, NJ: Rutgers University Press, 1988.

Harris, Susan K. "Extending and Subverting: The Iconography of Houses in 'The Deserted Wife.'" In *19th-Century American Women's Novels: Interpretative Strategies*. Cambridge: Cambridge University Press, 1990.

Noel, Mary. *Villains Galore: The Heyday of the Popular Story Weekly*. New York: Macmillan, 1954.

Papashvily, Helen Waite. *All the Happy Endings*. New York: Harper & Bros., 1956.

Pattee, Fred Lewis. *The Feminine Fifties*. New York: D. Appleton-Century Co., 1940.

THY. Introduction to *The Haunted Homestead*, by E. D. E. N. Southworth. Philadelphia: Peterson, 1860.

BIBLIOGRAPHY

Works by E. D. E. N. Southworth

Novels

Though many novels gained multiple titles when serialized, reprinted, and pirated in the United States and other countries, this list focuses on first U.S. book edition titles.

Retribution; or, The Vale of Shadows: A Tale of Passion. New York: Harper, 1849.

The Deserted Wife. New York: Appleton, 1850.

The Mother-in-Law; or, The Isle of Rays. New York: Appleton, 1851.

Shannondale. New York: Appleton, 1851.

The Curse of Clifton. Philadelphia: Peterson, 1852.

The Discarded Daughter; or, The Children of the Ilse: A Tale of the Chesapeake. Philadelphia: Hart, 1852.

Virginia and Magdalene; or, The Foster Sisters. Philadelphia: Hart, 1852.

Old Neighborhoods and New Settlements; or, Christmas Evening Legends. Philadelphia: Hart, 1853.

The Lost Heiress. Philadelphia: Peterson, 1854.

The Missing Bride; or, Miriam the Avenger. Philadelphia: Peterson, 1855.

India: The Pearl of Pearl River. Philadelphia: Peterson, 1856.

Viva; or, The Secret of Power. Philadelphia: Peterson, 1857.

The Lady of the Isle; or, The Island Princess. Philadelphia: Peterson, 1859.

The Haunted Homestead and Other Nouvellettes. With an Autobiography of the Author. Philadelphia: Peterson, 1860.

The Gipsy's Prophecy: A Tale of Real Life. Philadelphia: Peterson, 1861.

Hickory Hall; or, The Outcast: A Romance of the Blue Ridge. Philadelphia: Peterson, 1861.

The Broken Engagement; or, Speaking the Truth for a Day. Philadelphia: Peterson, 1862.

Love's Labor Won. Philadelphia: Peterson, 1862.

The Fatal Marriage. Philadelphia: Peterson, 1863.

The Bridal Eve. Philadelphia: Peterson, 1864.

Allworth Abbey. Philadelphia: Peterson, 1865.

The Bride of Llewellyn. Philadelphia: Peterson, 1866.

The Fortune Seeker; or, The Bridal Day. Philadelphia: Peterson, 1866.

The Coral Lady; or, The Bronzed Beauty of Paris. Philadelphia: C. W. Alexander, 1867.
    (Probably pirated unless Southworth broke her exclusive contract with Peterson)
The Widow's Son. Philadelphia: Peterson, 1867.
Fair Play; or, The Test of Lone Isle. Philadelphia: Peterson, 1868.
The Bride's Fate: A Sequel to "The Changed Brides." Philadelphia: Peterson, 1869.
The Changed Brides. Philadelphia: Peterson, 1869.
The Family Doom; or, The Sin of a Countess. Philadelphia: Peterson, 1869.
How He Won Her: A Sequel to Fair Play. Philadelphia: Peterson, 1869.
The Maiden Widow: A Sequel to the "Family Doom." Philadelphia: Peterson, 1870.
Cruel as the Grave. Philadelphia: Peterson, 1871.
Tried for Her Life. Philadelphia: Peterson, 1871.
The Lost Heir of Linlithgow. Philadelphia: Peterson, 1872.
The Noble Lord: The Sequel to "The Lost Heir of Linlithgow." Philadelphia: Peterson,
    1872.
A Beautiful Fiend; or, Through the Fire. Philadelphia: Peterson, 1873.
Victor's Triumphs: The Sequel to "A Beautiful Fiend." Philadelphia: Peterson, 1874.
Ishmael; or, In the Depths. Philadelphia: Peterson, 1876.
Self-Raised; or, From the Depths: A Sequel to "Ishmael." Philadelphia: Peterson, 1876.
The Bride's Ordeal: A Novel. New York: Burt, 1877.
Her Love or Her Life: A Sequel to "The Bride's Ordeal: A Novel." New York: Burt,
    1877.
The Red Hill Tragedy: A Novel. Philadelphia: Peterson, 1877.
Sybil Brotherton: A Novel. Philadelphia: Peterson, 1879.
The Trail of the Serpent; or, The Homicide at Hawke Hall. New York: Burt, 1880?
For Whose Sake? A Sequel to "Why Did He Wed Her?" New York: Burt, 1884.
Why Did He Wed Her? New York: Burt, 1884.
A Deed without a Name. New York: Burt, 1886.
Dorothy Harcourt's Secret: Sequel to a "A Deed without a Name." New York: Burt,
    1886.
A Leap in the Dark: A Novel. New York: Bonner, 1889.
Little Nea's Engagement: A Sequel to "Nearest and Dearest." New York: Burt, 1889.
Nearest and Dearest: A Novel. New York: Bonner, 1889.
Unknown; or, The Mystery of Raven Rocks. New York: Bonner, 1889.
For Woman's Love: A Novel. New York: Bonner, 1890.
The Lost Lady of Lone. New York: Bonner, 1890.
The Unloved Wife: A Novel. New York: Burt, 1890.
An Unrequited Love: A Sequel to "For Woman's Love." New York: Burt, 1890?
David Lindsay: A Sequel to Gloria. New York: Bonner, 1891.
Gloria: A Novel. New York: Bonner, 1891.
Lilith: A Sequel to "The Unloved Wife." New York: Bonner, 1891.
"Em": A Novel. New York: Bonner, 1892.
Em's Husband. New York: Bonner, 1892.
Brandon Coyle's Wife: A Sequel to "A Skeleton in the Closet." New York: Bonner,
    1893.
The Mysterious Marriage: A Sequel to "A Leap in the Dark." New York: Burt, 1893.
Only a Girl's Heart: A Novel. New York: Bonner, 1893.
A Skeleton in the Closet: A Novel. New York: Bonner, 1893.
Gertrude Haddon. New York: Bonner, 1894.

The Rejected Bride. New York: Bonner, 1894.
The Struggle of a Soul: A Sequel to "The Lost Lady of Lone." New York: Burt, 1904.
Sweet Love's Atonement: A Novel. New York: Burt, 1904.
Zenobia's Suitors: Sequel to "Sweet Love's Atonement." New York: Burt, 1904.
Her Mother's Secret. New York: Burt, 1910.
Love's Bitterest Cup: A Sequel to "Her Mother's Secret." New York: Burt, 1910.
When Shadows Die: A Sequel to "Love's Bitterest Cup." New York: Burt, 1910.
Fulfilling Her Destiny: A Sequel to "When Love Commands." New York: Burt, n.d.
The Initials: A Story of Modern Life. Philadelphia: Peterson, n.d.
To His Fate: A Sequel to "Dorothy Harcourt's Secret." New York: Street & Smith, n.d.
When Love Commands. New York: Burt, n.d.
When Love Gets Justice: A Sequel "To His Fate." New York: Street & Smith, n.d.
When the Shadows Darken: A Sequel to "The Unloved Wife." New York: Street & Smith, n.d.

Short Story Collections

Old Neighborhoods and New Settlements. Philadelphia: Hart, 1853.
The Haunted Homestead. Philadelphia: Peterson, 1860.
The Christmas Guest; or, The Crime and the Curse by Mrs. E. D. E. N. Southworth; and Stories by Her Sister, Mrs. Frances Henshaw Baden. Philadelphia: Peterson, 1870.
The Artist's Love by Mrs. E. D. E. N. Southworth; and Stories by her Sister, Mrs. Frances Henshaw Baden. Philadelphia: Peterson, 1872.
The Spectre Lover by E. D. E. N. Southworth; and Other Stories by Her Sister, Mrs. Frances Henshaw Baden. Philadelphia: Peterson, 1875.
The Fatal Secret by E. D. E. N. Southworth; and Other Stories by Her Sister, Mrs. Frances Henshaw Baden. Philadelphia: Peterson, 1877.
The Phantom Wedding; or, The Fall of the House of Flint by Mrs. E. D. E. N. Southworth; and Other Stories by Her Sister, Mrs. Frances Henshaw Baden. Philadelphia: Peterson, 1878.

Manuscripts and Archives

The major collections are at the Library of Congress and Duke University's Perkin's Library.

Studies of E. D. E. N. Southworth

Bardes, Barbara, and Suzanne Gossett. "Choosing Love Over Money." In *Declarations of Independence: Women and Political Power in Nineteenth-Century American Fiction.* New Brunswick, NJ: Rutgers University Press, 1990.
Boyle, Regis Louise. *Mrs. E. D. E. N. Southworth, Novelist.* Washington, D.C.: Catholic University Press, 1939.
Carpenter, Lynnette. "Double Talk: The Power and Glory of Paradox in E. D. E. N. Southworth's *The Hidden Hand.*" *Legacy* 10 (1993): 17–30.
Coultrap-McQuin, Susan. *Doing Literary Business: American Women Writers in the Nineteenth Century.* Chapel Hill: University of North Carolina, 1990.

Dobson, Joanne. "The Hidden Hand: Subversion of Cultural Ideology in Three Mid-Nineteenth-Century Women's Novels." *American Quarterly* 38 (1986): 223–242.

Habegger, Alfred. "A Well-Hidden Hand." *Novel* 14 (1981): 197–212.

Hudock, Amy E. "Challenging the Definition of Heroism in E. D. E. N. Southworth's *The Hidden Hand*." *ATQ: 19th C. Journal of American Literature and Culture* 9 (1995): 5–20.

———. " 'No Mere Mercenary': The Early Life and Work of E. D. E. N. Southworth." Ph.D. diss., University of South Carolina, 1993.

Merrill, Ann. "The Novels of E. D. E. N. Southworth: Challenging Gender Restrictions and Genre Conventions." Ph.D. diss., Emory University, 1993.

Silverblatt, Arthur. "E. D. E. N. Southworth and Southern Mythic Society." Ph.D. diss., Michigan State University, 1980.

HARRIET PRESCOTT SPOFFORD (1835–1921)

Alfred Bendixen

BIOGRAPHY

Harriet Elizabeth Prescott was born in Calais, Maine, on April 3, 1835, the oldest daughter of Joseph Newmarch Prescott and Sarah Bridges. Her father was at various times a merchant, lawyer, local politician, and officeholder, but he never managed to provide financial security for his large family, which included his mother and four sisters and eventually his five children. Nevertheless, the family encouraged young Harriet's active imagination and interest in literature. At the age of fourteen, she moved with her grandmother and an aunt to Newburyport, Massachusetts, where she relished the excellent education offered by the Putnam Free School. After graduating in 1852, she attended Pinkerton Academy in Derry, New Hampshire. She had substantially more formal education than most women writers of the period and a family that supported and nourished her literary interests. By the middle of the decade, the entire Prescott family reunited and established themselves in Newburyport, but poor health plagued both her father and her mother. The family faced a devastating financial plight, to which Harriet responded by becoming a writer of sensationalistic and melodramatic fiction.

The "story papers" of Boston were eager for her work, and she may have written hundreds of stories for them, receiving as little as $2.50 or $5.00 per tale. The experience made her into a professional writer who could turn out fiction quickly and prolifically, a habit that would eventually damage her reputation. Thomas Wentworth Higginson, who served as her mentor and later became known as Emily Dickinson's "preceptor," probably encouraged her to develop a richer form of narrative that could be published in more respectable venues. Her big break as a writer came when the *Atlantic Monthly* accepted "In a Cellar,'' a racy tale of crime, intrigue, and detection set in Paris. The elaborate plot is built around a series of dramatic confrontations that seem to reveal an intimate knowledge of European politics and society. The narrator's cosmopolitan tone, the sparkling dialogue, and the vivid descriptions of French scenes plunge the reader into a shockingly amoral universe. The story gained immediate acclaim.

She followed her first triumph with an even more ambitious narrative, ''The Amber Gods,'' which appeared in the *Atlantic* in January and February 1860. This daring tale featured a long, densely poetic and sensuous monologue by a completely self-absorbed woman, who recounts how she steals her virtuous cousin's fiancé. The story's lush prose and complex plot culminate in the final revelation that the narrator is speaking from beyond the grave. ''Circumstance,'' a story of a pioneer woman who fends off a savage beast by the power of her song, appeared in the May 1860 *Atlantic*, adding to the young writer's growing reputation. With these three tales, Harriet E. Prescott established herself as one of the most promising young writers of romantic fiction in the United States.

Her most interesting fiction is marked by an extravagance of language, an attempt to make fiction do the work normally ascribed to descriptive poetry. Fiction provided the most lucrative market for her talent, but she herself preferred poetry and probably would have devoted herself to verse if it were financially possible. The demands of the marketplace led her to the novel, a form she never fully mastered. Her first novel, *Sir Rohan's Ghost* (1860), a Gothic romance featuring an artist haunted by a ghost who ends up discovering that he has fallen in love with his own daughter, failed to make its characters come alive or fully develop its moral and psychological dimensions. Nevertheless, some of its descriptive passages were extraordinary; a chapter describing the contents of a wine cellar drew such admiration that the young author often found herself embarrassed when dining in public by some connoisseur sending over a bottle of wine in tribute. Her second novel, *Azarian: An Episode* (1864), which deals with a woman's foolish love for an egoist, provided further evidence of her willingness to sacrifice characterization, plot, and sometimes clarity to moments of lavish lyrical description that often threaten to engulf the work.

The volume that did the most to establish her reputation was *The Amber Gods and Other Stories* (1863), which collected seven tales. Short fiction proved to be the form most congenial to her talent and the most profitable, but she also sold poems and nonfiction pieces. Although she was relatively well paid by the standards of nineteenth-century magazines, the need for money remained a pressing problem and probably caused her to write too much too quickly. She became a prolific contributor to most of the major and many of the minor periodicals of her time—a pattern that would endure throughout her long life. While she gained a measure of financial security from this habit, she lost much of the critical esteem her earliest *Atlantic* contributions had generated and soon became known as a ''magazinist,'' a writer who could be counted on for an entertaining work but whose literary merits did not require serious consideration.

On December 19, 1865, she married Richard S. Spofford, a successful lawyer who admired and encouraged his new wife's literary achievements. By all accounts, the marriage was extremely happy and mutually supportive. His legal and political work often led the couple to divide their time between Newburyport and Washington, D.C. Their only child, a son, was born on January 30, 1867, but died the following September. In 1874, the Spoffords purchased Deer Island, five acres on the Merrimack River connected by bridges to Newburyport and Amesbury, and adapted the large house on the island into a gracious home for themselves and several members of both their families. They entertained extensively, and Harriet Spofford was occasionally held up as a model hostess who successfully balanced a literary career with social and family obligations. In 1885, the Spoffords became the legal guardians of Thomas and Marion Pierce, the orphaned children of friends. The death of her husband in 1888 was devastating to Spofford, but she found consolation in a deepening sense of religious faith and in the companionship of Marion Pierce and a niece, Katherine Prescott Moseley, both of whom became surrogate daughters to her. Spofford also became part of the circle of New England women writers that gathered around Annie Fields.

Spofford continued to write and publish throughout her long life, but her critical reputation did not survive the 1860s. Part of the problem can be attributed to the haste with which she wrote, but the shift to realism following the Civil War also had an enormous impact. Spofford found that there was little demand for the kind of romantic fiction she favored, that the American reading public preferred a relatively simple and plain style to the highly wrought poetic language that she lavished on her early tales. She adapted to the demands of the marketplace and focused much of her literary energy on the production of realistic stories but rarely achieved distinction in this mode. Furthermore, many of her strongest stories were not collected into book form, and most of the books she published did little to enhance her reputation. The novels *The Thief in the Night* (1872) and *The Marquis of Carabas* (1882) provided only a clumsy handling of romantic themes. The realistic stories collected in *A Scarlet Poppy and Other Stories* (1894) and the local color ones in *Old Washington* (1906) were largely forgettable. *Old Madame and Other Tragedies* (1900), however, rescued several tales in which Spofford successfully managed to blend romantic themes and realistic techniques, most notably the title story and "Her Story." Some of her most successful work in the realistic mode appears in the stories of New England village life, *The Elder's People* (1920), which were heavily influenced by the Dr. Lavendar stories of Margaret Deland. She also published several novelettes, of which only *A Master Spirit* (1896) rises above the superficial. An account of her publications in book form may reveal more about the nature of American publishing history than about the full extent of her talent. The bibliography in Halbeisen's biography lists about 275 stories, but many more remain buried away in the pages of nineteenth-century journals. Much of her best short fiction was never collected into book form during her lifetime. The 1989 collection of her stories in the Rutgers American Women Writers Series includes 10 stories, 5 of which had never before been collected.

Although Spofford herself valued her poetry over all her other work, her verse is generally conventional and unexciting, rarely displaying the flamboyant experimentation with language that marks her best prose. Her books for children, particularly *Hester Stanley at St. Marks* (1882) and *Hester Stanley's Friends* (1898), were successful in their time but have not endured. The nature of most of her nonfiction works can be accurately gauged from their titles: *New-England Legends* (1871), *Art Decoration Applied to Furniture* (1878), *The Servant Girl Question* (1881), *House and Hearth* (1891), and *Stepping Stones to Happiness* (1897). Spofford's domestic advice largely represents the platitudes of the time. *A Little Book of Friends* (1916) provides an affectionate but protective account of her friendships with Annie Fields, Rose Terry Cooke, Sarah Orne Jewett, Gail Hamilton, Celia Thaxter, and other women writers. *Four Days of God* (1905) has been almost completely ignored, but its graceful rendition of the search for God in nature and in each of the seasons testifies to the increasing religious faith that characterized Spofford's final years.

By the time of her death on August 14, 1921, Harriet Prescott Spofford had long reconciled herself to her position as a popular writer of magazine fiction, whose early romantic tales had once commanded attention and respect.

MAJOR WORKS AND THEMES

Spofford's importance rests largely on a relatively small number of tales, most notably the first three *Atlantic* stories: ''In a Cellar,'' ''The Amber Gods,'' and ''Circumstance.'' Several of her later stories merit more attention, especially the masterpiece ''Her Story,'' which appeared originally in *Lippincott's* in 1872 but was not collected into book form until 1900. ''Her Story'' anticipates Charlotte Perkins Gilman's ''The Yellow Wall-Paper'' in its treatment of a woman narrator driven beyond the edge of insanity by her marriage. Like ''The Amber Gods'' and several of her other romantic tales, this work focuses on the rivalry of two women—one, pure and virtuous, and the other, exotic, passionate, and demonic—as they struggle to win a man's love. Spofford's fiction often draws on the eagerness of a patriarchal society to relegate women to the roles of either Madonnas or whores, angels or demons, but her best work ultimately engages in a daring confrontation with the moral conventions of her day and raises complex questions about the ways in which a woman can find or create her identity. The pretensions of New England morality collapse or are rendered irrelevant in Spofford's fictional universe, a universe often ruled by intrigue, deception, and manipulation.

In the simplest terms, Spofford's primary fascination in all of her major work is with the nature of power—how power is gained or lost, how it can be used or abused. She is always aware of the limitations placed upon women, but her fiction also asserts that women always have the power to hurt or help other women. It is, however, in the relationships with men that Spofford's female characters end up losing or abusing whatever power they possess. This focus on power usually manifests itself in a concern with the way a woman can find or lose her voice. She insisted on exploring female voices in a culture devoted largely to silencing women. In the act of telling "Her Story" to a female friend in an asylum, the narrator may regain her sanity, but it is not clear that she will regain her freedom. The heroine of "Circumstance" employs the full range of her singing voice to ward off the demands of a savage beast, but at her most transcendent moment, she remains both helpless victim and triumphant artist. The long, sensual monologue of "The Amber Gods" draws the reader into the amoral world of its narrator, a woman whose voice will endure beyond the grave as it recounts both triumph and defeat. The lavish (and sometimes overwrought) style of her early tales represents Spofford's own desire to challenge the boundaries of language itself.

Like other writers of romantic fiction, Spofford was intrigued with the role of art and the artist, a theme that also runs throughout most of the major tales. Moreover, she shared with Hawthorne, Poe, and Melville a fascination with the dark corners of the human mind, with the dangers of egoism and monomania, with the capacity of human beings for evil, masochism, and self-destruction. In its focus on aberrational psychology as well as its use of exotic settings, extravagant plots, and extraordinary characters, Spofford's major tales represent both the final flowering of the romantic imagination in New England fiction and an intriguing feminine variation on genres and modes dominated by men.

CRITICAL RECEPTION

It is all too easy to characterize the critical reception of Spofford's work. The early works met with acclaim and enthusiasm, often from the finest literary minds in the United States. The initial enthusiasm was followed by disappointment as she turned out an abundant amount of work that failed to fulfill the promise of her first *Atlantic* pieces. For the rest of her long life, her books received polite reviews or occasional harsh criticism but no serious or extensive treatment from literary critics. These reviews are cited extensively in Halbeisen's biography. In the early twentieth century, only Fred Lewis Pattee and Arthur Hobson Quinn acknowledged her literary importance. There are, however, signs of a revival of interest in her work, especially by feminist critics.

A number of writers have testified to the impact of Spofford's early work. Rose Terry Cooke has explained the impact of "In a Cellar," noting that "this new and brilliant contribution dazzled us all with the splendors, the manners, the political intrigues, the sin-spiced witchery of Parisian life" (531). In her 1910 essay on "Stories That Stay," Elizabeth Stuart Phelps singled out "The Amber Gods" as one of the few stories that made a lasting impression on her, "a story which took a grip upon me deeper than taste or imagination" (119). Emily Dickinson was also among the readers who reacted passionately to Spofford's work. In a letter to her sister-in-law, Dickinson acclaimed "Circumstance" as "the only thing that I ever saw in my life that I did not think I could have written myself" and requested that she send "everything she writes." In a letter to Higginson, she paid a very different kind of tribute to the power of that tale, noting that "it followed me, in the Dark—so I avoided her—" (St. Armand 173). Although he acknowledged the weaknesses of *Sir Rohan's Ghost*, James Russell Lowell proclaimed: "It is our deliberate judgment that no first volume by any author has ever been published in America showing more undoubtful symptoms of genuine poetic power than this" (253). Lowell's judgment that the writer was "destined for great things" (254) was corroborated by other critics.

The change in Spofford's literary reputation can best be measured by the two reviews written by the young Henry James. In reviewing *The Amber Gods*, James ascribed her popularity to "the united strength and brilliancy of her descriptions," complained of her "morbid and unhealthful tone" and her willingness to explore "illicit love" (569), but concluded, "She has only to avoid a few faults, to breathe a healthier tone into her writings, and to cultivate her own capacity of original thought, in order to assume a foremost place in this department of letters" (568–570). When he reviewed *Azarian*, however, James found nothing to praise and almost everything to condemn, calling the book "a succession of forced assaults upon the impregnable stronghold of painting; a wearisome series of word-pictures, linked by a slight thread of narrative" (270). He urged the author to abandon "the ideal descriptive style" and to learn from the new realist school (269). The review is not only a manifesto for realism but an accurate account of the faults in Spofford's writing at its worst.

The decline in her critical reputation came quickly. Thomas Wentworth Higginson ascribed it to "that fatal cheapness of immediate reputation which stunts most of our young writers, making the rudiments of fame so easy to acquire, and fame itself so difficult—which dwarfs our female writers so especially" (Wells 194). Only two of the early twentieth-century critics acknowledged Spofford's importance in our literary history: Pattee's *Development of the American Short Story* (1923) and Arthur Hobson Quinn's *American Fiction* (1936). Halbeisen's 1935 biography of Spofford provided a useful survey of her work but failed to arouse much interest in her literary achievements.

There have been recent signs of a revival of interest in Spofford, including some excellent scholarly work. Anne Dalke's and Judith Fetterley's articles on "Circumstance" provide acute analyses of the psychological and sexual dimensions of that tale. Barton Levi St. Armand's essay on "The Amber Gods" and his book on Emily Dickinson do much to establish Spofford's importance within the cultural context of the times. He is also among the Dickinson scholars who credit Spofford with inspiring the poet to adopt the posthumous revery as an important technique. Eva Gold and Thomas H. Fick have collaborated on an insightful analysis of "Her Story" that recognizes both Spofford's feminism and artistry. The most comprehensive recent study of the short fiction is Alfred

Bendixen's introduction to the volume in the Rutgers American Women Writers Series. These works provide evidence that Harriet Prescott Spofford's literary achievements merit and will repay increased scholarly and critical attention.

WORKS CITED

Cooke, Rose Terry. "Harriet Prescott Spofford." In *Our Famous Women*. Hartford: A. D. Worthington, 1884. 521–538.
James, Henry. Review of *The Amber Gods*. *North American Review* (October 1863): 568–570.
———. Review of *Azarian*. *North American Review* (January 1865): 268–277.
Lowell, James Russell. Review of *Sir Rohan's Ghost*. *Atlantic Monthly* (February 1860): 252–254.
Phelps, Elizabeth Stuart. "Stories That Stay." *Century Magazine*, n.s., 59 (1910): 118–123.
St. Armand, Barton Levi. *Emily Dickinson and Her Culture*. Cambridge: Cambridge University Press, 1984.
Wells, Anna Mary. *Dear Preceptor: The Life and Times of Thomas Wentworth Higginson*. Boston: Houghton Mifflin, 1963.

BIBLIOGRAPHY

Works by Harriet Prescott Spofford

Poetry

Poems. Boston: Houghton, Mifflin, 1882.
Ballads about Authors. Boston: D. Lothrop, 1887.
In Titian's Garden and Other Poems. Boston: Copeland and Day, 1897.

Novels and Novelettes

Sir Rohan's Ghost. A Romance. Boston: J. E. Tilton, 1860.
Azarian: An Episode. Boston: Ticknor and Fields, 1864.
The Thief in the Night. Boston: Roberts Brothers, 1872.
The Marquis of Carabas. Boston: Roberts Brothers, 1882.
A Master Spirit. New York: Charles Scribner's Sons, 1896.
An Inheritance. New York: Charles Scribner's Sons, 1897.
Priscilla's Love-Story. Chicago: Herbert S. Stone, 1898.
The Maid He Married. Chicago: Herbert S. Stone, 1899.
That Betty. New York: Fleming H. Revell, 1903.
The Making of a Fortune. A Romance. New York: Harper Bros., 1911.

Collections of Stories

The Amber Gods and Other Stories. Boston: Ticknor and Fields, 1863.
A Scarlet Poppy and Other Stories. New York: Harper & Bros., 1894.
Old Madame and Other Tragedies. Boston: Richard G. Badger, 1900.
Old Washington. Boston: Little, Brown, 1906.

The King's Easter. Boston: World Peace Foundation, 1912.
The Elder's People. Boston: Houghton Mifflin, 1920.
"The Amber Gods" and Other Stories. Edited by Alfred Bendixen. New Brunswick: Rutgers University Press, 1989. (Different content than 1863 volume)

Essays and Nonfiction

New-England Legends. Boston: James R. Osgood, 1871.
Art Decoration Applied to Furniture. New York: Harper and Bros., 1878.
The Servant Girl Question. Boston: Houghton, Mifflin, 1881.
House and Hearth. New York: Dodd, Mead, 1891.
Stepping Stones to Happiness. New York: Christian Herald, 1897.
Four Days of God. Boston: Richard G. Badger, 1905.
A Little Book of Friends. Boston: Little, Brown, 1916.

Works for Children

Hester Stanley at St. Marks. Boston: Roberts Brothers, 1882.
Hester Stanley's Friends. Boston: Little, Brown, 1898.
The Children of the Valley. New York: Thomas Y. Crowell, 1901.
The Great Procession and Other Verses for and about Children. Boston: Richard G. Badger, 1902.
The Fairy Changeling: A Flower and Fairy Play. Boston: Richard G. Badger, 1911.

Studies of Harriet Prescott Spofford

Bendixen, Alfred. Introduction to *"The Amber Gods" and Other Stories*. Edited by Alfred Bendixen. New Brunswick: Rutgers University Press, 1989. ix–xxxix.
Dalke, Anne. " 'Circumstance' and the Creative Woman: Harriet Prescott Spofford." *Arizona Quarterly* 41, no. 1 (1985): 71–85.
Fast, Robin Riley. "Killing the Angel in Spofford's 'Desert Sands' and 'The South Breaker.' " *Legacy* 11, no. 1 (1994): 37–54.
Fetterley, Judith, ed. *Provisions: A Reader from 19th-Century American Women*. Bloomington: Indiana University Press, 1985. 261–268.
Garbowsky, Maryanne M. "A Maternal Muse for Emily Dickinson." *Dickinson Studies* 41 (December 1981): 12–17.
Gold, Eva, and Thomas H. Fick. "A 'Masterpiece' of the 'Educated Eye': Convention, Gaze, and Gender in Spofford's 'Her Story.' " *Studies in Short Fiction* 30, no. 4 (1993): 511–523.
Halbeisen, Elizabeth K. *Harriet Prescott Spofford: A Romantic Survival*. Philadelphia: University of Pennsylvania Press, 1935.
Pattee, Fred Lewis. *The Development of the American Short Story*. New York: Harper and Bros., 1923. 159–163.
Quinn, Arthur Hobson. *American Fiction: An Historical and Critical Survey*. New York: D. Appleton-Century, 1936. 208–214.
Shinn, Thelma J. "Harriet Prescott Spofford: A Reconsideration." *Turn-of-the-Century Women* 1, no. 1 (1984): 36–45.

St. Armand, Barton Levi. " 'I Must Have Died at Ten Minutes Past One': Posthumous Reveries in Harriet Prescott Spofford's 'The Amber Gods.' " In *The Haunted Dusk: American Supernatural Fiction, 1820–1920*, edited by Howard Kerr, John W. Crowley, and Charles L. Crow. Athens: University of Georgia Press, 1983. 101–119.

ANN SOPHIA STEPHENS (1810–1886)

Jennifer Hynes

BIOGRAPHY

Ann Sophia Winterbotham was born on March 30, 1810, in Humphreysville (now Seymour), Connecticut, the third child of ten born to Ann (Wrigley) and John Winterbotham, part owner and manager of a woolen mill owned by Connecticut poet-patriot Colonel David Humphreys. After her mother's death when she was young, she was raised by her mother's sister, Rachel, who became her stepmother. She was educated at the local dame school and in South Britain, Connecticut. Her first published compositions, poetry and prose, appeared under pen names in various newspapers.

In 1831 Ann Winterbotham married printer Edward Stephens of Plymouth, Massachusetts. They moved to Portland, Maine, where they founded the *Portland Magazine* (1834–1836), a women's magazine that included both reprinted material from other writers and their own work. Edward Stephens functioned as publisher, while Ann Stephens was editor. In 1837 the couple moved to New York, where Stephens wrote for the local popular magazines.

Stephens was to continue her editorial career—while she simultaneously wrote poetry, essays, and fiction—as associate editor of the *Ladies' Companion; and Literary Expositor* (1837–1841); associate editor of *Graham's Lady's and Gentleman's Magazine* (1841–1842); coeditor of the *Lady's World* (renamed *Peterson's Magazine* in 1849) (1842–1853); editor of *Frank Leslie's Lady's Gazette of Fashion and Fancy Needlework* (1854–1856); and founder and editor of *Mrs. Stephens New Monthly* (1856–1858).

Much of Stephens's own work appeared in the periodicals that she edited; her poems "My Natal Bowers" and "The Polish Boy" (which would be reprinted in anthologies throughout the century) ran in the *Portland Magazine*, while *Mary Derwent: A Tale of the Early Settlers* and *Malaeska* were serialized in the *Ladies' Companion*. Both novels were later issued separately. Early in her career, she also contributed to numerous other periodicals, including the *Lady's Wreath*, *Olive Branch*, and *Brother Jonathan*.

In 1850 Stephens left her two children, Ann (born in 1841) and Edward (born in 1845), with her husband while she toured Europe with her friends, Colonel George W. Pratt and his sister, Julia Pratt. While abroad she met several literary figures such as Charles Dickens and William Makepeace Thackeray. On this trip, she also gathered material that would appear in some later novels set in England, including *Zana; or, The Heiress of Clair Hall* (1854) and *Lord Hope's Choice* (1873). By the late 1850s Stephens's magazine writing and editing, as well as her books, had made her one of America's most popular writers.

Stephens's connection with the Philadelphia publishers Theophilus B. Peterson and his brother Charles Peterson furthered her career in several ways. Apart from editing *Peterson's Magazine* from 1842 to 1853, many of her serialized tales reached wide audiences through this publication. Significantly, these stories would be published as books later by the firm of T. B. Peterson. After about 1863 Stephens's most frequent publisher was the firm of T. B. Peterson, which also produced a twenty-three-volume edition of her collected works beginning in 1859.

But Stephens also enjoyed an important connection with the New York firm of Irwin P. Beadle. In 1860 Stephens's novel *Malaeska: The Indian Wife of the White Hunter* was reissued as the first volume of Beadle's Dime Novels series, a collection of inexpensive adventure novels. Although Beadle's Dime Novels have generally been remembered as the domain of men—both as writers and as readers—Stephens went on to contribute six more works to the series.

After her husband died in 1862, Stephens supported herself and children by writing fiction; twenty-seven more novels were to appear in the last twenty-four years of her life. Stephens died on August 20, 1886, of nephritis at the home of her friend and publisher, Charles Peterson, in Newport, Rhode Island.

MAJOR WORKS AND THEMES

As a savvy professional writer, Stephens created stories and novels that caught the public's interest. She capitalized on an interest in historical romances, especially dealing with Indians, starting with her prize-winning story *Mary Derwent: A Tale of the Early Settlers*, which first appeared in the *Ladies' Companion* in 1838. Other works that focused on turbulent relations between natives and white settlers included *Malaeska* (first serialized in the *Ladies' Companion* in 1839), *Mahaska, the Indian Princess* (1863), and *The Indian Queen* (1864). Although, as Nina Baym argues, Stephens appears to have been unconcerned with miscegenation, since several marriages take place between whites and Indians, these unions always end tragically. Perhaps Stephens realized that while her characters could be made to overlook differences, society was not yet ready to accept such intermarriages.

Stephens also was able to write the kind of domestic fiction that was devoured by women readers at midcentury. While Juliann Fleenor describes much of Stephens's popular fiction as stories intended to set off the heroine's attire and hairstyles, which receive ample attention even in the midst of thrilling plot turns, readers in a world lacking movies and television seemed to be drawn to such detailed visual asides. Stephens's *Fashion and Famine* (1854) and *The Old Homestead* (1855), both best-sellers and her greatest commercial successes, were a departure from the historical melodrama into the realm of sentimental women's fiction. Both novels foreshadow later realists' attempts to reproduce the suffering, poverty, and filth of modern urban life through graphic city scenes that contrast with wholesome country settings. As Stephens continued to reproduce the styles of fiction that fit the public taste, she persisted in writing sentimental works that focused on the difficulties of a young heroine—novels favorable to a largely female reading audience. Whether set in the United States, as they usually are, or in England or Europe, Stephens's novels champion women's individuality while supporting a domestic feminism (as defined by Kathryn Kish Sklar) that maintains separate gendered spheres.

In only one instance did Stephens wander into the realm of literary comedy. Her early *High Life in New York* (1843), which appeared under the pseudonym "Jonathan Slick, Esq.," was a spinoff from T. C. Haliburton's "Sam Slick" stories. This collection of stories and sketches, which had appeared originally in the *New York Daily Express*, satirized fashionable New York society. It was successful enough to be reprinted numerous times, both in the United States and abroad.

CRITICAL RECEPTION

Stephens made a name for herself as a popular writer and editor as early as the 1830s and grew to become one of the best-known American women writers both in the United States and abroad. By the time her most successful novels appeared in the mid-1850s, Stephens's name was in such demand that publisher Richard Bentley and *London Journal* editor Howard Paul campaigned to secure advance copies of her work for the British market. Stephens knew and worked with important writers and editors in America and England, from Charles Peterson and Lydia Sigourney to Charles Dickens and Edgar Allan Poe. Her New York literary salon attracted the most distinguished visitors to that city, while Henry Clay wrote a complimentary poem, "On the Departure of Mrs. Ann S. Stephens for Europe," in honor of her trip abroad.

Sarah Josepha Hale lauded Stephens in her entry in *Woman's Record* in 1855, commending the "picturesque detail" and "easy flow of language" in both poetry and prose (797). Hale included a lengthy passage of praise of Stephens by Charles J. Peterson, in which he cites the power of her description and gorgeousness of her style. Just a few years later, the 1875 edition of Evert A.

Duyckinck and George L. Duyckinck's *Cyclopaedia of American Literature* praised the energy of Stephens while it criticized some of her urban stories for their excess realism and "questionable taste" (2:395). While nineteenth-century readers enjoyed reading Stephens's work, fastidious critics were not always sure they should.

Critical opinion through the first two thirds of the twentieth century focused either on Stephens's financial success as a professional writer or on her importance as the author of the first Beadle Dime Novel. Fred Lewis Pattee in 1940 included Stephens in his list of members of the second flowering of New England writers, alongside such popular authors as Grace Greenwood, Fanny Fern, Caroline Lee Hentz, Sarah Josepha Hale, and Mary Jane Holmes. However, since Pattee's tone throughout *The Feminine Fifties* derided the sentimental style of many women of the period, his flippant classification of Stephens as a melodramatic writer of ephemera is not surprising. In contrast, Helen Waite Papashvily in 1956 credited Stephens with a superior business sense that secured her position as one of America's favorite writers—even if her work tended to be derivative of favorite plots and character types. In 1962, Madeleine Stern furthered Stephens's reputation by including her in a collection of historically important nineteenth-century women, again as the author of the first Beadle Dime Novel.

However, critical opinion in the last twenty years has turned to focus more closely on Stephens's work apart from the 1860 reprint of *Malaeska*. In particular, Nina Baym includes Stephens in her analysis of the subgenre she christens "woman's fiction"—popular fiction written by and for women during the mid-nineteenth century. Because many of Stephens's works focus on the trials of a female heroine—whether she is white, Indian, or of mixed ancestry—as she struggles to secure a position in a world of dangers and temptations, Baym includes her work in this subgenre. And while none of Stephens's works has found a place in the standard anthologies of American literature, she has become a fixture in guides and reference works on nineteenth-century women writers.

WORKS CITED

Duyckinck, Evert A., and George L. Duyckinck. *Cyclopaedia of American Literature.* 2 vols. Philadelphia: William Rutter & Co., 1875.

Hale, Sarah Josepha. *Woman's Record.* New York: Harper & Brothers, 1855.

Sklar, Kathryn Kish. *Catharine Beecher: A Study in American Domesticity.* New Haven: Yale University Press, 1973.

BIBLIOGRAPHY

Works by Ann Sophia Stephens

The Portland Sketch Book. Edited by Ann Sophia Stephens. Portland: Colman & Chisholm, 1836. Includes Stephens's poem "The Widowed Bride" and story "The Deserted Wife."

The Queen of a Week. New York: W. W. Snowden, 1839.

High Life in New York. By Jonathan Slick, Esq. New York: E. Stephens, 1843.

Alice Copley: A Tale of Queen Mary's Time. Boston: "Yankee" Office, 1844.

David Hunt and Malina Gray. Philadelphia: G. R. Graham, 1845.

The Diamond Necklace, and Other Tales. Boston: Gleason's Publishing Hall, 1846.

The Tradesman's Boast. Boston: Gleason's Publishing Hall, 1846.

Henry Longford; or, The Forged Will. A Tale of New York City. Boston: Gleason's
Publishing Hall, 1847.

The Red Coats; or, The Sack of Unquowa: A Tale of the Revolution. New York: Williams,
1848.

Fashion and Famine. New York: Bunce & Brother, 1854.

The Ladies' Complete Guide to Crochet, Fancy Knitting, and Needlework. New York:
Garrett, 1854.

Zana; or, The Heiress of Clair Hall. London: Ward & Lock, 1854. Republished as *The
Heiress of Greenhurst: An Autobiography.* New York: Edward Stephens, 1857.

Frank Leslie's Portfolio of Fancy Needlework. Edited by Ann Sophia Stephens. New
York: Stringer & Townsend, 1855.

The Old Homestead. New York: Bunce & Brother, 1855.

Myra, the Child of Adoption. A Romance of Real Life. New York: Beadle & Adams,
1856.

Mary Derwent. Philadelphia: T. B. Peterson and Brothers, 1858.

The Works of Mrs. Ann S. Stephens. 23 vols. Philadelphia: T. B. Peterson, 1859–1886.

Ahmo's Plot; or, The Governor's Indian Child. New York: Beadle, 1860.

Malaeska: The Indian Wife of the White Hunter. Beadle's Dime Novels No. 1. New
York: Irwin P. Beadle & Co., 1860.

Victor Hugo's Letter on John Brown, with Mrs. Ann S. Stephen's Reply. New York: I.
P. Beadle, 1860.

Sybil Chase; or, The Valley Ranche. A Tale of California Life. New York: Beadle, 1861.
Republished as *The Outlaw's Wife; or, The Valley Ranche.* New York: Beadle &
Adams, 1874.

Esther: A Story of the Oregon Trail. New York: Beadle, 1862. Republished as *Kirk, the
Guide. A Story of the Oregon Trail.* New York: Beadle & Adams, 1884.

Pictorial History of the War for the Union. 2 vols. New York: J. G. Wells, 1862.

Mahaska, the Indian Princess. A Tale of the Six Nations. London: Beadle, 1863. Republished as *The Indian Princess.* New York: Beadle & Adams, 1863.

The Rejected Wife. Philadelphia: T. B. Peterson, 1863.

The Indian Queen. New York: Beadle & Adams, 1864.

The Wife's Secret. Philadelphia: T. B. Peterson, 1864.

Silent Struggles. Philadelphia: T. B. Peterson, 1865.

The Gold Brick. New York: Lupton, 1866; Philadelphia: T. B. Peterson, 1866.

The Soldier's Orphans. Philadelphia: T. B. Peterson, 1866.

Doubly False. Philadelphia: T. B. Peterson, 1868.

Mabel's Mistake. Philadelphia: T. B. Peterson, 1868.

The Curse of Gold. Philadelphia: T. B. Peterson, 1869.

Ruby Gray's Strategy. New York: F. M. Lupton, 1869.

Wives and Widows; or, The Broken Life. Philadelphia: T. B. Peterson, 1869.

Married in Haste. Philadelphia: T. B. Peterson, 1870.

A Noble Woman. Philadelphia: T. B. Peterson, 1871.

Palaces and Prisons. Philadelphia: T. B. Peterson, 1871.
The Reigning Belle. Philadelphia: T. B. Peterson, 1872.
Bellehood and Bondage. Philadelphia: T. B. Peterson, 1873.
Lord Hope's Choice. Philadelphia: T. B. Peterson, 1873.
The Old Countess; or, The Two Proposals. Philadelphia: T. B. Peterson, 1873.
Phemie Frost's Experiences. New York: G. W. Carleton, 1874.
Bertha's Engagement. Philadelphia: T. B. Peterson, 1875.
Norston's Rest. Philadelphia: T. B. Peterson, 1877.
Lily. In Memoriam. New York: J. J. Little, 1884.
The Lady Mary. A Novel. New York: F. M. Lupton, 1887.
Rock Run; or, The Daughter of the Island. New York: F. M. Lupton, 1893.

Studies of Ann Sophia Stephens

Baym, Nina. "Ann Stephens, Mary Jane Holmes, and Marion Harland." In *Woman's Fiction: A Guide to Novels by and about Women in America 1820–70.* 2nd ed. Urbana and Chicago: University of Illinois Press, 1993. 175–207.

Eastman, James Alfred. "Ann Sophia Stephens." Master's thesis, Columbia University, 1952.

Fleenor, Juliann E. "Ann Sophia Winterbotham Stephens." In *American Women Writers: A Critical Reference Guide from Colonial Times to the Present*, edited by Lina Mainiero. Vol. 4. New York: Frederick Ungar, 1982. 163–164.

Gemme, Paola. "Rewriting the Indian Tale: Science, Politics, and the Evolution of Ann S. Stephens's Indian Romances." *Prospects: An Annual Journal of American Cultural Studies* 19 (1994): 376–387.

Morris, Linda Ann Finton. "Women Vernacular Humorists in Nineteenth-Century America: Ann Stephens, Frances Whitcher, and Marietta Holley." Ph.D. diss., University of California, 1978.

Myerson, Joel. "Ann Stephens, The *London Journal*, and Anglo-American Copyright in 1854." *Manuscripts* 35 (fall 1983): 281–286.

O'Brien, Frank P. Introduction to *Malaeska: The Indian Wife of the White Hunter*, by Mrs. Ann S. Stephens. New York: Benjamin Blom, 1971.

Papashvily, Helen Waite. *All the Happy Endings: A Study of the Domestic Novel in America, the Women Who Wrote It, the Women Who Read It in the Nineteenth Century.* New York: Harper, 1956.

Pattee, Fred Lewis. *The Feminine Fifties.* New York: D. Appleton-Century Co., 1940.

Pazicky, Diana Loercher. "The Orphan and the Other: Wanderings through the American Imagination, 1620–1855." Ph.D. diss., Temple University, 1995.

Stern, Madeleine B. "The Author of the First Beadle Dime Novel: Ann S. Stephens, 1860." In *We the Women: Career Firsts of Nineteenth-Century America.* New York: Schulte, 1962. 29–54.

MARIA STEWART
(1803–1879)

David Hicks

BIOGRAPHY

While unfamiliar to many Americans, Maria W. Stewart merits a distinct place in our history. Combining the moral zeal of a born-again Christian with the defiant radicalism of a feminist and abolitionist, Stewart was an inspiring speaker, teacher, and writer. The first American woman on record to speak before an audience of men and women (five years before the Grimké sisters did so), Stewart was probably also the first black American woman to lecture on women's rights. In her speeches and writings, she exhorted black Americans to wrest their freedom from oppression and advocated moral, social, economic, and spiritual responsibility.

Born in Hartford, Connecticut, Maria Miller was orphaned at age five and subsequently "bound out" as a servant in a clergyman's house, where she "had the seeds of piety and virtue early sown in [her] mind; but was deprived of the advantages of education" (*Productions* 3). There she lived for the next formative decade of her life, attending Sunday school and reading when she could. In 1826 she married James W. Stewart (at his suggestion, she took his middle initial), and they settled into a middle-class neighborhood in Boston.

But just a few years later came harrowing times. First, Stewart's young husband died from an illness in 1829. ("O God," she lamented, "was not my soul torn with anguish, and did not my heart bleed. . . . Come all ye that pass by, and see if there is any sorrow like unto my sorrow" [40–41].) A year later, her friend and mentor David Walker, the fiery abolitionist, was killed. Then, after a two-year litigation, Stewart, like other widowed black women, was conned by lawyers out of her legal inheritance.

The result of the grief, sudden poverty, and soul searching of these anguished times was a religious conversion; she was "brought to the knowledge of truth, as it is in Jesus, in 1830; in 1831, made a public profession of [her] faith in Christ" (4). This revitalized faith, which informed all her work, disdained fatalism and encouraged a self-reliance that, like Emerson's, was synonymous with God reliance.

Armed with the conviction that fighting for equality was the highest form of championing God on earth—since we are all equal in God's eyes—and with the manuscript of her first reveille to black Americans, Stewart visited the prominent abolitionist William Lloyd Garrison in 1831 at his New York City *Liberator* office. Garrison published her work as a pamphlet and would print her *Meditations from the Pen of Mrs. Maria W. Stewart*, a collection of fourteen poems and seven prayers—"perhaps Stewart's most self-consciously literary effort" (Fetterley 61).

In 1833 Stewart moved to New York, where she made the acquaintance of black intellectuals and became a member of a black Female Literary Society. There she began her long teaching career, in the public schools of New York and Brooklyn, culminating in her appointment to assistant principal in 1847. But by 1852 she had lost her Brooklyn job and moved to Baltimore, thinking that blacks in the South were more religious than Northern blacks. There she opened a school and taught for $.50 a month, until she learned that the going rate was twice that amount.

Sometime in the early 1860s, with the Rebel army rumored to be five miles from the city, Stewart moved to Washington, D.C. There she once again established a school, tirelessly recruiting poor children, helping many without compensation. During one stretch, she taught day school, night school, and Sunday school and held weekday prayer meetings. By the early 1870s Stewart had been appointed matron of the Freedman's Hospital. In this capacity, she presided over the housekeeping and spiritual needs of the homeless, needy, ill, and dispossessed. She eventually took up residence there.

In 1878 Congress passed new legislation that left Stewart eligible for a pension; her husband had been a seaman during the War of 1812. In order to procure proof of her marriage, she asked a friend to collect her personal papers, and in the process, her friend uncovered a copy of the book Stewart had published forty-three years earlier. Stewart returned to Boston and again met Garrison, forty-six years after their first encounter. With the pension money she was now receiving, she brought out a new edition of *Meditations* (actually an updated version of *Productions of Mrs. Maria Stewart*), adding a prefatory section of testimonials and a biographical essay, "Sufferings during the War." This essay, which depicts her life in melodramatic terms, at once embraces and resists the sentimentality of the times, providing both a text of a young woman fighting against the odds and a countertext of a black woman with very few options for beating them.

During her research, Stewart discovered her husband's will and realized that his executors had cheated her out of the inheritance he had left her. Her life of poverty and struggle, then, had been largely unnecessary. Stewart died a year later, at the Freedman's Hospital in Washington, D.C.

MAJOR WORKS AND THEMES

While her career as a public speaker was short-lived—barely a year—and the body of her writing thin, Stewart is an important figure of the nineteenth century—not only for the force and integrity of her work but for the very fact that she produced it as early as the 1830s. As Paula Giddings points out, the assertions contained in her writing and speeches gave black women social and political options that previously may have been unfathomable. Weighed down by their race and gender, black women found the ideas in Stewart's speeches liberating: "The moral urgency of being black and female—heightened especially in times when Black men were politically lethargic ('It is of no use for us to wait any longer for a generation of well educated men to rise,' she said scornfully)—suffused Black women with a tenacious feminism," one that predates that of whites like Sarah Grimké who are ordinarily credited with providing the first rationale for American women's political activism (Giddings 52). And her "tough love" applied as well to black men, whom she continually urged to overcome lethargy and take their rightful place in society.

Influenced, as Marilyn Richardson asserts, by the Bible and the incendiary writings of her Boston neighbor David Walker and of John Adams on women's history (*Maria W. Stewart* xvi), Stewart combined piety, rebellion, and feminism like no other early nineteenth-century writer or speaker. Like some white female activists, Stewart advocated both domestic responsibility and independence, paradoxically evoking patriarchal Christianity even while combating patriarchal social and political norms. But unlike her white contemporaries, she grounds her statements in racial as well as sexual identity; she speaks and writes almost invariably to black Americans—as in her best-known speech, "Why Sit Ye Here and Die?" As Sojourner Truth had shown, black women in America, unlike their white counterparts, had already proven their resilience, independence, and strength. Their convictions concerning the rights of women were deeply rooted in experience as well as theory (Giddings 55). While nineteenth-century white feminists were eager to rebel against patriarchy to achieve autonomy, black women had already achieved such autonomy, out of sheer necessity. And while white feminists were generally abolitionists as well, eager to link their fate with that of blacks, Stewart's feminism looks unblinkingly at the racism of white men and women and concludes that they are not to be trusted for help. Therefore, she calls on black people to lift themselves out of their condition by recalling and using their own physical and spiritual strengths.

Stewart's essays and speeches, often addressed to her "unconverted friends" (*Productions* 37) and repeating the same catchphrases and exhortations, collectively construct a comprehensive argument: No person has the right to suppress another, for in the eyes of God, we are all equal and loved. Whites will not willingly grant us our freedom. Therefore, invoking the will of God and the pride of our African heritage, and ignoring those who consider us a "hissing and a reproach" (55), we should cease being meek and submissive and instead work aggressively toward a common goal. "[We] have a great work to do. Never . . . will the chains of slavery and ignorance burst, till we become united as one, and cultivate among ourselves the pure principles of piety, morality and virtue" (6). So all of us, especially our young men wasting their lives in hopelessness, Stewart maintained, need to wake up and devote ourselves to the achievement of a stronger, more self-reliant, virtuous life.

Stewart's work seems embryonic in that her arguments, posturing, and themes anticipate that of—and were more extensively developed by—black women writers to follow. Writing about the evils of racism and the struggle for racial uplift, emphasizing the importance of education and the need to prepare a better, newer world for the next generation, championing Christian virtue and self-sacrifice, and demonstrating the uncompromising dignity, resourcefulness, and respectability of the black woman, Stewart provides the groundwork for the generation of black women fiction writers that includes Frances Harper, Emma Kelley, Alice Dunbar Nelson, and Pauline Hopkins (Richardson, *Maria W. Stewart* 83).

Such themes are especially evident in "Sufferings during the War," the essay that introduces the 1879 edition of *Meditations*. Opening with a description of her own dilemma as a black woman looking for a way out of Baltimore as the war encroached that city, Stewart weaves references to national events into accounts of her own financial difficulties, sorrows, and successes. "Through the minutiae of her daily life, the personal tally of losses and gains, triumphs and humiliations, she told the story of her life as a free black woman in the nation's capital during the war which brought about the end of slavery" (83). This is the mark of Stewart's accomplishment: Underlying all her speeches and writings, even her most melodramatic work, is a deliberate self-awareness, a personal argument grounded in and informed by her own hardships and distinct Christian faith.

CRITICAL RECEPTION

Stewart was not a prolific writer, speaker, or activist; the necessities of economic survival account for her scant productions. Moreover, her didacticism and frankness resist interpretive readings. Therefore, her work is seldom reprinted and even more rarely evaluated. Excerpts of her speeches appear in a few studies—histories of black American educators, inspirational figures, feminists, abolitionists. But scant critical attention has been paid to her work. Even anthologies and such encyclopedias as the *Columbia Literary History of the United States* and *Benet's Reader's Encyclopedia of American Literature* omit reference to her entirely. A notable exception is Marilyn Richardson's *Maria W. Stewart* (1987), which has for the first time collected Stewart's social and political writings; Richardson offers insightful introductions to Stewart's life and work as well.

WORKS CITED

Fetterley, Judith. "Maria W. Stewart." In *Provisions: A Reader from 19th-Century American Women*, edited by Judith Fetterley. Bloomington: Indiana University Press, 1985. 60–65.

Giddings, Paula. *When and Where I Enter: The Impact of Black Women on Race and Sex in America.* New York: William Morrow, 1989.

Stewart, Maria W. *Maria W. Stewart: America's First Black Woman Political Writer: Essays and Speeches.* Edited by Marilyn Richardson. Bloomington and Indianapolis: Indiana University Press, 1987.

———. *Productions of Mrs. Maria Stewart Presented to the First African Baptist Church & Society, of the City of Boston.* Boston: Friends of Freedom and Virtue, 1835.

BIBLIOGRAPHY

Works by Maria Stewart

Meditations from the Pen of Mrs. Maria W. Stewart. Boston: Garrison and Knapp, 1832.

Productions of Mrs. Maria Stewart Presented to the First African Baptist Church & Society, of the City of Boston. Boston: Friends of Freedom and Virtue, 1835.

Meditations from the Pen of Mrs. Maria W. Stewart. A reprint of *Productions*, with new introductory material. Washington, D.C.: Maria W. Stewart, 1879.

Maria W. Stewart: America's First Black Woman Political Writer: Essays and Speeches. Edited by Marilyn Richardson. Bloomington and Indianapolis: Indiana University Press, 1987. (Contains Stewart's political writing, available in its entirety for the first time since 1879.)

Studies of Maria Stewart

Giddings, Paula. *When and Where I Enter: The Impact of Black Women on Race and Sex in America.* New York: William Morrow, 1989. See esp. pp. 49–54, 195.

Sterling, Dorothy. *We Are Your Sisters: Black Women in the Nineteenth Century.* New York: W. W. Norton, 1984. 153–159.

Swan, Robert J. "A Synoptic History of Black Public Schools in Brooklyn." In *The Black Contribution to the Development of Brooklyn*, edited by Charlene Claye Van Derzee. Brooklyn: New Muse Community Museum of Brooklyn, 1977. 64.

Townsend, Thelma Marie. "Spiritual Autobiographies of Religious Activism by Black Women in the Antebellum Era." Ph.D. diss., Michigan State University, 1993.

ELIZABETH DREW BARSTOW STODDARD (1823–1902)

Sandra Harbert Petrulionis

BIOGRAPHY

Elizabeth Drew Barstow Stoddard was an unusually gifted and imaginative writer; unfortunately, critics agree that she suffered from writing for modern tastes during an age when her audience favored sentiment. Born on May 6, 1823, in the seafaring community of Mattapoisett, Massachusetts, Stoddard was the second of nine children born to Betsy Drew and Wilson Barstow. She descended from two old New England families, and her father continued the family business of shipbuilding. He earned a place in literary history not only by fathering Elizabeth but also by building the *Acushnet*, the whaler on which Herman Melville sailed. Her father's bankruptcies and business failures would figure prominently in Stoddard's best-known novel *The Morgesons* (1862), as would her preoccupation with the coastal setting in which she was raised.

James H. Matlack notes that the sea "might be . . . the closest thing to a god Elizabeth ever acknowledged" ("Literary Career" 23). She spent her days exploring the coast, sailing and skating, always entranced by the ocean, "so fixed and ever-varying," as she described it in a story (Buell and Zagarell 288). As a grown woman, Stoddard spent many summers in her native town where she relived her childhood and gathered inspiration for her literary endeavors.

Another pervasive influence upon the adolescent Stoddard, as with most New England writers during the nineteenth century, was the inheritance of the region's Puritan tradition. Like her literary neighbor Emily Dickinson, Stoddard refused to make a public profession of religious faith, an expected component of the Calvinist faith. She routinely scoffed at institutional religion in her newspaper columns and created fictional characters who reveled in their secular sensibility. Stoddard read voraciously, particularly the popular eighteenth-century novels and periodical fiction. She traveled occasionally with her father and often visited friends and relatives in Boston and in other New England states. For a time, she attended Wheaton Female Seminary in Norton, Massachusetts, but its emphasis on a Christian education for young ladies no doubt contributed to her decision to leave without earning a certificate of completion.

Her mother's death in 1849, following her sister Jane's the previous year, dealt Stoddard a tremendous emotional blow. As with the fictional sisters Cassandra and Veronica in *The Morgesons*, Elizabeth's and Jane's relationship suffered from their intense personality differences, yet losing her mother and sister left Stoddard alone with few friends. Her father's subsequent remarriage to a family servant only added to her devastation.

On December 6, 1852, Elizabeth Barstow married Richard Henry Stoddard, whom she had met in New York the previous year. Richard Stoddard was a fledgling poet whose literary ambitions remained unfulfilled. His career progressed through various hack writing assignments, editorships, and occasionally the published verse, but he never experienced any true literary success and certainly never earned a living by his pen. Eventually, he landed a job at the New York Custom House through the aid of Nathaniel Hawthorne—a favor he later passed on when he secured a position there for his friend Herman Melville. Throughout their lives, the Stoddards suffered tremendous financial insecurity and literary disappointment; life was a constant struggle, and rarely were they free from worry.

After their marriage, Richard and Elizabeth Stoddard made their home in New York, where they became close friends with other writers and poets who shared Richard's idealized, romantic style: Bayard Taylor, Thomas Bailey Aldrich, George Henry Boker, and Edmund Clarence Stedman, among others. Unfortunately, their poetry was derivative and hopelessly out of fashion in an age that soon ushered in Realism.

Tragically, the death of two young children increased the Stoddards' despair. Their elder son died when he was six years old, and a second son died in infancy. And although their third son, Lorimer, lived to enjoy relative success as a playwright, he died in 1901 at age thirty-seven, perpetuating his elderly mother's bitterness and continued sense of life's unfairness. She died the following year.

Elizabeth Stoddard's personality was difficult and often implacable. She took pride in her blunt manner and regularly quarreled with close friends, often severing relationships with a dismissive air. Caustic toward those she claimed to care about, she succeeded in alienating many loyal companions. Lamentably, the passion she celebrated in her fictional heroines was in life reduced to hostility and envy of those who enjoyed the success she never knew.

MAJOR WORKS AND THEMES

Like the popular women novelists of the nineteenth century whose work she ridiculed, Stoddard wrote prodigiously. But in contrast to many of them, she refused to compromise her desire to write serious, intellectually challenging fiction by pandering to the market's taste for sentiment, which, as Sybil Weir argues, Stoddard regarded "as false to the realities and complexities of the human experience" ("Our Lady Correspondent" 84). Stoddard's published work consists of three novels, *The Morgesons* (1862), *Two Men* (1865), and *Temple House* (1867); a book of children's tales, *Lolly Dink's Doings* (1874); a volume of poetry, *Poems* (1895); over eighty short stories and essays, published between 1852 and 1900; and seventy-five newspaper columns, written from 1854 to 1858, for the *Daily Alta California*. She displays more talent and originality than many of the nineteenth-century's best-selling authors, but the characters who inhabit her fiction—strong-willed, passionate, and wholly secular heroines, and tainted, Byronic males—did not appeal to her moralistic audience. Sandra Zagarell points out that Stoddard was "at odds with prevailing women's literary traditions" ("*Legacy* Profile" 39): She wrote domestic fiction, but in the vein of Nathaniel Hawthorne, not Susan Warner, Louisa May Alcott, or Harriet Beecher Stowe.

Stoddard's literary reputation received an enormous boost when she began writing a column for the San Francisco *Daily Alta California*, employment that provided the opportunity to develop and hone her style and to venture (and vent) her opinions on the day's literature, politics, and society. The *Daily Alta* was a popular paper, and Stoddard kept its West Coast audience abreast of New York happenings. She regularly included book reviews (of works by Fanny Fern, Henry David Thoreau, Walt Whitman, and Harriet Beecher Stowe), sketches of social gatherings and cultural events, and society gossip, all recounted in a witty, biting style. Here Stoddard registers her disdain for the sentimental works of her popular female peers. As one example, in her first column she lampoons Fanny Fern and wonders whether to write under her own botanical nom de plume: "I debate . . . how to appear most effectively, whether to present myself as a genuine original, or adopt some great example in style; such as the pugilisms of Fanny Fern, the pathetics of Minnie Myrtle, or the abandon of Cassie Cauliflower" (Matlack, "*Alta California*'s Lady Correspondent" 298).

The Morgesons, Stoddard's first novel, was published in 1862 and sold poorly, no doubt somewhat due to the unrest of war-torn America. Autobiographical in many respects, its heroine, Cassandra Morgeson, at least partially represents Stoddard, and Stoddard incorporates into the novel many elements of her childhood and adolescence. Growing up in a coastal New England town in a family of shipbuilders, Cassandra battles throughout her life with her elfinlike, sickly sister Veronica, whom critics regard as Cassandra's double. Cassandra's self-possession and at times almost demonic mood reflect the influence of the Brontë sisters, whose work Stoddard admired. As she matures into a young woman, Cassandra repudiates God, reads extensively, and feels embarrassed by her family's dwindling prosperity. After an unconsummated passion for her married cousin ends in his violent death and her physically scarred survival, Cassandra returns home. On a subsequent sojourn, she falls in love with a second dark man, Desmond Somers, but he insists on reforming before he will act on their love. Alone, she goes home again, and this time she finds her mother dying. Her father remarries shortly thereafter (a marriage that Cassandra violently opposes), and Veronica is unwilling and unable to share the familial responsibilities. Cassandra thus becomes lady of the house, entrapped within the tranquility and domesticity of the estate by the sea. Eventually, a rehabilitated Somers arrives; they marry and share their reclusive existence in the ancestral home with Veronica (now widowed) and her oddly silent infant.

Stoddard's other two novels, *Two Men* (1865) and *Temple House* (1867), reflect her continuing obsession with passionate heroines and their ultimate achievement of a true love match, but *Two Men* also brazenly attempts new ground. In *Two Men*, Stoddard becomes one of the earliest American authors to depict miscegenation when the wealthy and white Parke Auster becomes sexually involved with a young black woman, Charlotte Lang. Though Parke intends to marry Charlotte, he allows family and social considerations to delay the wedding, and Charlotte dies in childbirth.

Like *The Morgesons*, *Two Men* and *Temple House* feature attractive and ardent heroines whose uncontrolled passion often leads to acts of violence, revenge, or self-destruction. In *Temple House*, however, Matlack contends that Stoddard "becomes more conformist" by incorporating sentimental conventions ("Literary Career" 418), something Stoddard often does in her short fiction. Although the critical reception of *Two Men* and *Temple House* was largely favorable, with William Dean Howells comparing *Two Men* to *The Scarlet Letter* (Howells 366), the two later novels sold even worse than had *The Morgesons*, and Stoddard never wrote another one; instead, she turned her energies to short fiction.

Stoddard's stories and essays appeared from 1852 to 1894 in such popular venues as *Harper's, Saturday Evening Post, The Independent, Atlantic Monthly,* and *Putnam's*. Featuring regional settings populated with vivid New Englanders, many of these stories clearly belong to the local color tradition. Stoddard's narrative style is compelling, but stories frequently end abruptly or are frustratingly contrived. Like her novels, the stories typically center on a young heroine's marital woes or premarital quandaries. Popularly anthologized stories include "The Chimneys," "The Prescription," and "Lemorne *versus* Huell."

Stoddard's fiction nearly always fulfills her *Daily Alta* excoriation of sentimentality. Instead of woebegone females who seek salvation in a man and marriage, Stoddard depicts strong women who grapple with the critical dilemmas facing women in nineteenth-century America. She suggests that only by acknowledging a woman's sexual nature and her need for self-expression will relationships between the sexes improve. As does Cassandra Morgeson, the female characters in the stories discover their sexuality as an inseparable aspect of their human identity—a realization that contrasts pointedly with the demure women populating the fiction of Stoddard's female contemporaries.

Stoddard's poetry, like much of the nineteenth-century's blank verse, aspires to the Romantic, pastoral tradition, yet, like her fiction, modern readers may appreciate her poetic expression more than a nineteenth-century audience. Matlack writes that Stoddard's "profoundly original nature as a writer found its most revealing . . . utterance in poetry" ("Literary Career" 601). Many poems convey similar themes of loss, decay, hidden family secrets, and the haunted homes in which they are concealed. Others record a mother's joy in her children, and her grief at their death. Curiously, she writes those poems that center on the artist in the past tense—for Stoddard, the vocation of artist had become a closed door. In the first stanza of "Nameless Pain," she strikes a feminist chord and reveals the strain of attempting to combine her vocation as author with motherhood. Although she seems to rebuke herself for not being content with her roles as wife and mother, the stanza ends sarcastically as she asks, "What other blessing could be sent?" (*Poems*, 43). Though rarely anthologized, Stoddard's poetry contextualizes and broadens any examination of nineteenth-century American verse.

CRITICAL RECEPTION

During her lifetime, Stoddard's work received a largely favorable critical reception—and from those whose praise meant something to her: Nathaniel Hawthorne, James Lowell, George Ripley, Edmund C. Stedman, and William Dean Howells, among others. Hawthorne, a distant cousin of Stoddard's, wrote to her following the publication of *The Morgesons* and called it "a remarkable and powerful book" (Matlack, "Literary Career" 266), strong words from the man who otherwise scorned scribbling women. The reviewer in the *New York Post* praised *The Morgesons* for the " 'elaborate and truthful pictures it gives of everyday life' " (224); and in reviewing it for the *New York Tribune*, Ripley assessed the novel as " 'the outpouring of a singularly reflective nature—accustomed to brood over the mysteries of life,—with a remorseless habit of stripping the veil from the softest illusions' " (226). Yet the tributes often carried advice, as when Lowell urged her to tone down the eroticism of her work. Unfortunately, the critical acclaim only remotely influenced the book's sales, and Stoddard's ambitions for this first novel did not materialize.

The republication of all three novels in 1901, in the midst of the Realist literary era, brought renewed attention, although not from that period's most renowned novelist: Assailing Stoddard's *Two Men* as "cheap melodrama," Henry James lambasted *The Morgesons* and *Two Men* in unpublished reviews (Habegger 85, 95). His peers, however, disagreed. Stedman characterized Stoddard's writing as "essentially modern" (154), and he extolled her "strong original style" (156). Likewise, Howells remarked on Stoddard's "distinct and special quality" and lamented her inability to achieve the "recognition which her work merits" (87). Many scholars now consider Stoddard an appealing combination of Romanticism and Realism and find that she merges a Romantic sensibility with a Realist's fidelity to verisimilitude in setting and character. In her preface to the 1901 edition of *The Morgesons*, Stoddard accepts the label

" 'realist' " but adds that she "clothed [her] skeletons with the robe of romance" (iv).

From the turn of the century until the past few decades, Stoddard's works were largely ignored. Dismissed by sexist critics as yet another female scourge blighting the "American Renaissance," ironically she shared the fate of the popular women writers whose work she loathed. Not until James H. Matlack's 1967 dissertation, "The Literary Career of Elizabeth Stoddard," was Stoddard seriously examined, and this analysis remains the single best source for information about her life and writing. As his title indicates, Matlack investigates all aspects of Stoddard's biography and literary output. He tracks down much of her correspondence and pieces together the publication history of various stories and poems. In 1976, Sybil Weir cited the "neglect" of *The Morgesons* in her examination of it as a "female *bildungsroman*," and more recently, Weir has written about Stoddard's *Daily Alta* columns, and she notes the value of these years on the overall development of Stoddard's style ("Our Lady Correspondent" 90).

In 1984, Lawrence Buell and Sandra A. Zagarell edited a critical edition of *The Morgesons* that deserves much of the credit for renewing scholarly interest in Stoddard's literary achievement. They argue that Stoddard should be studied along with Hawthorne and Melville as "the most strikingly original voice in the mid-nineteenth-century American novel" (xi). Stoddard's steadfast focus on baring the essential motives and nature of her protagonists—male and female— and her intensity in following their passion for self-fulfillment through the course of their lives—is unprecedented among nineteenth-century female writers. Zagarell believes that Stoddard writes in a "male-derived Romantic model of the self-as-artist" and that, like all Romantics, she contends with the dilemma of how to remain an individual within a democracy ("*Legacy* Profile" 40). Additionally, however, Stoddard conveys the hopelessly gendered situation of the female Romantic: How does a woman confined by a patriarchal system authorize herself within the individual-versus-democracy paradigm?

Recent critical attention on Stoddard focuses primarily on *The Morgesons*, specifically on the passionate and openly sexual nature of Cassandra Morgeson. Weir compares Stoddard to Kate Chopin and her insistence that "women don't mature until they acknowledge their erotic nature" ("Neglected Feminist *Bildungsroman*" 434). Susan K. Harris calls *The Morgesons* "possibly the most radical women's novel of the 19th-century," and she notes the significance of its first-person narration, which robs the novel of an omniscient guide for the heroine's self-discovery ("Projecting" 152). Harris argues further that Stoddard "subverts the ideal of Victorian woman" (167) by failing to censure Cassandra for her passionate attraction to Charles Morgeson; she therefore "breaks through restrictions on 19th-century women's voices, insisting that women can take control of their environment" (170).

Less scholarship focuses on Stoddard's short fiction or poetry, although Zagarell writes about "The Chimneys," and John Humma analyzes sexual imagery in "Lemorne *versus* Huell." Critics comment on Stoddard's strong feminist voice in these two stories, both of which depict intense heroines who contemplate marriage but who feel trapped by their choices. Sadly, only a few of Stoddard's stories have been anthologized, and the majority of her short work remains uncollected, its richness unexplored.

In *New England Literary Culture*, Buell claims that Stoddard is "absurdly undervalued" (354), an assessment that is still true, although change is under way. Perhaps the very seriousness of Stoddard's work contributed to its delayed examination by those involved in the current recovery of nineteenth-century female texts, an effort that initially focused on writers of popular domestic fiction. Like Stoddard's own audience as well as our century's early critics of American literature, we, too, seem to set arbitrary criteria by which to gauge Stoddard's writing. Recent landmark studies of nineteenth-century American women's writing do not mention Stoddard, and she fails to appear in Blackwell's recently published *Nineteenth-Century American Women Writers: An Anthology* (1992).

Elizabeth Drew Barstow Stoddard's literary achievement encompasses nearly all literary genres: novels, poetry, short stories, essays, correspondence, and journalism. In an era that rewarded mediocre writers, Stoddard's steadfast refusal to join their ranks contributed to her literary oblivion. We are, however, reversing that trend and beginning to grant her the distinction that her works unquestionably merit. Her bold and imaginative narrative voice, her avowedly secular and sexual female characters, and her acerbic commentaries serve to enliven, enrich, and complicate our continuing reexamination of nineteenth-century American literature. Particularly as scholars reassess the diversity of women's writing and their correspondingly disparate ideologies during the nineteenth century, we should listen to and heed Stoddard's unique voice.

BIBLIOGRAPHY

Works by Elizabeth Stoddard

Book-Length Works

The Morgesons. New York: Carleton and Co., 1862. Republished with preface by Elizabeth Stoddard. Philadelphia: Coates and Co., 1901. Revised edition with a biographical and critical introduction by Lawrence Buell and Sandra A. Zagarell. Philadelphia: University of Pennsylvania Press, 1984.

Two Men. New York: Bunce and Huntington, 1865. Revised edition with preface by Edmund Clarence Stedman. New York: Cassell and Co., 1888. Republished, Philadelphia: Coates and Co., 1901.

Temple House. New York: Carleton and Co., 1867. Revised edition, New York: Cassell and Co., 1888. Republished, Philadelphia: Coates and Co., 1901.

Remember, a Keepsake. Edited by Richard H. and Elizabeth B. Stoddard. New York:

Leavitt, 1869. Republished as *Readings and Recitations from Modern Authors*. Chicago: Belford, Clark, and Co., 1886.

Lolly Dink's Doings. Boston: Gill, 1874.

Poems. Boston and New York: Houghton, Mifflin and Co., 1895.

Selected Short Prose

Following is a representative sampling of Stoddard's short prose. For a more inclusive list, see Matlack and Foster.

Seventy-five letters to the *Daily Alta California* from ''A Lady Correspondent'' and ''Our Lady Correspondent'' between October 8, 1854, and February 28, 1858.

''My Own Story.'' *Atlantic Monthly* 5 (May 1860): 526–547.

''Gone to the War.'' *Vanity Fair* 4 (21 December 1861): 275–276.

''Lemorne *versus* Huell.'' *Harper's* 26 (March 1863): 537–543.

''Tuberoses.'' *Harper's* 26 (January 1863): 191–197.

''The Prescription.'' *Harper's* 28 (May 1864): 794–800.

''The Chimneys.'' *Harper's* 31 (November 1865): 721–732.

''Collected by a Valetudinarian.'' *Harper's* 42 (December 1870): 96–105.

''A Study for a Heroine.'' *Independent* 37 (24 September 1885): 1246–1248.

Studies of Elizabeth Stoddard

Alaimo, Stacy. ''Elizabeth Stoddard's *The Morgesons*: A Feminist Dialogue of *Bildung* and Descent.'' *Legacy* 8 (spring 1991): 29–37.

Aldrich, Mrs. Thomas Bailey. *Crowding Memories*. Boston and New York: Houghton Mifflin, 1920.

Beatty, Richard Croom. *Bayard Taylor: Laureate of the Gilded Age*. Norman: University of Oklahoma Press, 1936.

Buell, Lawrence. *New England Literary Culture: From Revolution through Renaissance*. Cambridge: Cambridge University Press, 1986.

Buell, Lawrence, and Sandra A. Zagarell, eds. ''Biographical and Critical Introduction'' to *The Morgesons and Other Writings, Published and Unpublished by Elizabeth Stoddard*. Philadelphia: University of Pennsylvania Press, 1984. xi–xxix.

Cary, Richard. *The Genteel Circle: Bayard Taylor and His New York Friends*. Ithaca: Cornell University Press, 1952.

Croce, Ann Jerome. ''Phantoms from an Ancient Loom: Elizabeth Barstow Stoddard and the American Novel, 1860–1900.'' Ph.D., diss., Brown University, 1989.

———. ''A Woman Outside Her Time: Elizabeth Barstow Stoddard (1823–1902) and Nineteenth-Century American Popular Fiction.'' *Women's Studies* 19 (1991): 357–369.

Duffy, Charles, ed. *The Correspondence of Bayard Taylor and Paul Hamilton Hayne*. Baton Rouge: Louisiana State University Press, 1945.

Foster, Richard. Introduction to *The Morgesons*, by Elizabeth Stoddard. New York: Johnson, 1971. vii–li.

Habegger, Alfred. *Henry James and the ''Woman Business.''* Cambridge: Cambridge University Press, 1989.

Harris, Leila Assumpcao. ''The Marriage Tradition in the Novels of Elizabeth Stoddard.'' Ph.D. diss., Texas Technological University, 1991.

Harris, Susan K. "Projecting the 'I'/Conoclast: First-Person Narration in *The Morgesons.*" In *19th-Century American Women's Novels: Interpretive Strategies.* Cambridge: Cambridge University Press, 1992. 152–170.

———. "Stoddard's *The Morgesons*: A Contextual Evaluation." *ESQ* 31 (1st quarter 1985): 11–23.

Henwood, Dawn E. "Narrative Strategies and Narrative Challenges in the Novels of Elizabeth Stoddard." Ph.D. diss., Dalhousie University, 1992.

Howells, William Dean. *Literary Friends and Acquaintance: A Personal Retrospect of American Authorship.* New York: Harper & Brothers, 1900.

Humma, John B. "Realism and Beyond: The Imagery of Sex and Sexual Oppression in Elizabeth Stoddard's 'Lemorne *versus* Huell.' " *South Atlantic Review* 58 (January 1993): 33–47.

Kramer, Maurice. "Alone at Home with Elizabeth Stoddard." *ATQ* 47–48 (summer–fall 1980): 159–170.

Matlack, James Hendrickson. "The *Alta California*'s Lady Correspondent." *New York Historical Quarterly* 58 (1974): 280–303.

———. "Hawthorne and Elizabeth Barstow Stoddard. *NEQ* 50 (June 1977): 278–302.

———. "The Literary Career of Elizabeth Barstow Stoddard." Ph.D. diss., Yale University, 1968.

Reynolds, David S. *Beneath the American Renaissance: The Subversive Imagination in the Age of Emerson and Melville.* New York: Knopf, 1988.

Ruggles, Eleanor. *Prince of Players: Edwin Booth.* New York: W. W. Norton & Company, 1953.

Stedman, Edmund Clarence. *Genius and Other Essays.* New York: Moffat, Yard and Company, 1911.

Stedman, Laura, and George M. Gould. *Life and Letters of Edmund Clarence Stedman.* 2 vols. New York: Moffat, Yard, and Company, 1910.

Stoddard, Richard Henry. *Recollections, Personal and Literary.* Edited by Ripley Hitchcock with an introduction by Edmund Clarence Stedman. New York: A. S. Barnes and Co., 1903.

Taylor, Marie Hansen. *On Two Continents: Memories of Half a Century.* New York: Doubleday, Page & Company, 1905.

Weir, Sybil B. "*The Morgesons*: A Neglected Feminist *Bildungsroman.*" *NEQ* 49 (1976): 427–439.

———. "Our Lady Correspondent: The Achievement of Elizabeth Drew Stoddard." *San Jose Studies* 10 (spring 1984): 73–91.

Zagarell, Sandra A. "*Legacy* Profile: Elizabeth Drew Barstow Stoddard (1823–1902)." *Legacy* 8 (spring 1991): 39–49.

———. "The Repossession of a Heritage: Elizabeth Stoddard's *The Morgesons.*" *SAF* 13 (spring 1985): 45–56.

HARRIET BEECHER STOWE (1811–1896)

Denise D. Knight

BIOGRAPHY

Harriet Elizabeth Beecher was born on June 14, 1811, in the quaint New England town of Litchfield, Connecticut, the seventh child of stern and spirited Congregationalist minister Lyman Beecher and his wife, Roxana (Foote) Beecher. In 1816, when Harriet was just five, Roxana Beecher, a devoted helpmate and loving mother, died from tuberculosis. Shortly after Roxana's death, Lyman's half sister, Esther Beecher, moved into the rambling parsonage to assume the care of the household. Harriet's older sister Catharine, who later gained fame as a writer and educator, became a surrogate mother to her younger siblings. Lyman Beecher remarried the year following Roxana's death, and although his new wife's relationship with his children was cordial, Catharine remained their primary caretaker. Characterized by her new stepmother as an ''amiable, affectionate, and very bright'' child (Cross 1, 273), young Harriet's precocity revealed itself in her appetite for reading and in the easy fluency with which she wrote. She excelled at the Litchfield Female Academy, where she studied geography, history, arithmetic, grammar, chemistry, logic, and moral philosophy. Under the tutelage of one of her instructors, Harriet, by the age of nine, began writing weekly essays; at age twelve, her earliest extant composition—''Can the Immortality of the Soul Be Proved by the Light of Nature?''—was read before an assembly at the academy's annual exhibition of student work. In 1824, at the age of thirteen, Harriet enrolled in sister Catharine's Hartford Female Seminary, an innovative experiment in the education of women. Harriet stayed at the seminary until she was twenty-one, first as a student and later as a teacher of rhetoric and composition. Her classmates included Sara Willis, who would later gain fame as a writer using the pseudonym Fanny Fern. When Catharine

Beecher suffered a nervous breakdown in 1829, Harriet stepped in temporarily to assume the leadership of the school. In 1832, the Beechers moved en masse to Cincinnati, Ohio, after Lyman Beecher accepted the presidency of the Lane Theological Seminary. Homesick for the picturesque New England landscape she had left behind, Harriet eased the pain by immersing herself in writing. Her first publication, a textbook titled *Primary Geography for Children*, appeared in 1833. That same year she began contributing sketches, essays, and reviews to *Western Monthly Magazine*. She also became an active member of the Semi-Colon Club, a literary group that devoted itself to "the discussion of interesting questions belonging to society, literature, education, and religion" (quoted in Hedrick, *Harriet Beecher Stowe* 91). Among the members of the Club were Eliza Tyler Stowe, whom Harriet befriended, and her husband, Calvin Ellis Stowe, a theology professor at Lane. Shortly after Eliza's death from cholera in 1834, Calvin began courting Harriet; they married in January of 1836. In September of that year, while Calvin was traveling in Europe, Harriet gave birth to twin girls; five more children eventually followed. Despite the time devoted to child care, Harriet Beecher Stowe continued to write, publishing in such forums as *Godey's Lady's Book* and the *New-York Evangelist*. Calvin supported Stowe's writing and urged her to develop her talents as "a *literary woman*" (quoted in Hedrick, *Harriet Beecher Stowe* 138), in part because her earnings were needed to supplement his own modest income. Stowe's first book of fiction, *The Mayflower; or, Sketches of Scenes and Characters among the Descendents of the Puritans*, a collection of fifteen domestic sketches, was published in 1843 by Harper and Brothers, but it did not meet with critical success. In 1846–1847, Stowe spent fifteen months at the Brattleboro Water Cure, in Vermont, where she was treated with good results for exhaustion and mental fatigue, brought on by the care of her children and the management of her household. The Stowes left Cincinnati in 1850 for Brunswick, Maine, where Lyman accepted an appointment to the faculty of Bowdoin College. It was there that Stowe wrote her epic antislavery novel *Uncle Tom's Cabin* shortly after the passage of the Fugitive Slave Act of 1850. The publication of the novel thrust Stowe into the public eye; within months of its appearance she was an international celebrity. In 1852, the Stowes moved to Andover, Massachusetts, where Calvin joined the faculty of the Andover Theological Institute. A second antislavery novel, *Dred: A Tale of the Great Dismal Swamp*, was published in 1856, followed by several more books, including *The Minister's Wooing* (1859), *The Pearl of Orr's Island* (1862), *Agnes of Sorrento* (1862), *Oldtown Folks* (1869), *Lady Byron Vindicated* (1870), *Pink and White Tyranny: A Society Novel* (1871), *Palmetto-Leaves* (1873), and *Poganuc People* (1878). None of Stowe's subsequent works rivaled the power of *Uncle Tom's Cabin*; consequently, none were accorded the same degree of critical acclaim. The Stowes moved again when Calvin retired in 1864, this time to Nook Farm in Hartford, Connecticut. Between 1868 and 1884, the couple spent their winters in Florida. In 1884, Calvin's rapidly declining health forced the Stowes to return to Hartford, where Calvin succumbed to Bright's disease in 1886. Although Stowe herself became increasing ill and suffered from senility in her later years, she remained at Nook Farm until her death in 1896 at the age of eighty-five. She is buried next to her husband in the Andover Chapel Cemetery at the Andover Theological Seminary.

MAJOR WORKS AND THEMES

If Harriet Beecher Stowe had never written another word after the publication of *Uncle Tom's Cabin* in 1852, her place in American literary history would still be secure. A powerful polemic against the institution of slavery, *Uncle Tom's Cabin* has been called "the most influential novel ever written" and today "remains the world's all-time best-seller" (Donovan, "*Uncle Tom's Cabin*" 11).

During her eighteen years in Cincinnati, Stowe witnessed race riots and heard graphic accounts of conditions suffered by former slaves, which she later used to authenticate her depictions in *Uncle Tom's Cabin*. Before the passage of the Fugitive Slave Act of 1850, however, Stowe was not publicly active in the antislavery cause, although she published a handful of anonymous proabolition columns in the *Cincinnati Journal* and engaged in passionate discussions on the evils of slavery with friends and family members. It was Stowe's sister-in-law, Isabella Beecher, who in 1850 finally encouraged her to take action: "Now Hattie," she wrote, "if I could use a pen as you can, I would write something that would make this whole nation feel what an accursed thing slavery is" (quoted in Hedrick, *Harriet Beecher Stowe* 207). Several months later, Stowe reported that while attending a service at the First Parish Church in Brunswick, Maine, she was visited by the vision of a slave being beaten to death; thus was born the climactic scene of *Uncle Tom's Cabin* in which Tom is murdered by his brutal master, Simon Legree. Throughout her life, Stowe insisted that God was the author of the book; she was simply the instrument through which he spoke.

The plot of *Uncle Tom's Cabin* is held together by the journeys of two slaves, Eliza and Tom, who, when the novel opens, are the property of Mr. Shelby, a Kentucky plantation owner. Forced by an economic crisis to generate some quick cash, Shelby arranges to sell Eliza's young son, Harry, and his longtime slave, Uncle Tom. When Eliza learns of the impending sale, she plans an escape to Canada with her child. The novel follows her dramatic flight toward freedom, during which she receives assistance from various members of the Underground Railroad. The second journey, which Stowe develops in considerably more detail, involves Tom, a devout Christian who submits to his fate and is sold down the river through a succession of owners, until he meets his death at the hands of the evil Legree.

While Stowe wrote *Uncle Tom's Cabin* in part to make the "whole nation feel what an accursed thing slavery is"—indeed, she relied on her background in rhetoric to construct and sustain a compelling argument—other important themes emerge. Throughout the novel, for example, Stowe repeatedly questions the moral fiber of a nation that allowed the institution of slavery to exist. In nearly every chapter, she reminds the reader that Christian ethics are incompatible with a social system that tolerates human bondage. The moral drama is examined and developed through the responses of various characters to the existence of evil, which Stowe addresses on several levels: "theological, moral, economic, political, and practical" (Donovan, "*Uncle Tom's Cabin*" 33). Stowe also explores the power of Christian love—the antithesis of evil—most notably through little Eva St. Clare, an allegorical figure who exemplifies that love, and through her Christ figure, Uncle Tom.

Stowe's response to those who attacked *Uncle Tom's Cabin* as unsubstantiated propaganda was published in *A Key to Uncle Tom's Cabin* (1853), in which she passionately defended the novel, documented the facts behind it, and reaffirmed her commitment to the proabolitionist movement.

While *Uncle Tom's Cabin* is the major work in Stowe's oeuvre, others merit brief mention. *Dred: A Tale of the Great Dismal Swamp* (1856) is another antislavery novel set in North Carolina. Despite respectable sales in the months following its publication (it sold 150,000 copies in the United States during its first year in print), the novel is an inferior work in terms of both plot and structure. The title character, Dred, who does not appear until chapter eighteen, is an embittered and militant black man—the antithesis of Uncle Tom—who is driven by hatred in his quest for vengeance. A gloomy work with a contrived ending, *Dred* suffers from hasty writing and a slipshod plot.

The Pearl of Orr's Island (1862), set in New England, was a relatively minor work in Stowe's time but is now undergoing critical reappraisal. It is a powerful work in which Stowe explores the political and psychological dimensions of a young woman, Mara Lincoln, who hungers for adventure and opportunities in a world reserved solely for men. An insightful examination of the limitations imposed by socially prescribed roles, the novel is considered by some to be "as close as Stowe ever came to writing a fictionalized autobiography" (Hedrick, *Harriet Beecher Stowe* 297). In *The Minister's Wooing* (1859), also set in New England, Stowe draws upon her family's theological roots in her depiction of Dr. Samuel Hopkins, a prominent divine who pursues a young woman with the intention of marrying her. While the novel was well known in the years following its publication, it suffers from a thin and utterly predictable plot.

CRITICAL RECEPTION

Despite the fact that she was a prolific author with nearly two dozen books to her credit, Stowe's literary reputation rests almost exclusively on the reception accorded *Uncle Tom's Cabin*. Legend has it that when she met President Abraham Lincoln at the White House in 1863, he greeted her as "the little lady who started this big war" (quoted in Crozier 72). The controversy engendered by *Uncle Tom's Cabin* has been far-reaching: Supporters hail it as an important work of cultural realism, while detractors condemn it for promoting lies and distortions.

Initially appearing serially in the *National Era*, an antislavery newspaper, *Uncle Tom's Cabin* was published as a two-volume novel in 1852 and became an immediate best-seller. By the end of the first year, the novel had sold "300,000 copies in the United States and a million in England" (Donovan, "*Uncle Tom's Cabin*" 11). By the mid-1970s, it had been translated into fifty-eight languages.

Much of the early critical response to the novel was positive. British writer Charles Kingsley praised the book as "the greatest novel ever written" (quoted in Donovan, "*Uncle Tom's Cabin*" 16), a view that was shared by numerous critics on both sides of the Atlantic. Emerson applauded *Uncle Tom's Cabin* in his essay "Success" for its ability to speak "to the universal heart" (*Complete Works* 7, 286), and Frederick Douglass hailed the novel as "the *master book* of the nineteenth-century" (quoted in Foner 2, 227). Another former slave, Sella Martin, commented that in exposing details about slave auctions Stowe had "thrown sufficient light upon that horrible and inhuman agency of slavery" (quoted in Donovan, "*Uncle Tom's Cabin*" 17). Similarly, William Wells Brown, an African-American novelist, remarked that "*Uncle Tom's Cabin* has come down upon the dark abodes of slavery like a morning's sunlight . . . awakening sympathy in hearts that never before felt for the slave" (quoted in Donovan, "*Uncle Tom's Cabin*" 18). Throughout the remainder of the nineteenth century, the reception remained primarily positive, with some notable exceptions.

The Southern response to the novel, and to *A Key to Uncle Tom's Cabin*, was, predictably, generally hostile. William J. Grayson, a South Carolina poet, excoriated Stowe as "a moral scavenger" who "sniffs up pollution with a pious air" (quoted in Adams 39). In one of the most scathing reviews, William Gilmore Simms accused Stowe of possessing "a malignity so remarkable that the petticoat lifts of itself, and we see the hoof of the beast under the table" (quoted in Gossett 190). In addition, a review by George F. Holmes in the *Southern Literary Messenger* attacked Stowe for "intermeddl[ing] with things which concern her not—to libel and vilify people from among whom have gone forth some of the noblest men that have adorned the race" and for using her pen to bring forth "allegations of cruelty towards the slaves" that are "absolutely and unqualifiedly false" (quoted in Ammons, *Uncle Tom's Cabin* 468, 475). Stowe was also censured for suggesting colonization as a solution to slavery.

Throughout the early twentieth century, *Uncle Tom's Cabin* was either dismissed for its sentimentalism, criticized for its unpolished style, or considered too marginal for serious critical inquiry. Some critics, most notably James Baldwin, angrily denounced the novel for its racial stereotypes and accused Stowe of divesting Tom of his manhood. In the second half of the century, however, and particularly in recent years, *Uncle Tom's Cabin* has become firmly reassimilated into the American literary canon. Edmund Wilson proclaimed it in 1962 to be "a much more impressive work than one has ever been allowed to suspect" (5), and Leslie Fiedler in *Love and Death in the American Novel* characterized it as "an astonishingly various and complex work" (261). Kenneth Lynn argued that the negative characterization of the novel as "good propaganda" was "one of the most unjust clichés in all of American criticism" (quoted in Donovan, *"Uncle Tom's Cabin"* 21). More recently, Paul Lauter observed, "The restoration of *Uncle Tom's Cabin*—even despite its racial stereotypes—to a degree of literary grace in the last decades testifies more to the impact of the civil rights movement than, as yet, to a shift in our literary aesthetic" (107). Indeed, both the civil rights and women's movements of the 1960s set the stage for a critical reassessment of the novel. Feminist critics have come to see the novel as a revolt against male patriarchy and to recognize the political dimensions inherent in the power struggles that are depicted. Jean Fagan Yellin suggests that the "problems of slavery in [the novel are] finally inseparable from the issue of women's political impotence" (91).

While the bulk of criticism addressing Stowe's works has focused on *Uncle Tom's Cabin*, some of her other works, most notably *Oldtown Folks* and *The Pearl of Orr's Island*, are also beginning to receive scholarly attention. John R. Adams characterizes *Oldtown Folks* as "the best book [Stowe] ever wrote" and "the most comprehensive of her New England novels" (63). Judith Fetterley suggests that "next to *Uncle Tom's Cabin*," *The Pearl of Orr's Island* is "Stowe's most mythically charged and imaginatively compelling work" and that it "derives its deepest meaning from Stowe's vision of the value of the feminine principle in a masculine world" (379).

WORKS CITED

Cross, Barbara M., ed. *The Autobiography of Lyman Beecher*. 2 vols. Cambridge: Harvard University Press, 1961.

Emerson, Ralph Waldo. *The Complete Works of Ralph Waldo Emerson*. Cambridge: Riverside Press, 1903.

Fetterley, Judith, ed. *Provisions: A Reader from 19th-Century American Women*. Bloomington: Indiana University Press, 1985.

Fiedler, Leslie. *Love and Death in the American Novel*. New York: Criterion Books, 1960.

Foner, Philip S., ed. *The Life and Writings of Frederick Douglass*. Vol. 2. New York: International Publishers, 1950.

Lauter, Paul. *Canons and Contexts*. New York: Oxford University Press, 1991.

Wilson, Edmund. *Patriotic Gore*. New York: Oxford University Press, 1962.

Yellin, Jean Fagan. "Doing It Herself: *Uncle Tom's Cabin* and Women's Role in the Slavery Crisis." In *New Essays on "Uncle Tom's Cabin,"* edited by Eric J. Sundquist. New York: Cambridge University Press, 1986. 85–105.

BIBLIOGRAPHY

Works by Harriet Beecher Stowe

Primary Geography for Children. Cincinnati: Corey & Fairbank, 1833.
The Mayflower; or, Sketches of Scenes and Characters among the Descendents of the Puritans. New York: Harper and Brothers, 1843.
Uncle Tom's Cabin; Or, Life among the Lowly. 2 vols. Boston: John P. Jewett, 1852.
A Key to Uncle Tom's Cabin. Boston: John P. Jewett and Co., 1853.
Sunny Memories of Foreign Lands. 2 vols. Boston: Phillips, Sampson, 1854.
Dred: A Tale of the Great Dismal Swamp. 2 vols. Boston: Phillips, Sampson, 1856.
The Minister's Wooing. New York: Derby and Jackson, 1859.
Agnes of Sorrento. Boston: Ticknor and Fields, 1862.
The Pearl of Orr's Island: A Story of the Coast of Maine. Boston: Ticknor and Fields, 1862.
Little Foxes. Boston: Ticknor and Fields, 1866.
Oldtown Folks. Boston: Fields, Osgood, 1869.
Lady Byron Vindicated: A History of the Byron Controversy, from Its Beginnings in 1816 to the Present Time. Boston: Fields, Osgood, 1870.
Pink and White Tyranny: A Society Novel. Boston: Roberts Brothers, 1871.
Palmetto-Leaves. Boston: J. R. Osgood, 1873.
Woman in Sacred History: A Series of Sketches Drawn from Scriptural, Historical, and Legendary Sources. New York: J. B. Ford, 1873.
Footsteps of the Master. New York: J. B. Ford, 1877.
Poganuc People: Their Loves and Lives. New York: Fords, Howard, and Hulbert, 1878.
Religious Studies, Sketches, and Poems. Boston: Houghton, Mifflin, 1896.

Studies of Harriet Beecher Stowe

Adams, John R. *Harriet Beecher Stowe*. Boston: Twayne Publishers, 1989.
Ammons, Elizabeth, ed. *Critical Essays on Harriet Beecher Stowe*. Boston: G. K. Hall, 1980.
————. *Uncle Tom's Cabin*. A Norton Critical Edition. New York: Norton, 1994.
Ashton, Jean W. *Harriet Beecher Stowe: A Reference Guide*. Boston: G. K. Hall, 1977.
Baldwin, James. "Everybody's Protest Novel." In *Notes of a Native Son*. Boston: Beacon Press, 1955. 13–28.
Crozier, Alice C. *The Novels of Harriet Beecher Stowe*. New York: Oxford University Press, 1969.
Donovan, Josephine. "Harriet Beecher Stowe's Feminism." *American Transcendental Quarterly* 47–48 (summer–fall 1980): 141–157.
————. *"Uncle Tom's Cabin": Evil, Affliction, and Redemptive Love*. Boston: Twayne, 1977.
Fields, Annie. *Life and Letters of Harriet Beecher Stowe*. Boston: Houghton, Mifflin, 1898.
Foster, Charles H. *The Rungless Ladder: Harriet Beecher Stowe and New England Puritanism*. Durham, NC: Duke University Press, 1954.
Gilbertson, Catherine. *Harriet Beecher Stowe*. New York: D. Appleton-Century, 1937.

Gossett, Thomas F. *"Uncle Tom's Cabin" and American Culture*. Dallas: Southern Methodist University Press, 1985.

Graham, Thomas. "Harriet Beecher Stowe and the Question of Race." *New England Quarterly* 46, no. 4 (December 1973): 614–622.

Hedrick, Joan D. *Harriet Beecher Stowe: A Life*. New York: Oxford University Press, 1994.

———. " 'Peaceable Fruits': The Ministry of Harriet Beecher Stowe." *American Quarterly* 40, no. 3 (September 1988): 307–332.

Hildreth, Margaret Holbrook. *Harriet Beecher Stowe: A Bibliography*. Hamden, CT: Archon Books, Shoe String Press, 1976.

Holmes, George F. Review of *Uncle Tom's Cabin. Southern Literary Messenger* 18 (October 1852), n.p.

Kelley, Mary. "At War with Herself: Harriet Beecher Stowe as Woman in Conflict within the Home." *American Studies* 19 (fall 1978): 23–40.

Kirkham, E. Bruce. *The Building of "Uncle Tom's Cabin."* Knoxville: University of Tennessee Press, 1977.

Lynn, Kenneth S. Introduction to *Uncle Tom's Cabin: Or, Life among the Lowly*, by Harriet Beecher Stowe. Cambridge: Harvard University Press, Belknap Press, 1962.

McCray, Florine Thayer. *The Life-Work of the Author of "Uncle Tom's Cabin."* New York: Funk and Wagnalls, 1889.

McCullough, David. "The Unexpected Mrs. Stowe." In *Brave Companions: Portraits in History*. New York: Prentice-Hall, 1992.

Moers, Ellen. *Harriet Beecher Stowe and American Literature*. Hartford: Stowe-Day Foundation, 1978.

Stowe, Charles Edward. *Life of Harriet Beecher Stowe Compiled from Her Letters and Journals*. Boston: Houghton, Mifflin, 1889.

Stowe, Charles Edward, and Lyman Beecher Stowe. *Harriet Beecher Stowe: The Story of Her Life*. Boston: Houghton, Mifflin, 1911.

Stowe, Lyman Beecher. *Saints, Sinners, and Beechers*. Indianapolis: Bobbs-Merrill, 1934.

Sundquist, Eric J., ed. *New Essays on "Uncle Tom's Cabin."* New York: Cambridge University Press, 1986.

Terrell, Mary Church. *Harriet Beecher Stowe: An Appreciation*. Washington, D.C.: Murray Brothers, 1911.

Tompkins, Jane P. "Sentimental Power: *Uncle Tom's Cabin* and the Politics of Literary History." In *The New Feminist Criticism: Essays on Women, Literature, and Theory*, edited by Elaine Showalter. New York: Pantheon, 1985. 81–104.

Wagenknecht, Edward. *Harriet Beecher Stowe: The Known and the Unknown*. New York: Oxford University Press, 1965.

Wilson, Forrest. *Crusader in Crinoline: The Life of Harriet Beecher Stowe*. Philadelphia: J. B. Lippincott, 1941.

RUTH McENERY STUART
(1849–1917)

Charles Johanningsmeier

BIOGRAPHY

On May 21, 1849, Mary Routh McEnery was born in Marksville, Louisiana, to James and Mary Routh (Stirling) McEnery. Both her father, an Irish immigrant businessman, and her mother came from distinguished families whose members were quite successful in Louisiana business and politics. At some time in the early 1850s the family moved to New Orleans. Mary Routh lived there until August 1879, when she married Alfred Oden Stuart, a cotton planter twenty-eight years her senior, and she moved to his home in Washington, Arkansas. Her one son, Stirling, was born in 1882, but her husband died of a stroke shortly thereafter in 1883.

Following her husband's death, "Routh" McEnery Stuart returned to live in New Orleans and began to teach school and write in order to earn a living, since the postbellum economic depression had severely hurt the financial situation of her extended family. During a vacation to North Carolina in 1887, Stuart serendipitously met Charles Dudley Warner, the editor of *Harper's Monthly Magazine*, who invited her to submit some of her work to him. She did so shortly thereafter, and he helped place two stories, "Uncle Mingo's 'Speculatioms' " [*sic*] and "Lamentations of Jeremiah Johnson," in *The New Princeton Review* and *Harper's*, respectively; both were published in 1888. It was at this time that Stuart changed her first name to the more easily recognizable "Ruth."

Wishing to be closer to the publishing center of the United States, at some time around 1890 Ruth moved to New York City. The national magazines' appetite for "things Southern" in the late 1880s and 1890s appeared insatiable, and as a result, Stuart was much in demand as a contributor to all of the more famous periodicals. In addition, starting in 1893, Stuart spent a great deal of time traveling around the country delivering very popular readings of her short stories and verse; especially popular were those that included a great deal of Southern dialect.

By 1893 Stuart's reputation was substantial enough to prompt Harper's to issue a collection of her stories, *A Golden Wedding, and Other Tales.* In 1896 she published her enormously popular *Sonny,* a series of monologues by an aged farmer about his son, and this secured her place as a leading local color writer. Stuart's career suffered a serious setback, however, when in 1905 her son died from an accidental fall. For approximately four years Stuart was seriously depressed and did little work, but she finally did return to writing and continued to be quite successful. There are many indications of the high esteem in which Stuart was held by her contemporary reading public, especially in her home state of Louisiana. In 1907 a literary society called the Ruth McEnery Stuart Clan was founded in New Orleans (it still exists today), and in 1915, Tulane University conferred on her an honorary Doctor of Letters degree. Shortly after receiving this honor, however, Stuart died on May 6, 1917, in White Plains, New York.

MAJOR WORKS AND THEMES

Stuart rode to fame primarily on the basis of her stories about black ex-slaves in postbellum Louisiana. Most of the stories in her first short story collection, *A Golden Wedding* (1893), deal with black life during this era, as do such works as "Queen o' Sheba's Triumph" (1899), *Napoleon Jackson: The Gentleman of the Plush Rocker* (1902), and *George Washington Jones: A Christmas Gift That Went A-Begging* (1903). After the death of her son, Stuart returned to mine this territory as a source of a number of dialect poems, collected in *Daddy Do-Funny's Wisdom Jingles* (1913), and *Plantation Songs, and Other Verse* (1916). Many of her works dealing with African Americans present their subjects as stereotypical caricatures meant to be humorous: Lazy men and golden-hearted "mammies" abound. Contributing to this impression of African Americans is Stuart's frequent use of an educated narrator to frame the events in her local color fictions (a device she also often employs with stories about poor whites). Yet some works, most notably "Queen o' Sheba's Triumph" and *Napoleon Jackson*, portray blacks with greater subtlety. For example, the former story deals with a strong black woman from Arkansas named Queen o' Sheba Jackson, who moves to New York. She endures a hard life yet still retains control of her own representation, ironically by staging her own lavish funeral. In the latter work, Stuart uses Napoleon Jackson, an ostensibly lazy black man, to subvert white readers' stereotypes of black men. Local whites, thinking they are helping Napoleon's family, put him on trial in an attempt to get him to be more industrious and financially supportive. At the trial, however, his hardworking wife Rose Ann, his children, and an older black woman all defend Napoleon as an exemplary father and husband, and he is "acquitted."

Somewhat similar in tone are Stuart's works that deal with Italian immigrants in New Orleans: "Camelia Riccardo" (1893), *The Story of Babette* (1894), and *Carlotta's Intended* (1894). "Camelia Riccardo" and *Carlotta's Intended* are both primarily love stories. In the former a rich French butcher and a lazy Italian man nicknamed "Dago 'Manuel" compete for Camelia's hand in marriage; Manuel, inspired by Camelia's edict that he must work harder, becomes industrious and marries her. In the latter, Carlotta DiCarlo avoids marriage to a Mafia boss and instead marries an Irish immigrant named Patrick Rooney. In these stories Stuart's disdain of Italian Americans—especially what she saw as their ethos of male domination—is quite evident. Her portrayal of Italian characters is quite conventional for her time, exhibiting many of the misconceptions and fears about them that fueled the anti-Italian lynchings in New Orleans in 1891.

Most of Stuart's strongest works deal with rural whites from Arkansas. Drawing on her own experiences with small-town life there, Stuart modeled the fictional village of "Simpkinsville," the setting of many of these fictions, after Washington, Arkansas, where she lived briefly with her husband. Among the works dealing with rural white characters are *Sonny* (1896), *In Simpkinsville: Character Tales* (1897), *The Woman's Exchange of Simpkinsville* (1893), and *Sonny's Father* (1910). Stuart's portrayal of poor whites is generally more sympathetic than her portrayal of blacks. Her most popular work, for example, *Sonny*, includes seven monologues by Deuteronomy Jones, a poor, uneducated farmer in his seventies, in which he tells about events in his son's life, from his birth to his wedding. There is much humor in these monologues, but one also gathers that the narrator is symbolic of a type that Stuart much admired: simple, hardworking, faithful, and devoted to his family.

Stuart also had great respect and sympathy for rural and small-town white women. Possibly because of her own experiences, she portrayed a number of middle-aged women who find male soulmates and/or discover their own identities. "A Note of Scarlet" (1898), for example, involves a forty-one-year-old spinster named Melissa Ann Moore who spends her time knitting green moss mats for baby and wedding gifts. Suddenly, though, she rebels by knitting red mats, skipping church, and going fishing; in doing so she provokes from the deacon a confession of his admiration and affection. In *The Woman's Exchange of Simpkinsville* (1893), Stuart portrays the elderly twin sisters Sarey Mirandy and Sophie Falena Simpkins who, in response to their reduced circumstances, establish and run a successful cooperative hotel and bakery. *The Unlived Life of Little Mary Ellen* (1910), originally serialized in 1896, is possibly her most powerful work. In it, Mary Ellen is left alone at the altar on her wedding day when the groom does not appear. Psychologically devastated, she becomes extremely attached to a doll and treats it as if it were her own child. When the doll is chewed up by a dog, Mary Ellen mourns for it and orders that a funeral be conducted; in a highly symbolic scene at the end, Mary Ellen is found to have died at the funeral.

Although Stuart's works occasionally touch on quite serious issues (such as the fraudulent nature of rest cures in *The Cocoon: A Rest-Cure Comedy* [1915]), one must agree with the conclusion of one contemporary who wrote, "The anti-Christmas, anti-holiday, unchristianlike or unhappy side of life finds small expression from Mrs. Stuart's pen, for she is everywhere cheerful, looking on the bright side, and turning the flow of her drama away from tragedy and toward wholesome living, lightened by the play of comedy" (Stevens 11, 5148).

CRITICAL RECEPTION

In the late nineteenth and early twentieth centuries Stuart was regarded as one of the most important Southern writers and was compared favorably with other leading regionalists. One reviewer wrote regarding Stuart's first collection, *A Golden Wedding*, that she "is not at all inferior to Miss Grace King in her reproductions of Negro character and comedy and inconsistency" (*Critic* 22, 377). Kate Chopin was another admirer of Stuart's work, once commenting, "Sympathy and insight are the qualities I believe, which make her stories lovable, which makes them linger in the memory like pleasant human experiences" (quoted in Rankin 157).

Contemporary critics singled out Stuart's "realistic" portrayal of black life and speech for commendation, probably because she made blacks seem harmless and humorous. The condescending attitude evident in reviewers' comments grates the ears of modern readers, but they were actually meant to recommend Stuart's works. For example, Laurence Hutton of *Harper's* spoke of how Stuart portrayed "that picturesque, squalid, even-tempered, easy-going, unambitious, soft-voiced, warm-hearted, mendacious proletariat familiarly miscalled 'darkies,' no longer in derision, but in affectionate good-will" (Hutton 351). He also sounded a note common in other reviews of Stuart's work when he wrote, "The negro dialect can never have been better done than in these pages. All its grotesque exaggerations are observed, its sense of euphony, its use of superlatives, its sesquipedality, and its epigrammatic force, so that its very badness rises to the dignity of a quality" (Hutton 351). Kate Chopin, too, concluded, "Even [Thomas Nelson] Page and [Joel Chandler] Harris among the men have not surpassed her in the portrayal of that child-like exuberance which is so pronounced a feature of negro character" (quoted in Rankin 156).

What critics most admired in Stuart, though, was her ability to create believable characters and moving situations. Candace Wheeler, for example, wrote in 1899 that Stuart had "an ability to feel and to present every day phases of life in a manner inimitable for truth, kindness, humor and pathos" (Wheeler 1083). One reviewer of the collection *In Simpkinsville: Character Tales* commented that Stuart's "strength lies in her truthful and kindly discernment of the foibles and inconsistencies of human nature and in her shrewd perception of the picturesque possibilities of details which have been generally overlooked" ("Novel Notes" 164). Most appropriately, her portrayal of Mary Ellen in "The Unlived Life of Little Mary Ellen" received its due share of praise; one reviewer concluded that in it "a difficult theme is so simply and exquisitely handled that the reader forgets to regard the result as a work of art, and thinks of it only as most pitiful fact" ("Stories" 340).

Most of Stuart's works no longer appeal to readers because of the very qualities that her contemporaries admired: her representation of Southern blacks and her sentimentality. However, despite what one would now call her very conservative views (except in the area of women's role), her fiction in the last decade or so is beginning to receive a more appropriate amount of critical attention.

WORKS CITED

Hutton, Laurence. "Literary Notes." *Harper's* 86 (1893): 349–352.

"Novel Notes." *Bookman* 6 (1897): 164.

Rankin, Daniel S. *Kate Chopin and Her Creole Stories*. Philadelphia: University of Pennsylvania Press, 1932.

Review of *A Golden Wedding*. *Critic* 22 (n.s. 19) (1893): 377–378.

Stevens, Edwin Lewis. "Ruth McEnery Stuart." In *Library of Southern Literature*, edited by Edwin Anderson Alderman and Joel Chandler Harris. Vol. 11. New Orleans: Martin and Hoyt Co., 1909.

"Stories from Southern Life." *Critic* 31 (n.s. 28) (1897): 340–341.

Wheeler, Candace. "American Authoress of the Hour." *Harper's Bazar* 32 (16 December 1899): 1083–1084.

BIBLIOGRAPHY

Works by Ruth McEnery Stuart

A Golden Wedding, and Other Tales. New York: Harper and Brothers, 1893.

The Woman's Exchange of Simpkinsville. New York and London: Harper, 1893.

Carlotta's Intended and Other Tales. New York: Harper and Brothers, 1894.

The Story of Babette, a Little Creole Girl. New York: Harper and Brothers, 1894.

Gobolinks, or Shadow-Pictures for Young and Old. With Albert Bigelow Paine. New York: Century, 1896.

Solomon Crow's Christmas Pockets, and Other Tales. New York: Harper and Brothers, 1896.

Sonny. New York: Century, 1896.

In Simpkinsville: Character Tales. New York: Harper and Brothers, 1897.

The Snow-Cap Sisters: A Farce. New York and London: Harper and Brothers, 1897.

Holly and Pizen, and Other Stories. New York: N.p., 1898.

Moriah's Mourning, and Other Half-Hour Sketches. New York: Harper, 1898.

Napoleon Jackson: The Gentleman of the Plush Rocker. New York: Century, 1902.

George Washington Jones: A Christmas Gift That Went A-Begging. Philadelphia: H. Altemus, 1903.

The River's Children: An Idyl of the Mississippi. New York: Century, 1904.

The Second Wooing of Salina Sue, and Other Stories. New York: Harper and Brothers, 1905.

Aunt Amity's Silver Wedding, and Other Stories. New York: Century, 1909.
Sonny's Father. New York: Century, 1910.
The Unlived Life of Little Mary Ellen. Indianapolis: Bobbs-Merrill, 1910.
The Haunted Photograph, Whence and Whither, a Case in Diplomacy, the Afterglow.
     New York: Century, 1911.
Daddy Do-Funny's Wisdom Jingles. New York: Century, 1913.
The Cocoon: A Rest-Cure Comedy. New York: Hearst's International Library, 1915.
Plantation Songs, and Other Verse. New York: D. Appleton and Co., 1916.

Studies of Ruth McEnery Stuart

Brown, Dorothy H. "Ruth McEnery Stuart: A Reassessment." *Xavier Review* 7, no. 2
     (1987): 23–36.
Bush, Robert B. "Louisiana Prose Fiction, 1870–1900." Ph.D. diss., State University of
     Iowa, 1957.
Fletcher, Mary F. "A Biographical and Critical Study of Ruth McEnery Stuart." Ph.D.
     diss., Louisiana State University and Agricultural and Mechanical College, 1955.
Frisby, James R., Jr. "New Orleans Writers and the Negro: George Washington Cable,
     Grace King, Ruth McEnery Stuart, Kate Chopin, and Lafcadio Hearn, 1870–
     1900." Ph.D. diss., Emory University, 1972.
Hall, Joan Wylie. "Ruth McEnery Stuart." *Legacy* 10 (1993): 47–56.
Simpson, Ethel C. Introduction to *Simpkinsville and Vicinity: Arkansas Stories of Ruth
     McEnery Stuart.* Fayetteville: University of Arkansas Press, 1983. 1–20.
———. "Ruth McEnery Stuart: The Innocent Grotesque." *Louisiana Literature: A Re-
     view of Literature and Humanities* 4, no. 1 (spring 1987): 57–65.
Sneller, Judy Ellen. "Man-Figs and Magnolias, Ladies and Lariats: Humor and Irony in
     the Writings of Three New Orleans Women, 1865–1916." Ph.D. diss., Emory
     University, 1992.
Ruth McEnery Stuart Collection, Howard-Tilton Memorial Library, Tulane University,
     New Orleans.
Taylor, Helen. *Gender, Race, and Region in the Writings of Grace King, Ruth McEnery
     Stuart, and Kate Chopin.* Baton Rouge: Louisiana State University Press, 1989.

OCTAVE THANET
(ALICE FRENCH)
(1850–1934)

Charles Johanningsmeier

BIOGRAPHY

Alice French was born in Andover, Massachusetts, on March 19, 1850, the eldest daughter of George Henry French and Frances Wood Morton French, both of whom could trace their lineage back to the earliest settlement of Massachusetts in the 1630s. The family left its New England roots in 1856, however, and moved to Davenport, Iowa, where George Henry French became a successful businessman and civic leader.

From 1856 until 1866 Alice French attended public schools in Davenport, but from 1866 to 1868, she attended private schools in the East. Returning to Davenport after graduation, she entered a life of midwestern gentility and began to write occasional short stories and essays. Her first work published in a national periodical was a short story about railroad strikers entitled "Communists and Capitalists: A Sketch from Life," which appeared in *Lippincott's* in October 1878. This story is also important because it was the first to appear under the pseudonym "Octave Thanet." According to later interviews, French chose "Octave" because of a former roommate's name, Octavia, and because she liked the fact that it could be taken as either male or female; "Thanet" supposedly derived from some printing on the side of a boxcar that French once saw. Her first short story to gain national critical attention was "The Bishop's Vagabond," published in the *Atlantic Monthly* in January 1884. From this point until the end of the century, editors of the leading national magazines and managers of the major newspaper syndicates frequently solicited contributions from her, and she was among the highest-paid authors of the period.

An important turning point in French's life came in 1883. In this year she accompanied Jane Allen Crawford, a longtime friend and recent widow, to a plantation Crawford had inherited in northeastern Arkansas called "Clover Bend." From 1883 to 1909 French and Crawford spent every winter here, and during the summers, they lived together in Davenport. At Clover Bend, French wrote, gathered material about poor white and black residents, became conversant with the area dialects, and learned the local legends and history.

The popularity of French's short stories about western town life (Davenport) and Southern life (Clover Bend) that appeared in periodicals led eastern publishers to ask her to gather these stories in volume form. In 1887 Houghton Mifflin published the first such collection, *Knitters in the Sun*; eight more would follow, with the last, *Stories that End Well*, being published by Bobbs-Merrill in 1911. French also wrote six full-length novels during her career, with her first one, *Expiation*, appearing in 1890.

After the turn of the century French's popularity waned, although she remained quite active as a writer and speaker. Never married, she was a member of many social organizations and spent much of her time in Davenport distributing clothes and food to the poor. In Iowa she continued to be regarded as an important native writer, and in 1911, she received an honorary Doctor of Letters degree from the University of Iowa; another measure of her local fame was the Octave Thanet Society that existed at this university from 1899 to 1933. A staunch patriot and believer in traditional women's roles, French delivered numerous speeches criticizing the pacifist and suffragist movements in the years before and during World War I; her novelette *And the Captain Answered* (1917), for example, takes a decidedly antipacifist stand. In her old age, though, French's activities were restricted by a number of debilitating ailments, including diabetes, a hernia, and cataracts. Adding to her troubles was the postwar economic depression, which severely reduced the value of many of her stock holdings. Her final years were spent in near poverty, and by the time she died at age eighty-three in Davenport on January 9, 1934, she was an almost forgotten literary figure.

MAJOR WORKS AND THEMES

French's work is the product of a very divided sensibility. On the one hand, she came from a patrician, well-to-do New England background, with a father who was the head of a number of large business concerns. On the other hand, she divided most of her life between the midwestern city of Davenport, Iowa, and the Clover Bend plantation. All of these experiences shaped her work.

Many of her essays, short stories, and novels, for instance, draw on her life in Davenport and the relation between labor and capital in a rapidly industrializing city. Essays such as "The Tramp in Four Centuries" (*Lippincott's*, May 1879), "The English Workingman and the Commercial Crises" (*Lippincott's*, April and May 1880), "Sketches of American Types: The Provincials" (*Scribner's*, May 1894), "Sketches of American Types: The Working Man" (*Scribner's*, July 1894), and "The Contented Masses" (*Forum*, October 1894) demonstrate an interest in sociological observation, especially of working-class people. Yet the biases inherent in her own elevated social and economic class position are evident in all of her work on this subject. Her first published story, for example, "Communists and Capitalists" (1878), is generally critical of railroad strikers, which is not surprising given French's father's executive position with a railroad during this time. *The Heart of Toil* (1898) is composed of six stories about Northern laborers that show how easily they can be duped into believing that collective action will help their situation. Davenport appears (slightly disguised) in four stories of the collection entitled *Otto the Knight* (1891), and all of the works in *Stories of a Western Town* (1893) are set there. The latter collection is perhaps her strongest; her keen observations of life in a small midwestern town and depictions of the lives of its residents in some ways anticipates works such as Sherwood Anderson's *Winesburg, Ohio* (1919). French's novel *The Man of the Hour* (1905) also takes place in "Fairport" (Davenport) and features a labor organizer, John Winslow, who realizes the errors of his ways and becomes a capitalist. Although French often portrayed working men and women positively, all of her fiction about the relationship between workers and employers emphasizes that collective labor action is unnecessary and often harmful to the interests of both parties. Instead, she posits that enlightened, paternalistic action on the part of employers and society's well-to-do, along with individual hard work and adherence to traditional family virtues by the poor, will result in a better, stronger America.

French's stories about Davenport make her a midwestern local colorist, yet her time at Clover Bend enabled her to write many works of Southern local color. In these works, French exhibits a great deal of descriptive skill and a keen ability to depict the dialects of the region. As in the stories about labor unrest, however, French's own socioeconomically privileged position is evident in her attitudes toward the Arkansas natives. Her first story about this region was "Ma' Bowlin'," published in *Harper's Weekly* in 1887, and her first novel, *Expiation* (1890), is about an Arkansas man educated in England who comes back and defeats the "Graybacks," Confederate raiders during the last stages of the Civil War. French's second novel, *We All* (1891) concerns a young Chicago boy who visits an Arkansas plantation. In general, French portrays poor whites quite positively, commending their self-respect and willingness to work hard. Many of the stories, though, strike a condescending attitude toward African Americans, usually arguing that they are not fully capable of improving their situation by themselves. As the French writer Th. Bentzon (Marie Thérèse Blanc) wrote in 1896, "[The] habitual characteristic [of her 'negro stories'] is an inexpressible drollery" (Bentzon 43). French's philosophy is made especially clear in her late novel *By Inheritance* (1910). It is a thinly disguised autobiographical work about a New England spinster named Agatha Danforth who is almost sixty years old, drives a car, and visits Arkansas. As the plot unfolds she realizes that Sydney Danton, the black man who advocates higher education for African Americans and whose education at Harvard she had financed, is wrong about the capabilities of newly freed slaves. At the end of the novel, Danforth concludes that they are clearly not ready for higher education; instead, she ends up advocating a gradualist stance for their education very similar to Booker T. Washington's. Thus, French adopted the same type of paternalistic, condescending attitude toward blacks that she exhibited toward poor white Northern laborers; both needed more intelligent members of society to guide their progress.

CRITICAL RECEPTION

Until around 1900, contemporary reviewers were quite positive about French's work. Th. Bentzon (Madame Blanc) compared French's stories favorably to Maupassant's (39) and opined that "the scrupulous fidelity in the description of things and of people . . . makes of each one of Octave Thanet's short stories a little *chef-d'oeuvre* of truthful realism" (37). William Dean Howells wrote about her first collection, *Knitters in the Sun* (1887), that "it is . . . very well worth looking at" (644), and a review in the New York *Tribune* said it was "one of the best collections of short stories the reader can find anywhere. . . . As a story teller, Octave Thanet has no superior and very few peers" [Anonymous, quoted in McMichael 107]. Shortly thereafter, her first novel, *Expiation* (1890), received almost universal praise. William Morton Payne of the *Dial*, for example, wrote that "we may speak of the characters in this story as well drawn and vital, of the situations as interesting, and of the scenes as graphically described" (13). Contemporaries frequently ranked her along with Mary Wilkins, Sarah Orne Jewett, Hamlin Garland, Edward Eggleston, and Mary Noailles Murfree (Charles Egbert Craddock) as one of the leading local color writers of her day, and one reviewer, after listing a number of authors in this category, concluded that "none of them have Octave Thanet's sense of proportion, and none of them can chisel a character out of nature's quarry with her swift, unerring strokes" (Reid 108). The *Atlantic* reviewer of *Stories of a Western Town* (1893) concurred, adding that "Thanet recognizes the rawness of much of the material she is handling, but looks farther into it, and perceives certain signs of fundamental virtues which she is eager to introduce to the knowledge of others" ("A Few Story-Tellers" 698). In addition, as long as French's conservative views on labor and blacks were socially acceptable, reviewers praised her works on these subjects. One wrote of *The Heart of Toil* (1898) that French had "made the laboring man, the toiler in the mills, of the Middle West peculiarly her property, and it would be hard to pick out any other writer, man or woman, who writes at once so interestingly and with such entire understanding of both capitalist and laborer" ("Some American and English Women Novelists" 734). For the most part, though, after the turn of the century French's works were increasingly disparaged not only by the public and by publishers but also by critics.

Later literary historians and critics have generally ignored French's fiction;

quite possibly this is due to her conservative views, not only about labor, race, and women's issues but also about art. At an Authors' Congress session at the Columbian Exposition in 1893, when Hamlin Garland presented his theories about "veritism" and argued that local color fiction should be more realistic, French steadfastly defended the need to lighten such portrayals of midwestern and Southern life. French's distaste for gritty realism (and later, literary modernism), along with her anti-Union, anti–women's suffrage, anti-DuBoisian attitudes, clearly has not tended to make her an author favored by modern critics.

WORKS CITED

Bentzon, Th. [Marie Therese Blanc]. "In Arkansas. Apropos of Octave Thanet's Romances." *Midland Monthly* 6 (July and August 1896): 37–47, 136–145.

"A Few Story-Tellers, Old and New." *Atlantic* 72 (1893): 693–699.

Higginson, Thomas Wentworth. Letter to Bobbs-Merrill Co., 30 March 1910, Newberry Library. Quoted in McMichael 189.

Howells, William Dean. "Editor's Study." *Harper's Magazine* 76 (1888): 640–644.

McMichael, George. *Journey to Obscurity: The Life of Octave Thanet.* Lincoln: University of Nebraska Press, 1965.

Payne, William Morton. "Recent Fiction." *Dial* 11 (May 1890): 12–14.

Reid, Mary J. "The Theories of Octave Thanet and Other Western Realists." *Midland Monthly* 9 (February 1898): 99–108.

"Some American and English Women Novelists." *American Monthly Review of Reviews* 18 (December 1898): 734–735.

BIBLIOGRAPHY

Works by Octave Thanet

Knitters in the Sun. New York: Houghton Mifflin, 1887.

The Best Letters of Lady Mary Wortley Montague. Edited by Octave Thanet. Chicago: A. C. McClurg and Co., 1890.

Expiation. New York: Charles Scribner's Sons, 1890.

Otto the Knight and Other Trans-Mississippi Stories. New York: Houghton Mifflin and Co., 1891.

We All. New York: D. Appleton and Co., 1891.

An Adventure in Photography. New York: Charles Scribner's Sons, 1893.

Stories of a Western Town. New York: Charles Scribner's Sons, 1893.

A Book of True Lovers. Chicago: Way and Williams, 1897.

The Missionary Sheriff: Being Incidents in the Life of a Plain Man Who Tried to Do His Duty. New York: Harper and Brothers, 1897.

The Heart of Toil. New York: Charles Scribner's Sons, 1898.

A Slave to Duty and Other Women. New York: Herbert S. Stone, 1898.

The Captured Dream and Other Stories. New York and London: Harper and Brothers, 1899.

The Man of the Hour. Indianapolis: Bobbs-Merrill, 1905.

The Lion's Share. Indianapolis: Bobbs-Merrill, 1907.
By Inheritance. Indianapolis: Bobbs-Merrill, 1910.
Stories that End Well. Indianapolis: Bobbs-Merrill, 1911.
A Step on the Stair. Indianapolis: Bobbs-Merrill, 1913.
And the Captain Answered. Indianapolis: Bobbs-Merrill, 1917.

Studies of Octave Thanet

Bush, Robert. "The Literary Paternalism of Octave Thanet." *Newberry Library Bulletin* 6, no. 1 (November 1962): 24–28.

Dougan, Michael B. "Local Colorists and the Race Question: Opie Read and Octave Thanet." *Publications of the Arkansas Philological Association* 9, no. 2 (fall 1983): 26–34.

Harper, Clio. "Alice French." In *Library of Southern Literature*, edited by E. A. Anderson. New Orleans: Martin and Hoyt Co., 1909. 4:1713–1717.

Huse, Nancy. "Alice French (Octave Thanet)." In *American Short-Story Writers before 1880*, edited by Bobby Ellen Kimbel. Vol. 74 of *Dictionary of Literary Biography*. Detroit: Gale Research, 1988.

Rushton, Linda Elizabeth. "The Arkansas Fiction of Alice French." Ph.D. diss., University of Arkansas, 1982.

Shinn, Josiah H. "Miss Alice French of Clover Bend." *Publications of the Arkansas Historical Association* 2 (1906): 344–351.

Tigges, Sandra Ann Healey. "Alice French: A Noble Anachronism." Ph.D. diss., University of Iowa, 1981.

Tucker, Ruth. " 'Octave Thanet': A Biography of Alice French." Unpublished manuscript, Alice French Collection, Newberry Library, Chicago, IL, n.d.

The Alice French Collection at the Newberry Library in Chicago contains diaries, clippings, memorabilia, and literary manuscripts.

CELIA LAIGHTON THAXTER
(1835–1894)

Karen L. Kilcup

BIOGRAPHY

Celia Laighton was born on June 29, 1835, in the lively coastal city of Portsmouth, New Hampshire. Her civic-minded father, Thomas B. Laighton, was a local merchant who had a lumber business and engaged in West Indian trade; he also worked in the custom house and post office. After serving in the state legislature, he ran for governor and lost. Disappointed, and angry over the means by which he was defeated, Laighton, when Celia was four years old, moved his family to White Island, one of the Isles of Shoals off the coast, where he became the lighthouse keeper. The early part of Thaxter's childhood was an isolated one, with only her parents and two brothers for human company. Perhaps it was this isolation that enabled her to become the acute observer of nature revealed in her writing. Much later she would write to a friend, "Nobody knows how precious a word of kindness is, coming across the bitter sea to this howling wilderness of desolation, one lives so much on 'the weather' here; and when all out of doors turns your deadly enemy, it is hard to bear" (*Letters* 52).

This experience of isolation was mitigated somewhat when Laighton's family moved to Smutty Nose Island, one of the four Isles that her father had purchased, in 1841. Here, too, in spite of paying summer guests, the family was essentially alone during the hostile winter months, often confined to the house for weeks at a stretch. Nevertheless, the immense beauty of nature was something that she would recall with pleasure and awe in *Among the Isles of Shoals* (1873). Describing the subsidence of a thunderstorm, she wrote, "Presently this solemn gray lid was lifted at its western edge and an insufferable splendor streamed across the world from the sinking sun. The whole heaven was in a blaze of scarlet, across which sprang a rainbow unbroken to the topmost clouds . . . the sea answered the sky's rich blush, and the gray rocks lay drowned in melancholy purple. I hid my face from the glory—it was too much to bear'' (*Among the Isles of Shoals* 140).

A few years later, in 1847, Celia's father entered into a brief partnership with Harvard graduate Levi Thaxter, the man who would eventually become Celia's husband, and they began building the famous Appledore Hotel, one of the great resort hotels in nineteenth-century New England. Thomas Laighton soon bought out Levi's share, but Levi remained to tutor the Laighton children. Although Laighton recognized the unusual abilities of his daughter and took pains with her education himself, this tutoring, along with one term at Boston's Mount Washington Female Seminary, formed Celia's only formal education, and she was throughout her life ashamed of her lack of training, an absence that made her self-deprecating and allowed her to underestimate her own genius. Betrothed at the age of twelve, when she reached sixteen, she married her twenty-seven-year-old tutor, who was a college roommate of Thomas Wentworth Higginson and a familiar person in Boston literary circles that included many of the Transcendentalists.

Like many other nineteenth-century American women writers, Thaxter's marriage was for the most part unhappy, and the moody and often ill Levi was an uncongenial partner and a poor provider. Levi was unwilling to hire housekeeping help for Celia, even as she coped with the demands of a growing family, including a brain-damaged son for whom she cared throughout her life, and an active literary career. The difficulties of this period emerge in a letter to a friend: "Patience at my household tasks leaves me forlorn, ugly, and horrid'' (*Letters* 4) During the same period, she wrote to Annie Fields, "Oh, Annie, burn up this note straightway & do not breathe the madness to anybody, but do you know Mr. Thaxter refuses to have any servant at Newtonville, no not if I pay her wages & board besides. . . . I did beg so hard to be allowed to have one person to help do the work'' (Vallier 84). Levi's demands assuredly impaired her ability to begin and then to be wholly productive in her career as a writer.

In spite of his significant role in introducing his wife to literary notables, Levi was jealous of Celia's recognition, even though the family needed her income. Fortunately, Thaxter's poems, children's writing, and journalism sold well and were widely acclaimed. Thaxter's poems were first published in 1872, *Among the Isles of Shoals* in 1873, and *An Island Garden* in 1894. Later in her life, she also painted the illustrations for her work, as well as engaging in the considerably more lucrative art of china painting, of which she was proud. Gardening was the third art of this talented woman's life; her gardens were made famous by the paintings of her friend, the impressionist Childe Hassam.

Thaxter's marriage ultimately meant frequent periods of separation from her beloved family, especially her strong and loving mother. When Celia was facing the responsibilities of raising a young family, Levi moved them to Newtonville, Massachusetts. Because of a boating accident shortly after the marriage, Levi for the most part refused to travel to the Isles; the writer's sense of exile is apparent in a letter to Annie Fields of October 1862, written from Newtonville: "The leaves are falling, dry and sere after the sudden frost, and it looks pinched and cold out of doors, and the wind whistles. . . . Were I but a stork or a swallow! To have the fields locked up hard and fast, and the snow, blank, stiff, glaring, spread over all, months and months! . . . I long for the light and life, and ever shifting colors, and the delicious sound of the faithful old sea more in the winter than in the summer. No frost or snow can extinguish it'' (*Letters* 26–27).

The only periods that Celia spent with her birth family was summers, when she returned to help run the hotel. It was during this time that she hosted a famous salon that attracted eminent artists, musicians, and writers, including Childe Hassam, Sarah Orne Jewett, Annie and James Fields, Ralph Waldo Emerson, Lucy Larcom, Nathaniel Hawthorne, Thomas Wentworth Higginson, and Samuel Clemens. One frequent guest, John Greenleaf Whittier, was her friend and supporter for many years. As Jane Vallier observes, "[T]he remote Isles of Shoals gave the second generation Transcendentalists a place to contemplate the glories of nature and escape the growing pressures of urban American life'' (18). Ironically, although the salon and the friendships that it enabled offered Thaxter support and companionship, they also required enormous energy, and it is fortunate that Thaxter possessed a vigorous constitution. An important feature of her salons was the poetry readings that she gave beginning in the mid-1860s and continuing until her death; according to contemporaries, Thaxter was a highly gifted reader and speaker.

For most of her life, Thaxter held skeptical and unconventional religious beliefs and experimented with spiritualism and Buddhism, among other belief systems. After the death of her mother, she wrote to Fields, "[T]he 'consolations of religion' I cannot bear'' (*Letters* 88). Later in her life, she embraced a more traditional Christianity, tempered, perhaps, by her life experience. By the time that she moved to Appledore year-round to nurse her mother through her last illness in the 1870s, Thaxter's marriage was effectively over; but even among the Appledore family she sometimes felt alone and overworked. In March of 1876 she wrote to Annie Adams Fields, "I am so blue (let me whisper in your kind ear!) that I feel as if I bore the scar of Juggernaut upon my back day after day. I totally disbelieve in any sunrise to follow this pitch-black night. I believe I am going to see everything of a funereal purple color from this time forth and forever! But nobody guesses it. I don't tell anybody but you'' (71). On another occasion, she complained, "[O]ur family is so destitute of women it is really forlorn! No sisters, daughters, aunts, cousins, nothing but a howling wilderness of men!'' (50). Echoing the danger and pain expressed in the captivity narrative of her Puritan forebear Mary Rowlandson, who was imprisoned by those she deemed "savages,'' these words speak volumes about Thaxter's difficult, gifted life.

MAJOR WORKS AND THEMES

In all its guises, nature figures largely in Thaxter's work. Her first published poem, "Land-Locked," intimates the ambivalent relationship that she often depicted between humans and nature; in tandem with this theme is the sense of captivity also evident in "Imprisoned." Thaxter repeatedly depicted nature as beautiful and fearful, awe-ful and peaceful, both in her poems and in *Among the Isles of Shoals*. This conflict, or sense of realism, emerges in one passage in the latter when she describes the ocean as both nurturer and "enemy," "raging with senseless fury" (98): "In December the colors seem to fade out of the world. . . . The great, cool, whispering, delicious sea, that encircled us with a thousand caresses the beautiful summer through, turns slowly our sullen and inveterate enemy" (96).

The autobiographical *Among the Isles of Shoals* also highlights the isolation that was so prominent a feature of the writer's life, and it intimates a bleak view of gender relations and the cultural disempowerment of women. Thaxter's male islanders are strong and attractive, while her females are portrayed very differently: "It is strange that the sun and wind, which give such fine tints to the complexions of the lords of creation, should leave such hideous traces on the faces of women. When they are exposed to the same salt wind and clear sunshine they take the hue of dried fish, and become objects for men and angels to weep over" (61–62). Similarly, in a slightly later passage, she portrays "the women, many of whom have grown old before their time with hard work and bitter cares, with hewing of wood and drawing of water, turning of fish on the flakes to dry in the sun, endless household work and the cares of maternity," in wry contrast to their "lords," who "lounged about the rocks in their scarlet shirts in the sun, or 'held up the walls of the meeting-house' . . . with their brawny shoulders" (66). The women are "wrecks of humanity," and she concludes, "[D]espoiled and hopeless visions, it seemed as if youth and joy could never have been theirs" (66). A woman-identified woman, the writer explored women's perspectives in often indirect but powerful ways.

The apparently gratuitous or meaningless violence of both nature and human nature emerges as another theme in this volume; Thaxter tells the story, also published in *The Atlantic Monthly*, of the murder of two island women by a man whom they had assisted and employed. Asking why things happened as they did, and why the world was constituted as it was, whether implicitly or explicitly, was a frequent attitude of the writer's. A letter indicates this concern as it expresses another of her favorite themes, shipwreck: "It was perfectly still and bright. The huge vessel lay on the western side of the beach, not far from our morning-glory garden. Oh, such a sight! Crushed like an eggshell, broken in two, with the forward half standing upright and pointing to heaven with its splintered timbers. Her huge beams were snapped like sticks of macaroni . . . such a total and gigantic destruction is not to be described" (*Letters* 76–77).

Thaxter also wrote of nature in positive and loving terms. Her final book, *An Island Garden*, affirms the power of beauty as it refuses to portray a wholly romantic picture; her garden has both roses and slugs. Following the course of the seasons in her famous garden, Thaxter shares with the reader her labor and her love. The love of women, and especially of her mother, is a theme that Thaxter explores frequently in her poetry, where nature becomes an objective correlative for her feelings. These poems like "Alone" and "S.E.," often intense but rarely sentimental, were sometimes very modern in their restraint and attention to concrete image.

CRITICAL RECEPTION

William Dean Howells was one of the Thaxter's earliest supporters, pointing out that "something strangely full and bright came to her verse from the mystical environment of the ocean, like the luxury of leaf and tint that it gave the narrower flower-plots of her native isles" (124). Like many critics of the period, Howells characteristically highlighted the sunny aspects of Thaxter's poetry. Thaxter's work received a great deal of praise and admiration from other friends and contemporaries. Whittier, Jewett, Dickens, and Fields, among others, valued her work highly; the "sweet singer of the Isles of Shoals" (a title applied to Thaxter after her predecessor, Lydia Sigourney) was best known in her own lifetime as a poet.

As with many women writers, Thaxter's reputation waned after the turn of the century, as her work was dismissed or ignored by many New Critics, who failed to see its gendered modernity. Nevertheless, there were a few who took notice. Van Wyck Brooks valued her adult poetry. Writing in 1951, Perry D. Westbrook highlighted her unsentimental approach to nature; of "Tryst," he wrote: "The poem, though flabby in prosody, is not flabby in sentiment. It does not whine: it does not curse 'whatever brute and blackguard made the world.' It states a fact: nature is indifferent to man" (*Acres* 120). Comparing Thaxter to Emerson and Thoreau as well as to Wordsworth, Tennyson, and Arnold, he noted, "[N]o one, of course, would consider Celia Thaxter in any sense comparable to such men as Emerson, Melville, or Arnold." He proclaimed that "her achievement was small," and he values most her children's literature, calling it "exquisite" (*Acres* 137, 142). In 1964, Westbrook nevertheless acknowledged that "as a writer of prose, Celia Thaxter's position is unassailably in the first rank" ("Seeker" 506).

Contemporary work on the writer is still in the early stages. Barbara White's profile of the writer's life provides a discussion focusing on her life and making brief connections with the work of her contemporaries. Judith Fetterley and Marjorie Pryse situate Thaxter in the regionalist tradition, and they underscore her relationship with nature: "The mirroring and mothering that men and children expect to receive from women Thaxter finds as an adult in the landscape and in her imaginative recreation of place" (156). Karen Oakes focuses on the writer's alertness to both gender and class disadvantage in American society, while Pauline Woodward highlights "the essential femaleness of Thaxter's love poems" and gestures toward a new kind of critical approach with regard to the poet. The most complete analytical study of Thaxter is Jane Vallier's; in addition to providing details about the writer's life and highlighting, for example, her skill in conversation, Vallier assesses her poetry, folklore, children's writing, journalism, and naturalism; and she contextualizes Thaxter within her historical moment. The recent reissue of *An Island Garden* and the regular appearance of "popular" books on Thaxter suggest her continuing appeal to a contemporary audience.

WORKS CITED

Letters of Celia Thaxter. Edited by her friends A. F. [Annie Fields] and R. L. [Rose Lamb]. Boston: Houghton Mifflin, 1895.
Vallier, Jane. *Poet on Demand: The Life, Letters, and Works of Celia Thaxter*. Camden, ME: Downeast Books, 1982.

BIBLIOGRAPHY

Works by Celia Thaxter

Poetry and Children's Writing

Poems. New York: Hurd and Houghton, 1872.
Drift-Weed. Boston: Houghton, 1878.
Stories and Poems for Children. Boston: Houghton, 1878.
Poems for Children. Boston: Houghton Mifflin, 1882.
The Cruise of the Mystery, and Other Poems. Boston: Houghton Mifflin, 1886.
Idyls and Pastorals: A Home Gallery of Poetry and Art. Boston: Lothrop, 1886.
Verses. Boston: Lothrop, 1891.
The Poems of Celia Thaxter. Boston: Houghton Mifflin, 1896.
The Heavenly Guest. Edited by Oscar Laighton. Andover, MA: Smith and Coutts, 1935.

Prose and Journalism

Among the Isles of Shoals. Boston: J. R. Osgood & Co., 1873.
"A Memorable Murder." *Atlantic Monthly* (May 1875): 602–615.
An Island Garden. Boston: Houghton Mifflin, 1894.

Studies of Celia Thaxter

Armstrong, Tim. "Hardy, Thaxter, and History as Coincidence in 'The Convergence of the Twain.' " *Victorian Poetry* 30, no. 1 (1992): 29–42.
Brooks, Van Wyck. *New England: Indian Summer 1865–1915*. New York: Dutton, 1940.
Cary, Richard. "The Multi-Colored Spirit of Celia Thaxter." *Colby Library Quarterly* 6, no. 12 (1964): 512–536.

De Piza, Mary Dickson. "Celia Thaxter: Poet of the Isles of Shoals." Ph.D. diss, University of Pennsylvania, 1955.

Fetterley, Judith, and Marjorie Pryse, eds. *American Women Regionalists, 1850–1910.* New York: Norton, 1992.

Fields, Annie Adams. *Authors and Friends.* Boston: Houghton Mifflin, 1897.

Haugen, Einar. "Celia Thaxter and the Norwegians of the Isles of Shoals." In *Fin(s) de Siecle in Scandinavian Perspective,* edited by Faith Ingwersen and Harald S. Naess. Columbia, SC: Camden House, 1993.

Howells, William Dean. *Literary Friends and Acquaintance: A Personal Retrospect of American Authorship.* Edited by David F. Hiatt and Edwin H. Cady. Bloomington: University of Indiana Press, 1968.

Laighton, Oscar. *Ninety Years at the Isles of Shoals.* Boston: Star Island Corporation, 1971.

Myers, M. *Celia Thaxter: An Anthology in Memoriam (1835–1894).* Bristol, IN: Bristol Banner Press, 1994.

Oakes, Karen. ' "Colossal in Sheet-Lead': The Native American and Piscataqua Region Writers." In *A Noble and Dignified Stream: The Piscataqua Region in the Colonial Revival, 1860–1930,* edited by Sarah M. Giffen and Kevin M. Murphy. York, ME: Old York Historical Society, 1992. 165–176.

Older, Julia. *The Island Queen: Celia Thaxter of the Isles of Shoals.* Hancock, NH: Appledore Books, 1994.

Stubbs, M. Wilma. "Celia Laighton Thaxter, 1835–1894." *New England Quarterly* 8 (December 1935): 518–533.

Thaxter, Rosamond. *Sandpiper: The Life and Letters of Celia Thaxter, and Her Home on the Isles of Shoals, Her Family, Friends, and Favorite Poems.* Rev. ed. Francestown, NH: M. Jones, 1963.

Vaughn, Dorothy. "Celia Thaxter's Library." *Colby Library Quarterly* 6, no. 12 (1964): 536–550.

Walker, Cheryl, ed. *American Women Poets of the Nineteenth Century: An Anthology.* New Brunswick: Rutgers University Press, 1992.

Westbrook, Perry D. *Acres of Flint, Writers of Rural New England, 1870–1900.* Washington, D.C.: Scarecrow Press, 1951.

———. "Celia Thaxter: Seeker of the Unattainable." *Colby Library Quarterly* 6, no. 12 (1964): 499–512.

White, Barbara A. "*Legacy* Profile: Celia Thaxter (1835–1894)." *Legacy: A Journal of Nineteenth-Century American Women Writers* 7, no. 1 (1990): 59–64.

Woodward, Pauline. "Celia Thaxter's Love Poems." *Colby Library Quarterly* 23, no. 3 (1987): 144–155.

METTA VICTORIA FULLER VICTOR (1831–1885)

Katharine A. Parham

BIOGRAPHY

Metta Victoria Fuller Victor was born on March 2, 1831, the third of five children. Her parents were Adonijah Fuller and Lucy Williams Fuller. Victor was a precocious writer, publishing a historical novel, *Last Days of Tul* (1847), when she was fifteen. Befriended by the influential editor Nathaniel Parker Willis, Victor wrote poems and stories for the *New York Home Journal* while yet in her teens. Victor's older sister, Frances, was also a writer, best known today for her histories of the West. The two collaborated on *Poems of Sentiment and Imagination*, edited by Rufus Wilmot Griswold, editor and friend of Edgar Allan Poe.

In addition to her early work in Willis's journal, Victor published in numerous other periodicals throughout her career, including *The Saturday Evening Post* and *Godey's Lady's Book*. She also served as editor and contributor to *The Home*. In 1870, she contracted to write stories exclusively for *The New York Weekly*, for which she was paid $25,000 (Johannsen 279).

Although Victor was reported to have married a Dr. Morse in 1850, little is known about that marriage. In 1856 Victor married Orville J. Victor, an editor and writer often credited with developing the dime novel formula for Beadle. The marriage produced nine children and was productive professionally as well.

Metta Victor died on June 26, 1885. Despite her long and successful career, an obituary writer noted that at the time of her death she "was comparatively unknown to the present generation" (Taylor 520).

MAJOR WORKS AND THEMES

Best known as a dime novelist for the house of Beadle and Adams, Victor was a successful practitioner of nearly every popular nineteenth-century genre, publishing poetry and advice books in addition to sensational, sentimental, and humorous fiction.

Her fiction is marked by topicality and exciting plots. In the 1850s she wrote two temperance novels, *The Senator's Son* (1853) and *Fashionable Dissipation* (1853). *Mormon Wives* (1856) decried polygamy. Appearing in 1861, *Maum Guinea and Her Plantation "Children"* was the most popular of her dime novels and was credited by contemporaries with swaying British opinion to the Union cause. Twentieth-century critics recognize her as the author of the first detective novel, *The Dead Letter* (1864), written under the pseudonym Seeley Regester.

Victor also produced a number of humorous works, often under the pseudonyms Mrs. Mark Peabody and Walter T. Gray. These include *Miss Slimmens' Boarding House* (1882) and *A Bad Boy's Diary* (1880).

CRITICAL RECEPTION

Maum Guinea was well received by Union loyalists, deemed "as absorbing as *Uncle Tom's Cabin*" by Abraham Lincoln, and praised as a "telling shot" by Henry Ward Beecher (Harvey 39, 43). Like Stowe's novel, however, *Maum Guinea* has been criticized by twentieth-century critics for its use of stereotypes, particularly those associating black women with illicit sexuality (Carby 26, 33–34).

Presenting Victor's earliest work, Willis declared, in typically florid style, that her poetry bore "unquestionable marks of true genius" (Coggeshall 518). But what was perhaps most striking to both modern and contemporary readers is the range of work produced by Victor. As one nineteenth-century reader remarked, "Mrs. Victor is unusually endowed; her success has been remarkable in poetry of imagination and fancy; in humor and satire, prose and verse; in fiction and romance; in tales of purely imaginative creation; as well as in the departments of literary criticism and essays upon popular themes" (Coggeshall 519).

WORKS CITED

Carby, Hazel V. *Reconstructing Womanhood: The Emergence of the Afro-American Woman Novelist.* New York: Oxford University Press, 1987. 26, 33–34.

Coggeshall, William T. *The Poets and Poetry of the West: With Biographical and Critical Notices.* Columbus, OH: Follett, Foster & Co., 1860. 518–526.

Harvey, Charles M. "The Dime Novel in American Life." *Atlantic Monthly* C (July 1907): 37–45.

Johannsen, Albert. *The House of Beadle and Adams and Its Dime and Nickel Novels.* Vol. 2. Norman: University of Oklahoma Press, 1950.

Taylor, William R. "Victor, Metta Victoria Fuller." In *Notable American Women 1607–1950: A Biographical Dictionary,* edited by Edward T. James. Vol. 3. Cambridge, MA: Belknap Press of Harvard University, 1971.

BIBLIOGRAPHY

Works by Metta Victor

Poetry

Poems of Sentiment and Imagination. With Frances Foster Victor. New York: A. S. Barnes & Co., 1850.

The Arctic Queen. Sandusky, OH: N.p., 1856.

Novels and Short Story Collections

Last Days of Tul; a Romance of the Yucatan. 1847.

Fresh Leaves from Western Woods. Buffalo, NY: Derby & Co., 1852.

Fashionable Dissipation. New York: United States Book Co., 1853.

The Senator's Son, or, The Maine Law; a Last Refuge; a Story Dedicated to the Lawmakers. Also published under the title *Parke Madison; or, Fashion the Father of Intemperance, as Shown in the Life of the Senator's Son.* Cleveland, OH: Tooker and Gatchel, 1853.

Morman Wives; a Narrative of Facts Stranger than Fiction. Also published under the title *Lives of Female Mormons.* New York: Derby & Jackson, 1856.

Miss Slimmens' Window, and Other Papers. New York: Derby & Jackson, 1859.

Alice Wilde: The Raftman's Daughter. A Forest Romance. New York: Beadle & Co., 1860.

The Backwoods' Bride. A Romance of Squatter Life. New York: Beadle & Co., 1860.

The Emerald Necklace; or, Mrs. Butterby's Boarder. New York: Beadle & Co., 1860.

Myrtle; or, The Child of the Prairie. New York: Beadle & Co., 1860.

The Gold Hunters: A Picture of Western Character and Pike's Peak Life. New York: Beadle & Co., 1861.

Maum Guinea and Her Plantation "Children"; or, Holiday-week on a Louisiana Estate; a Slave Romance . . . New York: Beadle & Co., 1861.

Uncle Ezekiel and His Exploits on Two Continents. New York: Beadle & Co., 1861.

The Unionist's Daughter; a Tale of the Rebellion in Tennessee. Also published under the title *Turkey Dan; or, The Unionist's Daughter. A Tale of Tennessee.* New York: Beadle & Adams, 1862.

Jo Daviess' Client; or, "Courting" in Kentucky. New York: Beadle & Co., 1863.

The Country Cousin. New York: Beadle & Adams, 1864.

The Dead Letter, an American Romance. By Seeley Regester. New York: Beadle & Co., 1864.

The Two Hunters; or, The Cañon Camp. A Romance of the Santa Fé Trail. New York: Beadle & Co., 1865.

Who Was He? A Story of Two Lives. New York: Beadle & Co., 1866.

The Betrayed Bride; or, Wedded But Not Won. New York: Starr & Co., 1869.

The Figure Eight; or, The Mystery of Meredith Place. New York: Beadle & Co., 1869.

Nat Wolfe; or, The Gold Hunters. A Romance of Pike's Peak and New York. New York: Beadle & Adams, 1874.

Black Eyes and Blue; or, The Peril of Beauty and the Power of Purity. New York: Beadle & Adams, 1876.

Passing the Portal; or, A Girl's Struggle. New York: G. W. Carleton & Co., 1876.

Brave Barbara; or, First Love or No Love. New York: Beadle & Adams, 1877.
Dora Elmyr's Worst Enemy; or, Guilty or Not Guilty. New York: Street & Smith, 1878.
A Woman's Hand. New York: Beadle & Adams, 1878.
The Locked Heart; or, Sir Caryl's Sacrifice. New York: Beadle & Adams, 1879.
A Bad Boy's Diary. By Walter T. Gray. New York: J. S. Ogilvie, 1880.
The Black Riddle; or, Girlish Charms and Golden Dowers. A Story of Morley Beeches. New York: Beadle & Adams, 1880.
Madcap, the Little Quakeress; or, The Navel Cadet's Wooing. New York: Beadle & Adams, 1880.
The Mysterious Guardian; or, Little Clare, the Opera Singer. New York: Beadle & Adams, 1880.
Pretty and Proud; or, The Gold-bug of Fr'isco. A Story of a Girl's Folly. New York: Beadle & Adams, 1880.
Pursued to the Altar. New York: Beadle & Adams, 1880.
At His Mercy; or, A Woman's Fight for Honor. New York: Beadle & Adams, 1881.
The Blunders of a Bashful Man. New York: J. S. Ogilvie, 1881.
Miss Slimmens' Boarding House. By Walter T. Gray. New York: J. S. Ogilvie, 1882.
The War of Hearts. New York: Beadle & Adams, 1882.
A Wild Girl; or, Love's Glamour. New York: Beadle & Adams, 1882.
A Woman's Sorrow; or, The Blot on the Escutcheon. New York: Beadle & Adams, 1882.
The Bad Boy Abroad; the Funniest Book of the Age. New York: J. S. Ogilvie, 1883.
Morley Beeches; or, Girlish Charms and Golden Dowers. New York: Beadle & Adams, 1883.
Abijah Beanpole in New York: Detailing the Misfortunes and Mishaps of a Country Storekeeper on a Business Visit to the Great City of New York. New York: G. W. Carleton & Co., 1884.
Mrs. Rasher's Curtain Lectures. New York: J. S. Ogilvie, 1884.
A Naughty Girl's Diary. London: General Publishing Co., 1884.
The Bad Boy at Home and His Experiences in Trying to Become an Editor. New York: J. S. Ogilvie, 1885.
A Good Boy's Diary. New York: G. W. Carleton, 1885.
The Brown Princess. A Tale of the Death Cañon. New York: Street & Smith, 1888.
. . . *The Phantom Wife.* New York: Street & Smith, 1888.
A Bad Boy's Diary. Part Two. New York: J. S. Ogilvie, 1890.
. . . *Born to Betray; or, A Game Well Played.* New York: Street & Smith, 1890.
. . . *The Gay Captain.* New York: Street & Smith, 1891.
Who Owned the Jewels? Or, The Heiress of the Sandalwood Chest. New York: Street & Smith, 1891.
The Bad Boy in the Country. New York: J. S. Ogilvie, 1892.
The Georgie Papers, Giving the Humorous Adventures and Experiences of Georgie, Bill Johnson, Marie, and Several Other Persons. New York: J. S. Ogilvie, 1897.

Studies of Metta Victor

Baym, Nina. *Woman's Fiction: A Guide to Novels by and about Women in America 1820–1870.* 2nd ed. Urbana: University of Illinois Press, 1993. 267–268.
Biamonte, Gloria A. "Detection and the Text: Reading Three American Women of Mystery." Ph.D. diss., University of Massachusetts, 1991.

Evans, Clark. "*Maum Guinea*: Beadle's Unusual Jewel." *Dime Novel Roundup: A Magazine Devoted to the Collecting, Preservation and Study of Old-Time Dime and Nickel Novels* 63, no. 4 (August 1994): 77–79.

Johannsen, Albert. *The House of Beadle and Adams and Its Dime and Nickel Novels.* Vol. 2. Norman: University of Oklahoma Press, 1950. 278–285.

Nickerson, Catherine Ross. "The Domestic Detective Novel: Gothicism, Domesticity, and Investigation in American Women's Writing, 1865–1920." Ph.D. diss., Yale University, 1991.

Panek, Leroy Lad. *Probable Cause: Crime Fiction in America.* Bowling Green, OH: Bowling Green State University Popular Press, 1990. 20–24.

Rahn, B. J. "Seeley Regester: America's First Detective Novelist." In *The Sleuth and the Scholar: Origins, Evolution, and Current Trends in Detective Fiction*, edited by Barbara A. Rader and Howard G. Zettler. Westport, CT: Greenwood Press, 1988. 47–61.

Simmons, Michael K. "*Maum Guinea*: or, A Dime Novelist Looks at Abolition." *Journal of Popular Culture* 10 (summer 1976): 81–87.

ELIZABETH STUART PHELPS WARD (1844–1911)

Monika M. Elbert

BIOGRAPHY

One of the most prolific American writers of the nineteenth century, Elizabeth Stuart Phelps Ward was born on August 31, 1844. She was the first of three children born to Austin Phelps, a Boston minister and later a professor at Andover Theological Seminary, and to Elizabeth Wooster Stuart, a well-known and best-selling author. Though she was christened ''Mary Gray Phelps'' after a close friend of her mother, she changed her name to her mother's some time after her mother's death. In 1848, when Mary was four, the family moved to Andover, Massachusetts, and when Mary was only eight, her mother died of ''brain fever.'' Probably the name change occurred shortly after her mother's death, though the date has been disputed by her biographers. The legacy left by her mother and by her maternal grandmother, Abigail Clark Stuart, was a haunting vision of women authors sacrificing their own development and careers for the sake of husbands and children. Both mother and grandmother shared the similar fates of marriage to overbearing, self-centered ministers. Both women suffered ill health in their attempts to juggle their writing careers with household demands and familial obligations. In her autobiography, *Chapters from a Life* (1896), Phelps asserted, ''Her [mother's] last book and her last baby came together and killed her'' (12). Elizabeth Jr. would be spared the burdens of childbearing and child raising and would not get married until late in life (1888) to a journalist and aspiring (but second-rate) writer, Herbert Dickinson Ward, who was seventeen years her junior. However, the lives of her frustrated maternal forebears seemed to foreshadow her own unhappy marriage to a rather parasitic and insensitive young man.

As a child and adolescent, Elizabeth received her formal education at Mrs.

Edward's School for Young Ladies in Andover. But acquaintance with death also served as a formative influence on the young child. In a four-year period, from the ages of eight to twelve, Elizabeth lost her mother, paternal grandfather, maternal grandmother, and aunt/stepmother. This encounter with death at an early age would leave its mark on her later writings, especially in her *Gates* novels, in which the dead are resurrected to an infinitely better life than the one they experienced on earth—because it is based on feminine and feminist principles.

Her mother's life and death would prove a strong influence on her works, but her reading, at sixteen, of Elizabeth Barrett Browning's *Aurora Leigh* (published 1856) also had a profound effect upon Elizabeth. A blank-verse novel, *Aurora Leigh* exposes the problems facing a young single woman artist. To preserve her integrity as an artist and as a single woman, Aurora refuses to yield to a marriage proposal by her sexist and overbearing suitor, Romny, so that she can pursue her career as an artist. Only after he has become sensitized through an accident by fire (in which he is blinded) does Aurora accept him, knowing full well that he cannot expect dependence or subservience from her after this event. The problematics of a female artist, shared by Aurora Leigh and by Phelps's own mother, would be examined in Phelps's portraiture of her favorite heroine, Avis, in her favorite novel, *The Story of Avis* (1877).

Though Elizabeth Stuart Phelps Ward acknowledged the influence of her second stepmother, Mary Ann Johnson, whom her father Austin married in 1858, as positive, she was definitely more inspired by the example of her real writer-mother. According to her autobiography, Phelps, while at school in Andover, wrote three novels, which she shared with an anonymous friend, but these alleged works have been lost. In the early 1860s, when she completed and left school, Phelps became ill; this was one of the first of many times in her life when completion of a project would precede illness, and it was in keeping with a family pattern. However, at this time, she began to write various stories, and with its appearance in *Harper's New Monthly Magazine* in 1864, one particular Civil War story, "A Sacrifice Consumed," marked the beginning of her literary career.

In the 1860s Phelps began earning a living as a writer. Early in her career, she wrote didactic Sunday School works, which she herself later described as "hack work" (*Chapters* 81). Many of the works Phelps wrote at this time were children's stories and books. However, 1868 was a banner year for Phelps, as it established her as a best-selling author. She published one of her best-known early stories, "The Tenth of January" (*Atlantic Monthly*, later to be anthologized in *Men, Women, and Ghosts* [1879]). In this story Phelps renders a fictional account of a real event, the fire that raced through the Pemberton Mills and killed all the mill girls. The year 1868 also saw the publication of *The Gates Ajar*, arguably the most popular of her works in her time. This novel was the first of a series of three *Gates* novels and one *Gates* drama, which focus on the experiences of recently deceased characters enjoying a utopian afterlife. It was an apt theme for someone who had lost her loved ones at an early age, and on a national level, it would provide some consolation to a country that had just witnessed a bloody and turbulent Civil War. Phelps was always politically aware and responsible; private and public concerns converged in her works.

In the late 1860s and early 1870s, Phelps addressed women's rights in her fiction and in her journal essays. The causes she promoted were many: women's suffrage, women's education, improvement in women's working conditions, equal marriages, women's economic independence, compassion, and financial assistance for unwed mothers and for poverty-stricken women. The most famous works of this period are *Hedged In* (1870) and *The Silent Partner* (1871), in which women work against the odds and eventually turn down proposals by their suitors in order to lead a life of independence and dignity and to help others. Phelps spent various summers between 1869 and 1876 at several seaside retreats near Gloucester, Massachusetts, where she became interested in the welfare of Gloucester fishermen and became a temperance advocate from 1875 to 1879. Her experiences in Gloucester provided much of the material for her early local color short stories (as ''Jack the Fisherman'' and ''The Madonna of the Tubs,'' two of her favorite short stories, later anthologized in *Fourteen to One* [1891]) and for her semiautobiographical *An Old Maid's Paradise* (1879), a series of humorous sketches revolving around the life of a single woman who has no male protector, and its sequel, *Burglars in Paradise* (1886).

In the late 1870s and early 1880s, Phelps wrote novels and short fiction dealing with strong, rebellious, independent women, who, if they didn't avoid the burden of matrimony, were able to question the institution of marriage, among these, *The Story of Avis* (1877), *Friends* (1881), and *Doctor Zay* (1882). The mid-1880s were turbulent years for Phelps. She had suffered physical breakdowns after her completion of *The Silent Partner* (1871) and *The Story of Avis* (1877), but the decline in her health escalated rapidly in the 1880s. She had various infirmities, of which chronic insomnia might have been a symptom or a cause, and she experienced episodes of neuralgia, paralysis, and poor eyesight. She was also taxed psychologically by the continued sense of loss in her life. Her older brother, Stuart, a talented professor, died in a freak accident in 1883. Her father, whose approbation she had always sought (striking resemblance to the negative father-daughter relationship experienced by her mother), wrote two caustic essays against women's rights and women's suffrage, an obvious affront to Phelps's own writing. (After her father died in 1890, she wrote a loving tribute to him in *Austin Phelps: A Memoir* [1891], almost as if still looking for recognition from him in death.) Her own declining health from the 1880s on, too, might have contributed to her darkening vision and the sense of resignation common to her female protagonists in such later novels as *The Successors of Mary the First* (1901), *Avery* (1902), *Walled In* (1907), and *Though Life Us Do Part* (1908), in which women are actual invalids, dependent on their husbands for their physical well-being, or psychological cripples, dependent on men for emotional and economic sustenance.

In Phelps's own life, independence had graced her existence, but failing health made her take on a husband. Phelps's unfortunate marriage to Herbert Dickinson Ward in 1888 did not seem to bolster her spirits or her physical constitution. The marriage was apparently happy for the first couple of years, but after that, the couple spent much of their time separated, as Ward, clearly benefiting from his wife's financial security, spent months alone traveling, yachting, or in the winter, convalescing by himself in the South (as he, too, suffered from ill health). Along with her rapidly declining health, marriage to Ward seemed to detract from Phelps's writing career and from her earlier promising vision for women's progress. Out of this feeling of resignation emerges a more traditional woman protagonist and a negative plight for women. It is almost as if Phelps had foreseen her own future in *The Story of Avis* (1877), where a woman's creative powers rapidly deteriorate after marriage to a self-serving and insecure college professor. Phelps and her husband coauthored various unsuccessful novels; indeed, their collaborative ventures were dismal. In her own writings, Phelps became more conciliatory toward marriage and depicts more stereotypical roles for women. During this period, too, she wrote antivivisection essays, and two of her novels, *Trixy* (1904) and *Though Life Us Do Part* (1908), also speak out against animal cruelty. Compared to her earlier novels, these works are bland, dispassionate, and lifeless, and the plots are contrived and predictable. Only in *Confessions of a Wife* (1902) does Phelps recapture some of the earlier liveliness and passion (though not the style) of the best-seller *Avis*, but it is published under a pen name, Mary Adams, as if to ward off possible negative responses from an increasingly conservative female readership. From 1903 on, Phelps suffered from a serious heart condition, which prevented her from spending any winters with her convalescent husband in the South. Phelps died of myocardial degeneration in her Newton, Massachusetts, home on January 28, 1911. Like one of the protagonists in her novels, she found herself alone in life as in death.

MAJOR WORKS AND THEMES

Phelps wrote fifty-seven books (including five collections of short stories), as well as hundreds of essays and short stories, two collections of verse, and even two plays, though she did not fare well with the latter two genres. Then as now, she is best known for her novels, though the *Gates* novels were more popular then, and the most widely read of her novels today have been reprinted: *The Silent Partner* (1871), *The Story of Avis* (1877), and *Doctor Zay* (1882). She was an advocate of women's rights throughout her career, but she was also a champion for other social causes, as workers' rights, homeopathic medicine, temperance, and antivivisection. Many of her novels were serialized in journals, such as *Harper's New Monthly, Atlantic Monthly, Ladies' Home Journal, Independent, Woman's Home Companion*, and *Harper's Bazar*, before being published as novels. The "Female Bildungsroman" was the prototype and mainstay of her best works, but unlike many sentimental writers of her time, she did not celebrate ''true womanhood'' or depict marriage as the ultimate goal or reward for women. She insisted on a balance of power in marriage, and though she did not condemn marriage entirely, she frequently renders the tense relationship between the genders as a type of civil war.

The most famous of the marriage novels, *The Story of Avis*, tells the story of a thwarted woman artist, Avis Dobell, who has shown talent as a painter and has even studied art in Europe. However, she finally gives in to the marriage proposal of a persistent suitor, Philip Ostrander, a teacher at Harmouth University, and almost immediately loses her private space and both her time and inclination to paint. Once married, Avis finds herself totally responsible for child care and house management and eventually falls ill from exhaustion. But Philip, to do him justice, is just as overwhelmed with the obligations imposed upon the male breadwinner. His performance on the faculty of Harmouth University is poor, and he is forced out of his position; he has an affair, leaves for a convalescent vacation in France, and finally becomes ill with consumption. In the end, Avis loses her son to pneumonia and her husband to a freak accident and is forced to raise her daughter by herself and to begin a life not as a painter but as a teacher. She has not fulfilled her artistic goals, but she imagines a better life for her daughter, significantly named ''Wait,'' whom she educates in a nontraditional way to become independent and self-reliant.

Avis Dobell and Philip Ostrander can be perceived as the prototypes of many of Phelps's protagonists in her early ''marriage'' works. The novel *Friends* exposes the difficulties men and women face in being friends ''only.'' Reliance Strong, enjoying her widowhood and life as a philanthropist and temperance reformer, finally yields to her zealous suitor's proposal for marriage. Although Charles Nordhull is a kind friend of her deceased husband and a decent man who advocates equality between the sexes, the ending of the novel is rather foreboding in its suggestion that marriage will be far more advantageous to Charles than to Reliance. In *An Old Maid's Paradise*, the ''old maid'' Corona is able to ward off men's advances and to live harmoniously in a home of her own with her maid and friend, Puelvir. But in its sequel, *Burglars in Paradise*, the utopian feminine household deteriorates, the women squabble, and in the end, there is a suggestion that Corona will give in to a suitor's charm and companionship.

In *The Silent Partner* and in *Doctor Zay*, Phelps creates the only two women who are happy and fulfilled women, leading independent lives, devoted to their careers, not to men. *The Silent Partner* depicts Perley Kelso, a woman rising from the level of spoiled rich daughter to intelligent and beneficent businesswoman. After her father's accidental death in his mill, his two business partners try to oust Perley out, but she is naturally clever, educates herself in the world of work, and thus becomes a very powerful and independent voice in the business. Moreover, she uses her wealth and influence to help the poor mill people improve their working conditions and lots in life. She gives up her rich fiancé, one of the partners in the firm, and becomes the strong ''silent partner'' in the business. Because she is married to her job, helping the poor millworkers, Perley later turns down another proposal from a well-meaning, benevolent business-man, who has worked his way up from the working class and who also tries, with Perley, to improve the working conditions of the mill people.

Similarly, in *Dr. Zay*, Phelps portrays a strong, self-sufficient woman in Dr. Zay, a country doctor who cares infinitely more for the welfare of her patients than she does about marriage. When Waldo Yorke alights in Dr. Zay's village, it is literally by accident: He has been thrown off his horse and is in need of Dr. Zay's medical attention. Though trained as a lawyer, Waldo is a dilettante who practices no profession and who lives off his uncle's legacy. His inertia, even before the fall, is in stark contrast to Dr. Zay's mission to serve the women and children of the community. Waldo falls in love with her during a much-too-lengthy period of recuperation. Phelps masterfully reverses traditional gen-der expectations, as she renders him the feminized lovelorn patient. Dr. Zay finally accepts his marriage proposal, but she is worried about what marriage will mean for her career. The book ends with Dr. Zay's anxiety—before we see how an egalitarian marriage might work.

Hedged In, one of the most daring of Phelps's works, because it deals with a strong antimaternal sentiment and with the struggle of a poverty-stricken "fallen" woman, shows how single womanhood fares among the working class. Without the benefits of Perley Kelso's money or Dr. Zay's middle-class edu-cation, the protagonist, Nixy Trent, is literally "hedged in" a slum life. Sister-hood does not come easily in this world, and there are no suitors willing to protect Nixy, an orphaned sixteen-year-old girl who finds herself alone and pregnant. Nixy learns very quickly that her baby boy is a real liability when she is looking for a decent job as caretaker or servant, so she abandons her infant. She realizes the hypocrisy of so-called Christian women, who'll not grant her work when they find out about her past. Finally, a charitable woman, Mar-garet Purcell, takes Nixy in when she is on the brink of despair. In time, Nixy is educated and becomes a popular teacher in the town, only after many mis-givings of the hypocritical neighbors, when Nixy reclaims her lost child, who later dies. But in a middle-class, moralistic way, Phelps has Nixy become an invalid and die a martyr's death.

Though Phelps celebrates bonding between women in her early works, which might reflect her own close connection with her friend and personal physician, Mary Briggs Harris (who died in 1886), she depicts strained and imbalanced relationships between and among women in her later works. Even though Phelps does celebrate the memory of her many faithful servants and friends in her later work *The Successors of Mary the First* (1901), it is a romanticized and unequal relationship between women of different classes that is portrayed. This uneasy type of subordination/adoration is common to her narratives of friendships be-tween mistress and servant. In Phelps's later works, male physicians or close male relatives would often replace the trusted servant of eccentric or invalid women.

In fact, men become increasingly more important in her fictional works, so that they are indeed the focus in her later phase of writing (after the 1880s). Whether it was her father's declining position, professionally and healthwise, the accidental death of her brother, or the pathetic development of her husband as a man and writer, she began to sympathize more frequently with professional men's plight in the workplace. If marriages fail, it is because men become dissatisfied with their work, or they become ill, and it is up to the wives to redeem them. Marriages are only resuscitated when men are repentant and atone for their ills to the wives. Women themselves are portrayed victimized or invalid but patient and self-sacrificing, who are ready to help their husbands or brothers regain their professional standing or health. Thus, for example, in *The Gates Between* (1887), the workaholic doctor who ignores the welfare of his wife meets an untimely death and undergoes a process of rehabilitation in heaven, which allows him to see the feminine virtues of his wife. He does ultimately repent, and his wife does join him in heaven, but the final image of his creeping, clinging wife is disturbing. Similarly, in *Confessions of a Wife*, Marna Trent is deserted by her husband Dana when she becomes overwhelmed with child care and house care. After an affair, a desertion, and an addiction to opium, he returns home, and Marna accepts the wifely challenge of nursing him back to health. Cara Sterling, the female protagonist in *Though Life Us Do Part*, shares a similar fate. She marries the drinking, womanizing Dr. Chaunceford Dane, who soon becomes bored with her, has an affair, and abandons her and her child. She embarks on a new life as an independent woman and becomes a successful businesswoman. When Chaunceford returns, repentant and disfigured from a shipwreck, she accepts this new, improved version of a husband.

Most alarming about these later works is Phelps's readiness to blame the stereotypical superficial flirt for the men's indiscretions. From Barbara in *Avis* to Myrton's wife Tessa in *Walled In* to Mrs. Douce Marriot in *Though Life Us Do Part*, the frivolous seductress seems to become the bane of men's existence, when she is actually a way for them to escape their own thwarted ambitions. Instead of chastising the men for their own shortcomings, Phelps depicts a negative image of the sexually free woman and holds up as the preferred image the self-sacrificing woman. Thus, in *Walled In*, Professor Myrton becomes an invalid after falling off his steam carriage and finds himself totally disconnected from his impractical but fun-loving wife Tessa, who flirts with his students and drowns on a canoeing expedition with one of his ex-students. As an invalid, Myrton falls in love with his sister-in-law, Honor, who, conveniently, as a nurse, is able to cure him with excessive and blind devotion.

Though *A Singular Life* (1895) presents a more honorable man, the minister Emanuel Bayard, he also lets himself be spoiled by his housekeeper Jane and later his wife Helen, who seem to enjoy devoting themselves to him selflessly. Yet there is something redeeming and noble about Emanuel as he rebels against a patriarchal Church; he was, in fact, Phelps's favorite male protagonist (*Chapters* 273), and he was also perhaps an idealized version of what she wanted her father Austin to be. Though Emanuel has studied to be a minister under the direction of Helen's conservative father, Professor Carruth, he breaks with Church doctrine to become a true practicing Christian. He establishes a successful ministry in a poor fishing village, and his gentle and noncondescending temperance mission makes him loved by those he reforms, among them, the prostitute and the alcoholic wife-beater. The "Christian hero" is finally killed by the forces representing the liquor business.

Even early on in her career, Phelps recognized the potentially dehumanizing effect of the marketplace world. To this end, she created the "Gates" trilogy, Phelps's contribution to American utopian literature (which predated Bellamy's *Looking Backward*). The Christian sense of compassion and ethics that informs these works is in stark contrast to the way businesses are run, and the novels serve as antidotes to the evils of the man-made world. Whether one considers the novels religious or utopian, the ends are the same: to show how a more feminized perspective would ameliorate social conditions. The heavenly setting in *The Gates* works offers a feminist utopian lifestyle with extended child-care and communal support networks.

In *The Gates Ajar*, the bereaved Mary, who has lost her brother Roy in the Civil War, is nurtured back to emotional health by her Aunt Winifred Forceythe, who convinces her that spirits are reunited in an afterlife and that she will see her deceased relatives one day. The aunt goes against Church doctrine in elaborating on the utopian vision for women in an afterlife, but her message is more fulfilling than that of the dour clergymen. The system of support that Winifred advocates is only a presentiment of the loving community that awaits Mary, who inherits, literally, her aunt's daughter Faith and, figuratively, her aunt's faith. In *Beyond the Gates*, another Mary, the forty-year-old protagonist, unconscious with cerebral fever, has a vision that she dies and is led by her deceased father to a paradise where women are encouraged to cultivate their intellectual and sensory as well as spiritual sides and where women find reliable men as their partners and teachers. Mary, after having lived a charitable, unselfish life, learns the pleasures of rest in the afterlife. Moreover, she discovers that all the feminine qualities denigrated during her earthly life are valued above all others in heaven. Though this might be wishful thinking on Phelps's part, the society is an improvement over the urban wasteland that she criticizes in so many of her works. In *The Gates Between*, the last of the series, Phelps presents a male's introduction to a feminized heaven. The eminent workaholic physician, Esmerald Thorne, dies a fitting death when his rushing horse goes mad and causes an accident. He finds himself in a setting where his intelligence and prestige have little value; indeed, he discovers that the nurturing ability of his wife, Helen, has far greater effect than his intellect in the afterlife. Much of the time he spends mourning the absence of his wife, whom he has treated so shabbily and inconsiderately during his life. He learns the nurturing process when he has to take parental charge of his now-deceased son. The earthly physician undergoes a spiritual transformation, so that his increased kindness makes him deserving of a reunion with his wife in heaven.

Phelps also experimented with techniques and forms other than the female or male "bildungsroman" or feminist utopian fiction, and here, too, her collections of stories often replicate the concerns and subplots of the novels. For example, with their supernatural emphasis, the "Gates" novels approach the tone of the Gothic, and many of the stories in Phelps's *Men, Women, and Ghosts* have Gothic elements. In another vein, her local color works, *An Old Maid's Paradise* and *Burglars in Paradise*, and several of the stories in *Sealed Orders* (1880) and *Fourteen to One*, about the seafaring people she knew in Gloucester, Massachusetts, are precursors to the writings of Mary W. Freeman and Sarah Orne Jewett later on in the century.

Phelps wrote many elegiac tales and subplots in her novels about the devastating effects of the Civil War on the female psyche. In the late nineteenth century, there was a widespread tradition among male writers to write Civil War combat narratives from the male perspective, but Phelps would tell another story. From her first story "A Sacrifice Consumed" to her last novella, *Comrades* (1911), Phelps describes the process whereby women were abandoned by lovers and husbands in the Civil War. At times, it makes them stronger, more self-reliant women. But in many cases, as in "The Oath of Allegiance," the woman leads a life of self-abnegation in order to preserve the memory of her departed loved one. It has been speculated that Phelps herself lost a close male friend, Samuel Thompson, during the war. Perhaps the consolation narrative of *The Gates Ajar* is related to her own personal grieving process.

Throughout her career, Phelps's themes and interests focus on the creative woman's dilemma with marriage and motherhood; woman's bonding with female (and, later, male) friends, as an alternative family support system; a utopian/religious afterlife as a critique of contemporary social evils; the public's blindness toward the working class; alternative practices to patriarchal invasive medicine; and men's sense of imprisonment due to restrictive social roles. It is generally agreed that her themes are more innovative and interesting than her style.

CRITICAL RECEPTION

During her time, Elizabeth Stuart Phelps came to be known as the author of the "Gates" novels, which were more sentimental than her other works and well received by the public and by the critics; *The Gates Ajar* was the most popular and best-selling of the series. *The Story of Avis* might be among the most celebrated of her novels for modern readers, but during Phelps's time, it received hostile reviews and criticism for attacking and denouncing the sacred institutions of marriage and motherhood, and Phelps would never criticize marriage so blatantly in the future except for one last time, in *Confessions of a Wife*, which she wrote under a pseudonym. The more conservative and male-centered *A Singular Life* (1895) met with greater success. Perhaps an anonymous contemporary review (1897) in the *Woman's Journal* said it best: Whereas Howells puts men and women into separate spheres, Phelps "shakes up and wakes up" and makes both men and women interact in one world (quoted in Kessler, *Elizabeth Stuart Phelps* 102). John Greenleaf Whittier and T. W. Higginson praised her work, and the latter went so far as to say that Phelps showed "more genius" than Alcott or Stowe but that her zeal made her "literary execution" less successful (127). Other reviews compared her writing to Bret Harte's realism. In the early twentieth century, male recorders of literary history included Phelps in their works; Fred Lewis Pattee and V. L. Parrington give praise and criticize her in equal measure, while Arthur Hobson Quinn and Van Wyck Brooks point out her strengths as a realist writer, with Quinn going so far as to compare *The Silent Partner* to Dickens's fiction.

Phelps's reputation as a writer diminished after her death, and it took the feminist movement and the critics of the 1960s to resurrect her. Since then, a plethora of essays have been published, especially on *Dr. Zay, The Story of Avis, The Silent Partner*, and *Beyond the Gates.*

The first book-length biography, published in 1939 by Mary Angela Bennett, contains an excellent bibliography. Currently, the best, most thorough biography on Phelps is Carol Farley Kessler's *Elizabeth Stuart Phelps* (Twayne, 1982), while Lori Duin Kelly's work also serves as a valuable introduction to Phelps's life and work. Susan Coultrap-McQuin's introduction is also helpful: By placing Phelps in the context of a shifting literary marketplace, less receptive to women's struggle for selfhood, she accounts for the changes in Phelps's writing. Josephine Donovan, in her analysis of *Burglars in Paradise*, places Phelps within the context of New England women local color writers.

Susan Harris shows Phelps's importance among other nineteenth-century American women writers and commends her for showing the similarities between women's oppression and workers' exploitation in *The Silent Partner*. Mari Jo Buhle and Florence Howe also comment on the socioeconomic context of *The Silent Partner* and point out Rebecca Harding Davis's influence on Phelps. Barbara Bardes and Suzanne Gossett read Phelps's *The Silent Partner* as one of many attacks against the Gilded Age, with the solution being more charitable treatment of the poor by the upper classes. Deborah Carlin emphasizes the shortcomings of "Christian socialism" in relationship to "class difference" in *Hedged In* and *The Silent Partner* (217). The intersection of gender and class oppression is also foregrounded in Amy Schrager Lang's recent study of *The Silent Partner*. However, she problematizes her discussion by pointing to the discrepancy between the voice of a middle-class narrator and the realities of the working class; ultimately, it is the narrator's feminine consciousness, representative of an idealized middle class, that attempts to bridge the gap between the classes. More studies on Phelps's problematic relationship to class are warranted and are probably forthcoming. From a more psychological perspective, Judith Fetterley defines the quest in *The Silent Partner* in terms of women's empowerment through speech and silence. Frances Malpezzi reads *The Silent Partner* as it relates to the religion of Phelps's time, specifically to the Social Gospel movement.

Other critics are interested in the historical background of Phelps's fictional world, in terms of the work's relationship to an emerging female professional (businesswoman or physician) ethos, usually in such works as *The Silent Partner* and *Dr. Zay*. Some critics, like Susan Albertine, Barbara Bardes and Suzanne Gossett, and Jean-Carwile Masteller, place Phelps's work in a broader historical or literary context. Timothy Morris, however, focuses on how *Dr. Zay* might have assuaged suspicious middle-class readers because Dr. Zay did not support the stereotypical notion of the time that female physicians were abortionists; indeed, Phelps presents an antiabortionist perspective in her depiction of Dr. Zay. Susan Ward shows how Phelps goes beyond the formula of "True Womanhood" novels by making the love plot secondary to the career plots in *The Silent Partner* and *Dr. Zay*. Jack Wilson discusses the competing narratives of George Eliot's *Armgart* and Elizabeth Barrett Browning's "Aurora Leigh" as they define the problematics of the woman artist in *The Story of Avis*.

Finally, the "Gates" novels have received some attention recently, but not as much as in Phelps's day. Recent feminist critics, like Kessler, are less concerned with religious doctrine than with the feminist utopian communities revealed in these works. Barton Levi St. Armand suggests that Phelps's evocation of a feminized heaven in *The Gates Ajar* serves as inspiration for Dickinson. Nancy Schnog explains how *The Gates Ajar* allowed Phelps to write about very intimate feminine matters, couched under the condoned "social acts of mourning and condolence" available to middle-class women (42). Jay Martin praises Phelps for painting an accurate picture of the unconscious in *The Gates Ajar*, which, Martin maintains, served as a precursor to James's and Twain's representation of the supernatural realm.

Hopefully, a new generation of critics and feminists will turn to and appreciate the neglected oeuvres of Phelps; the stories, especially, warrant more attention. During her own time, *Sealed Orders* was lauded by Whittier, who compared the collection to Hawthorne's *Twice-Told Tales* (Kessler 1982, 124). On the whole, influences on other writers and connections between Phelps and other writers need to be studied.

BIBLIOGRAPHY

Works by Elizabeth Stuart Phelps Ward

Novels

The Gates Ajar. Boston: Fields, Osgood, 1868.
Hedged In. Boston: Fields, Osgood, 1870.
The Silent Partner. Boston: James R. Osgood, 1871.
The Story of Avis. Boston: James R. Osgood, 1877.

An Old Maid's Paradise. Boston: Houghton, Osgood, 1879.
Friends: A Duet. Boston: Houghton, Mifflin, 1881.
Doctor Zay. Boston: Houghton, Mifflin, 1882.
Beyond the Gates. Boston: Houghton, Mifflin, 1883.
Burglars in Paradise. Boston: Houghton, Mifflin, 1886.
The Gates Between. Boston: Houghton, Mifflin, 1887.
A Singular Life. Boston: Houghton, Mifflin, 1895.
The Successors of Mary the First. Boston: Houghton, Mifflin, 1901.
Avery. Boston: Houghton, Mifflin, 1902.
Confessions of a Wife. By Mary Adams. New York: Century, 1902.
Trixy. Boston: Houghton, Mifflin, 1904.
The Man in the Case. Boston: Houghton, Mifflin, 1906.
Walled In. Boston: Houghton, Mifflin, 1907.
Though Life Us Do Part. Boston: Houghton, Mifflin, 1908.
Comrades. New York: Harper & Brothers, 1911. (Published posthumously)

Collections of Short Stories

Men, Women, and Ghosts. Boston: Fields, Osgood, 1879.
Sealed Orders. Boston: Houghton, Osgood, 1880.
Fourteen to One. Boston: Houghton, Mifflin, 1891.
The Oath of Allegiance and Other Stories. Boston: Houghton, Mifflin, 1909.
The Empty House and Other Stories. Boston: Houghton, Mifflin, 1910.

Select Juvenile Literature

"Tiny" series. Boston: Massachusetts Sabbath Day School Society, 1864, 1866, 1867.
Up Hill; or, Life in the Factory. Boston: Henry Hoyt, 1865.
"Gypsy" series. Boston: Graves and Young, 1865, 1866.
"Trotty" series. Boston: Fields, Osgood and J. R. Osgood, 1870, 1873.
Donald Marcy. Boston: Houghton, Mifflin, 1893.

Other Works—Miscellaneous

Poetic Studies. Boston: James R. Osgood, 1875. (Verse)
Songs of the Silent World and Other Poems. Boston: Houghton, Mifflin, 1884.
Austin Phelps: A Memoir. New York: Charles Scribner's, 1891.
Chapters from a Life. Boston: Houghton, Mifflin, 1896.
The Story of Jesus Christ: An Interpretation. Boston: Houghton, Mifflin, 1897.

Studies of Elizabeth Stuart Phelps Ward

Albertine, Susan. "Breaking the Silent Partnership: Businesswomen in Popular Fiction." *American Literature* 62, no. 2 (1990): 238–261.
Bennett, Mary Angela. *Elizabeth Stuart Phelps*. Philadelphia: University of Pennsylvania Press, 1939.
Buhle, Mari Jo, and Florence Howe. Afterword to *The Silent Partner and "The Tenth of January,"* by Elizabeth Stuart Phelps Ward. New York: Feminist Press, 1983. 355–382.
Coultrap-McQuin, Susan. "The Demise of Feminine Strength: The Career of Elizabeth

Stuart Phelps (Ward)." In *Doing Literary Business: American Women Writers in the Nineteenth Century*. Chapel Hill: University of North Carolina Press, 1990. 167–192.

Donovan, Josephine. *New England Local Color Tradition: A Women's Tradition*. New York: Continuum, 1988. 82–98.

Fetterley, Judith. " 'Checkmate': Elizabeth Stuart Phelps's *The Silent Partner*." *Legacy: A Journal of American Women Writers* 3, no. 2 (1986): 17–29.

Harris, Susan K. *Nineteenth-Century American Women's Novels: Interpretive Strategies*. Cambridge: Cambridge University Press, 1990. 186–196, 201–210.

Kelly, Lori Duin. *The Life and Works of Elizabeth Stuart Phelps, Victorian Feminist Writer*. Troy, NY: Whitson Publishing Co., 1983.

Kessler, Carol Farley. *Elizabeth Stuart Phelps*. Boston: Twayne, 1982.

———. "The Heavenly Utopia of Elizabeth Stuart Phelps." In *Women and Utopia*, edited by Marleen Barr and Nicholas D. Smith. Lanham, MD: University Press of America, 1983. 85–95.

———. Introduction to *The Story of Avis*, by Elizabeth Stuart Phelps Ward. New Brunswick, NJ: Rutgers University Press, 1985. xiii–xxxiii.

———. "A Literary Legacy: Elizabeth Stuart Phelps, Mother and Daughter." *Frontiers: A Journal of Women's Studies* 5, no. 3 (1980): 28–33.

Lang, Amy Schrager. "The Syntax of Class in Elizabeth Stuart Phelps's *The Silent Partner*." In *Rethinking Class: Literary Studies and Social Formations*, edited by Wai-Chee Dimock and Michael T. Gilmore. New York: Columbia University Press, 1994. 267–285.

Malpezzi, Frances. "*The Silent Partner*: A Feminist Sermon on the Social Gospel." *Studies in the Humanities* 13, no. 2 (1986): 103–110.

Martin, Jay. "Ghostly Rentals, Ghostly Purchases: Haunted Imaginations in James, Twain, and Bellamy." In *The Haunted Dusk: American Supernatural Fiction, 1820–1920*, edited by Howard Kerr and John W. Crowley. Athens: University of Georgia Press, 1983. 123–131.

Masteller, Jean-Carwile. "The Women Doctors of Howells, Phelps, and Jewett: The Conflict of Marriage and Career." In *Critical Essays on Sarah Orne Jewett*, edited by Gwen L. Nagel. Boston: G. K. Hall, 1984. 135–147.

Morris, Timothy. "Professional Ethics and Professional Erotics in Elizabeth Stuart Phelps' *Doctor Zay*." *Studies in American Fiction* 21, no. 2 (1993): 141–152.

St. Armand, Barton Levi. "Heaven Deferred: The Image of Heaven in the Works of Emily Dickinson and Elizabeth Stuart Phelps." *American Quarterly* 29 (1977): 55–78.

Sartisky, Michael. Afterword to *Dr. Zay*, by Elizabeth Stuart Phelps Ward. New York: Feminist Press, 1987. 259–321.

Schnog, Nancy. " 'The Comfort of My Fancying': Loss and Recuperation in *The Gates Ajar*." *Arizona Quarterly* 49, no. 1 (1993): 21–47.

Segel, Elizabeth. "The *Gypsy Breynton* Series: Setting the Pattern for American Tomboy Heroines." *Children's Literature Association Quarterly* 14, no. 2 (1989): 67–71.

Spring, Elizabeth T. "Elizabeth Stuart Phelps." In *Our Famous Women, an Authorized Record of Their Lives and Deeds*. Hartford, CT: A. D. Worthington & Co., 1883. 560–579.

Stansell, Christine. "Elizabeth Stuart Phelps: A Study in Rebellion." *Massachusetts Review* 13 (1972): 239–256.

Ward, Susan. "The Career Woman Fiction of Elizabeth Stuart Phelps." In *Nineteenth-Century Women Writers of the English-Speaking World*, edited by Rhoda B. Nathan. New York: Greenwood, 1986. 210–219.

Wilson, Jack. "Competing Narratives in Elizabeth Stuart Phelps' *The Story of Avis*." *American Literary Realism* 26, no. 1 (1993): 60–75.

SUSAN WARNER
(1819–1885)

Jane Weiss

BIOGRAPHY

Susan Warner was born on July 11, 1819, the daughter of Henry Warner, a New York attorney, and Anna Bartlett. Indulged by her wealthy parents, Susan "had no doubt of her royalty," according to her sister and biographer Anna Warner (34). Although the death of their mother in 1826 must have been traumatic for seven-year-old Susan, Henry's sister, Frances Warner, joined the household to keep house for her brother, and Henry's law practice flourished throughout Susan's childhood. The Warners lived in spacious townhouses with gardens at fashionable addresses in New York City, summering in upstate New York or in rural Brooklyn. Warner's earliest journals mention visits to Betsy Jumel and Julia Ward (later Howe), dancing school, lavish parties with "champaigne" (170) and cotillions, and evenings at concerts or the opera.

Warner's formal education was desultory, stressing genteel accomplishments. Her lessons included French, Italian, singing, dancing, and piano; she read history, theology, and mathematics following a program designed by Henry but received little supervision. Daily household tasks included sweeping the parlors and rubbing the doorknobs.

Warner's fascination with language and storytelling began in childhood. Her favorite activity was "talking stories" (102): inventing tales with her sister or cousins as her audience. She read voraciously and responded emotionally to authors such as Sir Walter Scott, Fanny Burney, Hannah More, Maria Edgeworth, Mary Sherwood, and Amelia Opie, and she rewrote stories she read to suit herself. Warner began a journal at the age of thirteen, producing descriptions, dialogue, and similar writing exercises. She rigorously corrected her own grammar and phrasing, aiming for precision, accuracy, and felicitous phrases.

In adolescence Warner lost the ebullient confidence that Anna had identified as her childhood trait, while remaining judgmental and imperious. She grew self-conscious and awkward, with a hypercritical, charmless personality. Her journal recorded her "black ideas" (194), fits of weeping, and tongue-tiedness. At sixteen, Warner disparaged her beloved "talking stories" as a "nonsensical amusement" (187), like cutting out paper dolls. She began to recognize her privileges as a child of wealth and expressed a sense of superiority to the less refined who were unable to appreciate music or fine art.

On July 28, 1835, Warner first saw Constitution Island, New York, describing it as "rough and rude" and "poor-looking." This unprepossessing site was to be her home for the rest of her life. Henry Warner and his brother, Thomas, planned to develop the property as a luxury resort. When Thomas lost his position as chaplain at West Point Military Academy and moved to Europe, Henry was left with the mortgaged property, which consisted of some 400 acres of rocky land and saltmarsh extending into the Hudson River. Henry added new wings to the existing small farmhouse for use as a gentleman's summer residence and moved the family there in the spring of 1838.

But the next twelve years swept away the Warner family's privileges and dashed Susan's expectations. Perhaps in response to losses in the Panic of 1837, Henry sold his townhouse on St. Mark's Place and remained at Constitution Island. For several years, the family enjoyed a comfortable standard of living, continuing to acquire the latest books and keeping several servants. But a series of disastrous lawsuits damaged Henry's reputation as a lawyer and drained his assets. Anna lamented that "from dainty silks and laces, we came down to calicoes, fashioned by our own fingers" (*Susan Warner* 176).

For Susan and Anna, the most significant event of the 1840s was their conversion. They joined the Mercer Street Chapel on April 2, 1841, under the supervision of Rev. Thomas Harvey Skinner. Skinner, who later served on the faculty of Union Theological Seminary, was a sophisticated scholar who articulated Presbyterian doctrine through elaborate logical argument. Anna later attributed Susan's sudden resolve to become a church member to anguish at her growing isolation and sense of social inferiority, but Warner was also drawn by the intellectual rigor of Skinner's rhetoric.

In the summer of 1848 Henry's debts culminated in a bankruptcy auction in which was sold every remaining luxury item, including china, oil paintings, furniture, and Susan's cherished piano. Susan's and Anna's efforts to earn money began before the sheriff's auction: They transcribed legal documents for $.03 per sheet and invented a "Natural History" card game called "Robinson Crusoe's Farmyard." With the encouragement of Frances Warner, Susan began the first draft of her novel *The Wide, Wide World* during the winter of 1848.

By the fall of 1850, the family had exhausted their resources. Warner's journal of that year described her father's haplessness, the lack of money for necessities such as candles and sugar, her slim hope of winning a $50 prize for an essay on "Female Patriotism," and half-baked plans to become a governess. Far from bewailing homemade dresses, Warner wondered where the money would come from for material for winter cloaks. Doubtful of the success of her novel, Warner chose to publish it under the name Elizabeth Wetherell instead of using her own name; the manuscript was accepted by Putnam after a number of publishing houses had rejected it.

But *The Wide, Wide World* proved, as Warner had tentatively hoped in her journal on October 30, 1850, "a richer storehouse to us than it has been to most people." Appreciative reviews appeared immediately following the publication of the book in the last week of December 1850. Royalty payments followed, although Warner received no remuneration for pirated editions in both England and the United States. Profit from the book paid outstanding debts and replaced some household items. Warner began her second novel, *Queechy*, immediately upon the acceptance of *The Wide, Wide World*; it, too, became a best-seller. Warner used a portion of her royalties to purchase a riding horse and household comforts. At the same time, her diary of the period alluded to an unspecified personal crisis or temptation; an entry from the summer of 1851 complained that life had grown empty and "fame never was a woman's Paradise, yet" (285), and the following summer, she wrote mysteriously about "strange hope and fear" and "aches and pains and weariness of heart" (100). One biographer, Mabel Baker, speculated that "there had been a budding romance which had, for various causes, come to nothing" (8).

Warner's social life expanded as she and her sister gained recognition as authors. Mary Rutherford Garrettson, daughter of the prominent Methodist minister Freeborn Garrettson and Catharine Livingston, cultivated a friendship with the Warners. Garrettson's spectacular estate near Rhinecliff was a nexus for the Methodist denomination and for the prominent Livingston clan; the Warner family spent winters in a cottage on the estate and socialized with their new acquaintances in New York City. Under Garrettson's aegis Warner moved among a variety of people who shared her interests and who enjoyed the elite social position Warner continued to believe was her natural element. Her Methodist friends influenced Warner to change her own denominational affiliation in the mid-1860s, a doctrinal shift she explored in her later fiction.

But their success as authors did not restore wealth to the Warners. Henry's abortive attempts to reestablish his practice and ill-advised speculations prompted another financial crisis in 1858. "So we worked!" Anna wrote. "Big books, little books; now and then an article for some paper or magazine" (376). Susan and Anna continued to write in collaboration and separately. Although the Civil War disrupted book production and slowed book sales, Warner wrote another best-seller, *Daisy* (1868), immediately after the war.

A young African-American woman known as Bertha arrived at Constitution Island in the winter of 1869. A former slave, Bertha remained as a servant and grew to be a beloved companion to Anna. More class conscious than her unconventional sister, Warner resented the former slave's familiarity even while modeling fictional characters on her. Warner gradually came to value Anna's spontaneity, love of nature, and independence over their forty-six years at Constitution Island. Warner's relationship with her father evidently deteriorated over the years. In old age, Henry Warner strained the limits of filial duty. After sustaining injuries in a fall in 1872, Henry took to his bed, growing increasingly difficult; Warner came to resent his demands and caricatured him in her later novels.

Following Henry's death in 1875, Susan, Anna, and Frances took up annual winter residence north of West Point, facilitating closer ties between the Warners and the Military Academy. Warner began Bible readings and study sessions with officers' wives, and when cadets began to attend the sessions as well, she received permission to meet with them in the Cadet Chapel. In the summer months, the class met on Constitution Island, gathering on the lawn in front of the house; the afternoon's activities included textual analysis and doctrinal debate along with lemonade and cookies.

Warner's health began to fail in the winter of 1884–1885. While in the process of revising her last novel, *Daisy Plains*, she suffered a stroke on March 8, 1885, and died nine days later on March 16. She was buried in the military cemetery at West Point in a spot overlooking the house at Constitution Island.

MAJOR WORKS AND THEMES

The publication of *The Wide, Wide World* in 1850 in effect invented the concept of the best-seller. *The Wide, Wide World* remained in print continuously for eighty years after its first appearance through 106 editions and was translated into at least seven languages. Warner also edited a theological study and wrote some thirty additional novels for children and adults. Although Warner's fiction has been categorized as domestic, sentimental, or didactic, these labels misrepresent her. Her novels took place within middle-class homes, and Warner scrutinized ordinary houses, gardens, and farms microscopically. But no novelist ever hated housework more; Warner is unique among domestic novelists in never finding anything good to say about housekeeping. She wrote almost exclusively about hearth and parlor, but she did not celebrate them.

Nineteenth-century reviewers categorized Warner more accurately as a religious novelist and a realist. Unlike most midcentury American writers, Warner disliked allegory and exaggeration. She called Catharine Sedgwick's novels "dismally poor" (*Susan Warner* 305) because Sedgwick imposed romantic language and sensational occurrences upon historical settings. Indeed, Warner's fiction was almost awkwardly realist, eschewing not only unlikely events or exceptional people but even tropes such as extended metaphors or the pathetic fallacy. Although her characters often elucidate the significance of flowers, moonlight, Niagara Falls, and so on, Warner distinguished between interpreting existing phenomena, as one might do in real life, and manipulating reality from her position as author to construct didactic or romantic schemata. Warner set her stories among middle-class people in deliberately unromantic settings. She pioneered the use of vernacular dialogue and richly textured descriptions of household settings and tasks, techniques later imitated by writers such as Mark Twain and Sarah Orne Jewett. With the eye of an archaeologist, Warner recorded cornhusking and paring potatoes, shopping for clothing in a department store, wading through a marsh, or riding in a carriage down a cobblestone city street.

Paradoxically, Warner applied her scrupulously realistic style to explicate highly abstract theological and social issues. Her first novel, *The Wide, Wide World*, introduced the themes that would resonate throughout her work. Written after years of frustration and poverty, *The Wide, Wide World* voiced a scathing rejection of Emersonian autonomy. It depicted the travail of an adolescent girl, Ellen Montgomery, who is sent away from her invalid mother and indifferent father to live with a rigid, insensitive aunt on an isolated farm. Ellen's excruciating struggles to resign herself to her aunt's whims reflected Warner's application of Presbyterian theology to the situation of circumscribed and thwarted middle-class girls and women. *The Wide, Wide World* presented a drama of spiritual training through which a powerless and unhappy person could find an identity. Warner's positions would change over her career, but she continued to look in the marketplace of nineteenth-century dogmatic theology for possible solutions for isolation, scarcity, and disappointment.

Virtually all of Warner's subsequent fiction depicted young women, often orphaned or otherwise lacking resources, coping with adverse circumstances. Warner's only nonfiction work was a thematic anthology of Bible excerpts, *The Law and the Testimony* (1853), of which the Union Theological Seminary of New York acquired a copy. Considering the leverage exerted by doctrinal theology in the nineteenth century, Warner's validation as a theologian gave her a position of authority.

Warner's personal theology matured through her fiction. From treating resignation as a tool for female psychological survival, Warner moved to an analysis of ethics and praxis that offered women the hope of fulfilling lives. The fiction Warner wrote after 1865 centered on the question, How should a Christian live? Warner's later novels examined the obligation of Christians not only toward authority but also toward dependents and communities, concluding that genuine Christianity entailed not acquiescence to one's superiors but service to those in need and positive action in society.

Begun in 1861, *Melbourne House* (1864) reprised territory familiar from *The Wide, Wide World*, but Warner modified her formula to reflect her new theological stance. Daisy, the heroine, was an heiress instead of an orphan; she suffered not at the hands of self-reliant Aunt Fortune but from conflict between her conception of Christian ethics and her parents' nominally Christian doctrines. In *Melbourne House*, Warner examined the intersections of religious belief with power and authority in political as well as emotional terms.

In her next work, published late in 1863, Warner dramatized a conflict between conscience and authority. Set in England, Wales, and exotic Fiji, *The Old Helmet* depicted the heroine's choice between obedience to her Anglican parents' wishes and a marriage that would allow her to fulfill her vocation as a Methodist missionary. Unlike *The Wide, Wide World, The Old Helmet* redefined true Christianity as flouting the authority of parents and even clergymen. Warner was moving from the paradigm of her former mentor Thomas Harvey Skinner, stressing absolute submission to God and earthly authorities through rigorous training of the will, to the model of the dashing Methodist circuit riders, in which the action shifted outside the psyche and the home and into the larger world.

Ever fearful of class slippage, Warner felt little enthusiasm for the populist faction of Methodism. She admired Nathan Bangs, who had urged "scriptural restraint and moderation" and complained that Methodism "had been indifferent to the cause of literature and science" (Hatch 203–204). Although by the 1860s the Protestant Methodist sect denounced Bangs as an elitist, Warner placed herself squarely in Bangs's camp. In *The Old Helmet*, the hero's missionary call demanded the use rather than the suppression of his intellect (he carries a microscope to investigate Welsh flora while spreading the gospel), and Warner lavished praise on her heroine's "nice tastes" and delicate white dresses. The ending of the novel, describing the missionary couple's idyllic tropical honeymoon in Fiji, swerved drastically from her usual homespun realism, but it pointed the direction Warner's theology was taking.

The sequel to *Melbourne House, Daisy*, was a technically impressive book and an emotionally involving one. Although in *Melbourne House* the heroine had borne a family resemblance to Ellen Montgomery, Warner changed perspective in the sequel by the use of first-person narration, revealing her little angel of the house to be a moody, introspective, and manipulative adolescent. *Daisy* presented the title character's life as a series of negotiations to live up to her conception of Christian behavior in antagonistic environments: a Southern plantation, a fashionable school in New York, and abroad. In *Daisy* the obstacles faced by the heroine are not for the most part personal frustrations but encounters with ethical dilemmas demanding a choice between compliance and assertion. Confronting her parents' ownership of slaves, Daisy initially attempts to win small privileges for the slaves, but her convictions inevitably lead to a direct confrontation with her parents' ethics. When Daisy goes north, she decides to bring a slave with her across the Mason-Dixon Line, setting her free. The abstract issue recedes to the background during one of Warner's wonderful descriptions of clothes shopping, but after Daisy chooses inexpensive items so that she will be able to outfit her companion, her guardian chides her: " 'You must not take it on your heart that you have to teach all the ignorant and help all the distressed that come your way; because simply you cannot do it' " (187). Daisy's acts of charity challenge his authority.

Warner devoted a series of "juveniles" to the same question: How much can one do? The first volume describes Matilda Englefield's attempts to "love her neighbors" as a working-class child in Rhinebeck, New York. The next volume, ironically titled *Opportunities* (1870), describes Matilda's virtual imprisonment by her manipulative and sexually abusive aunt. In the last two volumes Matilda negotiates the temptations of complacency and selfishness when she is adopted by a rich and loving family. Throughout the series, Warner argued that patience and self-sacrifice were not goals in themselves; the goal was to "do what one can" to help the oppressed and exploited.

The emphasis on action was the hallmark of the Holiness movement within the Methodist Church, spearheaded by Phoebe Palmer. "Heroic holiness," Palmer dictated, required a Christian to devote virtually all of his or her resources and talents to "holy purposes" as angels of mercy. Palmer urged her followers to visit prisons, establish settlement houses, and adopt orphans (Raser 211–226). Although Warner did not perform such heroic acts, her books argued with increasing conviction that Christianity meant not self-abnegation or unquestioning resignation but redistribution of wealth and the development of social services.

Warner's last six years were her most productive. By the 1880s her style was regarded as old-fashioned; the realistic depiction of middle-class life that Warner had pioneered was being imitated by writers who omitted the now-dated dogmatic themes. But her publisher, Carter Brothers, still found a following for new Susan Warner titles, and the stories continued to sell briskly abroad. Warner produced a lengthy novel each year in a series of "true stories" based on anecdotes. Although the series is formulaic, it displays the virtues of professionalism, with neatly constructed plots, distinctive characters, and vivid detail. *My Desire* (1879), *The End of a Coil* (1880), *Nobody* (1882), *Stephen, M.D.* (1883), *A Red Wallflower* (1884), and *Daisy Plains* (1885) promoted the Holiness movement, featuring perfected, devout main characters meeting life's tribulations with fortitude. Surprisingly, *The Letter of Credit* (1881) presented a rebellious, stubborn, and very appealing heroine with a sense of humor, whose unrepentant arrogance recalls Warner's own personality as a young girl.

CRITICAL RECEPTION

The wild vicissitudes in the reception of Warner's works offers a case history in literary standards, thematic fads, and canon revision. Upon publication, *The Wide, Wide World* received highly respectful reviews, hailing Warner as a major literary talent and a religious polemicist comparable to John Bunyan. In contrast to Fred Pattee's and David Reynold's contention that writers like Warner were principally concerned with the marketplace, a number of reviewers remarked that Warner's style was innovative and distinctly uncommercial; several reviewers wondered at the lack of dramatic incident and the homely settings of *The Wide, Wide World* and *Queechy*. An anonymous reviewer for the *New York Tribune* called *Queechy* "free from inflation of sentiment and pomp of language" (undated review, Warner Family Archives). In 1865 in an essay in *The Nation*, Henry James compared Warner's handling of local color and realistic detail favorably with that of Flaubert (345). Although Warner's novels in the

1870s and 1880s excited less comment from reviewers, her works remained in print and sold steadily through the turn of the century.

Although Warner's realistic depictions of middle-class life might have won her a permanent place in the evolving canon of American literature, her fundamental themes—which took for granted the primacy of Protestant doctrine and the urgent importance of denominational distinctions—did not wear well in the midtwentieth century as the popularity of dogmatic theology skidded into decline. Indeed, these themes became invisible to scholars whose "universal values" prescribed secularism and Emersonian individualism and whose literary values demanded deliberately engineered plots and symbolic density. Along with other nineteenth-century American women novelists, Warner was dismissed by many Americanists in the 1940s and 1950s as a writer of weepy, preachy, and incoherent trash. She vanished altogether from anthologies and literary histories before reemerging in the 1980s amidst debate about the place of women in the canon.

Ann Douglas inadvertently began the rehabilitation of Warner's reputation in 1977, accusing *The Wide, Wide World*, *Queechy*, and *Daisy* of promoting "sentimental morality against [the forces] of theological scholarship" (171). Though contemptuous of Warner's literary ability, Douglas's acknowledgment of Warner's influence elicited responses from scholars eager to defend voices excluded from the canon. In *Woman's Fiction* (1978), Nina Baym discussed Warner's first three books in depth, identifying Warner as the finest exemplar of the domestic writer, a "literary talent unmarked by the alleged 'feminine' excesses of overblown imagery and inflated diction," while "Warner's subject and the angle from which she approaches it are relentlessly and deliberately feminine" (144). Jane Tompkins's *Sensational Designs*, appearing in 1985, devoted a chapter to the social and political subtexts of *The Wide, Wide World*, championing the novel's "tremendous original force," Warner's "millenial aims," and her rejection of escapism and fantasy. "Unlike their male counterparts," Tompkins wrote, "women writers of the nineteenth century could not walk out the door and become Mississippi riverboat captains, go off on whaling voyages, or build themselves cabins in the woods . . . 'escape' is the one thing that sentimental novels never offer. . . . The storms and winds of Warner's novel are those that nineteenth-century readers actually encountered in their lives" (174–185).

Warner has since become almost a metonymy for nineteenth-century popular fiction. *The Wide, Wide World* is mentioned passingly in *New York* and *Victoria Magazine* and scholarly studies such as David S. Reynold's *Beneath the American Renaissance* and Lawrence Buell's *New England Literary Culture*, a phenomenon noted grimly by D. G. Myers in *The New Criterion* in 1988. Several articles have addressed Warner's fictional strategies in greater depth. Susan Williams has examined the authority Warner claimed through the act of penning a novel; Mary Hieatt has discussed the political implications of the female-centered theology offered by *The Wide, Wide World*.

Less for any lack of intrinsic interest than because they are not readily available to scholars, Warner's later novels, theological writings, and journals have received far less attention than *The Wide, Wide World* and *Queechy*. Because they reached smaller audiences, these writings do not so neatly epitomize the politics of the best-seller and its exclusion from the literary canon; nor do they fit smoothly into existing theoretical approaches or curricula. However, Warner's lesser-known works have much to offer the historian of nineteenth-century literature. Her dramatizations of theological problems, however remote they may now seem, serve as a reminder of the central place Protestant doctrine held in nineteenth-century daily life; more important, her descriptions of piano lessons, housework, and Sunday school, "weaving" plots for novels, feeding the cow or having the minister to tea, celebrate the lasting value of historically bound, ordinary lives.

WORKS CITED

Baker, Mabel. *The Warner Family and the Warner Books*. West Point, NY: Constitution Island Association, 1971.

Baym, Nina. *Woman's Fiction: A Guide to Novels by and about Women in America 1820–1870*. Ithaca: Cornell University Press, 1978.

Douglas, Ann. *The Feminization of American Culture*. New York: Alfred A. Knopf, 1977.

Hatch, Nathan O. *The Democratization of American Christianity*. New Haven: Yale University Press, 1989.

James, Henry. "The Schonberg-Cotta Family." *The Nation*, 14 September 1865, 345.

Raser, Harold E. *Phoebe Palmer: Her Life and Thought*. Lewiston, NY: Edwin Mellen Press, 1987.

Tompkins, Jane P. *Sensational Designs: The Cultural Work of American Fiction, 1790–1860*. New York: Oxford University Press, 1985.

Warner, Anna. *Susan Warner*. New York: Putnam, 1909.

Weiss, Jane. *"Many Things Take My Time": The Journals of Susan Warner*. Ph.D. diss., City University of New York, 1995. Ann Arbor: University Microfilms, 1995. 9605681.

BIBLIOGRAPHY

Works by Susan Warner

Full-Length Novels

The Wide, Wide World. By Elizabeth Wetherell. New York: Putnam, 1850.

Queechy. New York: Putnam, 1852.

The Hills of the Shatemuc. New York: Appleton, 1856.

The Old Helmet. New York: Carter, 1863.

Melbourne House. New York: Carter, 1864.

Daisy. Philadelphia: Lippincott, 1868.

A Story of Small Beginnings:
    What She Could. New York: Carter, 1870.
    Opportunities. New York: Carter, 1870.
    The House in Town. New York: Carter, 1870.
    Trading. New York: Carter, 1872.
Diana. New York: Putnam, 1877.
My Desire. New York: Carter, 1879.
The End of a Coil. New York: Carter, 1880.
The Letter of Credit. New York: Carter, 1881.
Nobody. New York: Carter, 1882.
Stephen, M.D. New York: Carter, 1883.
A Red Wallflower. New York: Carter, 1884.
Daisy Plains. New York: Carter, 1885.

Theological Writings

The Law and the Testimony. New York: Carter, 1853.
Walks from Eden. New York: Carter, 1865.
The House of Israel. London: Routledge, 1866.
Broken Walls of Jerusalem. New York: Carter, 1870.
Lessons on the Standard Bearers of the Old Testament. New York: Randolph, 1872.
The Kingdom of Judah. New York: Carter, 1878.

Children's Books

Carl Krinken: His Christmas Stocking. New York: Putnam, 1853.
The Little Camp on Eagle Hill. New York: Carter, 1873.
Sceptres and Crowns. London: Goubard, 1874.
Willowbrook. New York: Carter, 1874.
Bread and Oranges. New York: Carter, 1875.
The Flag of Truce. New York: Carter, 1875.
The Rapids of Niagara. New York: Carter, 1876.
Pine Needles. New York: Carter, 1877.

Works Written with Anna Warner

Say and Seal. Philadelphia: Lippincott, 1860.
The Golden Ladder. New York: Randolph, 1862.
The Little American: A Series of Stories and Sketches for Young Folks, October 1862–
    December 1864.
The Gold of Chickaree. New York: Putnam, 1876.
Wych Hazel. New York: Putnam, 1876.

Studies of Susan Warner

Baker, Mabel. *Light in the Morning: Memories of Susan and Anna Warner.* West Point,
    NY: Constitution Island Association, 1978.
————. *The Warner Family and the Warner Books.* West Point, NY: Constitution Island
    Association, 1971.
Baym, Nina. *Novels, Readers and Reviewers: Responses to Fiction in Antebellum Amer-
    ica.* Ithaca: Cornell University Press, 1984.

————. *Woman's Fiction: A Guide to Novels by and about Women in America 1820–1870.* Ithaca: Cornell University Press, 1978.

Calabro, John A. "Susan Warner and Her Bible Classes." *Legacy* 4, no. 2 (fall 1987): 45–52.

Douglas, Ann. *The Feminization of American Culture.* New York: Alfred A. Knopf, 1977.

Foster, Edward Halsey. *Susan and Anna Warner.* New York: Twayne, n.d. [1978].

Harris, Susan K. *19th-Century American Women's Novels: Interpretive Strategies.* Cambridge: Cambridge University Press, 1990.

Hieatt, Mary P. "Susan Warner's Subtext: The Other Side of Piety." *Journal of Evolutionary Psychology* (August 1987): 250–261.

Kelley, Mary. *Private Woman, Public Stage: Literary Domesticity in Nineteenth-Century America.* New York: Oxford University Press, 1984.

Myers, D. G. "The Canonization of Susan Warner." *New Criterion* 7, no. 4 (1988): 73–78.

Oates, Joyce Carol. "Pleasure, Duty, Redemption Then and Now: Susan Warner's *Diana.*" *American Literature* 59, no. 3 (1987): 422–427.

Papashvily, Helen Waite. *All the Happy Endings: A Study of the Domestic Novel in America, the Women Who Wrote It, the Women Who Read It in the Nineteenth Century.* New York: Harper, 1956.

Sanderson, Dorothy Hurlbut. *They Wrote for a Living: A Bibliography of the Works of Susan Bogert Warner and Anna Bartlett Warner.* West Point, NY: Constitution Island Association, 1976.

Sehnog, Nancy. "Inside the Sentimental: The Psychological Work of *The Wide, Wide World.*" *Genders* 4 (1989): 11–25.

Stokes, Olivia E. Phelps. *Letters and Memories of Susan and Anna Bartlett Warner.* New York: Putnam, 1925.

Tompkins, Jane P. *Sensational Designs: The Cultural Work of American Fiction, 1790–1860.* New York: Oxford University Press, 1985.

Warner, Anna. *Susan Warner.* New York: Putnam, 1909.

Williams, Susan S. "Widening the World: Susan Warner, Her Readers, and the Assumption of Authorship." *American Quarterly* 42, no. 4 (1990): 565–586.

FRANCES MIRIAM BERRY WHITCHER (1814–1852)

Michael J. Kiskis

BIOGRAPHY

Frances Miriam Berry Whitcher was born in Whitesboro, New York, on November 1, 1814, the thirteenth of fifteen children born to Elizabeth and Lewis Berry. Lewis Berry, proprietor of Berry's Tavern, was active in Whig politics and a member of the Oneida Institute's board of trustees and the local Presbyterian Church; he broke with the Oneida Institute's second president Beriah Green when the institute's political and religious policy was linked with abolition. After Lewis's death in 1849, Elizabeth continued to control the family business until she and her daughters eventually sold the business.

Miriam, the only one of the children to move more than a day's journey from the homestead, was closest to her sister Kate (1817–1865), whose two-part biography of her sister, published in *Godey's Lady's Book*, remains a vital source for information about Miriam's childhood and final months. The family provided stimulation and protection for Miriam, who demonstrated an early talent for parody: she caricatured classmates—her first attempt came at age five—and those adults surrounding her whom she perceived as rude, unfair, or unfriendly. A shy child and a socially reticent adult, humor was her outlet for private pique and public dissent. At twenty-five she became a member of Whitesboro's Maeonian Circle, an active literary and social group, and presented a series of literary sketches featuring her first female protagonist, the Widow Permilla ("Permilly" or "Silly") Spriggins. She continued to write and develop her literary heroines until her death.

On January 6, 1847, Miriam married Reverend Benjamin William Whitcher, who was then pastor of Whitesboro's St. John's Episcopal Church. The marriage was clearly a love match: Surviving letters display a deep and playful affection.

In 1848 Miriam followed William to Elmira, New York, where he had taken an assignment as pastor of Trinity Episcopal Church. They returned to Whitesboro in 1850 after a particularly stressful time sparked by increasing financial pressures, the Elmira congregation's internal politics, and a stir created when Miriam was found to be the author of several "Aunt Maguire" sketches that the congregation interpreted as direct criticisms.

Family concerns were central from 1848 to 1850. On April 1, 1848, the Whitchers' first daughter (Mary) was stillborn; the baby's remains were exhumed in 1850 and reburied next to Lewis Berry, who died on March 25, 1849. A second daughter, Alice, was born on November 6, 1850. Mother and child were often separated from William as he took up several part-time pastorships: He was never to secure a full-time appointment after the debacle of Elmira. Miriam, always frail, suffered recurring bouts of illness after 1850. She was working on a novel (*Mary Elmer*) at the time of her death from consumption on January 4, 1852. She was buried in the Berry family plot in Whitesboro, New York.

MAJOR WORKS AND THEMES

Frances Miriam Berry Whitcher's professional writing career lasted roughly five years (1846–1851). She created three female first-person vernacular characters critical to the development of women's humor during the middle years of the nineteenth century as well as to the broader tradition of nineteenth-century American humor. Permilly Ruggles (the Widow Spriggins), Priscilla Bedott (the Widow Bedott), and Melissa Poole Maguire (Aunt Maguire, Priscilla Bedott's sister) are important markers in the evolution of vernacular humor, especially in their contribution to a social criticism that aimed at the American obsession with gentility.

The eleven Widow Spriggins sketches were the earliest. Originally presented to the Maeonian Circle in Whitesboro, the sketches were first published in 1839 in the Rome, New York, *Gazette* (Whitcher signed the sketches "Frank," a name that her family had used for her since childhood). Whitcher's tales burlesque Regina Maria Roche's eighteenth-century romance *Children of the Abbey*. The comic thrust comes from the attempts of an uncouth village woman to take on the language and props of romance. The Widow Spriggins has a good deal in common with other vernacular characters of the 1830s—her language is overblown and seasoned with malapropisms, mispellings, and gibberish. The burlesque is also aimed at aspects of contemporary women's writing: The Widow's adventures are punctuated with atrocious "occasional" poetry, and her zeal to create romance in the village of Podunk, New York, knows no boundaries. Widow Spriggins is obsessed with courtship and fashion; by the end of the series, Whitcher has taken aim at the growing fascination with the notion of gentility.

Whitcher's next creation—the Widow Bedott—would fire more effective volleys. The first Widow Bedott sketch was accepted in 1846 by Joseph Neal, editor of the *Saturday Gazette and Lady's Literary Museum* (after Neal's death, his wife Alice took over editorial duties and became a close friend to Whitcher). Later, Louis A. Godey asked Whitcher to submit Widow Bedott sketches to *Godey's Lady's Book*. No longer satisfied with the potential for humor in burlesquing literary convention, Whitcher turned a critical eye to the personalities and personal agendas that were common to Northeast village life. Unlike the Widow Spriggins's preoccupation with a fictional romance, Priscilla Bedott's primary aim is to find a new husband and end her tenuous social status as a widow. She is more complex because of her involvement in her community, and her observations carry a double edge. While "Silly" Spriggins bore the brunt of Whitcher's comedy of romance, the Widow Bedott was both a tart observer of village life and a supreme, if unconscious, example of the culture of gentility.

Whitcher's Widow Bedott is related to her vernacular siblings born during the thirty years between 1840 and 1870, including Seba Smith's "Jack Downing," Thomas Haliburton's "Sam Slick," even George Washington Harris's "Sut Lovingood." Whitcher, however, offers us a complex mix of sympathy and satire in a character whose fate is entangled with the social expectations that dominate small-town life. As we see in the messy tales developed as extended dramatic monologues ("Hezekiah Bedott" is among the more effective and is often linked to later monologues by Mark Twain, especially "Grandfather's Old Ram" from *Roughing It*), the Widow is hard-pressed to define herself in any way other than wife or not wife, which adds pathos to her search for a social identity. Her triumphant marriage to the Reverend Shadrack Sniffles at the end of the series drives home the Widow's main interests: Both "The Rev. Mrs. Sniffles Expresses Her Sentiments in Regard to the Parsonage" and "Extract from Mrs. Sniffles' Diary" describe her reliance upon the conventions of gentility and display a shallowness that prizes external appearance over family and meaningful human connection.

Though related to Priscilla Bedott, Melissa Poole Maguire, the third of the vernacular personae, allowed Whitcher an increased critical distance. Like the adventures of the Widow Bedott, Aunt Maguire's experiences also appeared in *Godey's Lady's Book*. Melissa Poole Maguire is an observer more than a participant; she is more sophisticated, more confident in her social position (she is married to the appropriately named Joshaway; their son Jefferson is more a tease than his father), and more interested in criticizing than in participating in the culture of gentility. More outward looking than her sister, Aunt Maguire's satire is aimed at social groups and community events. In "Parson Scrantum's Donation Party," "The Contemplated Sewing Society," and "The Sewing Society" (published in *Godey's* during 1848 and 1849) readers are introduced to the dynamics of small-town relations. The images of a penurious congregation's enthusiastic celebration at their minister's expense and of self-important, class-conscious social climbing tarnishes the genteel inhabitants of Scrabble Hill.

Whitcher uses character, setting, and situation to broaden her "domestic" humor to include both home and community.

Whitcher also wrote more conventional material. Her "Letters from Timberville," also published in *Godey's Lady's Book*, mix vernacular and conventional voices. Not as strongly satirical as the first-person narratives, the "Letters" explore household concerns as well as community issues; for example, "Letters from Timberville, III" concerns the difficulty of finding and hiring household help, a continual challenge for the Whitchers. The lack of a single perspective, however, works against the effectiveness of the series, especially in comparison to the Widow Bedott and Aunt Maguire adventures.

After moving back to Whitesboro in 1850, Miriam, by this time beginning to suffer more acute health problems, continued to write. Her novel *Mary Elmer* was more in line with the sentimental fiction then popular and remained unfinished at her death (Martha Ward Whitcher, William's second wife, completed the novel; it was published in 1867). The departure from the vernacular heroines of the early sketches may have contributed to the lackluster manuscript.

In the end, Whitcher's cautionary tales explode a social system that relies on genteel notions of fashion and behavior. She set the stage for Sara Willis Parton and Marietta Holley whose later personae (Fanny Fern; Betsy Bobbet and Samantha Allen, respectively) expanded the repertoire of women's humor to include women's economic and political rights.

CRITICAL RECEPTION

The Widow Bedott Papers (1856) sold 100,000 copies during ten years of sales and went through twenty-three editions; it was reprinted in 1880. The popularity of the first collection made the second, *Widow Spriggins, Mary Elmer, and Other Sketches* (1867) a certainty and reinforced Joseph Neal's early critical opinion of Miriam Whitcher's abilities as a humorist, satirist, and critic. The character Widow Bedott continued to be popular well into the 1880s, sparked by D. R. Locke's (Petroleum V. Nasby) production of the play *Widow Bedott, or a Hunt for a Husband*, which preserved much of the original dialogue. Well-known cross-dresser Neil Burgess played Bedott. He later took on the property and continued the successful production.

Early studies of American humor did not include Whitcher. She is not mentioned by Constance Rourke (1931). Walter Blair (1960) does include several of the Bedott sketches in his samples of the work of literary comedians; however, he (and later he and Hamlin Hill [1978]) focus on Whitcher's use of the stereotype (which is read as the acceptance of the stereotype) to reinforce an image of domestic calm. Such early work assumed that women's humor aimed at maintaining the status quo rather than subverting the dominant images of women available in the culture. More recent work in women's humor by Nancy A. Walker (1988) has been especially helpful in bringing Whitcher back into critical view. Linda A. Morris's literary biography (1992) places Whitcher within a context that takes into account the local influences that helped shape her humor and the personal experiences that gave rise to Whitcher's antigenteel positions. It is an important corrective that argues for Whitcher's value to American literary humor of the nineteenth century.

BIBLIOGRAPHY

Works by Frances Whitcher

Whitcher, Frances Miriam Berry. *The Widow Bedott Papers*. With an introduction by Alice B. Neal. New York: J. C. Derby, 1856.
————. *Widow Spriggins, Mary Elmer, and Other Sketches*. Edited with a memoir by M. L. Ward Whitcher. New York: George W. Carleton & Company, 1867.

Studies of Frances Whitcher

Berry, Kate. "Passages in the Life of the Author of Aunt Maguire's Letters, Bedott Papers, Etc." *Godey's Lady's Book* 47 (July 1853): 49–55; (August 1853): 109–115.
Blair, Walter. *Native American Humor*. San Francisco: Chandler Publishing Company, 1960.
Blair, Walter, and Hamlin Hill. *American Humor: From Poor Richard to Doonesbury*. New York: Oxford University Press, 1978.
Curry, Jane. "Yes, Virginia, There Were Female Humorists: Frances Whitcher and Her Widow Bedott." *University of Michigan Papers in Women's Studies* 1 (1974): 74–90.
Morris, Linda A. "Frances Miriam Whitcher: Social Satire in the Age of Gentility." *Women's Studies—An Interdisciplinary Journal* 15 (1988): 99–116.
————. *Women's Humor in the Age of Gentility: The Life and Works of Frances Miriam Whitcher*. Syracuse: Syracuse University Press, 1992.
Rourke, Constance. *American Humor: A Study of the National Character*. New York: Harcourt, Brace and Company, 1931.
Walker, Nancy. *A Very Serious Thing: Women's Humor in American Culture*. Minneapolis: University of Minnesota Press, 1988.

SARAH HELEN WHITMAN (1803–1878)

Noelle A. Baker

BIOGRAPHY

Sarah Helen Power Whitman was born the second of five children to Nicholas and Anna Marsh Power in Providence, Rhode Island, on January 19, 1803. In what Whitman considered an occult synchronicity, she shared her birthday with Edgar Allan Poe, whom she would champion fearlessly against his many detractors in *Edgar Poe and His Critics*, (1860). Such daring characterizes Whitman's career as feminist, Spiritualist, poet, essayist, translator, and journalist. Whitman audaciously claimed the motto "Break all bonds."

After Nicholas Power's mercantile business failed in 1813, he abandoned his family for nineteen years, leaving them to struggle with constricting legal and financial difficulties. Nevertheless, Sarah Power attended schools for young ladies, where she studied astronomy; geography; history; and French, German, and Italian literature. She read Byron feverishly and began composing her own verse.

In 1824 Sarah Helen Power was betrothed to John Winslow Whitman; they married in 1828. The literary-minded John Whitman wrote poetry and coedited the *Boston Spectator and Ladies' Album* and the *Bachelors' Journal*. He also promoted his fiancée's writing: Sarah Power first published her poetry in his *Spectator* (1827) as "Helen" (Varner 67). After their marriage, the Whitmans settled in Boston, where John Whitman practiced law.

After his death in 1833, Sarah Whitman returned to Providence. There, she flourished as a poet. Whitman continued to write poetry for the *Ladies' Magazine, Godey's Lady's Book, United States Magazine and Democratic Review*, and the *Providence Daily Journal* and gift books like *The Ladies' Wreath* (1837) and *The Token* (1842). Whitman's poetry also figured prominently in popular anthologies—Caroline May's *The American Female Poets* (1848), Rufus Griswold's *The Female Poets of America* (1849), and Sarah Josepha Hale's *Woman's Record* (1853), among others. Whitman published her own volume of poems, *Hours of Life and Other Poems*, in 1853.

Whitman adopted Transcendentalism with fervor. She met its major figures, including Ralph Waldo Emerson, Bronson Alcott, and Margaret Fuller. But even in her enthusiasms, Whitman followed the dictates of her own mind. Her *Boston Quarterly Review* essay on Emerson—signed "by a disciple"—elicited Emerson's comment that Whitman exercised independent thinking.

Whitman also kept abreast of European Romanticism. However, she decried American critics' moralistic censure of Romantic libertines. As "Egeria," Whitman launched defenses of Shelley, Goethe, and Byron—as well as her own evaluation of the "true nature of genius"—in the *Democratic Review, The Boston Pearl*, Providence's *Literary Journal* and *Daily Journal*, and the *Boston Quarterly Review*. Her essays so impressed editor Orestes Brownson that in 1840 he offered Whitman an equal share in the profits of his *Boston Quarterly Review* if she would contribute an article to each number (Varner 219).

In 1848 Whitman met Edgar Allan Poe. Poe scholar Edward Wagenknecht remarks that Poe pursued Whitman in part because of her literary standing; ambitiously, he hoped "they might preside over a distinguished literary salon and take their place with the intellectual leaders of America" (96). The couple's whirlwind romance produced engagement, estrangement, and literary scandal between the fall and December of 1848. Nevertheless, until her death, Whitman remained convinced that psychic forces determined and perpetuated her union with "The Raven."

Griswold's "Ludwig" attacks and pragmatic concerns about her own reputation further stimulated Whitman to resuscitate Poe's standing, primarily in the *New York Tribune* and in *Edgar Poe and His Critics* (1860). Tirelessly, Whitman rendered information to his biographers in the 1870s. Only a month before her death, she submitted a last vindication of Poe in the *Providence Daily Journal*.

Whitman also championed women's rights and other social issues—primarily in the *Tribune* and the *Providence Daily Journal*. For her service, the Rhode Island Suffrage Association elected Whitman vice president in 1868; moreover, New York suffragists honored her at national conventions in 1870 and 1871.

Additionally, Whitman achieved considerable renown as a Spiritualist. She held séances as a medium and became "one of [the movement's] most respected advocates" (St. Armand 5). Spiritualists believed that Whitman's literary reputation and forceful prose lent authority to their cause. In 1851, the *Tribune* printed her Spiritualist letters; they were "widely reprinted" (St. Armand 5) in texts like E. W. Capron's *Modern Spiritualism* (1855).

In life, Whitman exercised the full extent of her liberal mind; until the end, she "spent . . . her time casting off the bonds of convention and fighting for unpopular truths'' (Varner 210). In her last years, she defended friends engaging in ''free love'' and divorce; elaborated the rigorous journalistic prose for which she had become known; and supervised the arrangement of her verse for a posthumous collection, *Poems* (1879). She died at age seventy-five in Providence on June 27, 1878.

MAJOR WORKS AND THEMES

Whitman the poet represents aspects of the woman's personal and intellectual growth. In the early verse, characteristically, Whitman treats Romantic subjects—nature and its influence, idyllic children and solitary women, the power of art. She also composed verse fairy tales with her sister.

Whitman wrote philosophical poetry and verse translations also. *Hours of Life*, a spiritual and philosophical autobiography, serves as the most ambitious of the former. Her translations display Whitman's range and awareness of Romanticism beyond the States, from Goethe to Victor Hugo.

Arguably, the verse dedicated to Poe, however, made her reputation as a ''poetess.'' The six sonnets and miscellaneous others—like ''Resurgemus,'' ''Song,'' and ''The Raven''—replicate many of the strategies Whitman employed to defend Poe in prose. She casts Poe as a compelling prophet, a noble spirit. These poems also suggest Whitman's sensuous nature.

In later years, Whitman turned to less ethereal subjects. She exposes the century's enslavement to Progress in ''Science'' and reveals her unhappy skepticism about the fate of the woman's movement in ''Woman's Sphere'' and ''Minerva and the Doctors.'' Poems like ''Christmas Eve,'' ''Santa Claus,'' and ''A Pat of Butter'' exhibit a delightful directness and humor.

Whitman's journalistic correspondence indicates a dynamic intelligence that grappled with the major philosophies and social and literary interests of the day: American and European Romanticism, travel writing, metaphysical science, woman's suffrage, and civic reform. In two essays on Emerson— ''Emerson's Essays'' (1845) and ''Immortality as Viewed by Scholars and Scientists'' (1876)—Whitman demonstrates her growth from Transcendental disciple to independent philosopher. In maturity, Whitman held to her own ideological doctrines of personal identity, perfectibility, and universal salvation.

As a champion of literary blackguards, Sarah Whitman manifested considerable analytical expertise. John E. Reilly observes that she was ''perhaps, the only contemporary of Poe who recognized some of the larger dimensions of his work'' (120). Consistently, Whitman asked American critics to separate authors' acts from their literary production. The first book-length vindication of Poe, *Edgar Poe and His Critics*, pleads this defense. Whitman also argues in it that Poe's dark genius anticipated the skeptical Spirit of the Age; he perceived and transmitted its particular crisis through his work.

CRITICAL RECEPTION

By 1849, Whitman had established a reputation as a nature poet and essayist. Anthologist Caroline May particularly commends Whitman's prose, which "exhibit[s] much clearness of perception, and vigour of thought" (235).

Rufus Griswold singles out Whitman—with Elizabeth Oakes Smith, Maria Brooks, and Frances Sargent Osgood—as the premiere poet in his anthology. She "illustrate[s] as high and sustained a range of poetic art" as he believes women can achieve (8).

Whitman received mixed reviews for *Hours of Life* (1853). Generally, her Romantic verse appealed to the public more than her philosophical poetry. One reviewer disparages Whitman's avoidance of "feminine" poetic conventions: "[T]here is little of warm, genial, and sympathetic life in her poetry; the fastidiousness of the scholar has checked the impulsive cordiality of the woman" (quoted in Varner 524). Yet *The Shekinah* critic Fanny Green pronounces *Hours of Life* "a song of the soul" (291): "There is not only beauty in the poem, but a stateliness and dignity worthy of the old Masters" (294).

Although the book fared much better with popular magazines like *Godey's*, *Edgar Poe and His Critics* failed to convince Poe's antagonists. The *New York Advertiser* charges, "It is in fact a woman's argument, in assertion and declamation" (quoted in Varner 433). Whitman's philosophical angle scarcely tempted those anticipating a juicy exposé of the Poe-Whitman amour, nor did it shift the common opinion that Poe was a "bad man."

Scholars have remained vestigially aware of Whitman—generally, on the strength of her notorious romance with Poe. Several editions of her letters exist, of which John Carl Miller's *Poe's Helen Remembers* (1979) provides a recent example.

Poe biographer Kenneth Silverman offers a serious treatment of Whitman and some of her poetry. Silverman describes Whitman as "a woman with sophisticated philosophical and literary interests—after her friend Margaret Fuller, perhaps the leading female literary critic in America" (347).

Contemporary feminist critics recognize Whitman chiefly as a minor figure. Cheryl Walker suggests that "Whitman's poetic range was limited," but "her interests were broad" (*American Women Poets* 54). Similarly, Walker's *The Nightingale's Burden* denominates Whitman briefly as a poet derivative of Bryant and Tennyson. Emily Stipes Watts consigns Whitman to a similar footnote.

With the exception of John Varner's 1940 Ph.D. dissertation, Whitman has attracted only one scholarly monograph, Caroline Ticknor's *Poe's Helen* (1916). Ticknor offers helpful biographical information but little analytical rigor. Reilly's brief essay extols Whitman's critical abilities. Varner's study remains the most thoughtful and provocative analysis of every aspect of Whitman's life and work.

WORKS CITED

Green, Fanny. "Mrs. Whitman's Poems." Review of *Hours of Life and Other Poems*, by Whitman. *The Shekinah* 3, no. 290 (October 1853): 290–296.

Griswold, Rufus Wilmot. *The Female Poets of America*. Philadelphia: Carey and Hart, 1849.

May, Caroline. *The American Female Poets: With Biographical and Critical Notices by Caroline May*. Philadelphia: Lindsay & Blakiston, 1848.

Reilly, John E. "Sarah Helen Whitman as a Critic of Poe." *University of Mississippi Studies in English*, n.s., 3 (1982): 120–127.

St. Armand, Barton Levi. "Veiled Ladies: Dickinson, Bettine, and Transcendental Mediumship." In *Studies in the American Renaissance*, edited by Joel Myerson. Charlottesville: University of Virginia Press, 1987. 1–51.

Silverman, Kenneth. *Edgar A. Poe: Mournful and Never-Ending Remembrance*. New York: HarperCollins, 1991.

Varner, John Grier. "Sarah Helen Whitman: Seeress of Providence." Ph.D. diss., University of Virginia, 1940.

Wagenknecht, Edward. *Edgar Allan Poe: The Man behind the Legend*. New York: Oxford University Press, 1963.

Walker, Cheryl, ed. *American Women Poets of the Nineteenth Century: An Anthology*. New Brunswick: Rutgers University Press, 1992.

BIBLIOGRAPHY

Works by Sarah Helen Whitman

Poetry

Hours of Life and Other Poems. Providence: George H. Whitney, 1853.
"Woman's Sphere." *Providence Daily Journal*, 9 November 1871, 1.
"Minerva and the Doctors." *Providence Daily Journal*, 23 December 1873, 2.
Poems. Boston: Houghton, Osgood and Company, 1879.

Essays and Criticism

"Character and Writings of Shelley." *The Literary Journal, and Weekly Register of Science and the Arts* 1, no. 32 (1834): 352–353.

"On the Nature and Attributes of Genius." *The Boston Pearl* 5, no. 14 (1835): 108.

Review of *Conversations with Goethe, in the Last Years of His Life*. Translated by S. M. Fuller. *Boston Quarterly Review* 3, no. 9 (1840): 20–57.

"Emerson's Essays." *The United States Magazine, and Democratic Review* 16, no. 84 (1845): 589–602.

Edgar Poe and His Critics. New York: Rudd & Carlton, 1860.

"The Woman Question." *Providence Daily Journal*, 11 February 1868, 2.

"Woman's Suffrage." *Providence Daily Journal*, 10 December 1868, 2.

"Byronism." *Providence Daily Journal*, 18 October 1869, 2.

"Progressive Women and 'Average Young Men.' " *Providence Daily Journal*, 15 May 1869, 2.

"Immortality as Viewed by Scholars and Scientists." *Providence Daily Journal*, 20 March 1876, 2.

"Mr. Geo. W. Curtis on the 'True Mischief of Spiritualism.' " *Providence Daily Journal*, 29 September 1876, 1.

Letters and Reprinted Writings

Capron, E. W. *Modern Spiritualism*. Boston: Bela Marsh, 1855.

Miller, John Carl, ed. *Poe's Helen Remembers*. Charlottesville: University of Virginia Press, 1979.

Studies of Sarah Helen Whitman

See also Works Cited.

Ticknor, Caroline. *Poe's Helen*. New York: Scribner's, 1916.

Walker, Cheryl. *The Nightingale's Burden: Women Poets and American Culture before 1900*. Bloomington: Indiana University Press, 1982.

Watts, Emily Stipes. *The Poetry of American Women from 1632 to 1945*. Austin: University of Texas Press, 1977.

A. D. T. WHITNEY
(ADELINE DUTTON TRAIN
WHITNEY)
(1824–1906)

Debra Bernardi

BIOGRAPHY

A. D. T. Whitney spent her youth among the privileged classes of New England. Born on September 15, 1824, she was the daughter of Adeline Dutton and Colonel Enoch Train, a successful Boston shipping merchant. In her later works, such as the advice book for girls *Friendly Letters to Girl Friends* (1896), Whitney praised the traditional emphasis of her early education; at the respected girls' school run by George B. Emerson, she and her classmates were purportedly trained to be good daughters, sisters, neighbors, wives, and mothers.

After marrying Seth Whitney, a businessman over fifteen years her senior, Whitney moved to neighboring Milton, Massachusetts, and lived there until her death. She had four children (one died in infancy) and began her writing career only after her children were grown. Whitney's first major publication was *Mother Goose for Grown Folks* (1860), which explores adult lessons within the children's rhymes. According to one biographical essay, after the success of *Mother Goose*, her publishers urged her to write fiction (Halsey 182); the result was a series of more than twenty novels, most of them aimed at a young, female readership.

MAJOR WORKS AND THEMES

Whitney's first popular work, *Mother Goose for Grown Folks*, raises many of the major themes that her later novels explore: In "Little Jack Horner," for example, she pokes fun at the upper classes; "Missions" advises women to focus their energies in the home; and "Humpty Dumpty" considers the ways unmarried, older women might make themselves useful to society.

Following *Mother Goose*, Whitney published her first novel, *The Boys of Chequasset* (1862), supposedly inspired by her son. She eventually wrote a variety of works, including cookbooks, poetry, and an attack on Christian Science, but it was with her novels that focused on the lives of girls that she came to be ranked among the most popular writers of her time. In *Friendly Letters to Girl Friends*, Whitney classifies her novels as works of realism, which should "help us, best of anything, to find ourselves out" (26); her tales of young girls are indeed filled with lessons about life in American society. Among her best known are a series of four novels that compose the "Real Folks" series: *A Summer in Leslie Goldthwaite's Life* (1866), *We Girls* (1870), *Real Folks* (1871), and *The Other Girls* (1873). The female characters who reappear in these texts learn the emptiness of the pretensions of social rank while acknowledging the ways social position organizes society. In *We Girls*, for example, the heroines invite less fortunate girls to their parties, thereby helping others to move up socially; the novel thus notes the significance of social position and destabilizes rigid class structures.

Nineteenth-century readers of Whitney's work presumably also learned that women's happiness can be found in domesticity. The heroines of *We Girls* do without (most) hired help and enjoy performing household duties themselves. In *The Other Girls*, Whitney combines her critique of class distinctions with a celebration of domestic labor, drawing heroines who happily take on jobs as servants. She thereby promotes the idea that white American women in need of jobs should consider becoming domestics, offering a solution to the period's apparently nagging servant girl question—the widespread concern over the difficulty in finding good household help. It also points to Whitney's rather disturbing conviction, noted by Elinor Field, that untidy immigrants were crowding out American working girls who would be better off finding employment in the domestic sphere than in shops or dressmaking establishments (184).

Marriage is a frequent theme in Whitney's work (at least one marriage concludes almost all her novels), and several texts specifically explore the often rocky road to a good match. In *Faith Gartney's Girlhood* (1863), the heroine comes to realize that the man everyone expects her to marry is not right for her; she follows her heart and waits to discover her true love. In *The Gayworthys* (1865), one couple waits seventeen years before they can finally articulate their feelings for each other, and another, separated while the young man is at sea, has difficulty in reestablishing their connection after leading such different lives. *Hitherto* (1869), considered by some readers as perhaps too sophisticated for a young female audience, traces the loves of Anstiss Dolmeare. For many years, Anstiss is dissatisfied in her marriage to a hardworking, comfortable farmer. Finally, believing her husband is dying, Anstiss realizes how her love for him has grown. This was a match made in heaven all along. But, *Hitherto* asks, what about bad marriages, "where there is nothing to cling to"? (539). The answer promulgated here is that one can bear those because this living is "just a little bit" (539) of the larger spiritual plan. Bearing with the difficulties of life, trusting to divine providence, and knowing there is a world beyond earthly life are part of the lessons learned by characters worrying about their marital futures.

Patience Strong, an "old maid" of thirty-six, allows Whitney to explore another of her favorite themes—the place of older, unmarried women in society. The character is featured in *Patience Strong's Outings* (1868) and, later, in *Sights and Insights* (1876). One of Patience's points is that older women need to be appreciated: "People are so taken up with looking for the *coming* woman, that they forget all about the *going* one" (87). And from *Faith Gartney's Girlhood* to *We Girls, Hitherto*, and *Square Pegs* (1899), Whitney images worlds in which spinsters play crucial roles in their societies—dispensing wisdom, caring for the sick, and generally offering good company.

Overall, Whitney's works support the dominant gender narratives of white American, middle-class culture. Her novels are firmly entrenched in a domestic ideology that believes women affect the world by affecting the home. In a pamphlet entitled *The Law of Woman Life* (n.d.), Whitney argues against votes for women, asserting that women must influence "not at the polls, where the last utterance of a people's voice is given—where the results of character and conscience, and intelligence are shown . . . but where children learn to think and speak—where men love and listen, and the word is forming" (4). Her *Friendly Letters to Girl Friends* is filled with the advice her earlier novels dramatize—a woman's place is at home: "Make for this with all your power; the reestablishing of sweet, strong home centralities" (197). Supporting the idea of separate spheres for men and women, Whitney's novels celebrate female lives: Domestic work is described in such detail as to resemble spiritual rituals, prefiguring similar qualities in the work of Sarah Orne Jewett, who was an admirer of Whitney's.

If Whitney steps out of dominant ideology in any way, it is perhaps with her characters' attitudes toward economics and social positions. Where a number of Whitney heroines break social barriers by inviting unfortunate neighbors to their parties, the protagonist of *Square Pegs* goes further: Estabel Charlock questions the entire capitalist system. She conjectures, "I suppose if the men at the top—the money end—of the line didn't want so much, there would be more to go all the way down" (344). And later, she takes a nearly socialist position by thinking that the amount of money the rich can have should be regulated; as she puts it, "I don't think it ought to be so much credit to anybody to have *heaps* of money. It would be better to have a rule of giveaway" (346). It may be here that Whitney is at her most radical, causing the *New York Times* to chastise her for not thinking "her [economic] principles all the way through their working" ("New Novels" 740).

CRITICAL RECEPTION

Today A. D. T. Whitney is little known and little read. She appears in only one well-known contemporary critical work, Alfred Habegger's *Gender, Fantasy, and Realism*. But Whitney's contemporaries gave her a great deal of attention. An 1872 article in *The Nation* casts her as one of the three "most eagerly sought" (335) writers in a suburban Boston library, along with Harriet Beecher Stowe and Louisa May Alcott, with *We Girls* as a particular favorite. *Faith Gartney's Girlhood* was a national best-seller in 1863, selling upwards of 300,000 copies (Mott 309).

The popular press is mainly laudatory of Whitney's works, finding virtue in her female characters' demure qualities, which, perhaps, are the aspects of her novels most troubling to twentieth-century readers (especially feminists). The *New York Times* in 1896 praises the entire corpus of Whitney's novels for girls, comparing her work to those writers better known to us today: "Her books were as dear [to her readers] as Miss Edgeworth and Miss Sedgwick were to her— nay dearer, for they are full of the rich spiritual life. . . . We can imagine no better friends for girls than her Faiths, Says, Leslies, Barbaras. . . . We are at times distinctly conscious of a lack of fineness of fibre in Miss Alcott's girls, never in Miss Whitney's. . . . Miss Whitney's [characters] charm us by that sensitive withdrawal, that modest withholding we should like to see in our own girls" ("Mrs. Whitney's Letters" 3). Whitney, however, does suffer under the critical eye of Henry James, who reviewed *The Gayworthys* for the *North American Review*, criticizing Whitney's use of a young female character as a "degradation of sentiment." However, even James found in Whitney "much that is admirable and much that is powerful" (621–622).

WORKS CITED

"The Experience of a Public Library." *The Nation* 14 (May 23, 1872): 334–335.

Field, Elinor Whitney. "The Neighborhood Stories of Mrs. A. D. T. Whitney." *The Horn Book* 29, no. 3 (June 1953): 175–189.

Habegger, Alfred. *Gender, Fantasy, and Realism in American Literature.* New York: Columbia University Press, 1982.

Halsey, Francis Whiting. "Mrs. A. D. T. Whitney." In *Women Authors of Our Day in Their Homes.* New York: James Pott, 1903.

James, Henry. Review of *The Gayworthys. North American Review*, no. 109 (October 1865): 619–622.

Mott, Frank Luther. *Golden Multitudes: The Story of Best Sellers in the United States.* New York: Macmillan, 1947.

"Mrs. Whitney's Letters to Girls." *The New York Times Saturday Review of Books and Art*, 19 December 1896, 2–3.

"New Novels: Works by Marion Crawford, Mrs. Crockett, Blanche Willis Howard, Mrs. Whitney, and Margaret Sherwood." *The New York Times Saturday Review of Books and Art*, November 4, 1899, 740–741.

BIBLIOGRAPHY

Works by A. D. T. Whitney

Footsteps on the Seas: A Poem. Boston: Crosby, Nichols, and Co., 1857.
Mother Goose for Grown Folks. New York: Rudd and Carleton, 1860.

The Boys at Chequasset. Boston: A. K. Loring, 1862.

Faith Gartney's Girlhood. Boston: A. K. Loring, 1863.

The Gayworthys. Boston: A. K. Loring, 1865.

A Summer in Leslie Goldthwaite's Life. Boston: A. K. Loring, 1866.

Patience Strong's Outings. Boston: A. K. Loring, 1868.

Hitherto. Boston: A. K. Loring, 1869.

*That Night at Lower Eddy and Other Stories by Mrs. A. D. T. Whitney and Other Popular
     American Authors.* Boston: D. Lothrop, 1870.

We Girls. Boston: Fields, Osgood, 1870.

Real Folks. Boston: Fields, Osgood, 1871.

Zerub Throop's Experiment. Boston: Loring, 1871.

Pansies. N.p.: Strahan Publishers, 1872.

Six of One by Half a Dozen of the Other. With Harriet Beecher Stowe, Lucretia P. Hale,
     Frederic W. Loring, Frederic B. Perkins, and Edward Everett Hale. Boston: Rob-
     erts Brothers, 1872.

The Other Girls. Boston: Fields, Osgood, 1873.

Sights and Insights. Boston: J. R. Osgood and Co., 1876.

Just How: A Key to the Cook-books. Boston: Houghton, Osgood and Co., 1878.

Odd or Even? Boston: Houghton, Osgood and Co., 1880.

Bonnyborough. Boston: Houghton, Mifflin, 1886.

Homespun Yarns. Boston: Houghton, Mifflin, 1886.

Bird Talk. Boston: Houghton, Mifflin, 1887.

Daffodils. Boston: Houghton, Mifflin, 1887.

Ascutney Street. Boston: Houghton, Mifflin, 1890.

A Golden Gossip. Boston: Houghton, Mifflin, 1892.

White Memories. Boston: Houghton, Mifflin, 1893.

The Popular Tales of Mrs. A. D. T. Whitney. London: Simpkin, Marshall, Hamilton,
     Kent, and Co., 1895?

Friendly Letters to Girl Friends. Boston: Houghton, Mifflin, 1896.

The Open Mystery: A Reading of the Mosaic Story. Boston: Houghton, Mifflin, 1897.

Square Pegs. Boston: Houghton, Mifflin, 1899.

The Integrity of Christian Science. N.p., 1880(?).

Biddy's Episodes. Boston: Houghton, Mifflin, 1904.

The Law of Woman Life. N.p., n.d. (Pamphlet) 1880?

Studies of A. D. T. Whitney

Field, Elinor Whitney. "The Neighborhood Stories of Mrs. A. D. T. Whitney." *The
     Horn Book* 29, no. 3 (June 1953): 175–189.

Halsey, Francis Whiting. "Mrs. A. D. T. Whitney." In *Women Authors of Our Day in
     Their Homes.* New York: James Pott, 1903.

Seaton, Beverly. "Adeline Dutton Train Whitney." In *American Women Writers*, edited
     by Lina Mainiero. New York: Frederick Ungar, 1982.

Stowe, Harriet Beecher. "Mrs. A. D. T. Whitney." In *Our Famous Women.* Hartford:
     A. D. Worthington, 1884.

Vedder, Henry C. "Adeline D. T. Whitney." In *American Writers of To-Day.* New York:
     Silver, Burdett, 1894.

AUGUSTA JANE EVANS WILSON (1835–1909)

Shannon L. Nichols

BIOGRAPHY

When Augusta Jane Evans was born on May 8, 1835, in Augusta, Georgia, she seemed destined to assume all the traditional social and economic privileges of the antebellum "Southern belle." Her parents, Matthew Ryan Evans and Sarah Skrine Howard, were both from established Southern families with ties dating back to the Revolutionary War. In addition to extensive landholdings, Matt Evans co-owned a thriving mercantile firm in Columbus, Georgia; however, the depression of the late 1830s and the construction of a luxurious new home— dubbed "Matt's Folly" by his neighbors—forced him into bankruptcy in 1839. Life thereafter became a series of moves and economic setbacks for the growing family. These financial strains encouraged the young Augusta to try her hand at writing domestic fiction. Although she later became one of the wealthiest women in Alabama, the insecurity of her early life led Evans to return again and again in her fiction to the theme of a proud young woman forced to endure the slights and privations of poverty.

In 1845, in an effort to recoup the family fortunes, Matt Evans joined the westward migration, taking his family by covered wagon to San Antonio, Texas. General Zachary Taylor's troops kept the town relatively safe from attack during the Mexican War of 1846–1848, but the border town was scarcely quiet. A population made up of Mexicans, Spaniards, Germans, Indians, native Texans, and new immigrants, like the Evans, made for a volatile mix of cultural, religious, and social practices. Although Matt Evans's business prospered, Indian raids, street brawls, and busy brothels shocked and alarmed the new residents. Finally, in 1849, the dangers of frontier life led the family back east to settle in Mobile, Alabama.

During these years, Evans was tutored by her intelligent and devoted mother. Sarah Howard Evans was extremely well-read, and she shared her love of European literature with her serious, precocious eldest daughter. Outside of a brief period in Mobile, Evans received no formal schooling, however, as she was to say later, "[M]y mother was my Alma Mater, the one to whom I owe everything, and whom I reverence more than all else on earth" (quoted in Fidler 21). Also, during her childhood, Evans had been allowed free access to numerous well-stocked libraries, and her photographic memory absorbed an impressive knowledge of languages, literature, history, and Greek and Roman mythology, which she later incorporated liberally, if occasionally indiscriminately, into her novels.

In Mobile, the family's financial problems continued as illness and fire hampered Matt Evans's efforts to provide a consistent, adequate income for the household, which now contained eight children. In an attempt to aid the household finances, when she was not yet twenty, Augusta wrote her first novel, *Inez: A Tale of the Alamo*, which was published anonymously in 1855. Although *Inez* was ignored by readers and critics, her second novel, *Beulah* (1859), a spiritual bildungsroman, was a critical and financial success.

The Confederacy had few more loyal partisans than Evans. An uncompromising champion of secession, slavery, and Southern culture, she devoted her considerable organizational and literary talents to the cause. During the war, she nursed the wounded in a base near her home, affectionately nicknamed "Camp Beulah" after her second novel, wrote propaganda for the Mobile *Register*, and even, on occasion, advised senior Confederate officers and government officials such as General P. T. Beauregard and J. L. M. Curry. Her secessionist allegiances also prompted her to terminate her engagement to James Reed Spaulding, a pious, serious young Northerner, when he wrote a series of editorials in support of Lincoln and the Union in 1860. Her third novel, *Macaria; or, The Altars of Sacrifice* (1863; 1864), an impassioned defense of the Confederate cause, was so persuasive that one Northern general banned the book in camp and had all available copies burned. In late 1865, she claimed, "I believe I loved our cause *as a Jesuit his order*; and its utter ruin has saddened and crushed me, as no other event of my life had power to do so" (quoted in Fidler 119). After Appomattox, in her typical energetic, pragmatic fashion, she literalized her grief by memorializing the Confederate dead and fervently supporting the "Lost Cause."

For many Southerners, Reconstruction may have been the nadir of their fortunes, but for Evans, it was a period of both personal and public triumph. In 1867, *St. Elmo*, an erudite romance with many parallels to *Jane Eyre*, became an overnight sensation. Within four months of publication, over a million readers had read the rags to riches story of Edna Earl. Soon, steamboats, railway cars, villages, cigars, and children had been named after the Byronic titular hero or the pious young orphan who rescues him from his dissolute life. The following year, when she was thirty-three, she wed Colonial Lorenzo Madison Wilson, a wealthy widower twenty-eight years her senior, assuming management of his large home and four children. Despite the strictures of her heroines against women working after they assumed the moral and domestic duties of marriage, Evans produced five more novels at irregular intervals between 1869 and 1907. Although these later works never achieved the success of her early novels, she maintained a consistent following of readers until her death in Mobile, Alabama, in 1909.

MAJOR WORKS AND THEMES

Evans, like many Victorian Americans, believed literature "should elevate, should refine, should sanctify the heart" (quoted in Fidler 54). Although her novels have been categorized as domestic or sentimental fiction, the traditional romance plot is little more than a vehicle for the moral and intellectual education of her readers. All nine novels are set in the context of a specific political, intellectual, or moral conflict. Through the spiritual doubts of Beulah Benton, for example, she guides the reader through the major currents of early nineteenth-century European and American philosophical thought. *Beulah* is a semiautobiographical account of Evans's own struggle to reconcile rationalism and faith, written to "combat scepticism . . . and if possible, to help others to avoid the thorny path I have trod ere I was convinced of the fallibility of human reason" (quoted in Fidler 54). From her first work, *Inez*, an almost hysterical attack on Roman Catholicism, to her final work, *Devota* (1907), which supports capital punishment and women's domestic responsibilities, Evans was engaged in correcting what she perceived as the ills of modern democracy: demagogy, materialism, women's rights, moral laxness, and unfettered individualism. Invariably conservative in her political and social views, she nostalgically idealized the Old South's hierarchical gender, class, and race structure.

Her heroines exemplify the virtues of a selfless, unswerving loyalty to family and home, often risking love, reputation, and even their lives in their adherence to the values of "true womanhood." Their moral superiority is usually rewarded by an advantageous marriage, where they exchange self-actualization and independence for love, security, and moral influence. Although these young women can become tiresome in their unremitting goodness—they are invariably described as "pure," "proud," and "pious"—they are also ambitious, independent, and committed to advanced educational opportunities for women. In *St. Elmo*, Edna Earl is determined to earn her own living working in a factory and devotes her daylight hours, and much of her nighttime ones too, to intensive study of theology, philosophy, languages, and the sciences. Her diligence is rewarded when she becomes a literary cause célèbre. At the conclusion of the novel, however, her bridegroom declares, "To-day I snap the fetters of your literary bondage. There shall be no more books written! No more study, no more toil" (365). St. Elmo's words may deny the importance of women's education, but the novel implicitly endorses an alternate model as Evans's generous use of arcane language and literary allusions sent more than one female reader "running to the Dictionary or to an encyclopedia" (quoted in Harris 72).

CRITICAL RECEPTION

Until the early twentieth century, Evans had a sizable popular following, especially in the South. *St. Elmo* has been in print since it was published in 1867, despite being much abused, parodied, and dismissed by critics for its excesses of sentiment, rakish hero, and purple prose. Eight months after it appeared, a New York humorist, Charles Henry Webb, parodied the Byronic hero and the saintly Edna Earl and her erudition in *St. Twel'mo, or the Cuneiform Cyclopedist of Chattanooga*. Most nineteenth-century readers, however, admired the sincerity of its moral message, and many attested to its beneficial influence. In this century, despite her best-seller status, Evans has been virtually forgotten.

William Perry Fidler's *Augusta Evans Wilson, 1835–1909, a Biography* (1951) is the most extensive discussion of her life and works. More recently, there have been some radical rereadings of her major novels. As critics such as Susan K. Harris and Drew Gilpin Faust have observed, frequently there is a marked dissonance between the romantic overplot and reactionary views and the protagonist's drive for education and public recognition. As Harris says in her reading of *St. Elmo*, for female readers sympathetic to a quest for "intellectual parity . . . the most memorable portions of the novel would consist of Edna's intellectual triumphs, not her final submission" (76). Further, the heroines frequently exemplify a radical moral individualism that permits them to resist male domination.

It is not only twentieth-century readers who have noted these paradoxical elements in her novels. In 1881, Augusta Evans was listed among ten domestic novelists considered "questionable" by librarians at seventy large public libraries, probably because she implicitly criticizes the patriarchal family structure (Garrison 73). In more than one novel, the heroes are banished from the text for large periods or killed, and usually submission to the marriage bond is vigorously resisted until the final pages. Similarly, the ruthlessness and cruelty of her father figures raise questions about the beneficence of the Victorian family. In *Macaria*, Irene Huntingdon's father effectively disowns her after she refuses the suit of a dissolute cousin suitor, while in *A Speckled Bird* (1902), Eglah Kent is forced into a loveless marriage to save her swindling father from political ruin. These "moral exemplars," as David Reynolds suggests, live in "a world of devalued, amoral males" (342).

Beulah, Macaria, and *St. Elmo* have recently been reprinted, accompanied by excellent introductions. Although the didacticism and pedantry of her novels make it unlikely that Evans will become widely read again, they offer the student of American culture an important insight into the tastes and values of nineteenth-century readers.

WORKS CITED

Fidler, William Perry. *Augusta Evans Wilson, 1835–1909, a Biography*. University: University of Alabama Press, 1951.

Garrison, Dee. "Immoral Fiction in the Late Victorian Library." *American Quarterly* 28 (1976): 71–89.

Harris, Susan K. "Introduction to the Exploratory Text: Subversions of the Narrative Designs in *St. Elmo*." In *19th-Century American Women's Novels: Interpretive Strategies*. Cambridge: Cambridge University Press, 1990.

Reynolds, David S. *Beneath the American Renaissance: The Subversive Imagination in the Age of Emerson and Melville*. Cambridge: Harvard University Press, 1988.

BIBLIOGRAPHY

Works by Augusta Jane Evans Wilson

Inez: A Tale of the Alamo. New York: Harper, 1855.

Beulah. New York: Derby and Jackson, 1859.

Macaria; or, The Altars of Sacrifice. Confederate ed. Richmond: West and Johnson, 1863. Northern ed. New York: Lippincott, 1864.

St. Elmo. New York: Carleton, 1867.

At the Mercy of Tiberius. New York: Dillingham, 1869.

Vashti; or, Until Death Us Do Part. New York: Carleton, 1869.

Infelice. New York: Carleton, 1875.

A Speckled Bird. New York: Dillingham, 1902.

Devota. New York: Dillingham, 1907.

Studies of Augusta Jane Evans Wilson

Alderman, Edwin A., and Joel Chandler Harris, eds. *A Library of Southern Literature*. Atlanta: Martin and Hoyt, 1907. 13: 5841–5864.

Derby, J. C. *Fifty Years among Authors, Books, and Publishers*. New York: Carleton, 1884. 389–399.

Faust, Drew Gilpin. "Introduction: *Macaria*, a War Story for Confederate Women." In *Macaria; or, The Altars of Sacrifice*. Baton Rouge: Louisiana State University Press, 1992. xiii–xxix.

Fidler, William Perry. "The Life and Works of Augusta Evans Wilson." Ph.D. diss., University of Chicago, 1947.

Forrest, Mary [Mrs. Julia Deane Freeman]. *Women of the South Distinguished in Literature*. New York: Derby and Jackson, 1860. 328–332.

Jones, Anne Goodwyn. *Tomorrow Is Another Day: The Woman Writer in the South, 1859–1936*. Baton Rouge: Louisiana State University Press, 1981. 57–91.

Maurice, A. B. "*St. Elmo* and Its Author." *Bookman* 16 (September 1902): 12–14.

Moss, Elizabeth. *Domestic Novelists of the Old South: Defenders of Southern Culture*. Baton Rouge: Louisiana State University Press, 1992.

HARRIET E. WILSON
(1827?–1863?)

Cynthia J. Davis

BIOGRAPHY

There is a growing myth surrounding Harriet Wilson that goes something like this: No one knew of either her or her only novel's existence until Henry Louis Gates, Jr., resuscitated them in 1983. It was only then that Wilson was restored to her rightful place as the author of the first novel published by a black person in the United States and as one of the first two black women to publish a novel in English. And yet, while the information about "firsts" is correct, reports of Wilson's obscurity have been greatly exaggerated. In fact, Wilson's novel achieved a certain legendary status among rare booksellers over the years and even scored a mention in Herbert Ross Brown's seminal *The Sentimental Novel in America* (1940).

It isn't true, then, that Wilson was lost to history until Gates performed his heroic rescue effort; rather, what *is* true is that what was known about her was historically inaccurate. Until the sleuthing efforts of Gates and his researchers proved otherwise, many critics and collectors assumed that the author of *Our Nig* was a white male. The fact that the narrative's title page refers to its author only as "Our Nig" no doubt added to the confusion about authorial identity.

Of course, as Gates and subsequent scholars have demonstrated, Harriet Wilson was actually a black female. There is little else about Wilson, however, of which we can be certain. It is possible, as Gates contends in his introduction to the 1983 edition of the novel, that Harriet E. Adams was born in 1807 or 1808, if the age of fifty-two given on the 1860 Boston federal census is correct. However, it is also possible that she was born in 1827 or 1828, if the age of twenty-two recorded on the 1850 New Hampshire federal census is accurate (Gates xiv). To add to the confusion, these separate census reports also contradict each other as to Adams's place of birth: On the former, Wilson's birthplace is re-corded as being Fredericksburg, Virginia; in the 1850 census, her birthplace is listed as being New Hampshire. Finally, there is just as much mystery cloaking Wilson's death date. Although some sources list it as 1870, there is little to no written evidence of Wilson's existence beyond 1863 (White 26).

The decade of Wilson's life that is the most fully sketched is the 1850s, a decade that culminated in both the publication of her only novel, *Our Nig* (1859), and, the subsequent year, the death of her only son, George. In fact, George died less than six months after his mother published the story she hoped would save his (and possibly her own) life. Ironically, as Gates points out, it was his death certificate, unearthed more than 100 years after the boy's untimely demise, that definitively identified the racial identity of his mother and hence catapulted Wilson into literary history as the foremother of African-American novelists (Gates xiii).

To the extent that *Our Nig* is autobiographical, it seems certain that from a young age Wilson served as an indentured servant in the home of a white family in Milford, New Hampshire. There is even some question, however, as to that family's identity. The 1850 census lists a Harriet Adams as living in Milford with a white family, the Boyleses. It is this family that Gates contends serves as the model for the "Bellmonts" with whom Frado lives in *Our Nig*. Samuel Boyles, the head of the household, apparently supplemented his income as a carpenter by taking in boarders, including at one time Wilson.

More recent archival work by Barbara A. White, however, suggests that al-though Wilson may have resided with the Boyleses while in Milford, this oc-curred after she was finally released from her indentured servitude. Exonerating the Boyleses, White contends instead that the "Bellmonts" were actually mod-eled upon a family named Hayward. The information White has unearthed re-veals marked parallels between the Hayward family and farm and the family and locale described in Wilson's narrative (White 22–23).

What makes White's claim especially significant is that it means that the real-life figure upon whom Frado's she-devil mistress is based was Rebecca S. Hutchinson Hayward. Rebecca, besides being a direct descendant of Anne Hutchinson, was also a member of a prominent family of abolitionists (Milford itself was an abolitionist stronghold and a stop on the Underground Railroad). Rebecca Hayward was, in fact, related to a family that gained international recognition as the Hutchinson Family Singers, known for their efforts on behalf of abolitionism as well as women's rights and temperance. This revelation thus adds resonance to the hostility toward certain hypocritical abolitionists expressed in *Our Nig*. It certainly helps to explain this hostility, hitherto puzzling since abolitionists would undoubtedly have been Wilson's primary audience and hence the last group one would think the author, desperate to sell her novel, would want to alienate.

There may be another reason underlying Wilson's resentment of abolitionists: It is possible that she met her husband, Thomas Wilson, through his contacts within the abolitionist movement. It may be that the man Wilson married in the fall of 1851 is the author of one of that decade's several falsified fugitive slave narratives—narratives, ironically, that most abolitionists showed more interest in reading and promoting than they ever did in Wilson's *Our Nig: Sketches from the Life of a Free Black, in a Two-Story White House, North, Showing that Slavery's Shadows Fall Even There.*

The match between the Wilsons was short-lived: Thomas deserted his wife before their child was even born. Only nine months after her marriage, Harriet was forced to deliver George Mason Wilson (possibly named after her favorite of the Hayward children) in a "Country House" notorious for its intolerable conditions. According to a testimonial letter written by "Allida" and appended to *Our Nig*, Thomas returned once more after George's birth but eventually abandoned his family forever.

Thomas Wilson left behind him a wife and son who suffered not simply from his desertion but also from poverty and illness. Wilson's health was by this time broken, no doubt from the abuse she suffered as a servant that she so amply documents in *Our Nig*. George, it seems, was from birth a frail child. Furthermore, there is evidence that mother and son were so impoverished that they were forced on several occasions to rely on the town for aid. At least once, when George was three, he spent a month alone in another country farm than the one in which he was born before his mother—who had been very ill and hence unable to pay his board—could retrieve him.

The next time Wilson's whereabouts seem relatively certain she was living in Boston, the town in which she eventually published *Our Nig*. Beginning in 1856 and until 1863, Boston city records indicate a "Harriet E. Wilson, widow" as a resident of the city. Milford records, meanwhile, indicate that she had left her son behind in New Hampshire with a couple who provided for him with the help of town support. It was there that George died and was buried, despite his mother's desperate attempts to save him through her writing.

In 1859, some six months before George died of fever, Wilson registered the copyright for *Our Nig* in the Boston District's Clerk Office. She apparently paid for the publication of the novel out of her own pocket. Most likely she supported herself as a seamstress and/or dressmaker during this period and even managed to turn a profit for a time by selling hair dye. But with her own and her son's health failing, Wilson decided to write *Our Nig* in hopes of once and for all easing their lot. As she wrote in her preface to the narrative, "Deserted by kindred, disabled by failing health, I am forced to some experiment which shall aid me in maintaining myself and child without extinguishing this feeble life. . . . I sincerely appeal to my colored brethren universally for patronage, hoping they will not condemn this attempt of their sister to be erudite, but rally around me a faithful band of supporters and defenders" (n.p.).

Sadly, no such help came. After George's death, little is known of Wilson's activities. She seems to have continued to live in Boston until 1863, but after that date, Wilson virtually disappears from extant records (Gates; White).

MAJOR WORKS AND THEMES

Wilson's one and only novel is in some respects as difficult to pin down as is its author's background. When Gates reintroduced *Our Nig* to the reading public in 1983, he compared it to a sentimental novel, borrowing Nina Baym's definition of the form from her classic *Woman's Fiction* (Gates xli–xliii). Like most sentimental heroines, Frado, the mulatto protagonist of *Our Nig*, finds herself without parents, poor and friendless, abused by those who have power over her. She is hence forced to rely on her own strength of character and a select circle of friends who provide a surrogate family in order for her to find the sustenance to survive, even, perhaps, to triumph.

And yet there are marked differences between Wilson's narrative and the sentimental novel. For one thing, Frado considers, but eventually rejects, religion, especially once she learns that it is possible she and Mrs. B. might wind up sharing the same heaven. For another, there is so much anger in this narrative, and it is not repressed but righteous.

In addition, unlike the domestic novels so popular at the time Wilson was writing, Frado never finds anything resembling a home. In fact, as one recent critic points out, *Our Nig* resembles a Gothic novel far more than it does a domestic one, especially for the sadistic tormenting and silencing of its heroine and hence for the haunting, if not outright haunted, dimensions of her homelife and the "antinurture" she receives therein (Stern esp. 442–443).

Unlike in most women's fiction published during what one critic deemed "the feminine fifties" (Pattee), Wilson's protagonist is never rewarded, either materially or spiritually, despite her struggle to lead a virtuous life. The narrative does not have a happy ending; rather, it simply ends (although not without a rather ominous final paragraph describing the deaths of many of the Bellmont family and a promise that, for those still living, the narrator will "never cease to track them till beyond mortal vision" [131]).

Our Nig, published just one month after John Brown's raid on Harper's Ferry and virtually on the eve of the Civil War, almost inevitably invites comparisons to slave narratives, even though it does takes place "In a Two-Story White House, North." In fact, this seems to be precisely Wilson's point: Her narrative documents the extent to which—and not simply because of the passage of the 1850 Fugitive Slave Law—even the supposedly free North was not without real prejudice toward and dangers for blacks. *Our Nig* even appends the requisite testimonial letters that by now seemed obligatory to the slave narrative as a genre.

What's more, even though its setting and the supposedly "free" status of its protagonist disqualify it as a literal slave narrative, *Our Nig* functions quite nicely as an allegory for slavery. Not only does it focus on the struggles of its black protagonist for freedom from an oppressive master (or, in this case, mistress), like most antislavery writings it underscores the economic motivations that underwrite human relations within such a system—the tragedy of the fact that, to paraphrase Harriet Beecher Stowe's original subtitle for *Uncle Tom's Cabin*, humans were turned into things.

A final point worth mentioning about Wilson's narrative is its uneasy blending of autobiography and fiction. In his initial introduction to the text, Gates highlights its fictional aspects. But even there he notes how the autobiographical "I" keeps intruding on the third-person narrative, especially near its conclusion and in such chapter headings as "Mag Smith, My Mother." Ultimately, Gates's decision to underscore the narrative's literary dimensions enables him to claim Wilson as a first novelist rather than as but one in a succession of black female–authored autobiographies. Subsequent critics, however, appear divided over the extent to which the narrative is fictional, most resolving the conundrum by referring to the work as a fictionalized autobiography.

CRITICAL RECEPTION

Our Nig did not receive even one locatable review or notice when it was originally published. This is puzzling, given the reception of such novels as *Clotel* (1853) and the favorable response, especially within abolitionist circles, to black-authored narratives critical of enslaving conditions. Gates speculates that, in addition to the narrative's criticism of abolitionists, the controversial interracial marriage of Frado's parents might provide the explanation for this neglect (xxviii). Whatever the reason, the novel has been generally neglected by and in anthologies, bibliographies, criticism, or histories from the time of its publication up until the time of its rediscovery. Such neglect has now amply been remedied, for in the more-than-a-decade since its reissue, numerous critics have published chapters of books or articles in prominent journals about the novel, typically addressing issues of genre and/or of bodily representation. To date, however, there exists no book-length study of the author.

For close to 125 years, an audience for this powerful novel was virtually nonexistent. Contemporary critics have made much of the lack of response to *Our Nig*, its ultimate "failure" to be heard, claiming the text and its history as paradigmatic of a larger societal silence (silencing) of black women's lives and writings. However, these critics—and, for that matter, any reader of this novel—would concur that if there is a failure associated with *Our Nig*, it lies not in the narrative but in the audience—in their failure to listen. For ultimately, if Wilson's narrative found no audience, it was most certainly *not* because she did not speak and in ways that ought to have been heard.

WORKS CITED

Baym, Nina. *Woman's Fiction: A Guide to Novels by and about Women in America 1820–1870*. Ithaca: Cornell University Press, 1978.
Brown, Herbert Ross. *The Sentimental Novel in America, 1789–1860*. Durham, NC: Duke University Press, 1940.

Gates, Henry Louis. Introduction to *Our Nig*, by Harriet Wilson. New York: Random House, 1983. xi–lv.

Pattee, Fred Lewis. *The Feminine Fifties*. New York: D. Appleton-Century Co., 1940.

Stowe, Harriet Beecher. *Uncle Tom's Cabin; [The Man That Was a Thing.] Life among the Lowly*. 1852. Reprint, New York: Penguin, 1981.

White, Barbara A. " 'Our Nig' and the She-Devil: New Information about Harriet Wilson and the 'Bellmont' Family." *American Literature* 65 (March 1993): 19–52.

Wilson, Harriet. *Our Nig*. 1859. Reprint, New York: Random House, 1983.

BIBLIOGRAPHY

Work by Harriet E. Wilson

Our Nig. 1859. Reprint, New York: Random House, 1983.

Studies of Harriet E. Wilson

Carby, Hazel. *Reconstructing Womanhood: The Emergence of the Afro-American Woman Novelist*. New York: Oxford University Press, 1987.

Davis, Cynthia J. "Speaking the Body's Pain: Harriet Wilson's *Our Nig*." *African American Review* 27 (fall 1993): 391–404.

Ernest, John. "Economics of Identity: Harriet E. Wilson's *Our Nig*." *PMLA* 109 (May 1994): 424–438.

Gardner, Eric. " 'This Attempt of Their Sister': Harriet Wilson's *Our Nig* from Printer to Readers." *New England Quarterly* 66 (June 1993): 226–246.

Gates, Henry Louis. Introduction to *Our Nig*, by Harriet Wilson. New York: Random House, 1983. xi–lv.

Stern, Julia. "Excavating Genre in *Our Nig*." *American Literature* 67 (September 1995): 439–466.

Tate, Claudia. "Allegories of Black Female Desire: Or, Rereading Nineteenth-Century Sentimental Narratives of Black Female Authority." In *Changing Our Own Words: Essays on Criticism, Theory, and Writing by Black Women*, edited by Cheryl A. Wall. New Brunswick: Rutgers University Press, 1989. 98–126.

White, Barbara A. " 'Our Nig' and the She-Devil: New Information about Harriet Wilson and the 'Bellmont' Family." *American Literature* 65 (March 1993): 19–52.

SALLY S. WOOD
(1759–1855)

Barbara A. White

BIOGRAPHY

Sally Sayward Barrell Keating Wood pioneered in the development of U.S. fiction; she was one of the first Americans to publish more than a single novel and one of the earliest literary nationalists. Wood was born in York, Maine, the eldest daughter of Sarah Sayward and Nathaniel Barrell, a lieutenant in the French and Indian Wars. She spent much of her childhood living with her mother's father, who was known as the second richest man in Maine and to whom she was very close. Judge Jonathan Sayward, although a Tory during the Revolution, managed to retain most of his wealth and eminence. The Barrells had friends on the rebel side, and Nathaniel, son of a Boston merchant, became a delegate to the Constitutional Convention. Wood later wrote an antiwar novella, never published in her lifetime, with the title *War, the Parent of Domestic Calamity: A Tale of the Revolution.*

In 1778, when she was nineteen, Wood married Richard Keating, a clerk in her grandfather's office; they had three children before he died in 1783. During her widowhood, Wood began to write. She did not lack money to support her children, as would be the case later with many widows who took up writing, but she needed some occupation. She states in the preface to her first novel, *Julia* (1800), that her pen "soothed many *melancholy,* and sweetened many *bitter* hours" (n.p.).

Wood's first efforts were stories published anonymously in journals. Then, over a period of five years, she published four novels, again anonymously as "a Lady of Massachusetts" (Maine did not separate from Massachusetts until 1820). The novels were melodramatic adventure stories with Gothic elements borrowed from English writers, and all were consistent with her conservative background. In *Julia and the Illuminated Baron* (1800) she attacks the French Revolution and makes the villain a member of the secret society of the Illuminati, a supposed hotbed of atheists and radicals. *Dorval; or the Speculator* (1801) deals with the American scene and the evils of speculation and paper money. *Amelia; or the Influence of Virtue* (1802), again set in France, details the sufferings of a virtuous wife who accepts her husband's children by his mistress; Wood notes that Amelia is not a disciple of Mary Wollstonecraft and thus obeys her husband.

After the publication in 1804 of her fourth novel, *Ferdinand & Elmira: A Russian Story*, she married General Abiel Wood, a wealthy Tory who had been mobbed during the Revolution. They settled in Wiscasset, Maine, where Wood stopped writing and helped found the Female Charitable Society of Wiscasset. When her husband died in 1811, she moved to Portland and later to Kennebunk. "Madam Wood," as she was known, was something of a celebrity in Maine but published very little in her last fifty years—only *Tales of the Night* (1827), a collection of two novellas with Maine and New Hampshire settings. She again published anonymously, this time as "a Lady of Maine." Apparently Wood destroyed her projected sequel to *Tales*; it is unclear whether she preferred an active social life to writing or whether the rumor is true that she was so impressed by the novels of Sir Walter Scott she gave up writing. At any rate, Wood remained mentally alert into her nineties when she entertained her great-great-grandchildren with stories. She died in Kennebunk at age ninety-five.

MAJOR WORKS AND THEMES

Sally S. Wood's preface to *Dorval*, her second novel, is one of the earliest statements of American literary nationalism. "Why must the amusements of our leisure hours cross the Atlantic?" she asks. "Why we should not aim at independence, with respect to our mental enjoyments, as well as for our more substantial gratifications, I know not." Yet Wood's career illustrates the difficulties early novelists had in putting the nationalist impulse into practice. In her first novel, *Julia and the Illuminated Baron*, she adhered rather closely to the English Gothic tradition; Julia has to endure being kidnapped by the baron, imprisoned in a castlelike mansion, plagued by supernatural voices, and taken on a horrifying visit to a tomb. But Wood was clearly uneasy about presenting "foreign fashions and foreign manners to a people . . . capable of fabricating their own" (Preface to *Dorval*). In her preface to *Julia*, she apologizes for the foreign setting (France and England), explaining rather weakly that she chose it to avoid introducing living characters who might be recognized. Perhaps Wood's real problem was that her chosen form—the melodrama with Gothic touches—could not easily be adapted to the American scene; after all, America had few barons, illuminated or not.

Dorval; or the Speculator is set entirely in America, as Wood proudly announces: "The following pages are wholly American; the characters are those of our own country'' (Preface). But apparently it did not occur to her (as it did not occur to other novelists of the time) to set the book in her native state. Instead, the action takes place in Boston, New York, and Philadelphia, the most prestigious American sites but places Wood hardly knew; they are named but not described or distinguished from one another. Nor did Wood succeed in her attempt to, as she put it, ''catch the manners of her native land'' (Preface). The characters are stock characters of melodrama who behave like foul villains and fair heroines anywhere. Whatever American flavor the book has comes from references to the Revolution and actual financial practices in the new nation (Wood had an uncle who tried to increase his fortune through speculation and was swindled). Wood was a pioneer, but the difficulties in combining American manners and the melodramatic form proved too much for her. She set her subsequent novels, *Amelia* and *Ferdinand & Elmira*, in France and Russia and made no apology; the Gothic element, a prominent part of *Julia* but missing from *Dorval*, reappeared.

During the latter phase of her career, however, Wood made a more successful attempt to portray American manners. In the 1820s in *Tales of the Night*, she turned to historical romance and began to employ local settings. The first of the tales, ''Storms and Sunshine; or the House on the Hill,'' contains a description of a Maine snowstorm, and the second, ''The Hermitage or Rise of Fortune,'' draws on the life of her grandfather, though the focus is a conventional love story. Wood continued in this new direction, drawing on historical events and people and settings of her youth for *War, the Parent of Domestic Calamity: A Tale of the Revolution*, which she wrote after *Tales* but did not publish. Although *War* is flawed by a Websterian ending in which most of the characters suddenly kill themselves or each other, it contains some of Wood's best writing. There are effective descriptions of the ''brown frozen gloom'' (85) of a New England November and of the panic in Maine and New Hampshire caused by the British navy's burning of Falmouth (Portland). Wood mixes antiwar diatribes with positive assessments of the Revolution as ''that glorious cause, which terminated in establishing the freedom of millions'' (105), but the main point of the novella seems to be the ''domestic calamity'' or family divisions caused inevitably by war. Thus, even though Wood tended to be politically conservative, she expressed sentiments, here antiwar and in *Dorval* anticapitalist, that would become standard features of women's literary tradition.

Wood also created capable heroines in spite of her more traditional pronouncements on women. In her prefaces she assures the reader that women are better off attending to domestic duties rather than writing novels, and she disassociates herself from any suggestion of feminism by attacking Mary Wollstonecraft's *Vindication of the Rights of Women*, which had been published ten years before Wood began writing. Yet she also praises women writers, including the Americans ''Philenia'' (Sarah Wentworth Morton) and ''Constantia'' (Judith Sargent Murray). On the question of women, as well as in other matters, Wood was both traditionalist and pioneer. Her major female characters tend to have more spirit than many heroines of the time; they are capable of independent thought and frequently, like Aurelia of *Dorval*, triumph over the villain by their own efforts. Wood uses the technique of contrasting a passive and an active heroine, often sisters. In "Storms and Sunshine," for instance, the independent Cornelia is continually praised by the narrator over her obedient and conventional sister Emma.

CRITICAL RECEPTION

At the time they were published, Wood's novels and novellas were reviewed more favorably than not and became "reasonably popular" with readers (Sears 113). She is mentioned in most of the standard histories of American literature; the emphasis is on *Julia* and its introduction of Gothic elements to American fiction. Generally, Wood is criticized for her tortuous and sensational plots and her two-dimensional characters but acknowledged as a pioneer. Although she has never been well known outside her native Maine, several literary historians have agreed with Alexander Cowie's estimate in *The Rise of the American Novel*: "Although Mrs. Wood possessed only moderate ability, yet by virtue of her early position she repays attention in any study of the novel" (23).

Literary histories of the 1990s have omitted Wood, however. She does not appear in either *The Columbia History of the American Novel* or Richard Ruland and Malcolm Bradbury's history of American literature. In the lengthy *American Women Writers to 1800* she is mentioned only briefly as an author "whose works perpetuated patriarchal ideals of women's second-class citizenship" (171).

What little contemporary work there is on Wood foregrounds the contradictions in her attitudes and practices (Freibert and White; Scheick), instead of focusing solely on her conservatism. For instance, Scheick maintains that *Julia* presents a democratic Jeffersonian message; the same could be argued for *Ferdinand & Elmira*, Wood's last novel. Recently, more attention has been paid to the later work. In his assessment, Cowie stated that "Maine, her homestead, she never wrote of except tangentially" (26). But he did not know of her then-unpublished *War*. Ironically, Wood's literary reputation was established without reference to the work that by twentieth-century standards would be considered her best.

WORKS CITED

American Women Writers to 1800. Edited by Sharon M. Harris. New York: Oxford University Press, 1996.

The Columbia History of the American Novel. Edited by Emory Elliott. New York: Columbia University Press, 1991.

Cowie, Alexander. *The Rise of the American Novel*. New York: American Book Co., 1948.

Ruland, Richard, and Malcolm Bradbury. *From Puritanism to Postmodernism: A History of American Literature*. New York: Viking, 1991.

Sears, Donald A. "Maine Fiction before 1840: A Microcosm." *Colby Library Quarterly* 14 (September 1978): 109–124.

BIBLIOGRAPHY

Works by Sally S. Wood

Novels

Julia and the Illuminated Baron. Portsmouth, NH: Charles Peirce, 1800.
Dorval; or the Speculator. Portsmouth, NH: Nutting and Whitelock, 1801.
Amelia; or the Influence of Virtue. Portsmouth, NH: William Treadwell, 1802.
Ferdinand & Elmira: A Russian Story. Baltimore: Samuel Butler, 1804.

Novellas

Tales of the Night. Portland, ME: Thomas Todd, 1827. Reprinted with introduction by Herbert Ross Brown. Somersworth, NH: New England History Press, 1982.
War, the Parent of Domestic Calamity: A Tale of the Revolution. In *A Handful of Spice: A Miscellany of Maine Literature and History*, edited by Richard S. Sprague. Orono: University of Maine Press, 1968. 53–105.

Letter

"Madam Wood's 'Recollections.' " *Colby Library Quarterly* 7 (September 1965): 89–115.

Studies of Sally S. Wood

Dunnack, Henry E. "The First Novelist." In *The Maine Book*. Augusta: Maine State Library, 1920. 140–146.

Fife, Hilda M. "An Unpublished Manuscript by Madam Wood." In *A Handful of Spice: A Miscellany of Maine Literature and History*, edited by Richard S. Sprague. Orono: University of Maine Press, 1968. 41–51.

Freibert, Lucy M., and Barbara A. White, eds. "Sally Barrell Wood" and "*Dorval*." In *Hidden Hands: An Anthology of American Women Writers, 1790–1870*. New Brunswick, NJ: Rutgers University Press, 1985. 51–67.

Goold, William. "Madam Wood, the First Maine Writer of Fiction." *Collections and Proceedings of the Maine Historical Society*, 2nd ser., 1 (1890): 401–408.

Marston, Doris R. "A Lady of Maine: Sally Sayward Barrell Keating Wood, 1759–1855." Master's thesis, University of New Hampshire, 1970.

Scheick, William J. "Education, Class, and the French Revolution in Sarah Wood's *Julia*." *Studies in American Fiction* 16 (spring 1988): 111–118.

CONSTANCE FENIMORE WOOLSON (1840–1894)

Karen Tracey

BIOGRAPHY

Like many prominent nineteenth-century American writers, Constance Fenimore Woolson was born in New England. Unlike many of those writers, however, Woolson left New England when a child and never returned there to make a home. Throughout Woolson's life and within her stories and novels, we can see how profoundly these two facts influenced her: She thought of herself as a New Englander but had no New England home; she traveled widely in the United States and in Europe but always perceived herself as an outsider. The three major relocations in her life, from New England to Cleveland, from Cleveland to the American South, and from the South to Europe, were each driven by the death of family members.

Woolson was born in Claremont, New Hampshire, on March 5, 1840, but within weeks of her birth, three of her five sisters died of scarlet fever. To escape the pain of the losses, her parents moved with their surviving children to rapidly growing Cleveland, Ohio, where Constance attended Miss Hayden's School and the Cleveland Female Seminary before going to New York to finish her education at a fashionable boarding school, Madame Chegaray's, where she graduated at the head of her class in 1858. During the Civil War years and the remainder of the 1860s, she lived with her family in Cleveland and probably developed her writing skills. From this period of her life, she drew her knowledge of Mackinac Island in Lake Michigan and other Great Lakes regions, which became locations for sketches, stories, and novels. She did not publish, however, until after her father's death in 1869.

Woolson's publication history, which is interwoven with her continual relocations and travel, begins in 1870 with the appearance of her first sketches and stories in *Harper's New Monthly Magazine, Putnam's Magazine*, and the *Daily Cleveland Herald*. Her first book, published under the pseudonym Anne March, was a prize-winning juvenile entitled *The Old Stone House* (1872). Meanwhile, she traveled occasionally to New York and began taking her mother Hannah on extended trips in the southern United States, where they spent time in Virginia, the Carolinas, Tennessee, and Georgia. Their favorite location was St. Augustine, Florida, where they settled for the winter each year. Woolson published *Castle Nowhere: Lake-Country Sketches* (1875) and was absorbing knowledge of varied Southern regions that would become material for other work. After the death of her mother in 1879, Woolson began to travel in Europe rather than in the United States.

For the remainder of her life, she lived, wrote, and traveled in Europe, dwelling for extended periods of time in Italy (Florence, Venice, and Rome) and in England (London and Oxford). Woolson struggled with not only her loneliness and sense of exile but depression (which was a biological inheritance from her father and grandfather) and other health problems, including increasing deafness. But driven both by the desire to write and by the need to support herself, she wrote and published many stories, travel sketches, and her five novels: *Anne* (1880), *For the Major* (1883), *East Angels* (1886), *Jupiter Lights* (1889), and *Horace Chase* (1894).

Although Woolson became more reclusive as she grew more deaf and therefore less comfortable in company, she established close friendships that she maintained primarily by correspondence. Without a home or community she identified as her own, this network of friendships was centrally important to her. Included in these are significant literary friendships with poet and critic Edmund Clarence Stedman, an early supporter of her work whom she met while living in the American South, and with Henry James, whom she met when she relocated to Europe in 1880. Her friendship with James was particularly important to her development as an artist, because she found in him a kindred artistic spirit with whom she could talk at length about writing. They met frequently in Italy and England, corresponded regularly about their work, and developed a close friendship based on their shared perceptions of art. Sharon Dean concludes that ''James's willingness to champion Woolson's fiction . . . and his use of some of her ideas for his own work, indicate that Woolson was a valuable critic for him. She saw in him a soul mate and, because she was so blunt, he could use her as his ideal reader'' (87). James included an assessment of her work in *Partial Portraits* (1888), classifying her with prominent contemporaries including Ralph Waldo Emerson, Ivan Turgenev, and George Eliot.

Shortly after finishing *Horace Chase*, and suffering from both depression and influenza, Woolson died in Venice on January 24, 1894, when she fell from her window. Woolson was alone at the time and left no explanation, but because she had at times defended suicide as a rational and morally defensible choice, and because she did suffer from serious depression, some have concluded that she committed suicide. Two collections of her stories were published posthumously: *The Front Yard and Other Italian Stories* (1895) and *Dorothy and Other Italian Stories* (1896).

MAJOR WORKS AND THEMES

The prominent characteristics of Woolson's work grow out of her wandering life and from her struggle to gain respect as a serious author writing in an era when many women writers commanded huge popular audiences but few of them were taken seriously as artists. But Woolson's stories and novels do hold up to close literary analysis. Woolson has a wonderful sense of humor that often illuminates serious moments with ironic perspective, and a richly textured style, particularly evident in the scenic descriptions of the varied settings of her stories.

The psychology of her characters is complex and consistent, and in her novels, she allows these complexities to be drawn out gradually as events and as developing relationships illuminate them. Her plots tend to focus on the choices made by characters and the consequences of those choices, so that the reader sees logical, long-term results develop from psychological premises established early. In *For The Major*, the motivations of the enigmatic Madam Carroll are only gradually revealed to the reader; although the plot of Madam Carroll's history is sensational, the novel maintains interest by slowly revealing her character rather than by trading on her dramatic past.

Some of the characteristic qualities of Woolson's fiction grow from her close knowledge of different regions in the United States and in Europe and from her own lack of rootedness. She was able to bring multiple perspectives to the communities she observed and the characters she drew in her fiction. Unlike many writers classified as regionalist, Woolson was deeply interested in the ethnic diversity of different regions as much as in their cultural isolation and insularity. Always aware of the fragility of life and the rapidity with which families could be disrupted or communities could change, she also explored the search for a stable home or community. She was conscious of the plots and themes characteristic of popular fiction by women writers, and she drew upon and problematized these: romantic love, courtship, marriage, female self-sacrifice, family ties. As a woman artist fighting for respect, she was isolated in her professional as in her personal life, and she frequently wrote about women artists or, less directly, about women in search of some creative means of expression in communities that trivialized their efforts or demanded that their best energies be spent in service of others.

Woolson has been classified as a regional writer, but she is not associated with any particular area because she wrote about varied regions in the Great Lakes, the American South, and Europe. At times she uses an isolated setting to frame unusual characters and incidents, providing herself a space separated from the civilized and routinized world, a space where she can analyze the human in the guise of the exaggerated or the fantastic. "The Lady of Little Fishing," a doubly framed narrative set on an island in Lake Superior, tells the story of a woman missionary who temporarily revolutionized the rough behavior of a group of hunters. She imagined she converted them to her religion, but in fact they were only converted to idolatry of her, and they rejected her when she showed herself human by falling in love with one of them. The story exaggerates both the woman's elevation as an icon of purity and her fall into literally groveling at the feet of the man who rejects her; Woolson illuminates the impossible position women face when they are placed on a pedestal of moral purity that they did not seek and then denied the right to their own human feelings. "In the Cotton Country" describes how a Northern narrator persistently probes the privacy of a Southern woman, persuading her to reveal the intense isolation and bitterness she has suffered during the Civil War and its aftermath. The Southern woman may be an exaggerated portrait, but her bitter despair and the Northerner's awkward and intrusive efforts to comfort her suggest Woolson's insight into regional relations after the war.

Strikingly unlike regionalists such as New Englanders Mary Wilkins Freeman and Sarah Orne Jewett, writers whose work is grounded in a particular area and interested in the lives of an isolated and relatively homogenous community, Woolson was interested in the challenges and changes brought to communities by ethnic, racial, national, and religious difference. Woolson saw that when her contemporaries complacently identified "American" with "New England," they were ignoring the rapidly changing and widely heterogenous nature of many American communities. Her groups of characters are drawn from many backgrounds; their conflicts often derive from their differences, and at times, their successes involve growing to understand or at least accept without judgment those differences. As Sharon Dean notes, "The remarkable thing is that Woolson is so willing to recognize the inevitable cultural bias we all have. . . . Whatever its region, her fiction reveals a woman who deplores the divisiveness that turned diversity to hatred and war and who sees that cross-cultural understanding is both desirable and impossible" (50).

Two of Woolson's novels illustrate how the theme of ethnic diversity is often manifested in her work. In *Anne*, the Anglo-American protagonist confronts the challenge of living in a heterogenous family (she has biracial siblings) within a Mackinac Island community made up of characters drawn from French, Irish, and Native American backgrounds. *East Angels* is set largely in a small Florida town where New Englanders, Cubans, Americans of Spanish descent, and African Americans make up a close community despite the fact that language, custom, and religious differences often created misunderstandings and despite the fact that social and class distinctions were cautiously maintained. Woolson's own outsider perspective enabled her to note with irony the New England attitude that perceived Florida as virtually a foreign country, hardly "American" at all, and to draw a portrait of an impoverished but aristocratic Cuban who, though condescended to by most other members of the community, never questioned his own superiority to all of them and who eventually marries the heroine Garda Thorne, a child of New England and Spanish descent. Although like anyone Woolson participated in many of the biases and assumptions of her time; unlike many of her contemporaries she realized that ''America'' was profoundly characterized by cultural diversity, that ethnic difference and tension were central rather than marginal to American life.

Another pervasive theme in Woolson's work is that of the search for home, for stability, for rootedness, for security. Her letters frequently lament her lack of a home, and her fiction features characters who share that lack and who struggle to fill it or compensate for it. The search for home is, in Woolson's fiction, a long and arduous uphill struggle, and she does not complacently equate a happy home with marriage. Woolson longed to find a way to reconcile home with independence, but usually choosing marriage meant giving up independence. Sometimes her wandering characters eventually find fulfillment and stability in marriage, but she also explores issues of sexuality, violence, and betrayal, and her fiction is full of struggling marriages, estrangement, loss, and second partnerships. Even when characters do find a home, they have generally sacrificed or compromised to achieve that place of rest. The story ''The Street of the Hyacinth'' ends with a marriage that will free the heroine from the drudgery of supporting herself and her mother, but Woolson describes the heroine's long-delayed acceptance of her suitor as a fall, directing the reader's attention to the heroine's failure to fulfill her artistic aspirations rather than to her success in finding a secure marriage with a man she loves.

Connected to Woolson's interest in the search for home is her complex treatment of romantic love and courtship, the themes characteristic of most popular novels and no doubt expected by many readers. Her long poem *Two Women* (1862) tells of the rivalry and uneasy friendship between two women who love the same man and who embody opposed cultural definitions of love: the sentimental-domestic ideal, which stakes its claim to superiority on Christian principles, and the romantic-passionate ideal, which is authorized by spontaneous, overwhelming, all-consuming passion. As the complex characters and plots of her fiction demonstrate, Woolson was too much of a realist to subscribe unthinkingly to either version or to imply that characters who fell in love, whether they perceived their love from a sentimental or romantic perspective, were guaranteed happy marriages; on the contrary, though Woolson's novels generally follow a courtship plot, they are more likely to complicate than to exalt marriage. Far from idealizing her characters or their marriages, she frequently probes marriages in serious difficulties deriving from sexual manipulation, conflicts of loyalty, alcoholism, wife abuse, estrangement, or desertion. Margaret Harold, of *East Angels*, holds grimly to her sentimental-domestic ideal of marriage even though the man to whom she is married deserts her twice to pursue a love interest in Europe. She falls passionately in love with another character, who tries to persuade her to leave her husband, but she denies herself this possibility of romantic happiness to remain true to her marriage commitment, to serve the worthless husband she has chosen. *Jupiter Lights* explores at length a marriage in which the husband abuses his child and his wife, who despite fearing for her life tries to hold the marriage together. The title character of *Anne* is more fortunate, for her ill-chosen fiancé releases her from an engagement by eloping with her half sister; after considerable struggle and sacrifice, Anne marries the man to whom she is romantically attached. Madam Carroll, of *For The Major*, acts the part of childlike wife for years because the man who falls in love with her assumes she is much younger and more inexperienced than she is; he places her in the role of sentimental icon, and she plays that role perfectly until her aging husband's mind and eyesight fail, and she is free to quit maintaining her long golden curls, wearing makeup, and dressing in white frocks with gay ribbons. Madam Carroll sacrifices her own identity, replacing it with one that appealed to her husband, because she loved him and so needed a home.

Woolson's interest in women artists is often set in tension with the themes of love, marriage, and the search for home. Although Woolson herself achieved critical acclaim and earned a respectable living as a writer, the characters she draws who have artistic aspirations rarely match her success. To be a woman artist, in Woolson's stories, demanded that one deny oneself a home. The choice between art and marriage, as in the story "The Street of the Hyacinth," is presented as an either/or choice; she never imagines a character who is successful both in finding a home and in pursuing her art. Joan Myers Weimer argues that Woolson's women artists "seem to reflect her deepest feelings about women and art, convictions which persist from her earliest stories despite the improvement in her own circumstances" (4).

Instead of writing about successful, independent women artists, Woolson drew portraits of struggling artists, some gifted but most not, and virtually all of them are alienated and ultimately defeated. In "Miss Grief," a work Sharon Dean has labeled a "paradigmatic story of nineteenth-century women's artistry" (75), a poor, middle-aged, unpublished female writer approaches a young, successful, male writer and persuades him to read her manuscripts. Though he is moved by the power and originality of her writing, he also discovers flaws in the plot, structure, and expression, flaws that are also discerned by the male editors who reject the manuscripts. The protagonist Aaronna Moncrief is blind to the flaws that are so evident to the literary men, and Woolson leaves open the question of whether the flaws are in Aaronna's writing or in the standards of the male readers who reject it. Perhaps talented women writers cannot find publishers because no women mentors or women editors exist who might appreciate their work on its own terms. Instead, women's art is measured by male-defined standards of artistic excellence. In "The Chateau of Corinne," the American gentleman Mr. Ford indulges in long outbursts of outright hostility toward literary women, and he manages to persuade Katherine, who loses her fortune and therefore her independence, to give up writing and to marry him. Ford does not deny the possibility of genius in a woman, but he insists that such genius disfigures a woman, robs her of her true womanly qualities, and therefore makes her unfit to be a wife and to have a home.

CRITICAL RECEPTION

Woolson enjoyed critical acclaim during her lifetime but has been largely ignored throughout most of the twentieth-century; she has thus suffered the same fate she assigned to many of her own artist heroines, a fate that Cheryl Torsney calls "the grief of artistry" and that she describes as "the grief of silence, of having something important to say and then having it suppressed either because society does not want to hear the message itself or because the message is being communicated by a woman" (*Constance Fenimore Woolson* 4). Only very recently has Woolson begun to receive critical attention from academic scholars and therefore to be heard once again.

Nineteenth-century critics often praised Woolson for her descriptions of place, eye for detail, psychological realism, and moral rectitude. Henry James, while he noted certain flaws in her work, admired her writing overall and certainly treated her as a serious and talented artist: "[A]rtistically, she has had a fruitful instinct in seeing the novel as a picture of the actual, of the characteristic—a study of human types and passions, of the evolution of personal relations" (quoted in Woolson, *Women Artists, Women Exiles* 276). William Dean Howells, although he was less enthused by Woolson's novels, appreciated her sketches and short stories and offered this high praise of "The Lady of Little Fishing": "It has that internal harmony which is the only allegiance to probability we can exact from romance, and it has a high truth to human nature never once weakened by any vagueness of the moral ideal in the author" (quoted in Torsney, *Critical Essays* 18). Of course, Woolson received negative notices as well and was criticized for sensational episodes of murder and elaborate plot complications, or for writing descriptively at too great a length, or, at times, for perceived failures in psychological realism. She was generally treated seriously as a writer, not patronized with the condescending faint praise often given to "lady writers."

Twentieth-century academics have been slow indeed to give Woolson the respect accorded her by her contemporaries. Neither of two book-length studies of her work, the first written in 1934 by John Kern and the second in 1963 by Rayburn Moore, generated a response from other critics, and even when many other nineteenth-century women writers began receiving increased attention in the 1970s, Woolson was largely overlooked. But during the mid- to late 1980s, critics finally began publishing substantial articles exploring Woolson's fiction, and a collection of her short stories, edited by Joan Myers Weimer, appeared in the Rutgers American Women Writers Series.

While we still await a full biography and a collection of her letters, Woolson may, 100 years after her death, at last be on the verge of overcoming the critical neglect that has largely silenced her voice. A base from which critical dialogue about Woolson's work may develop has at length been established by three outstanding books: Two are individual studies, one by Cheryl Torsney (1989) and one by Sharon Dean (1995), and the third is a volume of the *Critical Essays* series (1992), edited by Torsney, that includes early critical assessments and both reprinted and new essays. Torsney studies Woolson's work in the context of her life story and nineteenth-century culture, paying particular attention to the dilemmas faced by the artist-heroines in her stories. Dean's study, subtitled *Homeward Bound*, employs a thematic approach to trace the pervasive idea of "home" through Woolson's life and work. Dean concludes by arguing that readers should study Woolson's writing for the insights it has to offer on nineteenth-century issues such as rising industrialism, demographic change, race relations, ethnic identity, and socially prescribed gender roles and that critics should at last build Woolson a home in the literary canon (199–200).

WORKS CITED

Dean, Sharon. *Constance Fenimore Woolson: Homeward Bound.* Knoxville: University of Tennessee Press, 1995.
Torsney, Cheryl B. *Constance Fenimore Woolson: The Grief of Artistry.* Athens: University of Georgia Press, 1989.
———, ed. *Critical Essays on Constance Fenimore Woolson.* New York: G. K. Hall, 1992.
Weimer, Joan Myers. "Women Artists as Exiles in the Fiction of Constance Fenimore Woolson." *Legacy* 3 (fall 1986): 3–15.
Woolson, Constance Fenimore. *Women Artists, Women Exiles: "Miss Grief" and Other Stories.* Edited by Joan Myers Weimer. New Brunswick: Rutgers University Press, 1988.

BIBLIOGRAPHY

Works by Constance Fenimore Woolson

Novels

Anne. New York: Harper, 1882.
For the Major. New York: Harper, 1883.
East Angels. New York: Harper, 1886.
Jupiter Lights. New York: Harper, 1889.
Horace Chase. New York: Harper, 1894.

Short Fiction

Castle Nowhere: Lake-Country Sketches. Boston: Osgood, 1875.
Rodman the Keeper: Southern Sketches. 1880. Reprint, New York: Harper, 1886.
Dorothy and Other Italian Stories. New York: Harper, 1896.
The Front Yard and Other Italian Stories. New York: Harper, 1895.

Poetry

Two Women. 1862. New York: Appleton, 1877, 1890.

Juvenile Literature

The Old Stone House. By Anne March. Boston: D. Lothrop, 1872.

Studies of Constance Fenimore Woolson

Dean, Sharon. *Constance Fenimore Woolson: Homeward Bound.* Knoxville: University of Tennessee Press, 1995.

Kern, John Dwight. *Constance Fenimore Woolson: Literary Pioneer.* Philadelphia: University of Pennsylvania Press, 1934.

Moore, Rayburn S. *Constance F. Woolson.* New York: Twayne, 1963.

Torsney, Cheryl B. *Constance Fenimore Woolson: The Grief of Artistry.* Athens: University of Georgia Press, 1989.

————, ed. *Critical Essays on Constance Fenimore Woolson.* New York: G. K. Hall, 1992.

Weimer, Joan Myers, ed. Introduction to *Women Artists, Women Exiles: ''Miss Grief'' and Other Stories,* by Constance Fenimore Woolson. New Brunswick: Rutgers University Press, 1988. ix–xliii.

————. ''Women Artists as Exiles in the Fiction of Constance Fenimore Woolson.'' *Legacy* 3 (fall 1986): 3–15.

BIBLIOGRAPHY

American Women Writers: A Critical Reference Guide from Colonial Times to the Present. Edited by Lina Mainiero and Langdon Lynne Faust. 4 vols. New York: Frederick Ungar, 1979–1982.

Ammons, Elizabeth. *Conflicting Stories: American Women Writers at the Turn into the Twentieth Century.* New York: Oxford University Press, 1991.

Baym, Nina. *American Women Writers and the Work of History, 1790–1860.* New Brunswick: Rutgers University Press, 1995.

———. *Woman's Fiction: A Guide to Novels by and about Women in America 1820–1870.* Ithaca: Cornell University Press, 1978.

Bloom, Harold. *The Western Canon.* New York: Harcourt Brace & Co., 1994.

Branch, Edward Douglas. *The Sentimental Years, 1836–1860.* New York: D. Appleton-Century Co., 1934.

Brooks, Van Wyck. *The Flowering of New England, 1815–1865.* New York: E. P. Dutton and Co., 1936.

Brown, Herbert Ross. *The Sentimental Novel in America, 1789–1860.* Durham, NC: Duke University Press, 1940.

Browne, Anita, ed. *The 100 Best Books by American Women, 1833–1933.* Chicago: Associated Authors Service, 1933.

Conrad, Susan P. *Perish the Thought: Intellectual Women in Romantic America, 1830–1860.* New York: Oxford University Press, 1976.

Cott, Nancy F. *The Bonds of Womanhood: "Woman's Sphere" in New England 1780–1835.* New Haven: Yale University Press, 1977.

Davidson, Cathy N. *Revolution and the Word: The Rise of the American Novel.* New York: Oxford University Press, 1986.

Deegan, Dorothy Yost. *The Stereotype of the Single Woman in American Novels.* New York: Columbia University Press, 1951.

Donovan, Josephine. "Toward the Local Colorists: Early American Women's Tradition."

In *New England Local Color Literature: A Women's Tradition*. New York: Frederick Ungar, 1983. 25–37.

Douglas, Ann. *The Feminization of American Culture*. New York: Alfred A. Knopf, 1977.

Fetterley, Judith. "Commentary: Nineteenth-Century American Women Writers and the Politics of Recovery." *American Literary History* 6 (1994): 600–611.

———, ed. *Provisions: A Reader from 19th-Century American Women*. Bloomington: Indiana University Press, 1985.

Fetterley, Judith, and Marjorie Pryse, eds. *American Women Regionalists, 1850–1910*. New York: Norton, 1992.

Fiedler, Leslie. *Love and Death in the American Novel*. New York: Criterion Books, 1960.

Forrest, Mary [Mrs. Julia Deane Freeman]. *Women of the South Distinguished in Literature*. New York: Charles B. Richardson, 1865.

Foster, Edward Halsey. *The Civilized Wilderness: Backgrounds to American Literature, 1817–1860*. New York: Free Press, 1975.

Foster, Frances Smith. *Written by Herself: Literary Production by African American Women, 1746–1892*. Bloomington: Indiana University Press, 1993.

Frederick, John T. "Hawthorne's 'Scribbling Women.' " *New England Quarterly* 48 (June 1975): 231–240.

Freibert, Lucy M., and Barbara A. White, eds. *Hidden Hands: An Anthology of American Women Writers, 1790–1870*. New Brunswick, NJ: Rutgers University Press, 1985.

Gates, Henry Louis, Jr. *The Schomburg Library of Nineteenth-Century Black Women Writers*. New York: Oxford University Press, 1988.

Geary, Susan. "The Domestic Novel as a Commercial Commodity: Making a Best Seller in the 1850s." *Papers of the Bibliographical Society of America* 70 (July–September 1976): 365–395.

Gilbert, Sandra, and Susan Guber. *The Madwoman in the Attic: The Woman Writer and the Nineteenth-Century Literary Imagination*. New Haven: Yale University Press, 1979.

Habegger, Alfred. *Gender, Fantasy, and Realism in American Literature*. New York: Columbia University Press, 1982.

Hale, Sarah Josepha. *Woman's Record; or, Sketches of All Distinguished Women, from the Creation to A.D. 1854*. New York: Harper and Brothers, 1855.

Harris, Susan K. *19th-Century American Women's Novels: Interpretive Strategies*. Cambridge: Cambridge University Press, 1990.

Hart, James D. "Home Influence." In *The Popular Book: A History of America's Literary Taste*. New York: Oxford University Press, 1950. 85–105.

Hart, John Seely. *The Female Prose Writers of America with Portraits, Biographical Notices, and Specimens of Their Writings*. Philadelphia: E. H. Butler and Co., 1852.

Henneman, John Bell. *The Nineteenth Century Woman in Literature*. N.p. [1892].

Higginson, Thomas Wentworth. "Woman in Literature." In *Woman: Her Position, Influence, and Achievement throughout the Civilized World*, edited by William C. King. Springfield, MA: King-Richardson Co., 1901. 493–505.

Hilldrup, Robert Le Roy. "Cold War against the Yankees in the Antebellum Literature of Southern Women." *North Carolina Historical Review* 31 (July 1954): 370–384.

Hofstader, Beatrice. "Popular Culture and the Romantic Heroine." *American Scholar* 30 (winter 1960–1961): 98–116.

Howe, Daniel Walker. "American Victorianism as a Culture." *American Quarterly* 27 (December 1975): 507–532.

Hubbell, Jay B. *The South in American Literature, 1607–1900.* Durham, NC: Duke University Press, 1954.

Hull, Raymona E. " 'Scribbling' Females and Serious Males: Hawthorne's Comments from Abroad on Some American Authors." In *The Nathaniel Hawthorne Journal 1975*, edited by C. E. Frazer Clark, Jr. Englewood, CO: Microcard Editions Books, 1975. 35–58.

Johannsen, Albert. *The House of Beadle and Adams and Its Dime and Nickel Novels.* 2 vols. Norman: University of Oklahoma Press, 1950.

Kelley, Mary. "The Literary Domestics: Private Woman on a Public Stage." In *Ideas in America's Cultures*, edited by Hamilton Cravens. Ames: Iowa State University Press, 1982. 83–102.

————. *Private Woman, Public Stage: Literary Domesticity in Nineteenth-Century America.* New York: Oxford University Press, 1984.

Kirkland, Joseph. "Realism versus Other Isms." *Dial*, 16 February 1893, 99–101.

Kolb, Harold H., Jr. *The Illusion of Life: American Realism as a Literary Form.* Charlottesville: University Press of Virginia, 1969.

Kolodny, Annette. *The Land before Her: Fantasy and Experience of the American Frontiers, 1630–1860.* Chapel Hill: University of North Carolina Press, 1984.

Lauter, Paul. *Canons and Contexts.* New York: Oxford University Press, 1991.

Loewenberg, Bert James, and Ruth Bogin, eds. *Black Women in Nineteenth-Century American Life: Their Words, Their Thoughts, Their Feelings*: University Park: Pennsylvania State University Press, 1976.

Loshe, Lillie Deming. *The Early American Novel.* New York: Columbia University Press, 1907.

McNall, Sally Allen. *Who Is in the House: A Psychological Study of Two Centuries of Women's Fiction in America, 1795 to the Present.* New York: Elsevier North-Holland, 1981.

Moers, Ellen. "Women's Lit: Profession and Tradition." *Columbia Forum* 1 (fall 1972): 27–34.

Mott, Frank Luther. *Golden Multitudes: The Story of Best Sellers in the United States.* New York: Macmillan Co., 1947.

————. *A History of American Magazines.* Vol. 1, 1741–1850. New York: D. Appleton and Co., 1930. Vol. 2. 1850–1865. Cambridge: Harvard University Press, 1939.

Nye, Russel B. "The Novel as Dream and Weapon: Women's Popular Novels in the 19th Century." *Historical Society of Michigan Chronicle* 11 (4th quart. 1975): 2–16.

————. *Society and Culture in America, 1830–1860.* New York: Harper and Row, 1974.

Papashvily, Helen Waite. *All the Happy Endings: A Study of the Domestic Novel in America, the Women Who Wrote It, the Women Who Read It, in the Nineteenth Century.* New York: Harper, 1956.

Parker, Gail. "Introduction." In *The Oven Birds: American Women on Womanhood, 1820–1920*, edited by Gail Parker. Garden City: Doubleday and Company, 1972.

Pattee, Fred Lewis. *The Feminine Fifties.* New York: D. Appleton-Century Co., 1940.

———. *First Century of American Literature*. New York: D. Appleton-Century Co., 1935.

Petter, Henri. *The Early American Novel*. Columbus: Ohio State University Press, 1971.

Quirk, Tom, and Gary Scharnhorst, eds. *American Realism and the Canon*. Newark: University of Delaware Press, 1994.

Raymond, Ida [Mary T. Tardy]. *The Living Female Writers of the South*. Philadelphia: Claxton, Remson and Haffelfinger, 1872.

———. *Southland Writers: Biographical and Critical Sketches of the Living Female Writers of the South. With Extracts from Their Writings*. 2 vols. Philadelphia: Claxton, Remson and Haffelfinger, 1870.

Rosenfelt, Deborah S. "The Politics of Bibliography: Women's Studies and the Literary Canon." In *Women in Print I*, edited by Joan E. Hartman and Ellen Messer-Davidow. New York: Modern Language Association, 1982. 11–35.

Ruoff, John C. "Frivolity to Consumption: or, Southern Womanhood in Antebellum Literature." *Civil War History* 18 (September 1972): 213–229.

Samuels, Shirley, ed. *The Culture of Sentiment: Race, Gender, and Sentimentality in Nineteenth-Century America*. New York: Oxford University Press, 1992.

Satterwaite, Joseph. "The Tremulous Formula: Form and Technique in *Godey's* Fiction." *American Quarterly* 8 (summer 1956): 99–113.

Shapiro, Ann R. *Unlikely Heroines: Nineteenth-Century American Women Writers and the Woman Question*. New York: Greenwood Press, 1987.

Smith, Henry Nash. "The Scribbling Women and the Cosmic Success Story." *Critical Inquiry* 1 (September 1974): 47–70.

Smith, Leslie. "Through Rose-Colored Glasses: Some American Victorian Sentimental Novels." In *New Dimensions in Popular Culture*, edited by Russel B. Nye. Bowling Green, OH: Bowling Green University Popular Press, 1972. 90–106.

Smith-Rosenberg, Carroll. "The Female World of Love and Ritual: Relations between Women in Nineteenth-Century America." *Signs* 1 (autumn 1975): 1–30.

"Some 'Lady Novelists' and Their Works: As Seen from a Public Library." *Literary World*, 3 June 1882, 184–186.

Stanford, Ann. "Images of Women in Early American Literature." In *What Manner of Woman: Essays on English and American Life and Literature*, edited by Marlene Springer. New York: New York University Press, 1977. 184–210.

Stearns, Bertha Monica. "New England Magazines for Ladies, 1830–1860." *New England Quarterly* 3 (October 1930): 627–656.

Sterling, Dorothy. *We Are Your Sisters: Black Women in the Nineteenth Century*. New York: W. W. Norton, 1984.

Stern, Madeleine B., ed. *Publishers for Mass Entertainment in Nineteenth Century America*. Boston: G. K. Hall and Co., 1980.

Tandy, Jeannette Reid. "Pro-Slavery Propaganda in American Fiction of the Fifties." *South Atlantic Quarterly* 21 (January 1922): 41–50; (April 1922): 170–178.

Thompson, Adele E. "Woman's Place in Early American Fiction." *Era* 12 (November 1903): 472–474.

Tompkins, Jane P. *Sensational Designs: The Cultural Work of American Fiction, 1790–1860*. New York: Oxford University Press, 1985.

Van Doren, Carl. *The American Novel, 1789–1939*. New York: Macmillan Co., 1947.

Voloshin, Beverly R. "The Limits of Domesticity: The Female *Bildungsroman* in America, 1820–1870." *Women's Studies* 10, no. 3 (1984): 283–302.

Walker, Cheryl, ed. *American Women Poets of the Nineteenth Century: An Anthology*. New Brunswick: Rutgers University Press, 1992.

Warren, Joyce W., ed. *The (Other) American Traditions: Nineteenth-Century American Women Writers*. New Brunswick: Rutgers University Press, 1993.

Watts, Emily Stipes. *The Poetry of American Women from 1632 to 1945*. Austin: University of Texas Press, 1977.

Welter, Barbara. "The Cult of True Womanhood, 1820–1860." *American Quarterly* 18 (summer 1966): 151–174.

———. *Dimity Convictions: The American Woman in the Nineteenth Century*. Athens: Ohio University Press, 1976.

Williams, Kenny. *They Also Spoke: An Essay on Negro Literature in America, 1787–1930*. Nashville: Townsend Press, 1970.

Wood, Ann Douglas. "The 'Scribbling Women' and Fanny Fern: Why Women Wrote." *American Quarterly* 23 (1971): 3–24.

Wright, Lyle J. "A Statistical Survey of American Fiction, 1774–1850." *Huntington Library Quarterly* 2 (April 1939): 309–318.

INDEX

Page numbers for main entries in the dictionary are set in **boldface** type.

ABOUT THE EDITOR AND CONTRIBUTORS

SUSAN ALVES is an Assistant Professor at Castleton State College, Vermont. Her doctoral dissertation from Northeastern University recovers and examines the poetic production of female factory workers in Great Britain and the United States from 1840 to 1914. She is preparing an anthology of British and American nineteenth-century working-class poetry.

NOELLE A. BAKER is the Editorial and Production Manager for the *Journal of The Writings of Henry D. Thoreau.* A doctoral candidate in nineteenth-century American literature at Georgia State University, she is editing the selected works of Sarah Helen Whitman for her dissertation.

ALFRED BENDIXEN is a Professor of English at California State University at Los Angeles and Executive Director of the American Literature Association. He has edited several books, including Spofford's *"The Amber Gods" and Other Stories* (1989) in the Rutgers American Women Writers Series.

DEBRA BERNARDI teaches English at the University of Wisconsin at Madison, where she earned her Ph.D. Her dissertation, titled "Domestic Horrors: Dis-figuring the American Home, 1860–1903," focuses on how political anxieties pervade nineteenth-century representations of domesticity.

VICTORIA BOYNTON teaches and writes fiction and poetry as well as articles on twentieth-century women writers. She uses a rhetorical and feminist approach, exemplified in her dissertation, "Sex-citing Ethos: Rhetorical Readings of North American Women Writers."

PATRICK W. BRYANT earned a B.A. in English from Mercer University in Macon, Georgia, and an M.A. in English at Georgia State University. Now pursuing a Ph.D. in English at Georgia State University, he studies American literature of the nineteenth century and textual editing.

SHELLE C. WILSON BRYANT earned a B.A. in English from Mercer University in Macon, Georgia, and a Master's of Theological Studies (M.T.S.) at Emory University in Atlanta. She is currently on staff in the English Department at Georgia State University.

JIM BURKHEAD writes poetry and fiction and is an independent scholar specializing in the American nineteenth century. He has taught English in high schools, prisons, colleges, and universities. He is currently working on a literary biography; on a collection of poetry, *East of Zebulon*; and on a novel, *Waiting for the Milkman*.

ALETA CANE is a recent Ph.D. recipient and an Adjunct Professor at Framingham State College and Northeastern University. She has published articles on Charlotte Perkins Gilman, Fay Weldon, and Gerard Manley Hopkins.

CYNTHIA J. DAVIS is an Assistant Professor of English at the University of South Carolina. The coauthor of *American Women Writers: A Timeline of Social, Cultural and Literary History* (1996) and the still-struggling author of a book manuscript on gender, genre, and medicine in late-nineteenth-century America, she has also written articles on Harriet Wilson and Sarah Orne Jewett and on topics ranging from feminist theory to television talk shows.

LYNN DOMINA is completing her dissertation on American women's autobiography and the construction of national identity at the State University of New York at Stony Brook. She has published several articles and a collection of poetry, *Corporal Works* (1995).

SAMANTHA MANCHESTER EARLEY is a Ph.D. candidate in American literature at Kent State University. She specializes in African-American literature.

GREGORY EISELEIN is an Assistant Professor of English at Kansas State University and the author of *Literature and Humanitarian Reform in the Civil War Era* (1996).

MONIKA M. ELBERT is an Associate Professor of English and Director of Graduate English at Montclair State University, as well as Associate Editor of *The Nathaniel Hawthorne Review*. She has published extensively on nineteenth-century American authors.

ERNELLE FIFE is a Visiting Lecturer at Georgia State University. She has authored articles on Jane Austen, medicine and literature, mythology in children's literature, and eighteenth-century medical rhetoric.

LOIS JOSEPHS FOWLER, Professor of English at Carnegie Mellon University, teaches courses in gender studies. Most recently, she has published *Revelations of Self* (1990), autobiographies of women in nineteenth-century America. She is currently working on a book focusing on women who have influenced political issues as the result of their sexual relationships with men in power.

LUCY M. FREIBERT, Professor Emerita of English at the University of Louisville, is the author of articles on Herman Melville, Hilda Doolittle, Margaret Atwood, and utopian fiction. With Barbara A. White, she edited *Hidden Hands: An Anthology of American Women Writers, 1790–1870* (1990). She is currently preparing an annotated bibliography of American wit and humor to 1876.

JANET GABLER-HOVER is an Associate Professor of nineteenth-century American literature at Georgia State University. Her publications include *Truth in American Fiction: The Legacy of Rhetorical Idealism* (1990) and essays and periodical articles on Henry James, Edith Wharton, Mark Twain, H. G. Wells, and nineteenth-century American periodical literature.

THERESA STROUTH GAUL is a Ph.D. candidate in American literature at the University of Wisconsin at Madison.

JENNIFER A. GEHRMAN is an Assistant Professor of English at Fort Lewis College in Durango, Colorado.

GRETCHEN HOLBROOK GERZINA is Associate Professor of English and Associate Dean of the Faculty at Vassar College. She is the author of *Carrington: A Life* (1989), a biography of the Bloomsbury figure Dora Carrington, and *Black London* (1995), about the black population of eighteenth-century England.

CATHERINE J. GOLDEN is an Associate Professor of English at Skidmore College. She is editor of *The Captive Imagination: A Casebook on "The Yellow Wallpaper"* (1992) and *Unpunished*, with Denise D. Knight (1997). She has published extensively on Victorian and American authors and illustrators.

JANETTE M. GOMES received an M.A. in English from Western Washington University, where she is currently studying American history.

KEVIN J. HAYES is an Associate Professor of English at the University of Central Oklahoma and the author of *A Colonial Woman's Bookshelf* (1996).

DAVID HICKS is the author of *Writing Through Literature* (1996) and is completing a book on the biographical/literary relationship of Nathaniel Hawthorne and Ralph Waldo Emerson. He is Associate Professor and Assistant Chair of the Literature and Communications Department at Pace University.

HILDEGARD HOELLER is a preceptor in the Expository Writing program at Harvard University. She has published articles on nineteenth- and twentieth-century American realist and sentimental fiction and on African women writers. She is currently completing a book entitled *Economy and Excess: Edith Wharton's Dialogue with Realism and Sentimental Fiction.*

AMY E. HUDOCK is a faculty member in the English Department at Marshall University. She has published articles on nineteenth-century women writers and is editing a collection of essays on the same topic. She is also currently writing a biography on E. D. E. N. Southworth.

LEE HUNTER is a doctoral candidate in American literature at Georgia State University. Her dissertation, ''Maids and Mammies: Black Women in White Fiction,'' examines interracial relationships in southern women's writings.

JENNIFER HYNES earned her doctorate from the University of South Carolina. Her current research focuses on personal and professional networks among nineteenth-century women writers. She lives in Morgantown, West Virginia, where she combines part-time teaching with freelance editing.

CHARLES JOHANNINGSMEIER is the author of *Fiction in the American Literary Marketplace, 1860–1900: The Role of Newspaper Syndicates* (1996) and articles on Sarah Orne Jewett, Mary E. Wilkins Freeman, and Frank Norris. He is a member of the English Department at the State University of New York at Cortland.

ROBERT E. KANTER is a Ph.D. candidate in English at the University of Illinois at Urbana-Champaign. His dissertation examines the representation of men and masculinity in nineteenth-century novels by American women.

GAIL C. KEATING has been Assistant Professor of English and Women's Studies at the Pennsylvania State University since 1970. Her doctoral dissertation from Temple University was titled ''Sarah Orne Jewett's Experiences with Mentoring and Communities of Women.'' She has published extensively on the New England local color writers.

KAREN L. KILCUP teaches American Literature at the University of North Carolina at Greensboro, and was recently a Visiting Professor at Westbrook College in Portland, Maine. Founder of the International Nineteenth-Century

American Women Writers Research Group, she has published widely on American literature, including *Nineteenth Century American Women Writers: An Anthology* (1997) and an accompanying critical collection by Blackwell Publishers.

LEIGH KIRKLAND in an Independent Scholar and writer living in Atlanta, Georgia. She holds a Ph.D. in American literature from Georgia State University.

MICHAEL J. KISKIS is Associate Professor of American Literature at Elmira College. He has published articles on nontraditional education and program development, adult students, and Mark Twain. He is editor of *Mark Twain's Own Autobiography: The Chapters from the North American Review* (1990). He also serves as editor of *Studies in American Humor: The Journal of the American Humor Studies Association.*

DENISE D. KNIGHT is an Associate Professor of English at the State University of New York at Cortland, where she specializes in nineteenth-century American literature. She is author of *Charlotte Perkins Gilman: A Study of the Short Fiction* (1997) and editor of *The Later Poetry of Charlotte Perkins Gilman* (1996), *The Diaries of Charlotte Perkins Gilman* (1994), *The Yellow Wall-Paper and Selected Stories of Charlotte Perkins Gilman* (1994), and other books appropriate to American literature. Her work has appeared in numerous journals and essay collections of American literature.

JACQUELYN N. LEONARDI is an Adjunct Instructor of freshman composition at Oklahoma State University.

MELANIE LEVINSON is a Visiting Assistant Professor in the English Department at Susquehanna University, where she teaches American and women's literature. She is currently working on a manuscript titled *From Uncle Tom's Cabin to Uncle Tom's Children: The ''Race'' Discourse in American Fiction.*

LISA LOGAN is Assistant Professor of English at the University of Central Florida, where she teaches courses in American literature. She writes on early American women's popular narratives, including captivities and domestic fiction.

LISA A. LONG is a doctoral candidate in American literature at the University of Wisconsin at Madison. Her dissertation is entitled ''The American Civil War and Cultural Revolution.''

DEBBIE L. LOPEZ received her Ph.D. in American literature from Harvard University. She is an Assistant Professor at the University of Texas at San Antonio.

JEAN MARIE LUTES is a Ph.D. candidate in American literature at the University of Wisconsin at Madison.

TERRY J. MARTIN is an Associate Professor of English at Baldwin-Wallace College, where he teaches and publishes in the areas of nineteenth-century American and African-American literature.

ELIZABETH A. MOOREHEAD is a Ph.D. candidate in English at the University of New Mexico.

SHANNON L. NICHOLS teaches at the Pennsylvania State University and is Managing Editor of *Legacy: A Journal of American Women Writers*.

KELLI OLSON is a Ph.D. candidate in American literature at Georgia State University.

KATHARINE A. PARHAM received her Master of Arts in English from the University of Illinois at Urbana-Champaign. She is writing a dissertation on nineteenth-century American women writers and working as a standards coordinator at the National Council of Teachers of English in Urbana.

SANDRA HARBERT PETRULIONIS is an Assistant Professor of English at Pennsylvania State University at Altoona. She has published on Louisa May Alcott and is the editor of *Journal 8:1854* in *The Writings of Henry D. Thoreau*, forthcoming.

TIMOTHY R. PRCHAL is a Ph.D. candidate in English at the University of Wisconsin at Milwaukee. He specializes in late nineteenth- and early twentieth-century American literature, popular genres, and creative writing.

LAURA ROGERS is an Adjunct and Writing Center Instructor at the Albany College of Pharmacy. She is a doctoral candidate in English at the State University of New York at Albany. She is also the coordinator of a creative writing workshop at a New York State correctional facility.

REBECCA R. SAULSBURY is a Ph.D. candidate in American Studies at Purdue University. Her dissertation is titled ''The Politics of Authorship: Maria Susanna Cummins and the Boston Literary Marketplace, 1820–1865.'' She has also written articles on Mary E. Wilkins Freeman and Constance Fenimore Woolson. She teaches American literature and composition.

GARY SCHARNHORST is Professor of English at the University of New Mexico, author of numerous books, coeditor of *American Literary Realism*, and editor in alternating years of *American Literary Scholarship*.

LAURA E. SKANDERA-TROMBLEY is the author of *Mark Twain in the Company of Women* (1994), winner of the 1995 *Choice* award for an outstanding scholarly work, and Assistant Provost at the State University of New York at Potsdam. She has lectured on Mark Twain nationally and internationally and has published numerous articles and reviews on Twain and on Chinese American women writers.

SUSAN BELASCO SMITH is an Associate Professor of English at the University of Tulsa. The author of several articles and reviews on nineteenth-century American women writers, she is the editor of *Summer on the Lakes, in 1843* by Margaret Fuller (1991); with Larry J. Reynolds, *"These Sad But Glorious Days": Dispatches from Europe, 1846–1850 by Margaret Fuller* (1991); and with Kenneth M. Price, *Periodical Literature in Nineteenth-Century America* (1995).

CAROLYN A. STATLER recently received a doctorate in Humanistic Studies from the State University of New York at Albany. She is an instructor in the Writing Center at Albany College of Pharmacy.

KAREN TRACEY is an Assistant Professor of English and Coordinator of Writing Programs at the University of Northern Iowa. She is writing a book about how nineteenth-century women writers manipulated courtship plots to address cultural concerns.

PATRICIA DUNLAVY VALENTI is an Associate Professor in the Department of Communicative Arts at Pembroke State University. In addition to her biography of Rose Hawthorne Lathrop, she has written about other members of the Hawthorne family and is currently writing a biography of Sophia Peabody Hawthorne.

NANCY A. WALKER is a Professor of English and former Director of Women's Studies at Vanderbilt University. Her publications include *Feminist Alternatives: Irony and Fantasy in the Contemporary Novel by Women* (1990), a critical edition of Kate Chopin's *The Awakening* (1992), *Fanny Fern* (1992), and *The Disobedient Writer: Women and Narrative Tradition* (1995). She is currently working on a study of the role of the women's magazine in defining domesticity from 1940 to 1960.

JOYCE W. WARREN teaches in the English Department at Queens College, City University of New York. She is the author of *The American Narcissus: Individualism and Women in Nineteenth-Century American Fiction* (1984) and *Fanny Fern: An Independent Woman* (1992). She edited *Ruth Hall and Other Writings by Fanny Fern* (1986) and *The (Other) American Traditions: Nineteenth-Century Women Writers* (1993).

JANE WEISS is currently editing Susan Warner's journals for publication and writing a critical biography of Warner. She is an Adjunct Assistant Professor at Hunter College of the City University of New York.

PERRY D. WESTBROOK is a Professor Emeritus of English at the State University of New York at Albany. Among his publications are a book on Mary E. Wilkins Freeman and one on Mary Ellen Chase. He has also published two volumes of literary history: *Acres of Flint: Sarah Orne Jewett and Her Contemporaries* (1981) and *A Literary History of New England* (1988).

BARBARA A. WHITE conducts research on nineteenth-century American women writers and has published six books on the subject; most recently, she edited *Wharton's New England: Seven Stories and "Ethan Frome"* (1995). She teaches at the University of New Hampshire and is book review editor of the National Women's Studies Association *Journal*.

KATE H. WINTER is the author of *Marietta Holley: Life with "Josiah Allen's Wife"* (1984) and *The Woman in the Mountain: Reconstructions of Self and Land by Adirondack Women Writers* (1989), as well as short fiction and two novels set in Hawaii. She teaches American literature and writing, dividing her time between the University of Hawaii and the University at Albany, New York.

NANCY R. WURZEL is an Assistant Professor in English at Baldwin-Wallace College. She recently completed work on "Willa Cather's Affirmative Modernism: Gender, Myth, and Nature."

ISBN 0-313-29713-4

9 780313 297137

HARDCOVER BAR CODE